THE BEST CANDIDATE

The way American citizens elect a president in November is enshrined in the Constitution and has remained unchanged for two hundred years. By contrast, the rules by which American political parties nominate their presidential candidates have evolved dramatically over this time. In recent years, these byzantine rules have allowed a number of unexpected candidates to win a party's presidential nomination. In *The Best Candidate*, a roster of leading election law scholars from across the political spectrum—true-blue Democrats, die-hard Republicans, and everyone in between—illuminate the law behind the modern presidential nomination process and offer ideas for how it can be improved. This book offers a blueprint for how American voters and their parties could nominate the best candidate for the presidency, and it should be read by anyone who cares about the occupant of the Oval Office.

Eugene D. Mazo is Visiting Associate Professor of Law at Rutgers University and a nationally recognized scholar of election law. He is the co-editor of several books, including *Democracy by the People: Reforming Campaign Finance in America* (2018) and *Election Law Stories* (2016). He is the chair of the Section on Election Law at the Association of American Law Schools (AALS), where he also serves on the executive committee of the Section on Constitutional Law. A graduate of Columbia College, Professor Mazo received his master's degree from Harvard University, a doctorate in politics from Oxford University, and his J.D. from Stanford Law School.

Michael R. Dimino is Professor of Law at the Widener University Commonwealth School of Law, where he also specializes in election law. He is the co-author of a major casebook in the field, *Voting Rights and Election Law* (2020), and of a leading treatise, *Understanding Election Law and Voting Rights* (2016). In 2011 and 2017, Widener University awarded Dimino its Douglas E. Ray Award for Excellence in Faculty Scholarship. A former Fulbright Scholar, Professor Dimino is a member of the American Law Institute. He received his B.A. from the State University of New York at Buffalo and his J.D. from Harvard Law School.

T0371452

The Best Candidate

PRESIDENTIAL NOMINATION IN POLARIZED TIMES

Edited by

EUGENE D. MAZO

Rutgers University

MICHAEL R. DIMINO

Widener University

CAMBRIDGE
UNIVERSITY PRESS

University Printing House, Cambridge CB2 8BS, United Kingdom

One Liberty Plaza, 20th Floor, New York, NY 10006, USA

477 Williamstown Road, Port Melbourne, VIC 3207, Australia

314–321, 3rd Floor, Plot 3, Splendor Forum, Jasola District Centre, New Delhi – 110025, India

79 Anson Road, #06–04/06, Singapore 079906

Cambridge University Press is part of the University of Cambridge.

It furthers the University's mission by disseminating knowledge in the pursuit of education, learning, and research at the highest international levels of excellence.

www.cambridge.org
Information on this title: www.cambridge.org/9781108835398
DOI: 10.1017/9781108883870

© Eugene D. Mazo and Michael R. Dimino 2020

First published 2020

A catalogue record for this publication is available from the British Library.

Library of Congress Cataloging-in-Publication Data
NAMES: Mazo, Eugene D. (Eugene David), 1973– editor. | Dimino, Michael, 1977– editor.
TITLE: The best candidate : presidential nomination in polarized times / edited by Eugene D. Mazo, Rutgers University; Michael R. Dimino, Widener University.
DESCRIPTION: Cambridge, United Kingdom ; New York, NY : Cambridge University Press, 2020. | Includes index. | Includes bibliographical references and index.
IDENTIFIERS: LCCN 2020015734 (print) | LCCN 2020015735 (ebook) | ISBN 9781108835398 (hardback) | ISBN 9781108793322 (paperback) | ISBN 9781108883870 (ebook)
SUBJECTS: LCSH: Election law – United States. | Presidents – United States – Nomination.
CLASSIFICATION: LCC KF4912 .B47 2021 (print) | LCC KF4912 (ebook) | DDC 324.273/15–dc23
LC record available at https://lccn.loc.gov/2020015734
LC ebook record available at https://lccn.loc.gov/2020015735

ISBN 978-1-108-83539-8 Hardback
ISBN 978-1-108-79332-2 Paperback

In memory of
Dr. Robert Clifton Parker
of Morrisville, Vermont
(1933–2020)

Contents

Contributors

RICHARD BRIFFAULT is the Joseph P. Chamberlain Professor of Legislation at Columbia Law School.

MICHAEL R. DIMINO is Professor of Law at the Widener University Commonwealth Law School.

JAMES A. GARDNER is the Bridget and Thomas Black SUNY Distinguished Professor of Law at the State University of New York at Buffalo.

EDWARD B. FOLEY is the Charles W. Ebersold and Florence Whitcomb Ebersold Professor of Constitutional Law and Director of the Election Law @ Moritz Program at The Ohio State University Moritz College of Law.

ANTHONY J. GAUGHAN is Professor of Law and Kern Family Chair in Law at Drake University Law School.

CHARLOTTE HILL is a Ph.D. candidate at the Goldman School of Public Policy at the University of California, Berkeley.

MICHAEL S. KANG is the William G. and Virginia K. Karnes Research Professor of Law at the Northwestern Pritzker School of Law.

EUGENE D. MAZO is Visiting Associate Professor of Law at Rutgers University.

MICHAEL T. MORLEY is Assistant Professor of Law at the Florida State University College of Law.

DEREK T. MULLER is Professor of Law at the University of Iowa College of Law.

RICHARD H. PILDES is the Sudler Family Professor of Constitutional Law at the New York University School of Law.

ANN M. RAVEL is Lecturer in Law at the University of California, Berkeley, School of Law and a former commissioner of the Federal Election Commission.

BRADLEY A. SMITH is the Josiah H. Blackmore II/Shirley M. Naught Professor of Law at Capital University Law School and a former commissioner of the Federal Election Commission.

CYNTHIA RICHIE TERRELL is the Executive Director of RepresentWomen.

RICHARD WINGER is the founder and editor of *Ballot Access News*.

SEAN J. WRIGHT is an attorney in private practice in Washington, D.C., and formerly worked at the Federal Election Commission's Office of General Counsel and as special counsel to FEC Commissioner Ann M. Ravel.

Introduction

Eugene D. Mazo and Michael R. Dimino

Every four years, citizens of the United States go to the polls to cast their votes for a new president. But the rules of electing a president in November and the rules governing how American political parties *nominate* their candidates for the presidency differ in important respects. In the general election, voters in each state choose electors, who subsequently vote for the president. The candidate who receives the majority of the electors' votes becomes president. Although there have been calls to abolish the Electoral College, Americans have largely relied on the same system since 1804—when the Twelfth Amendment altered important aspects of how the Electoral College works[1]—to decide the outcome of their general presidential election. In contrast to the relatively stable rules governing the general election, the rules by which American political parties nominate their presidential candidates have changed dramatically over the past two hundred years.

The American presidential nomination process has been able to evolve over time in part because it has no constitutional basis. The operation of the presidency and of Congress is controlled in many important respects by the Constitution, which regulates several aspects of how the occupants of each of these institutions are chosen and what qualifications they must have. By contrast, the basic structures of the presidential nomination process have developed largely outside of the confines of the Constitution's original design.[2] This is true of most features of the American presidential nomination process, including its system of primaries and caucuses, the role that political parties play in them, and the national party conventions that follow them. It is also true of the primary

---

[1] U.S. Const, amend. XII; *see also* Edward B. Foley, Presidential Elections and Majority Rule: The Rise, Demise, and Potential Restoration of the Jeffersonian Electoral College 27–42 (2020).

[2] *See* James W. Ceaser, Presidential Selection: Theory and Practice, at ix (1979).

debates that Americans watch, and of the campaigns that the country's presidential candidates wage.[3]

There are many worthy questions about the American presidential nomination process to which scholars do not have very good answers. Does the nomination process strengthen or weaken the country's political parties? Does it foster or impede the selection of presidents who are suitably skilled for the office? Is the presidential nomination process regarded as legitimate by the public? Is it sufficiently democratic? To what extent have the sequenced choices imposed by the presidential primary calendar been influential in determining the contest's final outcome? Would a redesign of the primary system lead to a different result? In the social sciences, institutional theories of politics often predict that political outcomes will result from the institutional settings in which they take place. For institutionally minded scholars, a primary system designed differently would result in a different outcome. There is no question that the institutional structure of the primaries and caucuses determines the outcome of the presidential nomination process in the United States, even if it does so in often unpredictable ways.

***

Part of the unpredictability comes from the fact that the United States maintains a unique presidential nomination system. It is the only democracy in the world that selects its nominees for the country's highest office by popular vote. Major parties in parliamentary democracies, including in the British Commonwealth, Western Europe, and Japan, choose their candidates for prime minister by a secret vote of party members. Though parties in these countries do hold annual conventions composed of delegates chosen by local or affiliated organizations, these conventions typically do not elect the parties' leaders. In other presidential democracies, such as those in Latin America, the presidential candidates of various political parties are also chosen in national delegate conventions, and these conventions resemble their American counterparts, but there is an important difference in that their delegates are elected by the dues-paying members of the parties' local and regional organizations or else given their seats by virtue of the executive or legislative offices they hold. No delegates are chosen through a presidential state primary or caucus in which ordinary voters actually participate.

The system used to work that way in the United States, too. For most of the country's history, a party's presidential nominee was chosen in a process that

[3]   *Id.*

was entirely closed to the public. Ordinary citizens had no say over who became their party's presidential candidate. Instead, this choice was left to party elites. People who had experience in government evaluated a nominee's credentials long before voters did—through a process that resembled a form of peer review. Then, in 1968, the American presidential nomination system was utterly transformed. The Democratic Party instituted new rules, put in place for the Democratic National Convention of 1972, that eliminated many of the backroom deals that had characterized the previous system. By 1976, the Republican Party followed suit and adopted similar rules. These new rules made the views of primary and caucus voters paramount. Over the next four decades, these new rules evolved, until they eventually yielded a presidential candidate—Donald Trump—who did not resemble any previous president in American history. Trump had no previous experience in government or the military and would never have been chosen under the prior system.

Nonetheless, during the 2016 primaries, Trump managed to beat out sixteen rivals on his way to winning the Republican Party's presidential nomination. At the Republican National Convention in Cleveland that year, a majority of the Republican Party's 2,472 delegates rallied around Mr. Trump to nominate him as their standard bearer. On the other side of the aisle, six candidates vied for the Democratic Party's nomination, although only two lasted until the Democratic National Convention in Philadelphia. Hillary Clinton won 34 primaries and caucuses while Bernie Sanders won 23 before a majority of the Democratic Party's 4,763 convention delegates nominated Clinton as their presidential candidate. While voters disagreed sharply on the preference for Trump or Clinton, most agreed that they did not like either candidate very much. Most voters told pollsters that they held unfavorable views of both candidates ahead of the 2016 election, leaving many to wonder how these two people managed to receive their party's nominations in the first place.

As election law scholars, we followed the 2016 election, including the nominations of Hillary Clinton and Donald Trump, very closely. Like the rest of the country, we also followed the field of two dozen candidates who announced in 2019 that they would vie for the Democratic Party's nomination and the chance to challenge Trump in November 2020.[4] While so doing, we came to realize that most American voters understand little about their country's presidential nomination process. For most people, the system used

---

[4] These candidates included Michael Bennet, Joe Biden, Michael Bloomberg, Cory Booker, Steve Bullock, Pete Buttigieg, Julián Castro, John Delaney, Tulsi Gabbard, Kirsten Gillibrand, Kamala Harris, John Hickenlooper, Jay Inslee, Amy Klobuchar, Beto O'Rourke, Bernie Sanders, Deval Patrick, Tom Steyer, Elizabeth Warren, Marianne Williamson, and Andrew Yang, among others.

in the United States to nominate presidential candidates remains rather opaque. Americans know, of course, that their fellow citizens vote in primaries and caucuses, and they also know that Iowa and New Hampshire proceed first in holding these contests. But few citizens can explain why these contests are staggered rather than held on a single day, how these contests result in the selection of convention delegates, or how many delegates are allocated to each state. Few citizens appreciate the patchwork of state laws and party rules that govern this byzantine process. Indeed, because the rules governing this process are so difficult to discern and understand, most Americans also fail to appreciate how significantly these rules have evolved since the country's founding.

***

Though the two major parties have used primaries and caucuses to nominate delegates to their national conventions since 1972, few people have a good grasp of the details concerning how this system works in practice. In 1974, the scholar Austin Ranney, who played a role in designing the modern presidential nomination system, wrote about how "in America, the presidential nominating game is played under by far the most elaborate, variegated, and complex set of rules in the world. They include national party rules, state statutes . . . and a wide variety of rulings by national and state courts."[5] Contemporary scholars have also commented on how little is known about these rules. "Every four years, the Democratic and Republican national parties each promulgate a long and detailed set of rules governing the composition and selection of national convention delegates," explains William G. Mayer, a scholar who has long observed the presidential nomination process. "In general, these rules are carefully studied by a very narrow slice of campaign managers, consultants, political activists, and reporters, while the vast majority of Americans—even those who follow politics rather closely—remain entirely unaware of them."[6]

Interest peaks in the Democratic and Republican nomination contests every four years, especially when the media begins covering these events. This interest increases during the primaries and national conventions and subsides once the national conventions end. Despite this periodic interest, there is little sustained discussion of the mechanics of the process by

---

[5] Austin Ranney, *Changing the Rules of the Nomination Game*, *in* CHOOSING THE PRESIDENT 72 (James David Barber ed., 1974).

[6] William G. Mayer, *Superdelegates: Reforming the Reforms Revisited*, *in* REFORMING THE PRESIDENTIAL NOMINATION PROCESS 85 (Steven S. Smith & Melanie J. Springer eds., 2009).

which the Democrats and Republicans—or, indeed, the country's minor political parties—nominate their presidential candidates. As the journalist Walter Shapiro perceptively explains, "The issue here is not *whom* the parties select, but rather *how* candidates should be chosen."[7] Is there a better, or perhaps fairer, way to nominate presidential candidates? Are there sensible ways to improve this system to make it more transparent and ultimately more democratic as a whole? If so, what are they?

Since the creation of the modern, primary-dominated nomination process, there has been little scholarly or public commentary devoted to large-scale reassessments of this system or consideration of major structural changes that might be made to it. Discrete issues within the nomination system have, of course, received a great deal of attention—such as what the appropriate sequencing of primaries in the states ought to be, or whether open rather than closed primaries ought to be used. But this attention has come mostly from political scientists, and it has focused mostly on issues surrounding party building, campaigning, voting, and the media. By comparison, almost no work on the presidential nomination process has been done by lawyers and legal scholars, who naturally approach this topic with a different set of lenses. There is no book, as far as we know, that explains the law—or the patchwork of laws—that drives presidential nomination in the United States. There is thus a gap in our collective knowledge that needs to be filled.

That's where we come in. We are two scholars of election law from opposite sides of the political spectrum. One of us is a Democrat, while the other is a Republican. Despite this, we happen to be good friends and close colleagues who have long been united in our belief that the American presidential nomination process can be designed to function in a better and simpler way. The process should be designed to function in a way that gives ordinary citizens the opportunity to nominate the candidate from their party for the presidency who is the best man or woman for the job. At the same time, we believe that our presidential nomination process should come with safeguards to ensure that only a person with the relevant qualifications, talent, integrity, and seriousness of purpose ascends to the presidency. It was with these goals in mind that we joined forces and decided to edit this book.

***

A few months after the historic presidential election of 2016, several of the contributors to this book gathered to participate in a discussion group called

---

[7] Walter Shapiro, *The Chosen One: Thoughts on a Better, Fairer, and Smarter Way to Pick Presidential Nominees* 5 (Brennan Ctr. for Justice, 2017) (emphasis in original).

"Reforming the Presidential Nomination Process." Our discussion initially focused on the following two questions: First, how did Hillary Clinton and Donald Trump, two candidates who were received negatively by most voters, manage to win their parties' respective nominations? Second, if we altered state voting rules, the primary calendar, the rules of the national conventions, the campaign finance rules, or the format of the presidential primary debates, might we have had a different outcome? Relatedly, our discussion group also sought to understand how well or poorly most Americans grasped the process by which our political parties select their presidential nominees. For example, do voters know who sets the rules of the presidential primary debates? Do they understand the mechanics of how the caucuses work? And do they know why our primaries are staggered over the course of many months rather than held on a single day? After probing these issues in depth, we turned to discussing two final issues: First, as election law scholars, do we have anything novel or unique to say about the American presidential nomination process? Second, if so, then how would we design this process to ensure that only the very best candidates get nominated for the presidency? Our discussion group met in Boca Raton, Florida, as part of the 2017 annual meeting of the Southeastern Association of Law Schools (SEALS). By the end of the day, we decided that a book should result from the fruits of our long discussion.

Each of our conference participants was asked to write about a different legal aspect of the nomination process and to suggest avenues for how it might be improved. From our discussion, which the two editors of this book organized, a set of long scholarly papers emerged. These papers discussed various aspects of the presidential nomination process that are not often covered by the news media and of which most citizens may not be aware.

Here are some examples of what our contributors submitted:

- A WOMAN AS PRESIDENT. Hillary Clinton wasn't the first woman to run for president. Since 1940, a full 40 women have been nominated by their parties for the highest office in the land. Ten of these women attracted more than 40,000 votes in the general presidential election. Female contenders have been similarly active in presidential primaries. Since 1964, ten women have campaigned in a major party primary or caucus. Despite this long history of women aspiring to the presidency, 2016 marked the first time that a woman participated in a general election presidential debate. What are the obstacles facing women candidates? How can we encourage more women to run?
- PRESIDENTIAL PUBLIC FUNDING. In 2020, Joe Biden ran for president for the third time. During his previous runs, in 1998 and 2008, he collected

public funding. In 2020, however, Biden was not using public funds. And he was not alone. Every single one of the two dozen Democratic candidates in 2020 was financed entirely by private contributions. How does a candidate running in the primaries qualify to receive public funding, and why do candidates today forgo this money in favor of private funds? What are Biden and the others thinking, and how can public funding be made attractive to candidates once more? Indeed, would it be a good idea to make it so?

- SUPER PACs. The non-use of public funding is not the only thing that has changed about the presidential nomination process. The deregulation of campaign finance law has upended the nature of private funding as well. Whereas candidates once relied on contributions from individuals and corporate and union PACs, today new kinds of political actors have entered the playing field whose spending cannot be capped. They include Super PACs, 501(c)(4), and 527 organizations. How has the deregulation of campaign funding changed the presidential nomination process? What can the law do about it?
- THE PRESIDENTIAL DEBATES. The Commission on Presidential Debates, a private, non-profit organization, sets the rules of the presidential debates and decides which candidates to invite, all on its own. Research shows that the exclusion of certain candidates has the effect of limiting the range of policy issues offered to American voters. Recently, the Federal Election Commission passed regulations to ensure that the debates are run more fairly, even though government oversight of the debates has traditionally been minimal. How are the debates regulated, and by whom? How should they be regulated?
- BINDING DELEGATES AT THE NATIONAL CONVENTIONS. Delegates elected to vote for one party candidate at the national conventions sometimes wind up casting a vote for another. This happens with presidential electors, too. In 2016, four Democratic electors from the state of Washington cast votes for president for Colin Powell and for Faith Spotted Eagle, rather than for Hillary Clinton. And rather than vote for Tim Kaine for vice president, they voted for Elizabeth Warren, Maria Cantwell, Susan Collins, and Winona LaDuke. The national media rarely reports on these faithless delegates and faithless electors, but scholars certainly study them. What should the law do about this?
- FRONT-LOADING. Iowa and New Hampshire have state statutes that grant their state officials discretion to move up the date of the their caucus and primary contests if any other state tries to hold an earlier contest. As a result, Iowa always holds the nation's first caucus, and New

Hampshire usually holds the nation's first primary. The national parties have tried to penalize these two states by refusing to seat their national convention delegates, a punishment Iowa and New Hampshire readily accept because the media attention showered on these states is more important to them than the small number of delegates they send to each party's national convention. Constitutionally, is there anything Congress can do to bring Iowa and New Hampshire in line?

Other contributors wrote chapters on how ranked-choice voting can be used for presidential primaries, what the impact of technology has been on the primary process, and related topics. In many cases, these chapters are written from a legal standpoint, and most of them uniquely try to engage with the law —state and federal, statutory and case law—that influences the presidential nomination process. Ultimately, each chapter provides recommendations for how that law might be changed or improved.

***

This book's importance springs from its historical moment. Presidential nomination reform is currently on the national agenda, and scholars and citizens alike are voicing their opinions about the process. Opinion polls show that most Americans overwhelmingly support efforts to reform their presidential nomination process, even though many of them do not know how to bring such reforms about.[8] The mechanics of the process are so complex that even most candidates do not fully understand them, and thus they resort to hiring expensive lawyers to help them navigate this labyrinth. Our goal for this book was to gather leading election law scholars from across the political spectrum to explain the myriad laws and rules that comprise this process.

We wish to thank all those who came to Florida to participate in our discussion, including several election law scholars who helped frame our thoughts but who did not contribute a chapter to our book: Joshua Douglas, Jacob Eisler, Atiba Ellis, and Ciara Torres-Spelliscy. We also thank those scholars who did not attend our gathering in Florida but nonetheless agreed to contribute a chapter after learning of our project. We thank our respective deans and associate deans for their support: Ronald Chen, Reid Weisbord,

---

[8] In 2016, there was profound disaffection with America's nomination system. Widespread accusations of unfairness accompanied the nomination fights of both major parties. The problems touched many aspects of the nomination process, including the sequencing of primaries, the oversight of the candidate debates, and, of course, the lackluster popular support that voters exhibited for Trump and Clinton, the two candidates who ultimately wound up winning each party's nomination.

David Lopez, and Rose Cuison Villazor at Rutgers, and Christian Johnson, Michael Hussey, and Juliet Moringiello at Widener. We are profoundly grateful to Richard Briffault, a senior scholar in our field, for offering us an abundance of behind-the-scenes wisdom and advice, as well as for generously agreeing to write two chapters for the book. We thank the NYU Law Review for granting us permission to republish portions of an article by Stephen Gardbaum and Richard Pildes, *Populism and Institutional Design: Methods of Selecting Candidates for Chief Executive*, 93 N.Y.U. L. REV. 647 (2018). Finally, we are extraordinarily grateful to Matt Gallaway, our talented editor, his colleagues Laura Blake and Cameron Daddis, our copy editor Helen Kitto and production manager Gayathri Tamilselvan, and three anonymous reviewers for championing this book. Each of these individuals shared our conviction that a bipartisan group of election law scholars might have something unique to say about the American presidential nomination process—and that fostering a deeper understanding of this process could help revitalize American democracy.

1

Presidential Selection: Historical, Institutional, and Democratic Perspectives

James A. Gardner[*]

It has been nearly two centuries since an American presidential election has evoked a crisis of confidence like that following the election of 2016. Not since the election of Andrew Jackson in 1828 has there been such a public display of anxiety concerning the methods by which we choose our chief executive. As in the contest of 1828 pitting the Democrat Jackson against his Federalist opponent John Quincy Adams, the presidential nominating process of 2016 produced a contest between a celebrity populist, widely seen as unqualified by experience or temperament, and a highly experienced and competent but deeply uninspiring political insider who had been anointed by establishment elites.

This anxiety ran deep in 2016: for the first time in the quarter-century during which such statistics have been recorded, neither major party candidate was viewed favorably by even half the electorate.[1] The emerging verdict appears to be that our system for selecting presidential candidates failed catastrophically in 2016, an impression many regard as confirmed by the damage subsequently inflicted on the office of the presidency and on our democratic institutions by the winner, Donald Trump. In offering a wide variety of suggestions about how to improve the nominating process, the contributors to this volume endorse the proposition that our presidential selection procedures now operate poorly and are in need of repair, if not wholesale rethinking.

Meaningful criticism of the current process requires, however, that existing procedures be judged against some baseline of what constitutes a good candidate selection process, yielding good candidates who, one presumes,

[*] James A. Gardner is Bridget and Thomas Black SUNY Distinguished Professor at the University at Buffalo Law School, State University of New York. He thanks Matt Steilen, Rick Su, Guyora Binder, and David McNamee for useful comments on a prior draft.

[1] William G. Mayer, *Was the Process to Blame? Why Hillary Clinton and Donald Trump Won Their Parties' Presidential Nominations*, 93 N.Y.U. L. REV. 759 (2018).

subsequently go on to become good presidents. If the current system works poorly, in other words, how *should* a good system of presidential nomination work? What kind of candidates should it produce, and how ought it to be structured so as to produce them? What kinds of improvements are needed, and how, if at all, can we obtain them? To address these questions, this chapter draws on three potential sources of guidance—history, institutional analysis, and democratic theory—and yields four broad conclusions.

First, an examination of the evolution of presidential nominating procedures since the founding reveals a steady historical trend of convergence in the identities of two critically important groups: the *selectorate*—the group authorized to choose officially recognized nominees[2]—and the *electorate*—the group that chooses the ultimate officeholder from among the nominees. Second, this convergence is significant because the design of nominating procedures has important consequences for the kinds of candidates likely to emerge as nominees. Third, although democratic theory can help a polity clarify the values it wishes its democratic institutions to promote, a turn to democratic theory does not relieve a polity of the antecedent need to make hard choices about its goals and commitments, which must come before it makes its hard choices about institutional design. Finally, although law is useful and important in structuring a presidential nominating process, citizen ethos—the collective internalization of consensual democratic norms—may well be the single most important factor necessary to the consistent production of high-quality presidential candidates.

I. EXPANSION OF THE PRESIDENTIAL SELECTORATE

A. *The Founding Era (1788–1799)*

How to choose a president proved to be the most difficult issue the Philadelphia Convention addressed. After several false starts and lengthy debate, the Founders finally settled on a system that soon pleased no one— the Electoral College. Conceived as an intermediate body of wise and virtuous men who would stand between the people and the presidency, the members of the Electoral College were meant to exercise a kind of Burkean trusteeship in which they would base their selection of a president on "the information and discernment requisite to such complicated investigations"[3]—that is, on their

---

2   *See, e.g.*, Reuven Y. Hazan & Gideon Rahat, Democracy within Parties: Candidate Selection Methods and Their Political Consequences 33–54 (2010).
3   The Federalist, No. 68 (Hamilton).

own sound, informed, and independent judgment. In so doing, the Electoral College would protect the people against their own human weakness and potentially poor judgment by assuring that excessively ambitious men, skilled in "low intrigue, and the little arts of popularity,"[4] would never attain the nation's highest office.

Interestingly, the Founders did not give much thought to the question of how qualified candidates for the presidency would come to the attention of the Electoral College. They did not provide for any system of nomination, nor did they grant the Electoral College any official authority to create one in the event that such a system should prove desirable. Instead, they seemed to assume that the nation's leading candidates for the presidency would simply be known, either personally or by reputation,[5] to the members of the Electoral College — a reasonable assumption, perhaps, in a world in which the ruling elite in any state might have numbered in the dozens, or at most, in the hundreds.[6]

In this system, where nominations for the presidency were to be self-generated by the same body authorized to elect the president, the selectorate was precisely co-extensive with the electorate. Such an arrangement, the Framers believed, would be most conducive to the election of presidents with the desired characteristics, namely, "preeminen[ce] for ability and virtue."[7] Certainly, the Founders would never have contemplated assigning the nominating function to political parties, an institution they considered detestably self-interested and factional, and indeed hoped would never appear on the American political landscape.[8]

B. *The First Party System (1800–1824)*

In less than two decades, of course, parties did appear on the scene, and they were quickly integrated into the presidential selection process. Parties of the Jeffersonian era were not like their modern counterparts; they did not conceive of themselves as representing a subset of the populace whose goal was to offer

---

[4] *Id.*

[5] James W. Ceaser, Presidential Selection: Theory and Development 66, 83 (1979).

[6] For example, due to property qualifications, the number of people eligible to serve as governor of South Carolina under its 1778 constitution was probably twenty-five or fewer. James A. Gardner, *Southern Character, Confederate Nationalism, and the Interpretation of State Constitutions: A Case Study in Constitutional Argument*, 76 Tex. L. Rev. 1219, 1273 n.275 (1998).

[7] The Federalist, No. 68 (Hamilton).

[8] Richard Hofstadter, The Idea of a Party System: The Rise of Legitimate Opposition in the United States, 1780–1840, at 9 (1970).

to the electorate a political vision or set of programmatic alternatives in a fair and equal competition for voter approval. Instead, parties of this era conceived of themselves as parties "of the whole people, not of any part or of any minority."[9] The Jeffersonian Democratic-Republicans, in particular, thought of themselves as embodying the original, animating spirit of the revolutionary nation, a spirit that they believed required restoration following what they viewed as the subversion of the established constitutional order by the Federalists during the administration of John Adams. Self-organization into parties, for the Jeffersonians, was an unpleasant but temporary expedient that could be abandoned following successful restoration of the true revolutionary order.[10]

To accomplish this task, the Jeffersonians deliberately exploited weaknesses in the design of the Electoral College to transform it into a vehicle of partisan mobilization. Their plan had two parts. First, they pre-selected their presidential candidate on partisan grounds, and through ground-level political activity promoted as candidates for the Electoral College individuals already committed to the party's candidate, an action that transformed members of the Electoral College into "instructed agents, not deliberative trustees."[11] Second, they de facto replaced the Electoral College as the instrument of candidate nomination with a newly devised, shadow organization, the congressional caucus. These caucuses consisted of informal meetings of members of Congress who shared party membership; at these caucuses, participants reached consensus on the identity of the party's candidate for the presidency.[12] The caucus choice went on to win the presidency in every election from 1800 to 1816.[13]

As a functional matter, the caucus system thus substituted the congressional caucus for the Electoral College as the nominating selectorate. As a result of this change, "[t]he ideological orthodoxy of the candidates ... became a decisive criterion for selection, while competence, virtue, and

---

[9] ALFRED DE GRAZIA, PUBLIC AND REPUBLIC 114 (reprint ed. 1985) (orig. ed. 1951).
[10] CEASER. *supra* note 5, at 91; GERALD LEONARD, THE INVENTION OF PARTY POLITICS 22–25 (2002).
[11] CEASER, *supra* note 5, at 88.
[12] Emmett H. Buell, Jr., *Presidential Nominations of the Pre-Convention Era, in* ENDURING CONTROVERSIES IN PRESIDENTIAL NOMINATING POLITICS 35–38 (Emmett H. Buell, Jr. & William G. Mayer eds., 2004); William G. Morgan, *The Origin and Development of the Congressional Caucus, in* ENDURING CONTROVERSIES, *supra,* at 60.
[13] Stephen Gardbaum & Richard H. Pildes, *Populism and Institutional Design: Methods of Selecting Candidates for Chief Executive,* 93 N.Y.U. L. REV. 647, 653 (2018).

service to the state—the Founders' intended criteria—receded into the background."[14]

C. *The Second Party System (1828–1912)*

The emergence of the Democratic party and the successful election of its 1828 candidate for president, Andrew Jackson, permanently and dramatically changed the American system of presidential selection in two important ways. First, under the ideological leadership of Martin Van Buren, Jacksonian Democrats developed for the first time a justification for a system of permanent party competition. Such a system, they contended, would institutionalize popular sovereignty by ensuring, first, that the people would always have a ready alternative to the government in power; and second, that they could hold incumbents accountable by voting them out and voting into power the opposition party. Second, Jacksonian Democrats advanced a very different conception of the presidency: the president, they claimed, was the only official in the United States who represented, and was accountable to, the entirety of the populace. To ensure presidential responsiveness to the appropriate constituency, the process of selecting presidential candidates had to be committed to a "mass" party of nationwide scale[15] whose members possessed a strong voice in the nominating process.

Jacksonian Democrats made good on these commitments by transferring the power to nominate from the congressional caucus to a national party convention.[16] In this system, each party nominated its candidate at a national convention whose members were party delegates chosen principally by state and local party organizations to represent their membership. During the nineteenth century, and well into the twentieth, the actual selection of convention delegates was typically made directly by state and local party leaders, who consequently exercised a great deal of control over the course of the convention and the ultimate nomination.[17] The selectorate, in this system, thus comprised convention delegates hand-picked by local party bosses.

---

[14] CEASER, *supra* note 5, at 96.
[15] JOHN ALDRICH, WHY PARTIES?: THE ORIGIN AND TRANSFORMATION OF POLITICAL PARTIES IN AMERICA 97–98 (1995).
[16] Emmett H. Buell, Jr., *The National Nominating Convention*, *in* ENDURING CONTROVERSIES, *supra* note 12, at 79.
[17] Gardbaum & Pildes, *supra* note 13, at 654.

D. *The Progressive Era (1912–1972)*

The Progressive movement arose in the 1880s, reaching the height of its influence in the early twentieth century. In their political views, Progressives echoed the founding-era distaste for political parties, but on different grounds: they viewed parties as captives of local machine bosses and corrupted by corporate interests for the benefit of the wealthy. As a result, on the Progressive view, parties had collaborated in bending government policies away from their true purpose—service to the common good—and toward a clientelistic system of local plunder of public assets. At the same time, Progressives saw the presidency as requiring enormous power in the modern world, and indeed as the one organ of government most capable of operating effectively in a dangerous world that often required swift and energetic national action, and in a manner genuinely responsive to mass public opinion.

Progressives implemented these views by leading a successful movement to require parties to nominate candidates through the use of direct primary elections. First introduced in 1899, when the Minnesota legislature enacted direct primaries for Minneapolis local elections,[18] the use of primary elections spread quickly: by 1916 over half the states utilized some form of primary, and by 1958 primary elections were nearly universally available,[19] though not always mandatory.

The movement toward primary elections continued a trend of expanding the nominating selectorate. From the members of the Electoral College, to the members of a congressional caucus, to delegates to a nationwide party convention, the presidential selectorate now increasingly included the rank and file membership of national political parties.

E. *Consolidation of the Mass Selectorate: The 1970s Reforms and Beyond*

By the mid-twentieth century, although most states offered the option of nomination by direct primary, parties were not necessarily required to select convention delegates according to the results of primary elections. Instead, the route to a party's presidential nomination typically lay through a mixed system in which candidates still had to seek privately the personal support of party

---

[18] Robert G. Boatwright, Congressional Primary Elections 27 (2014). There is some disagreement about where and when the first primary was introduced. Masket, for example, places it in Wisconsin in 1904. Seth Masket, The Inevitable Party: Why Attempts to Kill the Party System Fail and How They Weaken Democracy 127 (2016).

[19] Boatwright, *supra* note 18, at 27.

leaders, but could sometimes help their case by demonstrating their ability to win votes in advisory primary elections.[20]

This system was replaced, almost at a stroke, following the divisive 1968 Democratic convention in Chicago. There, while anti-Vietnam War protests were violently suppressed by the local political boss, Chicago Mayor Richard Daley, the convention proceeded to nominate the establishment, pro-war candidate, Vice President Hubert Humphrey, passing over a highly popular, anti-war candidate, Senator Eugene McCarthy. In response to the subsequent outcry from many quarters within the party—and the party's crushing defeat at the hands of Richard Nixon—the Democratic Party created the McGovern-Fraser Commission to recommend changes to the party's presidential selection procedure for the 1972 election. The Commission's principal charge was to recommend ways to improve representation at the convention of previously excluded groups, including women, minorities, and young people.[21]

The Commission responded with recommendations to open up the process by decreasing the proportion of convention delegates chosen directly by party leaders, requiring transparency in the selection of delegates, and imposing quotas that would increase the diversity of convention delegations. The Party adopted these recommendations, leaving the mode of compliance to state party organizations. In an unforeseen development, state parties—joined in many cases by state legislatures through the exercise of their Article II power to direct the manner of appointment of presidential electors—complied by moving to an almost entirely plebiscitary system of delegate selection through direct primary elections.[22] The Republican Party soon followed suit, in many cases under compulsion of state legislation. The changes were dramatic; as Gardbaum and Pildes explain, "[i]In 1968, the primaries had bound 36% of the delegates to each convention; just four years later, the primaries bound 58% of the Democratic delegates and 41% of the Republican ones, and by 1976, two-thirds of the Democrat delegates and more than half the Republican ones were bound."[23] Thus, by the late-twentieth century, the presidential selectorate had come to comprise essentially the entirety of the national parties' rank and file membership.[24]

---

[20] Gardbaum & Pildes, *supra* note 13, at 655–56.

[21] CEASER, *supra* note 5, at 277–84.

[22] Gardbaum & Pildes, *supra* note 13, at 659.

[23] *Id.*

[24] Political scientists disagree over the extent to which the move to direct primaries gave control over nominations to the party rank and file. According to one view, party elites continue to exercise a great degree of de facto control over the identity of nominees. *See, e.g.,* Hans J. G. Hassell, *Party Control of Party Primaries: Party Influence in Nominations for the U.S. Senate,* 78 J. POL. 75 (2015). Others, however, argue that the inclusiveness of nominating

Even this, however, did not represent the conclusion of the trend of expansion of the selectorate. In subsequent decades, some states began to experiment with opening up their primary elections *beyond* party rank and file. In a "semi-closed" primary, used by some parties for at least some offices in more than a dozen states, independent voters—those who have chosen not to affiliate formally with any party—may nevertheless vote in primary elections. In such a primary, the selectorate thus consists of the party rank and file *plus* any independent voters who choose to participate. In an "open" primary, used by some parties for some offices in more than twenty states, voters may vote in any party's primary, even if they have registered as members of a different party. In these primaries, the selectorate is expanded to include not only the party's rank and file, but also members of opposing parties. And in a "nonpartisan" primary, used in California, Washington, and Louisiana, all voters, regardless of prior registration, may vote for any candidate of any party. The two candidates with the most votes then run against each other in the general election, regardless of their partisan affiliation. In this kind of primary, the selectorate consists in principle of the entire electorate.[25]

Moreover, in response to dissatisfaction within the Democratic party over the 2016 nomination process, especially from supporters of Senator Bernie Sanders, the chief competitor to Hillary Clinton, the national Democratic Party recently announced it will consider further empowering the rank and file by reducing the role of "superdelegates" at the national convention. These

---

processes has contributed to the creation of a candidate-centered politics in which alliances of candidates and their supporters effectively control the nominating process. *See, e.g.,* HAZAN & RAHAT, *supra* note 2, at 148, 151. Some go even further, and argue that the polarity of party influence has reversed itself: instead of parties dictating the commitments of their nominees, it is candidates who now set the agenda to which their parties must then conform. *See, e.g.,* Richard S. Katz, *The Problem of Candidate Selection and Models of Party Democracy,* 7 PARTY POL. 277, 278 (2001); Austin Ranney, *Candidate Selection, in* DEMOCRACY AT THE POLLS: A COMPARATIVE STUDY OF COMPETITIVE NATIONAL ELECTIONS 103 (David Butler et al. eds. 1981); Gerald C. Wright, *Rules and the Ideological Character of Primary Electorates, in* REFORMING THE PRESIDENTIAL NOMINATION PROCESS 24 (Steven S. Smith & Melanie J. Springer eds., 2009).

[25] Another kind of primary, the so-called "blanket" primary, was invalidated by the Supreme Court in *California Democratic Party v. Jones,* 530 U.S. 567 (2000). In a blanket primary, every voter may vote in the primary election for any candidate of any party. The candidate of each party with the most votes is declared that party's nominee for purposes of the general election. The difference between a blanket and non-partisan primary is that in a blanket primary, each party is forced to include in its selectorate all other voters, a feature that the Court viewed as an unconstitutional interference with the right of party members to choose with whom to associate. In a non-partisan primary, in contrast, parties are stripped of the right to nominate candidates onto the general election ballot, so no party, in the Court's view, is forced to associate with anyone against its will in choosing a nominee.

delegates, who comprised about 15 percent of convention delegates in 2016, consist of party leaders and insiders whose presence at the convention had been thought to provide some ballast in the form of expertise and political experience.

In the march from semi-closed, to open, to non-partisan primary elections, the selectorate progressively becomes broader and broader to the point that it begins to converge with the electorate. History is thus in a sense circling back upon itself. During the founding era, the electorate and selectorate coincided, but both were extremely narrow in scope; in today's system, the electorate and selectorate also coincide, or nearly so, but both are broad-based, with the selectorate seemingly on a path soon to converge fully with the electorate. In the founding era version, nomination and election were the province of elites and party insiders, and non-elites and rank-and-file party members were excluded. Under today's system, nomination and election are the almost exclusive province of the mass electorate, and it is experienced, senior members of the party who lack a formal voice in the nominating process—a development that has been called, tellingly, the decline of "peer review."[26]

II. INSTITUTIONAL EFFECTS: THE CONSEQUENCES OF NOMINATING PROCEDURES

The United States is today a polity of more than 300 million, spread over thousands of miles of territory and, for purposes of presidential election, divided by law into 51 separate political communities. Because such an entity is incapable of spontaneously generating plausible candidates for national political office, some procedure for nominating candidates is therefore required. By *nominating procedure*, I mean simply mechanisms, established by law or by rules adopted by an officially recognized nominating entity, such as a political party, that distinguish candidates authorized to stand for office from those who are not. Moreover, because we want our presidents to be good ones, any procedure for generating presidential candidates should select them for the qualities we most wish our presidents to possess. The issue to which I now turn is the effect of nominating procedures on the characteristics possessed by candidates who successfully clear the hurdle of obtaining a nomination.

Variations in nominating procedures can in principle exert a triple screening effect on candidate characteristics. First, simply by establishing procedural

---

[26] The term dates at least to the 1980s. *See* Elaine C. Kamarck, *Returning Peer Review to the American Presidential Nomination Process*, 93 N.Y.U. L. Rev. 709 (2018).

requirements to obtain nomination, they can influence at the outset who might be tempted even to attempt a presidential run. Second, by manipulating the identity of the selectorate, nominating procedures tend to prescreen for the kinds of individuals who are most capable of making a successful appeal to the body doing the nominating. Third, by establishing the criteria that define the selectorate, and that distinguish one selectorate from another, nominating procedures can influence the substantive grounds along which the eventual candidates differentiate themselves.

A. *Self-Screening Effects*

Perhaps the most immediate impact of nominating procedures is their power to induce self-screening among potential candidates. The mere establishment of any set of nominating procedures will tend to attract candidates who are — or at least who think they are — more likely to succeed under the established procedures, and to deter those who are less likely to prosper under whatever procedures happen to prevail. For example, something as basic as a long primary season will tend to attract candidates who possess the physical robustness and mental and emotional stamina to traverse the entire process — characteristics in our day often spoken of, sometimes approvingly and sometimes not, as "fire in the belly." Potential candidates, even those well-qualified for the presidency on other grounds, are conversely likely to be deterred from attempting to run in a process that they suspect they will be either unlikely or unwilling to complete. Similarly, a nominating procedure that is expensive will tend to deter candidates who either do not possess or are unwilling to invest, substantial personal resources; or who are not well-positioned, either for lack of connections, pre-nomination public support, or native fund-raising ability, to raise the money necessary to make a presidential run.

B. *The Nature of Appeals to the Selectorate*

Selectorates may be defined in many different ways, for many different reasons, but one inevitable effect of defining a selectorate is to establish the characteristics of the group to which potential presidential candidates must appeal in order to secure nomination.[27] As a result, nominating procedures will tend to screen in candidates who possess personal characteristics that allow them to appeal successfully to the relevant selectorate, and to screen out those who lack the characteristics or ability to make such appeals.

---

[27] See Ceaser, *supra* note 5, at 18, 233; *see also id.* at 55, 62, 119.

This can have potentially significant consequences for the qualities possessed by candidates, because different qualities may be necessary to appeal
successfully to different selectorates, depending on their composition. For
example, if the selectorate is a congressional caucus, then the successful
candidate must be able to appeal to sitting members of Congress, an elite
group that is unusually well-informed about the qualities necessary for presidential success. Different characteristics and abilities, on the other hand,
may be necessary to appeal successfully to a selectorate consisting of the entire
party membership, the party activist base, local party bosses, rich donors, or
other groups. Indeed, a common complaint about the current process of party
nominations is that different qualities are necessary to appeal successfully to
the party rank and file when seeking the nomination than are required to
appeal to the electorate as a whole when running for the actual office.[28]

C. *Substantive Grounds of Nomination and Election*

Finally, and perhaps most importantly, nominating procedures establish the
cleavages along which the choice of nominees will be made, thus influencing
the issues that will be salient not only in the eventual choice of nominees, but in
the general election. The mechanism—unintended but inevitable—works like
this. The establishment of nominating procedures includes defining the selectorate. If the system divides the polity into multiple selectorates, each of which is
authorized to put forward nominees—if, that is, the bodies that do the nominating comprise some subset of the body that does the electing—then some criterion
will necessarily define the various selectorates, distinguishing them from one
another. The criteria that distinguish one selectorate from another in turn will
then influence (though they need not fully determine) the criteria by which
competing selectorates choose their nominees. And this in turn will influence the
qualities that distinguish the nominees from one another in the general election,
thereby influencing the grounds on which they are chosen by the electorate.

   This phenomenon may be easiest to see by analogy to a more familiar one:
dividing the electorate into legislative districts.[29] Tip O'Neill, Speaker of the

---

[28]   Richard Nixon reportedly offered the following advice to Bob Dole, the 1996 Republican
       candidate for President: "you have to run as far as you can to the right [during the primaries]
       because that's where 40% of the people who decide the nomination are. And to get elected you
       have to run as fast as you can back to the middle, because only about 4% of the nation's voters
       are on the extreme right wing." Jack Nelson, *Letters from Nixon Shape Dole's Campaign
       Strategy*, L.A. TIMES, May 7, 1995.
[29]   Here I draw on an argument made in James A. Gardner, *How to Do Things with Boundaries:
       Redistricting and the Construction of Politics*, 11 ELECTION L.J. 399 (2012).

U.S. House of Representatives from 1977 to 1987, famously quipped that "all politics is local."[30] O'Neill was accurate, but as political theorist Andrew Rehfeld subsequently observed, all politics is local only because we draw legislative districts territorially. If we drew districts based on occupation, Rehfeld argued, then "all politics would be 'vocational.'"[31] The important point is that in a contestatory political system, the contest often, even usually, will be won or lost along the cleavages that define the sorting of voters,[32] and the identity of those issue cleavages can be managed—or manipulated—in the process of drawing the districts.

The same holds for the process by which we divide the nationwide presidential electorate into competing selectorates, which might usefully be conceived as a kind of electoral "districting." If, for example, we defined selectorates by gender, with men entitled to nominate one candidate and women another, issues related to gender would be much more likely than under the present system regularly to rise to prominence in the nomination process. If selectorates were designated by race, ethnicity, or language, then those issues would likely be highly salient in the nominating and electoral phases. If the selectorates corresponded to income groupings— say, for example, the rich got to nominate one candidate, the middle class another, and so on—then issues of economic class would likely predominate in the selection of nominees. The point, again, is that the criteria used to define the selectorates will influence the cleavages that divide the candidates at the nomination phase, and thus the nature of the issues that confront the electorate in the general election. Thus, how we nominate influences not just the personal characteristics of the candidates, but the grounds on which they are likely to compete first for nomination, and then for election.

As it happens, we have for more than two hundred years assigned the job of producing nominations to national political parties, organizations that generally tend to distinguish themselves—at least in theory—along a spectrum of political ideology. By defining the selectorate in ideological terms, our system thus tends to produce—and, one presumes, is intended to produce—nominees who are distinguished from one another mainly on the basis of their ideological and programmatic commitments, thus presenting the electorate with a choice lying

---

[30] THOMAS P. O'NEILL, ALL POLITICS IS LOCAL AND OTHER RULES OF THE GAME (1993).

[31] ANDREW REHFELD, THE CONCEPT OF CONSTITUENCY: POLITICAL REPRESENTATION, DEMOCRATIC LEGITIMACY, AND INSTITUTIONAL DESIGN 8 (2005).

[32] Thomas W. Pogge, *Self-Constituting Constituencies to Enhance Freedom, Equality, and Participation in Democratic Procedures*, 49 THEORIA 26, 49 (2002); LANI GUINIER, THE TYRANNY OF THE MAJORITY 101 (1994).

along that axis. Although from many perspectives it may be desirable to design a system that tends to force voters into choosing among candidates on ideological grounds, ideology is not the only criterion salient to presidential success. Section D below takes up the question of whether it is possible to define selectorates so as to generate candidates who distinguish themselves along other salient dimensions.

D. *Congruence of Selectorate and Electorate*

As discussed earlier, a strong historical trend in the evolution of presidential nominating procedures has produced a growing convergence between presidential selectorates and the presidential electorate, with the former slowly expanding toward the boundaries of the latter. In light of the analysis set out above, what is the likely effect of such convergence on the grounds upon which selectorates nominate and electorates subsequently elect?

When the selectorate and the electorate are congruent, the potential benefits of deliberate institutional design are nullified: the system fails to nudge the choice of candidates into any particular orientation, so the choice of nominees is no longer channeled along any particular set of criteria or along any cleavage upon which the electorate might reasonably be thought—or hoped—to divide. As a result, nominations can much more easily be made upon any ground, whether or not relevant to the qualities presidential nominees ought to possess. Control over the criteria of nomination—that is to say, the advantage associated with the power to set the agenda—is thus abandoned by the polity and in a sense delegated to the discretion of individual actors within the system.

Consider, for example, a small committee or board the rules of which permit nominations for officers to be made by any member, without restriction. In those circumstances, the grounds for nomination will be determined entirely by the discretion of individual members. Board members might nominate on the basis of competence or experience, but they might just as easily nominate on the basis of family ties, personal friendship, hope of personal gain, race, gender, or religion. Any constraints on the grounds of nomination, if they exist at all, will be supplied by informal norms of the group, and the constraining effect of those norms will depend entirely on the willingness of members to observe them.[33]

---

[33] Hazan and Rahat argue that the inclusiveness of American parties' procedures for selecting legislative candidates is responsible for reducing party discipline within legislatures. Reuven

It is worth recalling here that the Framers designed the Electoral College, in which the selectorate and electorate coincided, for the express purpose of *impeding* nomination on the basis of partisan ideology. Such a system, they hoped, would promote selection on the basis of national reputation, a reputation they felt could be earned only by individuals of great virtue and ability and little personal ambition, on the model of a Patriot King, Cincinnatus, or George Washington.[34] But that reputation, they clearly believed, would be based on personal, non-partisan, non-ideological characteristics of the candidates. The Electoral College might have worked that way had the informal norms of the group remained stable. Those norms, however, changed radically when the Jeffersonians captured the process for electing members of the Electoral College and converted it into a system highly responsive to partisan considerations.

Moreover, even if the Framers were correct that congruence between the selectorate and electorate is likely to produce nominees with national reputations, the modern selectorate is very different from the Founding-era Electoral College, and changes in technology and political and social norms have drastically altered what it means to have a "national reputation," as well as the grounds upon which such a reputation can be made and the kinds of people who are capable of developing such a reputation. "Celebrity," in all its modern forms, simply did not exist in that era. In any case, both history and institutional logic demonstrate that congruence of the selectorate and the electorate creates institutional conditions in which the grounds of nomination are neither pressured by design incentives to lie along any particular axis of choice nor easily controlled by post-design regulatory measures.

E. *The Need for Intentional Design*

The foregoing historical and institutional analyses demonstrate, if nothing else, that a presidential nominating system might be built in many ways, and that details of design can exert some degree of influence—perhaps a considerable influence—on the criteria by which nominations are made, the qualities and characteristics of the nominees and ultimate officeholders, and even the grounds upon which the presidency is contested. There is thus no "natural" or even "best" way to structure a presidential nominating

---

Y. Hazan & Gideon Rahat, *Candidate Selection: Methods and Consequences, in* HANDBOOK OF PARTY POLITICS 116–17 (Richard S. Katz & William Crotty eds., 2006).

[34] *See* Henry St. John Bolingbroke, *The Idea of a Patriot King* (1738); RALPH KETCHUM, PRESIDENTS ABOVE PARTY: THE FIRST AMERICAN PRESIDENCY, 1789–1829, at 89 (1984).

procedure. On the contrary, the way such a system operates is highly contingent on its design, and it is therefore essential that a polity designing such a system for itself makes a clear and deliberate choice about the qualities it wants its candidates to possess, and then to build a nominating system adapted as well as possible to generating nominations of persons with those qualities.

But if, at the end of the day, we must make these kinds of hard choices, how should we do so? On what basis? Because nomination is an element of what has become a largely democratic process, one place to turn for assistance in making, or at least narrowing, the field of choices is democratic theory.

III. DEMOCRATIC THEORY AND PRESIDENTIAL CHARACTERISTICS

Over time, as we have seen, the process of presidential selection has become increasingly democratic, even plebiscitary. Since the founding, popular participation has increased dramatically during both the nomination phase, following the turn to direct primary elections, and during the election phase, following the conversion of the Electoral College into an institution that passes through, as far as its structure will allow, nationwide popular sentiment as expressed at the polls. To the extent that the process of presidential selection is democratic, then, democratic theory might offer some guidance about how best to structure it.

The guidance it offers, however, is limited. First, there are many competing theories of democracy, and each theory emphasizes different values and aspects of democratic practice. Consequently, democratic theory cannot definitively settle questions about democratic structure and practice, although it can help clarify the values among which polities must choose when designing democratic institutions. Second, most theories of democracy now in circulation do not readily generate concrete prescriptions for operationalizing their own commitments, so it is difficult to take guidance from them in designing appropriate implementing institutions. Third, even when democratic theories generate adequately specific prescriptions, those prescriptions often suffer from serious problems of infeasibility in actual implementation.

A. *Varieties of Democratic Theory*

"Democratic theory" is far from monolithic: many theories of democracy currently circulate. Below are a few of the most common.

- PROTECTIVE DEMOCRACY. From the time of the founding, one of the most common justifications for democratic forms of government is a set of theories that can be captured under the broad heading of "protective democracy."[35] Although the details sometimes vary, theories of protective democracy usually center on two core beliefs: that the ultimate purpose of government is to protect the rights and liberties of the citizenry; and that democracy is a form of government particularly well suited to accomplish that goal.
- DEVELOPMENTAL DEMOCRACY. Generally associated with thinkers such as Mill[36] and, later, with participationists such as Pateman and Barber,[37] theories of developmental democracy hold that the most important function of democracy is its capacity, by creating opportunities for popular participation in self-governance, to foster and maintain in the populace the skills of citizenship. These skills are critical because, as Mill wrote, "human beings are only secure from evil at the hands of others, in proportion as they have the power of being, and are, self-protecting; and they only achieve a high degree of success in [that] struggle . . ., in proportion as they are self-dependent, relying on what they themselves can do, . . . rather than on what others can do for them."[38]
- DEMOCRATIC MINIMALISM. Pioneered by the mid-twentieth-century political theorist Joseph Schumpeter, democratic minimalism holds that "the democratic method is that institutional arrangement for arriving at political decisions in which individuals acquire the power to decide by means of a competitive struggle for the people's vote."[39] On this view, the polity is fundamentally a passive observer of the political activities of elites, and its capacity to influence public affairs is limited to replacing one set of rulers with another.
- AGGREGATIVE THEORIES. More sophisticated versions of minimalism, aggregative or economic theories of democracy rest on the utilitarian premise that the good of society is achieved through the maximization of collective welfare. Democracy, in such theories, performs this function when parties and candidates offer competing programmatic commitments and voters then choose among the options by voting for the

---

[35] DAVID HELD, MODELS OF DEMOCRACY (1987).

[36] JOHN STUART MILL, CONSIDERATIONS ON REPRESENTATIVE GOVERNMENT (1861).

[37] CAROLE PATEMAN, PARTICIPATION AND DEMOCRATIC THEORY (1970); BENJAMIN BARBER, STRONG DEMOCRACY (1984).

[38] MILL, *supra* note 36, ch. III.

[39] JOSEPH SCHUMPETER, CAPITALISM, SOCIALISM AND DEMOCRACY 260 (1942).

candidate whose policy commitments will provide them with the greatest benefits.[40] Through the operation of forces similar to those prevailing in well-functioning markets, social utility is said to be maximized through the mechanical aggregation of the uncoordinated, self-interested decisions of voters.

- DELIBERATIVE THEORIES. The most recent entry into the field, deliberative theories of democracy reject the minimalist and aggregative premises that citizens have limited capacity to participate meaningfully in politics; and reject the contention that politics consists of the mere summing of individual utility preferences. Harkening back to earlier, thicker conceptions of democracy, deliberativists contend that citizens' preferences, and even their political self-understandings and identities, are formed in reasoned, self-conscious, and deliberative processes of political engagement; and that only viewpoints formed in this fashion are entitled to full consideration in the process by which a democratic society decides how best to govern itself.[41]

* * *

Each of these theories of democracy emphasizes different democratic values and aspects of democratic practice, and each thus offers distinct guidance as to the qualities that presidents and presidential candidates ought to possess. For example, under a theory of protective democracy, the most important quality a presidential candidate must possess would seem to be a substantive commitment to individual liberty. Aggregative theories, in contrast, seem to demand presidential candidates capable of balancing and adjusting competing voter preferences — a kind of talent for brokering.[42] Under deliberative theories, in contrast, the ideal presidential candidate would presumably be a skilled deliberator capable of leading the citizenry through a process of meaningful deliberation, who would respect, and exercise self-restraint in the face of, the outcomes of meaningful public deliberation.

For this reason, a turn to democratic theory cannot settle disputes over the qualities that presidential candidates ought to possess. It can, however, clarify the available choices and their consequences, and might therefore usefully assist a polity in recognizing those aspects of democracy that it most values and

---

[40] ANTHONY DOWNS, AN ECONOMIC THEORY OF DEMOCRACY (1957).

[41] *See, e.g.,* Joshua Cohen, *Deliberation and Democratic Legitimacy, in* THE GOOD POLITY: NORMATIVE ANALYSIS OF THE STATE (Alan Hamlin & Philip Pettit eds. 1989); JÜRGEN HABERMAS, BETWEEN FACTS AND NORMS: CONTRIBUTIONS TO A DISCOURSE THEORY OF LAW AND DEMOCRACY (William Rehg trans., 1996).

[42] *See* CEASER, *supra* note 5, at 158.

wishes to advance in its democratic institutions and practices. This may not be an easy task. First, no general consensus exists as to the descriptive accuracy, normative attractiveness, or pragmatic feasibility of any of these theories, so there is no default preference that might be invoked in the face of disagreement. Second, the process of choosing among democratic theories is complicated by the fact that the various theories have acquired over time a distinct ideological valence, even a partisan one: present-day conservatives and libertarians tend to gravitate toward protective and aggregative theories of democracy, while liberals tend to prefer developmental and deliberative conceptions. Thus, any enterprise of attempting to choose, in a sober, constitutional mode, among foundational democratic theories runs the risk of activating the habitual partisan cleavages of ordinary politics.

The need for affirmative choice is all the more urgent, however, because not all of these characteristics are equally likely to reside in the same individual. Aggregative brokering, for example, is in a sense the precise opposite of deliberative consensus-building. Brokering among competing interests requires facilitating logrolling and compromise, a task undertaken most effectively by according unquestioned validity to the merits of participants' demands and underlying beliefs. Deliberative consensus-building, on the other hand, requires leading participants through a process of potentially transformative self-reflection and self-interrogation as a means to achieving consensus. Thus, a willingness to take guidance from democratic theory cannot relieve us of the necessity of making hard choices about normative ends. Instead, it tends simply to push those choices down a level, converting them from choices about the desired qualities of presidential candidates to choices among competing conceptions of democratic practice.

B. *Prescriptive Vagueness*

Even if societal agreement on a theory of democracy is feasible, theories of democracy often have surprisingly little to say about how best to operationalize their own normative commitments. This is in part a consequence of the historic focus of democratic theory since the Enlightenment: the legitimacy of governmental authority. The great problem to which the Enlightenment political project addressed itself was undermining divine providence as the basis of governmental—which is to say, monarchical—authority, and refounding it on popular consent. As a result, democratic theories are typically, at bottom, theories of popular sovereignty in which the principal concern is whether the power exercised by rulers is legitimate, in the sense of authorized by popular consent.

Because of this focus, democratic theory often has little to say about how principles of popular sovereignty are operationalized. Consistent with the idea that the will of the popular sovereign must be formed freely, theories of democracy tend to assume a wide range of acceptable structural choices, and a correspondingly wide range of discretion among polities to choose a form of operationalization that best suits their goals and habits. No theory of democracy, for example, is so fine-grained at the operational level as either to prescribe or to prohibit very substantial yet commonplace variations in the format of democratic self-rule such as parliamentary or presidential systems, first-past-the-post or proportional electoral methods, short or long terms of office, closed or open party lists, and so forth; all such mechanisms are capable of satisfying the main requirement of democratic legitimacy. Insofar as democratic theory is concerned, the key criterion is thus popular sovereignty, not any particular instantiation of it.

A second reason why democratic theories typically offer little guidance at the operational level, particularly as relevant to the structure of candidate nominating systems, is their historic inattention to the role of political parties. More than 70 years ago, the great twentieth-century political scientist Elmer Schattschneider called parties "the orphans of political philosophy,"[43] and his description remains apt: "the current literatures on political parties and normative democratic theory continue to develop to an extraordinary degree in mutual isolation . . . . [M]odern democratic theory is noticeably silent on the question whether political parties have a legitimate place and function in a democracy."[44]

Indeed, political parties pose a singular challenge to democratic theory. Parties function as intermediate institutions which, though perhaps pragmatically necessary,[45] stand between the people and their elected representatives, thereby complicating the fulfillment of the principal condition of democratic legitimacy—that rulers must rule subject to some democratically meaningful form of popular consent. Over time, parties have come to exercise an important function in democratic practice by organizing an otherwise chaotic public sphere, filled with differing political views, into an intellectually coherent environment of ideologically competing partisan positions.[46] The party, in

---

[43] E. E. SCHATTSCHNEIDER, PARTY GOVERNMENT 10 (1942).

[44] Ingrid van Biezen & Michael Saward, *Democratic Theorists and Party Scholars: Why They Don't Talk to Each Other, and Why They Should,* 6 PERSP. ON POL. 21, 22 (2008).

[45] Schattschneider famously went so far as to declare that "the political parties created democracy and that modern democracy is unthinkable save in terms of the parties." SCHATTSCHNEIDER, *supra* note 43, at 1.

[46] Theorists as disparate as Downs and Rosenblum agree on this point. *See* DOWNS, *supra* note 40, at 25–26; NANCY L. ROSENBLUM, ON THE SIDE OF THE ANGELS: AN APPRECIATION OF PARTIES AND PARTISANSHIP 353–56 (2008).

other words, "coordinates the beliefs and intentions of activists [and] articulates a collective will."[47]

Democratic legitimacy requires that the popular will dictate the choice of rulers. Parties, however, by definition comprise only a portion of the electorate. If parties "assist" the electorate in formulating its will by defining the universe of options *before* the popular will is authoritatively formed, then it is not entirely clear that an expression of the popular will formed after parties have done their work is democratically equivalent to the formation of such a will in the absence of party intermediation. To put the matter differently, the role of parties in actively constructing the democratic will lays bare the hard truth, not always acknowledged by democratic theorists, that a democratic will is not an antecedently existing object to be discovered through the application of electoral procedures, but is rather an artifact of those procedures—such a will, in other words, is in large part constructed by the very procedures used to determine it.[48]

C. *Infeasibility of Selecting on the Necessary Criteria*

Finally, even where democratic theory is capable of producing concrete institutional prescriptions, it is often far from clear that nominating institutions can be designed to select candidates on the criteria demanded by the theory. Suppose, for instance, that Americans were to choose on normative grounds to accept guidance in their practice of democracy from some kind of theory of deliberative democracy. The ideal president, in that case, would presumably need to be not only a skilled, patient, and respectful deliberator him- or herself, but also someone capable of facilitating and leading normatively desirable deliberation among different groups, including cabinet officials, members of Congress, interest groups, and the general public.

Fair enough, but how might a nominating system be designed to select candidates on these qualities? One way, as we have seen, is to place a thumb on the scale by careful construction of the selectorate. Given the commitments of deliberative theories of democracy, an appropriate selectorate might thus be comprised of individuals who (1) value the skills of a good deliberative leader and (2) will be more responsive to appeals from potential candidates

---

[47] Jonathan White & Lea Ypi, The Meaning of Partisanship 85 (2016). In some societies this role has been formally acknowledged: the German Basic Law, for example, provides that parties "participate in the formation of the political will of the people." Const. of Germany, art. 22(1). To similar effect, see Const. of Switzerland, art. 137; Const. of Spain, art. 6.

[48] S. I. Benn & R. S. Peters, Principles of Political Thought 397–99 (1959).

who display those qualities than to appeals from candidates with other kinds of skills and virtues.

So far, so good. But of whom, then, would the selectorate actually be comprised? How do we identify individuals qualified to serve? Would they require specific kinds of experience or training? Certainly, the selectorate would likely have to be a small and exclusive group; the general public is not known for its great love and respect for genuinely deliberative politics,[49] particularly in the current era of partisan polarization. Similar problems arise under any of the various theories of democracy now in circulation. Suppose a collective commitment to a theory of protective democracy. To which rights and liberties would a qualified candidate have to be committed, and who decides? How would qualified members of a selectorate be identified, and by whom?

The problem quickly begins to swallow its own tail. Some theories of democracy, most notably democratic minimalism and associated aggregative theories, neither expect nor demand broad public participation during the nomination phase; such theories are satisfied by mass popular choice among whatever set of options may happen to be presented to a passive electorate.[50] Other theories, especially developmental and deliberative ones, often express a robust preference for wider public involvement at every stage of the process.[51] Thus, the theories that in principle require the greatest public participation at the nominating phase require in practice the most specific and exclusive selectorates, whereas the theories most readily amenable to practical implementation impose no particular requirements on nominating procedures.

Given the challenges associated with taking useful, concrete guidance from democratic theory in the design of nominating procedures, I turn to two other possible methods for guiding presidential nominations along desirable pathways: threshold qualifications and citizen ethos.

---

[49] ELIZABETH THEISS-MORSE & JOHN R. HIBBING, STEALTH DEMOCRACY (2002); JAMES A. GARDNER, WHAT ARE CAMPAIGNS FOR? THE ROLE OF PERSUASION IN ELECTORAL LAW AND POLITICS (2009).

[50] SCHUMPETER, *supra* note 39, at 260; SCHATTSCHNEIDER, *supra* note 43, at 53–64; DOWNS, *supra* note 40, at 36–38, 220–37; Thomas E. Mann, *Is This Any Way to Pick a President? Lessons from 2008*, *in* REFORMING THE PRESIDENTIAL NOMINATION PROCESS, *supra* note 24, at 168.

[51] *E.g.*, Fabio Wolkenstein, *A Deliberative Model of Intra-Party Democracy*, 24 J. POL. PHIL. 297 (2016); MIGUEL PÉREZ-MONEO, LA SELECCIÓN DE CANDIDATOS ELECTORALES EN LOS PARTIDOS (2012); Susan E. Scarrow et al., *From Social Integration to Electoral Contestation: The Changing Distribution of Power within Political Parties*, *in* PARTIES WITHOUT PARTISANS: POLITICAL CHANGE IN ADVANCED INDUSTRIAL DEMOCRACIES 130 (Russell J. Dalton & Martin P. Wattenberg eds., 2000).

IV. OTHER MECHANISMS OF PATH DEPENDENCY

A. *Candidate Qualifications*

Another common feature of institutional design capable of influencing the qualities of candidates for office is the use of constitutional qualifications and disqualifications. These mechanisms represent a classic form of constitutional self-restraint; they prevent the polity from doing something it might regret—in this case, electing an unqualified individual. At the federal level, the U.S. Constitution establishes qualifications of age, citizenship, and residency.[52] State constitutions typically establish the same three qualifications for governor, though some add the requirement that governors be qualified voters,[53] a provision that subjects candidates for executive office to standard grounds of disqualification applicable to voters, such as disqualification for mental incompetence or felony conviction. In some states, term limit provisions add an additional disqualification for having served some prior period in elected office.[54] The earliest state constitutions often contained property qualifications as well, but those provisions were gradually relaxed during the Jacksonian era, and are in any case of dubious constitutionality.[55]

These kinds of threshold screening requirements, however, do not in themselves identify qualities that officeholders must possess in order to be able to perform the job competently; there is no intrinsic reason why a foreign-born 34-year-old cannot be as good a president as a native-born 36-year-old. Rather, threshold screening requirements serve as proxies for other qualities on which the polity does place considerable weight—experience and maturity of judgment in the case of age; loyalty to the United States in the case of citizenship; knowledge of local needs and interests in the case of residency; and responsiveness to the electorate in the case of term limits.

The utility of qualification provisions, however, seems debatable. First, as with nominating procedures, the most desirable kinds of screening from the point of view of democratic theory pose serious difficulties of implementation.

---

[52] U.S. CONST. art. I, § 2, cl. 2 (Representatives); art. I, §3, cl. 3 (Senators); art. II, § 1, cl. 5 (President).

[53] *E.g.,* CAL. CONST., art. IV, § 2; FLA. CONST. art. III, § 5.

[54] *E.g.,* CAL. CONST. art. IV, § 2; COLO. CONST. art. IV, § 1.

[55] *See Turner v. Fouche,* 396 U.S. 346 (1970) and *Chappelle v. Greater Baton Rouge Airport District,* 431 U.S. 159 (1977), *summarily reversing* 329 So. 2d 801 (La. App. 1976) (both reversing state property qualifications for non-elective offices); *Harper v. Virginia Board of Elections,* 383 U.S. 663 (1966) (invalidating state property requirement for voting eligibility in the form of a poll tax).

It is no easier to design a threshold qualification to screen for commitment to individual liberty or aggregative or deliberative prowess than it is to design a nominating procedure to produce the same effect.

Second, threshold qualification provisions demonstrate a rather low regard for voter discernment and self-restraint; they presume that voters are sufficiently likely to be tempted by unqualified candidates to require that the electorate as a whole be affirmatively disabled from acting on those temptations. Even if that presumption is accurate, however, threshold qualifications do nothing to prevent voters from deploying this bad judgment by choosing inexperienced, immature, disloyal, ignorant, or corrupt candidates who clear the constitutional minima. Perhaps the most that might be said for qualification provisions is that they prevent voters from electing the most egregiously unqualified candidates, but even that assumption seems dubious: incompetence seems to be generously distributed in the population, even among native-born, lifelong residents over 35 years of age. If identifying a pool of solid, highly competent candidates is the goal, threshold qualifications perform only minimally useful work.

B. *Citizen Ethos*

To name citizen ethos as a procedure for screening presidential candidates is in a sense merely to name the condition of having no screening process at all, or at least no formal one. But the absence of a formal process for screening candidates does not mean that no screening criteria exist; it means only that citizens will base their choices among candidates on internalized, politically consensual criteria, if any exist; or in the absence of consensus, that citizens will apply their own personal views of good leadership. Thus, although formal screening and nominating procedures can influence the nature of the ultimate choice, they are not the only source of influence; citizens, as social beings living in a political community, will also respond to prevailing norms of politics. These norms, moreover, will not necessarily be dictated by democratic theory or by some other, presumptively authoritative source of formal principles of governance. Prevailing norms of political choice are just as likely to have their source in convention or in pragmatic considerations. Perhaps the leading example is the pre-Franklin D. Roosevelt norm of a two-term limit as a check on the private ambition of presidential candidates. The strength of this norm served for more than a century to screen out of the candidate pool individuals who had already served two terms as president, not because formal term limits had been imposed by law, but because the prevailing citizen ethos deterred voters from voting for any candidate who had the effrontery to run for a third term. During the period when the two-term norm prevailed, such candidates would have appeared to the electorate to be guilty of an overweening ambition inconsistent with successful continued service.

Because informal political norms supply the foundations of citizen decision-making in electoral politics, they are potentially the most important force for guiding the nomination of presidential candidates: only individuals whose qualifications comport with these norms will be plausible candidates for election. The great difficulty with relying on such norms, however, is that they are not easily controlled, or even influenced, by law. On the contrary, originating in what Habermas called the "'wild' complex" and "anarchic structure" of civil society,[56] they are vulnerable to social and political movements generated within civil society largely outside of the formal control of law. Indeed, many now argue that the main problem with politics in the United States—and, increasingly, throughout the world—is the deterioration in civil society of long-standing, previously stable norms of democratic citizenship.[57]

This does not mean that citizen ethos cannot be influenced by adjustments to legal and political institutions—the two undoubtedly shape one another in a dialectic process, so that institutional processes are in principle capable of inducing a kind of civic training. Aristotle, for example, argued that the kind of rotation in office typical of Athenian democracy helped to produce good rulers because the experience of being ruled taught citizens valuable lessons about how to rule well, lessons that they could apply when they later held office.[58] Much more recently, advocates of instant runoff voting argue persuasively that something as simple as allowing voters to indicate second and third choices on the ballot has altered the norms of political campaigning. When candidates stand to benefit by campaigning for voters' lower-ranked votes, they apparently no longer find it in their interest to campaign negatively by smearing and belittling opponents whom some voters might rank higher. This change in institutional incentives has thus produced more harmonious electoral campaigns in which candidates stress their positive attributes rather than their opponents' negatives so as to avoid alienating a slice of potential support.[59] Such a change in candidate behavior

---

[56] HABERMAS, *supra* note 41, at 307.

[57] *See, e.g.,* STEVEN LEVITSKY & DANIEL ZIBLATT, HOW DEMOCRACIES DIE (2018); Jamal Greene, *Trump as a Constitutional Failure*, 93 IND. L.J. 93 (2018); *Symposium, Is Democracy in Decline?*, 26 J. DEMOC. 5 ff. (2015).

[58] ARISTOTLE, POLITICS, bk. III, ch. iv, § 14–15, 1277b.

[59] *See, e.g.,* Jessie Van Berkel, *Ranked-choice Voting Alters Calculus in Minneapolis, St. Paul Races*, MINNEAPOLIS STAR-TRIBUNE, Oct. 7, 2017; FairVote, *Campaign Civility*, www.fairvote.org/research_rcvcampaigncivility (last visited Aug. 2, 2018).

might in turn generate more positive and less alienated sentiments among the electorate toward candidates and politicians. In this way, then, well-designed institutional structures can help "train" citizens to think and behave in desirable ways.

However, the most common form of pressure on citizen ethos and informal norms, at least in today's environment of cheap, easy communication, is ideological. At the moment, tremendous efforts are being made by communicative means, financed by enormous private fortunes, to alter prevailing social attitudes on a host of issues. Citizen ethos is now precisely the site of a titanic partisan battle, and for good reason. In addition, the arrival in power of the Trump Administration may well be providing a strong form of civic training: by normalizing behavior that conflicts radically with previously prevailing civic and democratic norms, the administration may well succeed in demolishing those norms and replacing them with others more congenial to non-democratic practices. Citizen ethos thus may well be by far the most significant battleground, quite possibly the only one that really matters.

V. CONCLUSIONS

Complaints about the low quality of presidential candidates are hardly new. One of the most astute nineteenth-century observers of American political institutions, Lord James Bryce, devoted a chapter of his 1893 book to the subject "Why Great Men Are Not Chosen President." In Bryce's view, all American presidents since Jackson, with the exception of Lincoln and Grant, had been "intellectual pigmies beside the real leaders of [their] generation."[60] Today, however, the stakes are much higher; unlike in Bryce's time, the United States is no longer merely one relatively advanced nation among many, but the richest and most powerful nation the world has ever known. The quality of its leadership is of concern not only to Americans, but to everyone on the planet.

The historical record shows that the procedures used for nominating presidential candidates have undergone significant change since the founding, and presumably could change again. The logic of institutional analysis shows that the design of nominating systems can influence strongly the qualities of candidates who successfully clear its screening procedures. Institutional logic also suggests that the current trend in nominations of expanding the selectorate to the point where it converges with the electorate tends to nullify the capacity of the nomination process to channel the choice of nominees along

---

[60] JAMES BRYCE, 1 THE AMERICAN COMMONWEALTH 84 (1893).

any particular axis of decision, no matter how desirable. Instead, convergence of the selectorate and electorate tends to result in a kind of functional delegation of the criteria of choice to self-appointed individuals, groups, and candidates, who may not fully share the collective norms of democratic practice that in the end comprise the most significant and effective constraint on the behavior of participants in the nominating process.

At the end of the day, reform of nomination mechanisms may not be the most effective site in which to invest reform energy. What we may need more than institutional reform is a systematic effort to renew, justify, and strengthen democratic norms, an effort that by definition must take place not in the halls of legislatures or party bureaucracies, but deep in the terrain of civil society.

2

The Historical Development of the U.S. Presidential Nomination Process

Richard H. Pildes[*]

The institutional framework and legal rules through which democracies choose the nominees who compete to become a nation's Chief Executive (the President or Prime Minister) are among the most important features in the institutional design of any democracy. Yet despite the considerable academic attention over the last thirty years to many other institutional and legal aspects of American democracy—redistricting, the regulation of money in politics, voting rights, election administration—surprisingly little scholarly focus has thus been devoted to the way we have come to structure the presidential nomination process. This scholarly gap is particularly striking because one of the most consequential and radical changes in the last fifty years to the way American democracy is structured is the change we made to the way the major party nominees for President are selected: the shift to a purely populist method in which primary elections (and a small dose of caucuses) completely determine the party's nominees. Yet as those of us focused on the institutional design of democracy know all too well, different selection methods inevitably shape choices about the kind of people who choose to run; the kind of political figures most likely to succeed in capturing nominations and the White House; and, most importantly, on the way government functions and the interests and political forces to which it is most likely to respond.

This chapter provides historical perspective on the evolution of the processes and institutions used to filter and present to the voters general-election presidential candidates since contested presidential elections began in the

[*] Richard H. Pildes is Sudler Family Professor of Constitutional Law at the New York University School of Law. This chapter draws from Stephen Gardbaum & Richard H. Pildes, *Populism and Institutional Design: Methods of Selecting Candidates for Chief Executive*, 93 N.Y.U. L. REV. 647 (2018). I wish to thank the editors of the law review for allowing me to reprint parts of that article here, to which I have added a new opening and made other modest modifications.

United States. Precisely because the dramatic new system put in place in the United States nearly fifty years ago has remained largely unchanged since then, most Americans undoubtedly have come to take for granted that our current system of presidential primaries and caucuses is the "natural" or the only "democratic" way to select nominees for President. Historical perspective can help destabilize that belief, and perhaps open up possibilities for considering changes to this system.

Part I briefly chronicles the historical development from the Founding until the 1970s of the different methods and institutional frameworks used for selecting presidential nominees. This Part demonstrates that for most of American history until the 1970s, this process included a significant role for what is called "peer review," in which those who were existing officeholders and party officials had significant weight in deciding who ought to represent the party as candidate for President. Part II then describes the radical change to this system that took place in the 1970s. That change can be characterized as the replacement of this "peer review" system with a purely populist selection process in which voters, through primaries and caucuses, completely determine the presidential nominees.[1] In recovering this history, this chapter suggests that we did not so much intentionally choose this new "modern" populist system as much as stumble inadvertently into it.

The current nominations process is unusual in two senses. Historically, we used various forms of "peer review" to select presidential nominees until relatively recently in our history. Comparatively, most democracies continue to use some form of peer review to filter candidates for chief executive before voters are given the final choice.[2] In strong form peer review, such as the center-right parties use in Australia and New Zealand, the party leaders are chosen exclusively by the elected party figures who serve in Parliament. Voters have no direct say in the choice. In mixed systems, members of Parliament filter potential party leaders down to a certain number of candidates, with voters then being given a choice only between these pre-selected candidates. When the Conservative Party in the United Kingdom selects a new party leader, for example, the Conservative members of Parliament winnow down the candidates to two; party members then choose between these two candidates. Thus, the current U.S. system is unusual in a comparative sense in now

---

[1] For clarification, I am using the term "populist" (versus "peer review") in a procedural sense, to mean a selection process in which the mass of voters select a party's candidate.

[2] For a full description of how many other major democracies structure the process of choosing party leaders or nominees for chief executive, see the Gardbaum and Pildes article referenced in the asterisked footnote.

opting for a system that completely bypasses elected members of the party and turns the process over to a purely popular vote process.

I. FROM THE BIRTH OF THE AMERICAN REPUBLIC UNTIL THE 1970S: THE DIFFERING FORMS OF PEER REVIEW

To put the current American presidential nomination process in historical perspective, we used a dramatically different system for all of American history until the 1970s. The change that took place in the 1970s was both radical, against this historical backdrop, and in many ways unintended, as described below.

The Framers of the Constitution devoted substantial attention to the final stage of how the President ought to be chosen, settling ultimately on the Electoral College, with the hope that the structure of the Electoral College would have significant selection effects on the kinds of figures who would become President. They expected the Electoral College to produce a non-partisan system of presidential election in which pre-existing national reputations of the candidates would play the decisive role.[3] But the Framers appear to have assumed that these potential credible candidates would emerge more or less spontaneously; they gave little thought to whether there was any need for a prior stage of filtering, in which potential candidates were somehow distilled down to a group amongst which voters (voting for the electors) would then choose.[4]

Yet starting in the early-nineteenth century, the first form of peer review and two-stage selection process emerged.[5] This was the congressional caucus, which arose as the de facto means of pre-selecting the most credible candidates for President in a world in which factional or partisan divisions had begun to emerge. In the caucus system, which lasted until 1824, members in Congress from a self-identified coalition—namely, the Republicans—would privately come to agreement on the candidate they would endorse to the public as the representative of their views. The birth of the caucus system reflected, in part, the fear that without such a filtering device, too many candidates would run,

---

[3] James W. Ceaser, Presidential Selection: Theory and Development 41 (1979).

[4] *Id.* at 86 ("[T]he Founders' thought remains vague on just how individuals would earn the 'continental reputations' of which they spoke. Their view was that such reputations would naturally emerge in a regime in which national politics played a large, if not the dominant, role.").

[5] The first caucus was in 1800, when Republicans were united behind Jefferson as their presidential candidate, but were uncertain about their vice-presidential candidate, and so gathered in private to forge agreement on Aaron Burr. 2 James Bryce, The American Commonwealth 843 (Liberty Fund 1995) (1888).

the Electoral College would not be able to select a clear winner, and the selection of the President would thus end up being decided in the House of Representatives (where each state delegation had one vote).

The emergence of the caucus system was ironic, for two reasons. First, it reflected the blossoming of the types of partisan divisions that the Framers most feared and that the Constitution had been designed to preclude.[6] Second, the Framers had specifically rejected having the President chosen by Congress, out of fear that the President would then be too dependent upon Congress.[7] But the entry of the caucus system at the "nomination" stage generated precisely that kind of dependency. To be sure, defenders of the caucus system argued that members of Congress were merely making recommendations to the public, with the choice still in the hands of the voters. And while scholars have debated how decisive the choice of the congressional caucus actually was, that choice became the President in every general election from 1800 to 1816.[8] For much of the first forty years, the role of the congressional caucus in the selection process meant that American government operated less as the system of separated powers originally envisioned and more as one involving a congressionally dominated fusion of legislative and executive powers.[9]

But critics derided the system as "King Caucus"—an elite capture of the presidential process—and soon the system began to lose its legitimacy. Within a couple of decades, it was replaced by the national, political-party nomination conventions that (in vestigial form) remain with us today. Though the party convention was not invented by Martin Van Buren, he quickly turned it into an enduring feature of American democracy, along with his brilliant creation and legitimation of the mass, national political party.[10] Of particular relevance here, Van Buren had concluded that, in the vacuum created by the demise of the congressional caucus as a way of filtering presidential nominees, competition for the presidency had devolved into a system of highly personalized and

---

[6] *See, e.g.,* Ceaser, *supra* note 3, at 77 ("Virtually all the Founders associated parties with seditious bodies.").

[7] *See, e.g., id.* at 65, 82.

[8] *Id.* at 117.

[9] Daryl J. Levinson & Richard H. Pildes, *Separation of Parties, Not Powers,* 119 Harv. L. Rev. 2311, 2321 (2006).

[10] The first national conventions were held in 1831, by the Anti-Masons and the National Republicans (who soon became the Whigs). In 1832, another national convention adopted the Whig nominations. In 1836, the Jacksonian Democrats selected through a national convention, but their opponents did not. But by 1840, the national convention had become used by all significant parties. *See, e.g.,* James S. Chase, Emergence of the Presidential Nominating Convention, 1789–1832, at 294–95 (1973).

factional politics which generated too many candidates and more extreme, demagogic campaign appeals, as individual candidates fought to find ways to distinguish their personal brands.[11] Unified, national political parties and party nominating conventions were thought to be vehicles for fostering broad consensus by forcing compromise among crosscutting cleavages and reining in the role of personalized, and hence more demagogic, politics. By 1836, as James Ceaser has written, "the idea of partisan nominations was never again seriously challenged; it became part of the living constitution."[12]

Though the conventions purportedly involved a larger and more representative group of selectors than the congressional caucus, the reality was that state and local party leaders effectively controlled the conventions and the nomination process. They had considerable capacity to influence the choice of delegates (who were chosen by means like party caucus, district convention, state convention, executive committee, or some combination of these and similar methods). These party leaders also led their own state delegations and essentially controlled how their state's delegation voted.[13] Party leaders, who included state and national officeholders, had thick ties to their party and its commitments; they had ongoing and long-standing ties to their parties and were professional politicians.[14] Thus, despite opening up the selection process to greater participation through the nominating conventions, through the dominance of these state and local party leaders, the conventions continued to provide peer review filtering of potential nominees, albeit in more attenuated form than the congressional caucus.

With certain incremental changes, these party conventions continued to provide this form of peer review and filtering all the way until 1972. The most significant adaption of this system came in 1912, with the advent of the Progressive Era's press for direct primaries as a general means of choosing party nominees for all levels of election. That movement introduced a limited role for a few direct presidential primaries to choose convention delegates. But in hindsight, what is most remarkable is how little effect the direct-primary movement had on the presidential nomination process, given how successful that movement turned out to be for elections at virtually every other level.

The direct primary was introduced as an element—but just an element—in the nomination system on behalf of former President Theodore Roosevelt's pursuit of the nomination in 1912. Disenchanted with his hand-picked

---

[11]   CEASER, *supra* note 3, at 132, 136.
[12]   *Id.* at 127.
[13]   For one description, see LEON EPSTEIN, POLITICAL PARTIES IN THE AMERICAN MOLD 90 (1986).
[14]   *Id.*

successor, William Howard Taft, Roosevelt, who had been President from 1901 to 1909, decided to challenge Taft in 1912 but realized that by this time President Taft had control of the party apparatus. To circumvent the party establishment, Roosevelt and his allies pressed states to adopt the direct primary for choosing delegates to the Republican Party convention, at the same time as the movement for direct primaries for choosing nominees for other offices was gaining steam. This support for increasing the direct role of "We the People" was purely strategic; before being convinced this was his only path to the nomination, Roosevelt had opposed direct primaries and other forms of more popular democracy.[15] Nonetheless, it is no surprise that one of the architects of the Democratic Party's post-1968 move to the "modern" system in which presidential primaries completely determine the party's nominee, Geoffrey Cowan, has recently written a book celebrating Roosevelt's role in inaugurating the first presidential primaries.[16] As a result of the pressure of Roosevelt and his allies, 13 states ended up choosing their delegates through the direct primary for the 1912 Republican convention.[17]

From this point on, our presidential nomination process is best understood as what scholars have characterized as a "mixed system." Primary elections to choose delegates from some states became an element in the process, alongside the continuing role for local, state, and national party figures selected in the more traditional ways. Although winning a primary could influence the selection process, the dominant power to determine the nominees continued to rest with the traditional party figures.[18]

---

[15] Geoffrey Cowan, Let the People Rule: Theodore Roosevelt and the Birth of the Presidential Primary 42 (2016) (noting that Roosevelt "refused to embrace popular democracy as the cornerstone of the progressive agenda"); *id.* at 43 (quoting Roosevelt's private letter remarking that every real supporter of democracy "acts and always must act on the perfectly sound (although unacknowledged, and often hotly contested) belief that only certain people are fit for democracy"). By the time he was running against Taft and pressing for primaries, he gave widely noticed speeches, including one he called "The Right of The People to Rule," in which he asserted: "The great fundamental issue now before the Republican Party and before our people can be stated briefly ... It is: Are the American people fit to govern themselves? I believe they are. My opponents do not." *Id.* at 99.

[16] Cowan, *supra* note 15.

[17] *Id.* at 1.

[18] In 1952, the American Political Science Association surveyed each state party organization in the country to find out how they selected delegates to the conventions and who effectively controlled that process. In carefully reviewing that survey data, the authors of *The Party Decides* concluded "that most party organizations were sufficiently insulated from popular pressures that the selection of delegates to the party conventions—and hence the choice of party nominee—was dominated by insiders." Marty Cohen et al., The Party Decides: Presidential Nominations Before and After Reform 118 (2008) [hereinafter The Party Decides].

Indeed, one might expect that once primaries were introduced into the system for Roosevelt, the pressure for the direct primary would only gain more momentum, particularly in light of the soon-common use of the direct primary to choose nominees for other national and state offices. But the presidential nomination process continued to resist the forces of complete populist control. President Woodrow Wilson believed a more empowered President was necessary, and that direct primaries would be a means toward that end; thus, he formally proposed in his first State of the Union speech in 1913 that Congress enact a national primary law.[19] But this proposal went nowhere. The high-watermark for primaries came in 1916: twenty states used one form or another of a presidential primary, and more than half the delegates for each party's convention were selected this way.[20] But even these primaries were not the primaries of today. Under many of these primary laws, state party leaders could still control their delegations by rules that permitted delegates to be elected as "unpledged" or to support "favorite son" candidates (the state's senator or governor, typically) who would be abandoned at the convention, as the party figures then bargained and negotiated over the serious nomination options.[21]

And by 1920, enthusiasm for the direct primary as part of the presidential nomination process had dissipated. Primaries settled into a contained feature of the system, with the dominance of the party organization re-solidified.[22] After 1920, only twelve to eighteen states in various years used some form of primary to select delegates.[23] Indeed, most readers will probably be surprised to learn that, as late as 1968, only fourteen states used primaries; they selected 37–38 percent of the delegates, well less than the majority needed to control the choice of nominee.[24]

The conventional negative story about this "old" system is that a cadre of party bosses got together in smoke-filled back rooms to choose the parties' nominees. But whether that characterization was accurate at one time, the

[19]   CEASER, *supra* note 3, at 173.
[20]   *See* HOWARD L. REITER, SELECTING THE PRESIDENT: THE NOMINATING PROCESS IN TRANSITION 3 (1985) (Table 1.1). However, Epstein reports that 26 states, not 20, used some form of primary. *See* EPSTEIN, *supra* note 13, at 91. The difference in these numbers probably reflects the range of structures that can arguably be considered some form of primary.
[21]   EPSTEIN, *supra* note 13, at 91; THE PARTY DECIDES, *supra* note 18, at 113.
[22]   EPSTEIN, *supra* note 13, at 91.
[23]   REITER, *supra* note 20, at 3. The one exception is the Democratic Party convention of 1956, when twenty states used primaries of some form. *Id.*
[24]   *Id.* at 3 tbl.1.1. Again, there is also some discrepancy in number between the sources on exactly how many states used primaries. Some sources report 16–17 states as using primaries in 1968. *See, e.g.*, EPSTEIN, *supra* note 13, at 91.

"mixed system" for nominations in the twentieth century functioned in considerably more complex and nuanced ways. In this system, the role of the popular primaries and that of the party figures turned out to perform a kind of checking and balancing function on each other's influence. The institutional party figures continued to have incentives to put their weight behind candidates likely to hold the party's factions together, run a competitive election, govern effectively, and reflect the party's general ideology. But primaries also kept the system from being too closed; "outsiders" could challenge existing party hierarchy and orthodoxy and force the parties to remain responsive, at least up to a point. No single institutional designer sat down in a single moment of synoptic rationality to create the "perfect" mix of populist and peer review sources of power; as often happens with democratic institutions, this system emerged from competing pressures over time. Yet the mixed system functioned surprisingly well.

Primaries enabled less tested candidates to show skeptical party leaders that they could win votes—as when John Kennedy won the West Virginia primary in May 1960 and proved that a Catholic could win votes even in heavily Protestant areas.[25] Even an insurgent candidate, like Barry Goldwater in 1964, could successfully work the mixed system.[26] But no candidate could succeed without also convincing enough institutional party figures throughout the country that they should throw their support behind him. In 1960, for example, Kennedy won only ten primaries. To win the nomination, he therefore had to persuade enough party regulars to back him. When candidates ran in the primaries they were thus always constrained to keep party regulars on board too. While personal appeal mattered, so did the ability to put together coalitions within the party. And party figures could bring to bear more personal knowledge than voters of how candidates actually functioned in government, which potentially could weed out nominees temperamentally unsuited to governing.

The selection effects of this mixed system were also balanced in a complex way. Under this system, some candidates chose to "run" on the inside track and make their appeal primarily or even exclusively to the party figures who controlled convention delegates; for instance, the Democrats nominated Adlai Stevenson in 1952, even though he had not run in any primary. The Democrats did so even though Estes Kefauver had run in and won 11 of the 12 the Democratic primaries he entered.[27] Others, such as John F. Kennedy,

---

[25] THE PARTY DECIDES, *supra* note 18, at 125–26.
[26] *Id.* at 142.
[27] COWAN, *supra* note 15, at 293; THE PARTY DECIDES, *supra* note 18, at 123.

effectively took advantage of the outside track to demonstrate their popular appeal. Whichever path a candidate took, this system combined populist and party-centered features. But the net effect was to keep the political parties (meaning party leaders from the national, state, and local levels) in control. As the most thorough recent study concludes about the convention process in the decades before it collapsed, in no nomination contest "was a party forced by strong candidates with large popular followings to choose a nominee it didn't want."[28] And, as this study of the convention process goes on to explain, "[w]ith the exception of the Republicans in 1964 and the Democrats in 1968, parties consistently attempted to find candidates who were broadly acceptable to party groups and able to compete well in the general election."[29] In other words, while the mixed system titrated peer review with a degree of populism, the power of peer review remained dominant.[30]

Thus, for the course of American history until the 1970s, the selection of credible nominees for the presidency typically involved a high degree of control and "peer review" from national, state, and local party leaders from throughout the country. "[P]arty leaders retained most of their customary power over presidential nominations,"[31] even as the precise form of this peer review evolved, from selection by a small caucus in Congress to nominating conventions that eventually created a partial role for direct popular input. But in the mixed system that emerged in 1912 and endured until the 1970s, peer review always played a central role in determining the major party presidential nominees.

II. STUMBLING INTO THE "MODERN" SYSTEM

This long-standing peer review system was destroyed, almost overnight, in the aftermath of the 1968 Democratic convention in Chicago. In its place was erected what has been called a pure "plebiscitary" system of selection. This change was radical. It took place almost overnight. And in many ways, it was unintended; indeed, it transpired despite the objective of its architects to forestall exactly the changes that their recommendations nonetheless brought

---

[28] THE PARTY DECIDES, *supra* note 18, 145.

[29] *Id.*

[30] Some scholars did argue in the 1950s that the parties' role in the conventions had already been weakened and that more populist forces had already taken control of the process. *See* William Carleton, *The Revolution in the Presidential Nominating Convention*, 72 POL. SCI. Q. 224–40 (1957). For a later reflection of this view, *see also* REITER, *supra* note 20. The analysis in *The Party Decides* rejects this view and provides strong empirical analyses for the opposite conclusion.

[31] EPSTEIN, *supra* note 13, at 91.

about. Within a decade, the American system had abandoned nearly two hundred years of a peer review selection system and replaced it (somewhat inadvertently) with a populist one. It is that system that now makes more likely nominations contested by 15 to 25 candidates, more frequent challenges to incumbent Presidents, the rise of celebrity candidates, and the nomination by a major party of figures, like Donald Trump, who have no prior experience in government and no meaningful ties to the party's leaders and traditional policy positions.

The catalyst for re-examining the nomination process, of course, was the explosive 1968 Democratic convention in Chicago, where the Democratic Party tore itself apart over political conflict, primarily over the Vietnam War. Outside the Convention hall, national television showed bloody, violent confrontations between the 30,000-strong police and security force Mayor Daley had unleashed for the Convention and the most violent wing of the anti-war activists, who had come to Chicago seeking such confrontations as a way to "heighten the contradictions" (as they saw it) of the American political system. Inside the Convention, some Democrats — particularly young, anti-war ones — were outraged that the Convention chose the establishment candidate, Vice President Hubert Humphrey, whom President Johnson strong-armed and intimidated into continuing to support the war. Humphrey had entered the race too late to make it onto the ballot for any of the primaries, and so he instead focused on winning over the party's political king-makers, such as the Democratic county chairmen who had the power to select the delegates to the national conventions. As one commentator put it, during the campaign Robert Kennedy was "going to the people, but Hubert's going to the party" — it was exactly the kind of approach, or the multiple, different approaches, available under the mixed system of nominations.[32] Inside the Convention hall, national television showed different factions among the Democratic delegates and party leaders at each others' throats, while in the streets the violent confrontations between demonstrators and police further contributed to the image of a Democratic Party completely divided and disordered. Indeed, the great campaign journalist, Theodore White, wrote as soon as he saw the violence that the Democrats were finished, and he would famously describe Humphrey as having been nominated "in a sea of blood."[33] It was hardly an auspicious start to the general election campaign.

---

[32]   The descriptions here of the 1968 Democratic Party convention and the turmoil surrounding it are drawn from NELSON W. POLSBY, CONSEQUENCES OF PARTY REFORM 9–53 (1983) and MICHAEL A. COHEN, AMERICAN MAELSTORM: THE 1968 ELECTION AND THE POLITICS OF DIVISION (2016).

[33]   POLSBY, *supra* note 32, at 33.

To appease the critics of his nomination, Humphrey agreed to a reform commission, eventually known as the "McGovern-Fraser Commission"— which turned out to be dominated by anti-war party reformers—to make recommendations for reforming the nomination process for the 1972 convention. These recommendations, which the Democratic National Convention accepted, led to the most centralized imposition ever by the national party of rules on the state parties for how they could select delegates to the Convention. The Supreme Court would then later hold that the Convention did indeed have the power to tell the state parties how they could select their delegates.[34] These top-down rules, described in a bit more detail below, were designed to open up participation in the nomination process.

To overstate the immediacy and significance of the changes made in the aftermath of the Commission's recommendations would be tough to do. As the author of the most thorough study of this reform process, Byron Shafer, puts it, these changes brought "the arrival of a revolutionary change in the mechanics of presidential selection, the greatest systematically planned and centrally imposed shift in the institutions of delegate selection in all of American history."[35] A mere four years later, by the time of the 1972 Democratic National Convention,

> every state was forced to amend the rules governing its delegate selection, and most did so in fundamental ways, to the point where half abandoned the basic institutional device they had used only four years before . . . . Along the way, and perhaps most crucially, the official party has been *erased* from what was still nominally the party's nomination process.[36]

Under the new rules, there was a dramatic decrease in the number of party leaders and elected officials who attended the convention.[37] As one commentator put it: "In less than four years, the Democratic Party discarded 130 years of political tradition."[38]

---

[34] See *Cousins v. Wigoda*, 419 U.S. 477 (1975), which upheld the power of the national credentials committee at the 1972 Democratic Convention to exclude delegates from Illinois that had been certified as the state's delegates but chosen under state rules that conflicted with the new rules the DNC had now established. In a later case analogous to a Supremacy Clause case for political parties, the Court upheld the power of the DNC to exclude delegates selected under state party rules that conflicted with the rules of the DNC. Democratic Party of the United States v. Wisconsin ex rel. La Follette, 450 U.S. 107 (1981).

[35] BYRON E. SHAFER, QUIET REVOLUTION: STRUGGLE FOR THE DEMOCRATIC PARTY AND THE SHAPING OF POST-REFORM POLITICS 4 (1983).

[36] *Id.* at 6.

[37] James I. Lengle, *Democratic Party Reforms: The Past as Prologue to the 1988 Campaign*, 4 J. L. & POL. 233, 237–38 (1988).

[38] *Id.* at 236.

Almost overnight, the United States moved toward a purely populist-dominated selection process. In 1968, the primaries had bound 36 percent of the delegates to each convention; just four years later, the primaries bound 58 percent of the Democratic delegates and 41 percent of the Republican ones, and by 1976, two-thirds of the Democratic delegates and more than half the Republican ones were bound.[39] By 1976, the system had changed completely: more than thirty states were using presidential primaries (today, more than forty states use primaries). Prior to the shift in the 1970s, primary elections were mechanisms for demonstrating electability to party leaders; in the new system, primaries directly determined delegate votes. "In the old system, candidates worked through the party regulars who habitually attended a caucus," explain the authors of a book on the primary system, while "in the new system, candidates try to flood party caucuses with their own people."[40] Among other effects, the greater number of candidates who ran signaled the loss of party control, as "party statesmen and spokesmen [were] replaced by 'cause candidates' espousing ideology (McGovern), the views of a discrete group (Jackson), and by 'anti-politics candidates' trumpeting political independence (Carter) or offering technical solutions to political problems (Hart)."[41] Primary challenges to sitting Presidents became more common.[42]

But strikingly, this radical change to one of our most important democratic institutions was not the intended aim of many reformers, which is the conclusion of the major studies of the post-1968 "reforms."[43] Indeed, these changes had, ironically, exactly the opposite effect of their intent. The Commission did not seek to create a primary-dominated selection system that essentially eliminated the voice of the institutional party figures altogether. In fact, the Commission wanted to save the party through reforms that would maintain a critical role for the party itself.

Among the Commissioners was Austin Ranney, a prominent political scientist who throughout his career had aimed to strengthen the parties, not hollow them out. He described the mismatch between what the Commission had meant to do and what happened in fact when its recommendations were implemented:

---

[39] POLSBY, *supra* note 32, at 64 tbl.2.3.
[40] THE PARTY DECIDES, *supra* note 18, at 160.
[41] Lengle, *supra* note 37, at 239 .
[42] *Id.* at 239–40.
[43] THE PARTY DECIDES, *supra* note 18, at 161; ELAINE C. KAMARCK, PRIMARY POLITICS: HOW PRESIDENTIAL CANDIDATES HAVE SHAPED THE MODERN NOMINATING SYSTEM 15 (2009); SHAFER, *supra* note 35, at 387.

I well remember that the first thing we members of the Democratic party's McGovern-Fraser commission (1969–72) agreed on ... was that we did not want a national presidential primary or any great increase in the number of state primaries. Indeed, we hoped to prevent any such development by reforming the delegate-selection rules so that the party's non-primary process would be open and fair, participation in them would greatly increase, and consequently the demand for more primaries would fade away ... But we got a rude shock ... We accomplished the opposite of what we intended.[44]

What had the Commission actually intended to do? And how did we end up instead with our current primary-dominated system?

The reforms largely sought to preserve the legitimacy of the party by making the caucus system more accessible, transparent, and open; until then, it had been governed by baroque rules designed to enable only party insiders to participate. Up until then, the caucuses were often open only to those who held party office. Some states chose delegates an entire year before the campaign began. Even when the caucuses were nominally open, anyone who was not a party official had a hard time finding out where and when the caucuses were being held; in some cases, different parts of the state might caucus on different days.[45]

Under the new rules, if states were going to use local caucuses or state conventions to select delegates, the process had to be open to all who claimed to be party members; the meeting times had to be widely publicized (a significant change) and they had to be held the same year as the presidential election (before, many states had held them a year or even two beforehand, which led only the most committed party members to participate). If states used primaries, they now had to be "candidate primaries"—meaning the name of the presidential candidate, rather than the potential delegate, would be listed.[46] But the McGovern-Fraser Commission was not seeking a greater role for primaries, nor to reduce the institutional party's role. The aspiration was that the recommended reforms would legitimate a continuing central role for the institutional party.

Yet as these new rules got implemented, they brought about the dramatic changes described above. Instead of opening up caucuses and conventions, the state parties—first on the Democratic side, then the Republican— responded by rapidly expanding the role of primaries, which had the effect

---

[44] Austin Ranney, Curing the Mischiefs of Faction: Party Reform in America 203–09 (1975).

[45] Epstein, *supra* note 13, at 90.

[46] The Party Decides, *supra* note 18, at 159–60.

of putting the nomination in the hands of primary voters once a majority of delegates were selected that way. Apparently, Democratic state parties were worried that if they failed to implement the new rules properly, their delegations would be subject to credentials challenges (of which there had been many at the 1972 Democratic convention). Party leaders in many states thought primaries would be simpler and safer. Of course, even the remaining caucuses were also no longer controlled by party insiders.

Republicans were pulled down the same path, partly because in many states in which Democrats controlled the legislature, they passed laws creating a primary for both parties. And as more open and participatory Democratic processes attracted greater media attention, Republicans also felt the need to move in the same direction.

To see how the Democratic Party stumbled into this profound change is troubling. As Shafer concluded, the committee members tended to overlook "practical effects in formally codified rules," which contributed to "the rapid and quiet acquiescence of these members in reforms which purported to alter the entire structure of national party politics."[47] Then, when the recommendations came to the Democratic National Committee for approval, they also failed to receive careful scrutiny, because the specter of the 1968 nightmare still loomed large. As one participant said: "There was still a lot of concern for having a nice, orderly, unified National Convention. These rules would help do that, but if there was foot-dragging on party reform, there would be disaffection on the left, and that would bring 1968 back, only worse."[48]

For a brief period of time, some argued that the radical change to the nominations process did not have significant practical effect, because "the political parties" found ways to effectively work within the new framework in a way that still enabled the party to have as its nominee the figure the party leaders or establishment most preferred. This view was partly based on a frequently referenced (if not carefully read) 2008 book by a distinguished quartet of political scientists, *The Party Decides: Presidential Nominations Before and After Reform*.[49] This book argued that, after the initial shock of the 1970s reforms, an informal, "invisible primary" had emerged that re-created the bargaining dynamics of the party conventions in the prior, mixed

---

[47] SHAFER, *supra* note 35, at 385.

[48] *Id.* at 390.

[49] *See generally* THE PARTY DECIDES, *supra* note 18. As the authors explain: "The reformers of the 1970s tried to wrest the presidential nomination away from party insiders and bestow it on rank-and-file partisans, but the people who are regularly active in party politics have regained much of the control that was lost." *Id.* at 7.

system.[50] In this "invisible primary," before the first formal primary takes place, "party elites" and "party insiders" effectively select the person who will in fact become the party's nominee. If this claim were right, it could be taken to mean that the 1970s changes made less practical difference than might be thought because "the party" still effectively determines its nominees.

But this interpretation is, first of all, a misunderstanding of what *The Party Decides* actually argues and purports to show. For one, "the party" that purportedly decides the nominee in the "invisible primary" is not the traditional party establishment from the days of meaningful "peer review." The authors redefine "the party" to include not just elected officials and formal party organizations, but also "religious organizations, civil rights groups ... organizers, fundraisers, pollsters, and media specialists" along with "citizen activists who join the political fray as weekend warriors."[51] Influential bloggers, politically activist talk radio and cable TV hosts, and other influential actors are all part of "the party" in this account. Once the party is redefined this expansively, it is clear that any "invisible primary" operates very differently from the "peer review" of elected party officials that dominated in the old, mixed system of nomination.

But even with this extremely loose conception of the party, it has become even less clear since this book was published whether the claim that "the party still decides" is accurate. The authors concede that the Democratic candidates of the 1970s, McGovern and Carter, were not the choice of the party establishment and would not have been chosen but for their ability to figure out how to work the new, populist-controlled nomination system.[52] Dismissing the significance of these nominations as transitional ones, the authors then rest their case on only ten nomination contests from 1980 to 2004. In eight of these, they conclude that "the party decided" the nominee, though they acknowledge two of those cases are questionable.[53] But nominations since then have been even less kind to their theory. They conceded at the time they wrote that if McCain were nominated in 2008 that would "rank as a clear breakdown of party control"[54] and be an "embarrassment" to their theory. He was and it is. And though they try to wriggle out a bit from the same conclusion concerning Obama's nomination, they have to start spinning epicycles to pull that off: they call Obama's nomination "unique" because "[t]he party changed its mind" *after* the voting had begun, with the Iowa caucus.[55] They candidly "confess

[50] *Id.* at 187.
[51] *Id.* at 4.
[52] *Id.* at 161–69.
[53] *Id.* at 175.
[54] *Id.* at 348, 352.
[55] *Id.* at 346.

that we did not anticipate this development" and call it "a problem" for "the party decides" claim.[56]

All that was before the 2016 election, which poses even more damaging challenges to their claim. Begin with the Democrats. If ever a party had decided on a candidate in the invisible primary that supposedly now substitutes for the party convention, it was the Democrats with their anointment of Hillary Clinton. Yet consider how close Bernie Sanders—a socialist and Independent, not even a member of the Democratic Party, who was widely disliked when he ran by the Democratic Party establishment, by the party's members in Congress, and by the party organization—came to a coup against the party's choice.[57] Had he won, it would be hard to imagine a more dramatic example of the populist-selection system completely displacing peer review. That Sanders came so close certainly poses another serious challenge to the theory. And then of course, there is the even more dramatic fact of Donald Trump having captured the Republican Party's nomination. Trump obviously represents the ultimate triumph of the populist nomination process over any role for peer review or for the newly constituted "invisible primary" through which "the party" purportedly still decides on the nominee. As a reminder, Trump abandoned many of the party's traditional policies; had no prior experience in government or the military; became a Republican only in recent years; and had virtually no support before the voting began from any traditional sources of authority and leadership in the party. He was essentially an independent free agent who successfully hijacked the party label for his own candidacy, as Sanders nearly did as well. For the authors of *The Party Decides*, "a central claim" about why the (broadly conceived) party still controls nominations is that, even in the primary-controlled process, the parties are able to "resist candidates who are unacceptable to important members of the coalition, even when those candidates are popular with voters."[58] For the Republicans in 2016 and 2008, the "party" has not been able to resist successfully the triumph of populist-fueled, insurgent candidates.[59]

***

---

56   *Id.* at 347.
57   This was recognized back in January 2016. *See* Daniel W. Drezner, *The Easy Test for 'The Party Decides' Suddenly Doesn't Look So Easy*, WASH. POST (Jan. 26, 2016), www.washington post.com/posteverything/wp/2016/01/26/the-easy-test-for-the-party-decides-suddenly-doesnt-lo ok-so-easy/?utm_term=.184de78c8a34.
58   THE PARTY DECIDES, *supra* note 18, at 339.
59   Using the accounting system of *The Party Decides* and totaling up all the post-reform contested nominations, we can say that the (broadly conceived) party has succeeded in determining the nominee between 9 and 11 times in the "modern" era, while insurgents, or the non-party candidates, have prevailed between 7 and 9 times.

As far back as the 1880s, astute observers of American politics rightly recognized the way a primary-dominated selection system could likely change the type of candidate who would be successful at competing to be the political parties' nominees for President. When the British Viscount, James Bryce, made his study of the American system in the years the first primaries were introduced, Bryce speculated that if the primary system ever became national, it might "eliminate all aspirants except those who possess conspicuous popular gifts."[60] Similarly, in more modern times, leading political scientists Nelson Polsby and Aaron Wildavsky warned that, at the time the primary system was being transformed to eliminate peer review altogether, a purely populist selection process "might lead to the appearance of extremist candidates and demagogues, who unrestrained by allegiance to any permanent party organization, would have little to lose by stirring up mass hatreds or making absurd promises."[61]

As these political scientists predicted when we changed to this system in the 1970s, this populist selection method makes it more likely that celebrity candidates would come to have significant advantages, that those who lack the relevant experience and competence would be more likely to emerge as successful candidates, and that we are likely to see a great number of candidates who are more politically extreme. To the extent small vestiges of peer review remain in our current system, even those vestiges are being eliminated. Thus, the Democratic Party had created a role for "super-delegates" after the party's debacles in the 1970s; these were party figures who served as unpledged delegates at the convention and had the capacity to use their votes to steer the party's choice in the direction that party figures thought made more sense. The creation of these super-delegates was designed precisely for the purpose of providing a check against the party adopting nominees who would be unlikely to win in the general election (McGovern) or be unable to govern effectively (Carter). But under pressure from the populist politics of Bernie Sanders' supporters, the Democratic National Committee—once again looking to buy peace between its competing factions, just as in the aftermath of the 1968 convention—agreed that, in 2020, the super-delegates would not be able to vote on the first ballot. Thus, if a candidate manages to win a majority of delegates, based only on the votes in the primaries and caucuses, that candidate will be the nominee.

---

[60] Bryce, *supra* note 5, at 850.
[61] Nelson W. Polsby & Aaron B. Wildavsky, Presidential Elections: Strategies of American Electoral Politics 230 (1964).

With the rise of populist politics in many democracies, including the United States, it is important to recognize that the old system of peer review made it far more difficult for populist figures to capture a party's nomination and put themselves into position to win highest political office.[62] Yet a few years ago, when Professor William Mayer surveyed the American literature and commentary on "peer review" in the nomination process, he wrote: "I cannot find a single, sustained attempt to defend the proposition that party leaders and elected officials deserve a larger role in what is clearly the most important decision the American parties make."[63] After events in more recent years, in the United States and elsewhere, such defenses are starting to appear.

---

[62] There is a good deal of debate currently taking place over how precisely "populist politics" ought to be conceptualized or defined. For the work which has received the most attention and inherently views populism as a substantive political ideology, linked to a rejection of political pluralism, see Jan-Werner Müller, What is Populism (2016). For a contrary view, which sees populism as a "thin" ideology that can take on various political substantive contents, and which sees populism as a politics premised on giving voice to ordinary people and curbing powerful "elites" who purportedly threaten "the people's interests," see Roger Eatwell & Matthew Goodwin, National Populism: The Revolt Against Liberal Democracy (2018).

[63] William G. Mayer, *Superdelegates: Reforming the Reforms Revisited, in* Reforming the Presidential Nomination Process 85, 104 (Steven S. Smith & Melanie J. Springer eds., 2009).

3

Constitutional Law and the Presidential Nomination Process

Richard Briffault[*]

I. INTRODUCTION

The Constitution says nothing about the presidential nominating process and has had little direct role in the evolution of that process from congressional caucuses to party national conventions to our current primary-dominated system of selecting convention delegates.[1] Yet, constitutional law is a factor in empowering and constraining the principal actors in the nomination process and in shaping the framework for potential future changes.

The constitutional law of the presidential nomination process operates along two axes: government-party, and state-national. The government-party dimension focuses on the tension between the states and the federal government in writing the rules for and administering the electoral process—which may include the primary elections that determine the nominees of the political parties—and the right of the parties to determine how to pick their nominees. This government-party axis affects all nominations of candidates for state and federal office. Presidential nominations, however, are distinct. For most elections, federal as well as state, most of the rules are determined by state law. But presidential nominations involve a national-level party decision for a nationwide office. As a result, national party rules and federal laws factor into shaping the nomination process and add the possibility of conflicts between national- and state-level rules to the more common government-party tensions.

This chapter reviews the constitutional context for the presidential nomination process and its implication for reforms. Part II considers the government-party axis, and especially the Supreme Court's efforts to reconcile the power of

[*] Richard Briffault is the Joseph P. Chamberlain Professor of Legislation at Columbia Law School.
[1] On the evolution of the presidential nomination process, see generally Stephen Gardbaum & Richard H. Pildes, *Populism and Institutional Design: Methods of Selecting Candidates for Chief Executive*, 93 N.Y.U. L. REV. 647, 652–66 (2018).

state governments to write the rules for state-run elections, including the primary elections that decide party nominations, with the freedom of political association guaranteed to the parties under the First Amendment.[2]

Part III adds national concerns to the mix. It examines the key Supreme Court rulings holding that national party rules and the decisions of the national party conventions take precedence over conflicting state laws and state party decisions. Part IV completes the treatment of the state-national dimension by considering the power of Congress to regulate the presidential nominating process. To date, Congress has played a minimal role in this area, and its authority to regulate the nomination process has been contested, but its powers are important to understand if Congress is to be involved in reforming this process.

Part V concludes by suggesting that although the multiplicity of constitutionally empowered actors may be—and has been—a source of conflict and complexity in the presidential nomination process, it may also be a strength. By permitting so many avenues for change, the constitutional framework creates multiple openings for reform.

II. THE POLITICAL PARTIES, PARTY NOMINATIONS, AND THE STATES

The Constitution says nothing about political parties. Indeed, as Madison's concerns in Federalist No. 10 about "the mischiefs of faction"[3] and Washington's denunciation in his Farewell Address of the "common and continual mischiefs of the spirit of party"[4] both suggest, the Framers were hostile to political parties. Nonetheless, political parties quickly emerged, and they played a crucial role in presidential elections as early as 1800. By the late-nineteenth century, our political process was thoroughly dominated by organized political parties. As private organizations, these political parties initially operated outside the scope of legal regulation. That began to change in the closing decades of the nineteenth century with the adoption of official state ballots.

---

[2]   Technically, in cases dealing with state law, the courts are applying the First Amendment as incorporated into the Fourteenth Amendment. For the sake of simplicity, this chapter will refer to these as First Amendment cases.

[3]   THE FEDERALIST NO. 10 (James Madison), https://avalon.law.yale.edu/18th_century/fed10 .asp.

[4]   *Transcript of President George Washington's Farewell Address,* OURDOCUMENTS.GOV (Sept. 17, 1796), www.ourdocuments.gov/doc.php?flash=false&doc=15&page=transcript.

A. *State Regulation of the Party Nomination Process*

At one time, it was common for the parties to print their own ballots and then try to persuade voters to take the party's ballot into the polls. As the Supreme Court put it, "[a]pproaching the polling place under this system was akin to entering an open auction place. As the elector started his journey to the polls, he was met by various party ticket peddlers 'who were only too anxious to supply him with their party tickets.' Often the competition became heated when several such peddlers found an uncommitted or wavering voter."[5] To combat the resulting problems of "voter intimidation and fraud," between about 1888 and 1896 virtually all of the states adopted the reform, first made popular in Australia, of requiring voters to use a ballot printed by the state.[6] But that meant the states had to decide which candidates or parties would be listed on that ballot. That, in turn, led the states to take a greater role in overseeing and, ultimately, mandating the procedures that the parties use to select their nominees.

In most states, that state-mandated procedure became the party primary. In the South, the party primary was a device for evading the Fifteenth Amendment's ban on racial discrimination in voting. As the primary was considered to be an internal party election, the Supreme Court held that a primary vote was not a "vote" within the meaning of the Constitution.[7] In the North and West, by contrast, the primary was a progressive reform that provided a means of challenging party bosses' control of the nomination process.[8] When challenged in state courts, primary requirements were generally sustained as promoting party integrity, preventing "fraud or oppression," and "increasing the power of the people to govern their parties."[9] The party primary also provided an opportunity for an actual competitive election in the many one-party states.[10] Primaries were hailed as a mechanism for combatting

---

[5] Burson v. Freeman, 504 U.S, 191, 202 (1992).

[6] *Id.* at 200–02.

[7] Grovey v. Townsend, 295 U.S. 45 (1935); *cf.* Newberry v. United States, 256 U.S. 232 (1921). States laws that *mandated* the exclusion of African-Americans from party primaries were held to violate the Fourteenth Amendment. *See* Nixon v. Herndon, 273 U.S. 536 (1927). But when the exclusion resulted from a party rule, it was a matter of private activity, not state action.

[8] *See, e.g.,* New York State Board of Elections v. Lopez Torres, 552 U.S. 196, 205 (2008) (states "set their faces against 'party bosses' by requiring party-candidate selection through processes more favorable to insurgents, such as primaries").

[9] *See* Stephen E. Gottlieb, *Rebuilding the Right of Association: The Right to Hold a Convention as a Test Case,* 11 HOFSTRA L. REV. 191, 196–200 (1982).

[10] *See* LEON D. EPSTEIN, POLITICAL PARTIES IN THE AMERICAN MOLD 129–30, 171 (1986). As the Pennsylvania Supreme Court observed in an 1886 decision, "[i]n many portions of the state, as is well known, a nomination by a convention of one of the parties is practically the

the corrupt domination of party bosses and for vindicating the right to vote by extending it to the nomination process.[11]

State primary laws were often accompanied by other measures that required certain forms of party organization, structures, and procedures for the selection of both party officers and party nominees but that also typically guaranteed the leading parties placement on state ballots. The states came to treat the major parties as institutions akin to public utilities—they were powerful entities that dominated political competition and provided an essential public service in organizing the electoral process but also needed to be overseen and regulated in order to protect the "democratic legitimacy" of that process.[12]

The Supreme Court implicitly recognized this "public utility" model in 1941, in *United States v. Classic*,[13] which disavowed the Court's prior position that a party primary is simply the internal procedure of a private organization. *Classic* held that the federal law criminalizing fraud in elections to federal office applied to Louisiana's congressional primary. As the Court explained, the primary "was conducted by the state at public expense,"[14] and was "an integral part of the procedure" that Louisiana had chosen for the election of members of Congress.[15] Indeed, "the practical influence of the choice of candidates at the primary may be so great as to affect profoundly the choice at the general election."[16] As a result, the Court in *Classic* held that Congress's power under Article I, Section 4 of the Constitution to regulate the "times, places, and manner of holding elections" for members of Congress includes the power to regulate the party primaries that select the nominees who run in congressional elections.[17]

Three years later, in *Smith v. Allwright*,[18] the Court observed that, due to *Classic*, "[i]t may now be taken as a postulate that the right to vote in ... a primary for the nomination of candidates without discrimination by the State, like the right to vote in a general election, is a right secured by the Constitution."[19] *Smith* held that the Texas Democratic Party could not

equivalent of an election. In some instances, it is the precise equivalent." Leonard v. Commonwealth, 4 A. 220, 225 (Pa. 1886).

[11] *See* Adam Winkler, *Voters' Rights and Parties' Wrongs: Early Political Party Regulation in the State Courts, 1886–1915*, 100 COLUM. L. REV. 873 (2000).

[12] *See* EPSTEIN, *supra* note 10, at 173–74.

[13] 313 U.S. 299 (1941).

[14] *Id.* at 311.

[15] *Id.* at 314.

[16] *Id.* at 319.

[17] *Id.* at 319–21.

[18] 321 U.S. 649 (1944).

[19] *Id.* at 661–62.

exclude African-Americans from participating in its primary. Although such exclusion was due to a party rule, and not a state law, it was still "state action," so that the Constitution's ban on racial discrimination in voting applied. Given the many state laws governing the internal structure of the party and the procedures for making party decisions, the party was "an agency of the state in so far as it determines the participants in a primary election."[20] Moreover, by making primaries "a part of the machinery for choosing officials, state and national" and "prescrib[ing] a general election ballot made up of party nominees ... chosen" in primaries, the state had effectively "endorse[d], adopt[ed], and enforce[d]" the party's racial discrimination.[21] The Court concluded that although, as a matter of internal autonomy, the party could set its own rules for membership, when party membership became "the essential qualification for voting in a primary to select nominees for a general election, the state makes the action of the party the action of the state."[22]

Nine years later, in *Terry v. Adams*,[23] the Court held that the internal elections of a Texas county political association which were open only to the county's white voters, and which, over a sixty-year period, effectively determined the winners of the Democratic primary and the general election, also constituted state action. There was no single opinion for the Court but the justices who composed the majority looked to the power of the party organization,[24] the state's acceptance and ratification of that power,[25] and its de facto incorporation into the decision-making of the county Democratic Party. The party organization had become part of the "electoral apparatus" of the state, and, thus, was subject to the constitutional anti-discrimination requirements that apply to state action.[26]

Four decades later, in *Morse v. Republican Party of Virginia*,[27] the Court held that the preclearance provision of Section 5 of the Voting Rights Act — which required Department of Justice approval of any new "standard, practice or procedure with respect to voting" adopted by a "covered jurisdiction" — applied to the Virginia Republican Party's decision to impose a registration fee on anyone who wanted to become a delegate to the party convention that was

---

[20] *Id.* at 662–63.
[21] *Id.* at 664.
[22] *Id.* at 664–65.
[23] 345 U.S. 461 (1953).
[24] *Id.* at 463–70 (opinion of Justice Black, joined by Justices Douglas and Burton); *id.* at 484 (opinion of Justice Clark, joined by Chief Justice Vinson and Justices Reed and Jackson).
[25] *Id.* at 468–70.
[26] *Id.* at 484.
[27] 517 U.S. 186 (1996).

called to nominate a candidate for the United States Senate.[28] Although there was no majority opinion for the Court, the two opinions that together made a majority relied on *Smith* and *Terry* in concluding that the party exercises a power delegated to it by the state when it chooses a nominee who will later appear, pursuant to state law, on the state's general election ballot. As a result, when the state places the candidate chosen by the convention on the ballot, "it 'endorses, adopts and enforces' the delegate qualifications set by the party."[29]

B. *First Amendment Protection of the Party Nomination Process*

Starting in the 1970s and 1980s, the Supreme Court began to voice a new theme in its treatment of the political parties by emphasizing that parties are political associations that enjoy the freedom of association guaranteed by the First Amendment. Moreover, the selection of a party's general election nominees was deemed to be at the core of the party's First Amendment rights.

In *Tashjian v. Republican Party of Connecticut*,[30] the Court held that the Connecticut law requiring that a party choose its nominees in a closed primary —that is, one limited to party members—unconstitutionally burdened the First Amendment rights of a party that wanted to open its primary to independent voters, that is, voters not registered with any party. The state law, the Court determined, "place[d] limits upon the group of registered voters whom the Party may invite to participate in the 'basic function' of selecting the Party's candidates."[31] The state's action "thus limit[ed] the Party's associational opportunities *at the crucial juncture* at which the appeal to common principles may be translated into concerted action, and hence to political power in the community."[32] The Court subjected the imposition of the closed primary requirement to strict judicial scrutiny, and concluded that it was not narrowly tailored to promoting a compelling state interest. The Court found one of the justifications the state offered—ensuring the administrability of the primary

---

[28] At the time *Morse* was decided, Virginia was a "covered jurisdiction," subject to the preclearance requirement of the Voting Rights Act. Two decades later, the Court struck down the provision of the Voting Rights Act setting the formula for the determination of covered jurisdictions, thus effectively terminating the preclearance requirement. *See* Shelby Co. v. Holder, 570 U.S. 529 (2013).

[29] *Morse*, 517 U.S. at 197–200 (opinion of Justice Stevens, joined by Justice Ginsburg). *See also id.* at 235, 239 (opinion of Justice Breyer, joined by Justices O'Connor and Souter, citing *Smith* as authority for application of Voting Rights Act to party nomination processes). *See also id.* at 212–18, 236–40 (citing *Terry*).

[30] 479 U.S. 208 (1986).

[31] *Id.* at 216.

[32] *Id.* (emphasis added).

system—was not compelling, while the others—avoiding voter confusion, and protecting the responsibility of party government—were not advanced by the closed primary requirement.[33]

In *Eu v. San Francisco County Democratic Central Committee*,[34] the Court struck down a law that barred the governing bodies of political parties from endorsing candidates in party primaries. The endorsement ban sought to reduce the role that the party organization had over the selection of party nominees, and it reflected the same goal that was the impetus behind forcing parties to hold primaries. But the Court nonetheless found that the ban interfered with the ability of the party to "select a 'standard bearer who best represents the party's ideologies and preferences.'"[35]

And in *California Democratic Party v. Jones*,[36] the Court invalidated California's blanket primary law, adopted by voter initiative, which would have allowed each voter to vote in any party's primary for each office on the ballot, including different party primaries for different offices (e.g., a voter could potentially vote in the Democratic primary for governor but in the Republican primary for attorney general). The Court reiterated that "states have a major role to play in structuring and monitoring the election process, including primaries,"[37] but emphasized that "the processes by which political parties select their nominees" are not "wholly public affairs that the state may regulate freely." Rather, the First Amendment "reserves" a "special place" and accords "special protection" to "the process by which a political party 'select[s] a standard bearer who best represents the party's ideologies and preferences.'"[38] The blanket primary severely burdened party First Amendment rights by allowing those who "at best, have refused to affiliate with the party, and, at worst, have expressly affiliated with a rival" to participate in the party's nomination process.[39] That could change both the identity of a party's nominee and the policy positions its candidates take, effectively "adulterat[ing]" the party's candidate selection process. "We can think of no heavier burden on a political party's associational freedom," the Court wrote. It then determined that the principal justifications advanced for the blanket primary—making party nominees more representative of the general electorate and allowing otherwise "disenfranchised voters" to participate in the

---

33   *Id.* at 217–24.
34   489 U.S. 214 (1989).
35   *Id.* at 224.
36   530 U.S. 567 (2000).
37   *Id.* at 572.
38   *Id.* at 572–75.
39   *Id.* at 577.

primary process—were not compelling.[40] Indeed, these justifications were actually inconsistent with the rights of parties and party members to select their own nominees. Other justifications—such as that the blanket primary would be "fairer" to non-party members in districts effectively controlled by one party, and that the blanket primary protected political privacy by enabling voters to participate in a primary without having to formally declare affiliation with a party—were dismissed as either non-compelling or capable of being satisfied by a less burdensome mechanism than the blanket primary.[41]

The Court in *Jones* stressed that its concern was with the state's opening *the party's nomination process* to non-party members. The state could still structure the ballot to facilitate participation by non-party voters in the selection of general-election candidates by creating a *non-partisan*—or "top two"—primary in which all candidates for an office run on the same ballot regardless of party affiliation, and all voters can vote in that election, with the top two vote-getters moving on to the general election.[42] In such a primary, non-party voters would not actually be picking a party's nominee, and the party would be free to use its own internal processes for endorsing its preferred candidate. Indeed, in 2010 California voters passed a ballot proposition creating such a top-two system for congressional and state-level elections.[43]

C. An Uncertain Synthesis

States have the constitutional power to regulate their elections, including elections for federal offices; to set the terms for the placement of parties and candidates on the state's ballot; and, as a result, to regulate the process by which parties determine their nominees. States can also use this power to promote other goals, such as the integrity and stability of the political party system.[44] Yet, the parties, as political associations, are protected by the First Amendment, and that protection extends to the party's selection of its nominees to contest the general election. These two constitutional norms do not easily fit together. In recent years, the doctrinal pendulum, which had swung first toward treating the parties as subject to state regulation and then toward a recognition of parties as bearers of First Amendment rights, appears to be swinging at least moderately back toward affirming state regulatory authority.

---

[40]   *Id.* at 579–82.
[41]   *Id.* at 582–86.
[42]   *Id.* at 585–86.
[43]   CAL. CONST. art. II, § 5.
[44]   *See, e.g.,* Storer v. Brown, 415 U.S. 724 (1974).

In *Timmons v. Twin Cities Area New Party*,[45] the Court upheld Minnesota's "anti-fusion" law that prohibited a party from nominating a candidate who had been nominated by another party. A few years later, in *Clingman v. Beaver*,[46] the Court rejected a party's argument that a state's semi-closed primary law, which permitted participation by party members and independent voters, but not voters registered with another party, violated the party's First Amendment right to choose to open its primary fully to voters registered with other parties. In both cases, the unsuccessful plaintiff was a minor party, so the results may be chalked up to the Court's preference for the two-party system[47] and its implicit hostility to minor parties.[48] But the Court's mode of analysis was not limited to minor parties. Instead, in both cases, the Court applied the so-called *Anderson-Burdick* balancing test, which it developed to deal with challenges brought by candidates and voters to state election regulations.[49] *Anderson-Burdick* reflects the judgment that "States may, and inevitably must, enact regulations of parties, elections, and ballots to reduce election- and campaign-related disorder,"[50] even though those regulations will also inevitably burden First Amendment associational rights. When an election regulation is challenged, the Court will first assess the "character and magnitude" of the burden of the state's rule. If the burden is severe, the law will have to be narrowly tailored to advancing a compelling state interest. But "[l]esser burdens ... trigger less exacting review" and "'important regulatory interests' will usually be enough to justify 'reasonable, nondiscriminatory restrictions.'"[51]

The preliminary determination of the magnitude of the burden of the state's law on protected associational freedom is key. In both *Timmons* and *Clingman*, the Court found the burdens to be relatively modest. *Timmons* reasoned that in light of the general laws that limit the eligibility of candidates, a party does not have an absolute right to nominate any particular candidate it wants. Moreover, although the anti-fusion law barred the party from nominating its preferred candidate, it was still free to endorse and support him.[52] This

---

[45]   520 U.S. 351 (1997).

[46]   544 U.S. 581 (2005).

[47]   *See, e.g.*, Timmons v. Twin Cities Area New Party, 520 U.S. at 367 (1997).

[48]   *See, e.g.*, Munro v. Socialist Workers Party, 479 U.S. 189 (1986); Jenness v. Fortson, 403 U.S. 431 (1971).

[49]   *Anderson-Burdick* derives from *Anderson v. Celebrezze*, 460 U.S. 780 (1983), in which an independent candidate sought a place on the general election ballot, and from *Burdick v. Takushi*, 504 U.S. 428 (1992), which considered a voter's claim to cast, and have counted, a write-in ballot in the state's general election.

[50]   *Timmons*, 520 U.S. at 358.

[51]   *Id.*

[52]   *Id.* at 359–60.

certainly seems in tension with the Court's prior decisions that had emphasized the vital importance of the party nominee as the "standard bearer who
best represents the party's ideologies and preferences."[53] In *Clingman*, four
members of the Court's majority did not find that the limit on the party's right
to open its primary to non-members was much of a burden on the associational
rights of the party at all.[54] The other two justices in the majority acknowledged
that some "significant associational interests [were] at stake" but thought the
burden imposed by a semi-closed primary was "modest and politically neutral"
as it barred only those voters who had chosen to affiliate with another party
from participating in the plaintiff party's primary.[55] Again, this is hard to square
with *Tashjian*'s emphasis on the party's interest in determining who can vote
in its primary. Both *Timmons* and *Clingman* found the laws at issue were
justified by the general state interests in the stability of the party system[56] and in
maintaining the integrity of political parties as "viable and identifiable interest
groups,"[57] even when political parties actually opposed those notionally pro-
party rules.

In *Washington State Grange v. Washington State Republican Party*,[58] the
Court employed the *Anderson-Burdick* standard to assess a First Amendment
challenge brought by a major party. In the aftermath of *California Democratic
Party v. Jones*, Washington voters adopted a top-two primary system, but that
law allowed a candidate to indicate a "party preference" on the ballot.[59] The
state's Republican Party sued, claiming that the "party preference" provision
violated the party's constitutional rights because voters would associate
a candidate with the party of his or her stated party preference even for "a
candidate who is unaffiliated with" the party "or even repugnant to" it.[60]
Stressing that the party was bringing only a facial challenge, the Court concluded that the party had failed to provide the evidence necessary to prove that
the "party preference" provision would inevitably be a severe burden on its
associational rights.[61] As a result, the state only had to show that the party
preference provision served an "important regulatory interest." The Court
agreed with the state that the interest in providing voters with information

---

[53] *See* Eu v. San Francisco County Democratic Central Committee, 489 U.S. 214, 224 (1989).
[54] Clingman v. Beaver, 544 U.S. at 587–91 (plurality opinion of Justice Thomas, joined by Chief
Justice Rehnquist and Justices Scalia and Kennedy).
[55] *Id.* at 602–04 (opinion of Justice O'Connor, joined by Justice Breyer).
[56] *Timmons*, 520 U.S. at 366–70.
[57] *Clingman*, 544 U.S. at 593–94.
[58] 552 U.S. 442 (2008).
[59] *Id.* at 444.
[60] *Id.* at 447.
[61] *Id.* at 454–58.

about the candidates on the ballot was such an interest.[62] *Washington Grange* was less clearly at odds with the view that the First Amendment protects party control over the nomination process than *Timmons* or *Clingman* but all three decisions certainly reflect the Court's continuing commitment to giving the states significant control over their primaries.

The strong statements in *Tashjian*, *Eu*, and *Jones* concerning the fundamental importance of the nomination process to party autonomy implicitly challenge the power of the states to mandate the use of a primary election to choose party nominees. In *American Party of Texas v. White*[63] — decided before the leading party autonomy cases — the Court declared that "it is too plain for argument . . . that the State . . . may insist that intraparty competition be settled before the general election by primary election or by party convention."[64] But the power to require a primary was not at issue in *White*, which concerned a Texas law that provided for different nomination processes for minor and new parties as opposed to the established major parties. The Court repeated *American Party*'s "too plain for argument" line in *Jones*[65] and more recently in *New York State Board of Elections v. Lopez Torres*,[66] although again a state's power to mandate a primary was not at issue in either case.[67] Indeed, the Court has never addressed a direct challenge to the constitutionality of the mandatory primary or explained how it squares with a party's powerful First Amendment interest in deciding the selection of its nominees. *Lopez Torres*, which turned back a challenge to New York's hybrid primary-and-convention system for selecting judicial candidates, gestured at a reason for the constitutionality of a primary requirement when it linked state regulation of the nomination process to the state's decision to "give[] the party a role in the election process . . . by giving certain parties the right to have their candidates appear with party endorsement on the general-election ballot."[68] But even then the Court noted that the state's power was limited by the First Amendment, citing the trio of *Tashjian*, *Eu*, and *Jones*.[69]

The constitutionality of the primary requirement was implicated in two post-*Jones* federal court of appeals decisions. In *Alaska Independence Party*

---

[62] *Id.* at 458.
[63] 415 U.S. 767 (1974).
[64] *Id.* at 781.
[65] California Democratic Party v. Jones, 530 U.S. 657, 572 (2000).
[66] 552 U.S. 196, 203 (2008).
[67] *See also* Tashjian v. Republican Party of Connecticut, 486 U.S. 208, 237 (1986) (Scalia, J. dissenting, quoting, and citing the line from *American Party*).
[68] *Lopez Torres*, 552 U.S. at 203.
[69] *Id.*

v. Alaska,[70] two minor parties challenged the Alaska law allowing any voter registered with a party—and any voter could choose to register with any party—to seek that party's nomination. The parties expressed the concern that because they could not control who registers with them and thus who may run for their nominations, the primary law prevented them from excluding candidates they found objectionable. The U.S. Court of Appeals for the Ninth Circuit, however, observed that the very purpose of the direct primary requirement is to shift control over the nomination process from "party leadership" to "rank-and-file party voters." As candidacy was limited to those who had chosen to affiliate with the party, and the party leadership remained free to endorse its preferred candidates and disavow undesired candidates, the court determined that the law's burden on party autonomy was modest. Even if it could be considered severe, "the state's interest in eliminating the fraud and corruption that frequently accompanied party-run nominating conventions is compelling."[71]

In 2018, *Utah Republican Party v. Cox*[72] vindicated a state's authority, in the face of a First Amendment objection, to alter a party's nomination process. Utah Republican Party rules provided for nominations by a convention composed of delegates elected at neighborhood caucuses. If a candidate won more than 60 percent of the convention vote, there would be no primary; if no candidate won 60 percent at the convention, there would be a primary limited to the two candidates who got the most convention votes. Utah's Republican-controlled legislature, however, passed a new law enabling any candidate who collected a qualifying number of petition signatures from party voters to participate in the primary, whether or not that candidate had sought the nomination in the convention or had been one of the top two convention candidates.[73] The Tenth Circuit rejected the state party organization's claim that this state-directed change to the nomination process severely burdened its freedom of association. In the court's view, the law was not an attack on party autonomy but a determination by the "overwhelmingly" Republican legislature of who actually spoke for the party—the relatively small group of activists who participate in the caucus-and-convention process, or the "roughly 600,000 registered Republicans"[74] eligible to participate in the primary.

---

[70]   545 F.3d 1173 (9th Cir. 2008).

[71]   *Id.* at 1179–80.

[72]   892 F.3d 1066 (10th Cir. 2018).

[73]   The law actually authorized two types of parties—"registered parties" and "qualified parties." All candidates for the nomination of a registered party would have to collect a certain number of signatures in order to qualify for placement on the primary ballot. Qualified parties—such as the Utah Republican Party—could also place their top convention candidates on the primary ballot without having to collect petition signatures. *Id.* 1072–73.

[74]   *Id.* at 1082.

With the primary limited to party voters, the court's majority saw little burden on associational rights,[75] and concluded the law was justified by the state's interests in increasing voter participation and access to the ballot.[76] However, the dissent found that by superseding the party's rules, the primary law necessarily interfered with party autonomy. The dissent also emphasized the tension between the mandatory primary and the Supreme Court's recognition of party autonomy in cases like *Jones*,[77] and contended that the "behemoth, corrupt party machines" invoked to justify mandatory primaries are a thing of the past. Indeed, the dissent urged the Supreme Court to directly address the constitutionality of the mandatory primary in light of the cases emphasizing party associational rights.[78] The Supreme Court, however, denied certiorari.[79]

Assuming a mandatory primary is constitutional, open primaries, as fifteen states require for at least some elections,[80] may be subject to challenge. *Jones* noted that an open primary "may be constitutionally distinct" from the invalidated blanket primary as "the voter is limited to one party's ballot," but *Jones* was also careful to say that it was not passing on the constitutionality of open primaries.[81] Moreover, the same concern of compelling party members to associate with non-members in the nomination process that was at issue in *Jones* is surely implicated by the open primary, in which any registered voter is entitled to vote, regardless of the voter's party affiliation. In the handful of challenges to open primary laws since *Jones*, the lower federal courts have generally been reluctant to find open primary laws facially unconstitutional,[82] but several have left open the possibility of as-applied challenges, and at least two courts have sustained those challenges when the parties provided evidence that there was likely to be a sufficiently high level of "cross-over voting"—that is, voting by members of other parties—to affect the nomination.[83] That would

---

[75]   *Id.* at 1081–83.
[76]   *Id.* at 1083–85.
[77]   *Id.* at 1110–11 (opinion of Tymkovich, C.J., concurring in part and dissenting in part).
[78]   *Id.* at 1072 (Tymkovich, C.J., concurring in denial of rehearing en banc).
[79]   Utah Republican Party v. Cox, 139 S. Ct. 1290 (2019).
[80]   *See State Primary Election Systems*, NAT'L CONF. OF STATE LEGISLATURES, www.ncsl.org /documents/Elections/Primary_Types_Table_2017.pdf.
[81]   California Democratic Party v. Jones, 530 U.S. 657, 577 n.8 (2000); *see also id.* at 576 n.6.
[82]   *See, e.g.*, Ravalli Co. Republican Central Comm. v. McCulloch, 154 F.Supp.3d 1063 (D. Mont. 2015); Democratic Party of Hawaii v. Nago, 982 F.Supp.2d 1166 (D. Hawaii 2013); Greenville Co. Republican Party Exec. Comm. v. State, 824 F.Supp.2d 655 (D.S.C. 2011); Miller v. Brown, 503 F.3d 360, 368 (4th Cir. 2007); Arizona Libertarian Party v. Bayless, 351 F.3d 1277 (9th Cir. 2003).
[83]   *See, e.g.*, Utah Republican Party v. Herbert, 144 F.Supp.3d 1263, 1270–82 (D. Utah 2015); Idaho Republican Party v. Ysursa, 765 F.Supp.2d 1266 (D. Idaho 2011).

be a "severe burden" on the party's freedom of association, not justified by any compelling state interest.

***

The constitutional tension between a state's control of its elections and a party's autonomy with respect to the selection of its nominees remains unresolved, at least in theory. In practice, the constitutionality of the mandatory primary seems settled. This may be due to the state's power to make the automatic listing of party nominees on the general election ballot contingent on the party's use of the primary to select its nominees. It may also reflect the sense that at least when the primary is limited to party voters, the state is not burdening freedom of association but protecting the rights of association members to be heard. The tension becomes sharper when the state requires the party to allow non-party members to participate in the primary process over the party's objection. There have been relatively few cases dealing with this issue, perhaps because the parties — or at least the major parties — are likely to have considerable influence with their state legislatures, so that laws the party organizations oppose will not often be enacted, although the recent Utah dispute is a clear counterexample. In the few cases that have arisen, courts have first looked to the states' power to structure their elections, including the regulation of party nominations, and have placed the burden on the challengers to prove that the state-determined voting rule severely infringes their associational rights. In a handful of cases, parties have been able to carry that burden, and it is possible that there will be more challenges in the future.

III. THE CONSTITUTIONAL STATUS OF NATIONAL PARTY RULES AND CONVENTIONS

Although the balance of constitutional power between government and party with respect to party nominations remains uncertain in state-level elections, in a trio of cases decided between 1972 and 1981, the Supreme Court made it clear that when it comes to the presidential nomination process, national party rules and the decisions of national party conventions take precedence over the rules and decisions of state-level actors. These decisions swept aside the nascent tendency, evidenced most clearly in a pair of decisions by the United States Court of Appeals for the District of Columbia Circuit in 1971, to extend the *Smith/Terry* treatment of the party nomination process as state action to the national conventions. Those D.C. Circuit decisions involved challenges, brought under the "one person, one vote" doctrine of the Fourteenth Amendment's Equal Protection Clause, to how the national parties allocated delegates across the states to the 1972 national conventions. Although the D.C. Circuit panels ultimately concluded the parties had not violated "one person, one vote," both cases agreed that a decision made by parties at the national level "is tantamount to a decision of the States acting in concert and therefore subject to constitutional standards applicable to state action," and that "there is no doubt that the allocation among the States of delegates to a party national convention is subject to the equal protection requirements of the Fourteenth Amendment."[84]

Beginning in 1972, however, the Supreme Court determined that the state action/public utility model does not apply to the national conventions and national party rules. In *O'Brien v. Brown*,[85] the Court addressed two controversies concerning the seating of competing delegations to the 1972 Democratic National Convention. The Illinois delegation had been elected in violation of guidelines adopted by the Democratic National Committee the year before, while the California delegation was entirely pledged to the winner of that state's winner-take-all primary, in violation of the mandate of the 1968 Democratic National Convention calling for the elimination of winner-take-all rules. The Convention's Credentials Committee had recommended unseating the Illinois delegation and 151 of the 271 California delegates. Suits were brought challenging both decisions. The D.C. Circuit sustained the district court's dismissal of the claim brought by the Illinois delegation, but reversed the district court's dismissal of the California claim, and petitions for certiorari and requests for stays were filed with the Supreme Court in both cases.

Acting on the very eve of the Convention, the Supreme Court stayed the judgments of the court of appeals. In a brief opinion, the Court underscored the status of "our national political parties ... as voluntary associations of individuals," and noted that whether there was either state action or a justiciable issue was uncertain "in this unique context." The Court cautioned against the judiciary acting "to interject itself into the deliberative processes of a national political convention." Instead, it found the "convention itself ... the proper forum for determining intra-party disputes as to which delegates shall be seated."[86]

The Illinois delegation's dispute was back before the Court more than two years later in *Cousins v. Wigoda*,[87] which grew out of the Illinois state court

---

[84]   Bode v. National Democratic Party, 452 F.2d 1032, 1304–05 (D.C. 1971); *accord* Georgia v. National Democratic Party, 447 F.2d 1271, 1274–78 (D.C. Cir. 1971).

[85]   409 U.S. 1 (1972).

[86]   *Id.* at 4.

[87]   419 U.S. 477 (1975).

litigation between the delegates who had won election in the March 1972 Illinois Democratic primary ("the Wigoda delegates") and the alternative delegation ("the Cousins delegates") who had argued that the procedures used to elect the Wigoda delegation violated the national party's guidelines. The Wigoda delegates won a state court order enjoining the Cousins group from serving as delegates at the Convention. Nonetheless, the Convention voted to seat the Cousins delegation. An Illinois appellate court subsequently affirmed the injunction previously issued by the state court, finding that the election of convention delegates was "governed by non-discriminatory state legislation" which reflected the "interest of the state in protecting the effective right to participate in primaries" and, thus, took "primacy ... over the decisions of a national political party convention."[88] The Supreme Court reversed in an opinion which emphasized the special nature of a presidential nomination as a nation-level decision.

The Court acknowledged that Illinois has "a compelling interest in protecting the right of its electoral processes and the right of its citizens ... to effective suffrage," but pointed to "the significant fact that the suffrage was exercised at the primary election to elect delegates to a National Party Convention." That necessarily reduced the weight of the state's interest, as convention delegates "perform a task of supreme importance to every citizen of the Nation regardless of their State of residence."[89] The Court minimized the state's stake in the selection of convention delegates, noting "[t]he States themselves have no constitutionally mandated role in the great task of the selection of Presidential and Vice-Presidential candidates," and then expressed the concern that requiring deference to state law left open the possibility of each state establishing its own qualifications without regard to party policy, "an obviously intolerable result." Instead, the matter ought to be left to the Convention, "which serves the pervasive national interest in the selection of candidates for national office, and this national interest is greater than any interest of an individual State."[90]

A third Supreme Court decision confirmed the primacy of national party decisions over state law and state parties with respect to the presidential nomination process. The national Democratic Party's rules for the selection of delegates to the 1980 National Convention provided that participation in the delegate selection process must be limited to registered Democrats. Since 1903, however, Wisconsin's election law had provided for state primaries to be open to all registered voters, and the state—including the state Democratic

---

[88] Wigoda v. Cousins, 302 N.E.2d 614, 627 (Ill. App. 1973).
[89] *Wigoda*, 419 U.S. at 489.
[90] *Id.* at 489–90.

Party—was unwilling to change this law. The state attorney general (a Democrat) sued the Democratic National Committee on behalf of the state, seeking a declaration that the national Democrats could not refuse to seat a Wisconsin delegation elected through an open primary. The Wisconsin Democratic Party, although technically a defendant, also sued the national party for an order requiring the national party to recognize the delegates selected according to Wisconsin law. The Wisconsin Supreme Court entered a judgment for the state and the state party.

In *Democratic Party of the United States v. Wisconsin ex rel. La Follette*,[91] the Supreme Court reversed, holding that "a State, or a court, may not constitutionally substitute its own judgment for that of the Party. A political party's choice among the various ways of determining the makeup of a State's delegation to the party's national convention is protected by the Constitution."[92] Wisconsin had a "substantial interest in the manner in which its elections are conducted"[93] and was free to hold an open primary, but it could not compel the national party to seat a delegation selected by a procedure that violated national party rules, nor could it compel Wisconsin delegates to vote according to the results of the state primary if that would violate party rules.[94]

La Follette was the last time the Supreme Court addressed the constitutional status of national party rules and national nominating conventions, and the message of *O'Brien*, *Cousins*, and *La Follette* taken together is clear. National political parties are unique entities, not analogous to the state actors in *White* and *Terry*, and their rules and decisions take precedence over conflicting state laws, state party preferences, and state court decisions. The doctrine resulting from these cases is so well-defined that there have been few significant cases dealing with national conventions or national parties since *La Follette*. Indeed, immediately following *Cousins*, the D.C. Circuit reconsidered its approach to the convention delegate allocation question, concluding that the "one person, one vote" doctrine did not apply to the parties at all and "reserving" the question of state action.[95] Subsequently, an Eleventh Circuit panel, relying on *La Follette*, dismissed as non-justiciable a challenge to

---

[91]   450 U.S. 107 (1981). While the case was pending, the Supreme Court stayed the Wisconsin Supreme Court's order, thus allowing the national party not to seat the Wisconsin delegates, but the Convention chose to seat the delegates. *Id.* at 114–15.

[92]   *Id.* at 123–24.

[93]   *Id.* at 126.

[94]   *Id.*

[95]   Ripon Society, Inc. v. National Republican Party, 525 F.2d 567, 580 (D.C. Cir. 1975) (en banc).

a Florida Republican Party rule, adopted pursuant to a national party directive concerning the apportionment of delegates within the state,[96] and the Fourth Circuit rejected a challenge to a 1984 Democratic National Committee rule requiring that state delegations to the national convention consist of equal numbers of men and women, observing in the course of its analysis that "the efforts of the states to regulate delegate selection have been consistently rebuffed."[97]

In short, the national parties' role in the presidential nomination process benefits from their status as private associations protected by the First Amendment, and even more so, at least relative to the states, as *national* actors engaged in a political process of national significance.

IV. THE CONSTITUTIONAL QUESTION OF A ROLE FOR CONGRESS

One aspect of the current presidential nomination system that has frequently been criticized is the presidential primary timetable. The early dates of the first caucuses and primaries (a problem known as front-loading);[98] the privileged position of small, demographically unrepresentative states like Iowa and New Hampshire; and the seemingly random and unstable nature of the caucus and primary schedules have led to calls for change. Possible reforms include a later start to the nomination calendar, rotating which states get to host the first contests, or regional primaries. Recognizing the difficulty of coordinating the laws of fifty states[99] and the rules of the state and national parties, some observers have called for federal legislation to address the presidential nomi-nation process while simultaneously also questioning whether Congress has the constitutional authority to enact legislation regulating presidential nominations.[100] This is not just a matter of whether the parties' First

---

[96] Wymbs v. Republican State Executive Comm. of Florida, 719 F.2d 1072 (11th Cir. 1983).

[97] Bachur v. National Democratic Party, 836 F.2d 837, 842 (4th Cir. 1987).

[98] *See, e.g.,* WILLIAM G. MAYER & ANDREW E. BUSCH, THE FRONT-LOADING PROBLEM IN PRESIDENTIAL NOMINATIONS (2003).

[99] There are typically far more than fifty jurisdictional delegations to the presidential nomina-tion conventions. There are regularly delegates from the District of Columbia, Puerto Rico, the Virgin Islands, Guam, American Samoa, and other overseas jurisdictions. The "fifty states" is merely convenient, if inaccurate, shorthand for the multiple subnational players involved in the process.

[100] *See, e.g.,* MAYER & BUSCH, *supra* note 98, at 131–39; ELAINE C. KAMARCK, PRIMARY POLITICS: EVERYTHING YOU NEED TO KNOW ABOUT HOW AMERICA NOMINATES ITS PRESIDENTIAL CANDIDATES 183–85 (2015).

Amendment protection precludes congressional regulation, but also whether as a matter of federalism Congress has any authority in this area at all.

The source of the asserted federalism difficulty is the text of Article II, Section 1 of the Constitution (as amended by the Twelfth Amendment), which establishes the procedure for electing a president through the Electoral College, especially when contrasted with the provisions of Article I, Section 4, which deals with congressional elections. Article II provides that "[e]ach State shall appoint, in such Manner as the Legislature thereof may direct, a Number of Electors" equal to the number of its members of Congress; limits the eligibility of who can serve as a presidential elector; lays out the procedure for the Electoral College to vote, and, if the Electoral College fails to produce a majority winner, for the House of Representatives to pick a president. (The Twelfth Amendment modified the procedure to provide for the separate election of a president and vice president.) Congress is authorized to "determine the Time of chusing the Electors, and the Day on which they shall give their Votes; which Day shall be the same throughout the United States." But other than this ability to set uniform days for the selection of Electors and for the Electors to vote, Congress is given no other power at all with respect to election of the Electoral College. Unless and until the Electoral College is unable to pick a majority winner, the presidential selection process established by the Constitution is very state-centered.

The argument for very limited congressional authority with respect to presidential elections is bolstered by a comparison of Article II with the Constitution's treatment of congressional elections. Although Article I, Section 4 begins by stating that "[t]he Times, Places and Manner of holding Elections for Senators and Representatives shall be prescribed in each State by the Legislature thereof" it then goes on to provide that "the Congress may at any time by Law make or alter such Regulations, except as to the Places of chusing Senators." As the Supreme Court recently emphasized, the "substantive scope" of congressional power to regulate congressional elections is "broad."[101] Its "comprehensive words embrace authority to provide a complete code for congressional elections"[102] and to supersede any inconsistent state law.[103] As previously noted, *United States v. Classic* extended that broad power to include the regulation of congressional primaries. The absence of any such constitutional power for Congress to regulate the election of presidential electors is striking, however, and has been cited as the basis for

---

[101] Arizona v. InterTribal Council of Arizona, Inc., 570 U.S. 1, 8 (2013).
[102] Smiley v. Holm, 285 U.S. 355, 366 (1932).
[103] Ex parte Siebold, 100 U.S. 371, 392 (1880).

doubting congressional authority to regulate the presidential nomination process.[104]

The textual silence of Article II, relative to Article I, notwithstanding, the Supreme Court has recognized Congress's power to regulate presidential elections. In *Burroughs v. United States*,[105] in 1932, the Court sustained the application of the campaign finance disclosure provisions of the Federal Corrupt Practices Act of 1925 to a presidential campaign committee. As the Court explained,

> The President is vested with the executive power of the nation. The importance of his election and the vital character of its relationship to and effect upon the welfare and safety of the whole people cannot be too strongly stated. To say that Congress is without power to pass appropriate legislation to safeguard such an election from the improper use of money to influence the result is to deny to the nation in a vital particular the power of self-protection. Congress, undoubtedly, possesses that power, as it possesses every other power essential to preserve the departments and institutions of the general government from impairment or destruction, whether threatened by force or corruption.[106]

Citing *Burroughs*, the Supreme Court again "recognized broad Congressional power to regulate in connection with the elections of the President and Vice President" in *Buckley v. Valeo*,[107] in which it generally upheld most of the contribution restrictions and disclosure requirements of the Federal Election Campaign Act without distinguishing between the law's application to congressional elections as opposed to presidential elections. Moreover, *Buckley* upheld the public funding provisions which dealt exclusively with presidential elections, including presidential primaries and the presidential nominating conventions.[108] Indeed, federal campaign finance law,[109] federal law dealing with fraud and misconduct in federal elections,[110] and other federal voting related measures have all been applied by Congress to presidential elections.

---

[104] *See, e.g.,* MAYER & BUSCH, *supra* note 98.

[105] 290 U.S. 534 (1934).

[106] *Id.* at 545.

[107] 424 U.S. 1 (1976).

[108] *See id.* at 85–109.

[109] On the consequences of federal campaign finance law for the ability of the national parties to sponsor debates among candidates for presidential nominations, see Bob Bauer, *A Debatable Role in the Process: Political Parties and the Candidate Debates in the Presidential Nominating Process,* 93 N.Y.U. L. REV. 589 (2018).

[110] *See, e.g.,* 18 U.S.C. § 594.

The Supreme Court also invoked the unique national nature of the presidency and presidential elections when it invalidated Ohio's early filing deadline for independent candidates in *Anderson v. Celebrezze*.[111] As the Court noted,

> in the context of a Presidential election, state-imposed restrictions implicate a uniquely important national interest. For the President and the Vice President of the United States are the only elected officials who represent all the voters in the Nation .... Similarly, the State has a less important interest in regulating Presidential elections than statewide or local elections, because the outcome of the former will be largely determined by voters beyond the State's boundaries.[112]

Although *Anderson* addressed only the limits on state regulatory power rather than the existence or scope of national regulatory power, its implication is that if there is going to be regulation of presidential elections it should at least in part be national in scope.

The foundation for congressional regulation of the presidential nomination process is ultimately structural rather than any specific provision of constitutional text. As Justice Black once put it, "inherent in the very concept of a supreme national government with national officers is a residual power in Congress to insure that those officers represent their national constituency as responsively as possible. This power arises from the nature of our constitutional system of government and from the Necessary and Proper Clause."[113] Scholars have also found constitutional authority for congressional action in Congress's power to count the electoral votes (combined with the Necessary and Proper Clause);[114] the Times, Places, and Manner Clause that authorizes federal regulation of congressional elections, as presidential elections are often held at the same time and on the same ballots as congressional elections;[115] and the Twelfth Amendment, which, it has been argued, implicitly recognizes the role of political parties in presidential elections.[116]

---

[111]   460 U.S. 780 (1983).

[112]   *Id.* at 794–95.

[113]   Oregon v. Mitchell, 400 U.S. 112, 124 n.7 (1970) (Justice Black, announcing the judgment of the Court in an opinion expressing his own views). *See also* Dan T. Coenen & Edward J. Larson, *Congressional Power over Presidential Elections: Lessons from the Past and Reforms for the Future*, 43 WM. & MARY L. REV. 851, 887–909 (2002).

[114]   *Id.* at 909–16.

[115]   *See id.* at 916–20; Vikram David Amar, *The Case for Reforming Presidential Elections by Sub-Constitutional Means: The Electoral College, the National Vote Compact and Congressional Power*, 100 GEO. L.J. 237, 260 (2011).

[116]   *See* Daniel H. Lowenstein, *Presidential Nomination Reform: Legal Restraints and Procedural Possibilities, in* REFORMING THE PRESIDENTIAL NOMINATION PROCESS 181–82 (Steven S. Smith & Melanie J. Springer eds., 2009).

Congressional power to regulate presidential nominations also likely includes the power to impose obligations on the states. Although the Supreme Court's anti-commandeering doctrine bars Congress from directing state legislatures to pass laws or from requiring state and local officials to implement federal laws,[117] several lower courts have held that the anti-commandeering principle does not apply to federal laws, such as the National Voter Registration Act, adopted pursuant to Congress's Times, Places, and Manner power.[118] Assuming, as the Supreme Court indicated in *Burroughs* and *Buckley*, that congressional power to regulate presidential elections is comparable to its power to regulate federal elections generally, the anti-commandeering doctrine ought not apply.

Congress, thus, ought to have as much power to regulate the presidential nomination process as it has to regulate federal elections generally. The real constraint on Congress, then, is not federalism but the First Amendment. As Part II has indicated, the extent of that constraint is uncertain. The Supreme Court would likely apply the *Anderson-Burdick* test, with the nature of the judicial review turning on the severity of the legislative burden that congressional regulations would have on a political party's freedom of association. As Part II has also shown, what counts as a severe burden—and what compelling interests might justify such a burden—is far from clear. It is tempting to speculate that some congressional regulation of the nomination process, such as changes to the timing and tempo of the nomination calendar, would not be seen as severe (especially if not opposed by the national parties) and could be justified by the "reasonable, nondiscriminatory" purpose of equalizing the influence of different states in the nomination process or giving candidates more time to bring their campaigns to more voters.[119] Conversely, it seems likely that a federal effort to regulate the inner workings of a Convention, such as by strengthening (or weakening) the influence of super-delegates, would be seen as a severe burden as such a change would likely change the type of candidate who gets nominated. But given the paucity of cases, and the tensions built into the Supreme Court's doctrine, these are necessarily speculative observations.

---

[117] *See, e.g.*, Printz v. United States, 521 U.S. 898 (1997); New York v. United States, 505 U.S. 144 (1992).

[118] *See, e.g.*, Association of Community Organizations for Reform Now ("ACORN") v. Miller, 129 F.3d 833 (6th Cir. 1997); ACORN v. Edgar, 56 F.3d 791 (7th Cir. 1995); Voting Rights Coalition v. Wilson, 60 F.3d 1411 (9th Cir. 1995).

[119] *Accord* Lowenstein, *supra* note 116, at 188–90; Richard L. Hasen, *"Too Plain for Argument?" The Uncertain Congressional Power to Require Parties to Choose Presidential Nominees Through Direct and Equal Primaries*, 102 Nw. U. L. Rev. 2009, 2017–19 (2008).

V. CONCLUSION

As a recent Congressional Research Service study concluded, "[t]he presidential nominating process is the single most complicated feature of the nation's electoral system, because it relies on national and state political party rules and practices, as well as aspects of federal and state election laws."[120] Political scientist Elaine Kamarck has also noted that "[n]o one is really in charge of the presidential nomination system; there is no 'decider.'"[121] This chapter's review of Supreme Court doctrine necessarily focused on the kinds of conflicts between participants in the process that generated contested cases, but the process is marked by cooperation and bargaining as least as much as it is by litigated conflict.[122] The national parties may make exceptions to their rules to accommodate recalcitrant states and state parties,[123] and states and state parties may change their practices in light of national party guidelines.

Moreover, although the lack of a single "decider" may complicate efforts to change the nomination process, changes to the process do occur on an ongoing basis. Although there has been no national solution to the front-loading problem, both national parties now provide incentives to their state parties to move back their delegate selection events. The national Democratic Party offers states that hold their primaries or caucuses later in the nomination process a 15–20 percent increase in delegates,[124] while the national Republican Party allows states that hold later nomination contests to allocate delegates on a winner-take-all basis rather than the proportional representation rule required for states that go earlier in the process.[125] This appears to have had some effect. The peak year for front-loading was 2008, and since then we have seen the caucus and primary calendar moved back a bit. Similarly, to promote "regional" primaries, which may reduce candidate costs and better focus voter attention, the Democratic party offers states that hold their delegate selection events on the same day as two other neighboring states a "cluster" bonus of 15 percent more delegates.[126]

---

[120] Kevin J. Coleman, *The Presidential Nominating Process and the National Party Conventions, 2016: Frequently Asked Questions*, Cong. Res. Serv., at 9 (Dec. 30, 2015).

[121] Kamarck, *supra* note 100, at 187.

[122] *See, e.g.*, Mayer & Busch, *supra* note 98, at 146.

[123] *See id.* at 142–46.

[124] Democratic Nat'l Comm., *Call for the 2020 Democratic National Convention*, § I.C.2.a.

[125] *Rules of the Republican Party*, Rule No. 16 (c), Republican Nat'l Comm., https://s3 .amazonaws.com/prod-static-ngop-pbl/docs/Rules_of_the_Republican+Party_FINAL_ S14090314.pdf.

[126] Democratic Nat'l Comm., *supra* note 124, at § I.C.2.b.

Following the sharp criticisms voiced concerning the caucus system, particularly the low rate of participation in caucuses (relative to primaries) and the difficulties of access to the caucus process,[127] the Democratic party changed its rules for the 2020 nomination to encourage greater use of primaries, and most of the caucus states have followed suit. As of the fall of 2019, at least ten of the fourteen states that held caucuses in 2016 have announced they will select their delegates to the 2020 convention by a primary,[128] so that the percentage of pledged delegates selected by caucus will drop from 14 percent to less than 5 percent.[129] These changes have also involved considerable innovation by state parties and cooperation between the state parties and state governments. For example, in four states—Alaska, Hawaii, Kansas, and North Dakota—the state Democratic Party will be holding party-run (or "firehouse") primaries. These will be conducted by party officials, and they will involve balloting in places and at times chosen by the party. Some of these party-run primaries will provide for unusual balloting mechanisms including ranked choice voting and early voting.[130]

Even the venerable Iowa caucus, although still a caucus, is being reformed by Iowa Democrats. The state party initially sought to expand participation by enabling Democrats to phone in absentee votes, rating their presidential preferences in a ranked choice style, with this virtual caucus taking place over six days. The Democratic National Committee ultimately vetoed the virtual caucus plan, concluding that it was too vulnerable to hacking.[131] The state party then came up with a new plan, which the national party approved, to create multiple "satellite" caucuses—which could be held in workplaces, nursing homes, out-of-state college campuses, and even overseas community

---

[127] See, e.g., Sean J. Wright, *Time to End Presidential Caucuses*, 85 FORDHAM L. REV. 1127 (2016).

[128] See Geoffrey Skelley, *How Will Democrats' Move Away from Caucuses Affect the 2020 Race?*, FIVETHIRTYEIGHT (May 17, 2019), https://fivethirtyeight.com/features/how-will-democrats-move-away-from-caucuses-affect-the-2020-race/.

[129] See Nate Cohn, *Fewer States Will Have Caucuses in 2020. Will It Matter?*, N.Y. TIMES (April 12, 2019), www.nytimes.com/2019/04/12/upshot/2020-election-fewer-caucuses-bernie.html.

[130] See Skelley, *supra* note 128; *Kansas Democrats Settle on May Party-Run Primary*, FRONTLOADING HQ (May 2, 2019), http://frontloading.blogspot.com/2019/05/; *Alaska Democrats Plan on April 4 Party-Run Primary*, FRONTLOADING HQ (March 31, 2019), http://frontloading.blogspot.com/2019/03/; *Hawaii Democrats Aim for an April Party-Run Primary in Lieu of Caucuses*, FRONTLOADING HQ (March 26, 2019).

[131] See Brianne Pfannensteil & Barbara Rodriguez, *DNC Recommends Scrapping Iowa's Virtual Caucuses. Iowa Democratic Party Chair Insists Iowa Will Still Be First*, DES MOINES REGISTER (Aug. 30, 2019), www.desmoinesregister.com/story/news/elections/presidential/caucus/2019/08/30/iowa-caucus-dnc-reject-virtual-plan-cyber-security-threat-2020-president-election-nevada-democratic/2163632001/.

gathering places and elsewhere—in addition to the precinct caucuses to accommodate people who cannot attend the traditional in-precinct caucuses.[132]

On the Republican side, the state parties have also been changing their rules, albeit with the focus not of expanding participation but of reducing the potential for opposition to the renomination of President Trump. Several state parties have eliminated the use of primaries or caucuses for selecting delegates or allocating them among candidates; some have raised the threshold of votes a candidate must receive in order to be allocated delegates, or some have cancelled their nominating procedures altogether.[133]

Overall, what is most striking when examining the actions of the national and state parties and the state legislatures in preparing for the 2020 nominations is the degree of cooperation among the various actors in writing and rewriting the rules for the selection of convention delegates. New state-run primaries,[134] changed primary dates,[135] authorization to cancel primaries,[136] the creation of party-run primaries,[137] and the expansion of participation in the caucus process in Iowa and Nevada,[138] have all gone forward without major

---

[132] *See* Brianne Pfannensteil, *DNC Approves Iowa's Plan to Hold "Satellite" Caucuses in Nursing Homes, College Campuses, and More in 2020*, DES MOINES REGISTER (Sept. 20, 2019), www .desmoinesregister.com/story/news/elections/presidential/caucus/2019/09/20/dnc-approves-iowa-caucuses-satellite-location-plan-2020-democrats-democratic-party/2387347001/

[133] *See, e.g., Alaska Republicans Scrap Presidential Preference Vote at 2020 Caucuses*, FRONTLOADING HQ (Sept. 23, 2019), http://frontloading.blogspot.com/2019/01/invisibleprimary-visible-republicans.html; *New Arizona Budget Contains a Presidential Primary Opt-Out for State Parties*, FRONTLOADING HQ (June 6, 2019), http://frontloading.blogspot.com/2019/06/; *North Carolina Republicans Have Tweaked Their Delegate Allocation Formula, but …*, FRONTLOADING HQ (May 16, 2019), http://frontloading.blogspot.com/2019/05/; *Massachusetts GOP Rules Change Adds an Element of Winner-Take-All to 2020 Delegate Allocation*, FRONTLOADING HQ (May 7, 2019), http://frontloading.blogspot.com/2019/05/massachusetts-gop-rules-change-adds.html.

[134] *On to the Governor: Maine House Passes Super Tuesday Presidential Primary Bill*, FRONTLOADING HQ (June 4, 2019), http://frontloading.blogspot.com/2019/06/; *Washington State Democrats Opt for Presidential Primary over Caucuses*, FRONTLOADING HQ (April 8, 2019), http://frontloading.blogspot.com/2019/06/ (April 8, 2019), http://frontloading .blogspot.com/2019/04/.

[135] *Utah Presidential Primary Shifts to Super Tuesday*, FRONTLOADING HQ (April 1, 2019), http:// frontloading.blogspot.com/2019/04/.

[136] *See, e.g., New Arizona Budget Contains a Presidential Primary Opt-Out for State Parties*, *supra* note 133.

[137] *See, e.g., Washington State Democrats Opt for Presidential Primary over Caucuses*, *supra* note 134.

[138] *See, e.g.,* Pfannensteil, *supra* note 132; *Nevada Delegates Release Draft Delegate Selection Plan*, FRONTLOADING HQ (March 21, 2019), http://frontloading.blogspot.com/2019/03/neva da-democrats-release-draft-delegate.html.

litigation. Although the course of changing the presidential nominating system is slow, messy, uneven, and uncertain, reforms do occur, even without a single "decider." Indeed, the process provides room for state-level and state- and party-specific innovations that reflect distinctive state and party preferences and also respond to and shape national trends.

***

Unlike the presidential election process—with its entrenched Electoral College—the Constitution itself imposes no constraints on changing the presidential nomination process. Moreover, the multiple potential actors empowered by constitutional law to address the nomination process provide multiple avenues for seeking change. The real obstacles to reforming the process are not constitutional but normative and political—deciding what would be a better process, and figuring out how to work the political system to get such a process adopted.

4

Winnowing and Endorsing: Separating the Two Distinct Functions of Party Primaries

Edward B. Foley[*]

With the increasing fear that democracy is faltering worldwide, it is perhaps naïve to think that there could actually exist a rational and well-ordered system for electing the president of the United States. Yet the opposite idea—that the process for picking the president is irrational and arbitrary, failing to reflect the real preferences of the electorate—is deeply unsettling. The American president wields too much power for the incumbent to be the product of an incoherent procedure. For the sake of humanity as a whole, as well as the people of the United States, it is essential to endeavor as best as is humanly possible to conceptualize what a coherent and sensible system for presidential elections might be.

This endeavor must encompass both the primary and general election phases of the overall process and, in doing so, must pay special attention to the interrelationship of the two phases. There is so much in need of fixing with respect to each of the two phases that it is easy to focus on the reform of each as a separate issue. But a rational primary process and a rational general election process does not guarantee rationality of the electoral system as a whole. The way in which the two components interact with each other, even though each is sensible by itself, may introduce incoherence into the system—and produce a winner that the electorate does not want, thereby undermining the democracy that the electoral system is intended to achieve.

Although this chapter focuses on the design of the presidential primary process, it will place particular emphasis on how a well-designed primary process must fit together with a well-designed general election process. This

* Edward B. Foley is the Charles W. Ebersold and Florence Whitcomb Ebersold Chair in Constitutional Law at The Ohio State University's Moritz College of Law, where he is also Director of the Election Law @ Moritz Program. The author thanks participants in Ohio State's colloquium on the Agendas and Procedures of Social Governance for their constructive critique of an earlier draft.

chapter cannot offer a complete blueprint for the entire presidential election system; that would require a whole other book. But the chapter can begin to sketch what that blueprint would entail. It does so by starting with an extreme example of how the relationship between the primary process and the general election can breakdown: when the loser of a primary wants to "bolt" from the party and run in the general election. The point of starting with this example is not to claim that it is especially likely to occur, either in 2020 or any other year. But in the same way that a stress test enables doctors to detect a heart problem that is asymptomatic at rest, examining how the system would handle a "bolt" scenario exposes incoherence in the overall system that is otherwise masked.

I. A "BOLT" FROM A BROKERED CONVENTION

In 2019, there had been talk about the possibility of the Democrats having a "brokered convention" in 2020—which would result if no candidate managed to win a majority of the convention's delegates on the first ballot, as required for the party's nomination. This talk had been accompanied by the recognition that pundits early in each presidential cycle invariably raise the brokered convention idea, but this time they insisted it really could happen. Pointing to a constellation of factors, including the unusually crowded Democratic field, the party's use of proportional delegate allocation, and the front-loading of the primary schedule, with California and other big states holding their primaries earlier than usual, sober prognosticators like Nate Silver had warned that this possibility was much higher than in the recent past.[1]

Although a brokered convention did not actually happen, the idea allows us to consider a variation of that possibility: a rift in the party that causes a candidate who is denied the nomination at a brokered convention to "bolt" and run as an independent in the general election. The chance of this occurring is small but always latent, and its potentiality raises important issues concerning the relationship of primary and general elections. To illustrate the general point with a concrete example, all we have to do is think of a vivid scenario that captures how the electoral process could go haywire in terms of making an orderly sensible transition from the primaries to the general election. Imagine that Bernie Sanders had not dropped out of the

---

[1] *See* Ed Kilgore, *Yes, a Contested Convention Could Actually Happen in 2020*, N.Y. MAG. (Mar. 14, 2019); Noah Millman, *How Bernie 2020 Could Lead to a Brokered Convention*, THE WEEK (Feb. 21, 2019); Paul Bledsoe, *Jam-packed Primary Poses a Serious Threat to Democrats in 2020*, THE HILL (Mar. 25, 2019); David Rutz, *Nate Silver: 'High Probability' of Brokered Democratic Convention in 2020*, WASH. FREE BEACON (Dec. 8, 2017).

race in April 2020. Instead, imagine that he arrived at the convention with a plurality, but not majority, of delegates—say 37 percent. Joe Biden was next, with 33 percent. Then came, say, Amy Klobuchar, with 20 percent. The remaining 10 percent of delegates were split among candidates who had already bowed out of the race and had endorsed one of the three finalists (for example, Elizabeth Warren endorsing Sanders, Kamala Harris endorsing Biden, and Beto O'Rourke endorsing Klobuchar). After Sanders fails to win the nomination on the first ballot, Biden and Klobuchar strike a deal: Biden will be the top of the ticket, with Klobuchar his running mate. Pooling their delegates this way, Biden wins the nomination on the second ballot.

Bernie and his supporters, according to this hypothetical account, are outraged and leave the convention vowing to continue their fight on to the general election. In reality, Sanders signed a pledge in April of 2019 to support the Democratic nominee "period"—with "[n]o third-party threats."[2] But this pledge could be broken more than a year later, in light of subsequent developments, and Bernie's history as an independent socialist rather than a Democrat would make that situation plausible.

Continuing with the hypothetical speculation, we can imagine that Biden, Klobuchar, and other Democrats plead for Bernie not to split the party, virtually guaranteeing Trump's re-election. Nonetheless, Sanders is not dissuaded, and he announces that his progressive cause is bigger than the party or any one election. Several minor parties have candidates of their own on the ballot—Libertarian, Green, and the like—as is routinely true (and there may be other independent candidates as well).[3] Bernie observes that the general election would be fragmented among multiple candidates anyway and therefore the American people ought to have a chance to support his progressive vision, and not let that opportunity be "stolen" from them by a "corrupt bargain"[4] among Biden, Klobuchar, and other "establishment-types" within the Democratic Party.

---

[2] Ed Kilgore, *2020 Candidates Begin Signing Unity Pledge, with Sanders Taking the Lead*, N.Y. MAGAZINE, April 26, 2019.

[3] For example, in July 2019, former Republican and now independent Representative Justin Amash of Michigan would not rule out an independent bid for the presidency in 2020. *See* Robert Costa, *Amash Doesn't Rule Out 2020 Bid, Potentially Complicating Trump's Path to Reelection*, WASH. POST (July 7, 2019). In April 2020, Amash actively sought the presidential nomination of the Libertarian Party. *See* Rachel Bitecofer, *Justin Amash's Libertarian Candidacy May Act as a Spoiler—But That Could Help Biden*, GUARDIAN (April 30, 2020), www.theguardian.com/commentisfree/2020/apr/30/justin-amash-libertarian-candidacy-spoiler-f or-whom.

[4] The reference to a "corrupt bargain" is not accidental. It invoked Andrew Jackson's allegation of a "corrupt bargain" between John Quincy Adams and Henry Clay to deprive Jackson of the

Quite clearly, whatever one thinks of the primary process that leads to this kind of bolt from the convention, the general election is going to be entirely different depending on whether (1) the Democratic party nominee, here hypothetically Biden, is the only Democratic candidate on the general election ballot, or (2) the Democratic party nominee is joined on the general election ballot by a disgruntled Democratic candidate, here hypothetically Sanders, who has bolted from the party and is now running as an independent. Unless the system as a whole is prepared for both possibilities, and figures out how to handle the latter as well as the former sensibly, it has not woven together the primary and general election processes into a unified and coherent whole.

II. THE RELATIONSHIP OF PRIMARIES AND THE GENERAL ELECTION

This division in the Democratic Party may need only be sufficiently realistic to demonstrate the interdependent connection between the party nomination process and the general election. Evaluating the success or failure of the nomination process requires not only a judgment about the quality of the nominee whom the process produces, but also an assessment of how the nomination process fits into the overall enterprise of producing a president from the entire field of candidates.

This observation builds upon a new book I have written that addresses the need for the presidential election system to adopt reforms for handling the role of third-party and independent candidates on the general election ballot.[5] The book advocates for states to adopt Instant Runoff Voting, or some other mechanism, to assure that no presidential candidate wins all of a state's Electoral College votes without winning a majority of the state's popular votes. Instant Runoff Voting, also known as ranked choice voting, enables voters to rank candidates in order of preference, and these preferences permit a computer to tabulate an "instant runoff" winner if no candidate receives a majority of first choice votes. For example, the 2016 presidential election had several candidates besides Donald Trump and Hillary Clinton: Gary Johnson,

---

presidency in the 1824 election, after Jackson wins a plurality but not a majority of Electoral College votes, and the election goes to the House of Representatives, according to special procedure set forth in the Twelfth Amendment of the Constitution. I discuss the 1824 election and its relevance to understanding how the Electoral College operates today in EDWARD B. FOLEY, PRESIDENTIAL ELECTIONS AND MAJORITY RULE: THE RISE, DEMISE, AND POTENTIAL RESTORATION OF THE JEFFERSONIAN ELECTORAL COLLEGE (2020).

[5] *Id.*

the Libertarian; Jill Stein, the Green; and Evan McMullin, an independent. The use of Instant Runoff Voting would have permitted a voter to rank Johnson first and Clinton ahead of Trump, or vice versa, and this type of ranking would have enabled a calculation of whether Trump or Clinton was preferred by a majority of voters in those states where neither Trump nor Clinton was the first choice of a majority. Because Trump won 107 of his 304 electoral votes in states where he failed to receive more than half of the popular votes cast in the state, the minor party and independent candidates were significant factors in the race, and the use of Instant Runoff Voting might have made a difference in the outcome (if Clinton was preferred over Trump by enough of the voters who cast their ballots for these other candidates).

Instant Runoff Voting solves what is sometimes derisively called the "spoiler" effect of third-party and independent candidates, who distort the choice that the electorate would make if the ballot were confined to the top two candidates. "Spoiler" is an unfair label, given the right of all candidates and political parties to compete on equal terms without any presumption at the outset about who is entitled to win—or even who is entitled to be considered as one of the top two contenders. But one can understand the use of the term when one realizes that the presence of a third candidate can determine which of the two other candidates ends up winning. To crystalize this point most lucidly, recall the sheer terror that Democrats had when it looked like Howard Schultz, the former CEO of Starbucks, was seriously considering an independent run in 2020. The realistic fear among Democrats was that Howard Schultz would "siphon" enough votes from the Democratic nominee to alter the outcome, in the same way that Ralph Nader did in 2000.[6] Instant Runoff Voting lets third-party and independent candidates run without the risk of being "spoilers": voters can rank these candidates first, if they wish, with one of the major-party candidates as a backup preference. If these additional candidates fail to attract enough support to be one of the two candidates with the most first choice rankings, then all these extra candidates are eliminated and thus do not distort the determination of which candidate—between the top two—is the one preferred by the majority of the voters.

The question to be considered here is how to view the nomination process if Instant Runoff Voting were adopted for the general election presidential vote. In this regard, one point is obvious: if Bernie Sanders were to run as an independent in the general election after losing the Democratic nomination in a brokered convention, as in the scenario described above, Instant Runoff

---

[6]   Kevin Kruse & Julian Zelizer, *Historians: Howard Schultz could re-elect Donald Trump*, CNN
      OPINION (Jan. 29, 2019).

Voting could "handle" the addition of this independent candidacy in the same way as it could "handle" any other independent candidacy.[7] In other words, if they wished, voters could list Bernie Sanders as their first choice and then, begrudgingly, list Joe Biden as their second choice. The split in the Democratic Party as a result of the brokered convention would not cripple the party in the general election. If voters generally agreed with the convention's decision to give Biden the nominee, and this level of support was enough to win in November, then the disappointment of Bernie's supporters would not drag Biden down. Alternatively, if Bernie were actually a stronger general election candidate than Biden, and the convention had made a mistake in not recognizing this, then Instant Runoff Voting could "protect" against this mistake as well: Biden's general election voters could list Bernie as their second choice, and if this level of support were enough, he would win the election (without, again, Biden's presence on the ballot dragging Bernie down).

But even though it is easy to see that Instant Runoff Voting could protect against a rupture within a party resulting from a convention fight, questions remain concerning what role a party nomination should have if the general election ballot uses Instant Runoff Voting. Is there a point to having party nominations at all, if multiple candidates from the same party can appear on the general election ballot with the use of Instant Runoff Voting? Alternatively, even if Instant Runoff Voting can "handle" multiple candidates from the same party, is there a reason to limit the general election ballot to only one candidate from each party (along with any independent candidates), and, if so, does that mean that in the hypothetical rift following the brokered convention Bernie Sanders should be denied a spot on the general election ballot, because Biden received the party's nomination (even if controversially)? And should Bernie be denied a spot on the general election ballot even though independent candidates (like, potentially, Howard Schultz) get a spot, and even assuming Bernie has far greater support among voters than these independent candidates do? These questions require us to think carefully about the function of party nominations in a system where, because of Instant Runoff Voting, it is possible for the general election ballot to accommodate multiple candidates.

---

[7] For example, independent candidate Howard Schultz suspended his incipient quest for the presidency in June of 2019 but did not foreclose the possibility of resuming it. *See* Pia Deshpande, *Back Surgery Sidelines Howard Schultz's Exploratory Campaign*, Politico (June 12, 2019).

III. TWO-PARTY VERSUS MULTIPARTY COMPETITION, IN THEORY AND IN AMERICAN HISTORY

In a two-party electoral system, where, according to its idealized conception, there are only supposed to be two candidates in contention at the general election stage of the process, the essential function of each party's nomination procedure is to identify one of those two candidates. There are only two teams, red and blue. All potential candidates must choose which team they wish to play for. Each team must then pick which, among its many contenders, should do battle against the other team's chosen gladiator.[8]

Given this conception of the electoral process, we can debate the method that each team should use to pick its chosen gladiator for the general election battle against the other team.[9] There might be a difference of opinion on what makes for a good general election candidate, with a team's members having a different view on this point from the public as a whole. But however we decide to resolve this particular procedural conflict, we would all agree that in a strict two-party system (where the general election is indeed confined to the candidates of just the two parties) the task of each party's nomination process is fundamentally to select a single candidate to duel against the other party's single candidate. Nomination, in other words, is all about winnowing the field in this way, casting aside all the other potential competitors but one for each of the two teams.

Although America has conceived of itself as having a two-party system ever since the Jeffersonians squared off against the Federalists, most momentously in the election of 1800, in reality presidential elections since the 1840s have featured several notable third-party and independent candidates.[10] Some of these have been defectors from one of the two main parties at the time. Spurned at their own party's nominating convention, these defectors felt compelled to take their case directly to the American electorate as a whole in the general election.

Martin Van Buren was the first, and perhaps most ironic, of these defectors when he accepted the nomination of the newly formed Free Soil party in 1848, after having been passed over for the Democratic party's nomination that year. Two decades earlier, Van Buren had been a principal architect of

---

[8] For a canonical statement of this model, see William H. Riker, *The Two-party System and Duverger's Law: An Essay on the History of Political Science*, 76 AM. POL. SCI. REV. 753 (1982).

[9] The U.S. Supreme Court addressed this issue most significantly in *California Democratic Party v. Jones*, 530 U.S. 567 (2000), but for reasons we shall discuss the Court's decision in that case is highly questionable.

[10] *See* FOLEY, *supra* note 4.

America's second two-party system, solidifying competition between Democrats under the leadership of Andrew Jackson and Van Buren himself against their Whig opponents. Having won the presidency as Jackson's successor in 1836, but then after losing reelection in 1840 against William Henry Harrison, Van Buren was denied the chance for a comeback by his own Democratic party in 1844 and again in 1848. Spurned in this way, and lamenting the sharp proslavery shift of the Democrats in 1844 and increasingly thereafter, Van Buren agreed in 1848 to head the new Free Soil ticket against his old party's nominee, Senator Lewis Cass of Michigan, as well as the Whig candidate, General Zachary Taylor.[11]

Although Democrats viewed Van Buren as disloyal, Van Buren did not view himself this way. Rather, he saw the faction in control of the party's national convention at Baltimore in 1848 as disloyal to the party's roots and values, and thus he viewed his reluctant Free Soil candidacy as the only way to save the true Democratic Party from its new false self.[12] This psychology of defection is important to keep in mind as one considers the hypothetical possibility of a similar defection from the Democratic Party in 2020.[13]

Martin Van Buren is not the only former president to run as a third-party candidate after having been denied another chance to run as the nominee of his own (former) party. Teddy Roosevelt did the same thing in 1912. He had been elected as a Republican in 1904, after ascending to the presidency as William McKinley's vice-president upon McKinley's assassination in 1901. Having served almost two full terms, and mindful of the two-term tradition set by George Washington and followed ever since (up to that point), Roosevelt declined to run again in 1908. Instead, he anointed William Howard Taft as his successor. Taft's performance in office, however, disappointed Roosevelt. The former was becoming increasingly conservative, while the latter was growing increasingly progressive. Roosevelt decided to challenge Taft for the Republican nomination in 1912. The fight between these former friends was titanic, going all the way to the convention, with challenges over the credentialing of competing slates of delegates from several states. After Taft

---

[11] DANIEL WALKER HOWE, WHAT HATH GOD WROUGHT: THE TRANSFORMATION OF AMERICA, 1815–1848 (2007); JOHN NIVEN, MARTIN VAN BUREN: THE ROMANTIC AGE OF AMERICAN POLITICS (2000); DONALD COLE, MARTIN VAN BUREN AND THE AMERICAN POLITICAL SYSTEM (2014).

[12] HOWE, *supra* note 11, at 832; COLE, *supra* note 11, at 418.

[13] For Sanders, the psychology of defection would be complicated by the fact that he has considered himself an independent rather than a Democrat, but that fact could make it psychologically easier (rather than harder) to defect from the Democrats, who wrongfully deprived him of their nomination, because there would be less sense of disloyalty to long-standing ties of party affiliation.

secured the Republican nomination, Roosevelt "bolted" from the convention and formed the Progressive Party.[14] Although Roosevelt's "Bull Moose" run, as it was colloquially known, was technically a third-party candidacy, Roosevelt won more general election votes than Taft did as the Republican nominee. Indeed, had Instant Runoff Voting been available for the general election in 1912, Roosevelt most likely would have won. By gaining the second choice votes of Taft's supporters, Roosevelt would have pulled ahead of Woodrow Wilson, the Democratic candidate who was then governor of New Jersey and who won the presidency in 1912.

Roosevelt, never one to think modestly of himself, did not view his "bolt" from the Republican party as disloyal. Instead, he viewed himself as the superior Republican candidate to Taft, who had gone astray in Roosevelt's eyes. The party should have supported him. Indeed, Roosevelt felt robbed of the party's nomination by the party's bosses at the convention. Far from betraying the party by his "Bull Moose" run, Roosevelt believed he was remaining faithful to the party's true cause.[15]

In 2016, for a while it appeared that there might be a major schism in the Republican party not unlike what happened in 1912. As Donald Trump upended the GOP establishment and clinched the Republican nomination heading into the party's Cleveland convention, there was increasing talk among "true conservatives" about bolting from the party to form a separate general election candidacy. There was hope that Mitt Romney, or someone of his stature, might be willing to make such a move. In the end, it fell to little known Evan McMullin to serve as the renegade Republican candidate in the general election for the "never Trump" wing of the party.[16] McMullin, who had not run in the primaries and had almost no following in the electorate, obviously could not pull off the same kind of separate campaign that Roosevelt had in 1912 or that Mitt Romney might have had. By contrast, if Bernie Sanders bolted from the Democrats in 2020, after being "deprived" of the party's nomination despite (hypothetically) finishing first in the 2020 Democratic primaries with 37 percent of the delegates, his separate general election

---

[14] The story of the split between Taft and Roosevelt is beautifully told in DORIS KEARNS GOODWIN, THE BULLY PULPIT: THEODORE ROOSEVELT, WILLIAM HOWARD TAFT, AND THE GOLDEN AGE OF JOURNALISM (2013).

[15] *See* GEOFFREY COWEN, LET THE PEOPLE RULE: THEODORE ROOSEVELT AND THE BIRTH OF THE PRESIDENTIAL PRIMARY 250 (2016).

[16] Maggie Haberman, *Evan McMullin, Anti-Trump Republican, Mounts Independent Presidential Bid*, N.Y. TIMES (Aug. 8, 2016); Maggie Haberman, *Conservative Donor's Group Presses Ballot Access for a Third-Party Candidate*, N.Y. TIMES (June 14, 2016); Philip Rucker & Robert Costa, *Inside the GOP Effort to Draft an Independent Candidate to Derail Trump*, WASH. POST (May 14, 2016).

campaign would be nothing like Evan McMullin's. Instead, it would be a lot more prominent, and in this respect more like Teddy Roosevelt's, with Sanders claiming that he, too, had been "robbed" of the nomination. He would claim that he was going into the general election as the "authentic" voice of the party's voters.

IV. DISTINGUISHING TWO FUNCTIONS OF A PARTY PRIMARY

Although monumental defections of the kind committed by Van Buren and Roosevelt are relatively rare, other candidates besides former presidents have run as independents after failing to achieve their own party's nomination. Senator Robert La Follette ran as a Progressive in 1924 after losing the Republican nomination, and Senator Storm Thurmond ran as a Dixiecrat in 1948 after the southern segregationists bolted from the Democratic National Convention that year. In 1980, John Anderson started running in the Republican primaries but abandoned that effort early in the process, never taking his candidacy to the GOP convention, in favor of an independent bid in the general election against Ronald Reagan as the Republican nominee and Jimmy Carter as the incumbent Democrat.

More frequent are independent and third-party candidacies that emerge not from splits within one of the two major parties, but instead from movements that never attempted to capture either of the two major-party nominations. Ross Perot's run in 1992 is a prominent example of an entirely separate candidacy, as was James Weaver's run as a Populist a century earlier, in 1892. This category also includes the myriad minor-party candidacies, like Ralph Nader's in 2000 or Gary Johnson's and Jill Stein's in 2016, which, despite winning very low percentages of the total vote, can end up having a major impact, potentially even one that is outcome-determinative, on the race.

A sensible presidential election system must deal with both types of separate candidacies. While it is important for the system to manage a truly independent candidacy like Ross Perot's, it is equally imperative to manage a rupture, or splinter, candidacy like Teddy Roosevelt's in 1912 or John Anderson's in 1980. One cannot ignore the fact that, from time to time, there may be a breakdown in a major party's nomination process, leading to an internal fissure within the party that produces two (or potentially more) general election candidates from the same party. From the perspective of handling multiple candidates on the general election ballot, it matters not whether an independent candidate competed briefly for a major-party nomination as John Anderson did in 1980, or had been the governor of a state as a major-party nominee but did not pursue a major-party presidential nomination, which was Gary Johnson's status in 2016.

Since Instant Runoff Voting can handle a splinter or rupture candidacy just the same as a truly independent candidacy, in an electoral system that includes Instant Runoff Voting it becomes possible to think of party nominations as performing not so much a *winnowing* function, as required in a strict two-party system, but instead as a separate *endorsement* function. It is no problem that both Taft and Roosevelt appear on the general election ballot, but only Taft is entitled to have the Republican Party's endorsement next to his name, because Taft is the one who received the Republican nomination. The same point would apply if there were indeed a rupture in the Democratic Party in 2020, as hypothetically described above: both Biden and Sanders would get their spots on the general election ballot, but only Biden would have the Democratic Party's endorsement next to his name. If one is a member of the party, one hopes that such a rupture never occurs: even in a system with Instant Runoff Voting, a party would prefer that the attention of voters not be distracted from the party's nominee by other names of the ballot, especially not prominent candidates who just competed for and lost a major fight for the party's nomination. From the party's perspective, of course the preference would be for the losing candidate to bow out gracefully and support the party's nominee. But if this kind of rupture does occur, and the losing candidate will appear on the general election ballot alongside the party's nominee, then from the party's perspective it is advantageous both that the system uses Instant Runoff Voting and that the party's nominee is identified with the party's official endorsement on the ballot. In that way the party would be in the best possible position to have its nominee prevail in the general election, despite the rupture that occurred at the party's convention.

V. THE PARTY'S RIGHT TO CONTROL
THE ENDORSEMENT PROCESS

If the party nomination process serves an endorsement function, without the additional need to winnow the field, then the First Amendment interest of the party having the right to control the nomination process is especially strong. The party should be able to decide for itself how it wants to go about endorsing whichever candidate it thinks is the best or strongest, according to whatever criteria the party considers most important. Presumably, the party will want to win and thus will try to endorse a candidate with a reasonable chance of prevailing in the general election. But in making this judgment, the party needs to weigh a complex set of factors in evaluating what might make a candidate most electable in the context of this particular election — and also how much to trade off the goal of winning against the party's policy and ideological commitment insofar as there may be a conflict between electoral competitiveness and philosophical purity.[17] Added to this complex substantive judgment, there is also the procedural question of what process the party should use to make its endorsement.

This procedural question contains many subparts. Should the endorsement be made by the party's convention delegates, or be determined conclusively in advance by the pure counting of ballots cast in the party's primaries? If the endorsement is to be made at the convention, should it be made pursuant to a majority rule requirement, or a supermajority requirement (as the Democratic Party used in the past),[18] or even a mere plurality requirement? Should there be any form of delegates, like so-called "superdelegates," whose right to vote at the convention does not derive from the result of primary elections? What should be the voting rules for primaries? Winner-take-all or proportional allocation of delegates? District-based or statewide? Ranked choice or regular (first-choice-only) ballots? Caucuses instead of primaries? And what should be the schedule, including order, of the primaries? And so on and so forth?

With respect to all these questions, there could be reasonable differences of opinion on what would be best. But as long as the party's nomination process serves only an endorsement function, and no winnowing function, then the party's own opinion on all of these questions should control. The government simply has no overriding interest to stipulate the procedure by which a political party determines which candidate it wishes to endorse for which public office. Settling upon the procedure for making that determination is an essential element of the party's freedom of association.

In this respect, political parties are no different from other ideological associations that might wish to endorse a preferred presidential candidate during the primary process. The Sierra Club, the NRA, NARAL, and a whole host of advocacy organizations may wish to express a preference on which presidential candidate would be best from their perspective. Because

---

[17] Lisa Lerer, *What Does "Electable" Mean in the 2020 Race? Here Are 5 Theories*, N.Y. TIMES, May 6, 2019; Chelsea Janes, *Who Is the Most Electable? Candidates Point to Themselves*, WASH. POST, May 6, 2019.

[18] William G. Mayer, *How Parties Nominate Presidents, in* THE OXFORD HANDBOOK OF AMERICAN POLITICAL PARTIES AND INTEREST GROUPS 189 (L. Sandy Maisel, Jeffrey M. Berry & George C. Edwards III eds., 2010) ("Democratic [Party] rules insisted that a candidate receive two-thirds of the convention votes before being declared the winner.").

these non-party interest groups have no formal role in the winnowing process, the First Amendment requires that they be free to determine their own internal governance procedures for deciding which candidate to endorse. Likewise, insofar as a political party's endorsement of a candidate has been separated from the winnowing process, there is no reason to treat a political party differently than any other ideological organization in terms of upholding its First Amendment right to control the internal governance method by which it makes this endorsement.

VI. THE GOVERNMENT'S INTEREST IN REGULATING THE WINNOWING PROCESS

Even with the use of Instant Runoff Voting in general elections, there remains a strong interest in the winnowing of candidates in order to determine which should qualify for a place on the general election ballot. Just try to imagine a single Instant Runoff ballot with all of the candidates wanting to run for president. As of April 30, 2020, more than 1,000 individuals—1,079, to be exact—had filed papers with the Federal Election Commission (FEC) as candidates for president: 313 Democrats, 156 Republicans, 63 Libertarians, 22 Greens, and hundreds of others.[19] Even with a system that would have the parties conduct their own separate processes for endorsing a single one of these candidates, and which would permit that partisan endorsement to appear on the Instant Runoff ballot, it would be entirely unwieldy to give voters a ballot with 1,079 candidates. There must be some process for narrowing the field to a manageable number for an Instant Runoff ballot.

Conceptually, it might be possible to design a kind of non-partisan process that does not give parties automatic spots on the general election ballot, but instead simply awards spots to a designated number of candidates who received the most votes in an earlier stage of the process. For example, the general election ballot could contain the names of five finalists, the ones who did the best among a much larger pool of names on a preliminary ballot. The preliminary vote could occur on or around Labor Day, giving state and local election officials time to prepare the November general election ballot. Even this much larger pool on the preliminary ballot must have its limits, perhaps no more than 25 candidates, culled from the full list of candidates by means of

---

[19] *See Candidates for President*, FED. ELECTION COMM'N (April 30, 2020), www.fec.gov/data/can didates/?election_year=2020&office=P; *see also* List of Registered 2020 Presidential Candidates, BALLOTPEDIA (April 27, 2020), //ballotpedia.org/List_of_registered_2020_presidential_candidates.

a signature requirement or some other threshold showing of strength. The FEC, which maintains the official list of all presidential candidates, could work with states to administer a process in which any registered voter could "nominate" one of the candidates listed on the FEC's website. Using modern technology, these voter-submitted "nominations" could be made electronically, over the internet, with any registered voter able to click the name of the nominated candidate (in a manner similar to clicking a Doodle, or other internet-based, poll). Those candidates with the 25 largest number of these voter-submitted "nominations" would receive a spot on the preliminary ballot.

Ranked choice voting could be used with this preliminary ballot of 25 candidates to generate the five finalists, so that rather than just selecting the five candidates with the most first choice votes initially, the least popular candidates could be eliminated one-by-one with ballots redistributed to remaining candidates based on lower-ranked preferences until five finalists remain. (This kind of "bottom-up" approach, which would cause candidates to seek support from voters beyond just those for whom the candidate is their first choice preference, would tend to produce a more consensus-based politics than prevails in today's hyperpolarized environment.) Parties could be permitted to endorse one of the 25 candidates, with these endorsements appearing on the ballot next to the endorsed candidate's name. But a party's procedure for determining which candidate would receive this endorsement would be entirely separate from the government's winnowing process. Under this system, the winnowing process would be non-partisan insofar as it would remain distinct from each party's endorsement process. For example, if a party's endorsed candidate on the preliminary ballot of 25 names was not one of the five finalists on the general election ballot, the party might be permitted to endorse one of the five finalists as its most preferred among this much narrower group, and this new endorsement could appear on the general election ballot.[20]

Even though this kind of non-partisan winnowing process is conceptually feasible for presidential elections, it is not necessarily the most desirable form of a winnowing process. Instead, it might be better to give the parties a more formal role in the winnowing function, and this is true even with the use of Instant Runoff Voting for general election ballots. Rather than having the five most popular candidates overall regardless of party, which a non-partisan

---

[20] As this example illustrates, the conceptual distinction between a political party and any other ideological association would be simply that a party would be entitled to have its endorsements appear on the ballot next to the endorsed candidate's name, whereas the endorsements of other groups would not appear on the ballot.

winnowing process would produce, maybe it would be better to have the most popular Democrat, the most popular Republican, the most popular Libertarian, the most popular Green, and so forth, with each of these finalists selected as a result of an internal competition within each party.

Insofar as each party stands for something distinctive, it might be best for the general election voters to select among the best version of each distinct brand of politician. In this respect, presidential elections might be something like a dog show competition: rather than having "best in show overall" selected among five finalists regardless of breed (so that at least in theory all five finalists might come from the same breed, say Labrador), it might be better to have "best in show overall" chosen from among all the "best in breed" winners, so that there is one candidate from each breed in the final round of competition.[21] In the same way, it might be best to have one candidate from each party in the general election, with each of these candidates having been selected at a preliminary stage as the best candidate from each party.

If parties are to perform this winnowing function (and not just an endorsement function) for purposes of determining which candidates are on the Instant Runoff ballot for the general election, then it might no longer make sense to give parties complete control over the mechanics of the winnowing process. Since the winnowing process is designed to serve the purposes of the general election ballot itself, it makes sense to design the winnowing process in a way that most promotes the proper functioning of the general election ballot.[22] Since we are assuming that the general election ballot will use Instant Runoff Voting, it might make sense that the winnowing process within each party also uses Instant Runoff Voting in order to identify the best candidate within each party to put on the general election ballot.

The political parties, however, might prefer not to use Instant Runoff Voting to identify their presidential nominees. For whatever reason, a particular

---

[21]   Dog shows use two stages to winnow from "best in breed" to "best in show": there is an intermediary step in which breeds are divided into seven "groups" of breeds—Sporting, Hound, Working, Terrier, Toy, Non-Sporting, and Herding—with seven "best in group" dogs selected, who move on to compete for overall "best in show." *See Dog Show 101*, WESTMINSTER KENNEL CLUB (April 28, 2016), www.westminsterkennelclub.org/dog-show--101.

[22]   In this respect, the *White Primary Cases* become relevant again. If the goal is to put on the general election ballot a single Democrat and a single Republican, each of whom best serves the overall purposes of the general election ballot, then it becomes unconstitutional for the internal competition among Democrats and Republicans to have racial, religious, or other forms of exclusions incompatible with the values of the Constitution itself. A political party, like the Nazis, unwilling to accept the obligation to conduct its internal competition according to rules consistent with the values of the Constitution itself would be appropriately denied a designated spot on the general election ballot.

political party might consider Instant Runoff Voting an undesirable method of choosing a nominee. They might think Instant Runoff Voting unnecessary if they use a proportional system for awarding delegates to candidates, or they might think Instant Runoff Voting unsuitable for a convention-based process of picking a nominee. No matter what the party's reason, if the government insists that a party use Instant Runoff Voting in order to identify the candidate who will occupy the party's spot on the general election ballot, but the party prefers to use another method to identify the candidate to occupy this spot, then there is a clash between (1) the government's interest in shaping the winnowing function to serve its goals as being a preliminary step to the general election ballot and (2) the party's interest in choosing the method for identifying its candidate on the general election ballot.

The Supreme Court, most notably in *California Democratic Party v. Jones*,[23] has recognized the right of a political party to resist the government's rules for determining a party's nominee.[24] But it is possible that the Court's decisions on this topic are distinguishable if the government carefully separates the winnowing function from the endorsement function. While the government has no business in interfering with the party's own chosen procedures for exercising the endorsement function, the government's interest in structuring the winnowing function is another matter.

VII. THE OLYMPICS ANALOGY

To understand this point, it helps to consider another analogy. This time think of the general election as equivalent to the Olympic Games and a party's primary elections as equivalent to a nation's Olympic-qualifying tournament, held for the purpose of determining which athletes will represent the nation at the Olympic Games.[25] As part of participating in the Olympics, each nation might have a view about how these Olympic-qualifying tournaments should

---

[23] 530 U.S. 567 (2000).

[24] For discussions of this jurisprudence, see Michael Kang, *The Problem of Irresponsible Party Government*, 119 COLUM. L. REV. ONLINE 1 (2019); Wayne Batchis, *The Political Party System as a Public Forum: The Incoherence of Political Parties as Free Speech Associations and a Proposed Correction*, 52 U. MICH. J. L. REFORM 437 (2019); Tabatha Abu El-Haj, Networking the Party: First Amendment Rights and the Pursuit of Responsive Party Government," 118 COLUM. L. REV. 1225 (2018).

[25] For example, in swimming each National Olympic Committee (NOC) is limited to two individual swimmers per event. *See International Swimming Federation – Qualification System – Games of the XXXII Olympiad–Tokyo 2020*, INT'L SWIMMING FED. (March 19, 2018), www.fina.org/sites/default/files/general/final - 2018-03-19 - tokyo_2020 - qualification_ system - swimming - eng.pdf.

be structured and/or which of its own athletes might be the best to send from the nation to the Olympic Games, but ultimately the International Olympic Committee (IOC) itself sets the rules for these Olympic-qualifying tournaments. The Olympics invites each nation to participate according to the rules that the IOC stipulates. Each nation must abide by these rules in order to send athletes to the Olympics. A nation might prefer these rules to be different, or that a different one of its own athletes prevailed in the qualifying tournament conducted according to the Olympics rules, but the nature of the qualifying tournament is such that the winning athlete may not be the one that the nation itself prefers, but instead the athlete who prevailed according to the Olympics' rules for conducting the qualifying tournaments.[26]

Similarly, we can understand the government as inviting political parties to participate in preliminary qualifying elections in order for a candidate belonging to that party to receive a spot on the general election ballot. The party can accept this invitation, or not, as it wishes. If it does, then the party must hold the preliminary qualifying election in accordance with the rules that the government sets forth. Acceptance of this process does not mean that the candidate winning the party's preliminary qualifying election receives the *endorsement* of the party as its most preferred candidate. Rather, all it means is that the winning candidate is the one who is most successful in the particular form of competition that the government has adopted as the preliminary stage for determining which candidate from that party is the one entitled to appear on the general election ballot at that ultimate stage of competition. Indeed, the party could hold an entirely separate process for determining which of its own candidates is the one it wants to endorse. (Imagine, for example, a nation deciding that its own national championship in a sport—like gymnastics or diving—would be conducted by using somewhat different rules for judging that competition than those used by the Olympics and its qualifying tournaments.) The key point is that, as long as the Olympics analogy is sound, the primary election is a qualifying tournament for the purpose of determining the contestants in the general election, according to what best serves the general election itself, and this is true even though each primary is confined to members of political parties.

---

[26] For the 2020 Olympics, the international rules have been changed in a way that limits each nation's discretion even further, in a way that has cause some consternation among some nations and athletes. Robert Johnson, *Here's How the New 2020 Olympic Qualifying Rules Would Impact the Sprints, Field Events, and Walks in the United States*, LetsRun (March 18, 2019), www.letsrun.com/news/2019/03/heres-how-the-new-2020-olympic-qualifying-rules-would-impact-the-sprints-field-events-and-walks-in-the-united-states/.

Thus, if the government determines that Instant Runoff Voting is the procedure best suited for identifying a winner in competitive elections involving multiple candidates, the government could decide to adopt a two-stage process analogous to Olympic competition. Stage one would be for the candidates to organize themselves into partisan teams, corresponding to the national teams in Olympic competition. Each partisan team in the first stage of the process would conduct a competition among its candidates using Instant Runoff Voting, in accordance with the rules set forth by the government responsible for the overall electoral process. Stage two would be for all of the stage one winners to compete in the main event—the electoral Olympics—using Instant Runoff Voting again to determine the ultimate winner.

It is possible to imagine what a well-designed two-stage process would look like. Each state would hold a series of party primaries using ranked choice ballots. Starting with smaller states first and ending with larger states, and also maintaining demographic and regional balance among the states holding these primaries in any given week of this schedule, the process would unfold with a nationwide accumulation of ranked choice ballots that could be tallied using the Instant Runoff Voting procedure. The winning candidate from each party would be the one to represent the party on the general election ballot.[27]

If such a system existed, should there be a way to get on the general election ballot other than winning one of the partisan preliminary qualifying elections? In other words, should independent candidacies be permitted? And if so, should candidates who compete in, but do not win, one of the partisan preliminary qualifying elections be permitted to earn a spot on the general election ballot as an independent candidate?

Even the Olympics permits some independent athletes to compete without representing a national team.[28] While the analogy is not perfect, there is no good reason to categorically preclude all independent candidates even if a two-stage electoral process is structured so that in the first stage candidates compete as members of a team in order to represent that team at the second stage. It helps voters to understand and assess candidates on the general election ballot if these candidates are identified as affiliated with a political party, but that fact does not mean that one or more unaffiliated candidates should not be able to

---

[27]　This process would eliminate the need for the nominating conventions. Although the primary votes would occur state-by-state, the winning candidate would be identified by the national accumulation of all those primary votes nationwide (based on the IRV calculation).

[28]　Alex Gladu, *What Are Independent Olympic Athletes? They Aren't Very Common in the Games,* Bustle (August 11, 2016) www.bustle.com/articles/178067-what-are-independent-olympic-athletes-they-arent-very-common-in-the-games.

earn a spot on the general election ballot if they exhibit a sufficient indication of strength. An appropriately demanding petition signature requirement would weed out independent candidates who should not clutter the general election ballot, while at the same time permitting the few independents who deserve a chance to compete against the winners of the party primaries.

VIII. A SECOND CHANCE AFTER LOSING A PRIMARY?

But what of a candidate who loses a party primary yet still wants a spot on the general election ballot as an independent candidate? Suppose the candidate is capable of satisfying whatever signature requirement exists for independent candidates. Should the candidate still be disqualified by virtue of having attempted to win one of the party spots on the general election ballot?[29] After all, one generally cannot go to the Olympic Games as an independent athlete if one failed to qualify for the Olympics earlier as a member of a national team.

The analogy, however, need not control in all respects. As a general matter, candidates who lose a party primary will not want to compete in the general election. The norm of party loyalty will cause them to back down and support the party's candidate on the general election ballot. They may want the chance to win the party's primary the next time and thus earn the right to the party's spot on the general election ballot. In a system where party affiliation is important, earning the party's spot on the ballot next time may be more valuable than obtaining an independent spot on the ballot this time.

But this general proposition will not apply in all circumstances. Sometimes the contest to represent a party on the primary ballot will be so intense that the runner-up will feel compelled to seek a spot on the general election ballot.[30] Even if the primary process is as well designed as possible, so that the winner of the party primary is undeniably the overall favorite of the party's primary voters—as would be true with the use of Instant Runoff Voting in the primary process—there may be a perceived need for another candidate who competed in the primary to make a case to the general election's voters. In effect, there would be such a schism within the party that those who did not support the party's winning candidate would feel

---

[29]   *See generally* Michael Kang, *Sore Loser Laws and Democratic Contestation*, 99 GEO. L.J. 1013 (2011).

[30]   Incumbent U.S. Senator Lisa Murkowski's independent candidacy in 2010, after losing the Republican primary to a "Tea Party" insurgent, is a major example. Because of Alaska's ballot access rules, Murkowski was required to run as a write-in candidate. *See* William Yardley, *Lisa Murkowski Wins Alaska Senate Race*, N.Y. TIMES (Nov. 17, 2010).

unrepresented in the general election unless another candidate was included. These disaffected voters would be claiming the need to sever from their previous party and begin the process of forming a new one, if only by supporting an independent candidacy in this election as a first step. Or it might be the party's old guard feeling that their party was "hijacked" by insurgents and thus needing to support an establishment candidate, who did not win the party primary, as an independent. Although this independent candidate would not be entitled to the party's label on the general election ballot, having lost the party's primary, any party organization (including its established national committee) could endorse this independent candidate as its preferred choice despite having lost the primary.

For the 2020 election, the internal competition within the Democratic Party shaped up to be a major fight between the party's progressive and moderate wings. It might be appropriate to have the leading candidates of both wings on the general election ballot, even though only one candidate would be the officially designated winner of the Democratic primary. Even if the fissure between the party's two wings might not be so deep as to precipitate the kind of "bolt" envisioned at the outset, there still may be a strong belief that general election voters deserve a choice between the leading candidates from each of the party's two wings.

The use of Instant Runoff Voting in the primary election helps to avoid the need for multiple candidates from the same party on the general election ballot. But it may not be able to eliminate this need entirely. One can imagine either a progressive or a moderate prevailing as a result of Instant Runoff Voting in the primary—and still the other wing of the party wanting its chance to compete for general election votes. For example, suppose a progressive (like Elizabeth Warren) won a primary process that employed ranked choice ballots. Moderates might still feel that a progressive would be unable to defeat Donald Trump in the general election, and therefore would want a moderate Democrat on the November ballot alongside Elizabeth Warren. Even though Warren would be the one with the official designation as winner of the Democratic primary, moderates might still consider it advantageous to have one of their own on the ballot as an independent. (This kind of strategy, again, necessarily assumes the existence of Instant Runoff Voting for the general election. Otherwise, the moderates would recognize that such a move would be counter-productive, given their overriding goal of defeating Trump's reelection.)

Thus, even in a well-designed system involving the use of Instant Runoff Voting at both the primary and general election stages of the process, there is the need for a "safety-valve" mechanism that permits a candidate who loses a primary election to secure enough signatures to appear on the general election ballot as an independent candidate. This kind of safety-valve mechanism will not often be invoked. None of Trump's primary election opponents in 2016 — not Cruz, Rubio, or Kasich — attempted to run in the general election as independent candidates. But a safety valve needs to be there, so that, as with the Taft–Roosevelt contest of 1912, the system can accommodate a rupture with a kind of backup mechanism.

If there ever developed a fear of candidates who lose their party's primaries too frequently taking advantage of this safety-valve option, the signature requirement for these candidates to get on the general election ballot could be increased. Indeed, there is no necessity that the signature requirement for these "party defectors" (a term that is far preferable to "sore losers") be set at the same level as genuinely independent candidates, those who never participate in any party primary. For example, it could be twice as hard to get on the ballot as an independent having participated in but lost a party primary than as an independent not having participated in any primary. But setting the bar higher in this way is a far more sensible procedure than making a categorical rule that would prohibit any such candidate from appearing on the general election ballot, no matter what the circumstances.[31]

When a primary has truly produced a pronounced fissure between two wings of a party, then in a system that uses Instant Runoff Voting for the general election it may be necessary for that general election to include candidates representative of both of the party's wings. In this context, it is worth recalling that the winnowing process has been structured to give a role to the parties because, as a general rule, parties help narrow the field in a coherent way. But when a party's role in this winnowing process breaks down, because two factions within the party feel that they cannot accept each other's candidate as their own representative, then the general election ballot must allow for the possibility of both factions having their candidates included.

---

[31] Ideally, there would be a uniform national standard for determining when an independent presidential candidate is eligible for the general election ballot. But given the current reality that state law controls access to the ballot in the decentralized Electoral College system, as required by the constitutional provision that gives each state legislature the authority for determining the method of appointing the state's presidential electors, the rules for determining when a "party defector" would be eligible to run as an independent in the general election would need to be set by state law. If a state did decide to make it more difficult for "party defectors" to get on the general election ballot than "entirely independent" candidates, it would not be difficult for state law to administer this distinction. A "party defector" could be defined as any candidate who was on the ballot at the party primary stage of the process, whereas an "entirely independent" candidate was not. Thus, to invoke the opening hypothetical of Bernie Sanders bolting after the convention, he would be a "party defector" because he participated in the Democratic party primary, and the fact that he calls himself an "independent" rather than a "Democrat" would be irrelevant.

This point applies even more when parties are permitted to control the procedures for their primary elections. They may use procedures more likely to produce schisms or otherwise cause a significant portion of the party's electorate to believe that the party's chosen candidate does not genuinely reflect the will of the party's electorate. In this situation, as might prove true with the Democrats in 2020, there is all the more need for a safety-valve mechanism that enables this disgruntled portion of the electorate to put its preferred candidate on the general election ballot. Of course, this point presupposes that the general election ballot can handle independent candidates or, indeed, candidates representing parties other than just the two major ones. But if the system cannot handle any candidates beyond two, then the inclusion of a candidate because of a schism within one of the two major parties is no more (or less) problematic than the addition of an independent or third-party candidate for any other reason.

IX. CONCLUSION: PROTECTING THE PUBLIC INTEREST

Presidential elections are too important to permit the political parties to mess them up. It is easy to believe that in 2016 the Republican Party mishandled its own internal procedures for identifying its presidential nominee and, as a result, let Donald Trump prevail, whereas a different internal procedure may have produced Marco Rubio or Ted Cruz as the nominee.[32] This self-afflicted wound, however, affected not just the party itself, but the nation as a whole. With the Democratic nominee being especially flawed herself (or at least particularly unpopular by historical measures), the internal Republican procedures that produced Trump instead of Rubio or Cruz made a difference for the relatively unpalatable choice that the general electorate was required to make in November of 2016. Had the Republicans used a better nomination process, the general electorate might have been presented with alternatives that did not seem like the most acute form of selecting between the lesser of two evils.[33]

---

[32] Eric Maskin & Amartya Sen, *How Majority Rule Might Have Stopped Donald Trump*, N.Y. TIMES (April 28, 2016). *See also* Andrew Douglas, Rob Richie & Elliot Louthen, *Simulating Instant Runoff Flips Most Donald Trump Primary Victories*, FAIRVOTE (March 4, 2016), www .fairvote.org/simulating_instant_runoff_flips_most_donald_trump_primary_victories.

[33] Melina Delkic, *Voters Choosing Among "Lesser of Two Evils," Survey Finds*, ABC NEWS (Sept. 29, 2016), //abcnews.go.com/Politics/voters-choosing-lesser-evils-survey-finds/story? id=42460153.

During the 2020 primary season, there was a fear that the Democrats would make a mess of their internal deliberations, just as the Republicans did in 2016.[34] With over twenty candidates to choose from (at least at the outset of the process), some thought the Democrats would splinter into multiple factions and be unable to coalesce around a single choice. Others feared they would go hard left, producing a nominee who was unable to compete for the median voter in the general election. There was a widespread sense that the Democratic Party could not be trusted to produce an option that was appropriate for the general election.

Given the risks of the political parties producing nominees that are less than fully suitable as general election candidates, there is good reason to rethink the role of the parties in the process of winnowing candidates for presentation on the general election ballot. Parties never should be deprived of their right to endorse whichever candidate they would most prefer, but the party's preferred candidate should not necessarily be the one to occupy the party's spot on the general election ballot. Instead, the candidate whom the voters themselves most prefer might be the most suitable occupant of the party's general election spot, just as a nation's athlete at the Olympics is the one who wins the qualifying race and not necessarily the one that the nation most wants to send.

If this Olympics analogy determines which of the party's candidates appears on the general election ballot, then the system avoids the risk that the parties themselves will mess up their internal nomination process to the detriment of the public as a whole, as well as to the party. The stakes of letting the parties endorse their preferred candidates are considerably lowered if these endorsement decisions do not determine which candidates actually appear on the general election ballot. The stakes are lowered even more if the party's preferred candidate can also occupy a slot on the general election ballot alongside the party's candidate whom the voters most prefer. Providing both alternatives gives the general electorate a greater opportunity to pick the candidate that it considers best—depending on whether that general election uses a system, like

---

[34] *See, e.g.*, Paul Starr, *Did Democrats Just Set Themselves Up for a Fiasco?*, AMER. PROSPECT (Sept. 6, 2018), https://prospect.org/article/did-democrats-just-set-themselves-fiasco. On April 14, 2019, the noted political analyst Dave Wasserman tweeted: "Potentially one of Trump's biggest reelection allies: DNC rulebook." This tweet was in response to one from fellow analysis Nate Silver, who observed: "I continue to think Democrats' extremely proportional delegate allocation rules are a big problem for them, making it much more likely that a nominee must be chosen at the convention."

Instant Runoff Voting, that permits the voters to rank their preferences among multiple options.

Designing a presidential election system is not easy. The process must narrow the field of an inordinately large number of candidates into a sensible set of options for the electorate. The goal should be to structure that process in a way that maximizes the chances that the electorate will be able to select a candidate whom it genuinely wants to win. Separating the winnowing and endorsement functions, and thereby letting both the most popular and the party-preferred candidates from the same party on the general election ballot, increases the chances that the general electorate will choose a winner that is not merely the least evil of the alternatives, but one that garners genuine enthusiasm among the voters.

Perhaps most significantly, allowing for two candidates from each major party on the general election ballot increases the chances that the winning candidate will be one of the more moderate ones, capable of attracting support from across the middle of the political spectrum. If the general election ballot contains a left-wing Democrat, a moderate Democrat, a moderate Republican, and a right-wing Republican, and if the general election uses ranked choice voting, then there is a greater likelihood that either the moderate Democrat or moderate Republican will receive second choice votes, both from the other moderate candidate's supporters as well as the more extreme candidate from the same party. As a result, presidential politics will tend to be less polarizing.

For this reason, if we get to the point where we use ranked choice voting for the general election in presidential races, then we should adopt the additional reforms of requiring the parties themselves to use ranked choice voting insofar as they participate in the process of winnowing candidates for inclusion on the general election ballot. At the same time, we should continue to permit parties to make their own separate endorsements according to whatever internal procedures they wish to adopt, and we should permit these party-endorsed candidates to occupy a spot on the general election ballot in addition to party-nominated candidates as a result of winning the government's ranked choice primary process.

Often, the party-endorsed candidate will be the same as the primary winner, and there will be no need for a second candidate from the same party on the general election ballot. But when the party, through its own chosen procedures, determines it necessary to field a second of its own candidates, the option should exist. Consider, again, the possibility that Democratic voters might want Warren, while the party itself might want all general election voters—not just those participating in the primary—to have the option of Biden as well. Giving the general election voters this greater choice will produce outcomes that better reflect what the American electorate as a whole wants in choosing a president. Accordingly, this combination of reforms should be recognized as creating an overall electoral system superior to the status quo.

5

Simplifying Presidential Primaries

Derek T. Muller[*]

I. INTRODUCTION

Presidential primaries have a simple purpose: they are the elections to select a party's presidential candidate for the general election. But they are often much more than that. In some states, they also serve as the first step in a series of steps that political parties use to handle other assorted types of business.

When voters go to the polls during a primary election, they are not voting for a presidential candidate. Instead, they may be helping to choose representatives to attend the party's national nominating convention, a meeting where the actual presidential candidate is chosen. Or they may be choosing representatives to attend local conventions, like a county convention or a state convention, who will in turn go on to choose the representatives to attend the national convention. Or voters may be choosing representatives who will later meet to help choose presidential electors, the individuals who formally elect the next president and vice president.

This system has not developed in a thoughtful manner that best reflects the will of the voters. Instead, too often, state political parties cobble together steps without fully considering the greater impact of the system they have created.

The system is needlessly messy. Most voters are unclear about the discrete stage of the process that marks their participation in a presidential primary. Their votes may not translate into expected results. The process is also opaque— voters casting ballots at a presidential primary or caucus for Donald Trump or Hillary Clinton likely have little idea that other processes are happening in other states. The state party leadership may also be surprised that delegates or electors

[*] Derek T. Muller is Professor of Law at the University of Iowa College of Law. Special thanks to Gene Mazo for his important work in helping bring this volume together, and for his extraordinarily helpful comments as I drafted this chapter. Beau Carter provided valuable research assistance.

selected through this process fail to meet the party's expectations. The decision to muddle stages of the political process has led to unanticipated and undesirable consequences.

This chapter examines these deficiencies through the lens of the 2016 presidential primaries. Many of these deficiencies arose because of confusing primary processes, which often involved state parties transacting other kinds of business through primaries as well. Delegates and electors, believed to be loyal to certain candidates, peeled off to express their independence. If presidential primaries ought to be a way for voters to translate their political preferences into a presidential candidate, the existing process has significant curable weaknesses. If the parties had used more careful and discrete processes for selecting nomination delegates and presidential electors, some problems parties faced in 2016 would have likely been avoided.

This chapter categorizes flaws in the needlessly complicated presidential primary process as it relates to the selection of presidential delegates and presidential electors. It then suggests ways to resolve some of these flaws.

II. INDIRECT ELECTIONS

A presidential primary might function quite simply. Voters arrive at the polling place for a presidential primary and cast a vote for a preferred presidential candidate. The presidential candidate who receives the greatest number of votes in that primary becomes the party's presidential nominee. If we had a simple, national, direct primary election, this is how it would function. This kind of primary election has been a common feature of legislative, gubernatorial, and state officer elections in the United States for over one hundred years.[1] *See* Figure 5.1.

But we do not have that system. Today, the political parties formally exercise control over the presidential nomination process. Those parties reformed the presidential nomination process in the 1970s to provide for much greater public participation by voters. They managed to do so in part by implementing an indirect electoral process.[2]

FIGURE 5.1

Voters ➡ Presidential Nominee

---

[1] John A. Lapp, *Legislative Notes and Reviews*, 9 AM. POL. SCI. REV. 309 (1915).
[2] *See, e.g.*, John C. Greer, *Rules Governing Presidential Primaries*, 48 J. POL. 1006 (1986).

Republicans and Democrats use similar processes. The nomination of a party's presidential candidate formally occurs at a nominating convention, often late in the summer before the presidential election. The convention hosts hundreds of party members—called "delegates"—authorized to vote for a presidential nominee. Those delegates—and not the millions of voters who show up to the polls over the course of the primaries—have the *actual* power to choose a party's presidential nominee.

Voters, then, play an indirect role in the selection of a presidential candidate. When the voters cast ballots in a presidential primary, they are usually choosing party delegates. Those delegates then choose the nominee. *See* Figure 5.2.

Indirect elections are unremarkable in the United States. Before the Seventeenth Amendment, state legislatures chose United States senators, while the people of each state chose the members of the state legislatures. The people did not directly elect senators; instead, they were indirectly elected by the people through their state representatives.[3] The Constitution was later amended to allow the people to elect senators to Congress directly.

Today, while we directly select most of our elected officials, most of our laws are enacted indirectly. We elect representatives, who then enact laws. But many states have the initiative or referendum process to allow direct enactment of statutes, which allows voters to bypass their representative government.[4]

And the presidential election itself is an indirect election. When voters show up on Election Day to cast votes for a presidential ticket, they formally cast votes for presidential electors. The ballot may list the names of the presidential and vice presidential candidates, but those names are proxies for the presidential electors who are behind the candidates.[5] Then, those presidential electors later vote for the president and the vice president. Voters rarely think of this system as an indirect election, because presidential electors' names are rarely

FIGURE 5.2

Voters ➡ Delegates ➡ Presidential Nominee
(at the party's National Convention)

[3] *See, e.g.*, Vikram David Amar, *Indirect Effects of Direct Election: A Structural Examination of the Seventeenth Amendment*, 49 VAND. L. REV. 1347 (1996).

[4] *See, e.g.*, THOMAS E. CRONIN, DIRECT DEMOCRACY: THE POLITICS OF INITIATIVE, REFERENDUM, AND RECALL (1989); Kenneth P. Miller, *Constraining Populism: The Real Challenge of Initiative Reform*, 41 SANTA CLARA L. REV. 1037 (2001).

[5] *See, e.g.*, Tara Ross, THE INDISPENSABLE ELECTORAL COLLEGE (2017).

on the ballot anymore. Presidential electors also almost invariably cast their votes in a manner consistent with the popular vote in each state, and the totals tallied on election night almost perfectly resemble the formal, final result.[6] Almost—more on that later.

Some scholars have proposed abolishing this presidential primary process altogether and holding a national presidential primary.[7] That said, indirect selection of presidential nominees may make sense for constitutional and practical reasons—it is uncertain whether Congress has the power to create a uniform presidential nomination process,[8] and the political parties appear to have little appetite for a dramatic overhaul of their presidential nomination process.

III. OBJECTIVES IN SIMPLIFYING PRESIDENTIAL PRIMARIES

Let us open with a few premises about how a presidential primary *ought* to operate. By presidential primary, I include caucuses, even though there are disputes about whether they are the same or whether one is preferable to another.[9] Indeed, I simply address any system where voters participate in the selection process for a party's presidential nominee.

Presidential primaries ought to minimize confusion. While we cannot expect any system of voting to be entirely understandable to everyone, we can do our best to make it as comprehensible to as many voters as possible. We should aspire to develop elections where voters have confidence in those elections, because low confidence leads to questions of legitimacy and the erosion of social norms.[10]

---

[6] Vasan Kesavan, *The Very Faithless Elector?*, 104 W. VA. L. REV. 123 (2001).

[7] *See generally* Elaine C. Karmarck, *Why is the presidential nominating system such a mess?*, Center for Effective Public Management, Brookings Institution, Jan. 2016, www.brookings.edu/wp-content/uploads/2016/07/primaries.pdf (describing complexities in reforming the presidential nomination process).

[8] *See, e.g.*, Richard L. Hasen, *"Too Plain for Argument?" The Uncertain Congressional Power to Require Parties to Choose Presidential Nominees Through Direct and Equal Primaries*, 102 NW. U. L. REV. COLLOQUY 253 (2008).

[9] *See, e.g.*, Thomas R. Marshall, *Turnout and Representation: Caucuses Versus Primaries*, 22 AM. J. POL. SCI. 169 (1978); Costas Panagopoulos, *Are Caucuses Bad for Democracy?*, 125 POL. SCI. Q. 425 (2010); Etian Hersch, *Primary Voters Versus Caucus Goers and the Peripheral Motivations of Political Participation*, 34 POL. BEHAVIOR 689 (2012).

[10] *See, e.g.*, Jack Citrin, *The Political Relevance of Trust in Government*, 68 AM. POL. SCI. REV. 973 (1974); Arthur H. Miller, *Political Issues and Trust in Government: 1964–1970*, 68 AM. POL. SCI. REV. 951 (1974); WHY PEOPLE DON'T TRUST GOVERNMENT (Joseph S. Nye, Jr., Philip D. Zelikow & David C. King eds., 1997).

To begin, presidential primaries are already indirect elections. Voters are casting votes that will lead to delegates being sent to a national convention. The delegates formally choose the party's presidential nominee at the national convention. If we want a system that minimizes confusion, then an optimal presidential primary system in a state should look like that process—voters should cast votes for delegates, who will be sent to the national convention.

That means we should aspire to reduce or eliminate intermediary steps between voting during the primary and choosing the presidential candidate at the national convention. Intermediary steps introduce opportunities for results that do not reflect the preferences of voters. When those intermediary steps lead to outcomes that do not reflect voter preferences, voters might feel disconnected from the process and question the fairness of the results.[11] A more streamlined process would better meet voters' expectations.[12]

IV. A LOOK AT PRESIDENTIAL PRIMARIES AND DELEGATE SELECTION

While indirect elections of political candidates are not unusual, they are likely not how most voters understand the presidential primary process to operate. When voters show up to the polls on the day of a presidential primary and cast a vote for "Hillary Clinton" or "Bernie Sanders," or for "Donald Trump" or "Ted Cruz," there is a natural expectation that voters are casting votes for these candidates.

But they are not doing that. They are usually casting votes for delegates, who then attend the nominating convention months later and who formally vote for the party's presidential nominee. In 2016, there were 2,472 voting delegates who attended the Republican National Convention and 4,763 voting delegates

---

[11] *Cf.* Alan Agresti & Brett Presnell, *Misvotes, Undervotes and Overvotes: The 2000 Presidential Election in Florida*, 17 STATISTICAL SCI. 436 (2002) (highlighting errors in ballot design that confused voters in contested election); R. Michael Alvarez, Melanie Goodrich, Thad E. Hall, D. Roderick Kiewiet & Sarah M. Sled, *The Complexity of the California Recall Election*, 37 PS: POL. SCI. & POL. 23 (2004) (examining problems in complicated recall election and its potential effect on confused or overwhelmed voters).

[12] Of course, some may object to presidential primaries in the first place, or support systems that allow for party leaders or others to intervene at intermediate stages of the primary process. If that is the case, then perhaps we should not have primaries. As long as the primaries exist as the system for translating voters' preferences into a party's presidential nominee, the results of those primaries ought to reflect those preferences.

In addition, Democrats have historically had a group of delegates who are not chosen through the presidential primary process—"superdelegates," consisting of party leaders who automatically qualify to participate in the presidential nominating convention. This chapter looks only at the deficiencies of choosing delegates during the primary process.

at the Democratic National Convention. Donald Trump and Hillary Clinton each received a majority of votes from the delegates in attendance and became the presidential nominee of their respective parties.

When voters cast their presidential primary votes for delegates for Donald Trump or Hillary Clinton, those delegates may not ultimately choose to cast their votes for Donald Trump or Hillary Clinton in turn. Some states bind delegates and compel them to vote for the candidate they pledged to support. Other states do not, and these delegates may well cast votes for someone else. Indeed, one group of delegates successfully sued in 2016 to ensure the right to cast a vote for any nominee, despite a pledge to support a particular candidate.[13]

The public may be surprised to learn that these delegates may cast votes for someone else. To that end, Michael Morley has explored one important dimension of public expectations when it comes to delegate commitments. When the people vote for delegates who are ostensible supporters of a particular presidential candidate, Morley proposes that these delegates ought to be bound to support that candidate at the national convention, and that candidates should be permitted to veto delegates who are purportedly chosen to support them but who in fact do not.[14] Suppose Delegate A, a Candidate A supporter, is chosen. Delegate A changes her mind and wants to vote for Candidate B. Candidate A could veto that delegate because Delegate A should be bound to the particular candidate that got her chosen as a delegate. And Candidate A can replace the delegate, or the party must pick another delegate, knowing that Candidate A could veto that next delegate, too.

These are useful recommendations that help meet voters' expectations, or, as Professor Morley explains, to "ensure that the tens of millions of votes cast in primaries and caucuses are not effectively nullified through backroom convention machinations."[15]

The political parties develop these rules for their presidential nominating process. But the parties' rules — even if well-intentioned and developed years ahead of a nominating contest — can lead to outcomes that surprise the public. For instance, Ron Paul's 2012 bid for the Republican presidential nomination never had wide popular support. But his supporters managed to navigate the complex rules of the nomination process to elect far more delegates than he

---

[13] Correll v. Herring, 212 F. Supp. 3d 584 (E.D. Va. 2016).
[14] Michael T. Morley, *Reforming the Contested Convention: Rethinking the Presidential Nomination Process*, 85 FORDHAM L. REV. 1073, 1094–95 (2016).
[15] *Id.* at 1095.

would otherwise receive from an allocation based purely on the primary results.[16]

During the Iowa caucuses in 2012, Rick Santorum and Mitt Romney each earned 25 percent of the popular vote, and Paul 21 percent of the vote. Paul's campaign recognized that delegates to the national convention were actually selected in a later process that began with county conventions followed by a state convention. Delegates chosen at the state convention went on to the national convention and cast votes for the presidential candidate. While other campaigns moved on to other states after the Iowa caucuses, the Paul campaign stayed to focus on the county conventions, where the delegates would actually be selected. Paul supporters showed up in large numbers to the county conventions and dominated these meetings—meetings where the delegates were actually selected. Paul ultimately secured 22 of Iowa's 28 delegates, despite placing third at in the popular caucus vote. Voters' preferences at the caucuses never translated into that state's delegate totals.

Because Paul's campaign had figured out how to navigate the complicated party rules, he managed to secure far more delegates than his popular vote totals otherwise suggested. His supporters recognized that the mismatch between the caucuses (where voters expressed their preferences) and the county conventions (the beginning of the actual delegate selection process) provided an opportunity for the campaign. Consistent with his strategy from Iowa, Paul also secured 33 of Minnesota's 40 delegates despite winning just 27 percent of the vote in Minnesota's caucuses, and he grabbed 17 of Nevada's 28 delegates despite winning just 19 percent of the vote in Nevada's caucuses.[17]

Paul never came close to threatening Romney's nomination, but he so sufficiently disrupted the nomination process that the party changed the rules. The Republican National Committee streamlined some of these processes in 2016 to help ensure that candidates who win a state's caucuses have more control over the state's delegates.[18] But complexity remained in 2016. Supporters of Donald Trump and Bernie Sanders complained that the system

---

[16] Paul Harris, *How Ron Paul's Far-reaching Delegate Strategy Is Starting to Pay Off*, GUARDIAN May 4, 2012, www.theguardian.com/world/2012/may/04/ron-paul-delegate-strategy-gop-nomination (explaining how "Paul's strategy relies on using his campaign's enthusiastic followers and impressive organisation to dominate the complex and time-consuming delegate selection process in ways the Romney campaign struggles with.").

[17] *See* Richard E. Berg-Andersson, 2012 *Presidential Primaries, Caucuses, and Conventions*, THE GREEN PAPERS, www.thegreenpapers.com/P12/R.

[18] James Hohman, *Mitt Asserts Control over '16 Dates*, POLITICO, Aug. 24, 2012, www.politico.com/story/2012/08/mitt-asserts-control-over-16-dates-080110.

was unfair, sometimes going so far as to suggest the process was "rigged," in part because of this complexity.[19]

"Rigged" goes too far. The processes by which the votes of those who participate in primaries are translated into delegate seats at the national conventions were established well before the primaries. But the critique that the processes are too complicated—or, I would argue, too needlessly complicated—rings true.

V. NEEDLESS COMPLEXITY IN PRESIDENTIAL PRIMARIES

The indirect process of choosing a presidential nominee adds one layer of process between the participation of voters in the primary and the actual selection of a party's presidential nominee. Some presidential primaries, however, move beyond Figure 5.2's illustration of indirect elections. Some state parties require *multiple* interim steps to take place between the popular vote and the selection of delegates. In 2016, those multiple interim steps were where problems arose.

To frame this issue, take a straightforward process like the New Hampshire primary. Under the New Hampshire primary rules in 2016, voters go to the polling place and cast votes identifying which presidential candidate they support.[20] Those votes are then totaled across the state. New Hampshire had 32 Democratic delegates, and 24 of them were allocated based on the percentage of the vote each candidate received. Bernie Sanders received 60 percent of the vote, so he received 60 percent of the delegates.[21] Those delegates then go on to the national convention and formally vote for the Democratic Party's presidential candidate.

The act of participating in the New Hampshire primary has a direct effect on the delegate selection process. While not as smooth as a direct selection of delegates, New Hampshire primary voters express preferences at the primaries that are later translated into delegates. Voters are not looking at a list of names of delegates on their ballots. Instead, they are looking at the names of

---

[19] Pam Fessler, *Amid Long Voting Lines and Claims of A 'Rigged System,' Does My Vote Matter?*, NPR, June 14, 2016, www.npr.org/2016/06/14/481582413/amid-long-voting-lines-and-claims-of -a-rigged-system-does-my-vote-matter (noting "unusually high" levels of voter distrust in the primary process).

[20] *See* N.H. REV. STAT. § 659:14 (permitting eligible voters who declare their affiliation with a political party to cast a ballot in that party's presidential primary election).

[21] In New Hampshire, the Democratic Party technically awards some delegates based on the percentage of the vote in each of the two congressional districts, and the rest of the delegates based on the statewide vote totals. Sanders's support was roughly 60% in each congressional district and statewide.

a presidential candidate. Meanwhile, each presidential candidate has filed a list of 24 delegates who are pledged to support that candidate.[22] After the primary, the Democratic Party determines that Sanders received 60 percent of the vote, is entitled to 60 percent of the delegates, and awards him 15 delegates from the list of those pledged to support him. The process looks something like Figure 5.3—a modified version of Figure 5.2.

Figure 5.3 resembles Figure 5.2. But unlike Figure 5.2, where the voters are directly choosing delegates, Figure 5.3 is a model where the voters preferences are later translated into the choosing of delegates—60 percent of the popular vote, 60 percent of the delegates. And to be frank, this might actually be *better* than Figure 5.2. Voters likely do not particularly care if Jane Smith is a Sanders delegate or John Jones is a Clinton delegate. They simply want to express a preference for Sanders or Clinton, and the party can make sure its rules turn those preferences into delegates.

The process can be confusing, particularly when it comes to determining how the results on primary night are translated into delegates. But the primary process still has a direct effect on delegate selection—voters cast votes for Sanders, and those preferences are translated into Sanders-supporting delegates, who will go on to attend a national convention. At the Democratic National Convention, those 15 delegates will, in all likelihood, cast votes for Sanders.

In contrast, consider how Colorado's Republican Party went about choosing its 37 delegates to the national convention in 2016.[23] Three delegates attended the national convention because of their role as party leaders, but 34 were selected by voters in staggered stages. In March 2016, the Colorado Republican Party held precinct caucuses. Registered Republicans visited a local precinct caucus and chose delegates. But these delegates who were selected at the

FIGURE 5.3

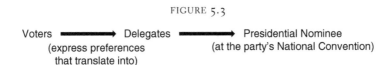

Voters ⟶ Delegates ⟶ Presidential Nominee
(express preferences   (at the party's National Convention)
that translate into)

---

22 See N.H. Rev. Stat. § 655:50–51.

23 A useful summary may be found at *The Green Papers*. *See* Richard E. Berg-Andersson, *2016 Presidential Primaries, Caucuses, and Conventions*, The Green Papers, www.thegreenpapers.com/P16/CO-R. The Adams County Republican Party offers its own summary of the multilayered process. *See* Caucus/Primary Process in Colorado, AdamsCountyGOP.com, www.//adamscountygop.com/files/AdCo_Caucus-Primary_Process1.pdf.

precinct caucuses were not delegates for the national convention. Instead, they were delegates to the county assemblies and district conventions.

County assemblies are meetings for members of the Colorado Republican Party in each county. Country assemblies take place in each county in Colorado in the weeks after the precinct caucuses. Party members give speeches and discuss how to support the party at these county assemblies. Delegates attending the county assemblies in turn elected delegates to the district conventions and to the state convention.

In April, district conventions were held across Colorado's seven congressional districts. Like at the county assemblies, party members gave speeches and discussed party activity. Delegates at those district conventions chose 21 delegates for the Republican National Convention, and other delegates for the state convention.

At the state convention in April, a meeting for the entire Colorado Republican Party took place. Among other business—speeches, party support activities, reviewing the party's bylaws, and so on—13 more delegates were chosen for the Republican National Convention.

In short, after the precinct caucuses took place, various groups of Colorado Republicans had additional meetings, took votes, and elected delegates for other meetings—21 delegates at district conventions, 13 delegates at the state convention, and 3 delegates by virtue of their role as party leaders for a total of 37 delegates. This multilayered process looked something like Figure 5.4.

This process is hardly transparent to the typical Colorado voter, who may be up to *four steps removed* from the final process of choosing a presidential nominee.

Admittedly, one problem with this process may simply be inherent to the caucus model. There was not a presidential primary in Colorado like in New Hampshire, where voters show up during a typical Primary Day and cast ballots in the voting booth. Instead, the process begins with precinct caucuses, low-turnout affairs that require the party faithful to attend a meeting that lasts about 90 minutes on a Tuesday night.

FIGURE 5.4

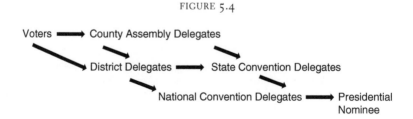

If there is a commitment to broader popular participation in the selection process of presidential nominees, then moving to presidential primaries is one solution. But caucuses can also be well-attended affairs. The Iowa and Nevada caucuses, influential because of their early placement in the Republican presidential nominating cycle, are well-attended affairs. (We lack data about the number of participants in Colorado's precinct caucuses precisely because they are such insular affairs.) Colorado's precinct caucuses, however, *felt* much more removed from the actual selection of national convention delegates—because they *were* much more removed. The results of the precinct caucuses had no direct effect on delegate selection.

The distant nature of this process left a political outsider like Donald Trump frustrated, and he called it a "rigged" and "crooked" system.[24] That's largely because the multilayered process worked against Mr. Trump. Virtually all of Colorado's delegates ultimately were awarded to Ted Cruz. Why? Simply because Mr. Cruz's supporters showed up at each stage of the process to ensure that his delegates continued on to the next round. By the later rounds—the actual opportunities to choose delegates to the national convention—Cruz supporter's controlled the process. When the Colorado process moved into its later stages, where delegates to the national convention were selected, a candidate like Donald Trump felt left out.

If Colorado simply abolished its caucus and expected the state's political insiders to choose a nominee, perhaps the results wouldn't disrupt the expectations of the voting public.[25] But if the thought is to hold a caucus in which any Republican in the state could participate, it ought to have a closer nexus to the actual selection of delegates to the national convention.

The Colorado process is hardly the only unusual process we have. Illinois Republicans, for instance, hosted what is commonly known as a "loophole primary." Voters cast two sets of votes. First, they cast votes in a "beauty contest," an advisory vote about which presidential candidate they prefer.[26]

---

[24]   John Whiteside, *Trump blasts 'rigged' rules on picking Republican delegates*, REUTERS, Apr. 11, 2016, www.reuters.com/article/us-usa-election/trump-blasts-rigged-rules-on-picking-republican-delegates-idUSKCN0X81HE.

[25]   John Frank, *Colorado Republicans Cancel Presidential Vote at 2016 Caucus*, DENVER POST, Aug. 25, 2015, www.denverpost.com/2015/08/25/colorado-republicans-cancel-presidential-vote-at-2016-caucus/ (noting that Colorado changed its process to hold a caucus but would no longer directly hold a presidential vote).

[26]   It was thought that such advisory votes could influence the state's delegation at the national convention. *See Primary/Caucus/Convention Glossary*, THE GREEN PAPERS (Sept. 20, 2015), www.thegreenpapers.com/Definitions.html. In Illinois, 12 statewide delegates and 3 party leaders in the state are bound to the candidate with the largest number of votes—so it

FIGURE 5.5

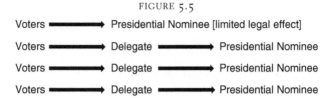

They then cast votes for individual presidential delegates, three per district. The ballot looks like Figure 5.5.

Illinois's decision to use this system exploited a "loophole" in the party's rules for allocating delegates. Most other primaries allocate delegates proportionally—that is, delegates are awarded roughly in proportion to the percentage of the popular vote a candidate receives in the state. If a candidate receives 30 percent of the state popular vote, that candidate receives 30 percent of the delegates. (Republican candidates who receive more than 50 percent of the vote may win all the delegates if the state party chooses to allow this.) Suppose that Donald Trump receives 40 percent of the vote and Ted Cruz 30 percent of the vote. Trump should receive 40 percent of the delegates and Cruz 30 percent.

In contrast, Illinois Republicans' loophole primary allows direct selection of delegates rather than assigning delegates by proportion to the candidate's name. Voters could vote for Cruz, and then voters could vote for three specific Cruz-affiliated delegates. There's no proportional allocation that later takes place. Instead, voters are voting for specific delegates—and if they are voting for delegates, they are not subject to proportional allocation rules.

Illinois is divided into a number of districts, and voters in each district get to vote for up to three delegates in the loophole primary. Cruz and Trump each file a slate of three delegates in each district. In one district, suppose Cruz's delegates receive support from 41 percent, 40 percent, and 39 percent of voters in Figure 5.5. Trump's delegates received support from 31 percent, 30 percent, and 29 percent of the voters in each district. Illinois could award Cruz three delegates and Trump zero, because it has a system of choosing delegates instead of candidates. And Illinois has just circumvented the proportional allocation requirement.

While the system appears to simplify the process in one regard—voters know that they are casting votes directly for a delegate—it adds complexity in another.

technically does have *some* legal effect. But 54 of the state's 69 delegates are awarded without regard to the results of this top-line advisory vote.

Voters are casting four votes in a single presidential primary race (one in the "beauty contest," then three for delegates). And many voters undervote—they fail to vote for all three delegates, perhaps because of "ballot fatigue" and growing weariness from checking so many boxes, or perhaps because they incorrectly believe that they only need to vote in the beauty contest or for one delegate. But the loophole primary is designed to get around the proportional allocation of delegates. The state party has added complexity to avoid national party rules. And if our objective is to simplify presidential primaries, the added complexity of loophole primaries is an apparent problem.

Republicans are not alone in these complicated processes. Democrats in the state of Washington provide an illustrative example of how both parties engage in this kind of activity. The Washington State Democratic presidential caucuses took place on March 25, 2016. Bernie Sanders won about 73 percent of the vote and the lion's share of delegates; Hillary Clinton won about 27 percent of the vote and far fewer delegates.[27] Washington State's Democrats participate in a multistaged presidential primary process. Greatly simplified, first come precinct caucuses to choose delegates to the legislative district caucuses and county conventions. The legislative district caucuses and county conventions choose delegates for the congressional district caucuses and often to the state convention. The congressional district caucuses choose delegates for the national convention. And the state convention also chooses a final, second group of delegates for the national convention.[28] This process is depicted in Figure 5.6.

But Washington also held a separate "beauty contest" on May 24, almost two months after the caucuses, in which over 800,000 voters participated and

FIGURE 5.6

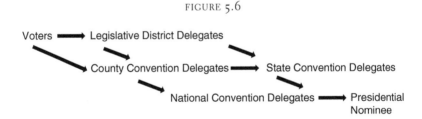

---

27 *Washington State Results, Election 2016*, N.Y. TIMES, Sept. 29, 2016, www.nytimes.com/ele ctions/2016/results/primaries/washington.

28 Washington State Democrats, 2016 *Caucus and Convention Cycle Guide*, www.wa-democrats.org /sites/wadems/files/documents/2016%20Caucus%20and%20Convention%20Party%20Leader%20 Guide.pdf.

preferred Clinton over Sanders 52 percent to 48 percent, a "symbolic" reversal of the caucus results.[29]

Holding several contests on different dates for the same office assuredly injects additional confusion into the process. As one Democratic Party official explained, primaries tend to reflect the ability of candidates to raise money for television advertising, while caucuses show grassroots support.[30] In 2016, Sanders had stronger grassroots support and won the caucus, while Clinton won the popular vote in the primary. The state holds both to reflect two different ways of determining candidate strength. But if that's the case, then delegates ought to be awarded at both contests if the party believes that they reflect the different strengths of the candidates. Otherwise, the state party should decide which process is better and only hold one.

Admittedly, these multilayered contests have never ultimately affected the outcome of a presidential nomination process. But the uncertainty and confusion they introduced into elections are enough to raise questions about why these multilayered contests exist in the first place. And they leave the impression in the minds of many voters—often those on the short end of these contests—that the presidential primaries are unfair.

VI. FURTHER CONFUSION FOR PRESIDENTIAL ELECTORS IN COMPLEX PRIMARIES

These multilayered proceedings do other things, too. For example, they often serve as an opportunity for the political parties to transact additional business. A county or state party meeting could vote on amendments to the party's bylaws, amend the state party's platform on particular issues, elect state or local party officers, or choose presidential electors for the general election. When they choose presidential electors, these proceedings—run by the state political parties and not the presidential candidates themselves—offer another opportunity for trouble.

Most states entrust the responsibility for choosing presidential electors to a political party, not to the putative presidential and vice-presidential candidates.

---

[29] Clare Foran, *An Awkward Reality in the Democratic Primary*, ATLANTIC, May 25, 2016, www.theatlantic.com/politics/archive/2016/05/washington-primary-bernie-sanders-hillary-cli nton/484313/ (explaining how "Hillary Clinton won the state's Democratic primary, symbolically reversing the outcome of the state's Democratic caucus in March where Sanders prevailed as the victor.").

[30] *Why Does Washington State Hold Both a Caucus and a Primary?*, SEATTLE POST-INTELLIGENCER, Dec. 9, 2007, www.seattlepi.com/local/article/Why-does-Washington-state-hold-both-a-caucus-and-a-1259305.php.

(Independent candidates file their own slates of electors, as do non-ballot-recognized parties.) The party, then, must gather and meet in some formal sense to choose electors. Parties are typically already gathering in the spring to choose delegates for the party's national convention, or to ratify the results of a presidential primary. They often choose presidential electors at that same meeting.

But the purpose of the presidential primary is to choose delegates to the national nominating convention, not presidential electors. The presidential primaries are, in theory, *unrelated* to the party's selection of presidential electors. When state parties operate these two essential and distinct functions related to presidential elections, lumping them together, it has often led to disastrous results—as in 2016.

Let us return to the Washington State Democrats. In Washington, each congressional district caucus chose delegates for the national convention. But at the same meeting, each congressional district caucus also elected one presidential elector and one alternate—these caucuses were held on May 21, 2016.[31] The state convention also chose delegates for the national convention. And that same state convention, which took place June 17–19, 2016, also chose presidential electors.[32]

Recall that Sanders won the overwhelming number of delegates in Washington's caucuses, who then participated in the legislative district conventions, congressional district conventions, and state conventions. Those conventions might have simply been additional layers of the presidential primary delegate selection process. But they were doing something else, too—participants in those intermediate-level conventions chose presidential electors who would ostensibly support the party's presidential nominee.

There were two problems with this model. First, these state-level conventions were meeting well before anyone knew who the Democratic nominee would officially be—the Democratic National Convention was held July 25–28, 2016. Second, these state level conventions were not necessarily filled with those loyal to the Democratic Party. They were filled with those loyal to a particular candidate—here, Mr. Sanders—and could run into problems if some friction arose between a losing candidate and the party's eventual nominee.

After the November presidential election, presidential electors prepared to meet in state capitals around the country in late December. Those electors would formally cast votes for a presidential and a vice-presidential candidate.

---

[31] Washington State Democrats, 2016 *Caucus and Convention Cycle Guide*, *supra* note 28.
[32] *Id.*

Washington's twelve electors were twelve Democratic electors, in accordance with the results of the November presidential election. Because Hillary Clinton and Tim Kaine were the Democratic Party's presidential nominees, one would have expected the presidential electors from Washington to cast votes for them.

But that was not the case. Four of Washington's twelve electors cast votes for someone other than Ms. Clinton: three voted for Colin Powell, and one voted for Faith Spotted Eagle. Rather than vote for Tim Kaine for vice president, they voted for Elizabeth Warren, Maria Cantwell, Susan Collins, and Winona LaDuke.[33]

The four faithless presidential electors had been chosen in the March district caucuses, while the other eight electors who faithfully voted for Democratic nominees Hillary Clinton and Tim Kaine were chosen at other meetings. The faithless electors were supporters of Mr. Sanders — understandable, given that Sanders won the caucus and that the district caucuses preferred him.[34] But the choice to award electors at those district caucuses proved detrimental to Clinton when the electors met in December to cast their vote for president. While electors are typically faithful to the party, rancor in 2016 prompted these unusual defections.

The district caucuses were designed for a major purpose: to choose delegates for the national convention. And those caucuses were filled with Washington Democrats who preferred Mr. Sanders. The caucuses were not necessarily filled with party leaders, nor with Washington Democrats who were chosen by some process after the national convention nominated Ms. Clinton as the Democratic candidate. The presidential electors chosen in March, then, arose from a process that had been loyal to a candidate who was not the party's eventual nominee.[35]

One can understand why a party might want to choose presidential electors at the district caucuses. Parties must convene to choose delegates to the

---

[33] Jim Brunner, *Four Washington State Electors Break Ranks and Don't Vote for Clinton*, SEATTLE TIMES, Dec. 19, 2016, www.seattletimes.com/seattle-news/politics/four-washington-electors-break-ranks-and-dont-vote-for-clinton/.

[34] The 2016 election highlighted how the indirect nature of the Electoral College might also be lost on the typical voter. As described above, when voters cast votes for a presidential ticket during the general election, they are actually casting votes for presidential electors who will later cast votes for that ticket. Electors rarely stray from the preferences of voters, *see* Kesavan, *supra* note 6, but the number of faithless electors in 2016 shows that an indirect system still includes additional steps that could differ from the original preferences of voters.

[35] Jim Brunner, *1 Washington State Democratic Elector Won't Support Clinton, Another Won't Commit*, SEATTLE TIMES, Nov. 4, 2016, www.seattletimes.com/seattle-news/politics/hes-a-sta te-democratic-elector-but-robert-satiacum-says-he-wont-vote-for-clinton/.

national convention, and parties must convene to choose presidential electors. Rather than meet twice in a single calendar year, why not simply collapse the two events into a single event? Parties can then choose both convention delegates and presidential electors at once. That the convention to nominate presidential electors occurs at the same time as the convention to choose delegates for the party's national nominating convention is a matter of convenience. That convenience cost Clinton four Electoral College votes.[36]

Consider Colorado's process. In Colorado, presidential electors are chosen by members of the political party at state and local conventions.[37] Each presidential elector meets in December and must vote for the presidential candidate who received the most votes in the state in the general presidential election in November.[38] Refusal of an elector to vote for the winner of the state's popular vote creates a vacancy in the Electoral College, which the other presidential electors will fill by a vote.[39]

In early April 2016, the Colorado Democratic Party held precinct caucuses, the first in a multilayer process to choose delegates to the national convention.[40] Each congressional district also held a convention to choose delegates for the national convention. Those conventions each also chose a presidential elector. That same month, a state convention elected additional delegates to the national convention. But at the same meeting, it chose two at-large presidential electors.[41] The nominated presidential electors pledged to vote for the Democratic Party candidates and bound themselves to that vote when they accepted their nominations.[42]

But like Washington's state-level conventions, Colorado's state-level convention was filled with Sanders supporters. Three of Colorado's nine presidential electors attempted to cast votes for someone other than Clinton—two cast votes for Clinton under protest after trying to vote for someone else, and

---

[36] It doesn't have to work this way. Washington law requires a far different timeline for choosing electors. Presidential candidates certify their names to the Secretary of State "no later than the third Tuesday of August" along with their slate of presidential electors. REV. CODE OF WASH. § 29A.56.360. The party chooses a slate of presidential electors, and the timing of those choices is left to the parties, as long as they provide names by the third Tuesday in August. Id. § 320.

[37] COLO. REV. STAT. § 1-4-302(1).

[38] COLO. REV. STAT. § 1-4-304(5). The Supreme Court is currently considering the issue of whether state statutes may lawfully bind presidential electors to cast their votes in accordance with the candidate they were pledged to support. *See* Colorado Dep't of State v. Baca, No. 19–518.

[39] COLO. REV. STAT. § 1-4-304(1), adopted Aug. 11, 2017.

[40] Colorado Democratic Party, *Plan of Organization and Rules*, www.coloradodems.org/wp-content/uploads/2018/02/CDP_Rules_and_Bylaws_Amended_20171209.pdf.

[41] *Id.*

[42] *Id.*

one tried to vote for John Kasich before he was replaced for violating his duty. It took significant effort and litigation to get Democratic electors to cast votes for Clinton,[43] because these electors had been chosen at a convention filled with Sanders supporters. These electors ended up not as party faithful but as disloyal dissenters, and they cast votes for Clinton only under compulsion of state law.

One way to ensure loyal electors might be to include a law like Colorado's, which requires presidential electors to cast votes consistent with their earlier pledge or risk being replaced.[44] But parties have other options at their disposal. Presidential nomination rules about the selection of delegates and state laws governing the selection of electors provide far more flexibility than state parties have used. While these rules and laws provide opportunities for much later decision-making, parties have, out of convenience, moved their decision-making to these spring dates at a time when other party business is being transacted. As a result, the conventions chose presidential electors who can be loyal to the losing primary candidate.

VII. PROPOSED SOLUTIONS

There are several solutions to streamline and simplify the presidential primary process. These solutions would help meet the expectations of voters and minimize confusion to the public. They would also allow campaigns to operate under a simpler set of rules.

At the outset, these solutions are committed to the principles articulated at the beginning of this chapter about the goals of primaries. That is, if we are going to hold primaries or caucuses in the first place where parties invite the public to participate, the process should aspire to be as simple and straightforward as possible. Eliminating confusion and minimizing intermediate steps would help. So, too, would decisions that most directly convert voters' preferences into national convention delegates.

First, state parties should eliminate intermediate steps between the voters and the choice of delegates. As it is, the presidential nomination process is an indirect selection process; voters choose each party's convention delegates, and these delegates choose the presidential nominees. Indeed, if delegates are

---

[43] Brian Eason, *Colorado's Electoral Votes Go to Hillary Clinton After One Is Replaced*, DENVER POST, Dec. 19, 2016, www.denverpost.com/2016/12/19/colorado-electors-new-motion-federal-appeal-denied/.

[44] There are disputes about these laws' constitutionality, which is a reason why informal mechanism may be preferable. *See, e.g.*, Ray v. Blair, 343 U.S. 214 (1952).

bound to support a particular presidential candidate, the selection process is essentially a system of direct election and only formally indirect.

County, congressional district, and state party meetings may serve essential state party-building functions. But their role in the contemporary presidential primary process is, at best, questionable. If state parties choose to hold such meetings, they could develop recommendations for the party's platform, or choose state party officials to serve for the next year or election cycle. But they should not serve as an intermediary step between the primary and the actual selection of delegates for the national convention.

Instead, candidates should submit the names of delegates who will be chosen. That process could be a winner-take-all, a proportional allocation, or something else. But whatever it is, it would flow directly from the results of the primary or caucus. In the alternative, if delegates purportedly pledged to support a certain candidate are chosen, the candidate should have the right to strike and replace them with alternates.[45]

This solution would rarely need legislation and could usually be accomplished by the parties writing new internal rules. If a party holds a caucus or a primary under state law, it is usually up to the party to decide the effect of a caucus or primary.[46] And parties could simply adopt rules that award delegates proportionately with a winner-take-all possibility: candidates receive delegates in proportion to the percentage of the state's popular vote they receive, unless the candidate wins a majority of the state vote, in which case that candidate receives all of that state's delegates. The outcome of a primary or caucus leads to the selection of delegates that are sent to the national convention — not to an intermediate district or county or state convention.

Second, parties should end loophole primaries and beauty contests like Illinois holds. Loophole primaries are simply ways to circumvent proportional allocation when party rules prefer proportional allocation. And beauty contests give the illusion to voters that they are participating in the political process when voters are really engaging in the equivalent of a state-run (and costly) public opinion poll to "advise" delegates.

Primaries and caucuses should have a material impact, not simply an advisory one. If state statutes require one kind of contest and the party wants to hold another kind of contest, state laws should be amended to the party's preference.

---

[45] *See* Morley, *supra* note 14, at 1094–95.

[46] *See, e.g.*, Democratic Party of the United States v. Wisconsin ex rel. La Follette, 450 U.S. 107, 126 (1981) ("The National Party rules do not forbid Wisconsin to conduct an open primary. But if Wisconsin does open its primary, it cannot require that Wisconsin delegates to the National Party Convention vote there in accordance with the primary results, if to do so would violate Party rules.").

For instance, if Washington State Democrats want to hold a caucus, they should not be obligated to hold a primary, which they end up treating as advisory only.

If state parties in states like Illinois are instituting rules to exploit loopholes in the national party's rules or to circumvent those national party rules, then national parties should expressly punish state parties that do so and get them in line. Punishing recalcitrant state parties can be a challenge. For instance, Florida and Michigan Democrats in 2008 held their primaries earlier than state rules permitted. The national party leaders voted to strip the states of their delegates.[47] After protest, the national party restored half their total number of delegates.[48] And on the eve of the convention, the presumptive nominee Barack Obama moved that the states' full delegations be recognized.[49] It was a fragile and contested process, but one that ultimately prevented any other states from thwarting the national party's calendar in 2016.

Third, parties should disassociate their selection of presidential electors for the general election from the mechanisms surrounding the party's presidential primaries. The presidential elector selection process should be moved closer to, if not after, the nominating conventions. Granted, the incidents listed above are largely only a problem if there is intraparty squabbling. Given how rarely presidential elector rebellions actually occur, these concerns may appear overstated. But as 2016 demonstrated, an effort to find dissatisfied electors in both parties fueled the fire for faithless electors across the country. It exposed a potential problem that, while historically rare, remains a real threat for political parties' presidential nominees in the future.

Sometimes the state legislature must change the law to improve this process. For instance, Arizona formerly required that parties name presidential electors at least 90 days before the primary; now they may do so up to ten days after the primary.[50] That pushes back the deadline from around late May to early September.[51] In late May, the party's presidential nominee may still be

[47] Associated Press, *Democrats punish Michigan for early primary*, Dec. 1, 2007, www.nbcnews.com/id/22054151/ns/politics-decision_08/t/democrats-punish-michigan-early-primary/; Richard Simon, *Democrat Is Still at Odds over Florida Delegates*, S. Fla. Sun-Sentinel, Mar. 10, 2008, www.sun-sentinel.com/news/fl-xpm-2008-03-10-0803090 054-story.html.

[48] Katharine Q. Seelye & Jeff Zeleny, *Democrats Approve Deal on Michigan and Florida*, N.Y. Times, June 1, 2008, www.nytimes.com/2008/06/01/us/politics/01rules.html.

[49] Katharine Q. Seelye, *Obama Wants Full Voting Rights for Florida and Michigan Delegates*, N.Y. Times, Aug 3, 2008,https://thecaucus.blogs.nytimes.com/2008/08/03/obama-wants-full-voting-rights-to-florida-michigan-delegates/.

[50] Ariz. Rev. Stat. § 16-344 (amended by 2017 Ariz. Legis. Serv. Ch. 262 (SB 1307), 2017).

[51] Arizona's primaries are held the tenth Tuesday before the general election. Ariz. Rev. Stat. § 16-201. These differ from the presidential preference election, held on the first Tuesday after March 15. Ariz. Rev. Stat. § 16-241.

uncertain. But by September, the national party conventions have been held and the parties have official presidential and vice-presidential candidates. A September selection of presidential electors, then, occurs with full knowledge of the candidates and the opportunity to vet electors to ensure they support the party's nominees.

But many states need no legislation to change these deadlines. Instead, it is a question of the practices of the political parties in choosing their electors. In Washington, Democrats did not need to choose their electors until much later than they actually did. State parties can simply move their process for choosing electors to the late summer, even after the nominating conventions, if state law allows the naming of electors that late. Alternatively, state parties could institute rules that allow presidential nominees to strike and replace the names of presidential electors.

It is understandable why the parties choose their electors early, rather than hold a second (later) convention to choose electors. Given the formal requirements in some states of a convention, rather than simply a proxy vote or selection by party leaders, changes to the process could be somewhat onerous—particularly if the party's members have met once in the spring before the convention, then traveled sometime in the late summer to the convention itself, and are later expected to hold yet another meeting to choose electors after the convention.

Some states also have much stronger measures, like the law that calls for replacing faithless electors in Colorado. But this solution avoids drastic legislative measures: it simply requires state parties to choose presidential electors at some later date, after the nominee is made known, and increases the likelihood that the electors are faithful to the national party's nominee.

VIII. CONCLUSION

The state-by-state presidential primary system is unlikely to disappear anytime soon, and parties accept that primary rules can vary from state to state. But needless complexity exists in the current structure. When voters attend a primary or caucus, they should do one thing only: choose delegates who will attend the national convention in support of a particular candidate. Simplifying presidential primaries will help reduce unnecessary surprises and allegations of "rigged" elections. It will also more closely reflect the actual preferences of voters.

6

The Case for Standardizing Primary Voter Eligibility Rules

Michael R. Dimino[*]

I. INTRODUCTION

National convention delegates are chosen through a bewildering array of procedures that vary from state to state.[1] Because states, for the most part, determine not only whether parties hold a primary or caucus, but also which voters are eligible to participate, delegates arrive at the national convention having been selected by very different constituencies that have very different policy ideas and very different levels of commitment to their respective parties.

The result is that neither the Republican Party nor the Democratic Party is able to express a clear ideological message through its presidential nominations. Presidential candidates seeking to win delegates in different state elections must appeal to the electorate in each state—and the state electorates differ greatly because the state-imposed voter eligibility rules differ greatly from state to state. As a result, candidates who articulate a clear and consistent message will draw different levels of support from the primary electorate in the various states, even when their messages appeal to similar proportions of party members and non-party members in each state. Party loyalists in closed-primary states see the effect of their votes canceled by independents' votes in open-primary states, while independents know that while they might influence the selection of delegates in some states, they will be excluded from the delegate-selection process in others. In the end, we wind up with two major-party presidential nominees who can be said to represent no single constituency's views. They do not represent the views of the party loyalists who

[*] Michael R. Dimino is Professor of Law at Widener University Commonwealth Law School. He wishes to thank Gene Mazo for his leadership, hard work, and energy in pursuing this project, and Gregory Darr and Evelyn Stoner for their research assistance.
[1] See *Primaries: Who Can Vote in Presidential Primaries*, FAIRVOTE (May 2016), www.fairvote .org/primaries#presidential_primary_or_caucus_type_by_state.

contributed to their campaigns, the views of the party members who nominated them, or the views of the American voters who may have voted for them though not party members themselves. Rather, the presidential nomination process combines these distinct constituencies in a crazy quilt of different state rules that, when aggregated, lack any coherent or logical basis.

There is a better way. The parties should develop their own rules for choosing nominees, and those rules should apply in every state. Having a single uniform rule for each party would provide clarity for voters and candidates that is currently lacking. It would also protect the speech and association rights of the parties, enabling them to determine the rules by which they choose their leaders, who in turn will act as their faces and will take their messages to the public.

II. THE PROBLEM: DIFFERENT RULES, ONE ELECTION

A. *The Variety of Delegate Selection Rules*

Like other associations, both major political parties choose leaders who represent their members and advocate for their ideals. The parties nominate presidential candidates and agree on their party platforms at national conventions that are held during the summer before the general presidential election takes place in November. Unlike other associations, however, political parties are not free to set their own rules concerning who is eligible to participate in their nomination processes. Instead, state law typically dictates the rules that parties must follow. State law decrees whether a party shall choose its convention delegates through a caucus or a primary. If a primary is used, state law determines whether the primary will be open or closed — and thus determines whether non-members of the party will be permitted to vote for the party's delegates. As a result of this decentralization, the delegate selection rules vary widely from state to state.

Thirteen states use open primaries or caucuses, allowing voters to participate in these contests regardless of whether or not they have any partisan affiliation. In a state that employs open primaries, all of a state's registered voters may participate in a party's primary, irrespective of whether they are members of the party, unaffiliated voters, or members of another party. By contrast, fifteen jurisdictions hold closed primaries or caucuses. In these states, voters must be affiliated with the party in order to be able to participate in the party's primary. The deadlines for party affiliation differ greatly from state to state. New Hampshire, a closed primary state, allows voters to affiliate with the party or indeed to switch affiliations up to the day before the primary. Four more states (Hawaii, Iowa, Ohio, and Utah) also have closed systems but permit participants to switch their affiliations on the very day that the primaries or caucuses are held. Meanwhile, New Jersey permits unaffiliated voters to join a party on the day of the primary, but affiliated voters intending to switch parties must do so more than fifty days before the primary. And that is not all of the variation. Illinois, another closed primary state, permits each voter to declare his or her party affiliation at the polling place. The affiliation is then loudly announced, and the voter is permitted to vote in his choice of primary if there is no challenge.

Meanwhile, three states (Massachusetts, North Carolina, and Rhode Island) employ semi-closed primaries. In these states, all party members and all unaffiliated voters may participate in party's primary, but members of other parties may not. Some states hold variations of semi-closed primaries. For example, they might require voters who participate in a primary to show some support for but not necessarily hold membership in a political party. Indiana does not require partisan affiliation, but purports to limit voters to the primary ballot of the party that the voter supported in the previous general election.[2] Tennessee does not require partisan affiliation, but purports to require voters to declare their support for the party.[3]

Eight states permit parties to exercise some control over the selection system that the party in that state uses for its delegate selection process. Five states (California, Louisiana, Oklahoma, South Dakota, and West Virginia) provide for closed selection systems but give parties the option of inviting independents and making it a semi-closed system. Two more (Maine and Maryland) provide for closed systems but permit parties to have open primaries if they wish. Idaho establishes closed primaries but allows parties to opt for either semi-closed or open primaries. As a result of this freedom, five states use different systems for different parties. Idaho Democrats run an open caucus, but Idaho Republicans require participants to be affiliated with the party (although they permit same-day affiliation). In California and South Dakota, Republicans run a closed primary, while Democrats run a semi-closed one. Finally, two states, Nebraska and Nevada, limit participation to party members

---

[2] If the voter did not vote in the previous general election, the voter is supposed to choose the ballot of the party he intends to support in the next general election.

[3] In practice, Tennessee uses an open primary, because it makes no attempt to enforce the requirement of an intention to support the party in the general election. Until 2017, Mississippi had the same (unenforced) requirement. On Mississippi's primary, see generally *Mississippi State Democratic Party v. Barbour*, 491 F. Supp. 2d 641 (N.D. Miss. 2007) (holding that Mississippi's primary system unconstitutionally prevented the party from excluding non-members from participating in its primary), *vacated as unripe*, 529 F.3d 538 (5th Cir. 2008).

but permit parties to decide *when* voters need to affiliate with the parties. As a result, Nevada and Nebraska voters intending to vote Republican must have affiliated with the party in advance, but voters may switch their affiliation to the Democratic side on the day that delegates are chosen.

Ordinarily such pluralism is an unobjectionable—and perhaps even desirable—effect of federalism. If states use a variety of different election rules in selecting or nominating their officials (or even if states disagree about whether to have elections at all for certain offices, such as judges and attorneys general), there is no harm to the candidates, the parties, or the electorate. Whenever the electorate is wholly located within one state, candidates need only consult that one state's laws in developing an effective strategy to appeal to voters. The election winner will have been chosen by a process that applies the same rules throughout the jurisdiction, so that the winner can be said to represent a singular class of eligible voters. Because voter eligibility rules tend to be uniform statewide, a single constituency selects each party's nominee for state offices and Congress. As a result, there is no confusion about what it means to be a party's nominee—or what interests he or she was chosen to represent.

The presidency is different—uniquely so. Although technically convention delegates—not presidential candidates—are chosen at primaries and caucuses, those delegates are chosen because of their anticipated votes for the presidential candidates they intend to support at the party's national convention. Thus, presidential candidates are the focus of the primary elections, and they—not the delegates—run campaigns. The presidential candidates, not the candidates seeking to be convention delegates, need to decide on a strategy to appeal to voters, and that strategy must be reasonably consistent across states. Even though primary elections are spaced out both geographically and temporally, much campaign activity through radio and television programs, as well as the Internet, is directed at a national audience. If each state's delegate selection process had the same voter eligibility rules, presidential candidates could treat the nomination as a single election, analogous to the general election, and could employ a consistent strategy to appeal to likely participants in primaries and caucuses across the country.

As it is, however, presidential candidates are forced to run different campaigns in more than fifty different jurisdictions. Such a system forces them not only to appeal to voters in different states and territories who have very different interests, but to compete for support by appealing to party members in some places and to voters irrespective of party membership in others. It is one thing to say that Republicans in Iowa may care more about farming than do Republicans in Rhode Island; it is quite another to force primary candidates

TABLE 6.1 *State Qualifications for Voters in Primaries and Caucuses, 2020*

Selection System	States
Open Primary/Caucus	Alabama Arkansas Georgia Michigan Minnesota Mississippi Missouri Montana North Dakota South Carolina Texas Vermont Virginia Wisconsin
Closed Primary/Caucus	Alaska Arizona Colorado Connecticut Delaware District of Columbia Florida Kansas Kentucky New Hampshire New Jersey (for former members of other parties) New Mexico New York Oregon Pennsylvania Wyoming
Closed Primary or Caucus with Election-Day Affiliation	Hawaii Illinois (if announced affiliation is not challenged) Iowa New Jersey (for previously unaffiliated voters) Ohio Utah
Closed Primary or Caucus with Party Option of Affiliation in Advance or on Election Day	Nebraska Nevada
Semi-Closed Primary	Massachusetts North Carolina Rhode Island
Requires Support for, but Not Membership in, Party	Indiana Tennessee

TABLE 6.1 (*continued*)

Selection System	States
Closed Primary with Party Option for Semi-Closed	California Louisiana Oklahoma South Dakota West Virginia
Closed Primary with Party Option for Open	Maine Maryland
Closed Primary with Party Option for Semi-Closed or Open	Idaho

to appeal to an exclusively Republican electorate in New Hampshire but to all voters, irrespective of party, in Vermont.

Candidates then face a dilemma: if they change their message too much from state to state, they lose credibility and undermine the power that their message would have if it were expressed more consistently. On the other hand, if they adopt a consistent message, they will have a hard time demonstrating a high level of support across states where the primary electorate is comprised of different constituencies. Candidates that appeal to the party faithful may succeed in states with closed primaries but not succeed in states with open primaries. Candidates that appeal to the median voter will have the opposite problem; they may succeed in open primaries but struggle in closed ones. And candidates that split the difference may not succeed in either; they may be too moderate for closed primaries and too ideological for open ones.[4]

---

[4] Typically, closed primaries will favor candidates with relatively extreme ideologies and open primaries will tend to favor candidates with more moderate ideologies because party members (who are the only ones eligible to participate in closed primaries) will have more extreme ideologies than the entire general electorate (who would be eligible to participate in open primaries). In certain situations, however, the candidates favored by party members may not be the more ideologically extreme ones. They might be the candidates who have a longer or closer connection to the party, for example. It is even possible that party members will favor the less ideologically extreme candidates, if the independents participating in the primary come from the ideological fringes (e.g., if independents voting in the Democratic primary are disproportionately socialist or if independents participating in the Republican primary are Tea Partiers or religious conservatives). In most cases, however, ideological candidates will have an advantage in closed primaries and moderate candidates will have an advantage in open ones.

The point, however, is not which candidates will succeed under certain sets of electoral rules. Rather, the point is that there will be a difference, and that difference will manifest itself in candidates receiving different percentages of the vote in two states where they may appeal to the same proportion of party members but the voter eligibility rules differ, so that in one state the result will be affected because non-party members can vote. Further, if the choice of electoral rules is made by the state instead of by the party, then the state will have given an

In addition, the mishmash of voter eligibility rules denies the party conventions the ideological coherence that they could have if all the delegates were selected according to the same rules. Most clearly, if all delegates were selected in closed primaries or caucuses, nominees could justifiably claim to be the choice of the party members and would owe their nominations to party members. If all delegates were selected in open primaries, nominees could similarly claim to be the choice of a broad coalition of voters, and they would owe their nominations to voters that were interested in choosing the party's nominee but who might not be committed to the party's ideology. As it is now, however, nominees do not represent the views of either group of voters. The nominee, rather than being the candidate who most effectively appeals either to party members or an open-primary coalition, is the candidate who amasses more delegates in the states with voter eligibility rules most closely suited to his candidacy. That is, the party will be represented by a candidate who appeals to a portion of the electorate not chosen consciously by the party to reflect its identity, image, or strategy, but by each state on an individual basis, for reasons that may have nothing to do with the party's beliefs or its prospects for success.

Such ideological incoherence is particularly apparent today, given that both major parties have significant internal factions. The Democratic Party has a substantial element of generally new, young, radically left-wing party members and legislators, some of whom openly embrace the label "socialist." Those far-left elements of the Democratic Party are competing against the more traditional elements of the party that are reluctant to sign on to the more extreme parts of the left-wing agenda.

The Republican Party likewise faces a significant internal division. A substantial portion of the party adheres to the right-wing populism identified with President Trump and his emphasis on trade policy and immigration — and that populist element is likely the reason for Trump's success in 2016. (These right-wing populists are in some ways heirs to the Tea Party movement, but the modern populists seem less interested in the Tea Party's focus on small government and reduced spending.) Many other members of the Republican Party favor the party's more traditional free-market agenda and still others are primarily motivated by social or religious conservatism. Because both parties face crises of identity, both will have significant decisions to make in the coming years concerning the ideological directions they will take. The parties should make those decisions themselves, according to rules that they set for themselves.

advantage to certain kinds of candidates seeking to lead the party—perhaps contrary to the preference of the party itself.

It is fundamentally important that state governments respect party autonomy and let parties make their own decisions. As the Supreme Court said forty-
five years ago, "[i]f the qualifications and eligibility of delegates to National
Political Party Conventions were left to state law, 'each of the fifty states could
establish the qualifications of its delegates to the various party conventions
without regard to party policy, an obviously intolerable result.'"[5] Government
should not interfere by telling the parties *who* should participate in their
decisions, or *how* those decisions should be made, any more than the government should tell the parties *what* their decisions should be.

B. *Impact on the 2016 Election*

In the 2016 Democratic race for President, former Secretary of State
Hillary Clinton was the clear choice of Democratic voters, but she faced
stiff opposition from Senator Bernie Sanders, who had great support from
independents. Among Democratic primary voters identifying as
Democrats, Clinton was the preferred candidate by a two-to-one margin.
Voters not identifying as Democrats preferred Sanders by a similar margin.
Unfortunately for Sanders, however, 75 percent of Democratic primary
voters were Democrats, and so Clinton was the clear winner in the
primaries—even without considering the unpledged "superdelegates,"
who overwhelmingly preferred Clinton.[6]

Sanders's strength showed most clearly in states that used caucuses; of the 22
contests won by Sanders, 12 (55 percent) were caucuses. Considering that there
were only 14 caucuses, Sanders's victory in 12 of them (86 percent) is particularly striking. By contrast, of the 31 contests won by Clinton, only 2 (6 percent)
were caucuses.[7] Because caucus participants tend to be more intense than the
average party member and unrepresentative of their state populations, enthusiastic young supporters of Sanders's "democratic socialism" had an advantage
in caucuses. Again, however, Clinton had the advantage overall because more

---

[5] Cousins v. Wigoda, 419 U.S. 477, 490 (1975) (quoting Wigoda v. Cousins, 342 F. Supp. 82, 86
(N.D. Ill. 1972)).

[6] *See* William G. Mayer, *The Nominations: The Road to a Much-Disliked General Election, in*
THE ELECTIONS OF 2016, at 44 (Michael Nelson ed., 2018).

[7] Results and election types (e.g., primary versus caucus, closed versus open) are helpfully, if
unofficially, collected at *Results of the 2016 Democratic Party Presidential Primaries*,
WIKIPEDIA, https://en.wikipedia.org/wiki/Results_of_the_2016_Democratic_Party_presidenti
al_primaries. The results discussed above include races in states and the District of
Columbia, but do not include races in territories. The combined victories for Clinton and
Sanders total 53 because Nebraska and Washington are counted twice; each holds both
a primary and a caucus. Clinton won each state's primary; Sanders won each state's caucus.

states used the format (primaries) that favored her mainstream appeal among Democratic voters. Clinton lost only 10 of 39 primaries — 5 open ones (including Sanders's home state of Vermont), 1 closed one, and 4 semi-closed ones.

The Republican race showed a similar disparity between the candidates' fortunes in primaries and caucuses. Businessman Donald Trump, the eventual nominee, was particularly strong in primaries, winning a plurality of votes in 33 of the 38 primaries (24 of the 29 primaries that were held before May 4, when his final two opponents dropped out). His opponents were stronger in the caucuses, with Trump winning a plurality in only 4 of the 13 caucuses. Trump's success in primaries was almost as strong in closed as in open primaries. Of the five primaries that Trump lost, two (Texas and Ohio) were in his opponents' home states. The other three were Oklahoma (closed), Idaho (closed), and Wisconsin (open).

While one might expect closed primaries and caucuses to advantage party-faithful "insiders," the results in 2016 do not appear to support such a hypothesis. The insider Republican candidates did show more strength in caucuses than the outsider (Trump) did, but the same effect did not appear on the Democratic side, where it was the outsider, Bernie Sanders (who, until recently, was not even a member of the Democratic Party), who saw more success in caucuses. The relative success in caucuses by Sanders and by Trump's principal opponent, Senator Ted Cruz, may be due to the way that caucuses depend on energizing committed participants. Because caucus voters tend to be committed ideologues, candidates appealing to relative ideological extremes may have an advantage in caucuses, whereas primaries favor candidates whose supporters are willing to vote but unwilling to caucus.

Perhaps neither the Democratic nor Republican nomination would have turned out differently in 2016 had different primary systems been employed. But there is no doubt that different electoral rules — including the choice of primaries or caucuses, and the choice of open, closed, or semi-closed selection processes — can favor certain candidates. To have those choices forced on a party threatens to force parties to accept leaders and messages that they would not prefer to embrace. The state governments should not interfere with a party's ability to decide its own leaders and messages — including by deciding the way in which those leaders and messages are chosen.

In sum, there are two problems with the current system: First, the myriad different rules for selecting delegates make it difficult for candidates and parties to promote a consistent and coherent message that will appeal to similar proportions of eligible voters in different states' primaries. Second, rules that interfere with parties' decisions about how to select their own leaders — and especially who will be able to participate in those decisions—interfere with the parties' ability to formulate their own messages.

III. SOLUTIONS

The two problems identified above—one stemming from the states' disuniformity of electoral rules and the other stemming from the states' interference with parties' nomination decisions—call for multiple potential solutions. Nationally mandated closed or open primaries would produce uniformity, but at the cost of interfering with parties' liberty to choose their own delegate selection methods. By contrast, permitting parties to set their own rules might produce disuniformity in multiple ways. The Democratic and Republican parties might choose different rules, creating disuniformity between parties (although a single national rule for the Democrats and a single national rule for the Republicans would surely be less confusing than the current mess). Each party might even permit disuniformity between states, leading to a jumble of rules similar to that which we have now.

Uniformity would improve the presidential selection system in important ways. It would make it easier for candidates and parties to express a consistent message and create a consistent identity, which might permit parties to regain some of the strength they have lost to the more ideologically consistent interest groups. Uniform rules would also aid voters, as parties, candidates, and others could more easily explain one national voter eligibility rule than different rules for different states.

Ultimately, however, parties (both major parties and minor parties) should have the authority to decide whether to adopt nationwide rules for selecting their own leaders, or whether instead to permit (or to impose) different rules in different states.[8] Uniformity is valuable and important, but the choice to have national uniformity should be made by the parties. Parties might be granted this autonomy through either of two means: legislatively or through court decisions recognizing parties' First Amendment rights to structure themselves and their messages as they see fit.

Legislative solutions come in several forms. Most easily, states could pass laws enabling each party to select its delegates through the means

---

[8] National parties would also have the freedom to decide how much autonomy to grant to their state affiliates. Thus, if, under state law, a state party has the ability to decide on a delegate selection method, the national party could demand that the state party exercise that discretion by choosing a particular method, or the national party could leave the choice with the state party. Obviously, the advantages of uniformity would be achieved only if the national party chose to insist that each state adopt the same system.

chosen by the party. As noted above, eight states already have laws that give parties at least some freedom to decide for themselves the qualifications of participants in their delegate-selection processes. This proposal would simply expand that freedom across the country and allow parties to make more decisions for themselves about how they select their own leaders. Under such a system, parties would have the option to use primaries, caucuses, conventions, or other systems, and would have the ability to set their own qualifications for participating in whatever processes they adopt. For example, the states, individually or as part of an interstate compact,[9] could enact laws providing that

> the governing body of each national party shall have the right, power, and authority to fix and prescribe the political or other qualifications of its own members as well as the method for selecting delegates to its national convention, and shall, in its own way, declare and determine who shall be entitled and qualified to vote in such selection process or to be candidates therein.

A more fundamental solution rests with the First Amendment. Parties, like other individuals and associations, have the right under the First Amendment to speak, which includes the ability to develop one's own message and to be free of government control of that message.[10] Both the methods of choosing nominees and the eligibility rules for participating in the nomination processes can affect the results of those processes and, therefore, the parties' messages. As explained above, open primaries might lead to different results than closed caucuses and might cause parties to support different policies or to have different priorities than they would have under a different set of rules. Because delegate selection processes have such a manifest possibility of affecting parties' speech,[11] the parties have a First Amendment interest in

---

[9] *See* U.S. CONST. art. I, § 10, cl. 3 ("No State shall, without the Consent of Congress, . . . enter into any Agreement or Compact with another State.").

[10] *See* California Democratic Party v. Jones, 530 U.S. 567, 573 (2000) ("[W]e have continually stressed that when States regulate parties' internal processes they must act within limits imposed by the Constitution.") (citing Eu v. San Francisco County Democratic Central Comm., 489 U.S. 214 (1989), and Democratic Party of United States v. Wisconsin ex rel. La Follette, 450 U.S. 107 (1981)). On the right of individuals to be free of government compulsion to speak a message chosen by the government, see, e.g., National Inst. of Family & Life Advocates v. Becerra, 138 S. Ct. 2361 (2018); Wooley v. Maynard, 430 U.S. 705 (1977); West Virginia Bd. of Educ. v. Barnette, 319 U.S. 624 (1943).

[11] As the Court noted with respect to California's unconstitutional blanket primary, manipulating parties' speech and their choice of leaders may be the whole point of the state laws, rather than an unintended side-effect. *See California Democratic Party*, 530 U.S. at 580 ("[T]he whole *purpose* of Proposition 198 was to favor nominees with 'moderate' positions.") (emphasis in original).

being free of government influence in the choice of delegate selection methods.

Alternatively, the states could band together to choose a single selection method rather than deferring to the parties' choices. Even if there were to be variations among states, concerted nationwide action could produce a system that has some rationale for its variations. Lastly, Congress could exercise its power to make or alter the manner of federal elections and require states to adopt a consistent delegate selection method, or to defer to the parties' choices.

A. *Parties' First Amendment Rights to Choose Their Own Delegate Selection Rules*

The Supreme Court has already laid the groundwork for recognizing political parties' First Amendment right to select the methods for choosing their own leaders.[12] Parties exist to promote political ideals, and therefore their activities occupy the core of the First Amendment, which guarantees Americans the freedom to discuss and debate public affairs and candidates—a necessary freedom for a self-governing people. Not only is a party's expression constitutionally protected, but the Court has recognized a First Amendment interest in an expressive association's ability to limit its membership, because the ideological message that a group chooses to express is determined by the identity of the persons who form the group and who make the group's decisions.[13]

Further, the ability of the group to articulate its message, as well as the style in which that message will be articulated, are affected by the people the association selects as its leaders and spokespeople. If the government were able to prohibit an association from choosing its own leaders, or if the government were able to insist that an association's leaders would be chosen by non-members of the group, the association's ability to speak its own message would be hindered. Thus, the Supreme Court has recognized that parties must have some constitutional protection against "forced association"—the government's insistence that the parties accept the participation of outsiders in their decisions, including decisions about whom to nominate for public office.[14]

---

[12] *See* Democratic Party of the United States v. Wisconsin ex rel. La Follette, 450 U.S. 107, 124 (1981) ("A political party's choice among the various ways of determining the makeup of a State's delegation to the party's national convention is protected by the Constitution.").

[13] *California Democratic Party*, 530 U.S. at 574 ("[A] corollary of the right to associate is the right not to associate.").

[14] *See id.* at 575 ("In no area is the political association's right to exclude more important than in the process of selecting its nominee.").

If parties' right to autonomy were fully protected, parties would have the constitutional right to insist on their own choice of delegate selection methods; state laws attempting to impose a particular system on an unconsenting party (for example, an open primary imposed on a party that wants to use a closed primary, or a primary imposed on a party that wants to choose its delegates through caucuses) would be unconstitutional.

Under the current system of state-imposed rules for parties' selection of delegates, not only are parties' nominees chosen in part by people unwilling to join the parties, but the decision to invite the participation of non-members is usually made not by the parties but by the states. Such a practice interferes with party members' freedom of association. Each party should have the constitutional right to decide for itself not only whom to nominate, but which processes to use to nominate candidates. Thus, whether or not the states or Congress pass legislation giving parties the ability to select their own rules for choosing their delegates, parties should be able to insist on their liberty to do so.

Although the Supreme Court has recognized that political parties have First Amendment rights to speak and to associate, its treatment of parties' First Amendment rights has been extremely inconsistent.[15] In the series of cases collectively known as the *White Primary Cases*, the Court held that parties were state actors and thus had an obligation under the Fifteenth Amendment to refrain from racial discrimination in conducting primary elections.[16] Thus, not only did parties not have a First Amendment right to determine who should be eligible to participate in their primaries, but the Fifteenth Amendment required parties not to discriminate even if state law permitted them to do so.

Decades later, however, when overt racial discrimination was much less of a concern, the Court held in *Democratic Party of the United States v. Wisconsin ex rel. La Follette* that parties did, in fact, possess First Amendment associational rights that protected their autonomy in "limiting those who could participate in the processes leading to the selection of delegates to their National Convention."[17] *La Follette* recognized that "the inclusion of persons unaffiliated with a political party may seriously distort its

---

[15] *See generally* MICHAEL R. DIMINO, BRADLEY A. SMITH & MICHAEL E. SOLIMINE, UNDERSTANDING ELECTION LAW AND VOTING RIGHTS 87–113 (2016); MICHAEL DIMINO, BRADLEY A. SMITH & MICHAEL E. SOLIMINE, VOTING RIGHTS AND ELECTION LAW 419–97 (2nd ed. 2015).

[16] *See* Terry v. Adams, 345 U.S. 461 (1953); Smith v. Allwright, 321 U.S. 649 (1944); Nixon v. Condon, 286 U.S. 73 (1932); Nixon v. Herndon, 273 U.S. 536 (1927).

[17] *La Follette*, 450 U.S. at 122.

collective decisions,"[18] and thus that party messages could be altered by laws that forced parties to take into account outsiders' views. For that reason, the Court held that Wisconsin could not require delegates to the Democratic National Convention to vote in accordance with the results of that state's open primary.[19]

La Follette's view of parties' right to autonomy was echoed in *Tashjian v. Republican Party of Connecticut*,[20] *Eu v. San Francisco County Democratic Central Committee*,[21] and *California Democratic Party v. Jones*.[22] In *Tashjian*, the Supreme Court held that parties have the right to invite independents to participate in their primaries, even where state law requires that primaries be closed. In *Eu*, the Court struck down two provisions of California law, one prohibiting parties' governing bodies from issuing endorsements and the other limiting parties' ability to organize their governing structure. And in *Jones*, the Court invalidated California's blanket primary—a kind of wide-open primary, according to which voters could participate in multiple parties' primaries in different races in a single visit to the polls (for example, a voter could participate in the Republican primary for governor and the Democratic primary for the state assembly).

From these four cases, it appeared that parties had the right to organize themselves and their primaries as they saw fit. The Court repeatedly stressed the importance of party autonomy in the selection of nominees: "The moment of choosing the party's nominee . . . is 'the crucial juncture at which the appeal to common principles may be translated into concerted action, and hence to political power in the community.'"[23] As the Court explained, laws forcing parties to accept the influence of non-members could have an effect on the messages that the party adopts as its own:

> "[R]egulating the identity of the parties" leaders,' we have said, "may . . . color the parties' message and interfere with the parties' decisions as to the best means to promote that message." . . . Even when the person favored by a majority of the party members prevails, he will have prevailed by taking somewhat different positions – and, should he be elected, will continue to take somewhat different positions in order to be *re*nominated.[24]

---

[18] *Id.* (citing Ray v. Blair, 343 U.S. 214, 221–22 (1952)).

[19] *See id.* at 126. *See also* Cousins v. Wigoda, 419 U.S. 477 (1975) (holding that national conventions have the constitutional right to credential delegates as they see fit, regardless of the state law under which the delegates were chosen).

[20] 479 U.S. 208 (1986).

[21] 489 U.S. 214 (1989).

[22] 530 U.S. 567 (2000).

[23] *Jones*, 530 U.S. at 575 (quoting *Tashjian*, 479 U.S. at 216).

[24] *Jones*, 530 U.S. at 579–80 (quoting *Eu*, 489 U.S. at 231 n.21) (emphasis in original).

Accordingly, governmental interference with a party's selection of nominees or national convention delegates would have the maximum possible impact on a party's message, and it was therefore essential that the parties be able to determine for themselves how to organize and how to choose their leaders.

Other cases, however, have not read the principle of those cases quite as broadly. Logically, a principle of party autonomy would extend not only to allowing the party to determine who shall be permitted to vote in its primaries, but also to the decision whether to have a primary at all. But the Court has never questioned its dictum in *American Party of Texas v. White* that "[i]t is too plain for argument . . . that the State . . . may insist that intra-party competition be settled before the general election by primary election or by party convention."[25] Likewise, if parties really have the right to exclude non-members from participating in their decisions, open primaries—and even semi-closed primaries—should be disallowed when the party rules call for closed primaries.[26] Yet approximately half of the states use open or semi-closed primaries.

Further, the Supreme Court has explicitly limited *Tashjian* by holding in *Clingman v. Beaver* that states may hold a semi-closed primary despite the party's desire to hold an open primary.[27] Thus while parties have the right to invite unaffiliated voters to participate in their primaries, they do not have the right to invite members of other parties. The Court held that there were strong First Amendment associational interests involved in cases such as *Jones*, where the party wished to *exclude* non-members from participating in its decisions. But in cases where the party wished to *include* members of other parties, the Court held that there was much less of an associational interest because the parties and the non-member voters "associated" with the party only as to participation in the primary.[28]

---

[25] American Party of Texas v. White, 415 U.S. 767, 781 (1974).

[26] In *Jones*, the Court half-heartedly suggested that perhaps state-mandated open primaries would be distinguishable from state-mandated blanket primaries because in an open primary at least the voter affiliates with the party to the extent of voting in its (and only its) primary. 530 U.S. at 577 n.8. That rationale, however, is quite inconsistent with the rationale of the rest of the *Jones* opinion, which finds a constitutional violation when the party is forced to associate with non-members. To the extent that a voter's participation in an open primary is an association, it is a violation of the party's right *not* to associate with that voter—regardless of whether the voter is a member of a different party.

[27] 544 U.S. 581 (2005).

[28] *See also* Timmons v. Twin Cities Area New Party, 520 U.S. 351 (1997) (holding that a state may limit a party to placing on the ballot only candidates who do not simultaneously appear as the nominee of another party).

Such a limitation on party autonomy is misguided and represents an overly narrow interpretation of parties' First Amendment rights. Parties and individuals should have the right to "associate" with each other to the extent that both are willing, even if that association stops well short of the individual's membership in the party. The Supreme Court should re-examine its jurisprudence and hold that parties have the right to decide for themselves who should be entitled to participate in their nomination processes.[29]

Even without such a re-examination, however, the Court's current doctrine allows parties to insist that party decisions be made by only party members. Thus, parties may have the right to impose a uniform system of closed primaries, even if (under *Beaver*) parties do not have the right to impose a uniform system of open primaries.

The extent of the rule stemming from *La Follette* and *Jones* is uncertain and some courts have read those decisions narrowly,[30] but their core insight is clear and should be easy to apply: parties have the right to determine their own messages, and when the government forces parties to accept non-member influence, the messages of parties may be affected. Accordingly, if a party wishes to run a closed primary and to exclude non-members from choosing national convention delegates, states should not be able to force parties to use open or semi-closed primaries. Similarly, if parties wish to run semi-closed primaries, states should not be able to insist that delegates be chosen through open primaries. Thus, parties have the power to make states' delegate selection rules consistent—at least if they insist that the process be closed to non-members.

B. *Legislative Solutions*

The United States has a confusing variety of delegate selection systems because each state has claimed the power to choose for itself the method that is used in that state. The last section argued that such an exercise of power is unconstitutional—that parties have a First Amendment right to decide for themselves the methods they use to select their leaders. Even if states have authority to regulate party primaries, however, there are possible legislative

[29] *See* Michael R. Dimino, Sr., *It's My Party and I'll Do What I Want To: Political Parties, Unconstitutional Conditions, and the Freedom of Association*, 12 FIRST AMEND. L. REV. 65 (2013).

[30] *See* Utah Republican Party v. Cox, 885 F.3d 1219, *reh'g en banc denied*, 892 F.3d 1066 (10th Cir. 2018) (holding that a state could permit candidates to qualify for the primary ballot by gathering signatures, despite the party's desire to use a convention as the sole means of earning a position on the primary ballot), *cert. denied*, 139 S. Ct. 1290 (2019).

reforms that could create a uniform standard for voter qualifications in primary elections in every state, or which could give parties the ability to set such uniform rules for themselves.

The greatest impediment to uniformity in states' primary voter qualifications is the fact that states act individually rather than in concert. Fifty separate state decisions are bound to lead to disuniformity, but there are several methods that could be employed to counter the tendency to entropy. First, states could enact uniform laws providing that delegates will be chosen by one particular system—closed primaries, for example. That solution would bring uniformity, however, only if all states adopted the "uniform" law. Second, states could band together by forming an interstate compact, according to which all of the states participating in the compact would agree to adopt a particular selection method. Again, however, such a solution depends on the voluntary participation of each state, plus the consent of Congress. While some states might agree to put aside their individual preferences and agree on a uniform nationwide rule for delegate selection, it seems unlikely that all states would do so.

Rather than having state law determine the method of choosing delegates, a third option is for states to enact laws delegating the choice of method to the parties. In other words, state laws could provide that parties

> wishing to hold ... a presidential preference primary shall, not less than [number] days before such primary is to be held, adopt and file with the Secretary of State, or with the state officer charged with overseeing the state's elections, a resolution stating that intention, the method by which electors are to indicate one or more preferences, [and] the method by which delegates are to be selected, elected, chosen, and replaced.[31]

This proposal already has some support in the states: Alaska, Idaho, Kansas, South Dakota, and Utah currently permit the parties to choose whether to use open or closed selection processes. Under this proposal, it would be within the parties' control whether to have different delegate selection methods in different states, or whether to insist that each state employ the same method. Parties might wish to continue the tradition of holding a caucus in Iowa, for example, but might otherwise want open primaries, even though such a decision would prevent the party and its voters from realizing the benefits of uniformity. Or perhaps the parties would want only party members to participate in the selection of their nominees, and would opt for closed primaries in every state. The choice, however, would be for the parties; the

---

[31] ALA. CODE § 17-13-10.

parties and the candidates would not have to conform to choices made by fifty different state governments.

However attractive these options may be on the merits, each requires the voluntary participation of each state, and thus each state would have the power to undermine the uniformity of any new rule for delegate selection. We need not rely on each state's voluntary participation, however; Congress has the power to "make or alter ... Regulations" respecting the "Manner" of federal elections.[32] Thus, if party primaries qualify as federal elections, a fourth option is for Congress simply to require that a uniform standard for voter eligibility apply throughout the country.

While it is not completely clear that party primaries should be considered federal elections (primaries select nominees, rather than federal officeholders, and therefore primaries might be thought to be private affairs), the Supreme Court has permitted Congress to regulate primaries by punishing fraud occurring in primaries.[33] Further, if primaries are private affairs immune from congressional regulation, then the First Amendment should give them the autonomy to be free from state regulation as well. Thus, either parties should have the First Amendment freedom to set primary-voter qualifications for themselves, or Congress should be able to impose a uniform national standard for voter quali-fications. And even if Congress could not set uniform procedures for party primaries because parties are private associations, Congress could assuredly force states to adopt *non-partisan* primary elections, under which states would hold a "primary" that would whittle down the field of candidates to two without designating those two candidates the nominees of particular parties. Such a national mandate for non-partisan primaries would have the effect of imposing

---

[32] U.S. CONST. art. I, § 4. *See generally* Richard L. Hasen, *"Too Plain for Argument?": The Uncertain Congressional Power to Require Parties to Choose Presidential Nominees Through Direct and Equal Primaries*, 102 NW. U. L. REV. 2009 (2008). Although the constitutional provision, by its terms, would appear to apply only to "Elections for Senators and Representatives," Justice Black's controlling opinion in *Oregon v. Mitchell*, 400 U.S. 112 (1970), held that "[i]t cannot be seriously contended that Congress has less power over the conduct of presidential elections than it has over congressional elections." *Id.* at 124 (opinion of Black, J.).

[33] *See* United States v. Classic, 313 U.S. 299 (1941). Classic was accused of violating others' constitutional rights by committing fraud in a primary election for the U.S. House of Representatives. The Court held that there was a constitutional right to vote in the primary election because the primary was an integral part of the electoral process. *See id.* at 318. *See also* Terry v. Adams, 345 U.S. 461 (1953); Smith v. Allwright, 321 U.S. 649 (1944); Nixon v. Condon, 286 U.S. 73 (1932); Nixon v. Herndon, 273 U.S. 536 (1927) (collectively, the *White Primary Cases*) (striking down race discrimination in primaries as violating the Fifteenth Amendment). If, as *Classic* held, there is a federal constitutional right to vote in a primary, then there is a strong argument that the primary is a federal election, such that Congress would have the power to "make or alter" electoral rules governing primaries.

a uniform rule of open primaries across the country, because all voters would be eligible to participate in the non-partisan primaries.

This analysis suggests that even if the states have the initial authority to set delegate selection procedures, Congress can simply override any state laws that are not to its liking. Regardless of states' preferences, then, Congress could likely impose closed or open primaries on all fifty states,[34] or Congress could require states to accept the parties' choices of delegate selection methods. Once parties have the ability to determine their own rules for delegate selection, they should impose uniform rules on all fifty states (with perhaps a small number of nostalgic exceptions, such as the Iowa caucuses, and even those should be open or closed to non-party members to the same extent as the delegate selection processes in other states).

IV. CONCLUSION

The fifty states employ a confusing, seemingly random jumble of rules setting out which persons are permitted to participate in parties' delegate selection processes. Because delegates to the parties' national conventions are chosen as the result of so many different processes, candidates may receive vastly different percentages of the vote in different states, even where the candidates' support among party members and non-party members is relatively consistent across states. Further, the diversity of delegate selection processes muddles the endorsement message that the party is able to give its nominees. The core question is which individuals make up the party—which persons' support does a nomination signify? The diversity of state rules makes it difficult to give a clear answer to that question.

Party identity, like party ideology and party messaging, should be up to the party itself. Yet most states give the parties very little ability to choose their own delegate selection methods. States should change their rules to give parties more autonomy, but parties should not need to wait for states to give them permission to make their own decisions. The First Amendment gives parties the right to independence from the government, both in creating their messages and in defining their own associations. The parties themselves can make the nomination process simpler and more coherent simply by insisting on one national rule. And while current doctrine may not give parties the right to insist on open primaries in every state, they may well have the right to insist on closed primaries in every state.

---

[34] Congress might be limited by the First Amendment if it attempted to impose closed or (especially) open primaries on unwilling parties. But states would have no substantial federalism-based objection to such an assertion of congressional power.

7

Primary Day: Why Presidential Nominees Should Be Chosen on a Single Day

Eugene D. Mazo[*]

I. INTRODUCTION

Why do we have an Election Day but not a Primary Day? No aspect of the presidential nomination process causes as much controversy as the primary calendar. The calendar starts off in January or February and ends in June of each election year. A total of 57 states and territories hold their primaries and caucuses over the course of these months. The Iowa caucuses always start off the calendar, followed by the New Hampshire primaries. The results of these contests invariably eliminate some candidates and bestow momentum on others. Many more candidates participate in the first few presidential nomination contests than in the many later ones. As a result, disproportionate power is given to voters whose states hold early nomination contests, while the citizens of states with later nomination contests have less or sometimes no voice in choosing their party's presidential nominee. In most years, a party's presidential nomination contest ends months before citizens in the late-voting states have ever had a chance to cast their ballots. To gain more influence and a greater voice, a number of ambitious states have tried to move their primaries and caucuses forward, creating a phenomenon that has come to be known as "front-loading."[1] This dynamic repeatedly leads to calls for reform, as politicians, journalists, scholars, and citizens all try to rethink the primary calendar.

---

[*] Eugene D. Mazo is Visiting Associate Professor of Law at Rutgers University. He thanks Michael Dimino and Richard Winger for providing comments on this chapter and his colleagues at Rutgers for allowing him to test out several of its ideas at a Half-Baked Ideas Workshop held on May 16, 2019.

[1] *See* Andrew E. Busch & William G. Mayer, *The Front-Loading Problem, in* THE MAKING OF PRESIDENTIAL CANDIDATES 2004, at 2 (William G. Mayer ed., 2004) (defining front-loading as "the name that has been given to an important recent trend in the presidential nomination process, in which more and more states schedule their primaries and caucuses near the very beginning of the delegate selection season.").

This chapter examines the primary calendar and what can be done to change it. It begins by explaining why Iowa and New Hampshire hold their nomination contests first, as well as how other states have tried to match the power of these two small states through front-loading. The chapter also briefly examines the 2020 primary calendar and the way both major parties have recently tried to play with their rules to bring some stability to the presidential nomination process. After examining front-loading in depth, the chapter turns to look more closely at the one reform that a majority of American voters consistently support: holding all primaries and caucuses on a single day. Scheduling a national Primary Day is important not only because the current staggered nature of the calendar privileges some candidates over others, but also because it favors voters and party members in some states over those in other states. One way to remedy this problem and to ensure that all voters are treated equally is to hold our 57 nomination contests on the single day.

Scheduling a national Primary Day would appear to be a simple, direct, and fair way of selecting a party's presidential nominee. But a national primary also comes with its own challenges. A national primary would change the nature of presidential campaigns by shifting the resources and spending of candidates from low-population states like Iowa, New Hampshire, and South Carolina to high-population states like California, Texas, and Florida. It would also diminish the aspirations of candidates with less money and name recognition by denying them the opportunity to build momentum in the early primary and caucus states. A related concern has to do with how the votes from different states would be tallied and added in a national primary, especially when the list of candidates running could potentially be very large, as well as what should happen if no single candidate manages to wins a majority of the votes cast. Finally, there is the thorny issue of how a single primary date could ever be imposed on the states. Whether Congress has the power to set the date on which the states hold their primaries is a constitutional question that remains unresolved. Meanwhile, whether the national parties have the willpower to impose a national primary on the states also remains in doubt. As a result, while it seems that the benefits of a national Primary Day may be substantial, the path to getting there comes with its own challenges.

II. THE MODERN PRIMARY CALENDAR

Very few scholars are fans of the modern primary calendar. "It is a peculiarity of American government that after 200 years no fixed system exists for selecting the president of the United States," writes James W. Ceaser, a well-known scholar of the presidential nomination process. "Almost every nomination contest brings with it a different arrangement for the schedule of primaries ... No one can get used to the system before it has changed again."[2] Ever since the modern calendar began in 1972, Iowa has almost always held the first presidential nominating contest, and it has usually been followed by New Hampshire. After that, other states have jostled and jockeyed for better pole position and have attempted to move their nominating contests earlier and earlier in the calendar, only to have Iowa and New Hampshire respond. In the 1980s, a related problem emerged when some states began clustering their primaries on a single day that came relatively early in the primary calendar. This day eventually came to be known as Super Tuesday.

A. *Iowa and New Hampshire*

Iowa and New Hampshire acquired their privileged position at the front of the calendar through happenstance. Prior to 1972, Iowa had held its precinct caucuses in March or April. In 1972, however, a series of unrelated decisions by the major parties and Iowa's state legislature forced the state to hold its precinct caucuses in January.[3] That year, the Democratic National Committee decided to hold its national convention from July 10–13. The rules of Iowa's Democratic party required at least thirty days to pass between the different stages of the Iowa caucuses, which consisted of precinct caucuses, county conventions, congressional district conventions, and the Democratic state convention. This thirty-day rule was adopted for practical reasons; party workers needed that much time to certify paperwork between each caucus stage.[4] In 1972, the final stage of the caucuses, the Democratic state convention, was set to be held on May 20. That day was chosen because it was the first date that a convention hall could be found large enough to hold all of Iowa's Democrats, who needed to meet to elect delegates before the party's national convention began on July 10.[5] Working backward from May 20, Iowa's precinct caucuses were set for January 24.

Iowa's caucuses happened to be the first nominating event in the nation in 1972, which itself was the first year of the modern nomination system. At the

---

[2] James W. Ceaser, *The Presidential Nomination Mess*, 8(4) CLAREMONT REV. OF BOOKS 21 (2008).

[3] *See* DAVID P. REDLAWSK, CAROLINE J. TOLBERT & TODD DONOVAN, WHY IOWA? HOW CAUCUSES AND SEQUENTIAL ELECTIONS IMPROVE THE PRESIDENTIAL NOMINATION PROCESS 47 (2011); Peverill Squire, *Iowa and the Nomination Process, in* THE IOWA CAUCUSES AND THE PRESIDENTIAL NOMINATION PROCESS 1 (Peverill Squire ed., 1989).

[4] Squire, *supra* note 3, at 2.

[5] *See* Nelson W. Polsby, *The Iowa Caucuses in a Front-Loaded System: A Few Historical Lessons, in* THE IOWA CAUCUSES AND THE PRESIDENTIAL NOMINATION PROCESS 152 (Peverill Squire ed., 1989).

time, most observers did not attribute any importance to the January date. Though George McGovern campaigned in Iowa ahead of the precinct caucuses, the state's caucuses received only a small amount of national attention. Still, whatever attention Iowa did receive was noticed by the parties.[6] In 1972, Iowa's Republicans held their precinct caucuses in April. However, by 1976, the state's Republicans were cooperating with the Democrats, and both parties held their caucuses on January 19.[7] Since then, Iowa has never relinquished its starting position in the nomination calendar. In 1976, Jimmy Carter's campaign heavily concentrated its resources in Iowa. Carter's success there led the state's caucuses to attain national stature.[8] Subsequently, doing well in Iowa became necessary for winning the presidential nomination, or rather, and perhaps more accurately, doing poorly in Iowa has proven to be a death knell. Those who fail in Iowa quickly find that the media loses interest in them, so serious candidates ignore Iowa at their peril.

Iowa's rise blindsided officials in New Hampshire, which until that point had long had the privilege of holding the first primary in the nation. But New Hampshire's early primary was itself an anomaly. When the state enacted its primary law back in 1913, its legislature set the date of the state's primary elections in May. Then, in 1916, the state moved its primaries to the second Tuesday in March. This date was chosen so that the primary could coincide with New Hampshire's town meetings; the legislature wanted to save money by avoiding the expense of an extra election.[9] From 1920 to 1952, no one seemed to mind that New Hampshire's primary was the first in the nation because this contest was merely used to select delegates to the parties' national conventions. The election did not give voters an opportunity to vote for the presidential candidates themselves.[10] However, in 1952, a non-binding presidential preference poll was added to the delegate ballot. Voters going to the polls during the primary could now also voice their preference for a presidential candidate, although this vote was only a "beauty contest."[11] It did not translate into the selection of delegates, and the elected delegates were not bound at the parties' national conventions to cast their votes for the candidate who won New

6   Squire, *supra* note 3, at 2.
7   *Id.*
8   *Id.* at 3; *see also* REDLAWSK, TOLBERT & DONOVAN, *supra* note 3, at 47–48.
9   William G. Mayer, *The New Hampshire Primary: A Historical Overview, in* MEDIA AND MOMENTUM: THE NEW HAMPSHIRE PRIMARY AND NOMINATION POLITICS 10 (Gary R. Orren & Nelson W. Polsby eds., 1996).
10 *Id.*
11 Emmett H. Buell, *The Changing Face of the New Hampshire Primary, in* IN PURSUIT OF THE WHITE HOUSE 2000, at 93 (William G. Mayer ed., 2000); *see also* CHARLES BRERETON, FIRST IN THE NATION: NEW HAMPSHIRE AND THE PREMIER PRESIDENTIAL PRIMARY 4 (1987).

Hampshire's presidential preference ballot. But this contest brought new media attention to New Hampshire, and before long the state decided to link the presidential preference vote to the selection of delegates.[12]

In the ensuing years, the legislatures of Iowa and New Hampshire have worked hard to protect their first-in-time status. In 1978, Iowa's legislature adopted a statute to regulate the date of the state's precinct caucuses. Today, that statute requires that the caucuses take place at least eight days earlier than the presidential nomination contest of any other U.S. state or territory.[13] In 1979, New Hampshire's legislature adopted a similar statute. Initially, it set New Hampshire's primary for the Tuesday immediately preceding the date on which any other New England state had scheduled a similar election.[14] Subsequently, this statute was amended, and today it grants discretion to New Hampshire's secretary of state to set the date of the primary for the Tuesday immediately preceding the date on which any other state is scheduled to hold a similar election.[15] (Iowa's caucuses are not considered to be a similar election.) The expectation is that New Hampshire's secretary of state will always exercise the discretion afforded to him. After all, as the state's legislature explains in its statute: "The purpose of this section is to protect the tradition of the New Hampshire first-in-the-nation presidential primary."[16]

B. *Front-Loading and Super Tuesday*

Going first in the primary calendar bestowed enormous benefits on Iowa and New Hampshire, including increased press coverage, greater attention from candidates, unmatched influence in shaping public opinion, various economic benefits, and important policy concessions.[17] Soon other states began

---

[12] BARBARA NORRANDER, THE IMPERFECT PRIMARY: ODDITIES, BIASES, AND STRENGTHS OF THE U.S. PRESIDENTIAL NOMINATION PROCESS 107–08 (2015).

[13] IOWA CODE §43.4(1) (requiring that the date of Iowa's caucuses "shall be at least eight days earlier than the scheduled date for any meeting, caucus, or primary which constitutes the first determining stage of the presidential nominating process in any other state, territory, or any other group which has the authority to select delegates in the presidential nomination.").

[14] Buell, *supra* note 11, at 92.

[15] N.H. R.S.A. §653:9 ("The presidential primary election shall be held on the second Tuesday in March or on a date selected by the secretary of state which is 7 days or more immediately preceding the date on which any other state shall hold a similar election, whichever is earlier, of each year when a president of the United States is to be elected or the year previous.").

[16] N.H. R.S.A. §653:9.

[17] WILLIAM G. MAYER & ANDREW E. BUSCH, THE FRONT-LOADING PROBLEM IN PRESIDENTIAL NOMINATIONS 24–30 (2004); *see also* Randall E. Adkins & Andrew J. Dowdle, *How Important Are Iowa and New Hampshire to Winning Post-Reform Presidential Nominations?*, 54 POL. SCI. Q. 431, 440 (2001).

envying Iowa and New Hampshire and moving up their own primary and caucus dates.[18] This phenomenon became known as "front-loading." As William G. Mayer and Andrew E. Busch explain, the term refers to the trend of states moving to schedule their contests at the beginning of the primary calendar.[19] The consequence of front-loading "is a nomination calendar in which a large portion of the delegates are selected within a few weeks after the process formally commences, as opposed to having the primaries and caucuses spread out evenly or having them concentrated near the end of the process."[20] Front-loading turned out to be one of the major unforeseen consequences of the McGovern-Fraser Commission's reforms.

The major parties initially did little to combat front-loading. Eventually, however, they put in place timing rules to govern when state primaries and caucuses could occur.[21] Each year, Iowa and New Hampshire have sought exemptions from these timing rules or else have violated them outright. The national parties have consistently threatened to punish Iowa and New Hampshire for their violations by refusing to seat their national convention delegates, or by reducing the number of delegates allocated to these states.[22] But there have been no sticks behind the national parties' carrots. The parties have consistently refused to follow through with their punishments, and the seating of Iowa's and New Hampshire's convention delegates has never been challenged. For decades, this phenomenon has exasperated party insiders and scholarly observers alike.

It is worth exploring how the timing window has worked. In 1984, the Democratic Party set the second Tuesday in March as the opening window of the primary calendar. When Vermont scheduled an earlier contest, Iowa and New Hampshire responded by moving their contests to even earlier dates.[23] In 1988, the Democrats again set the calendar's start date as the second Tuesday in March, only this time they issued Iowa and New

---

[18]   MAYER & BUSCH, *supra* note 17, at 23.

[19]   *Id.* at 4.

[20]   *Id.*

[21]   After the McGovern-Fraser Commission's (1969) recommendations created our modern presidential nomination system, several other Democratic primary reform commissions have tried to address the problem of front-loading. These have included the Winograd Commission (1975), the Hunt Commission (1982), the Fowler Commission (1986), the Price-Herman Commission (2004), the Democratic Change Commission (2009), and the Unity Reform Commission (2017). Since 1984, a timing rule has been used to determine when the primary contests may begin, as recommended by several of these commissions.

[22]   LISA K. PARSHALL, REFORMING THE PRESIDENTIAL NOMINATION PROCESS: FRONT-LOADING'S CONSEQUENCES AND THE NATIONAL PRIMARY SOLUTION 24–28 tbl.1.3 (2018).

[23]   *Id.* at 21–22.

Hampshire exemptions from the timing window. When South Dakota scheduled its nomination contest to fall on the same date as New Hampshire's, New Hampshire moved its contest up and Iowa then did the same.[24] In 1992, the pattern repeated. When South Dakota refused to move its primary to within the window allocated to non-exempt states, Iowa and New Hampshire responded, each by moving its own contest forward. In 1996, Delaware was the culprit. When it tried to claim the lead-off spot, Iowa and New Hampshire put pressure on the candidates to skip Delaware's primary.[25]

It took until 2000 for the Republican Party to enact a timing window. When it did so, it set the first Tuesday in February as the opening date of the Republican primaries. As a result, Iowa and New Hampshire pushed their nomination contests into January. Many states followed by scheduling their contests for the very beginning of the primary window in early February. The process of states pushing their nomination contests to the first allowable date in the primary window was first witnessed in 1980. It was created by the Democratic Party's initial timing window. By 1988, this phenomenon became known as Super Tuesday. Super Tuesday often saw more than a dozen nomination contests take place on a single day. In 1988, 40 percent of the Democratic Party's delegates were elected by Super Tuesday, a number that rose to 54 percent in 1996.[26] In 2008, the peak year of front-loading, 56 percent of the Democratic Party's delegates and 60 percent of the Republican Party's delegates were chosen by Super Tuesday, which that year took place on February 5.[27] A total of 22 nominating contests occurred on that day.[28]

The major parties have tried to institute various measures to ameliorate front-loading. One calls for bonus delegates to be awarded to states that agree to hold later nomination contests. Another involves stripping convention delegates from states that violate a party's timing rules. How this would work was tested in 2008, when the Democrats set the first Tuesday in February as the opening date for the party's timing window. That year, the party also decided to allow additional states to apply for permission to hold their nomination contests in the pre-window period, joining Iowa and New Hampshire. Nevada and South Carolina won the right to hold earlier contests, in part because of their large populations of Latino and African American voters, only to witness Michigan and Florida, two states not chosen, unilaterally move their contests

[24]   *Id.* at 22.
[25]   *Id.*
[26]   *Id.* 30.
[27]   *Id.* at 31–32, 39–40.
[28]   *Id.* at 40.

forward. Of course, Iowa and New Hampshire responded in predictable fashion.

To punish Michigan and Florida, the Democratic Party stripped each state of its convention delegates and instructed the presidential candidates not to campaign there.[29] Most of the candidates abided, but Hillary Clinton's name still appeared on Michigan's ballot, and she wound up "winning" Michigan's primary with 55 percent of the vote. In Florida, both Clinton's and Barack Obama's names appeared on the ballot. As Clinton tried to catch Obama in the race for the Democratic Party's nomination in 2008, her campaign argued that the voting rights of Michigan's and Florida's delegates should be restored. The Democratic National Committee (DNC) soon reversed course and ruled that each of Michigan's and Florida's delegates should be afforded a half vote, as opposed to a full vote, at the national convention.[30] When Obama was assured of winning the nomination, he urged the DNC to restore the full voting rights of these states' delegates, and the DNC complied.[31]

The front-loading shenanigans of the states appear during almost every election cycle. In 2012, the Democratic Party decided that its primary window would open in March, but it allowed the exempted states to hold their pre-window contests in February.[32] In addition, the states were encouraged to cluster their primaries by region. Both parties again threatened to punish states that did not abide by their timing rules, this time by reducing their delegate allotment in half.[33] Despite this, Michigan and Florida pushed the envelope again and held earlier nomination contests, this time joined by Arizona. In response, Iowa, New Hampshire, and South Carolina moved their contests forward, although Nevada abided by its original caucus date.[34] As punishment, the Republican Party cut the number of delegates allotted to Michigan, Florida, Arizona, Iowa, New Hampshire, and South Carolina in half. As usual, this punishment had little effect. The Republican presidential candidates in 2012 continued to campaign as usual in each of these states and continued to make appeals to their voters.[35]

In 2016, Michigan again threatened to jump ahead in the calendar, this time along with Utah, but in the end that did not happen. In 2016, as Lisa Parshall

---

[29]   NORRANDER, *supra* note 12, at 129–31.
[30]   PARSHALL, *supra* note 22, at 56.
[31]   *Id.* at 57.
[32]   NORRANDER, *supra* note 12, at 129.
[33]   *Id.* at 130.
[34]   *Id.*
[35]   *Id.* at 131.

explains, "the jockeying of states was less pronounced, front-loading was muted, and no penalties for timing violations were imposed."[36] However, 2016 brought a new surprise when Donald Trump, a candidate unlike any other in American politics, won the Republican Party's presidential nomination. A total of seventeen Republican candidates had entered the 2016 race, and this time the primary calendar worked to fuel the rise of an insurgent. The long schedule of Republican primaries and caucuses—together with the Republican Party's many primary debates—helped Trump attract media attention for months on end. As he amassed new delegates in each state, angry Republican voters in states that had not yet held their nomination contests, rather than feel disenfranchised, found a voice in supporting Trump.

C. *The 2020 Calendar*

In 2020, the parties managed to tame front-loading, although unexpected twists and turns led the calendar to develop in ways that could not have been foreseen. After the parties kept January free of any nomination contests, the Iowa caucuses began the calendar on February 3. They were followed by a primary in New Hampshire on February 11, a caucus in Nevada on February 22, and a primary in South Carolina on February 29. Joe Biden failed to finish among the top three in either Iowa or New Hampshire and came in a very distant second place behind Bernie Sanders in Nevada. But Biden roared to a resounding victory in South Carolina, setting up Super Tuesday as the day the Democratic presidential nomination would be decided. Super Tuesday occurred on March 3 and saw sixteen Democratic primary contests take place on a single day. In 2020, California joined the fray and moved its primary up from its traditional June date to March 3, making Super Tuesday an even more important event than it had been in previous years, as California's 495 convention delegates, the most of any state, were now chosen three months earlier. By Super Tuesday, 38 percent of the pledged Democratic delegates were elected. A week after Super Tuesday, six more states held their presidential nomination contests on March 10, and four more states were set to do so on March 17. By the end of March, 65 percent of the pledged Democratic delegates were scheduled to be elected. This meant, of course, that the nomination contests that were set to take place in April, May, and June would have little impact on the nomination.[37]

---

[36] Parshall, *supra* note 22, at 92.
[37] *See 2020 Democratic Presidential Nomination*, 270TOWIN.COM (2019), www.270towin.com/ 2020-democratic-nomination/?view=total.

In mid-March, however, a national health care crisis, the Covid-19 pandemic, presented an unprecedented threat to voters. Voting in-person suddenly became dangerous, and many states began postponing their nomination contests — back-loading them instead of front-loading them now. Ohio, one of the four states that had originally been scheduled to vote on March 17, moved its primary election to April 28 and allowed nearly all voting to be conducted by mail. Wisconsin's governor also tried to allow his state's residents to vote by mail during that state's primary on April 7, but his efforts were opposed by the the Wisconsin legislature and quickly became the subject of litigation.[38] The long and hotly contested Democratic nomination process of 2020 ended with a whimper when Bernie Sanders dropped out of the race on April 8, leaving Biden to campaign against Trump from the confines of his home because of shelter-in-place orders. At that point, voters in more than twenty jurisdictions still had not voted, either because their scheduled primary had not yet taken place or because it had been postponed due to Covid-19, meaning that, once again, the Democratic nomination contest would end before millions of voters could exercise a voice in choosing their party's nominee.[39]

The Democrats were scheduled to elect 3,979 pledged national convention delegates through primaries and caucuses in 2020. These 3,979 pledged delegates were to be joined at the Democratic convention by an estimated 776 superdelegates. The Republicans were scheduled to elect a total of 2,550 delegates for their national convention. Rule-tinkering by the Democratic Party ahead of the 2020 nomination contests determined how voting would proceed at the party's national convention. Bowing to criticisms that unelected superdelegates had been too influential in 2016, the Democratic Party implemented new convention voting rules for 2020. Only pledged delegates could vote on the first ballot,[40] meaning that a majority of the 3,979 pledged delegates — or 1,990 votes — were needed to win the nomination. If no candidate won the party's nomination on the first ballot, the Democratic Party's new voting rules allowed superdelegates to vote on the second ballot.[41] The

---

[38] *See* Richard Briffault, *COVID-19 and the Law: Elections, in* LAW IN THE TIME OF COVID-19, at 36–40 (Katharina Pistor ed., 2020).

[39] *See 2020 Primary Election Dates,* NAT'L CONF. OF ST. LEGISLATURES (April 27, 2020), www.ncsl.org/research/elections-and-campaigns/2020-state-primary-election-dates.aspx; Rob Richie & David Daley, *A Post-Pandemic Voting Reform Agenda,* DEMOCRACY: J. OF IDEAS (April 20, 2020), https://democracyjournal.org/arguments/a-post-pandemic-voting-reform-agenda/.

[40] Democratic Nat'l Comm., *Call for the 2020 Democratic National Convention,* § IX.C.7.b, at 16 (Aug. 25, 2018), https://democrats.org/wp-content/uploads/2019/02/2020-Call-for-Convention-WITH-Attachments-2.26.19.pdf.

[41] *Id.* at § IX.C.7.c, at 16.

approximately 776 superdelegates appointed by the party brought the number of total convention delegates to 4,745, so half of that number — or 2,373 — were needed to win the nomination if it went beyond one round of voting.

The Democratic Party in 2020 also decided to use bonus delegates to reward any state or territory that scheduled its nominating contest for later in the calendar. Under the new rules, a 10 percent bonus was to be given to states that held their nomination contests in April, while a 20 percent bonus was to be awarded to states that opted to wait until May or June.[42] Separately, states that held their contests after March 24 would get a 15 percent bonus for participating in a "regional cluster," which was defined as a contest held on the same date as at least two neighboring states.[43] These bonuses could be added, so that if a state held a primary in May or June and simultaneously participated in a regional cluster, it would receive a 35 percent bonus in delegates (the total when its 20 percent and 15 percent bonuses are added). As this book went to press, it was unclear how the Democratic Party planned to allocate bonus delegates to states that changed their primary dates due to Covid-19.[44]

The fact that the Democratic contests dominated the conversation in 2020 allowed the Republicans to begin quietly cancelling their primaries and caucuses altogether. After maneuvering by Trump's loyalists, state Republican parties in Nevada and South Carolina announced that they were calling off their nomination contests.[45] They were followed by state Republican parties in Alaska, Arizona, Hawaii, Kansas, and Virginia cancelling their primaries and caucuses as well. In total, seven state Republican parties decided not to hold any nomination contest. While this saved money for state officials and for these state Republican parties, it served to deprive voters in these states from having any say over their party's presidential nominee.

---

[42]   *Id.* at § I.C.2.a, at 1–2.

[43]   *Id.* at § I.C.2.b, at 2.

[44]   *See* Josh Putnam, *How Could All Those Primary Postponements Change the Delegate Math?*, FIVETHIRYEIGHT (April 10, 2020), https://fivethirtyeight.com/features/how-could-all-those-primary-postponements-change-the-delegate-math/; *Bonus Delegates*, 270TOWIN.COM (2020), www.270towin.com/content/2020-democratic-nomination-bonus-delegate-allocation.

[45]   Alex Isenstadt, *Republicans to Scrap Primaries and Caucuses as Trump Challengers Cry Foul*, POLITICO (Sept. 6, 2019), www.politico.com/story/2019/09/06/republicans-cancel-primaries-trump-challengers-1483126; *Canceled No More? South Carolina GOP Decision to Cancel Presidential Primary Challenged in Court*, FRONTLOADING HQ (Oct. 1, 2019), https://frontloading.blogspot.com/2019/10/canceled-no-more-south-carolina-gop.html; *Nevada Republic Presidential Nominating Process*, THE GREEN PAPERS: 2020 PRESIDENTIAL PRIMARIES, CAUCUSES, AND CONVENTIONS (2020), www.thegreenpapers.com/P20/NV-R.

D. *The Consequences of Front-Loading*

Many aspects of the primary calendar have been repeatedly criticized. Some scholars believe that front-loading has turned the presidential nomination process into "a televised horse race," one that happens to focus more on media appeal than on the competing ideas, policy programs, or character of the candidates.[46] The outcomes of primaries and caucuses are reported by the media according to the percentage of the vote that each candidate receives. But this is often deceiving, given that the popular vote results of a primary or caucus do not always faithfully reflect how party delegates are elected in these contests or how they are allocated to the presidential candidates. "The popular vote totals are *not* really what matters in the primaries," explains John Haskell. "What matters is how many delegates from that state the candidate will get in his quest to secure enough delegates to be the presidential nominee."[47] But this number is often ignored. "Even in a famous caucus state such as Iowa, only the first round of voting in the dead of winter draws attention," according to Rhodes Cook. "By the time the delegates are actually selected during the spring, the candidates and the media are long gone."[48]

Busch and Mayer, two of our most serious scholars of the nomination process, argue that front-loading makes presidential nominations "less deliberative, less rational, less flexible, and more chaotic."[49] One of the negative consequences of a front-loaded calendar, they note, is that is leads to accelerated voter decision-making.[50] This conclusion seems counterintuitive, given that most serious presidential candidates start their campaigns many months before the first nomination contests begin. But polling data suggests that early candidate campaigning takes place when voters are not paying serious attention to the candidates or the details of their policy proposals. During this early phase, most voters say they still do not have enough information about their party's candidates to make up their minds. It is only when the primaries and caucuses begin in earnest that voter learning accelerates and voter opinions stabilize. But by then, the front-loaded system hits voters like a bus, and they "are forced to reach a final decision about their party's next presidential

---

[46] Thomas Cronin & Robert Loevy, *The Case for a National Pre-Primary Convention Plan*, in ENDURING CONTROVERSIES IN PRESIDENTIAL NOMINATING POLITICS 271–72 (Emmett H. Buell Jr. & Willian G. Mayer eds., 2004).

[47] *See* JOHN HASKELL, FUNDAMENTALLY FLAWED: UNDERSTANDING AND REFORMING THE PRESIDENTIAL PRIMARIES 34–35 (1996).

[48] RHODES COOK, THE PRESIDENTIAL NOMINATION PROCESS: A PLACE FOR US? 45 (2004).

[49] MAYER & BUSCH, *supra* note 17, at 56.

[50] *Id.* at 56–60.

nominees in a remarkably short period of time."[51] This criticism, though it sounds contrary to intuition, has been echoed by other scholars as well.[52]

The impact of front-loading on voters, of course, is only one side of the story. Mayer and Busch find that a front-loaded calendar has a negative impact on candidates as well. For one thing, it leads to worse campaigns.[53] By the time Super Tuesday arrives, campaigns become artificial. By this point, the very first contests have usually locked in the front-runners. Those not anointed as such find it difficult to attract media attention and a continuing flow of campaign cash.[54] The winners of the early contests gain media attention and momentum that become impossible for rivals to overcome.[55] For this reason, many presidential candidates drop out of the primaries after doing poorly in the first few contests.[56] Mayer and Busch find that these dropouts have an effect on voters. As the field of candidates narrows, voters are discouraged from coming out in subsequent contests. Unsurprisingly, scholarly studies on voter turnout reveal that voter participation rates decrease as the primary calendar unfolds.[57]

There is yet another harm that is profound but that has not received much scholarly attention. It is that the sequenced primary calendar may violate the equal protection rights of voters by treating them differently in different states. Voters in the early primary states are presented with one slate of candidates, while voters in the later primary states confront an entirely different slate, after the presidential candidates who fared poorly drop out. Thus, American voters are not comparing apples to apples when they cast their ballots in sequenced primaries and caucuses. This important point was made in a recent book by Lisa Parshall, who argues that when states hold open or semi-closed primaries and their citizens vote before states that hold closed primaries, some voters who are not affiliated with any party, or indeed who are

---

[51] *Id.* at 63.

[52] *See, e.g.*, NORRANDER, *supra* note 12, at 109–10.

[53] MAYER & BUSCH, *supra* note 17, at 63–64.

[54] *Id.* at 67–71.

[55] *See* LARRY BARTELS, PRESIDENTIAL PRIMARIES AND THE DYNAMICS OF PUBLIC CHOICE (1988) (chronicling the phenomenon of "momentum" and how it influences the presidential nomination process).

[56] Indeed, many would-be candidates drop their presidential bids before the calendar even begins because they cannot compete in the "invisible primary," which is based on fundraising. *See* MICHAEL J. GOFF, THE MONEY PRIMARY: THE NEW POLITICS OF THE PRESIDENTIAL NOMINATION PROCESS 3–13, 87–92 (2004). In the 2020 cycle, a total of 17 candidates dropped out before voters ever went to the polls in Iowa, including Cory Booker, Kirsten Gillibrand, Kamala Harris, Beto O'Rourke, and Julián Castro, among them.

[57] MAYER & BUSCH, *supra* note 17, at 83–86.

members of competing parties, are given the opportunity to cast a more effective and meaningful vote than actual party members.[58]

The regulation of party membership itself, of course, is not uniform throughout the United States. Indeed, the rules regulating party membership, voter registration, and primary participation all vary significantly from state to state. In some states, primaries are open to non-members; in others, they are not. However, as Parshall notes, the concern is not so much that variations exist. Rather, it is that sequential voting exacerbates the inequality of party membership. The system gives greater influence to party members who have to meet lower thresholds of membership or even to non-members in the early voting states, while it may leave others who have to satisfy higher thresholds of membership in the later states "with a constrained choice."[59]

The sequential nature of the primary calendar thus creates meaningful participation disparities among different portions of the electorate. These disparities have until now largely been ignored, even though, as Parshall points out, "there is something profoundly troubling about a presidential nomination process that leaves millions of voters with a limited or ineffectual choice in the selection of their parties' presidential nominees."[60] Recently, some have argued that the consequence of having to cast an ineffectual vote in the nomination process due to the sequencing of the calendar may violate the equal protection rights of voters and party members in late-voting states.[61] A sequenced calendar treats the voices of different voters differently. It serves to amplify some voices while silencing others. The only way to remedy this

---

[58]   PARSHALL, *supra* note 22, at 124.
[59]   *Id.* at 125.
[60]   *Id.* at 169.
[61]   *See, e.g.*, Lisa Parshall & Franco Mattei, *Challenging the Presidential Nomination Process: The Constitutionality of Front-Loading*, 26 HAMLINE J.L. & PUB. POL'Y 1, 21 (2004). This argument is based on the belief that even though the right to vote is conferred by the states, that does not preclude it from having federal constitutional protections when it is exercised to nominate a *national* candidate. In other words, because the presidency is a national office, denying the right to vote to someone based on his state of residency would be unconstitutional. Of course, there is a strong counterargument to this. After all, the Equal Protection Clause prohibits each state from depriving its residents of the equal protection of the laws. But there is no requirement that each state treat its residents the same as a different state treats its residents. And while the national government is also bound by equal-protection principles, there is no national law governing the current nomination process that would deny anyone equal treatment. If one were to argue that national parties are state actors, then perhaps they are treating different states' residents differently, but it is not certain whether such different treatment would be a constitutional violation, and it is not clear that the parties would be state actors when encouraging states to set primaries in a certain order. The author thanks Michael Dimino for clarifying these points. Email from Michael Dimino (Feb. 5, 2020).

problem is to design a nomination system that would require all primaries and caucuses to be held on a single day.

III. HOLDING A SINGLE PRIMARY DAY

The idea of holding a national primary on a single day is not new. Both Theodore Roosevelt and Woodrow Wilson promoted it over a century ago. In 1912, Roosevelt, who had already served eight years as president, decided to seek the Republican Party's nomination once again, this time by running against his chosen successor, incumbent William Howard Taft. But Taft controlled the Republican Party's machinery, so Roosevelt decided to challenge him by forming a new party. "We should provide by national law for presidential primaries," Roosevelt told his audience at the Progressive Party's national nominating convention.[62] Indeed, the platform of the Progressive Party demanded that a national presidential primary be held.[63] Of course, Woodrow Wilson won the presidency in 1912, beating both Roosevelt and Taft. A year later, in his first State of the Union address, Wilson also endorsed the idea of holding a national primary.[64] He urged "the prompt enactment of legislation which will provide for primary elections throughout the country at which the voters of the several parties may choose their nominees for the Presidency without the intervention of nominating conventions."[65] Since then, every time Americans have been polled on the idea of holding a national primary, approximately two-thirds of respondents have said they support the idea.

A. *The Advantages*

There are a number of advantages of holding a single Primary Day. The first and most important is that every voter's voice would count equally. Gone would be the current staggered system that disadvantages voters and party members in states that hold their nomination contests in May or June, effectively rendering the voices of these individuals meaningless in most election years. In 1996, 2000, and 2004, both major party candidates clinched their nominations in March. In 2008, the Republican nominee, John McCain, clinched in March, and in 2012, the Republican nomination contest was effectively over by early April.[66] In 2020, the

---

[62] Ceaser, *supra* note 2, at 25 (quoting Roosevelt).
[63] *See* DONALD BRUCE JOHNSON & KIRK H. PORTER, NATIONAL PARTY PLATFORMS, 1840–1972, at 176 (1975).
[64] *See* ARTHUR S. LINK, 29 THE PAPERS OF WOODROW WILSON 7 (1979).
[65] Ceaser, *supra* note 2, at 25 (quoting Wilson).
[66] See PARSHALL, *supra* note 22, at 18.

Democratic nomination contest was effectively over by early April as well. If the primaries were held on a single day, the early states would no longer have this kind of winnowing function.

Another benefit of Primary Day is that it would shorten the length of presidential campaigns. Currently, presidential campaigns start a year before the Iowa caucuses, if not even earlier than that. For the 2020 presidential race, Cory Booker, Amy Klobuchar, Bernie Sanders, and Elizabeth Warren all launched their campaigns in February of 2019, a full year before the Iowa caucuses began. Julián Castro, Tulsi Gabbard, Kamala Harris, and Marianne Williamson launched their campaigns even earlier, in January. Joe Biden and Pete Buttigieg launched in April of 2019. By the time of the 2020 general election, the Democratic Party's nominee will have campaigned for over a year and a half. By contrast, if a single day in June, July, or August of an election year were used to hold all state primaries and caucuses, campaigns would be much shorter. An "invisible primary" would still exist, no doubt, and provide a period of time when candidates raise the bulk of their money, but even that would start much later.

One common objection to a national primary is that it would increase the costs of campaigning for the presidency. To participate in a one-day national primary, candidates will have to run national campaigns from the beginning, and they will have to raise a lot more money up front.[67] A corollary to this criticism is that a national primary will also change the nature of primary campaigns.[68] Unlike the Iowa and New Hampshire campaigns of yesterday, which were driven by face-to-face contact between candidates and voters, a national primary would lead to so-called "tarmac campaigns" in which candidates fly from one airport to the next, spending as little time as possible in each place. Instead of engaging in retail politics, candidates would rely on superficial TV and Internet advertising to reach their targeted audiences on a mass scale.[69] Relatedly, another common objection is that a national primary would prevent a little-known or dark-horse candidate from winning the nomination.[70] The example often provided is of Jimmy Carter, who built momentum in small states and used it to become his party's nominee.[71]

[67] Michael Nelson & Andrew E. Busch, *Resolved, Political Parties Should Nominate Candidates for the Presidency Through a National Primary*, in Debating the Presidency: Conflicting Perspectives on the American Executive 51–52 (Richard J. Ellis & Michael Nelson eds., 2018).

[68] Haskell, *supra* note 47, at 125.

[69] *Id.* at 126.

[70] Robert E. Altschuler, *Selecting Presidential Nominees by National Primary: An Idea Whose Time Has Come?*, 5(4) Forum 1, 6 (2008).

[71] *Id.*

Those who advance the criticisms above, however, forget the significant extent to which the modern presidential nomination process has evolved since 1972. Today, campaigns not only begin earlier than ever, but they are also more expensive than ever. In 2016, Donald Trump raised $333,127,164 to fuel his presidential bid, and he was supported by another $119,430,779 in spending by outside groups. Hillary Clinton raised even more, an astounding $563,756,928, and she was supported by another $206,122,160 in outside spending.[72] Presidential campaigns become significantly more expensive with each election cycle, and it is hard to imagine this trend changing, regardless of whether the primaries are staggered or held on a single day. Campaigns also become more technologically sophisticated with each cycle. Even in places like Iowa and New Hampshire, the face-to-face campaigns of the past have been replaced with high-priced digital marketing extravaganzas that voters watch on their phones, not on television. Keeping the current primary calendar will do little to change the acceleration of this trend. Finally, given the sheer expense and marketing savvy that goes into a modern presidential campaign, it is hard to imagine a little-known candidate ever gaining traction with voters today. Serious candidates either have a national profile these days or else raise the money necessary to establish one.

If there were any downsides to holding a national primary a few years ago, they probably no longer exist, given that the advances in technology, fundraising, and campaigning make it unlikely that a dark-horse candidate could emerge through the primaries today. On the other hand, holding a national primary would improve the nomination system in many ways. For example, it would certainly increase voter turnout.[73] The corrosive effects that staggered primaries currently have on voter participation would simply disappear, given that there would no longer be early or late primaries. Voters would finally be treated equally, or at least more equally than they have been.[74]

Relatedly, having a national primary would reduce the role of media pundits in shaping people's perceptions of the winners and losers. Staggered primary contests vest the media with an outsized role in determining who's up and who's down in a presidential race. Even before the vote takes place in Iowa and New Hampshire, media coverage whittles down the field by shaping who

---

[72] *See Donald Trump (R): Winner, 2016 Presidential Race*, Ctr. for Responsive Pol. (2016), www.opensecrets.org/pres16/candidate?id=N00023864; and *Hillary Clinton (D), 2016 Presidential Race*, Ctr. for Responsive Pol. (2016), www.opensecrets.org/pres16/candidate?id=N00000019.

[73] *See* Michael Nelson, *Two Cheers for the National Primary, in* Enduring Controversies in Presidential Nominating Politics 283 (Emmett H. Buell Jr. & Willian G. Mayer eds., 2004).

[74] *Id.* at 284.

the contest's front-runners are. Voters too busy to tune in rely on media pundits to dissect the presidential vote in the early contests for them. A national primary would change that. The resources of the press would now be stretched across the country, just like the resources of the campaigns themselves would be. Moreover, candidates in a national primary would bring national issues to the forefront of campaigns, as opposed to issues that concern only voters in the early states. A national primary would feel much more like a general election, with a long crescendo building up to it, rather than like one horse race followed by another and then another.

Perhaps the best argument for holding a national primary is that most voters support the idea. For nearly 70 years, polls have indicated that roughly two-thirds to three-fourths of Americans have been in favor of holding a national primary to select each party's presidential nominee.[75] In 1952, before the modern primary system was adopted, 73 percent of respondents told Gallup they would prefer that presidential candidates be chosen in a national primary instead of by political party conventions (which at the time had the power to select presidential nominees).[76] From the time when the modern presidential nomination system first came into place in 1972 until Gallup ceased polling on this question in 1988, the percentage of Americans in favor of holding a national primary consistently hovered at above two-thirds.[77] Over time, these percentages have shifted only slightly. In 1996, 69 percent of voters preferred a national primary, while 75 percent did so in 2000[78] and 73 percent did so in 2008.[79] To be fair, how the question has been put to voters has differed,[80] and the percentages supporting the national primary have varied over time and by region. In 2015, 64 percent of those polled in the Northeast supported a direct national primary, whereas the percentage of support fell to 55 percent in the Midwest and 50 percent in the

[75]   Barbara Norrander, *Public Support for Presidential Nomination Reform*, 73(3) PUB. OP. Q. 578, 587–88 (2009) (examining public opinion on a national primary from 1968 to 2007 and finding that the idea has consistently received about 70% support, when it is presented without also offering other alternatives).

[76]   Robert E. Altschuler, *supra* note 70, at 3. In 1952, Gallup asked: "It has been suggested that presidential candidates be chosen by the voters in a national primary instead of by political party conventions as it present. Would you favor or oppose this?" *Id.*

[77]   *Id.*

[78]   *Id.*

[79]   Caroline E. Tolbert, David P. Redlawsk & Daniel C Bowen, *Reforming Presidential Nominations: Rotating State Primaries or a National Primary?*, 49 PS: POL. SCI. & POL. 71, 75 (2009).

[80]   *See* Caroline J. Tolbert, Amanda Keller & Todd Donovan, *Modified National Primary: State Losers and Support for Changing the Presidential Nominating Process*, 125 POL. SCI. Q. 393 (2010).

South.[81] In January 2020, a poll conducted by Monmouth University confirmed that most Democratic voters thought that Iowa and New Hampshire had too much control over the presidential nomination process, and 58 percent of Democratic voters said they would rather hold a single national primary in which every state held its nomination contest on the same day.[82] A mere 11 percent wanted to keep the current calendar, with Iowa, New Hampshire, South Carolina, and Nevada leading off.[83]

B. *Timing and Technicalities*

While the merits of holding a national primary have been debated, the technicalities of how such a proposal would work have received much less attention. How candidates would qualify for a national primary, which voters would be given the right to participate in this contest, and when the national primary should take place are all questions that do not have uniform answers. Most of the commentators who have championed the idea of a national primary have not given nearly enough thought to the specifics of how their proposal would work in practice. Indeed, most commentators have tended to promote one aspect of the idea—that it should take place on a single day—at the expense of outlining how its mechanics should function. As with most such arrangements, the devil is found in the details. Here, most importantly, these details must address how the ballots of voters in different states should be counted and aggregated to select a party's presidential nominee.

Two dominant national primary models have been advanced. One calls for holding a direct national *primary*; the second calls for holding a series of state *primaries* on the same day. These two models differ from each other in important respects. The first seeks to establish a single national contest. The proposals for how it would be run vary in their details, but they all share in common the idea that individual delegate-electing state primaries should be abolished in favor of a one-day event during which a single election would be used to select a party's presidential nominee.[84] The vote totals from the states would be added together in a direct primary, and the party's presidential nominee would be the candidate who won the most popular votes nationwide. Such an election would look like a presidential election in which the popular

---

[81]   *Majority Support for a National Primary*, YOUGOV.COM (March 5, 2015), https://today
       .yougov.com/topics/politics/articles-reports/2015/03/05/primaries.
[82]   *Democrats Want a National Primary*, MONMOUTH U. POLLING INST. (Jan. 22, 2020),
       www.monmouth.edu/polling-institute/reports/monmouthpoll_us_012220/.
[83]   *Id.*
[84]   See PARSHALL, *supra* note 22, at 199–200.

vote determined the winner. Because the nomination would go to the winner of the popular vote, the need to hold a national nominating convention would disappear—although conventions might be retained to transact other party business, apart from choosing a presidential candidate.[85]

A direct primary raises several important technical issues. First, what should happen if the leading candidate emerges from the direct national primary with only a plurality, but not a majority, of the national popular vote? Presidential nomination contests have historically tended to attract a large number of candidates. In 2016, twelve Republican candidates participated in the state primaries and caucuses, and another five participated in the debates leading up to these contests but withdrew before the primary calendar began. In 2020, more than two dozen candidates ran for the Democratic Party's nomination, although again many withdrew before any votes were cast. If a direct national primary was implemented, chances are that a dozen or more ambitious candidates would participate in it each year, but it might turn out that none of them receive more than 50 percent of the popular vote. Ranked choice voting would not solve this problem. This is because ranked choice voting would be extremely cumbersome to implement on a national scale. Even if ranked choice voting were adopted by all 57 primary and caucus jurisdictions and each elected a winner with the majority of that jurisdiction's ranked choice votes, it is not clear that adding these distinct victories would lead to a candidate receiving a majority of the overall popular vote.

To get around this problem, some advocates of a direct primary have suggested that a second-round runoff should be held between the top two candidates, if no candidate secures a majority of the vote in the first round.[86] Haskell, in slightly reformulating the runoff proposal, suggests that a second-round runoff should be held only if no candidate wins at least 40 percent of the vote in the first round.[87] This runoff election would be held three weeks after the first round of voting and would produce a clear majority winner. However, under Haskell's proposal, a candidate who wins the most votes and obtains a plurality above 40 percent could still receive his party's nomination without the need for a runoff.[88]

Relatedly, another issue concerns who would vote in a direct national primary. The states currently employ very different participation rules for their primary elections. Some states allow any citizen to participate in a party's primary. Other states have rules that allow only party members to

---

[85] Thomas Durbin, *Presidential Primaries: Proposals Before Congress to Reform Them and Congressional Authority to Regulate Them*, 1(2) J. L. & POL. 381, 391–92 (1984).

[86] NORRANDER, *supra* note 12, at 119–20.

[87] HASKELL, *supra* note 47, at 74.

[88] *Id.* at 73–74.

participate. Yet other states allow party members and so-called unaffiliated voters to participate but not voters who are registered as members of other parties. There are several variations on these voter eligibility rules as well. For a direct national primary to work, there may have to be some unification of these eligibility rules so that the primary electorate does not consist of different kinds of voters in different states.[89]

Then there is the problem of how the candidates would qualify for a direct primary. Presidential candidates currently qualify for the ballot in the states in various ways. In some states, candidates pay a fee to qualify for the ballot. In others, they gather a certain number of signatures to demonstrate that their primary candidacy has enough support among potential voters to appear on the state ballot. The candidate qualification rules may need to be made more uniform if a direct primary is to be a truly national contest.[90] Otherwise, a candidate may qualify in one state but not in another. Modern, sophisticated presidential campaigns have experienced staff to make sure that a major party candidate does not fail to qualify for the ballot in a state, but this fate could affect minor-party presidential candidates who are not well-financed, if minor parties are also forced to hold their nomination contests through a direct national primary. Because of these complicated dynamics, most proposals to hold a national primary apply only to the two major parties.[91]

Yet another problem concerns how a direct national primary would accommodate states with caucuses. Voting in caucuses takes place over the course of many rounds, and the results are tabulated and re-tabulated as caucus-goers

---

[89] See Barbara Norrander & Jay Wendland, *Open versus Closed Primaries and the Ideological Composition of Presidential Primary Electorates*, 42 ELECTORAL STUD. 229 (2016).

[90] Lowell Weicker, the Senator from Connecticut, had once introduced a bill proposing that to get on the national primary ballot, a candidate would have to obtain signatures equal to 1% of the turnout in the most recent presidential election. *See* Nelson, *supra* note 73, at 281.

[91] The reason minor parties are not included in my presidential primary reform proposal is that, traditionally, minor parties (apart from the Green Party) have not considered any of their presidential primaries to be binding. Also, most states do not allow small qualified parties to have their own presidential primaries, and even when they do, minor parties frequently decide not to use their primaries. In 2020, there were more states with minor party presidential primaries in which the party was not holding a primary than there were states in which a minor party was holding a primary. In addition, minor parties often wind up holding their presidential nominating conventions before some states have held a presidential primary for any party. A minor party needs to hold its nominating convention early because in some states the party may not be on the ballot. And sometimes when a minor party is not on the ballot at the beginning of the year, it cannot get on the general election ballot until after it has completed a petition that must include the names of its presidential and vice-presidential candidates. The author thanks Richard Winger for explaining and clarifying these points concerning how minor parties select their presidential nominees. Email from Richard Winger (Feb. 4, 2020).

either leave the caucus or throw their votes in favor of a different candidate, after their first-choice candidate fails to receive 15 percent of the vote. The initial precinct caucuses typically represent only the first stage in a complex multistage contest, one that takes place over many months. For a direct primary to succeed, a primary election would have to replace the state caucuses in states like Iowa, Nevada, and Wyoming, or else the results of the precinct caucus would have to be conclusive. The results of the caucuses would have to have a way of being calculated and added to other states' results on the day of the national primary, without the need for additional stages to be held.

Given these and other complexities, a question arises as to whether a national primary should consist of one national election or of 57 state and territorial delegate-selecting contests that would simply be held on the same day.[92] The latter option constitutes the second dominant model for holding a national primary. It calls for retaining our current state primaries and caucuses—in the plural sense. In doing so, this national primary model attempts to get around the formidable hurdles associated with the direct primary described above. Under this second model, states and territories would continue to hold their unique state nomination contests as they have previously—except they would now hold them all on the same day.[93]

The mandatory uniformity regarding the timing of these 57 contests would eliminate front-loading. Under this model, the states would continue to elect delegates to national party conventions, where these delegates would continue to select a presidential nominee. The unique delegate selection rules, candidate qualification rules, and voter eligibility rules of the individual states could be retained under this system. Votes would be counted as they are now in most states for each primary. Of course, some anomalies of the current system would have to be reconsidered. For instance, precinct caucuses would again have to be held on the same day as the state primaries (now plural), but for states holding multistage caucus contests, later-stage caucus dates could be held later, as long as the contests wrapped up before the national conventions.

Whereas the primaries and caucuses now begin in January or February of an election year, most proposals for a national primary—whether in the singular or plural sense—suggest that the one-day contest should take place later. Most commentators chose a day in June, July, or August of an election year as the ideal day.[94] Enough time needs to be factored in for a possible second-round

---

[92]   Nelson & Busch, *supra* note 67, at 49.
[93]   *See* THOMAS GANGALE, FORM THE PRIMARIES TO THE POLLS: HOW TO REPAIR AMERICA'S BROKEN PRESIDENTIAL NOMINATION PROCESS 95–97 (2008).
[94]   Nelson & Busch, *supra* note 67, at 44.

runoff take place if a direct primary is held, or for convention delegates to meet, deliberate, and vote on a presidential nominee if individual state primaries and caucuses continue to elect delegates (even if these delegates all happen to be chosen on a single day). Michael Nelson recommends that the ideal time to hold the national primary would be the first week in August. To win, a candidate would have to win more than 50 percent of the vote on primary day, and if no one managed to do so, a runoff election would be held.[95] Thereafter, the national party conventions would be held to hear acceptance speeches and to attend to other matters, such as selecting a vice-presidential candidate.

C. *Constitutional Challenges*

One reason the presidential primary system remains a hodgepodge is because of the controversies surrounding who should take responsibility for reforming it. Three different actors could pursue reforms to the primary calendar. These are Congress, the two major national political parties, and the individual states acting in concert through coordinated action.[96]

Let us begin with Congress, the most obvious possible regulator of the presidential nomination process. Since 1911, hundreds of bills have been introduced in Congress to reform our presidential primary system.[97] These bills have sought to do many different things, including establish a system of regional primaries, a direct national primary, and a commission to study the presidential nomination process.[98] In 1976, Joseph Gorman conducted one of the earliest studies of these proposals.[99] In 2018, Gorman's research was updated to include all proposals to reform the nomination process introduced in Congress from 1911 to 2017.[100] During this time period, 322 bills were introduced in Congress that have sought to reform the presidential nomination process, although only a subset of them have sought to create a direct national primary.[101] According to Lisa Parshall, 173 of these 322 bills

---

[95] *Id.* at 43.

[96] A fourth way to reform the presidential nomination process is through a constitutional amendment, and this idea has for a very long time received attention in the literature. *See, e.g.*, P. Orman Ray, *Reform of Presidential Nominating Methods*, 106 ANNALS OF AM. ACAD. OF POL. & SOC. SCI. 68–69 (1923).

[97] *See* Thomas Durbin, *supra* note 85, at 386 (1984).

[98] *Id.*

[99] Joseph B. Gorman, *Federal Presidential Primary Proposals, 1911–1976*, CONG. RES. SERV., Report 80–53 GOV, JK 2071 A (March 27, 1976).

[100] PARSHALL, *supra* note 22, at 199–219.

[101] *Id.* at 200–01.

(53.7 percent) concerned a direct national primary, and of these, only 111 called for primaries to take place on a single day.[102]

Most of these bills, however, have witnessed little legislative activity, and they have not advanced very far in the legislative process. Moreover, most of them lacked specific instructions or provisions that would make them workable in practice. According to Parshall's analysis, only 65 of these bills included requirements that would make a true national primary work: a method for nominating candidates that was national in scope, the call for a single election to take place on the same day across the country, and eligibility rules that would restrict voting solely to party members. Parshall also found many of these bills to be "duplicative measures (the same bill) introduced in multiple Congresses by a relatively small number of sponsors."[103] Few of these bills advanced out of committee or were given a hearing in Congress. Indeed, only five proceeded to some action on the House floor, and only three of these were ever voted on, and they were all quickly defeated.[104] The belief that the national primary plan has been often debated in Congress is not confirmed by the congressional record, Parshall explains; rather, it is an idea that Congress has frequently mentioned, but then has largely ignored.[105] Other scholars who have looked at these bills have come to similar conclusions, finding that no national primary bill has ever come close to being enacted by Congress.[106]

While Congress may be the most obvious actor to implement a national primary, it is also the most controversial. Scholars have argued at length over whether Congress has the power to regulate presidential primaries. The framers did not contemplate the development of political parties, and the Constitution does not explicitly authorize Congress to regulate primary elections. This is partly why the presidential nomination process has been able to evolve so significantly over the past two hundred years, despite the fact that Americans have been governed by the same Constitution the entire time. Opponents of a national primary argue that is it impossible for Congress to impose a national primary date on the states. They see the presidential nomination process as being "outside the Constitution," given that "no constitutional provision touches nominations."[107] Only two provisions govern the

---

[102]   *Id.* at 202.
[103]   *Id.*
[104]   *Id.* at 214.
[105]   *Id.*
[106]   *See, e.g.,* Emmett H. Buell Jr., *Back to the Future? Proposals for Change, in* ENDURING CONTROVERSIES IN THE PRESIDENTIAL NOMINATION PROCESS 260–61 (Emmett H. Buell Jr. & William G. Mayer eds., 2004).
[107]   Nelson & Busch, *supra* note 67, at 53.

timing of federal elections. Article I grants the states the ability to regulate the "Times, Places, and Manner" of congressional elections but allows Congress to "make or alter" such regulations,[108] while Article II only grants Congress the power to determine the "time" of choosing presidential electors and the day they shall vote.[109] No language grants Congress the power to regulate the "manner" of choosing presidential electors. Based on this textual difference between Articles I and II, some scholars have argued that Congress lacks the power to regulate presidential primaries or the nomination process.[110]

Conceding that a purely textual argument cannot carry the day, several scholars have tried to advance other arguments for why Congress has the power to regulate primaries. One of these relies on the Necessary and Proper Clause,[111] which grants Congress the power "to make all laws" that might be necessary and proper to carry out its enumerated powers.[112] In 1981, Antonin Scalia, at the time a law professor at the University of Chicago, argued that since Congress had the power to select the time of choosing presidential electors, it also has "at least the authority to choose the *dates* of primaries,"[113] since these contests are a necessary antecedent to choosing presidential electors. Further, Daniel Lowenstein argues that congressional action in this realm should be upheld not only because of the Necessary and Proper Clause, but also based on the structural design of the Constitution.[114]

Lowenstein rests his argument on the Twelfth Amendment, which changed the way the way electors selected the president.[115] Under the original Constitution, the candidate for the presidency who received the most electoral votes became president and the candidate who received the second-most became vice president. In 1800, two candidates received the same number of votes, forcing the election to be decided by the House of Representatives and causing a constitutional crisis. As a result, the Twelfth Amendment was adopted. It called for electors to cast a separate vote for the president and

---

[108]   U.S. CONST. art. I, §4.
[109]   U.S. CONST. art. II, §1, cl. 3.
[110]   *See, e.g.*, William G. Mayer & Andrew W. Busch, *Can the Federal Government Reform the Presidential Nomination Process?*, 3 ELECTION L.J. 613 (2004).
[111]   U.S. CONST. art. I, § 8.
[112]   See Richard L. Hasen, *"Too Plain for Argument?": The Uncertain Congressional Power to Require Parties to Chosen Presidential Nominees through Direct and Equal Primaries*, 102 Nw. U. L. REV. 2009, 2016–17 (2008).
[113]   Antonin Scalia, *The Legal Framework for Reform*, 4 COMMONSENSE 40, 47 (1981) (emphasis in original); *see also* Hasen, *supra* note 112, at 2017.
[114]   Daniel H. Lowenstein, *Presidential Nomination Reform: Legal Restraints and Procedural Possibilities, in* REFORMING THE PRESIDENTIAL NOMINATION PROCESS 176–77 (Steven S. Smith & Melanie J. Springer eds., 2009).
[115]   U.S. CONST. amend. XII.

vice president. The framers of this amendment implicitly understood that the old method of selecting a president had been "displaced by the reality of a party-based, nationally coordinated process."[116] They also likely understood that if parties came up with a new way to nominate their presidential candidates, this process would need to be subject to congressional regulation. Thus the Twelfth Amendment is one provision where Congress's structural authority to regulate the presidential nomination process can be found.[117]

One other promising place where scholars might look for Congress's structural authority to regulate the presidential nomination process is the Fourteenth Amendment. Under its power to enforce the Equal Protection Clause, Congress likely has the power to impose a uniform primary date on the states in order to ensure that there is fairness and uniformity in the nomination process. This power of Congress also trumps the provisions of Article II, given that the Fourteenth Amendment was adopted later in time. After all, a proper structural understanding of the Constitution must consider its amendments and not just be confined to the original document. Despite this intuitive logic, a structural argument for regulating the presidential nomination process based on the Fourteenth Amendment has gone largely unexplored by legal scholars.[118]

A second and perhaps easier way to achieve a national primary is through the national parties. Some scholars have advised Congress to consider facilitating solutions devised by the national parties rather than imposing its own solutions on the parties and the states. In a way, that makes sense, especially since several important Supreme Court rulings in this area have reaffirmed the parties' First Amendment right of association when it comes to regulating various aspects of party primaries.[119] Any regulation not supported by the

---

[116] Lowenstein, *supra* note 114, at 182.

[117] *See, e.g.*, Dan T. Coenen & Edward J. Larson, *Congressional Power over Presidential Elections: Lessons from the Past and Reforms for the Future*, 43 WM. & MARY L. REV. 851, 887–909 (2002).

[118] For some notable exceptions to this, see Hasen, *supra* note 112, at 2018; Peter Shane, *Disappearing Democracy: How* Bush v. Gore *Undermined the Federal Right to Vote for Presidential Electors*, 29 FLA. ST. U. L. REV. 535 (2001). Although the argument that Congress can regulate the presidential primary process under the Fourteenth Amendment has largely gone unexplored, it deserves to be noted that the Supreme Court has previously upheld, on other constitutional grounds, federal provisions that regulate different aspects of the primary process. *See, e.g.*, United States v. Classic, 313 U.S. 299 (1941) (holding that Article I, Section 4 of the Constitution allows Congress to prevent the corruption of congressional primaries); Buckley v. Valeo, 424 U.S. 1, 85–109 (1976) (upholding the public funding provisions of the Federal Election Campaign Act, including their application to presidential primaries and nominating conventions).

[119] *See, e.g.*, Eu v. S.F. County Democratic Cent. Comm., 489 U.S. 214 (1989) (holding that a state law cannot prohibit parties from endorsing their preferred candidates in party

parties would surely see a First Amendment challenge. It also deserves to be noted that, thus far, all prior reforms to the presidential nomination process have been initiated by the parties themselves. Although they have proceeded incrementally and often in piecemeal fashion, these reforms *have* changed the presidential nomination process. This happened most dramatically in 1972. But it has also happened since, such as when the two major parties started working together to create an opening window for the primary calendar.

However, even though the parties have worked together to play with the timing rules of the caucuses and primaries, their attempts to prevent front-loading, as the discussion earlier illustrated, have not been entirely successful. This is because the national parties face several structural challenges when it comes to imposing discipline and uniformity on the states. One such challenge is that the national parties have no way to enforce their rules against state parties and state governments. Our nation's two major parties have also traditionally had difficulty coordinating with one another. After many fits and starts, the national parties learned to rely on a combination of sticks and carrots to encourage compliance with their preferred primary calendars. In some election years, they have created primary windows outside of which the states would be prevented from holding their nomination contests. States that violated a party's rules were threatened with a loss of convention delegates, while party rules rewarded states scheduling late nomination contests with bonus delegates. However, these attempts at regulating the presidential nomination calendar have been rather modest in nature and have proven not to be terribly effective at preventing front-loading.[120]

The other way that a national primary could be set is through the coordinated action of state governments. After all, primary dates are set by state law. Of course, the states are unlikely to participate in coordinated action on their own, given the huge incentives they have to hold their nomination contests ahead of the pack. And history has shown that the national parties have limited options for punishing the states if they refuse to abide by party directives, so it is not clear that the parties can coax the states into accepting a national primary date. There may be a workaround, however. Congress could encourage the states to adhere to a national primary date through various legislative soft

---

primaries); *Tashjian v. Republican Party of Connecticut*, 479 U.S. 208 (1986) (holding that states cannot mandate a closed primary system because it denies a political party its right under the First Amendments to enter into political association with individuals of its own choosing); *see also* Michael R. Dimino, *It's My Party and I'll Do What I Want To: Political Parties, Unconstitutional Conditions, and the Freedom of Association*, 12 FIRST AMEND. L. REV. 65 (2014).

[120] PARSHALL, *supra* note 22, at 23.

power schemes. For example, Congress could earmark funds to the states to reimburse them, at least in part, for the cost of holding their primary elections, but a state would only be eligible for these funds if it agreed to hold its primary on a certain date. There are other types of soft power schemes that Congress could propose. Such congressional conditioning constitutes the best hope of rationalizing and systemizing the primary calendar.

State legislatures often have their own goals in scheduling their primaries and caucuses. This makes predicting the consequences of any reform difficult. Presidential nomination politics involve many more moving pieces than just the date on which a primary or caucus takes place. The candidates, their staff, and their donors have their own priorities. The media have separate priorities. Each voter has his or her own priorities as well. Barbara Norrander, a longtime observer of the presidential nomination process, cautions that any "new nomination system may come close to the goal of . . . reformers, or it may deviate significantly from what they intended."[121] An important lesson we have learned from past efforts at reforming the nomination process is that new reforms often come with unintended consequences.

IV. CONCLUSION

There are a host of problems with the primary calendar and any given list of them is a bound to be lengthy. The system suffers from many flaws. It fails to educate voters, empowers the media, and makes presidential campaigns so long that only rich and established candidates can run for office.[122] Change, however, is difficult to implement. "Far from being a model, our presidential selection process is unworthy of a banana republic," writes James W. Ceaser.

> To add insult to injury, it is unclear where, if anywhere, the effective authority resides to implement any serious reform. Each state can change its own laws, but not the laws of any other state. Each national party — or, in the ideal case, the two of them working together — can influence state laws, but they are loathe to take on this assignment; and the states, in any case, are not obliged to listen. As for the federal government, it is disputed to this day whether Congress has the constitutional power to legislate in this domain.[123]

---

[121]   NORRANDER, *supra* note 12, at 128.
[122]   *See* NICHOLAS CARNES, THE CASH CEILING: WHY ONLY THE RICH RUN FOR OFFICE – AND WHAT WE CAN DO ABOUT IT (2018).
[123]   Ceaser, *supra* note 2, at 21–22.

Ceasar's take on the calendar is pessimistic for good reason. Still, reforming the primary calendar is a worthy goal. Voters would be better off if the country's presidential nomination contests were all held on a single day. Whether the political will exists for Congress, the parties, and the states to change our byzantine system is another question.

8

A Eulogy for Caucuses

Sean J. Wright[*]

I. INTRODUCTION

In 1976, the Iowa caucuses launched a Georgia governor and peanut farmer into the White House. In 2008, Barack Obama ran up delegate scores across the country during the Democratic nomination contest in caucus states characterized by high-intensity voting. The presidential caucuses have long been a staple of American democracy. In 2020, however, only three states — Iowa, Nevada, and Wyoming — hosted a presidential caucus. Overnight, the caucuses suddenly became obsolete.[1] This chapter explains how and why this happened.

The major parties have repeatedly tinkered with the presidential nomination process over the past two hundred years. Since the 1968 Democratic National Convention, when rioting over an exclusionary nomination process led to a series of important reforms (primarily to the detriment of caucuses), the major parties have sought to balance ways to include ordinary individual voters in the nomination process while not necessarily excluding the party establishment. After each presidential election cycle, the parties reassess the presidential nomination system. Following 1968, reforms were enacted to take away power from party leaders and backroom dealers.[2] In the 1980s,

---

[*] Sean J. Wright is an attorney in private practice in Washington, D.C. He formerly worked in the Policy Division of the Office of General Counsel at the Federal Election Commission and served as Special Counsel to FEC Commissioner Ann M. Ravel. He wishes to thank Dania for her support and encouragement.

[1] Geoffrey Skelley, *How Will Democrats' Move Away from Caucuses Affect the 2020 Race?* FIVETHIRTYEIGHT (May 17, 2019), https://fivethirtyeight.com/features/how-will-democrats-move-away-from-caucuses-affect-the-2020-race/.

[2] *See* Steven S. Smith & Melanie J. Springer, *Choosing Presidential Candidates, in* REFORMING THE PRESIDENTIAL NOMINATION PROCESS, at 1, 6–7 (Steven S. Smith & Melanie J. Springer eds., 2009).

the pendulum swung back and the importance of party leaders was promoted once again, or at least in the Democratic Party through its super-delegate rule.[3]

Following the 2016 election cycle, new reforms implemented by the Democratic Party sought to expand the use of primaries while at the same time making caucuses less burdensome and more inclusive. As a result of these changes, more states were incentivized to abandon caucuses and to substitute primaries in their place. All told, eleven of the eighteen U.S. states and territories that held caucuses in 2016 decided to hold a primary election in 2020 instead. These eleven jurisdictions, however, were not monolithic. Several of them chose to hold party-run primaries, raising the question of whether state parties have the capacity to take on the administrative burden of hosting higher turnout primaries without the financial and logistical support of state governments.

This chapter chronicles the transformation of the presidential caucuses from the congressional caucuses of the early nineteenth century to the well-known caucuses of today. It identifies the strengths of using caucuses and reviews the criticism that caucuses have received. In doing so, this chapter reflects on the greatest vestigial remnant of a bygone era — one known more for "smoke-filled back rooms" than inclusivity and access for rank-and-file voters. Caucuses have been derided as undemocratic electoral mechanisms that exacerbate polarization, but they have also long been a fixture of our demo-cratic process. The decline of the caucus system in 2020 signifies a historic transformation for the presidential nomination process in the United States.

II. THE PRESIDENTIAL PREFERENCE CAUCUSES:
A SHORT HISTORY

The presidential nomination process in the late-eighteenth and early-nineteenth centuries worked differently from the modern presidential nomi-nation process. During the early Republic, a markedly different caucus system was utilized. Known as the "congressional caucus," it involved members of Congress from one of the congressional caucuses gathering and jointly select-ing a candidate to endorse for the presidency.[4] By 1840, the system had evolved, and every major party soon began selecting its candidates through a caucus followed by a national convention.

---

[3] *Id.* at 6.
[4] Stephen Gardbaum & Richard H. Pildes, *Populism and Institutional Design: Methods of Selecting Candidates for Chief Executive*, 93 N.Y.U. L. Rev. 647, 653 (2018).

In the early-twentieth century, the public came to view the caucus and convention system as a tool of party control. This perception drove some states away from holding caucuses and toward holding primaries instead.[5] This wave of reform subsided during the 1920s, and for the next forty years state and national party elites largely controlled delegate selection through the caucus system. While primary elections were held, they largely played a symbolic role. John F. Kennedy's victory in the West Virginia primary in 1960, for instance, addressed the concerns that many people had at the time about the viability of a Catholic presidential candidate, but West Virginia's primary had very little influence over whether Kennedy would be able to secure his party's presidential nomination. Rather, that was determined by the votes of party insiders who attended the party's national convention in 1960. These convention delegates were party insiders who were chosen through state caucuses and party conventions. For rank-and-file voters, the nominating caucuses made participation exceedingly difficult. For example, there was no requirement that rank-and-file voters had to receive notice of an upcoming caucus.

The public's frustration with the presidential nomination process came to a boil during the 1968 Democratic National Convention. When the Democratic Party nominated Vice President Hubert Humphrey for the presidency, riots broke out.[6] The selection of Humphrey crystalized the problems of the caucus and convention system. Humphrey had won the Democratic nomination without setting foot on the campaign trail or participating in any state's primary. Instead, he worked with party leaders through the more traditional state party committees to gain the support of state delegates, who then attended the national convention.[7] In an instant, the disastrous 1968 Democratic National Convention became a symbol of the need to reform what had been an efficient yet patently undemocratic presidential nomination process.[8] To address these concerns, the Democratic Party authorized the creation of the McGovern-Fraser Commission after that year's national convention,[9] and the Commission's reforms had the effect of encouraging

---

[5] Heather R. Abraham, *Legitimate Absenteeism: The Unconstitutionality of the Caucus Attendance Requirement*, 95 MINN. L. REV. 1003, 1006 (2010) (explaining how "[i]n the 1910s and shortly thereafter, the voting public came to regard the caucus system as an instrument of party leader control; this perception stimulated a shift in many states from caucuses to primaries.").

[6] Smith & Springer, *supra* note 2, at 5.

[7] *Id.*

[8] *See* Sean Wilentz & Julian E. Zelizer, *A Rotten Way to Pick a President*, WASH. POST (Feb. 17, 2008), www.washingtonpost.com/wp-dyn/content/article/2008/02/14/AR2008021401595.html.

[9] *See* Smith & Springer, *supra* note 2, at 5.

states to move away from caucuses towards holding primaries. Not all leaders within the Democratic Party were pleased to see presidential primaries take precedence over caucuses.[10] In fact, members of the McGovern-Fraser Commission were surprised by the results of their proposed reforms.

During the 1970s, the Republican Party followed suit and implemented several of the reforms originally proposed by the McGovern-Fraser Commission.[11] Having broken the absolute power of the party bosses, the Republican reforms resulted in elevating the voices of the Republican Party's right wing, leading to Ronald Reagan's near upset of President Gerald R. Ford during the 1976 presidential nomination contest through his surprise wins in the North Carolina and Texas primaries.[12] Similarly, Jimmy Carter used a stunning victory in the 1976 Iowa caucuses to transform himself from a little-known governor into a viable Democratic front-runner.[13]

Iowa has always been an anomaly in the presidential nomination contest. Rising from obscurity due to a quirk in the 1972 nomination calendar, the Iowa caucuses firmly established themselves as a critical gatekeeper in the nomination process. The caucus system dates back to the earliest days of statehood in Iowa. During the Progressive Era's rush toward primary elections, Iowa officials were swept up in reform fever and briefly substituted the state's long-standing caucus for a primary. The state then held one presidential primary election, in 1916, but it was marked by low turnout. None of the major candidates were even listed on the state's ballot.[14] Iowa reverted back to its former caucus and convention model, which it continues to use today.

Unlike other states that responded to the McGovern-Fraser Commission's reform proposals by instituting primaries, Iowa maintained its caucus system, although the state also sought to reduce the power of party bosses in using it. The reform proposals advanced by the McGovern-Fraser Commission required caucuses and primaries, starting in 1972, to provide a thirty-day notice before each stage of the nomination process could take place. Because Iowa's caucus and convention system has four stages—precinct caucuses, county conventions, congressional district conventions, and finally the state convention—the notice requirement forced the precinct caucuses to be scheduled early in the calendar year. In 1972, this meant that the Iowa Democratic caucuses would

---

[10] *Id.* at 6 (explaining how "[t]he rapid shift to primaries, particularly in most of the big states, surprised Democratic reformers and even disappointed some.").

[11] *See* Wilentz & Zelizer, *supra* note 8.

[12] *Id.*

[13] *Id.*

[14] Lily Rothman, *How the Iowa Caucuses Became a Big Deal*, Time (Feb. 1, 2016), https://time.com/4196949/caucus-history/.

be the first contest of the presidential nomination cycle. To meet the thirty-day notice requirement for each stage of Iowa's complex nomination process, the state Democratic Party had to notify eligible voters early about the next stage in the process. Iowa's state convention was typically held in June, but in 1972 there were no available hotel rooms in Des Moines on the weekend in June when the Democrats planned to hold their state convention. This forced the party to move the state convention to May. This scheduling change, combined with the thirty-day notice requirement, meant that Iowa's precinct caucuses had to be held in 1972 as early as January 24, which was even before that year's New Hampshire primary was scheduled to take place.[15]

By 1976, both major parties were holding their Iowa caucuses on the same day, and Jimmy Carter's surprise second place finish in Iowa and the corresponding media attention it received helped launch him to the White House. Today, Iowa state law requires that caucuses be held "at least eight days earlier than the scheduled date for any meeting, caucus, or primary which constitutes the first determining stage of the presidential nominating process in any other state, territory, or any other group which has the authority to select delegates in the presidential nomination."[16] Thus, Iowa cements its place in the nomination calendar through legislation.

III. THE PRESIDENTIAL CAUCUSES IN 2016

Generally, a caucus system relies on a series of meetings to choose a state's national convention delegates.[17] First, rank-and-file voters participate in precinct caucuses. These are local meetings where a presidential preference vote is taken and delegates are elected to the next stage of the caucuses based on those preferences. The precinct caucus is often followed by county conventions, then congressional district conventions, and, ultimately, a state convention, which is where national convention delegates are actually elected.[18] Each state runs its caucus differently, and it is difficult to make sweeping generalizations about the process. However, one key feature that differentiates the state caucuses from one another has to do with whether the initial

---

[15]   Ezra Klein, *Why Iowa Gets to Go First, and Other Facts About Tonight's Caucus,* WASH. POST (Jan. 3, 2012), www.washingtonpost.com/blogs/ezra-klein/post/why-iowa-gets-to-go-first-and-other-facts-about-tonights-caucus/2011/08/25/gIQAJtygYP_blog.html.

[16]   Iowa Code § 43.4 (2019).

[17]   KEVIN J. COLEMAN, CONG. RESEARCH SERV., REPORT NO. R42533, THE PRESIDENTIAL NOMINATING PROCESS AND THE NATIONAL PARTY CONVENTIONS, 2016: FREQUENTLY ASKED QUESTIONS 3 (2015).

[18]   *Id.*

preferences of the rank-and-file voters bind the national convention delegates to vote a certain way or not.

Taken together, caucuses also work in markedly different ways from primaries. While a voting precinct may be used to host a caucus, other caucus venues could also include schools, fire stations, government buildings, private businesses, community centers, and private residences.[19] And whereas primaries are often held in thousands of precincts across each state, caucuses are typically held only in a handful of locations. Once voters arrive at their caucus location, supporters of various presidential candidates are given an opportunity to speak on behalf of a candidate. Once this process is complete, the caucus goers separate themselves into groups, according to their preferred candidates.[20] To select delegates moving forward, a group of voters who support a specific candidate must attain the votes of a certain percentage of all caucus goers (e.g., 15 percent). Some caucus states—typically larger jurisdictions like Minnesota—use voting procedures during the precinct caucus that also resemble a traditional primary.

What is it like for a caucus goer on caucus night? To understand this, we might examine the Iowa caucuses of 2016. In Iowa, once the caucus has been called to order, supporters for the various presidential candidates begin to voice their support—literally. Then the caucus goers separate into groups of like-minded supporters in the corners of the room.[21] Domenico Montanaro of National Public Radio has described this process as being akin to "a junior high dance, if the kids weren't so petrified of each other."[22] An elected chair assesses the number of supporters of each candidate.[23] During the initial round, each presidential candidate needs the support of at least 15 percent of the participants to remain in contention.[24] For candidates deemed non-viable, their supporters are forced to choose another candidate to support.[25] This "re-caucus" necessitates shuffling and realignment, and encourages the cajoling and persuading of supporters of non-viable candidates to join other groups.[26] Once re-caucusing is settled, the numbers are tallied again.[27]

---

[19] *Id.*
[20] *Id.*
[21] Domenico Montanaro, *How Exactly Do the Iowa Caucuses Work?*, NPR (Jan. 30, 2016), www.npr.org/2016/01/30/464960979/how-do-the-iowa-caucuses-work.
[22] *Id.*
[23] *Id.*
[24] *Id.*
[25] *Id.*
[26] *Id.*
[27] *Id.*

During the 2016 Iowa caucuses, there were 1,683 precinct caucuses initially held across the state. These 1,683 precinct caucuses wound up selecting 11,065 delegates to attend the state's county conventions. In turn, there these 11,065 delegates were divided, for the Democratic Party at least, proportionately to the percentage of support that each viable presidential candidate received at the precinct caucuses. The number of delegates who attended the congressional district conventions and state conventions was whittled down to 1,406 delegates, and these 1,406 delegates were responsible for selecting the majority of Iowa's delegates to the Democratic National Convention.[28] The process of selecting delegates to the national convention takes months. Forty-four delegates and seven super-delegates were ultimately sent to the national convention.[29]

What the media reports on caucus night are the "state delegate equivalents," which is an imprecise estimate of the proportional share of how many delegates per candidate, out of the 11,065 available, would attend the county, congressional district, and state conventions.[30] Yet in the months and weeks that follow, these proportions could change dramatically. This is so because, under the 2016 delegate selection rules, delegates could realign at the county conventions with a different presidential preference group. They typically do so simply by signing a short statement that says they now support someone else for the Democratic nomination for President.[31] Thus, while the results of the Iowa caucuses garner lots of media attention and provide candidates with much-needed momentum, these results are also often not reflective of the overall delegate share that may be secured by the "winning" candidate on the night of the precinct caucuses.

Several controversies arose during the Iowa caucuses in 2016. One was that the media reported a slim margin of victory for Hillary Clinton. However, the Iowa Democratic Party had no way to confirm this by holding a recount. This sparked an outcry from Bernie Sanders's supporters, who felt that the caucuses were rigged to favor Clinton. Similar concerns were expressed during Utah's caucuses in 2016. Utah's Republican caucuses were plagued with extremely long lines, insufficient parking, and ballot shortages. The Republican Party

---

[28] *Id.* While the majority of delegates are selected through the caucus and convention process, Iowa's 2016 delegate selection plan provided for seven unpledged "party leaders and elected officials," also known as super-delegates.

[29] *Id.*

[30] *Id.*

[31] Iowa Democratic Party, Iowa Delegate Selection Plan For the 2016 Democratic National Convention 12 (2019), https://iowademocrats.org/wp-content/uploads/sites/3/201 9/02/2020-Iowa-DSP-DRAFT-2.11.19.pdf.

tried to permit online voting at these caucuses, a measure designed to increase access, but technical problems prevented one-fourth of the state's Republican voters who signed up to participate in voting online from ever casting a caucus ballot (roughly 10,000 of nearly 40,000 voters were affected).[32]

The problems exposed during the 2016 election cycle were neither new nor novel. In 2012, Nevada's Republican officials elected to add a special late-night session to their caucuses in order to accommodate religious observers. This decision infuriated several candidates because the late-night voters who participated were required to sign a statement indicating that religious obligations— rather than health or work commitments—prevented them from voting earlier. The decision to extend the time for caucusing based on religious and not other reasons caused controversy. Making matters worse, one Nevada county needed an extra day to count its late ballots. It was also forced to resolve a "trouble box" of questionable and disputed ballots.[33]

As is evident, holding caucuses can be a complex endeavor. Many observers have questioned why states continue to hold presidential preference caucuses in the first place. Although the overwhelming trend since 1968 has been for states to use primary elections for their presidential nomination contests, during the 2016 election cycle a total of fourteen states and four U.S. territories still held a presidential caucus, as Table 8.1 below demonstrates.[34]

Many of the presidential caucuses were held in smaller states in 2016. Because the caucus tends to be an intimate and engaging event, the administrative burdens of hosting a caucus tend to increase when the number of caucus goers rises. In 2016, as mentioned, the Democratic Party in Iowa held 1,683 precinct caucuses at over one thousand locations. Iowa's total population is in the bottom third of all states nationally. Of course, larger states have held caucuses as well. For instance, about 230,000 voters participated in Washington's Democratic presidential caucuses, which Democrats in Washington used to select their party's delegates for the Democratic National Convention. The Republican Party in Washington holds a government-run primary, and the Democratic

---

[32] Lee Davidson, *After Chaos in Utah's Last Presidential Caucuses, Bill Advances to Replace Them with a Super Tuesday Primary*, SALT LAKE CITY TRIB. (Mar. 8, 2019), www.sltrib.com /news/politics/2019/03/08/after-chaos-utahs-last/.

[33] Anjeanette Damon, *Nevada GOP Dealing with "Trouble Box" of Questionable Ballots*, LAS VEGAS SUN (Feb. 5, 2012), https://lasvegassun.com/news/2012/feb/05/nevada-gop-dealing- trouble-box/.

[34] FED. ELECTION COMM'N, 2016 PRESIDENTIAL PRIMARY DATES AND CANDIDATE FILING DEADLINES FOR BALLOT ACCESS (2016), www.fec.gov/pubrec/fe2016/2016pdates.pdf; LastWeekTonight, *Primaries and Caucuses: Last Week Tonight with John Oliver*, YOUTUBE (May 22, 2016), www.youtube.com/watch?v=_S2G8jhhUHg (discussing the State of Washington's use of an uncounted caucus).

TABLE 8.1 *Jurisdictions holding caucuses in 2016*

Jurisdiction	Democratic Caucus	Republican Caucus
Alaska	Yes	Yes
American Samoa	Yes	Yes
Colorado	Yes	Yes
Guam	Yes	Yes
Hawaii	Yes	Yes
Idaho	Yes	No
Iowa	Yes	Yes
Kansas	Yes	Yes
Kentucky	No	Yes
Maine	Yes	Yes
Minnesota	Yes	Yes
Nebraska	Yes	No
Nevada	Yes	Yes
North Dakota	Yes	No
Northern Mariana Islands	Yes	Yes
Utah	Yes	Yes
U.S. Virgin Islands	Yes	Yes
Washington	Yes	No
Wyoming	Yes	Yes

presidential candidates are listed on the ballot there as well, but for Democrats this is a "beauty contest" and its results are substantively meaningless. However, notably, over 800,000 people voted in Washington's primary, dwarfing the turnout of Washington's caucuses.[35]

U.S. territories happen to make up a high proportion of the jurisdictions that hold caucuses. In 2016, U.S. territories made up over one-fifth of all caucus jurisdictions. Under the Electoral College system, voters in the territories are not able to cast a vote for the President in the general election.[36] Thus, participating in the presidential nomination process through caucuses is the only opportunity that the nearly four million U.S. citizens and U.S. nationals who reside in U.S. territories have to influence the outcome of the American presidential contest.

---

[35] Jim Kessler, *Want to help End Voter Suppression? Junk the Caucuses*, WASH. POST (June 21, 2016), www.washingtonpost.com/opinions/want-to-help-end-voter-suppression-junk-the-caucuses/2016/06/20/2dfe75b0-372a-11e6-8f7c-d4c723a2becb_story.html?utm_term=.3851f22b56ea.

[36] Matt Kwong, *Americans can vote from space, so why not from U.S. island territories?*, CBC NEWS (Nov. 7, 2016), www.cbc.ca/news/world/us-election-island-territories-1.3840319.

IV. DEBATING THE MERITS OF CAUCUSES

The rules of the presidential nomination process matter a great deal. While a chorus of commentators has recently advocated replacing all caucuses with primary elections,[37] the caucuses also provide concrete benefits to our political system. This section of the chapter evaluates the benefits of the caucus system and also offers some criticism of caucuses.

A. *Arguments in Favor of Caucuses*

Proponents of caucuses identify two primary advantages that caucuses have: first, they provide various benefits to political parties, benefits not available in primary elections; second, they enhance social and community ties.[38] The caucuses benefit political parties, as Thomas Marshall has noted, by "identifying potential activists and volunteers, permitting grass-roots issue debates, and allowing face-to-face meetings of party activists."[39] State parties in Iowa, Colorado, and Washington have routinely conducted other business on their caucus nights, separate and apart from debating who should be their party's presidential nominee. This other routine business might include holding elections for members of local county central committees, selecting delegates and alternative delegates for county conventions, reviewing party bylaws, engaging in party support activities, debating local policies, and so on. So while the presidential nomination process is by far the most important component of caucus night, caucuses also have other functions.

In arranging for party faithful to meet at one particular place and time, caucuses play a crucial role in encouraging party building. Political parties have always played a central role in American democracy.[40] Parties encourage Americans to participate in politics, educate voters, and counterbalance narrow special interests.[41] However, there is a growing consensus that political parties today are being displaced, especially now that social media and

---

[37] See Sean J. Wright, *Time to End Presidential Caucuses*, 85 FORDHAM L. REV. 1127 (2016); Kessler, *supra* note 35.

[38] See Brief for Sen. Mike Lee, Sen. Ted Cruz, Rep. Raul Labrador & Rep. Bob Bishop as Amicus Curiae Supporting Petitioners at 23, *Utah Republican Party v. Cox*, No. 18–450 (Nov. 13, 2018), *available at* www.supremecourt.gov/DocketPDF/18/18–450/72032/2018111414561533 6_18–450%20Amici%20Curiae%20Brief.pdf.

[39] Thomas R. Marshall, *Turnout and Representation: Caucuses Versus Primaries*, 22 AM. J. POL. SCI. 169, 180 (1978).

[40] See IAN VANDEWALKER & DANIEL I. WEINER, STRONG PARTIES, STRONGER DEMOCRACY: RETHINKING REFORM 1 (Brennan Ctr. for Justice, 2015).

[41] *Id.* at 5.

technology permit candidates to connect directly with voters without relying on a party's army of operatives and volunteers.

Over the past century, the transition away from the caucuses and convention model to holding more primary elections has served to erode the power and control that political parties once had over voters. Primaries tend to take more decision-making authority out of the hands of party insiders and give it to grassroots voters. But this has not been as true in the caucus states. As such, caucuses serve an important role in sustaining political parties. During a caucus, the party engages with voters, secures future volunteer commitments, and helps disseminate important information about upcoming elections. While alternative proposals to strengthen the political parties have failed to gain traction, the caucus system remains an important party-building event.[42]

In addition, caucuses come with a strong social component. Caucuses, in the words of political scientist Eitan Hersh, are "an *event*," one that is often "accompan[ied] by potluck snacks."[43] The social aspect of a caucus is a critical motivator that gets citizens to participate. Hersh disputes the conventional wisdom that believes caucuses disproportionately draw extreme partisans out to vote. Instead, drawing upon national survey data, Hersh finds that the predominant rationale for attending a caucus is that "the public setting of the caucus attracts people who are not foremost concerned with expressing a political opinion, but voters who want to see the spectacle and be seen."[44] Because many caucuses are held in small states, there is corresponding pressure to attend a caucus and a social cost to abstaining. If you fail to attend, your neighbors will surely know. Caucus goers are more engaged in their local communities. According to the National Election Study, a national survey of voters in the United States, caucus goers indicate that they are 29 percent more likely to attend a public meeting than a non-caucus goer.[45] As such, caucuses play a role in promoting civic mindedness. Christopher Karpowitz and Jeremy Pope found that citizens who participate in the caucuses tend to find them "more fair, more open to different points of view, more likely to result in the best choice, and less prone to bias toward special interests."[46] Caucus goers find their fellow caucuses attendees to be more engaged, rather than more partisan.

---

[42] *Id.* at 3.
[43] Eitan D. Hersh, *A caucus-goer's community*, REUTERS (Jan. 3, 2012), http://blogs.reuters.com/great-debate/2012/01/03/a-caucus-goers-community/ (emphasis in original).
[44] *Id.*
[45] *Id.*
[46] Christopher F. Karpowitz & Jeremy C. Pope, *Who Caucuses? An Experimental Approach to Institutional Design and Electoral Participation*, 45 BRIT. J. POL. SCI. 329, 340 (2013).

Supporters of the caucus system also point to the organizational efforts witnessed at caucuses: candidates who are better organized and have stronger grassroots support tend to be victorious.[47] Ever since 1972, when George McGovern's campaign invested time, energy, and resources in the Iowa caucuses, campaigns of lesser-known candidates have looked to Iowa to help elevate their fortunes. Succeeding in Iowa requires candidates to have personal conversations with voters, to invest in local community interests, and to cultivate passionate volunteers. These tactics ultimately benefit the campaigns that have the most organic, grassroots support. Thus, the final aspect of caucuses is that they have a democratizing effect on campaigns. They offer campaigns that may not have the biggest budgets a somewhat more level playing field than primaries do.

B. Arguments against Caucuses

Not everyone supports caucuses, however. Opponents of caucuses argue that the caucuses can be highly undemocratic — not for the citizens of the caucus state, but for the rest of the country.[48] While the reforms initially ushered into the presidential nomination process in the 1970s have produced a far more fair and democratic process than existed beforehand,[49] the power of the Iowa caucuses to set the tone of the presidential nomination contest have not been lost on residents of other states.[50] The first caucus in Iowa (like the first primary in New Hampshire) has had a disproportionately strong influence on selecting which candidate each party will chose as its eventual presidential nominee.[51] Moreover, Iowans hardly reflect the values of the rest of the country. Many have bemoaned the racially unrepresentative composition of the voters in Iowa's caucuses,[52] not to mention the fact that Iowa is not culturally reflective of most of America.

---

[47] A notable exception to this rule was the 2016 Nevada Republican caucus, which Donald Trump won without significant on-the-ground support.

[48] Wilentz & Zelizer, *supra* note 8.

[49] Richard Pildes, *Two Myths About the Unruly American Primary System*, WASH. POST (May 25, 2016), www.washingtonpost.com/news/monkey-cage/wp/2016/05/25/two-myths-about-the-unruly-american-primary-system/ ("The recommended reforms aimed to make the caucus system more open, more transparent and more accessible to all Democrats.").

[50] *See* Justin Driver, *Underenfranchisement: Black Voters and the Presidential Nominating Process*, 117 HARV. L. REV. 2318 (2004).

[51] Lisa K. Parshall & Franco Mattei, *Challenging the Presidential Nomination Process: The Constitutionality of Front-Loading*, 26 HAMLINE J. PUB. L. & POL'Y 1, 1 (2004) (explain how "[p]erhaps the most egregious deficiency of a front-loaded calendar is that by the time many voters cast their preferences, nominations have already been mathematically determined.").

[52] *See, e.g.*, Anthony Johnstone, *The Federalist Safeguards of Politics*, 39 HARV. J. L. & PUB. POL'Y 415, 444 n.140 (2016); Gerald C. Wright, *Rules and Ideological Character of Primary*

Holding Iowa's caucuses early in the presidential nomination calendar provides the state with enormous agenda-setting power.[53] The problem, of course, is that the issues that matter to Iowans do not necessarily resonate with other Americans. To succeed in Iowa, candidates tend to emphasize issues of concern to Iowa residents.[54] The 2020 presidential campaign, particularly among Democratic candidates, sought to change this trend to some extent, and several candidates came to Iowa advocating national policies and talking about how they would increase economic prosperity for African-Americans and other minority groups.[55] However, the fact that this happened is more a testament to changing dynamics within the Democratic Party than a rejection of Iowa-centric thinking. Indeed, the vast majority of the leading 2020 Democratic candidates continued to support the Renewable Fuel Standards and biofuels (e.g., ethanol), policies that were at odds with the larger climate change platform that the Democratic Party had adopted, because these issues were of interest to Iowa's farming communities and agrarian interests.[56]

Critics often claim that caucuses in general are at odds with many of the deeply held notions of free and fair elections that Americans have. Sean Wilentz and Julian Zelizer have argued that by "eliminat[ing] the secret ballot," voters in states like Iowa, which hold caucuses, are forced "to declare their loyalties publicly, and are thus vulnerable to intimidation and manipulation."[57] The public nature of caucuses distinguishes them in profound ways from the private nature of primaries, where voting is done in secret. If a voter does not attend the caucuses in person, he generally cannot participate. The attendance requirement leads to another criticism: it places a heavy burden on lower and middle-class voters, who may have fixed shifts at work or may be unable to leave home or work for extended periods of time to caucus with others.[58]

Electorates, *in* REFORMING THE PRESIDENTIAL NOMINATION PROCESS 27 (Steve S. Smith & Melanie J. Springer eds., 2009).

[53]   Driver, *supra* note 50, at 2322–23.

[54]   *Id.*

[55]   *See, e.g.*, Rachel Franzin, *Buttigieg Puts Forth "Douglass Plan" to Improve Black American Prosperity*, THE HILL (June 12, 2019), https://thehill.com/homenews/campaign/448250-buttigieg-puts-forth-douglass-plan-to-improve-black-american-prosperity.

[56]   Michael Grunwald, *How the 2020 Democrats Learned to Love Ethanol*, POLITICO MAG. (Mar. 5, 2019), www.politico.com/magazine/story/2019/03/05/2020-democrats-ethanol-225517.

[57]   Wilentz & Zelizer, *supra* note 8.

[58]   *See* Ian Millhiser, *Ban the Iowa Caucus*, THINKPROGRESS (Jan. 25, 2016), https://thinkprogress.org/ban-the-iowa-caucus-1be63c1c6bdb#.4m9vuj3oo.

Recent research has demonstrated how the caucuses disproportionately disenfranchise minorities, lower-income earners, and young people, who are much less likely to show up to caucus with their neighbors than older, whiter, and wealthier voters. Costas Panagopoulos observes "that voters, especially new voters, will have difficulty navigating caucuses' arcane rules and procedures and that participation will be discouraged by the strenuous and time-consuming demands (one time, location) caucuses place on voters."[59] The requirement of physical attendance also disproportionally impacts various constituencies like deployed service members, religious observers, persons who have disabilities or are in poor health, students attending far-away schools, and shift workers unable to leave work.[60] The result is that the voters who participate in a caucus often represent a narrow range of backgrounds, interests, and experiences.[61]

Another problem is that voter turnout has historically been much lower in caucus states, particularly compared to primary states. In fact, in 1976, turnout for the Iowa caucuses stood at a measly 2.5 percent of the voting-eligible population. This was in comparison to the 33.4 percent turnout rate of that year's New Hampshire primary. Since 1976, studies have consistently shown that caucuses tend to have significantly less voter participation than primaries. As a result, only a small subset of the voters in states with caucuses meaningfully participate in selecting the delegates that those states send to the national conventions. This phenomenon has a direct impact on the types of candidates who make it through the caucus process. The 2016 presidential election continued the long-standing trend of lower voter turnout in caucuses. According to one study, only one caucus state in 2016, Idaho, had a higher voter turnout rate than the lowest turnout rate of any primary state.[62] Table 8.2 below provides the voter turnout rates from 2016 in all jurisdictions that held caucuses, rounded to the nearest tenth of

---

[59] Costas Panagopoulos, *Are Caucuses Bad for Democracy?*, 125 POL. SCI. Q. 425, 427 (2010) (citing TOVA WANG, HAS AMERICA OUTGROWN THE CAUCUS? SOME THOUGHTS ON RESHAPING THE NOMINATION CONTEST 4 (2007)).

[60] Abraham, *supra* note 5, at 1004 (detailing the experience of Felipe Goodman, who after serving a decade as a rabbi in Nevada, became a citizen intending to vote, but was unable to because the state's scheduled caucus was held on a Saturday and required attendance); *see also* Richard L. Hasen, *Whatever Happened to "One Person, One Vote"?*, SLATE (Feb. 5, 2008), www.slate.com/id/2183751/ (recounting how "Orthodox Jews complained that they couldn't vote in the Saturday morning Nevada caucuses").

[61] *See* Guy-Uriel E. Charles, *Corruption Temptation*, 102 CAL. L. REV. 25, 36 (2014).

[62] *See* Jeff Stein, *The Real Obstacle to Voter Turnout in Democratic Primaries: Caucuses*, VOX (May 2, 2016,), www.vox.com/2016/5/2/11535648/bernie-sanders-closed-primaries-caucuses.

TABLE 8.2 *Turnout rates in jurisdictions with caucuses in 2016*[63]

Jurisdiction	Democratic Turnout rate	Republican Turnout Rate	Total Caucus Turnout Rate
Alaska	6.2%	4.2%	10.4%
American Samoa	N/A	N/A	N/A
Colorado	3.1%	1.5%	4.6%
Guam	2.6%	N/A	2.6%
Hawaii	3.3%	1.3%	4.6%
Idaho	21.9%	No Caucus	21.9%
Iowa	7.5%	8.2%	15.7%
Kansas	1.9%	3.5%	5.5%
Kentucky	No Caucus	7.0%	7.0%
Maine	4.4%	1.8%	6.1%
Minnesota	5.2%	2.9%	8.1%
Nebraska	2.5%	No Caucus	2.5%
Nevada	4.3%	3.9%	8.2%
North Dakota	0.7%	No Caucus	0.7%
Northern Mariana Islands	N/A	N/A	N/A
Puerto Rico	3.3%	1.5%	4.8%
Utah	4.2%	10.2%	14.3%
Virgin Islands	3.3%	N/A	3.3%
Washington	4.5%	No Caucus	4.5%
Wyoming	1.6%	N/A	1.6%

[63] The figure listed for the Republican turnout rate in Colorado (1.5%) should be regarded with some caution. The percentage was generated by using the spreadsheet data for total Voter Eligible Population (VEP) in Colorado (3,928,790) and compared against media reporting of the Chairman of the Colorado Republican Committee's claim that approximately 60,000 Colorado Republicans attended the state's caucuses. This claim is difficult to verify. 60,000 divided by 3,928,790 results in turnout rate for Colorado's Republican caucus. The Guam data was acquired from a government report and estimates the number of "Registered Voters" (49,363). This is presumably a smaller figure than the traditional "Voting Eligible Population," meaning that the turnout figure listed for Gaum is artificially inflated. See GUAM ELECTION COMM'N, 2016 ELECTION COMPARATIVE ANALYSIS 55 (2017), https://drive .google.com/file/d/1BP7zs7zwV7s-w773tpoy-hrt2hRotYof/view. In Guam, 1,305 ballots were cast for a Democratic candidate during the caucus. See Richard E. Berg-Anderson, *Guam Democrat*, GREEN PAPERS: 2016 PRESIDENTIAL PRIMARIES, CAUCUSES, AND CONVENTIONS, www.thegreenpapers.com/P16/GU-D (last visited Aug. 8, 2019). The data for Puerto Rico includes Voting Age Population (VAP) instead of Voter Eligible Population (VEP), since VAP could not be determined; the VAP in Puerto Rico in 2016 was 2,686,177. Using VAP instead of VEP for the denominator will make Puerto Rico's caucus turnout rates be slightly lower than they may have actually been. *Citizen Voting-Age Population: Puerto Rico*, U.S. CENSUS BUREAU, www.census.gov/library/visualizations/2016/comm/citizen_voting_age_po

a percent.[64] As the table makes clear, campaigns looking to pick up votes in the small caucus states have a narrow window of supporters to woo.

There are also measurable differences between the kind of people who vote in primaries and caucuses. A 2010 study by Costas Panagopoulos found that across severa demographic characteristics, including race, gender, educational attainment, and degree of religious observance, the traits of caucus participants and primary voters substantially resembled that of the U.S. population as a whole. However, there were also characteristics which distinguished caucus participants from the population as a whole, at least in comparison to primary voters.[65] "Generally speaking, there is clear evidence that caucus voters held more-extreme views" on contentious political issues "compared to both primary voters and to the population at large," writes Panagopoulos, and he finds "that the public's policy preferences overall were more congruent with those of primary voters than with those of caucus voters."[66] If this finding is true, it is significant: it suggests that precinct caucus goers may select delegates for their county and state-level caucuses who will be more polarized than the rest of the voting population, and this in turn may lead to the election of national delegates who are more extreme in their views than

pulation/cb16-tps18_pr.html (last accessed Aug. 8, 2019). The total number of ballots cast for a Democratic candidate in Puerto Rico was 89,188. *See* Richard E. Berg-Anderson, *Puerto Rico Democrat*, Green Papers: 2016 Presidential Primaries, Caucuses, and Conventions, www.thegreenpapers.com/P16/PR-D (last visited Jan. 8, 2019). The total number of ballots cast for a Republican candidate in Puerto Rice was 39,656. *See* Richard E. Berg-Anderson, *Puerto Rico Republican*, Green Papers: 2016 Presidential Primaries, Caucuses, and Conventions, www.thegreenpapers.com/P16/PR-R (last visited Jan. 8, 2019). The Virgin Islands data were acquired from a government website and demonstrate the number of "Registrants" on the various islands (46,084). Presumably this refers to a "Registered Voter," which is a smaller number than the traditional "Voting Eligible Population." This means that the turnout figure provided here for the U.S. Virgin Islands will be inflated. *See Cross Reference Report for Jurisdictions: A Breakdown of Age Within Gender*, Election Sys. of the V.I., www.vivote.gov/sites/default/files/Voters%20Statistical%20Report%20Nov.pdf. A total of 1,522 ballots were cast for a Democratic candidate during the caucus in the Virgin Islands. *See* Richard E. Berg-Anderson, *Virgin Islands Democrat*, Green Papers: 2016 Presidential Primaries, Caucuses, and Conventions, www.thegreenpapers.com/P16/VI-D.

[64] For a relatively complete spreadsheet of turnout in all fifty states, see Michael P. McDonald, *2016 Presidential Nomination Contest Turnout Rates*, U.S. Elections Project, www.electproject.org/2016P. These data include best estimates for caucuses, as well as vote totals for states with primary elections. Data for the territorial islands are harder to obtain. It is difficult to determine turnout in party caucuses, since caucus attendance is not recorded or reported in a reliable fashion. *See* Drew DeSilver, *Turnout Was High in the 2016 Primary Season, but Just Short of 2008 Record*, Pew Research Ctr. (June 10, 2016), www.pewresearch.org/fact-tank/2016/06/10/turnout-was-high-in-the-2016-primary-season-but-j ust-short-of-2008-record/. *See also* Stein, *supra* note 62.

[65] Panagopoulos, *supra* note 59, at 431.

[66] *Id.* at 436.

the general public. This phenomenon has been witnessed in Iowa's recent Republican presidential caucuses, where more socially conservative candidates have recently been more successful.[67]

American political polarization has been the subject of increasing study and debate among scholars. The phenomenon has affected all kinds of political institutions, including our parties. As our major parties have become more polarized, as Gerald Wright observes, "the voices of the two parties come from increasingly distant positions, leading to polarizing political candidates as well."[68] That is troubling because 39 percent of Americans consider themselves to be independents and are turned off by the partisanship they see in their politics.[69] Regardless of the purported benefits of party unity that caucuses may provide, any process that furthers polarization discourages political participation on the part of Americans who consider themselves to be independents.

It also does not help that many caucuses, because they are front-loaded, assume a level of importance that is out of proposition to their delegate count.[70] In 1972, Iowa moved up its caucus schedule to January.[71] Iowa is not alone, however. Since 2008, Nevada's caucuses have also been frontloaded, and today the Nevada caucuses constitute one of the first four presidential nomination contests. Since the 1980s, the first few frontloaded nomination contests have received significantly more media attention. Candidates who do not do well in those contests are forced to exit the presidential race early when their popularity and fundraising ability wane.[72] For this reason, campaigns spend outsized energy focusing on these early contests, and on Iowa in particular. In 2008, Barack Obama famously developed a winning coalition strategy for Iowa. As Redlawsk, Tolbert, and Donovan's national survey data show, winning Iowa "was critical to [the] perception that Obama could win the nomination . . . and that viability was in turn the most important factor predicting a vote for Obama in subsequent primaries and caucuses."[73]

---

[67] *Results from the 2016 Iowa Caucus*, WALL ST. J. (Feb. 2, 2016), graphics.wsj.com/elections/2016/iowa-caucus-results/ ("On the Republican side, social conservatives have asserted their influence in recent years.").

[68] Wright, *supra* note 52, at 37.

[69] Joshua Holland, *What Everyone Gets Wrong About Independent Voters*, THE NATION (May 18, 2016), www.thenation.com/article/what-everyone-gets-wrong-about-independent-voters/.

[70] Wright, *supra* note 52, at 27.

[71] Anthony J. Gaughan, *Five Things You Should Know About the Iowa Caucuses*, NEWSWEEK (Jan. 24, 2016), www.newsweek.com/five-things-know-iowa-caucuses-418948.

[72] *See* Smith & Springer, *supra* note 2, at 7.

[73] DAVID P. REDLAWSK, CAROLINE J. TOLBERT & TODD DONOVAN, WHY IOWA? HOW CAUCUSES AND SEQUENTIAL ELECTIONS IMPROVE THE PRESIDENTIAL NOMINATING PROCESS 5–6 (2016).

The fact that two out of our first four nomination contests (Iowa and Nevada) now happen to be caucuses only exacerbates the problems referred to above.[74] Almost by design, the caucus system—with its multiple-round tallies, cajoling and persuading voters to change position, and re-tallying of votes—makes resolving electoral disputes impossible in any meaningful sense. Practically speaking, it may impossible to determine the results of a caucus with any great degree of accuracy. Iowa in particular has been problematic. The results of Iowa's precinct caucuses were incredibly close in 2016, but because the state did not provide a paper ballot it was nearly impossible to verify the votes taken to determine the accuracy of the official results.[75] And in 2020, Iowa's precinct caucuses proved to be a debacle. Because of technological failures, Iowa's results could not be determined, and no winner was announced for weeks. The candidates and the media left for the next contest in New Hampshire without knowing who had won in Iowa.

Compared to traditional primary elections, the caucuses are a ticking time bomb of ballot-casting and ballot-counting controversies. It is true that no electoral system is impervious to dispute, no matter how well-designed or -administered it may be. But our political parties could reduce the risk of controversy further by moving away from caucuses, which—given their unique nature—are especially prone to disputes. The lack of safeguards in the caucus process means that the public lacks the ability to ensure errors do not occur during the counting of votes. During the Iowa Democratic presidential caucus of 2016, the editors of the *Des Moines Register* wrote about how "[t]oo many accounts have arisen of inconsistent counts, untrained and overwhelmed volunteers, confused voters, cramped precinct locations, a lack of voter registration forms and other problems."[76] Reporters from the newspaper who observed Iowa's caucuses found plenty "opportunities for error."[77] It would be exceedingly difficult to resolve a challenge alleging counting errors in caucuses. Given the disproportionate value placed on the Iowa caucuses, ensuring that ballots are accurately counted is something that matters a great deal.[78]

---

[74]   *See* Parshall & Mattei, *supra* note 51, at 1.
[75]   *Id.*
[76]   *Something Smells in the Democratic Party*, DES MOINES REG. (Feb. 5, 2016), www.desmoinesregister.com/story/opinion/editorials/caucus/2016/02/03/editorial-something-smells-democratic-party/79777580/.
[77]   *Id.*
[78]   EDWARD B. FOLEY, BALLOT BATTLES: THE HISTORY OF DISPUTES ELECTIONS IN THE UNITED STATES 340 (2016).

V. THE 2020 CAUCUSES

After the Democratic presidential nomination process was repeatedly criticized in 2016 for being rigged to favor Hillary Clinton, the Democratic National Committee (DNC) engaged in an extensive and at times contentious restructuring of the nomination rules. During this process, the DNC sought to amend its nomination rules to make the nomination contest more inclusive, much like it had done at the time of the McGovern-Fraser Commission. However, this time the DNC broke from the model set by the McGovern-Fraser Commission and expressly encouraged state parties to hold primary elections instead of caucuses. As a result, many states that had held Democratic caucuses in 2016 decided to hold primaries instead in 2020. In part, this change was implemented to increase voter turnout. In total, eleven states switched from running a caucus to holding either a government-run or party-run Democratic primary in 2020. Only three states in total retained caucuses. Two of these were two of the earliest states in the nomination calendar, Iowa and Nevada. The third state that retained its caucuses in 2020 was Wyoming. All four U.S. territories that held Democratic caucuses in 2016 also retained caucuses as their method of selecting their convention delegates in 2020. It is important to understand what changes states have made to their caucuses since 2016 and the impact these changes had in 2020.

A. *Changes Implemented by the Democratic National Committee*

In the wake of President Donald Trump's election in 2016, the DNC formed the Unity Reform Commission (URC) to "re-examine" the Democratic Party's presidential nomination process.[79] The URC released a report in late 2017 recommending several procedural changes to the nomination process, including some changes that would significantly affect states that had held caucuses in the past.[80] The URC recommended that caucuses be made "less

---

[79] Adam Hilton, *The Democratic Party's Latest Reform Commission Just Met. It's Likely to Slash the Power of Superdelegates*, WASH. POST (Dec. 12, 2017), www.washingtonpost.com/news/monkey-cage/wp/2017/12/12/the-democratic-partys-latest-reform-commission-just-met-its-likely-to-slash-the-power-of-superdelegates/. The URC was created to "heal the rifts between supporters of Bernie Sanders and Hillary Clinton" after the Democratic Party's loss in 2016. *Id.* Many Sanders supporters believed that party procedures unjustly favored Clinton—despite grassroots support for Sanders—thereby making Clinton the 2016 presidential nominee.

[80] *See generally* REPORT OF THE UNITY REFORM COMMISSION, DEMOCRATIC UNITY REFORM COMM. (Dec. 9, 2017), https://democrats.org/wp-content/uploads/2018/10/URC_Report_FINAL.pdf.

burdensome" and "more inclusive, transparent, and accessible to participants."[81] Moving forward, the DNC required caucus states to provide for absentee voting, same-day registration, and party-affiliation changes at all caucus sites.[82] The rationale behind these proposals was to alleviate concerns that certain voters who cannot participate in the hours-long deliberations of the caucuses—such as overseas service members, seniors, and those with work-related conflicts—may be prevented from participating in the presidential nomination process. Although the recommendation to provide for absentee voting could theoretically expand caucus participation, some commentators expressed concern that absentee balloting might also favor the candidates who have more financial resources. Better-funded candidates could contact prospective voters with direct mail advertising, as well as hire canvassers to "harvest" absentee ballots.[83] Others worried that absentee balloting was fundamentally incompatible with caucusing.[84] Indeed, accepting absentee ballots could discourage the most committed voters from getting together to deliberate physically if such voters know their votes would count equally to those who failed to show up.

To make the caucuses more transparent, the DNC also required votes in caucus states to be cast in writing. This reform was meant to address the earlier administrative concerns about how to recreate or recount a unique, one-day event meaningfully. In addition, all caucus states were henceforth required to report publicly the total statewide vote each candidate received, and for this to be cross-referenced with written ballots so as to be able to resolve ballot disputes.[85]

Importantly, the revised DNC delegate selection rules expressly stated that state parties should strive to use primary elections.[86] However, the preference of the DNC was to have state parties use government-run primaries. Holding government-run primaries would not prove to be feasible in all jurisdictions, however, and especially in those states that did not already have a government-

---

[81]   *Id.* at 18.

[82]   *Id.*

[83]   Seth McLaughlin, *Iowa Caucuses' Character at Odds with New Push for Absentee Voting,* WASH. TIMES (Jan. 10, 2019), www.washingtontimes.com/news/2019/jan/10/iowa-caucuses-character-at-odds-with-new-push-for-/.

[84]   *Id.*

[85]   REPORT OF THE UNITY REFORM COMMISSION, *supra* note 80, at 18.

[86]   *Id.* at 8 ("The Unity Reform Commission was mandated to encourage the expanded use of primaries in the presidential nominating process to increase voter participation and inclusion of grassroots engagement," and "the Commission believes that state-run primaries are often the most efficient, open, and transparent means of voting"); Skelley, *supra* note 1.

run primary scheduled to be run in the spring of 2020. In such cases, a party-run primary, caucus, or convention would be permissible under the new rules, although the DNC required that additional inclusive measures be adopted for these types of contests, like absentee and early voting, same-day voter registration, and a process for handling recounts.

Notwithstanding the potential worries posed by caucuses, the Iowa Democratic Party decided to continue to hold a caucus. However, it also adopted new rules that would allow voters to cast absentee ballots in 2020. In addition, it planned to host six virtual caucuses.[87] In August 2019, the DNC's Rules and Bylaws Committee rejected the virtual caucus proposal, despite the fact that the Iowa Democratic Party had worked on it for months. The Iowa Democratic Party was then forced to evaluate alternative methods of expanding accessibility to its caucus so that it did not have to ask for a waiver to be granted exempting it from the DNC's new requirements.[88]

The Iowa Democratic Party also committed itself to releasing raw vote tabulations for each candidate. These would permit the public to have a much clearer sense of the actual vote tallies received by each candidate during the caucuses.[89] At least for the Iowa caucuses, this was a significant change from 2016. In 2020, the Democratic Party in Nevada decided to provide four days of early voting and to host two virtual caucuses. Both efforts were designed to encourage higher voter turnout.[90] Given the challenges that online caucusing experienced in 2016, the advent of virtual caucuses in 2020, designed specifically to expand voter turnout, promised to test whether our caucuses were really prepared for the twenty-first century (or not). Unfortunately, just as in Iowa, Nevada's plan to host virtual caucuses had to be abandoned because of security concerns.

As mentioned, a total of eleven states that held Democratic caucuses in 2016 switched to primaries for 2020. These states that switched to primaries may be

---

[87] Jason Noble, *In Major Reform, 2020 Iowa Caucuses Would Include Absentee Voting, Public Vote Totals*, DES MOINES REG. (Dec. 9, 2017), www.desmoinesregister.com/story/news/2017/12/09/major-reform-2020-iowa-caucuses-include-absentee-voting-public-vote-totals/934913001/; *see also* McLaughlin, *supra* note 83; Grace Segers, *Iowa Democratic Party adds six "virtual" caucuses*, CBS NEWS (Feb. 12, 2019), www.cbsnews.com/news/iowa-caucuses-2020-iowa-democratic-party-adds-six-virtual-caucuses/.

[88] Brianne Pfannenstiel, *Iowa Democrats Not Giving Up on Expanding Caucus Accessibility even as DNC Formally Scraps Virtual Option*, DES MOINES REG. (Sept. 6, 2019), www.desmoinesregister.com/story/news/elections/presidential/caucus/2019/09/06/election-2020-iowa-caucus-democrats-dnc-accessibility-virtual-caucuses-rules/2234481001/.

[89] Noble, *supra* note 87.

[90] Elena Schneider, *Nevada Dems Revamp Caucuses After 2016 Clashes*, POLITICO (Mar. 20, 2019), www.politico.com/story/2019/03/20/nevada-dems-caucuses-1229982.

divided into two groups, depending on whether they held government-run primaries or party-run primaries. The Democrats in Colorado, Maine, Minnesota, and Utah abandoned caucuses and made the party's presidential candidates compete in newly established government-run primaries. Meanwhile, Democrats in Idaho, Nebraska, and Washington opted to use their states' existing government-run primaries, which were already used by the Republicans, rather than hold a Democratic caucus again.[91] By contrast, Democrats in Alaska, Hawaii, Kansas, and North Dakota decided to hold party-run primaries. In each of these states, the state government did not hold a primary of its own. Thus, the primary contest was organized and conducted by the state parties.

The differences between government-run and party-run primaries can be drastic. "While state governments might open hundreds or thousands of polling places statewide for 12 hours or more" in government-run primaries, as Geoffrey Skelley notes, the party-run primaries "might provide less than one voting location per county or keep the polls open for just four hours on primary day."[92] Under the DNC's rules, party-run primaries had to offer early and absentee voting in 2020. However, it is also the case that the state party had to assume the logistical burden of managing these voting processes without the assistance of the government-run logistical support systems that typically handle these kinds of election administration issues.

B. *Changes Implemented by the Republican National Committee*

Until mid-2019, it appeared that the Republican Party primaries and caucuses would be a pro forma exercise for President Trump as he sought his party's re-nomination. Given his historically low levels of popular support, the President faced at least one primary challenger in former Massachusetts Governor Bill Weld.[93] Though they have received less attention than the DNC's changes, various Republican state party committees also made substantive changes to their rules. In 2020, Republicans in Minnesota switched from holding a caucus to a primary after being caught unprepared for the massive enthusiasm and turnout of Republican voters during the 2016

---

[91] Skelley, *supra* note 1.

[92] *Id.*

[93] *See* Kris Schneider, *Ohioans Eyeing 2020? Kasich, Brown "Very Seriously" Consider Runs Against Trump*, ABC NEWS (Nov. 25, 2018), https://abcnews.go.com/Politics/outgoing-ohio-gov-kasich-2020-presidential-run/story?id=59394035 (also discussing former Ohio Governor John Kasich's potential primary challenge).

presidential race.[94] Voters in Minnesota thus selected their preferred Republican candidate through primary ballots instead of caucuses. Likewise, Republicans in Colorado also opted to hold a primary over a caucus.[95] Finally, the Republican Party in Nevada decided to poll its central committee members to nominate President Trump instead of holding a caucus.[96]

C. *The Impact of the New Rules on the 2020 Race*

As states shifted from caucuses to primaries, higher levels of voter participation were expected, particularly in the Democratic nomination contests. That was because turnout tends to be higher in primaries than caucuses.[97] One of the key features of the new government-run primaries is that they allow voters to cast their ballots during a lengthy open period of voting. Increased flexibility in voting—for example, by having several hours to vote instead of having to linger around during a caucus—draws more voters to the polls and makes the switch from caucuses especially dramatic. According to Caitlin Jewitt, whose research evaluates the effects of election rules on turnout, the transition away from caucuses increases voter turnout by 17–18 percent.[98] And turnout increased drastically. In Colorado, turnout in 2020 was more than six times higher than in 2016, and in both Maine and Minnesota it was more than four times higher than in 2016.[99]

This difference in turnout between caucuses and primaries, however, was blunted in states that held party-run primaries, where party rules and the more limited financial resources allocated by the parties to run these contests impacted the ease of casting a ballot.[100] Accordingly, the story of the 2020 presidential nomination contest, at least from the standpoint of voter participation, concerned

---

[94] Briana Bierschbach, *Why Minnesota's Caucuses Are So Important This Year*, MINNPOST (Feb. 5, 2018), www.minnpost.com/politics-policy/2018/02/why-minnesotas-caucuses-are-so-important-year/; Dave Orrick, *New Minnesota Law May Bring Change to How State Handles Presidential Primaries*, WEST CENT. TRIB. (Dec. 13, 2018), www.wctrib.com/news/govern ment-and-politics/4543798-new-minnesota-law-may-bring-change-how-state-handles.

[95] *Primary Election FAQs*, COLO. SEC'Y OF STATE, www.sos.state.co.us/pubs/elections/FAQs/primaryElectionsFAQ.html (last accessed Jan. 8, 2019).

[96] Debra J. Saunders, *Nevada GOP May Use Poll to Endorse Trump, Not Caucus*, LAS VEGAS REV.-J. (Aug. 1, 2019), www.reviewjournal.com/news/politics-and-government/nevada/neva da-gop-may-use-poll-to-endorse-trump-not-caucus-1816702/.

[97] Skelley, *supra* note 1; *cf.* Marshall, *supra* note 39.

[98] Skelley, *supra* note 1.

[99] German Lopez, *Voter Turnout Surged in Super Tuesday States That Ditched Caucuses*, VOX (Mar. 4, 2020), www.vox.com/policy-and-politics/2020/3/4/21164591/super-tuesday-election-results-voter-turnout-caucus.

[100] *See* Skelley, *supra* note 1.

the burgeoning divide between government-run primaries and party-run primaries, with the limited states still holding caucuses remaining an afterthought. Josh Putnam of the publication *Frontloading HQ* had predicted that turnout in party-run primaries would be higher than it would have been for traditional caucuses but low enough that there would still be measurable a gap between the government-run and party-run primaries in 2020.[101] And Putnam's prediction was right. While states that held new party-run primaries, like Alaska and North Dakota, may have doubled their 2016 turnout rates, states that held government-run primaries saw even greater increases.[102]

As mentioned earlier in this chapter, Democrats in Colorado, Minnesota, Utah, and Maine decided that the presidential candidates would compete in new government-run presidential primaries in their states in 2020.[103] Democrats in Idaho, Nebraska, and Washington State also opted to use government-run primaries in 2020, but rather than have new primaries, they added their candidate's names to the state's existing primary process, which was already being used by Republicans.[104] By contrast, Democrats in Alaska, Hawaii, Kansas, and North Dakota decided to host party-run primaries because these states did not already have government-run primary elections that they ran on their own or that were scheduled.[105]

[101] *Id.*

[102] Nathaniel Herz, *Biden wins Alaska Democratic presidential primary, claiming 8 of 15 delegates*, Alaska Public Media (Apr. 11, 2020), www.alaskapublic.org/2020/04/11/biden-wins-alaska-democratic-primary-claiming-9-of-17-delegates/.

[103] Colorado Democrats, Draft Colorado Delegate Selection Plan (Mar. 1, 2019), www.coloradodems.org/wp-content/uploads/2019/03/2020-DelegateSelectionPlan-Draft.pdf; Minnesota Democratic-Farmer-Labor Party, Minnesota Delegate Selection Plan for the 2020 Democratic National Convention (May 4, 2019), www.dfl.org/wp-content/uploads/2019/05/2020-Minnesota-NDSP-2019–05-05-National-Delegate-Selection-Plan-Rev-A-FINAL.pdf; Utah Democratic Party, Utah Delegate Selection Plan For the 2020 Democratic National Convention (Apr. 1, 2019), https://drive.google.com/file/d/16Z-IBuUuGIZQ56cvI8X4UPXJYY-FwKQL/view; *Maine Democratic Party, Maine Democrats Replace Caucus with Primary Set for Super Tuesday* (Jun 21, 2019), www.mainedems.org/media/maine-democrats-replace-caucus-primary-set-super-tuesday.

[104] Betsy Z. Russell, *Idaho Dems to Switch to Presidential Primary, Rather Than Caucuses*, Idaho Press (Jun. 20, 2019), www.idahopress.com/news/local/idaho-dems-to-switch-to-presidential-primary-rather-than-caucuses/article_36285da4-e7ee-5024-91a3-ba07e91cc373.html; Roseann Morning & Mitch Mertes, *Nebraska Democratic Party votes to discontinue caucuses and return to primary system*, APNews (Dec. 9, 2018), www.apnews.com/b91bb832d73a4d0295b4908a4b47446a; Rachel La Corte, *Washington Democrats to use results of presidential primary*, APNews (Apr. 7, 2019), www.apnews.com/c80d80adfcee40db9e82295873cd9cb.

[105] Alaska Democrats, 2020 Alaska Presidential Preference Party-Run Primary, https://static1.squarespace.com/static/54beeoc9e4b0441ce96c4681/t/5d1668743c57e500015e874b/1561749621416/2020+Pres+Primary+Process+%282%29.pdf ("Alaska Democrats will

The most worrying aspect of the shift from caucuses to primaries involves the administrative headaches associated with party-run primaries. Although the switch to primaries was meant to increase voter turnout, as a general rule state Democratic parties typically do not have the resources to administer a statewide primary. Consider Hawaii's delegate selection plan. It provided for only "approximately 20 polling locations around the state" that would be open only from the hours of 7:00 a.m. to 3:00 p.m.[106] In addition, the state was required to permit absentee and early voting. The state party was also obligated to manage and administer these systems, without the assistance of a state board of election or a similar entity experienced at handling an influx of ballots.

On a positive note, many of the delegate selection plans for states holding party-run primaries forced the party to incorporate ranked choice voting (RCV) into its primary. RCV permits voters to indicate their first choice candidate and then rank-order the remaining candidates on the ballot.[107] If a candidate has not secured a majority of the vote, an instant runoff occurs until a winner secures a majority of the votes. Ideally implemented, RCV ensures that all voters cast a meaningful vote for their preferred candidate. Yet RCV presents a new logistical challenge for counting votes. In light of a state party's new responsibility of hosting a primary election and its responsibility to count absentee and early votes as well, the party needs to engage in a series of administratively challenging instant-runoffs if a candidate does not secure a majority of the votes and if RCV is employed—and some parties are ill-equipped to do this.

---

not use a Presidential Preference Caucus in 2020 and will use a primary system with rank-choice voting for the 2020 Delegate Selection Process."); DEMOCRATIC PARTY OF HAWAII, HAWAII DELEGATE SELECTION PLAN FOR THE 2020 DEMOCRATIC NATIONAL CONVENTION (Mar. 25, 2019), https://hawaiidemocrats.org/wp-content/uploads/2019/03/2020-Hawaii-Delegate-Selection-Plan_DRAFT_2019-3-25.pdf ("A Party-run Presidential Preference Poll will occur on April 4, 2020"); KANSAS DEMOCRATIC PARTY, KANSAS DELEGATE SELECTION PLAN FOR THE 2020 DEMOCRATIC NATIONAL CONVENTION (May 2, 2019), https://kansasdems.org/wp-content/uploads/sites/6/2019/05/2020-Kansas-Delegate-Selection-Plan-1.pdf ("District-level delegates and alternates shall be elected by a Party-Run Primary with the first determining step occurring on May 2, 2020"); NORTH DAKOTA DEMOCRATIC-NPL, DELEGATE SELECTION PLAN FOR THE 2020 DEMOCRATIC NATIONAL CONVENTION (2019), https://demnpl.com/wp-content/uploads/2019/04/North-Dakota-Democratic-NPL-2020-Delegate-Selection-Plan.pdf ("North Dakota refers to the party-run event as a firehouse caucus"); *see also* Skelley, *supra* note 1.

[106] DEMOCRATIC PARTY OF HAWAII, *supra* note 105, at 8.

[107] Rob Richie, *The Case for a One-Person, One-Vote National Primary to Nominate Our Presidential Candidates in 2020*, IN THESE TIMES (June 2, 2016), http://inthesetimes.com/article/19163/the-case-for-a-one-person-one-vote-national-primaryto-elect-our-presidenti.

Why did Iowa, Nevada, and Wyoming retain their caucuses? For Iowa, it was about tradition. The Iowa caucuses have taken on an outsized role in the nomination process, and they are firmly cemented into our political milieu. Meanwhile, Nevada's diverse electorate serves as a helpful early foil to Iowa. In 2020, both Iowa and Nevada decided to select their delegates for the national convention based on the preferences exhibited by voters during the precinct caucuses, which was a significant change from 2016. Both Iowa and Nevada also tried to incorporate a form of ranked choice voting in 2020. Their initial Delegate Selection Plans called for these states to hold a virtual caucus in which voters submitted rankings of their candidate preferences, and instant rounds of runoffs and realignment would then continue until candidates were sorted as either viable (i.e., above 15 percent) or not. For security reasons, the DNC ultimately rejected both Iowa's and Nevada's requests to hold ranked-choice virtual caucuses. Wyoming released a draft delegate selection plan in early 2019 and made only modest changes to its caucus as compared to Iowa and Nevada. Wyoming did not initially decide to host virtual caucuses or incorporate RCV.

Notably, the four U.S. territories that held Democratic caucuses in 2016 — Guam, the Northern Mariana Islands, American Samoa, and the U.S. Virgin Islands — decided to hold territorial caucuses again in 2020.[108] The territories that held Republican caucuses in 2016 likewise retained their caucuses. Because caucuses tend to have significantly less voter participation than primaries, retaining caucuses in the territories perpetuates the dismal representation of American citizens and nationals who live there when it comes to the presidential election process. As Bryan Whitener notes, the "the Electoral College system does not provide for residents of U.S. Territories (Puerto Rico, Guam, the U.S. Virgin Islands, Northern Mariana Islands, American Samoa, and the U.S. Minor Outlying Islands) to vote for President."[109] Lower turnout in the territories exacerbates the already undemocratic aspects of caucuses. It

---

[108] DEMOCRATIC PARTY OF GUAM, GUAM DELEGATE SELECTION PLAN FOR THE 2020 DEMOCRATIC NATIONAL CONVENTION (July 6, 2019), https://drive.google.com/file/d/1x3RKH MN24wZ7fEu4vsMQqGiFHxnumij6/view; *Northern Mariana Island Democrats Will Caucus on March 14*, FRONTLOADING HQ (July 30, 2019), https://frontloading.blogspot.com/2019/07/n orthern-mariana-island-democrats-will.html; DEMOCRATIC PARTY OF AMERICAN SAMOA, AMERICAN SAMOA DELEGATE SELECTION PLAN (July 3, 2019), https://drive.google.com/file/d /1BWoYnzqdoUW6QFr4tQao6t8pd_IhaY4J/view; VIRGIN ISLANDS DEMOCRATIC PARTY, VIRGIN ISLANDS DELEGATE SELECTION AND AFFIRMATIVE ACTION PLAN FOR THE 2020 DEMOCRATIC NATIONAL CONVENTION, https://drive.google.com/file/d/1R6kZ_X4v4hU6O_B z9eN3TVnPl8OdZVMg/view.

[109] Maria Murriel, *Millions of Americans can't vote for president because of where they live*, PRI (Nov. 1, 2016, 2:45 P.M.), www.pri.org/stories/2016–11-01/millions-americans-cant-vote-president-because-where-they-live.

also works to consolidate decision-making in the hands of a few party-connected officials in the territories.

Consider the delegate selection process for the U.S. Virgin Islands. The U.S. Virgin Islands is allocated thirteen delegates to the Democratic National Convention in total. Six of these are automatic delegates who are selected because of the role they play in the party—and they include the territory's governor, its delegate to Congress, the party chair, the party vice chair, the national committeeman, and the national committeewoman. The territory's remaining seven delegates are selected at-large, but rather than being elected territory-wide, these delegates are elected from subsets of the territory. Based on how the delegate allocation rules of the U.S. Virgin Islands work, candidates receiving a smaller percentage of vote are unlikely to receive pledged delegates. Josh Putnam explains how, in the U.S. Virgin Islands, the presidential candidate must receive at least 16.67 percent of the vote to ensure a presidential delegate is allocated to him, which is a high bar.[110] Compounding this situation, the U.S. Virgin Islands does not use RCV or a similar mechanism to ensure that caucus goers can cast a meaningful vote for their preferred candidate.

In the end, the move away from caucuses to primaries in 2020 likely changes what it means to be a successful candidate. In 2016, Senator Bernie Sanders won 12 of the 18 states and territories that employed caucuses, whereas he won only 11 of the 39 states and territories that had held primaries. Without the influx of caucus-oriented delegates, Sanders's presidential campaign would have folded much earlier. Another valuable point of comparison is the 2008 campaign, when Barack Obama famously ran up the numbers in caucus states.[111] After the Iowa caucuses and the New Hampshire primary, Hillary Clinton, as a general rule, won the primaries in more populous states, while Obama's team focused on amassing delegates in smaller states—particularly caucus states—to help secure his victory.[112] The 2020 presidential campaigns were surely cognizant of the new rules and well aware that the strategy of hording delegates from caucus states would no longer be a viable option to secure the Democratic Party's presidential nominations.

---

[110] Josh Putnam, *Virgin Islands Democratic Caucuses Slated for June*, FRONTLOADING HQ (July 11, 2019), https://frontloading.blogspot.com/2019/07/virgin-islands-democratic-caucuses.html.

[111] Andrew Prokop, *7 Charts That Explain Why Hillary Clinton Lost in 2008 – and Why She's Winning in 2016*, VOX (June 10, 2015, 3:55 P.M.), www.vox.com/2015/2/20/8062125/hillary-clinton-lost-2008.

[112] *Id.*

D. *Iowa's 2020 Caucus Calamity*

Proponents of the move away from caucuses to primaries felt validated by the outcome of the 2020 Iowa caucuses, which turned out to be a complete disaster. As noted by the Associated Press, the caucuses were plagued by technological challenges, which led to delays in reporting the precinct-level results.[113] As a result, no clear winner was announced on caucus night, when rival candidates, unsure of the results, all gave tepid "victory" speeches. The main culprit of Iowa's reporting challenges was a technological reporting application developed by a Democratic Party operative that was meant to give Iowa's precinct chairs an easy way to calculate delegate totals and report results. When caucus volunteers were unable to download or properly use the application, the Iowa Democratic Party ignored the warning signs. When precinct chairs were unable to report results using technology, they tried to use the phone to report their results, but they were met with hours-long waits to connect with the central party's machinery.

Attempting to resolve the serious administrative failings of election night, the Iowa Democratic Party began to release results in batches. The party's decision to release piecemeal caucus results, instead of waiting to release a verified and confirmed final total, was widely criticized. In the end, the reporting of Iowa's caucus results was tainted by mistakes that required corrections, and purported mathematical errors occurred that may never be resolved. The event proved to be a national debacle, and the state's caucuses received widespread negative media coverage. The Iowa Democratic Party continued to recount votes and update the results of the caucuses in the weeks that followed, finally releasing a tally that indicated that Pete Buttigieg had won the state's Democratic caucuses. These final, recounted results were released nearly a month after the state's caucuses had taken place. After reviewing them, the Associated Press decided not to declare a winner due to concerns that the results were not fully accurate.[114]

Unsurprisingly, many high-ranking officials in the Democratic Party called for the Iowa caucuses to be replaced by a primary election. For instance, Senator Dick Durbin (D-IL), the Senate minority whip, announced that "[t]he Democratic caucus is a quirky, quaint tradition that should come to an end."[115] The chaotic results in Iowa set off a scramble in the states holding subsequent

[113] Ryan J. Foley, *How the Iowa caucuses "broke down in every way possible,"* Assoc. Press (Feb. 11, 2020), https://apnews.com/ee095683c85f6c97e51b6589b412f674.

[114] *AP decides not to declare Iowa caucus winner after recount*, Assoc. Press (Feb. 27, 2020), https://apnews.com/fc6777e93b8c50b2fd20e0d31fcc43b3.

[115] John McCormick, *Democrats Call for End of Iowa Caucuses After Results Debacle*, Wall St. J. (Feb. 4, 2020), www.wsj.com/articles/democrats-call-for-end-of-iowa-caucuses-after-results-debacle-11580834954.

contests to avoid using the same application that derailed reporting in Iowa. Instead states like Nevada resorted to using a combination of Google Forms and paper back-ups.[116] The Nevada caucus results were untainted by the same reporting errors and were returned swiftly.

VI. CONCLUSION

Commentators have long believed that the caucus system was on its deathbed. While previously praised for promoting party unity, the caucuses, typified by what happens every four years in Iowa, are generally no longer in vogue. With only three states and four U.S. territories holding caucuses in 2020, the ultimate ascent of the primaries has now occurred. Yet the states and territories that have held onto their caucuses have also shown that caucuses have some resiliency. Reforms imposed following the 2016 presidential election, predominately by the DNC, sought to address the most critical concerns about caucuses—that they are burdensome, time-consuming, and uninviting to large segments of society. Proposals to change the caucuses to include early and absentee voting, same-day registration, and virtual caucusing were all improvements designed to address the undemocratic aspects of the system. Even with such reforms, however, it remains unlikely that voter turnout in caucus states can increase to the level of voter turnout witnessed in primaries. Going forward, the caucus process will remain largely the same: voters will be required to spend hours cajoling and persuading supporters of non-viable candidates to realign, and this process will continue until the viable candidates are finally selected.

One truism of the American presidential nomination process is that its rules are ever-changing and candidates must adapt their strategies and messages to suc-ceed. Ideally, the transformations ushered in by the 2020 election cycle will prompt increased voter participation and turnout, and the new reforms will address the failings of caucuses. It is especially important to understand and assess what has happened in states that decided to hold party-run primaries. In the future, the jurisdictions that adopted party-run primaries in 2020 may flourish along with the more famous Iowa and Nevada caucuses or they may be ridiculed for their administrative troubles. It is also important to assess whether these new contests ultimately strengthen or weaken the role of political parties in the states. Some commentators believe that the transition away from the caucuses may serve to expedite the decline of the influence of parties, but only time will tell.

---

[116] Juweek Adolphe, Seán Clarke & Peter Andringa, *Nevada Caucus Results in Full*, GUARDIAN (Feb. 22, 2020), www.theguardian.com/us-news/ng-interactive/2020/feb/22/nevada-results-live-tracker-latest-votes-by-county-latest.

9

Floor Fight: Protecting the National Party Conventions from Manipulation

Michael T. Morley[*]

The Democratic and Republican parties select their presidential nominees through a complex, fundamentally unstable process. It is an awkward amalgamation of disparate components, each designed to empower different constituencies within the party and pursue different goals. Each party ultimately chooses its nominee at a national convention comprised of delegates from each state.[1] The mechanisms for selecting delegates to the national convention, however, are distinct from the procedures for determining the presidential candidates for whom those delegates must vote.[2] National convention delegates are often selected at statewide or congressional-district conventions or through other intra-party mechanisms. They are typically pledged or "bound" to presidential candidates based on the outcomes of presidential preference contests, such as primaries and caucuses. Because of the complicated relationship among these components, the national convention need not nominate the person who received the most primary and caucus votes nationwide, won the most delegates, or prevailed in the most primaries and caucuses. Indeed, the convention may decide to nominate someone who did not run in the primaries and caucuses at all.[3]

---

[*] Michael T. Morley is Assistant Professor of Law at Florida State University College of Law. Special thanks to Barbara Kaplan and Mary McCormick of the Florida State University College of Law Research Center for their assistance in gathering sources.

[1] DEMOCRATIC NAT'L COMM., *Charter of the Democratic Party of the United States* [hereinafter *Democratic Charter*], *in* THE CHARTER AND BYLAWS OF THE DEMOCRATIC PARTY OF THE UNITED STATES, 1, 2, art. 2, § 3 (Aug. 25, 2018) [hereinafter CHARTER AND BYLAWS], https://democrats.org/wp-content/uploads/2018/10/DNC-Charter-Bylaws-8.25.18-with-Amendments.pdf [https://perma.cc/V6LV-QARF]; REPUBLICAN NAT'L COMM., THE RULES OF THE REPUBLICAN PARTY 41, R.40(d) (July 20, 2018) [hereinafter REPUBLICAN RULES], https://prod-cdn-static.gop.com/media/documents/2016-Republican-Rules-Reformatted2018_1533138132.pdf [perma.cc/T3RZ-WD5V].

[2] *See* Michael T. Morley, *Reforming the Contested Convention: Rethinking the Presidential Nomination Process*, 85 FORDHAM L. REV. 1073, 1076 (2016).

[3] *Id.* at 1076.

The entire process is ultimately governed by the national convention's rules. Among other things, the convention rules specify the number of delegate votes a presidential candidate must receive to win the nomination, the candidates for whom delegates may validly cast votes, the effects and enforceability of delegates' pledges or binding to particular candidates, and the applicability of restrictions such as the "unit rule." The rules are not definitively established until the beginning of the conventions themselves, however—long after the presidential preference primaries and caucuses, as well as statewide and congressional-district conventions, have concluded.[4] National convention delegates not only vote on the rules that will govern the convention, but may vote later to suspend them.[5]

Each party should establish permanent convention rules at the outset of each presidential nomination cycle, before any step of the nomination process begins.[6] The rules should not be subject to rejection, amendment, or suspension at the convention itself. Basic principles of fairness and due process dictate that the rules governing the presidential nomination process should not be changed after millions of votes have been cast in presidential preference contests,[7] delegates have been selected, and the presidential candidates who will benefit from potential changes are known.[8]

This chapter begins by explaining the details of the presidential nomination process for both the Democratic and Republican parties. It then discusses important convention rules most susceptible to manipulation late in the process, and concludes by discussing historical examples of attempts by delegates to change the rules at the last minute to manipulate the convention's results. Granting national convention delegates the power to change or

---

[4] *See, e.g.,* Democratic Nat'l Comm., *Call for the 2020 Democratic National Convention*, 13, § IX (Aug. 25, 2018) [hereinafter *Democratic Call*], https://democrats.org/wp-content/uploads/2019/02/2020-Call-for-Convention-WITH-Attachments-2.26.19.pdf [https://perma.cc/LN4C-7RYW]; Republican Nat'l Comm., *Call for the 2016 National Convention*, 43, R.42 (Nov. 30, 2015) [hereinafter *Republican Call*], https://prod-cdn-static.gop.com/media/documents/Call%20of%20the%202016%20Convention_1448920406.pdf [https://perma.cc/59J6-BMZ4]; *see also* Democratic Nat'l. Comm., *Bylaws, in* Charter and Bylaws, *supra* note 1, at 11, 11, art. I, § 2 [hereinafter *Democratic Bylaws*]. As of the date this chapter was drafted, the Democratic National Committee has issued its call for the 2020 Democratic National Convention. *Democratic Call, supra* at 1. Because the Republican National Committee has not yet issued its call, this chapter uses the Call for the 2016 Republican National Convention for comparison purposes.

[5] *Cf. Democratic Call, supra* note 4, at 19, § IX(J); Republican Rules, *supra* note 1, at 37, R. 32.

[6] Morley, *supra* note 2, at 1092–93.

[7] Fed. Election Comm'n, Federal Elections 2016: Election Results for the U.S. President, U.S. Senate and the U.S. House of Representatives 45 (Dec. 2017).

[8] *See, e.g.,* Roe v. Alabama, 43 F.3d 574, 581–82 (11th Cir. 1995); Griffin v. Burns, 570 F.2d 1065, 1075–76 (1st Cir. 1978); Briscoe v. Kusper, 435 F.2d 1046, 1055 (7th Cir. 1970).

suspend convention rules at the eleventh hour destabilizes and undermines the legitimacy of the entire nomination process. Allowing such last-minute rule changes to secure a particular candidate's nomination also defeats the point of having millions of people throughout the nation participate in presidential preference contests. And it encourages backroom machinations and intraparty discord at the very time the party would prefer to be coalescing around a standard-bearer and fostering unity for the general election.

I. THE PRESIDENTIAL NOMINATION PROCESS

The presidential nomination process officially begins for each major political party when its national committee issues a call to hold a national convention.[9] The call serves four main purposes. It announces the time and place of the convention,[10] sets forth temporary rules to govern the convention until the convention itself adopts permanent rules,[11] specifies the number and type of national convention delegates allocated to each state,[12] and sets the deadline by which state parties must nominate and, if applicable, bind their delegates.[13]

A. *Size and Composition of the National Conventions*

Both national conventions are comprised of several types of delegates. The Democratic Call specifies that the 2020 Democratic National Convention will consist of 4,533 delegates falling into four categories: 2,437 pledged district-level base delegates, 841 pledged at-large base delegates,[14] 490 pledged "party leader and elected official" delegates ("PLEOs"), and 765 unpledged "automatic delegates," colloquially referred to as superdelegates.[15]

---

[9]   *Democratic Charter, supra* note 1, at 3, art. 3, § 1(a); *Democratic Bylaws, supra* note 4, at 11, art. 2, § 1(a); REPUBLICAN RULES, *supra* note 1, at 15, R.13.

[10] *See, e.g., Democratic Call, supra* note 4, at 1; *Republican Call, supra* note 4, at 2.

[11] *See, e.g., Democratic Call, supra* note 4, at 13–21, § IX; *Republican Call, supra* note 4, at 3–43; *see also Democratic Bylaws, supra* note 4, at 11, art. I, § 2; REPUBLICAN RULES, *supra* note 1, at 43, R.42.

[12] *See, e.g., Democratic Call, supra* note 4, App. B, *2020 Democratic National Convention Delegate / Alternate Allocation* (Feb. 26, 2019); *Republican Call, supra* note 4, at 47–58. Both parties generally treat the District of Columbia and U.S. territories as states. *See, e.g., Democratic Call, supra* note 4, at 1, § I(B); *id.* at 2 & n.4–5, § I(E)–(F), (H) & n.4–5, *id.* at 16, § IX(C)(7)(a), (f); *Republican Call, supra* note 4, at 2; *id.* at 4, R.14(a)(2), (4).

[13] *Democratic Call, supra* note 4, at 4, § III; *Republican Call, supra* note 4, at 10, R.16(c)(1); *id.* at 24, R.20(a).

[14] Between the district-level base delegates and at-large base delegates, there is a total of 3,278 pledged base delegates.

[15] *Democratic Call, supra* note 4, App. B.

States and the District of Columbia are allocated both district-level delegates and at-large delegates (collectively called "base delegates") based on their respective populations and the number of votes they cast for the Democratic candidate for president in the last three presidential elections.[16] States also receive bonus base delegates for scheduling their nomination activities later in the cycle.[17] States' base delegate allocations range in size from Wyoming's 11 to California's 362.[18] Three-quarters of each state's base delegates are "district-level delegates," to be chosen "at the congressional district level or smaller," while the remaining quarter is comprised of "at-large" delegates, elected on a statewide basis.[19] U.S. Territories, as well as Democrats Abroad, also receive specified numbers of base delegates.[20]

Each state also receives PLEO slots equaling 15 percent of its total number of district-level and at-large base delegates.[21] PLEO slots are reserved for "big city mayors and state-wide elected officials," state legislative leaders and other legislators, and "other state, county and local elected officials and party leaders."[22] Finally, the Democratic Call designates all current Democratic National Committee (DNC) members; current Democratic Senators, Representatives, and Governors; and current and former "Distinguished Party Leaders" (including Democratic Presidents, Vice Presidents, Senate and House chamber leaders, and DNC chairs), as automatic delegates, or superdelegates.[23] Unlike PLEOs and other pledged delegates, automatic delegates are not pledged to any particular presidential candidate and may vote for whichever presidential candidate they wish at the national convention.[24]

In contrast, it is estimated that the 2020 Republican National Convention will be comprised of 2,550 delegates, divided into three categories: 1,077 at-large delegates, 1,305 congressional district delegates, and 168 automatic

---

[16]   *Democratic Charter, supra* note 1, at 3, art. 2, § 5(a); *Democratic Call, supra* note 4, at 1, § I(B).

[17]   *Democratic Charter, supra* note 1, at 3, art. 2, § 5(b); *Democratic Call, supra* note 4, at 1–2 § I(C)(2).

[18]   *Democratic Call, supra* note 4, App. B.

[19]   Democratic Nat'l Comm., *Delegate Selection Rules for the 2020 Democratic National Convention*, 10, R.8(C) (Aug. 25, 2018) [hereinafter, *Democratic Delegate Selection Rules*], https://democrats.org/wp-content/uploads/2019/01/2020-Delegate-Selection-Rules-12.17.18-FINAL.pdf [https://perma.cc/Z54A-8E4L].

[20]   *Democratic Call, supra* note 4, at 2, § I(E); *see also id.* App. B.

[21]   *Democratic Call, supra* note 4, at 2, § I(D); *Democratic Delegate Selection Rules, supra* note 19, at 10, R.8(D).

[22]   *Democratic Delegate Selection Rules, supra* note 19, at 11, R.10(A)(1).

[23]   *Democratic Call, supra* note 4, at 2, § I(F)-(H); *accord Democratic Charter, supra* note 1, at 2–3, art. 2, § 4(h); *Democratic Delegate Selection Rules, supra* note 19, at 10–11, R.9(A).

[24]   *Democratic Call, supra* note 4, at 18, § IX(F)(3)(a).

delegates.[25] Each state is allocated a minimum of ten at-large delegates,[26] along with bonus at-large delegates for states that voted for the Republican candidate in the last presidential election or that have Republican governors or U.S. Senators, a majority-Republican delegation to the U.S. House of Representatives, or Republican-controlled chambers of the state legislature.[27] Each state also receives three congressional district delegates for each district it has.[28] Finally, each state has three "automatic" delegates: the state Republican party chair, as well as its national committeeman and national committeewoman.[29] Delegations sizes are estimated to range from 16 for Delaware to 172 for California.[30] The rules provide between six and twenty at-large delegates each to the District of Columbia, Puerto Rico, and other U.S. territories.[31]

B. *Selection of National Convention Delegates*

The Democratic Party's Delegate Selection Rules allow state Democratic parties to authorize the selection of district-level delegates to the national convention in one of two ways. First, the state party may allow eligible voters in each congressional district (or smaller jurisdictional units within each district) to vote directly on that district's base delegates on the presidential preference primary ballot.[32] Each candidate for district-level delegate must either specify the presidential candidate to whom they wish to be pledged or identify as "uncommitted."[33] If a state party chooses this method, each presidential candidate has complete discretion to prevent someone from running to become one of his or her pledged district-level delegates.[34] Under this approach, the presidential preference primary election determines both the identity of the state's district-level base delegates to the national convention and the presidential candidate to whom each is pledged.

---

[25]   Richard E. Berg-Anderson, *2020 Presidential Primaries, Caucuses, and Conventions*, GREEN PAPERS (Feb. 22, 2019), www.thegreenpapers.com/P20/R [perma.cc/ADZ8-RYHN].

[26]   REPUBLICAN RULES, *supra* note 1, at 16, R.14(a)(1).

[27]   *Id.* at 16–17, R.14(a)(5)–(6).

[28]   *Id.* at 16, R.14(a)(3).

[29]   *Id.* at 16, R.14(a)(2).

[30]   Richard E. Berg-Anderson, *The Math Behind the Republican Delegate Allocation – 2020*, GREEN PAPERS (Jan. 16, 2017), www.thegreenpapers.com/P20/R-Alloc.phtml [https://perma .cc/X7VP-EXKS].

[31]   REPUBLICAN RULES, *supra* note 1, at 16, R.14(a)(4).

[32]   *Democratic Delegate Selection Rules*, *supra* note 19, at 14, R.13(G).

[33]   *Id.* at 12, R.13(B).

[34]   *Id.* at 13, R.13(D), (E), (E)(1).

Second, a state party may instead choose to separate its presidential preference contest from the process for selecting district-level delegates. In that
case, any presidential candidate who receives at least 15 percent of the vote
within a congressional district in a presidential preference primary or caucus is
entitled to have a proportionate share of the district-level delegates for that
district pledged to him or her.[35] A caucus of eligible voters from the district
who sign "statements of support" for each such presidential candidate then
chooses the district-level delegates to fill that candidate's slots.[36] A presidential
candidate may prohibit the caucus from considering certain people to be
selected as district-level delegates pledged to him or her, so long as three or
more candidates for each of that presidential candidate's district-level delegate
slots remain.[37] Thus, presidential candidates have less control over determining the district-level delegates pledged to them when delegate selection occurs
independently from presidential preference contests than when the delegates
themselves run on the presidential preference primary ballot.

A state Democratic party may allow that state's at-large delegates[38] and
PLEOs[39] to be selected in one of three ways: at the state convention (by state
convention delegates selected from municipalities and counties), by that state's
district-level delegates to the national convention, or by the state party committee itself. Candidates for at-large or PLEO delegate slots must pledge themselves
to a particular presidential candidate or identify as "uncommitted."[40]
A presidential candidate may prevent a person from seeking to become an at-
large or PLEO delegate pledged to him or her, so long as there are at least one or
two candidates remaining for each such slot, depending on the state party's
rules.[41] There is no separate selection process for automatic delegate seats, since
they are granted to certain current and former Democratic leaders and party
officials by virtue of their positions.

Each state Republican party may decide whether its at-large and district-
level delegates will be directly elected in a presidential preference primary,
appointed by the state party committee, chosen at state and district-level party
conventions, or selected through other methods previously used by that state.[42]
Presidential candidates have no input into the identity of the delegates to be

---

[35]   *Id.* at 15, R.14(B), (D).
[36]   *Id.* at 14, R.13(G).
[37]   *Id.* at 13, R.13(D), (E), (E)(1).
[38]   *Democratic Delegate Selection Rules, supra* note 19, at 12, R.11(B).
[39]   *Id.* at 11, R.10(B).
[40]   *Id.* at 12, R.13(A); *see also id.* at 11, R.10(A)(3); *id.* at 12, R.13(B).
[41]   *Id.* at 13–14, R.13(E)(2).
[42]   Republican Rules, *supra* note 1, at 20–21, R.16(d)(1).

pledged to them, unless the state party allows it.[43] Accordingly, people opposed to a certain presidential candidate may be chosen as delegates pledged to that candidate. While such delegates are required to vote for that candidate on the first (and, depending on the state party, possibly subsequent) rounds of balloting at the national convention, they may otherwise work to undermine that candidate's chances of receiving the nomination.

C. *Allocation of National Convention Delegates among Presidential Candidates*

The parties differ in how they allocate national convention delegates among presidential candidates based on the results of presidential preference contests. As discussed above, the Democratic Party's Delegate Selection Rules allow each state party to decide for itself whether to combine or separate its process for selecting district-level delegates from its mechanism for allocating them among presidential candidates. On the one hand, a state party may allow the voters of each congressional district (or smaller jurisdiction) to elect district-level delegates directly on the presidential preference primary ballot.[44] Because each candidate for district-level delegate must pledge himself or herself to a particular presidential candidate,[45] the outcome of the presidential preference primary determines both which district-level delegates are elected and the presidential candidates to whom they are pledged.

Alternatively, state Democratic parties may select district-level delegates independently of presidential preference contests. In such states, voters choose their preferred presidential candidates through a primary or caucus. Some states hold open primaries and caucuses, in which any voters may participate (so long as they did not participate in another party's nomination process that year). Other states' primaries and caucuses are open only to members of each political party, or to party members and independents.[46] Any presidential candidate who receives at least 15 percent of the vote within a congressional district is allocated a proportionate share of the district-level delegates for that district.[47] At-large[48] and PLEO[49] delegates are likewise generally allocated proportionately among presidential candidates who receive at least 15 percent

---

[43] *Id.* at 19, R.16(a)(2).
[44] *Democratic Delegate Selection Rules, supra* note 19, at 14, R.13(G).
[45] *Id.* at 12, R.13(B).
[46] Morley, *supra* note 2, at 1084.
[47] *Democratic Delegate Selection Rules, supra* note 19, at 15, R.14(B), (D).
[48] *Id.* at 12, R.11(C); *id.* at 15, R.14(E).
[49] *Id.* at 11, R.10(A)(2).

in the statewide presidential preference vote. Automatic delegates, or super-delegates, are never allocated among presidential candidates, but rather are free to vote for whomever they wish at the national convention.[50]

The Republican rules similarly provide that a state's delegates must be allocated among presidential candidates based on the results of that state's presidential preference contest, except for delegates, if any, elected directly on a statewide presidential preference primary ballot.[51] A state party may choose to conduct its presidential preference contest through a primary, caucus, or state convention.[52] If a state party holds its presidential preference contest before March 15 of the convention year (except for Iowa, New Hampshire, South Carolina, and Nevada), delegates must be allocated proportionately among presidential candidates based on the results.[53] In such states, at-large delegates must be allocated based on the statewide results, and district-level delegates based on the results within each congressional district.[54] State parties have great flexibility in satisfying these requirements. They may allocate their delegates among presidential candidates completely proportionately; allocate delegates only among candidates who receive more than a specified percentage of the vote (up to 20 percent) within a district or statewide; or establish modified winner-take-all rules awarding a candidate who exceeds a specified level of support (at least 50 percent) all of the state's delegates.[55] States that hold their presidential preference contests on or after March 15 are free to decide whether to allocate their delegates through any of these proportionate methods or on a winner-take-all basis.[56]

The effects of delegate binding differ from state to state. Most state Republican parties specify that the state's delegates must vote for a specific candidate only during the first round or two of balloting at the national convention.[57] Others bind delegates for additional rounds of balloting unless the candidate to whom they are bound withdraws from the race or releases them.[58] Binding applies only to the actual selection of a presidential nominee and not other potentially critical issues upon which delegates may vote, such as the convention rules. That means that a delegate may vote on questions before

---

[50] *Democratic Call, supra* note 4, at 18, § IX(F)(3)(a).
[51] REPUBLICAN RULES, *supra* note 1, at 19, R.16(a)(1).
[52] *Id.*
[53] *Id.* at 20, R.16(c)(1)–(2).
[54] *Id.* at 20, R.16(c)(3).
[55] *Id.* at 20, R.16(c)(3)(i)–(ii).
[56] *Id.* at 19, R.16(a)(1).
[57] Morley, *supra* note 2, at 1086.
[58] *Id.*

the convention in a way that harms or even assures the defeat of the candidate to whom he or she is bound.

Thus, for the Republican Party and, to a lesser extent, the Democratic Party, this untidy fusion of primaries, caucuses, state conventions, and national conventions may result in the selection of national convention delegates who oppose the presidential candidates to whom they are pledged or bound.

D. *National Convention Committees*

Each party's national convention features several standing committees, including a Rules Committee and Credentials Committee.[59] For the Democratic Convention, each of these committees is comprised of 162 base members[60] and an additional 25 PLEO members.[61] Committee members must be Democrats, but need not be convention delegates.[62] The committee base members from each state are allocated among presidential candidates proportionately based on the outcome of the statewide presidential preference primary or, in non-primary states, the allocation of the state's at-large delegates.[63] A presidential candidate submits one or more names for each committee slot allocated to him or her, and that state's national convention delegates formally select committee members from among those submissions.[64] The Chair of the DNC nominates, and the DNC's Executive Committee confirms, each convention committee's chair and co-chairs,[65] as well as its PLEO members.[66]

For the Republicans, each committee is comprised of one man and one woman from each state.[67] Each state's national convention delegation determines which of its members shall serve on each committee.[68] The Chair of the RNC appoints each convention committee's chair and co-chair.[69]

In advance of each party's national convention, the Credentials Committee prepares a report containing resolutions concerning each challenge to the

---

[59]   *Democratic Call, supra* note 4, at 8, § VII; REPUBLICAN RULES, *supra* note 1, at 41–42, R.41(a).
[60]   *Democratic Call, supra* note 4, at 8, § VII(A)(1); *see also id.* App. D.
[61]   *Id.* at 8, § VII(A)(2).
[62]   *Id.* at 8, § VII(A)(3)–(4).
[63]   *Id.* at 9–10, § VII(C)(1).
[64]   *Id.* at 9–11, § VII(B)(1), (C)(4), (D)(2).
[65]   *Id.* at 11, § VII(F)(1).
[66]   *Id.* at 9, § VII(B)(2).
[67]   REPUBLICAN RULES, *supra* note 1, at 41, R.41(a).
[68]   *Id.*
[69]   *Id.*

credentials of delegates to the national convention.[70] Dissenting members may prepare a minority report recommending different conclusions.[71]

E. *Proceedings of the National Conventions*

Both parties conduct their national conventions similarly. The convention is called to order by the chair of the national party committee[72] and governed by temporary rules until the convention itself adopts permanent rules.[73] Similarly, a temporary roll of delegates is used to determine who is eligible to vote until the permanent roll is adopted. For the Democratic Party, the temporary roll includes all delegates certified by their state parties who have not been challenged, as well as any delegates whom the Credentials Committee's proposed report recommends be seated.[74] For the Republican Party, the temporary roll is comprised of all delegates certified by their state parties,[75] regardless of whether they have been challenged, though a challenged delegate may not vote unless the RNC or Credentials Committee allows it.[76]

After the convention is convened, the chair of the Credentials Committee presents the committee's report, along with any minority reports.[77] The convention then holds a voice vote on whether to adopt the credentials report, amend it, or replace it with the minority report, unless a roll-call vote of each state delegation is validly requested.[78] Under the Democratic Party rules, a roll-call vote must be held whenever the chair is uncertain about the results of a voice vote or more than

---

[70] *Democratic Call, supra* note 4, at 29, App. A, §§ 9(F)(2), 10; Republican Rules, *supra* note 1, at 35, R.27(a); *see also id.* at 34, R.25(b).

[71] *Democratic Call, supra* note 4, at 29–30, App. A, § 11; *see also id.* at 13, § VII(J)(3)–(4); *id.* at 20, § IX(M); Republican Rules, *supra* note 1, at 37, R.34(b).

[72] *Democratic Call, supra* note 4, at 13, § IX(A)(1); Republican Nat'l Comm., *Order of Business, 2016 Republican National Convention,* at 8 (July 2016), www.politico.com/story/2016/07/rnc-2016-schedule-of-events-and-speakers-225704 [https://perma.cc/SU2J-25PM].

[73] *Democratic Call, supra* note 4, at 13, § IX; *Democratic Bylaws, supra* note 4, at 11, art. 1, § 2; Republican Rules, *supra* note 1, at 43, R.42.

[74] *Democratic Call, supra* note 4, at 14, § IX(B)(1). A delegate on the temporary roll may not vote on his or her own credentials contest. *Id.* at 14, § IX(B)(2).

[75] Republican Rules, *supra* note 1, at 29–30 R.20(c); *id.* at 31, R.22(a).

[76] *Id.* at 31, R.22(b). As with the Democratic rules, a challenged delegate on the temporary roll may not vote on his or her own credentials challenge. *Id.*

[77] *Democratic Call, supra* note 4, at 14, § IX(C)(1)(a); Republican Rules, *supra* note 1, at 35, R.27(a).

[78] *Democratic Call, supra* note 4, at 18, § IX(F)(3)(b); Republican Rules, *supra* note 1, at 39–40, R.39.

a quarter of the delegates demands it.[79] Republican Rules require a roll-call vote whenever a majority of delegates from seven delegations demands it.[80] A majority vote of eligible delegates on the temporary roll is required to adopt a credentials report.[81] Whichever report the convention adopts constitutes the permanent roll of delegates who may vote on all subsequent issues, including nominating a presidential candidate.

The chair of the Rules Committee then presents the Rules Committee's report proposing permanent rules to govern the remainder of the convention,[82] along with any minority reports.[83] The convention votes on the rules report in the same manner as the credentials report.[84] Once adopted, the permanent rules from the rules report displace the temporary rules in the convention's Call.[85] After electing a Permanent Chair, Co-Chairs, and Secretary, the convention then votes on adopting the party's platform, specifying its principles and positions on various political, social, and economic issues.[86]

Finally, the convention accepts nominations for the party's presidential candidate.[87] To be eligible to seek the Democratic nomination, a person must be a "bona fide Democrat" as determined by the Chair of the DNC; file a written statement with the DNC; be registered to vote in the upcoming presidential election and have been registered to vote in the previous one; satisfy the Constitution's eligibility requirements for President; and have "established substantial support" for his or her nomination, including having pledged delegates.[88] A nominating petition for an eligible candidate must be signed by at least 300 delegates, no more than 50 of whom may come from the same delegation; a delegate may not sign multiple petitions.[89] Under the temporary

---

[79]   *Democratic Call, supra* note 4, at 18, § IX(F)(3)(b).
[80]   Republican Rules, *supra* note 1, at 39–40, R.39.
[81]   *See Democratic Call, supra* note 4, at 14, § IX(C)(1)(c).
[82]   *Democratic Call, supra* note 4, at 15, § IX(C)(2); *id.* at 12, § VII(I)(1); Republican Rules, *supra* note 1, at 35, R.27(a).
[83]   *Democratic Call, supra* note 4, at 15, § IX(C)(2); Republican Rules, *supra* note 1, at 37, R.34(a).
[84]   *See Democratic Call, supra* note 4, at 15, § IX(C)(2).
[85]   *Democratic Bylaws, supra* note 4, at 11, art. 1, § 2; Republican Rules, *supra* note 1, at 43, R.42.
[86]   *Democratic Call, supra* note 4, at 15, § IX(C)(3)-(5); Republican Rules, *supra* note 1, at 35, R.27(a).
[87]   *Democratic Call, supra* note 4, at 15, § IX(C)(6); Republican Rules, *supra* note 1, at 35, R.27(a).
[88]   *Democratic Call, supra* note 4, at 7, § VI; *accord Democratic Delegate Selection Rules, supra* note 19, at 14, R.13(K)(1)(a)–(b), (2).
[89]   *Democratic Call, supra* note 4, at 15, § IX(C)(6)(b).

rules for the 2020 Republican National Convention, a candidate must submit a certificate signed by a plurality of delegates from at least five states to be eligible for nomination.[90]

After the nomination and seconding speeches,[91] the Convention chair conducts an alphabetical roll-call vote of the delegations.[92] In a roll-call vote under the Democratic rules, each delegation's chair announces the vote tally for that jurisdiction's delegates.[93] Any delegation member may challenge the accuracy of the chair's announcement.[94] The Convention chair or parliamentarian must then poll that delegation's members and record their votes "without regard to any state law, party rule, resolution or instruction binding the delegation or any member thereof to vote for or against any candidate or proposition."[95] Although the Convention Call specifies that delegates "pledged to a presidential candidate shall in good conscience reflect the sentiments of those who elected them,"[96] it appears the Democratic Party lacks an effective mechanism to enforce this requirement at the national convention. In other words, delegates may vote for someone other than the candidate to whom they are pledged. Convention officials will accept and count votes cast for any person who satisfies the eligibility requirements for the Democratic nomination (discussed above), regardless of whether that person's name was placed in nomination.[97] Any vote cast for an ineligible candidate is deemed a vote of "Present."[98]

The rules governing the 2020 Democratic National Convention contain a new provision specifying that only pledged delegates may participate in the first round of balloting for the presidential nominee; automatic delegates (superdelegates) are excluded.[99] All delegates, including automatic delegates, are eligible to participate in the second and subsequent rounds of balloting.[100]

---

[90] REPUBLICAN RULES, *supra* note 1, at 40, R.40(b)(2). At the 2016 convention, a candidate was required to submit a certificate signed by a majority of delegates from eight or more states. *Id.* at 40, R.40(b)(1).

[91] *Democratic Call*, *supra* note 4, at 16, § IX(C)(6)(d); REPUBLICAN RULES, *supra* note 1, at 41, R.40(c).

[92] *Democratic Call*, *supra* note 4, at 16, § IX(C)(7)(a); REPUBLICAN RULES, *supra* note 1, at 40, R.40(a).

[93] *Democratic Call*, *supra* note 4, at 18, § IX(F)(3)(c).

[94] *Id.* at 18, § IX(F)(3)(f)–(g).

[95] *Id.* at 18, § IX(F)(3)(f).

[96] *Id.* at 18, § IX(F)(3)(d); *accord Democratic Delegate Selection Rules*, *supra* note 19, at 14, R.13(J).

[97] *Democratic Call*, *supra* note 4, at 16, § IX(C)(7)(e).

[98] *Id.*

[99] *Id.* at 16, § IX(C)(7)(b). Unpledged delegates (superdelegates) may participate in the first round only if a presidential candidate has enough pledged delegates to guarantee the nomination mathematically. *Id.*

[100] *Id.* at 16, § IX(C)(7)(c).

To win the nomination, a candidate must receive "[a] majority of all Convention delegates eligible to vote on the ballot in question."[101] This means that a candidate may win during the first round of voting by receiving a majority of only pledged delegate votes (i.e., 1,885 votes); to win during later rounds, a candidate must receive a majority of all delegate votes (i.e., 2,267 votes). The convention holds as many rounds of balloting as necessary until a candidate wins the nomination.[102]

The Republican rules for conducting a roll-call vote are similar, but its method of binding delegates is much more effective. The name of each state and territory is called in alphabetical order, and the delegation's chair responds by announcing the number of votes from that delegation for each presidential candidate.[103] If any member of the delegation objects to the delegation chair's announcement, the convention chair must poll the delegation's members and record their votes.[104] The Republican Rules specify, however, that a delegate's vote for President shall be recorded in accordance with his or her binding, regardless of the candidate for which the delegation chair or delegate attempts to cast it.[105] A vote cast in accordance with a delegate's binding must be counted, even if the candidate for whom it was cast did not have his or her name entered into nomination at the national convention.[106] A candidate must receive a majority of all votes entitled to be cast at the convention to win the nomination,[107] and the convention holds as many rounds of balloting as necessary until that occurs.[108]

For both parties, after the presidential candidate is nominated, the vice-presidential candidate is nominated through substantially the same process, except the Democratic Party allows automatic delegates to participate in the first round of voting.[109] Usually, both conventions simply approve the President's desired running mate by acclamation.

---

[101]   *Id.* at 16, § IX(C)(7)(d).

[102]   *Id.* at 16, § IX(C)(7)(f).

[103]   REPUBLICAN RULES, *supra* note 1, at 38, R.37(a)–(b).

[104]   *Id.* at 38, R.37(b).

[105]   *Id.* at 38, R.37(b); *see also id.* at 19, R.16(a)(2) ("The Secretary of the Convention shall faithfully announce and record each delegate's vote in accordance with the delegate's obligation under Rule No. 16(a)(1), state law, or state party rule.").

[106]   *Id.* at 19, R.16(a)(2).

[107]   *Id.* at 41, R.40(d).

[108]   *Id.* at 41, R.40(e).

[109]   *Democratic Call, supra* note 4, at 17, § IX(C)(9), (10); REPUBLICAN RULES, *supra* note 1, at 40–41, R.40.

II. MANIPULATING THE CONVENTION RULES

A national convention's rules govern numerous critical issues that can directly impact the convention's outcome and determine the effects of the millions of votes cast throughout the nation in presidential preference primaries and caucuses. This part explores the rules most likely to affect a party's nomination.

A. *Rules Governing Delegate Voting, Binding, and Candidate Eligibility*

Most basically, national convention rules determine which delegates to the convention may vote on the presidential nominee, and when they may do so. The Democratic rules, for example, presently prohibit unpledged automatic delegates (superdelegates) from participating in the first round of voting on the nominee.[110] The rules further specify that a candidate needs to receive votes from only a majority of "Convention delegates eligible to vote on the ballot in question" to win the nomination.[111] Thus, a presidential candidate who is supported by a majority of pledged delegates could become the Democratic nominee, even if a majority of all delegates to the convention opposed him or her.

All delegates, however — including superdelegates — are entitled to vote on the rules governing the convention.[112] Superdelegates may attempt to use this power to remove the constraints on their participation in the nomination process. For example, at the convention's outset, a narrow majority of pledged delegates may support a presidential candidate whom most of the superdelegates oppose. Those superdelegates are free to join with the pledged delegates who also oppose that candidate to change the convention's rules so that superdelegates may participate in the first round of voting. Through one small tweak, the convention's outcome could be completely changed.

The rules likewise govern the effects of the presidential preference contests held throughout the nation in the months leading up to the convention. In most states, the only function of the presidential preference contest is to determine the presidential candidates to which some or all of that state's delegates to the national convention will be pledged or bound. The national convention's rules ultimately control the enforceability and consequences of such pledging or binding. Those rules specify whether national convention delegates may vote contrary to their pledges or binding, as well as the manner

---

[110]   *Democratic Call, supra* note 4, at 16, § IX(C)(7)(b); *see supra* note 99 and accompanying text.
[111]   *Democratic Call, supra* note 4, at 16, § IX(C)(7)(d).
[112]   *Id.* at 14–15, § IX(C)(1)(c), (C)(2).

in which pledging or binding will be enforced. Without enforceable binding rules, delegates are free to vote for whichever candidates they wish despite the results of presidential preference contests.

Binding rules are especially important in the Republican nomination process because the Republican rules generally give presidential candidates little, if any, voice in selecting the national convention delegates to be bound to them. Delegates may be bound to presidential candidates whom they actively oppose, and work to undermine those candidates' chances of success through their votes on the convention rules and credential disputes. The Democratic rules, in contrast, give presidential candidates a substantial voice in approving the delegates to be allocated or pledged to them. Even then, however, delegates may be "faithless" or change their minds about the candidates they support, though the risk is far less.

Consider a scenario in which a candidate enters the convention with a narrow majority of pledged or bound candidates. If some of those delegates oppose the candidate, they may join with delegates pledged or bound to other candidates to change the convention rules to eliminate pledges or binding. Alternatively, many Republican state parties currently bind their delegates for only the first round of voting. Delegates to the national convention could adopt the "two-thirds rule" for the first round of balloting, raising the percentage of votes a candidate needs to win the nomination in that round to 66.67 percent—a threshold the leading candidate may be unable to meet. Delegates whose binding expires after the first round of voting would be free to vote for whomever they wished during second and subsequent rounds. These strategies allow national convention delegates to effectively nullify the entire presidential preference process leading up to the convention. Due process and fundamental fairness suggest that delegates should not be able to alter the consequences of presidential preference contests after those contests have been held and the number (and identities) of delegates pledged or bound to each candidate are known.

Convention rules also have a substantial impact on whether so-called "white knight"[113] or "dark horse"[114] candidates, who did not do well or potentially even participate in presidential preference contests, may compete for the nomination. The rules determine who is eligible to be recognized as a potential candidate for the presidential nomination, the procedural requirements for

---

[113]   *See, e.g.*, Ralph Z. Hallow, *RNC Rules Panel Rejects Proposal to Simplify Convention Procedures*, WASH. TIMES, Apr. 22, 2016, www.washingtontimes.com/news/2016/apr/21/rnc-rules-panel-rejects-proposal-simplify-conventi/ [https://perma.cc/39S7-DS3P].

[114]   *See generally* LOUISE A. MAYO, PRESIDENT JAMES K. POLK: THE DARK HORSE PRESIDENT (2006).

potential candidates to be placed into nomination, and whether delegates may vote for eligible candidates who have not been formally placed into nomination. These procedures and requirements should be firmly established in advance, before the beneficiaries of any changes are definitively known.

Delegates at either convention also may vote to "suspend" the convention rules.[115] Thus, no matter what the rules provide, a sufficiently large coalition of delegates may simply decline to follow them if the convention takes an unexpected turn.

B. *The Unit Rule*

The unit rule is another measure that party leaders have applied over the years to tilt convention results in their favor. When a national convention adopts a unit rule, it typically allows each state party to decide whether its delegation must vote as a unit, meaning a majority of delegates from that state determine how all of the votes assigned to that state's delegates will be cast on each issue.[116] Early Democratic national conventions adopted the unit rule, but there is some debate over whether Republican national conventions ever did so.[117] Some claim the Republican Party employed the rule until 1880,[118] but historian Carl Becker has dismissed such contentions as "wide of the mark."[119]

As originally adopted at the first Democratic National Convention, the unit rule stated, "[I]n taking the vote[,] the majority of the delegates from each state [shall] designate the person by whom the votes for that state shall be given."[120] This provision required each state delegation to cast its votes through its chairman, who could decide for himself whether to cast the state's votes as

---

[115] *Democratic Call, supra* note 4, at 19, § IX(J); REPUBLICAN RULES, *supra* note 1, at 37, R.32. The rules of the Democratic National Convention may be suspended only by a two-thirds vote "of delegates voting." *Democratic Call, supra* note 4, at 19, § IX(J). A two-thirds requirement to suspend the rules likewise applies at the Republican Convention by virtue of the *Rules of the U.S. House of Representatives* (which the Republican convention rules incorporate by reference). *See* REPUBLICAN RULES, *supra* note 1, at 36, R.30; U.S. HOUSE R. XV(1)(a), 116th Cong. (Jan. 11, 2019).

[116] CQ PRESS, NATIONAL PARTY CONVENTIONS 1831–2008, at 38 (2010); *see also* EDWARD STANWOOD, A HISTORY OF THE PRESIDENCY FROM 1788 TO 1897, at 173 (new ed. 1926).

[117] Carl Becker, *The Unit Rule in National Nominating Conventions*, 5 AM. HIST. REV. 64, 80 (1899).

[118] STANWOOD, *supra* note 116, at 173–74.

[119] Becker, *supra* note 117, at 80.

[120] *Id.* at 66.

a unit.[121] In 1835, for example, at the second Democratic National Convention in Baltimore, Ohio cast all 21 of its votes for Richard M. Johnson.[122] An Ohio delegate protested that some of the state's delegates had not voted for Johnson, but the chair of the national convention ruled that it "was a matter for the delegation to decide for itself."[123]

Starting with the 1848 Democratic National Convention, the rule's wording was changed to provide, "[I]n voting upon any questions which may arise in the proceedings of the convention[,] the vote shall be taken by states at the request of any one state ... [T]he manner in which said vote is cast to be decided by the delegation of each state for itself."[124] Again, this provision authorized each state to decide for itself whether to apply the unit rule. Many state parties took advantage of this option, instructing their delegations to vote as units.[125] A qualification was added in 1860 specifying that, if a state party convention did not "provid[e] or direct[]" that the unit rule would apply to that state's delegates, the national convention "will recognize the right of each delegate to cast his individual vote."[126] Under this formulation, only a state convention—not the delegation itself or the delegation chair—could adopt unit voting for the state.[127]

In 1872, the rule was amended to empower state delegation chairs to implement unit voting for their respective states, at least when voting on nominations. It stated, "[I]n casting the vote for president and vice-president, the chairman of each delegation shall rise in his place and name how the delegation votes, and his statement alone shall be considered the vote of such state."[128] Thus, even if a state convention had not instructed its delegates to apply the unit rule, the state delegation's chairman could adopt it and the national convention was bound by his decision. Nevertheless, during the 1896 convention, the national convention chair suggested that the unit rule applied only if the state convention had instructed its delegation to use it.[129]

Early Democratic National Conventions had adopted the rule because they lacked control over the number of delegates each state party sent. At the second Democratic National Convention held in 1835, for example, 422

---

[121]   Daniel Klinghard, The Nationalization of American Political Parties, 1880–1896, at 47 (2010).

[122]   Becker, *supra* note 117, at 66.

[123]   *Id.*

[124]   *Id.*

[125]   Klinghard, *supra* note 121, at 47; *see also* Stanwood, *supra* note 116, at 173.

[126]   Becker, *supra* note 117, at 67.

[127]   *Id.* at 67–68.

[128]   *Id.* at 69.

[129]   *Id.* at 72–73.

of the 620 delegates were from four nearby states.[130] The Maryland Democratic state convention had elected all of its members as delegates to the national convention.[131] Allocating a vote to each delegate would have unfairly allowed those four states to control the outcome.[132] The national convention therefore voted that each state would be allocated the same number of votes it had in the Electoral College, and a majority of delegates from each state would determine the candidate for whom all of its votes would be cast.[133] Because Tennessee had failed to send any delegates to the convention, a Tennessee resident named Mr. Rucker, who happened to be visiting Baltimore that day, cast all fifteen of the state's votes.[134]

Even after the size of state delegations to the Democratic National Convention was better regulated, conventions continued to adopt the unit rule for political purposes. It prevented state delegation members from effectively canceling out each other's votes, thereby diluting the state's influence over selecting a nominee. The rule also enhanced the ability of state delegation chairs to influence the nomination process, enabling them to "silence political minorities" and either "double or eliminate entirely the influence of a faction or a group within a delegation."[135] By persuading just a few delegates from his state, a state delegation chair could swing the state's entire vote.[136] Conversely, the rule precluded a delegate who preferred a different candidate than the rest of his or her delegation from joining with other delegates across state lines to form a national coalition.[137]

A main justification for the unit rule was that "national delegates were agents of the state conventions, nor direct representatives of the people."[138] A state convention therefore had the right to determine how votes allocated to that state would be counted. One problematic consequence of the unit rule, however, is that a presidential candidate could be nominated with the support of only a minority of national convention delegates.[139] It allowed a candidate supported by slim majorities of delegates in a few large states

---

[130]   C. S. Potts, *The Unit Rule and the Two-Thirds Rule: Undemocratic Devices Used by the Democratic Party*, 45 AM. REV. OF REVS. 705, 706 (1912); STANWOOD, *supra* note 116, at 181–82.
[131]   Potts, *supra* note 130, at 706; STANWOOD, *supra* note 116, at 181–82.
[132]   KLINGHARD, *supra* note 121, at 47; *see also* STANWOOD, *supra* note 116, at 173.
[133]   Potts, *supra* note 130, at 706; STANWOOD, *supra* note 116, at 181–82.
[134]   Potts, *supra* note 130, at 706; *see also* STANWOOD, *supra* note 116, at 182.
[135]   KLINGHARD, *supra* note 121, at 48; *see also* STANWOOD, *supra* note 116, at 173.
[136]   Potts, *supra* note 130, at 707.
[137]   KLINGHARD, *supra* note 121, at 48.
[138]   *Id.* at 47.
[139]   *Id.*

to receive all of those states' votes, which could be enough to secure the nomination.

In recent years, both the Democratic[140] and Republican[141] parties have prohibited state delegations from imposing a unit rule. Nothing stops national convention delegates from adopting the rule at the convention's outset, however, when it appears politically advantageous.

C. *The Two-Thirds Rule*

One of the most fundamental rules for a presidential nominating convention concerns the percentage of votes a candidate must receive to win the nomination. As its name suggests, the two-thirds rule provides that a candidate must receive votes from two-thirds of the delegates at the convention to win. The rule was exclusively a Democratic Party innovation;[142] the party retained it until the 1968 convention.[143] The Republicans, in contrast, never adopted it.[144]

President Andrew Jackson's allies introduced the rule at the first Democratic National Convention in 1832.[145] Due to Jackson's overwhelming popularity, the convention's primary purpose was to determine the Democrats' nominee for Vice President. The delegates barely debated the two-thirds rule since most were willing to defer to Jackson's wish to have Martin Van Buren as his running mate,[146] and Van Buren easily cleared the two-thirds threshold on the first ballot.[147]

Some supporters of the rule claimed it ensured that the nominee reflected the consensus of the party and gave the nomination "a more imposing

---

[140] *Democratic Delegate Selection Rules, supra* note 19, at 17, R.18(A) ("The unit rule, or any rule or practice whereby all members of a Party unit or delegation may be required to cast their votes in accordance with the will of a majority of the body, shall not be used at any stage of the delegate selection process."); *see also Democratic Call, supra* note 4, at 17, § IX(F)(3)(f) (requiring national convention leaders to poll a state's delegates and record their votes whenever one of the delegation's members objects to the delegation chair's announcement of their votes).

[141] REPUBLICAN RULES, *supra* note 1, at 39, R. 38 ("No delegate or alternate delegate shall be bound by any attempt of any state or congressional district to impose the unit rule."). The Republican Rules define "unit rule" as "a rule or law under which a delegation at the national convention casts its entire vote as a unit as determined by a majority of the delegation." *Id.* The prohibition on the unit rule does not prevent enforcement of delegate binding requirements. *Id.*

[142] Becker, *supra* note 117, at 64.

[143] CQ PRESS, *supra* note 116, at 38.

[144] Becker, *supra* note 117, at 64.

[145] *Id.*

[146] STANWOOD, *supra* note 116, at 159–61; *see also* Potts, *supra* note 130, at 706.

[147] STANWOOD, *supra* note 116, at 161.

effect."[148] It also helped dampen the effects of the unit rule, which allowed a majority of a state's delegation to determine the candidate for whom all of that state's votes would be cast. Under the unit rule, as discussed above, a delegate supported only by a bare majority of delegates in a few large states could secure the nomination, even though a majority of delegates across the convention opposed him. By requiring candidates to receive a supermajority of delegates' votes to win, the two-thirds rule offset some of the artificially inflated support the unit rule might provide and encouraged candidates to amass geographically wider support.[149]

Critics, on the other hand, complained the two-thirds rule allowed a determined minority to frustrate the will of the majority and sometimes resulted in the selection of compromise candidates whom neither faction preferred.[150] It also was inconsistent with basic majority-rule principles of Jeffersonian democracy. Moreover, the rule frequently "produced protracted, multiballot conventions, often giving the Democrats a degree of turbulence the Republicans, requiring only a simple majority, did not have."[151] Neither party currently uses the rule, though delegates remain free to re-introduce it, should it provide a strategic advantage.

III. HISTORICAL EXAMPLES OF CONVENTION RULE DISPUTES

Over the years, party leaders and delegates have attempted to manipulate national convention rules to benefit candidates they supported. Sometimes, rule changes were intended primarily to improve the optics of the convention, rather than affect its outcome. For example, in 2012, Mitt Romney entered the convention with an overwhelming majority of delegates. At the time, Republican Rule 40(b) required a potential candidate to demonstrate support from a plurality of delegates from only five or more states to have his or her name placed into nomination.[152] Romney's supporters amended the rule to require a candidate to "demonstrate the support of a majority of the delegates from each of eight (8) or more states"[153] to be placed into nomination. The amendment prevented Ron Paul's supporters from including his name on the

---

[148] Potts, *supra* note 130, at 707; *see also* Becker, *supra* note 117, at 64.
[149] Becker, *supra* note 117, at 65.
[150] Potts, *supra* note 130, at 707.
[151] CQ PRESS, *supra* note 116, at 38.
[152] Alan Fram, *Candidates with the Muscle Could Alter GOP Convention Rules*, ASSOC. PRESS (Apr. 11, 2016), www.startribune.com/candidates-with-the-muscle-could-alter-gop-convention-rules/375219751/ [perma.cc/A8R3-M76A].
[153] REPUBLICAN RULES, *supra* note 1, at 40, R.40(b)(1).

ballot and consuming valuable convention time with speeches supporting him that would highlight divisions within the party and deflect public attention from Romney.[154]

Far more pernicious are rule changes that directly impact the selection of a nominee. This part of the chapter examines historical examples of how political insiders have changed, or attempted to change, key rules to control the outcome of nominating conventions. It begins by explaining how the two-thirds rule led to the nomination of dark horse candidate James K. Polk at the Democratic National Convention of 1844. It then discusses disputes over the unit rule underlying the nominations of James Garfield at the Republican National Convention of 1880 and Hubert Humphrey at the Democratic National Convention of 1968. Finally, this part concludes by discussing how delegate binding rules ensured Jimmy Carter's nomination at the 1980 Democratic National Convention.

A. *The Two-Thirds Rule and the Democratic National Convention of 1844*

The two-thirds rule played a prominent role at the 1844 Democratic National Convention, leading to the nomination of dark horse candidate James K. Polk, a former Speaker of the U.S. House and Governor of Tennessee.[155] Throughout most of the Democratic Party's nomination process, former President Martin Van Buren was heavily favored to win the party's nomination,[156] having prevailed in 16 out of 26 state conventions.[157] A few weeks before the convention, however, President John Tyler signed a treaty to annex Texas.[158] Van Buren's public opposition to the annexation made him unelectable to many delegates and Members of Congress.[159] It also "offered a most convenient excuse for party leaders who had been cool or secretly hostile to his candidacy to repudiate his pretensions openly."[160]

Although a majority of delegates still supported Van Buren, the controversy precluded him from winning a supermajority of delegate votes.[161] Accordingly,

---

[154] Fram, *supra* note 152.
[155] Robert S. Lambert, *The Democratic National Convention of 1844*, 1 Tenn. Hist. Q. 3, 3 (1955).
[156] Stanwood, *supra* note 116, at 191; Lambert, *supra* note 155, at 3–4.
[157] 1 Gil Troy, et al., History of American Presidential Elections 1789–2008, at 334 (4th ed. 2012); *see also* John Niven, Martin Van Buren: The Romantic Age of American Politics 523 (1983).
[158] Troy, *supra* note 157, at 339.
[159] Niven, *supra* note 157, at 531; *see also* Stanwood, *supra* note 116, at 210.
[160] Lambert, *supra* note 155, at 6.
[161] Niven, *supra* note 157, at 534.

his opponents "labored day and night" lobbying delegates to adopt a two-thirds rule to block his nomination.[162] The rule was especially attractive to delegates who were personally opposed to Van Buren, but whose state parties had instructed them to vote for him since he had won their state conventions.[163]

Twenty minutes before the convention's official start time and before all of the delegates had even arrived,[164] Congressman Romulus Saunders of North Carolina tried to rush through adoption of the two-thirds rule before Van Buren's supporters could put up a fight.[165] Saunders unilaterally called the convention to order and declared that an ally, Hendrick Wright, had been elected by voice vote as temporary convention chair.[166] Saunders then immediately moved that the convention adopt the same rules as the 1832 and 1835 conventions, which included the two-thirds rule.[167] Another delegate objected, however, that the convention could not vote on rules until it approved an official roster of delegates.[168] Wright agreed; after prayers, he formed committees on credentials and permanent organization.[169]

One of Van Buren's allies subsequently moved that the convention create a Rules Committee, but Saunders responded by proposing an amendment that would instead simply adopt the rules governing the previous Democratic conventions.[170] Desperate to defeat the two-thirds rule, Van Buren's supporters moved that the convention apply the unit rule in counting the votes on those pending issues.[171] The convention rejected the unit rule, and the chair ruled that each state delegation could instead decide for itself whether to vote as a unit or instead allow individual delegates to vote how they wished.[172] Applying that voting procedure, the convention adopted the two-thirds rule by a small majority, 148 to 118 [173] (some reports claim 148 to 116).[174] Northern delegates from states that Van Buren had won—who were pledged to vote for

---

[162]   TROY, *supra* note 157, at 342.
[163]   Potts, *supra* note 130, at 708.
[164]   Lambert, *supra* note 155, at 8.
[165]   NIVEN, *supra* note 157, at 535.
[166]   *Id.* at 535–56; TROY, *supra* note 157, at 343–44.
[167]   TROY, *supra* note 157, at 344. Stanwood and Lambert contend that Saunders referenced the rules of the 1832 convention, *see* STANWOOD, *supra* note 116, at 212; Lambert, *supra* note 155, at 9, while Niven asserts that he referred to the conventions of 1836 and 1840. NIVEN, *supra* note 157, at 536.
[168]   NIVEN, *supra* note 157, at 536; TROY, *supra* note 157, at 344.
[169]   TROY, *supra* note 157, at 344; Lambert, *supra* note 155, at 9.
[170]   NIVEN, *supra* note 157, at 537. TROY, *supra* note 157, at 344.
[171]   TROY, *supra* note 157, at 344.
[172]   Lambert, *supra* note 155, at 10.
[173]   CQ PRESS, *supra* note 116, at 53, 204; Potts, *supra* note 130, at 708.
[174]   TROY, *supra* note 157, at 344; *see also* NIVEN, *supra* note 157, at 538.

his nomination—could have defeated the rule, but they voted to adopt it specifically to prevent his nomination.[175]

In the first round of voting on the presidential nomination, Van Buren received a majority with 146 votes, but fell short of the 177 necessary under the two-thirds rule.[176] Lewis Cass, former Secretary of War and Ambassador to France, won 84 votes.[177] Over the next several rounds of balloting, Cass took increasing numbers of votes from Van Buren.[178] Desperate to block Cass's nomination, Van Buren's supporters convinced the New York delegation to switch their votes from Van Buren to former Tennessee Governor James K. Polk.[179] Polk was an acceptable choice because he was a firm Jacksonian and Van Buren supporter, but also supported the annexation of Texas.[180] Once word spread of New York's decision, other states switched their votes to Polk, and he overwhelmingly won the nomination on the ninth ballot.[181]

Senator Thomas Hart Benton of Missouri complained that, due to the convention's machinations, the people had "no more control over the selection of the man who is to be President than the subjects of a king have over the birth of the child who is to be their ruler."[182] Historian C. S. Potts agreed, declaring, "The will of the people, as expressed by the instructions to a majority of the delegates, was ruthlessly disregarded and a man upon whom the voters had had no opportunity to pass was put forward as the party's choice for President."[183]

B. *The Unit Rule and the Republican National Convention of 1880*

The unit rule was a major focus of the Republican National Convention of 1880.[184] Because President Rutherford B. Hayes had declined to run for a second term, the three major contenders for the Republican nomination were former President Ulysses S. Grant, Maine Senator James G. Blaine, and Treasury Secretary John Sherman.[185] Grant, a renowned Civil War general,

---

[175] STANWOOD, *supra* note 116, at 212; Lambert, *supra* note 155, at 10.
[176] TROY, *supra* note 157, at 344; *see also* NIVEN, *supra* note 157, at 538.
[177] TROY, *supra* note 157, at 344.
[178] NIVEN, *supra* note 157, at 538; TROY, *supra* note 157, at 344; CQ PRESS, *supra* note 116, at 204.
[179] NIVEN, *supra* note 157, at 539; TROY, *supra* note 157, at 347; CQ PRESS, *supra* note 116, at 204.
[180] NIVEN, *supra* note 157, at 539; TROY, *supra* note 157, at 342.
[181] NIVEN, *supra* note 157, at 540; TROY, *supra* note 157, at 347.
[182] Potts, *supra* note 130, at 708.
[183] *Id.* at 709.
[184] For additional background on the 1880 convention, see Frank B. Evans, *Wharton Barker and the Republican National Convention of 1880*, 27 PA. HIST. J. MID-ATL. STUD. 28 (1960).
[185] HERBERT J. CLANCY, THE PRESIDENTIAL ELECTION OF 1880, at 35 (1958); KENNETH D. ACKERMAN, DARK HORSE: THE SURPRISE ELECTION AND POLITICAL MURDER OF PRESIDENT JAMES A. GARFIELD 21, 31 (2003).

had already served two terms as President from 1869 through 1876. His tenure had been marked by corruption and political patronage, and a third term would have violated the precedent set by George Washington of serving only two terms.[186] Among Grant's most important supporters were New York Senator Roscoe Conkling and Republican National Committee chair Don Cameron.[187] Senator-elect James Garfield of Ohio, another Civil War general and former House Minority Leader, instead supported Sherman and had agreed to place his name into nomination at the convention.[188]

The convention was comprised of 756 delegates; a candidate needed 379 votes to secure the nomination.[189] Entering the convention, Grant and Blaine each were supported by approximately 300 delegates, with many of the remaining delegates backing Sherman.[190] Sherman's only hope was that Grant and Blaine would deadlock and one would eventually release his delegates to Sherman.[191]

Grant hoped to win on the first ballot, with Cameron's assistance, by having the convention impose the unit rule on all state delegations.[192] While individual states had imposed the unit rule on their own delegations in earlier conventions, no previous Republican national convention had ever adopted it as a compulsory requirement.[193] Several states had instructed their delegations to vote as units at the 1880 convention, but many delegates announced that they intended to ignore those instructions.[194] If the convention did not impose a unit rule, Grant would lose 63 votes from Pennsylvania, Illinois, and New York, preventing him from reaching a majority.[195] With the unit rule in place, however, Grant would be able to sweep the nomination on the first round of balloting, despite being supported by only a minority of delegates.

As RNC chair, Cameron would be responsible for opening the convention and running it until the delegates selected a temporary convention chair.[196] He planned to apply the unit rule unilaterally when the delegates voted on a temporary convention chair, in order to ensure the election of a Grant supporter. A friendly chair could then continue to apply the unit rule to all

---

[186]   ACKERMAN, *supra* note 185, at 49.
[187]   *Id.* at 49.
[188]   CLANCY, *supra* note 185, at 35; ACKERMAN, *supra* note 185, at 26.
[189]   CLANCY, *supra* note 185, at 83.
[190]   ACKERMAN, *supra* note 185, at 19.
[191]   CLANCY, *supra* note 185, at 87.
[192]   *Id.* at 51, 83; ACKERMAN, *supra* note 185, at 54.
[193]   ACKERMAN, *supra* note 185, at 34 & n.3.
[194]   Becker, *supra* note 117, at 77.
[195]   CLANCY, *supra* note 185, at 83–84.
[196]   *Id.* at 84.

subsequent votes, including any attempts to reject or repeal the rule, as well as the ultimate vote on the nomination.[197]

A majority of RNC members opposed Grant, however, and worked together to frustrate Cameron's plans.[198] The RNC met in late May 1880, a few days before the convention began.[199] Grant's opponents on the committee moved to prevent the convention from adopting a unit rule. As RNC chair, Cameron ruled any motions concerning the convention's rules out of order, on the grounds that the convention itself was the proper forum for determining them.[200] He likewise rejected all efforts to appeal his rulings on the issue.[201] His actions antagonized the RNC's anti-Grant majority, leading many members to consider ousting him as chairman.[202] To prevent his removal, Cameron compromised with the anti-Grant members by agreeing that Senator George F. Hoar, who did not support any of the candidates for the presidential nomination, would serve as both temporary and permanent convention chair.[203] Cameron also conceded that the unit rule would not apply at the convention unless the delegates voted to adopt it.[204]

When the convention began, Hoar was duly elected as chair[205] and Garfield was selected as chair of the Rules Committee.[206] Senator Conkling, a Grant supporter, offered a resolution declaring that "every member of [the national convention] is bound in honor to support its nominee, whoever that nominee may be; and that no man should hold a seat here who is not ready to so agree."[207] Although the measure received overwhelming support in a voice vote, Conkling heard a few people opposing it and demanded a roll-call vote.[208] The resolution passed 716 to 3; only three delegates from West Virginia went on record opposing it.[209]

Conkling then overplayed his hand by moving to strip the votes of the three delegates who had voted against the resolution.[210] Garfield rose in opposition

---

[197] *Id.*

[198] *Id.* at 83, 85.

[199] *Id.* at 85.

[200] *Id.* at 84-85; ACKERMAN, *supra* note 185, at 59.

[201] ACKERMAN, *supra* note 185, at 59.

[202] CLANCY, *supra* note 185, at 85; Becker, *supra* note 117, at 78.

[203] CLANCY, *supra* note 185, at 85–86; ACKERMAN, *supra* note 185, at 63.

[204] CLANCY, *supra* note 185, at 86; ACKERMAN, *supra* note 185, at 65.

[205] PROCEEDINGS OF THE REPUBLICAN NATIONAL CONVENTION HELD AT CHICAGO, ILLINOIS 5, 22 (1881) [hereinafter CONVENTION PROCEEDINGS].

[206] CLANCY, *supra* note 185, at 88–89.

[207] CONVENTION PROCEEDINGS, *supra* note 205, at 34.

[208] *Id.* at 35.

[209] *Id.* at 35–36.

[210] *Id.* at 36.

to the motion, declaring that the convention was "about to commit a great error."[211] He argued that delegates must be free to vote however they wished on any resolution, and "are responsible for those votes to [their] constituents, and to them alone."[212] Garfield added that he knew one of the three dissenting delegates, and the convention could not reasonably disenfranchise or expel him. For over twenty years, during the "dark days of slavery," the unnamed delegate had "stood up for liberty with a clear-sighted courage and a brave heart equal to that of the best Republican who lives on this globe."[213] When Conkling resumed the podium, the convention booed and hissed at him, and he withdrew his motion.[214] Garfield's defense of the delegates was a stinging defeat for Conkling[215] — and, by extension, Grant — and made Garfield "the man of the hour."[216]

As chair of the Rules Committee, Garfield then presented the committee's majority report.[217] The committee proposed the same rules that had governed the previous convention, except it recommended a new Rule 8.[218] The proposed new rule provided that, in any recorded vote, each state delegation chair would "announce the number of votes cast for any candidate or for or against any proposition."[219] If any of that state's delegates objected to the "correctness of such announcement," he could demand a roll-call vote of the delegation's members "and the result shall be recorded in accordance with the votes individually given."[220] The Rules Committee also presented a minority report which sought to preserve the unit rule.[221] The minority report's recommendation was similar to the proposed Rule 8, except it omitted the proviso allowing delegates to object to the vote tallies announced by their state chairs.[222]

After a delegate unsuccessfully moved to "proceed immediately to ballot for candidates for President and Vice-President of the United States" without adopting any rules,[223] the convention adopted the majority report, including Rule 8, by voice vote.[224] In doing so, Hoar did not apply the unit rule, as

[211]   *Id.* at 40.
[212]   *Id.*
[213]   *Id.* at 41.
[214]   ACKERMAN, *supra* note 185, at 83.
[215]   *Id.* at 83–84.
[216]   CLANCY, *supra* note 185, at 92.
[217]   CONVENTION PROCEEDINGS, *supra* note 205, at 43.
[218]   *Id.* at 44.
[219]   *Id.*
[220]   *Id.*
[221]   *Id.*
[222]   *Id.*
[223]   *Id.* at 158.
[224]   *Id.* at 160; *see also* Becker, *supra* note 117, at 79.

Cameron had planned to do, but rather allowed delegates to vote individually.[225]

When the convention turned to selecting a presidential candidate, Grant won 304 votes in the first round of balloting, far short of the 379 he needed to win.[226] Blaine received 284 votes; Sherman got 93; and other candidates a total of 74.[227] Garfield did not receive any.[228] The convention held 27 more rounds of balloting throughout the day. By the evening, Grant's vote tally had grown slightly to 307, Blaine's had fallen to 279, and Sherman's eroded to 91.[229] Garfield, who had not declared himself as a candidate, received two votes.[230]

On the 34th ballot, Wisconsin shocked the convention by casting sixteen of its twenty votes for Garfield.[231] One history of the convention explains that "a rich harvest of conspiracy theories has grown up around what actually might have preceded the Wisconsin break."[232] Garfield himself objected to the votes on the grounds he had not consented to be nominated, but Hoar ruled the objection out of order.[233] In the next round of balloting, most of Indiana's thirty delegates, as well as a few delegates from some other states, joined Wisconsin's delegates, bringing Garfield's vote total up to fifty.[234] Due to the ongoing deadlock and Garfield's growing support, Blaine and Sherman both released their delegates to him.[235] Bolstered by Blaine's and Sherman's former supporters, Garfield went over the top on the 36th ballot, winning the nomination.[236] Had Cameron been able to impose the unit rule at the outset of the convention, Grant would have won in the first round of balloting.

C. *The Unit Rule and the Democratic National Convention of 1968*

Candidates also strategized over the unit rule at the 1968 Democratic National Convention. President Lyndon B. Johnson had withdrawn from the

---

[225] ACKERMAN, *supra* note 185, at 80; *see also* CONVENTION PROCEEDINGS, *supra* note 205, at 32.
[226] CONVENTION PROCEEDINGS, *supra* note 205, at 197.
[227] *Id.*
[228] *Id.*
[229] ACKERMAN, *supra* note 185, at 101.
[230] *Id.*
[231] *Id.* at 108; CONVENTION PROCEEDINGS, *supra* note 205, at 268.
[232] ACKERMAN, *supra* note 185, at 101.
[233] CONVENTION PROCEEDINGS, *supra* note 205, at 269.
[234] *Id.* at 269–70.
[235] ACKERMAN, *supra* note 185, at 110–11.
[236] CONVENTION PROCEEDINGS, *supra* note 205, at 270. Even in victory, Garfield made it a point to emphasize that he had not sought the nomination and had done everything possible to help Sherman win it. ACKERMAN, *supra* note 185, at 113–14.

presidential race in early 1968 because public opposition to the Vietnam War had grown dramatically following the Vietcong's Tet Offensive.[237] His decision left Vice President Hubert Humphrey free to seek the nomination, but it was too late for Humphrey to run in most primaries. Humphrey's main strategy was to win over national convention delegates pledged to states' "favorite sons" who were not running serious national campaigns.[238]

Senator Eugene McCarthy was running as an anti-war candidate.[239] After seeing McCarthy's success early in the nomination process, Senator Robert Kennedy also entered the race opposing Vietnam.[240] He lost the Oregon primary, however, and was assassinated the night he won the California primary.[241]

To win the Democratic nomination, a candidate had to receive 1,312 votes at the national convention.[242] Because only 14 states had held presidential preference contests, none of the candidates entered the convention with anything close to a majority of pledged delegates.[243] Governors and party officials controlled most of the other delegations' votes.[244]

McCarthy's supporters on the Rules Committee attempted to bolster his candidacy by prohibiting state delegations from imposing the unit rule.[245] By 1968, only Southern states retained it.[246] McCarthy thought that, without the rule, he could build a coalition comprised of the delegates he had won in the primaries and uncommitted delegates from states where the majority of the delegation supported Humphrey. Southern leaders opposed his proposal, believing that abolishing the unit rule during the convention "would be like 'changing the rules in the final quarter of the game.'"[247]

The Rules Committee left the issue for the convention to resolve.[248] After a "furious floor fight" over the rule, the convention voted 1,350 to 1,206 to

---

[237] LAWRENCE O'DONNELL, PLAYING WITH FIRE 95, 126, 228 (2017).

[238] *Id.* at 244, 246, 250–51, 319.

[239] *Id.* at 20–23, 94–95.

[240] *Id.* at 183.

[241] *Id.* at 271. Only two weeks before the convention, Senator George McGovern entered the race as another peace candidate, backed by many of Kennedy's former supporters. *Id.* at 261, 340. Having not run in any presidential preference contests, he counted on appealing directly to individual delegates. *Id.* at 340.

[242] *Id.* at 121.

[243] O'DONNELL, *supra* note 237, at 121.

[244] *Id.* at 224; *see also id.* at 327.

[245] *Id.* at 325.

[246] LEWIS CHESTER, ET AL., AN AMERICAN MELODRAMA: THE PRESIDENTIAL CAMPAIGN OF 1968, at 556 (1969).

[247] *Id.* at 557.

[248] O'DONNELL, *supra* note 237, at 326.

eliminate it not only at the national convention, but for future state and local conventions, as well.[249] Despite McCarthy's procedural victory in abolishing the unit rule, Humphrey still won the nomination by 1,760.25 votes to McCarthy's 601.[250] The 1968 Democratic National Convention is a vivid example of a successful last-minute rule change that exacerbated internal divisions within the party, yet fell far short of allowing its intended beneficiary to win the nomination.

D. *Delegate Binding and the Democratic National Convention of 1980*

Senator Edward M. Kennedy attempted to wrest the presidential nomination from President Jimmy Carter at the 1980 Democratic National Convention by unbinding delegates. Carter had started the nomination cycle strong, beating Kennedy in almost every primary. As the Iranian hostage crisis dragged on and economic stagflation persisted, however, Carter's support eroded and Kennedy won several primaries, including those in California and New York. Carter also faced a scandal shortly before the convention when the public learned that his brother, Billy Carter, misled government investigators about his work as an agent for Muammar Gaddafi's Libyan government.[251] Carter's 22 percent Harris poll rating was "a new low for him or any modern President."[252]

Carter was slated to enter the convention with 1981.1 of the convention's 3,331 delegates—well over half—pledged or "bound" to him.[253] Kennedy had only 1,225.8 delegates pledged to him.[254] 122.1 delegates were uncommitted, and two were committed to other candidates.[255] If delegates were required to vote in accordance with their pledges, Carter would win. Kennedy's only hope was to free delegates to vote for whomever they wished.

In the weeks before the convention, a group of Democratic members of the U.S. House of Representatives formed the "Committee to Continue the Open

---

[249] CHESTER, *supra* note 246, at 558.
[250] O'DONNELL, *supra* note 237, at 373. George McGovern claimed 146.5 votes and other candidates received a total of 80.25. *Id.*
[251] Peter Elkind, *The Many Faces of Billy Carter's Side of the Libya Affair*, WASH. POST, Aug. 1, 1980, www.washingtonpost.com/archive/politics/1980/08/01/the-many-faces-of-billy-car ters-side-of-the-libya-affair/e0660ofb-c060-4aef-b7fd-9c4445e0a667/?utm_term=.40 d584a27d87 [https://perma.cc/N7QA-BDMW].
[252] Peter Goldman, *The Drive to Dump Carter*, NEWSWEEK, Aug. 11, 1980, at 18.
[253] *Divided Democrats Renominate Carter, in* CQ ALMANAC 1980, at 85-B, 89-B (36th ed., 1981) [hereinafter *Divided Democrats*].
[254] *Id.*
[255] *Id.*

Convention," chaired by nationally renowned litigator Edward Bennett Williams of Williams & Connolly LLP.[256] At the press conference announcing the committee, Williams declared that binding delegates "would undo 148 years of Democratic history and reduce [delegates] to 'nothing more than robots or automatons.'"[257] Delegates, he argued, should not be "led like lemmings to the sea" or "be required to wear 'gags, earmuffs and blinders.'"[258] The Committee raised $200,000; opened offices in Washington, D.C. and New York City, where the convention would be held;[259] and operated telephone banks to persuade delegates to vote to unbind themselves.[260]

The convention's Rules Committee met several weeks prior to the convention to prepare a report proposing permanent rules for the convention. Approximately two-thirds of the Committee's members were Carter supporters, and it voted 87 to 66 in favor of binding delegates.[261] The measure, Proposed Rule F(3)(c), provided that "All delegates to the national convention shall be bound to vote for the Presidential candidate whom they were elected to support for at least the first convention ballot," unless that candidate released them to vote for someone else.[262] If a delegate violated this rule, the candidate to whom they were pledged could replace them with an alternate delegate pledged to that candidate.[263] A minority report accompanying the proposal contained Minority Rule #5, which rejected Proposed Rule F(3)(c) and left delegates free to vote for whichever candidate they wished.[264]

At the convention, Dianne Feinstein, then Mayor of San Francisco, cogently argued that unbinding delegates "would deny the 19 million voters in the Democratic primaries their rightful voice at the convention. She charged that the Kennedy forces were 'the losing team,' demanding extra innings after losing the primaries and caucuses."[265] Echoing these sentiments,

---

[256] Evan Thomas, Edward Bennett Williams: The Man to See 373 (1991).

[257] Goldman, *supra* note 252, at 18.

[258] *Id.*

[259] *Id.*

[260] Bill Peterson & T. R. Reid, *Democratic Warriors Knuckle Down*, Wash. Post, Aug. 2, 1980, www.washingtonpost.com/archive/politics/1980/08/02/democratic-warriors-knuckle-down/9bc65975-e354-4913-848e-1fa3cd9265f0/?utm_term=.0c443d2f9a18 [https://perma.cc/99GE-E8HJ].

[261] James Doyle, *Vowing Defiance to the End*, Time, July 21, 1980, at 21.

[262] A. O. Sulzberger Jr., *Democrats Weigh Rule Binding Delegates*, N.Y. Times, July 31, 1980, at A1.

[263] *Id.*

[264] CQ Press, *supra* note 116, at 260 n.1 (2010).

[265] David S. Broder & Edward Walsh, *Kennedy Ends Fight for Nomination*, Wash. Post, Aug. 12, 1980.

Senator Abraham A. Ribicoff of Connecticut emphasized "that both the candidates had competed through the primaries with the understanding that delegate commitments were binding and 'it isn't fair to change the rules now.'"[266] Williams, in contrast, exhorted President Carter to "[b]e confident" and "trust the delegates.... . Let them vote for you in freedom and not in compulsion."[267]

The convention voted 1,936.4 to 1,390.6 to reject Minority Rule #5, then adopted the Rules Committee report containing Proposed Rule F(c)(3), binding delegates.[268] Most of the uncommitted delegates had sided with Kennedy by voting for Minority Rule #5 to prevent binding, but very few delegates pledged to Carter did so.[269] Following the vote, Kennedy withdrew his candidacy, leaving Carter unchallenged for the nomination.[270] Carter won with 2,123 votes, far exceeding Kennedy's 1,150.5 votes and the 54.5 votes split by assorted other candidates.[271]

IV. CONCLUSION

National convention rules should be established before a presidential election cycle begins. A national party should not allow delegates to adopt, amend, or suspend the rules at the convention itself, after the outcomes of the presidential preference contests and identities of the delegates are known.[272] Convention delegates who disagree with the results of primaries and caucuses should not be able to nullify them after the fact by eliminating delegate binding, altering the rules for delegate voting, or modifying the requirements for a candidate to win the nomination. Determining or changing the consequences of votes in an election after they have been cast is unfair, manifests disrespect for the millions of voters who participated in presidential preference contests, and undermines the public legitimacy of the nomination process.

Allowing the convention rules to be manipulated also fosters discord within a political party at the very time it should be coalescing around a presidential candidate. The opportunity to craft or change convention rules creates incentives for presidential candidates who lost in the primaries and caucuses, or did

---

[266] *Id.*

[267] *Id.*

[268] *Divided Democrats, supra* note 253, at 85-B, 89-B.

[269] *Id.*

[270] David S. Broder & Edward Walsh, *Kennedy Ends Fight for Nomination*, Wash. Post, Aug. 12, 1980.

[271] CQ Press, *supra* note 116, at 163.

[272] Stanwood, *supra* note 116, at 175; Morley, *supra* note 2, at 1092.

not run at all, to continue intraparty intrigue and manipulation, rather than rallying together behind a standard-bearer. Additionally, a political party's choice of particular rules allows it to structure its nomination process in ways it believes are fair, empower certain elements of the party, or facilitate the nomination of certain kinds of candidates. Allowing delegates to circumvent those rules to nominate a different candidate defeats the values and goals the party sought to promote in crafting its nomination process. Political parties should not permit delegates to destabilize their presidential nomination processes in this way. Instead, they should adopt binding convention rules at the outset of the process, before presidential preference contests are held and convention delegates are selected.

10

A Better Financing System? The Death and Possible Rebirth of the Presidential Nomination Public Financing Program

Richard Briffault[*]

I. INTRODUCTION

In the spring of 1974, the 31-year-old junior Senator from Delaware, Joseph R. Biden, Jr., published a law review article in which he decried the traditional system of privately financed election campaigns. Private financing, Senator Biden contended, "affords certain wealthy individuals or special interest groups the potential for exerting a disproportionate influence over both the electoral mechanism and the policy-making processes of the government." Moreover, Biden urged, private funding poses an obstacle to the candidacies of "individuals of moderate means" and so was at odds with the "concept of American democracy [that] presumes that all citizens, regardless of access to wealth, have equal access to the political process." In addition, he argued that private funding favored incumbents.[1] To address the "Political Darwinism"[2] of private financing, Biden called on Congress to adopt a system of public funding for all federal candidates.

Biden's article grew out of a long tradition of treating public funding as integral to campaign finance regulation. As far back as 1907, President Theodore Roosevelt, in his Seventh Annual Message to Congress, had called for public funding of candidates, and in the late 1960s and early 1970s Congress began to take tentative steps in that direction.[3] Congress created

---

[*] Richard Briffault is the Joseph P. Chamberlain Professor of Legislation at Columbia Law School.

[1] Joseph R. Biden, Jr., *Public Financing of Elections: Legislative Proposals and Constitutional Questions*, 69 Nw. U. L. Rev. 1, 2–3 (1974).

[2] *Id.* at 2.

[3] *See* Richard Briffault, *Reforming Campaign Finance Reform: The Future of Public Financing*, in Democracy by the People: Reforming Campaign Finance in America 103–04 & nn. 4–5 (Eugene D. Mazo & Timothy K. Kuhner eds., 2018).

a Presidential Election Campaign Fund, with a mandate initially limited to funding general election candidates. In October 1974, Congress went further and authorized, starting in the 1976 election, the use of public funds to finance the party nominating conventions and the campaigns of the candidates running for their nominations.[4] The pre-nomination public funding system differs from the general election program, however. The general election system authorizes large flat grants for the major party nominees who agree to limit their spending to the government grant. The pre-nomination program was designed to match small donations, so that even with public funding, candidates would still need and be able to use private contributions, albeit subject to a spending limit.

True to his principles, Senator Biden twice turned to the public funding program when he ran for the Democratic presidential nomination. In the 1987–88 election, he obtained $901,213 in federal matching funds, which were added to the $3.8 million in private contributions he received in his short-lived campaign. Counting loans and transfers from his other campaign committees, public funds accounted for about 22.3 percent of Biden's total campaign spending.[5] When Biden ran again in 2007–08, he collected $2,033,471.83 in public funds, compared to less than $8.6 million in private individual contributions to his campaign. With transfers and loans factored in, public funds accounted for about 14 percent of Biden's 2008 campaign spending.[6] Biden's 2008 campaign also ended early, with him dropping out after placing fifth in the Iowa caucuses held on January 3, 2008.

Biden's 2020 campaign for the Democratic presidential nomination, however, did not use public funds. Instead, the campaign relied entirely on private contributions, along with substantial support from independent committees. In relying entirely on private funding this time, Biden was not alone. Every single one of the nearly two dozen Democratic candidates was entirely financed by private contributions. Nor was the absence of public funding in the 2020 race unusual. In 2016, exactly one of the 23 major party primary contenders — across both parties — took public funds, with both of the major party nomination winners — Donald Trump and Hillary Clinton — wholly privately funded. So, too, both major party nominees in 2012 — Barack

---

[4] *See* Federal Election Campaign Act Amendments of 1974, Pub. L. 93–443 (Oct. 15, 1974), section 408, creating the Presidential Primary Matching Payment Account, chapter 96 of subtitle H of the Internal Revenue Code, 26 U.S.C. 9031 *et seq.*

[5] Biden, Joseph, R. Jr., *Financial Summary (1988)*, FED. ELECTION COMM'N, www.fec.gov/data/candidate/P80000722/?cycle=1988&election_full=true.

[6] Biden, Joseph, R. Jr., *Financial Summary (2008)*, FED. ELECTION COMM'N, www.fec.gov/data/candidate/P80000722/?cycle=2008&election_full=true.

Obama and Mitt Romney—and all the other 2012 contenders financed their nomination campaigns from private funds; so did both major party nomination winners and the runners-up in 2008. Indeed, the last Democratic candidate who used public funds in winning his party's presidential nomination was Al Gore in 2000, and the last successful publicly funded candidate for the Republican nomination was Bob Dole in 1996.

It is not as if the public funding program was always a flop. Indeed, public funding was an important factor in major party nomination campaigns in the first quarter-century after the program was adopted. Public funding was critical to the emergence of Jimmy Carter in 1976 and to Ronald Reagan's near-successful 1976 campaign, which helped position him for his successful 1980 run. Public funding has also been credited with shaping and sustaining nomination contests over several decades, by helping to finance the candidates who were the principal challengers to their party's front-runners—George H. W. Bush in 1980, Gary Hart in 1984, Jesse Jackson in 1988, Pat Buchanan in 1992, John McCain in 2000, and John Edwards in 2004.[7]

So, what happened? What caused the collapse of the presidential nomination public funding program, beginning in 2000 and culminating in its complete irrelevance by 2012? What have the consequences been for presidential nomination campaigns? Should the presidential nomination public funding program be re-created, and if so, how?

Part II of this chapter reviews the structure and legal framework of the presidential nomination public funding system. It tracks the declining use of public funds over the last two decades, and examines the reasons for the public funding program's collapse.

Part III then considers whether a presidential nomination public funding program should be re-created, and, if so, how. Notwithstanding young Senator Biden's concern about the inability of candidates to raise the funds needed to mount competitive campaigns without public funding, both parties in 2008, the Republicans in 2012, and both parties in 2016 had highly competitive nomination contests, with the 2008 Democratic race and especially the Republican 2016 nomination campaign joined by what were then record numbers of contestants. The 2020 Democratic nomination had even more entrants than the Republicans did in 2016. Also, many of these candidates managed to receive significant support from low-dollar donors. Nonetheless, most of the truly competitive candidates have been largely dependent on large

---

[7] *See* Campaign Finance Institute Task Force on Financing Presidential Nominations, So the Voters May Choose ... Reviving the Presidential Matching Fund System 2–4 (2005) (hereinafter "CFI 2005").

donors or, like Mitt Romney in 2008, Donald Trump in 2016, or Michael Bloomberg in 2020, their personal wealth. With the exception of Bernie Sanders in 2016 and 2020, the candidates who relied primarily on low-dollar donations usually exited their races early.

As a result, there remains a need for public funding to counter the role of large donors and to help sustain the campaigns of outsider candidates. Moreover, the growing experience of many states and cities with forms of public funding that depart from and improve on the failed presidential model provide some guidance as to how to create a workable reformed system.

Part IV will conclude by sketching out the elements necessary for a reinvigorated public funding system.

II. THE PRESIDENTIAL NOMINATION PUBLIC FUNDING PROGRAM IN BRIEF

A. *Structure*

The presidential nomination public funding program provides qualified candidates with public funds by matching small individual donations. To qualify, a candidate must raise at least $100,000, consisting of at least $5000 in individual contributions—counting only $250 from any individual's donation—from residents of at least twenty states.[8] These numbers have not been changed since the program's enactment in 1974. The program will then match on a dollar-per-dollar basis each individual contribution the candidate receives, up to $250 per donor. The law sets a spending limit—which is adjusted for inflation—as a condition for public funding and also caps the amount of public funds the candidate can receive to half the spending limit. In 2016 the pre-nomination spending limit was $48.07 million (although additional funds could be spent for legal, accounting, and fundraising costs), so the maximum grant in 2016 was effectively $24 million. By comparison, Democratic nominee Hillary Clinton raised more than $500 million for her nomination campaign in 2016, her runner-up Bernie Sanders raised $237 million, and Republican nominee Donald Trump raised $350 million. Moreover, although the law provides for the matching of any eligible contributions received starting the year before the year of the presidential election, no matching payments can actually be made to a candidate until the start of the year of the presidential election.[9]

---

[8]   26 U.S.C. § 9033 (b)(3), (4).
[9]   26 U.S.C. § 9032 (6).

The law also limits how much a candidate can spend in each state to $200,000, adjusted for inflation, or to a specified inflation-adjusted amount based on the number of voters in each state.[10] That meant that in 2016 a publicly funded presidential contender would have been allowed to spend just $961,400 in the all-important New Hampshire primary.[11] In addition, the law limits a candidate to spending no more than $50,000 in personal or immediate family funds.[12] A candidate ceases to be eligible for matching funds thirty days after he or she receives less than 10 percent of the vote in two consecutive primaries that the candidate contested, unless he or she rebounds by obtaining 20 percent of the vote in another primary.

The program, along with general election public funding, is funded voluntarily by taxpayers who choose to check-off a box on their tax form that will dedicate a small portion of their tax liability to the Presidential Election Campaign Fund. The check-off was originally $1 (or $2 for a couple filing a joint tax return) and was raised to $3 (and $6 for couples filing jointly) in 1993.

As the one-to-one match and the cap on public funds at half the spending limit indicate, the nomination public funding program was intended to be a hybrid of public and private. Candidates need to raise private funds in order to receive public funds, and the program assumes that private funds will constitute a significant portion of campaign treasuries. Public funding was intended to reduce candidate dependence on large donors, but not fully to replace private donations.

B. *Constitutional Framework*

In the foundational case of *Buckley v. Valeo*,[13] the Supreme Court sustained both the general election and pre-nomination public funding programs, holding that the public financing of campaigns advances the general welfare goals of reducing "the deleterious influence of large contributions on the political process," "facilitat[ing] communication by candidates with the electorate," and "free[ing] candidates from the rigors of fundraising."[14] The Court went on to find that "public financing as a means of eliminating the influence of large private contributions furthers a significant government interest."[15]

---

[10] 26 U.S.C. § 9035.
[11] *Presidential Spending Limits for 2016*, FED. ELECTION COMM'N, https://transition.fec.gov/pages/brochures/pubfund_limits_2016.shtml.
[12] 26 U.S.C. § 9035.
[13] 424 U.S. 1 (1976)
[14] *Id.* at 91.
[15] *Id.* at 97.

Buckley held that candidates could be required to accept spending limits —
which are otherwise unconstitutional — as a condition for receiving public
funds.[16] The Court also upheld the specific eligibility requirements for obtaining pre-nomination campaign funding and rejected the contention that the
matching funds format favors wealthy voters and candidates.[17]

In subsequent cases — which focused on general election presidential public funding, rather than the pre-nomination program — the Court rejected the
argument that candidates are somehow coerced into accepting public funds,[18]
but the Court in 1985 also invalidated a provision of the public funding law
that limited independent expenditures in support of or opposed to a publicly
funded candidate.[19] As a result, spending-limited publicly funded candidates
have to contend with both non-spending-limited privately funded opponents
and non-spending-limited hostile independent committees — although
a publicly funded candidate could also benefit from the unlimited spending
of a supportive independent committee.

In 2011, in a case known as *Arizona Free Enterprise* — involving a state public
funding program — the Court held that the government could not provide
a publicly funded candidate with additional public funds to respond to high
levels of spending by a privately funded opponent or hostile independent
committee.[20] The Court determined that such a "fair fight" or "rescue"
mechanism burdens the speech of the candidate or committee whose spending triggered the payment of the additional public funds, and that the burden
is not justified by the interests that support public funding.[21] Although the
presidential public funding program does not have such a trigger mechanism,
Arizona Free Enterprise limits the ability to make public funding more attractive to candidates and so has important implications for any re-design of the
presidential nomination public funding program.

C. *History: Rise, Decline, and Fall, 1976–2016*

In the first six presidential election cycles after the public financing program
was enacted — 1976, 1980, 1984, 1988, 1992, and 1996 — virtually every major
presidential contender in both parties participated in the public funding

---

[16] *Id.* at 57 n. 65, 107–08.

[17] *Id.* at 105–08.

[18] Republican Nat'l Comm. v. FEC, 445 U.S. 955 (1980), *aff'd* Republican Nat'l Comm. v. FEC, 487 F.Supp. 280 (S.D.N.Y. 1980).

[19] FEC v. Nat'l Cons. PAC, 470 U.S. 480 (1985).

[20] Arizona Free Enterprise Club's Freedom Club PAC v. Bennett, 564 U.S. 721 (2011).

[21] *Id.* at 736–55.

program, and, typically, federal matching funds constituted a significant fraction of their total contributions. In 1976, Jimmy Carter's $8 million in private individual contributions was matched by $3.6 million in public funds. On the Republican side, a third of Gerald Ford's primary receipts and 40 percent of Ronald Reagan's funding consisted of public funds.[22] The funds were particularly valuable at the start of the campaign season to the virtually unknown Jimmy Carter and to Ronald Reagan, who was challenging an incumbent president of his own party, as each had less than $50,000 on hand before the public funds began to flow at the beginning of 1976.[23] Again, in 1980, both for Reagan and his principal opponent George H. W. Bush on the Republican side, and for Carter and his challenger Senator Ted Kennedy on the Democratic side, matching payments accounted for about a third of their total funds.[24] The payment of public funds at the start of 1980 has been credited with saving Bush from financial elimination and enabling him to become the runner-up to Reagan and Reagan's pick for vice-president.[25]

The pattern continued through the 1984, 1988, and 1992 elections, with both major party nomination winners and their principal opponents taking public funds.[26] So, too, the infusion of public funds at the start of the election year enabled candidates who were virtually out of cash—Gary Hart (1984), Jesse Jackson (1988), Paul Tsongas (1992), Pat Buchanan (1992)—to keep in their races and mount major challenges against the frontrunners.[27] In this period, matching funds accounted for a quarter to a third of the war chests of participating candidates.[28] Things began to change in 1996. President Clinton's Democratic nomination was essentially uncontested, but he still participated in the public funding program, and public funds accounted for almost one-third of his primary period receipts. On the Republican side, however, although the ultimate nomination winner Bob Dole participated in the primary matching program, as did his principal runner-up Pat Buchanan, Dole's other main opponent, millionaire Steve Forbes, opted out of the program and committed nearly $40 million of his own funds to his campaign, thereby virtually equaling Dole's combination of private

---

[22] Michael J. Malbin & Brendan Glavin, CFI's Guide to Money in Federal Elections: 2016 in Historical Context, at 27 (Table 1–1) (Camp. Fin. Inst. 2018).

[23] See CFI 2005, *supra* note 7, at 2.

[24] Malbin & Glavin, *supra* note 22, at 27 (Table 1-1).

[25] See CFI 2005, *supra* note 7, at 3.

[26] Malbin & Glavin, *supra* note 22, at 26 (Table 1-1).

[27] CFI 2005, *supra* note 7, at 3.

[28] Michael J. Malbin, *Small Donors, Large Donors and the Internet: The Case for Public Funding After Obama*, Campaign Finance Institute, at 5 (2009), www.cfinst.org/president/pdf/PresidentialWorkingPaper_April09.pdf.

contributions and public funds.[29] By winning two early primaries and ultimately about 11 percent of the primary vote,[30] Forbes became the first serious
primary candidate to opt out of public funding since the program was
adopted.[31]

In 2000, the initial crack in the public funding program began to widen, as
George W. Bush became the first candidate to win a major party nomination
without public funding since the public funding program was enacted. To be
sure, public funding enabled John McCain to mount a serious challenge to
Bush,[32] winning seven primaries and 31 percent of the Republican primary
vote.[33] But Bush's $103 million in private primary contributions was more than
double McCain's total receipts; indeed, it was more than double the pre-
nomination campaign receipts of any major party candidate in the preceding
quarter-century.[34] Although both major Democratic contenders—Al Gore
and Bill Bradley—opted to take matching funds, which accounted for roughly
30 percent of their receipts,[35] the writing was on the wall. In 2004, the winners
of both major party nominations—George W. Bush and John Kerry—
declined public funding. Each raised well over $200 million, or far more
than he could have raised if he had chosen to rely on public funding. Again,
public funding sustained a number of other Democratic contenders through
the early primaries, and public funding arguably enabled John Edwards to
become Kerry's longest-lasting opponent, first runner-up, and vice-
presidential pick.[36] But 2004 was the last election in which public funding
played any significant factor in the party nomination contests.

In 2008, the two leading Democratic contenders—Barack Obama and
Hillary Clinton—opted out of public funding, as did all of the principal
Republican candidates—John McCain, Mitt Romney, Rudy Giuliani, Rand
Paul, and Mike Huckabee. To be sure, a handful of prominent Democratic
contenders—John Edwards, Joe Biden, Christopher Dodd, and Dennis

---

[29]   CFI 2005, *supra* note 7, at 25 (Table 1-1).

[30]   1996 *Republican Party presidential primaries*, WIKIPEDIA, https://en.wikipedia.org/wiki/
       1996_Republican_Party_presidential_primaries.

[31]   In 1980, John Connally, the former Governor of Texas and Secretary of the Treasury, ran for
       the Republican presidential nomination without taking public funds. Although he spent
       $11 million on his campaign, he did not win a single primary and secured the support of
       only a single delegate. *See John Connally*, WIKIPEDIA, https://en.wikipedia.org/wiki/
       John_Connally.

[32]   *See* CFI 2005, *supra* note 7, at 3.

[33]   *See* 2000 *Republican Party presidential primaries*, WIKIPEDIA, https://en.wikipedia.org/wiki/
       2000_Republican_Party_presidential_primaries.

[34]   See CFI 2018, *supra* note 22, at 25–27 (Table 1-1).

[35]   *Id.* at 25.

[36]   *See* CFI 2005, *supra* note 7, at 3–4.

Kucinich—qualified for public funds, but only Edwards came in as high as second in any state primary or caucus contest. With the publicly funded candidates mostly dropping out early, the total allocation of matching funds in 2008 came to just $20 million, or less than 2 percent of the $1.2 billion raised by all of the presidential hopefuls in the nomination phase of that year's election.[37] In 2012, the public funding program ceased to play any role in the pursuit of the major party nominations.[38] Matching funds payments dropped to a little more than $350,000 in 2012, with all the funds going to candidates for third-party nominations. In 2016, the program played a marginally larger role, with Maryland Governor Martin O'Malley, a candidate for the Democratic nomination, qualifying for public funds, and obtaining a little over $1 million in matching funds, or about one-sixth of his campaign receipts. O'Malley, however, placed a very distant third place in the Iowa caucuses and dropped out of the race early. By comparison, the two leading Democratic contenders, Hillary Clinton and Bernie Sanders, together raised in excess of $630 million in private contributions.[39] None of the Republican candidates took public funds.[40]

D. Why Did Public Funding Fail?

The public funding system failed for two reasons, which are essentially two sides of the same coin: public funding became incapable of providing candidates with enough money to cover the drastically increased costs of the major party nomination contests, and, conversely, it became much easier to raise the necessary funds from private sources. More fundamentally, public funding fell victim to the interplay of the dramatic changes in the nomination process, developments in the campaign finance system, and public funding's own unchanged rules.

Turning first to the failure of public funding to keep up with the costs of running for a major party nomination, perhaps the most significant development in the four decades since public funding was adopted is the changed nature of the nomination contest itself. In 1972, the last election before public

---

[37] *See* John C. Green & Diana Kingsbury, *Financing the 2008 Presidential Nominating Campaigns, in* Financing the 2008 Election: Assessing Reform 86, 96–97 (David B. Magleby & Anthony Corrado eds., 2011).

[38] *See Presidential Campaign Receipts Through December 31, 2012*, Fed. Election Comm'n, https://transition.fec.gov/press/summaries/2012/tables/presidential/Pres1_2012_24m.pdf.

[39] *See Presidential Table 1: Presidential Pre-Nomination Campaign Receipts Through December 31, 2016*, Fed. Election Comm'n (April 7, 2017), https://transition.fec.gov/press/summaries/2016/tables/presidential/PresCand1_2016_24m.pdf.

[40] *Id.*

funding was enacted, Democratic candidates contested just 21 primaries and 11 caucuses,[41] and just 61 percent of Democratic convention delegates and 54 percent of Republican delegates were chosen in primaries.[42] By 1976, the percentage of delegates chosen in primaries had risen to 73 percent and 68 percent, respectively.[43] Those numbers continued to rise in the 1980s, so that by 1988, virtually every jurisdiction conducted a primary or caucus and used these contests to select or bind convention delegates.

Not only did the number of state contests rise sharply, but primaries were increasingly frontloaded. In 1972, the New Hampshire primary took place on March 7. In 2004, it was held on January 27. In 2008, it was on January 8. Moreover, whereas in the 1970s, primaries were sequenced "at what now seems like a leisurely pace,"[44] with major contests often several weeks apart, starting in 1984 and 1988, they began to be bunched together in ever-more "super" Tuesdays. In 2004, there were 18 contests in February and another 10 on March 2, when John Kerry effectively secured the Democratic nomination.[45] In 2008, there were 23 Democratic contests and 21 Republican contests on a single day—and a very early day at that, February 5.[46] Although the Obama–Clinton race continued until late spring, by March 4, 2008, John McCain had effectively triumphed over a crowded Republican field and secured his party's nomination.[47]

The public funding program has become an anachronism. Provisions that worked in the 1970s and 1980s are simply incapable of handling the timing, pace, and intensity of the twenty-first-century nomination process. The small size of the grant and the low spending limit were not designed for a system with more than fifty state campaigns (as well as campaigns in the District of Columbia and other jurisdictions that select convention delegates). The prohibition on the payment of funds before January 1 of the election year fails to deal with the early dates of the first contests and their crucial

---

[41] 1972 *Democratic presidential primaries*, WIKIPEDIA, https://en.wikipedia.org/wiki/ 1972_Democratic_Party_presidential_primaries.

[42] See Michael J. Malbin, *A Public Funding System in Jeopardy: Lessons from the Presidential Nomination Contest of 2004*, in THE ELECTION AFTER REFORM: MONEY POLITICS AND THE BIPARTISAN CAMPAIGN REFORM ACT 220 (Michael J. Malbin ed., 2006).

[43] *Id.*

[44] *Id.* at 221.

[45] See John C. Green, *Financing the 2004 Presidential Nomination Campaigns*, in FINANCING THE 2004 ELECTION, at 96–97, 115–17 (David B. Magleby, Anthony Corrado & Kelly D. Patterson eds., 2006).

[46] Green & Kingsbury, *supra* note 37, at 89.

[47] 2008 *Republican presidential primaries*, WIKIPEDIA, https://en.wikipedia.org/wiki/ 2008_Republican_Party_presidential_primaries.

importance in framing the race. The state-specific spending limits make no sense, particularly when low-population (and low-spending limit) states like Iowa and New Hampshire loom so large in the nomination calendar. These limits are also fundamentally at odds with the national scope of the Super Tuesday elections.

The law's limit on total pre-nomination spending poses other problems. One is the so-called "bridge period." With the candidates furiously spending in the crucial early contests, a winning candidate is likely to hit the spending limit—and be barred from further campaign expenditures—months before his or her party's national convention. This is essentially what happened to Bob Dole in 1996. Pushed by the intense spending by his privately funded (and largely self-funded) primary opponent Steve Forbes, Dole had "to spend almost the legal limit during the primaries, leaving him legally unable to raise and spend money from late March until the convention in July."[48] This left Dole vulnerable to an intensive negative advertising campaign in the March–July period by his general election opponent, President Bill Clinton,[49] who, running unopposed for re-nomination, had accumulated a substantial war chest that included more than $13 million in matching funds.[50] Dole's inability to spend during this bridge period between winning the primaries and being formally nominated at the national convention is one of the factors that led George W. Bush to opt out of public funding in 2000,[51] and forced John Kerry to make a similar decision in 2004.

Of course, not every nomination fight is settled early enough to create a bridge period problem. The nomination battles between Barack Obama and Hillary Clinton in 2008 and between Hillary Clinton and Bernie Sanders in 2016 truly went the distance, with hotly contested primaries and caucuses happening as late as June. There is no way Clinton and Sanders could have competed as long and as intensely as they did under an aggregate primary spending ceiling of less than $50 million. Indeed, Sanders spent nearly five times that amount, and Clinton more than ten times the primary spending limit.[52] On the Republican side, Donald Trump, Ted Cruz, Ben Carson, and

---

[48] Wesley Joe & Clyde Wilcox, *Financing the 1996 Presidential Nominations: The Last Regulated Campaign?*, in FINANCING THE 1996 ELECTION 57 (John C. Green ed., 1999).

[49] *Id.* at 58–59.

[50] CFI 2018, *supra* note 22, at 26 (Table 1-1).

[51] *See* John C. Green & Nathan S. Bigelow, *The 2000 Presidential Nominations: The Costs of Innovation*, in FINANCING THE 2000 ELECTION 58 (David B. Magleby ed., 2002).

[52] *Presidential Table 2: Presidential Pre-nomination Campaign Disbursements through December 31, 2016*, FED. ELECTION COMM'N (April 7, 2017), https://transition.fec.gov/press/summaries/2016/tables/presidential/PresCand2_2016_24m.pdf.

Marco Rubio all spent above the public funding spending limit,[53] even though both Carson and Rubio had withdrawn from the race by early March.

Contemporary nomination contests simply cost far too much for candidates to be able to abide by the aggregate primary spending limit. With the matching fund payments statutorily capped at half the spending limit, the program provides far too little money to enable a candidate to fund the kind of campaign needed to win a nomination. As one leading campaign finance scholar pointed out a decade ago, "the cost of running has far outpaced the amount a candidate is allowed to spend."[54]

The other side of the coin is that it has become far easier for candidates to obtain private funds or to benefit from the spending of wealthy supporters. One not fully appreciated consequence of the McCain-Feingold law (formally the Bipartisan Campaign Reform Act or BCRA) is that in exchange for placing limits on political party soft money, the law doubled the contribution limits for private donations, and then indexed them for inflation. In other words, the cap on individual contributions, which had been $1,000 per donor per election from 1976 through 2000, jumped to $2,000 for the 2004 election, and was set at $2,800 for the 2020 election. However, the law increased neither the size of the contribution that could be matched with public funds nor the match ratio. As a result, private financing has become far more attractive relative to public funding.

Candidates also have become more adept at raising large amounts of private contributions. George W. Bush in 2000 demonstrated what the aggressive use of bundlers—individuals who commit to raising the maximum amount of individual donations from a large number of friends and associates—can accomplish. Bush recruited 226 "Pioneers" who each raised $100,000 or more from donors who gave the then-maximum of $1,000 per person. These bundlers alone accounted for a quarter of Bush's pre-nomination funds.[55] Bush did even better in 2004, with two tiers of bundlers—Rangers who brought in $200,000 or more, as well as the $100,000 Pioneers—raising $77 million or 30 percent of his total donations.[56] Obama, Clinton, and McCain in 2008,[57] and Obama and Romney in 2012, also benefited significantly from fundraising by bundlers.[58]

---

[53] *Id.*

[54] David B. Magleby, *Adaptation and Innovation in the Financing of the 2008 Elections, in* Financing the 2008 Election: Assessing Reform 11 (David B. Magleby & Anthony Corrado eds., 2011).

[55] *See* Green & Bigelow, *supra* note 51, at 59–60.

[56] *See* Green, *supra* note 45, at 104.

[57] *See* Green & Kingsbury, *supra* note 37, at 98, 101.

[58] See John C. Green, Michael E. Kohler & Ian P. Schwarber, *Financing the 2012 Presidential Nominating Contests, in* Financing the 2012 Election 90, 92 (David B. Magleby ed., 2014).

The numbers just cited referred only to contributions collected by a candidate's official campaign committee. Candidates have other means of benefiting from large private donations. A prospective presidential candidate may defer entering the race and engage in a protracted "testing the waters" period, using a leadership PAC, a supportive albeit nominally independent political committee, or a friendly social welfare organization to pay for travel, public appearances, fundraising, political research, polling, and generally laying the groundwork for a campaign.[59] A leadership PAC is a political action committee established or controlled by a candidate that is supposed to be used to support the campaigns of *other* candidates but can be used to cover some of the expenses of the candidate who controls the PAC. A donor can give up to $5,000 per year to a leadership PAC—including non-election years—which is considerably higher than the cap on donations to the candidate's campaign committee, and, of course, donors can give to both. As a leading study of the "testing the waters" provision found, "[h]istorically, leadership PACs have been very popular vehicles for federal officeholders testing the waters of a presidential campaign."[60]

Outside groups, such as 527 organizations and 501(c)(4) organizations have played an important role in funneling big money into nomination campaigns at least since the 2000 election.[61] Both types of organizations take their names from provisions of the Internal Revenue Code that exempt their income from taxation. 527s are dedicated to political activities; they can accept unlimited contributions and engage in unlimited independent spending, but they are subject to disclosure requirements. 501(c)(4)s are supposed to be primarily non-electoral, but can engage in some election-related activities. However, even their technically non-electoral spending may focus on issues that can affect elections. They can accept unlimited contributions and make unlimited expenditures—subject to the requirement that their expenditures are primarily non-electoral—but they are not required to disclose their donors. Initially, most of the spending by these outside groups occurred in the so-called bridge period and was aimed either at helping the presumptive nominee of the party that the outside group supported or attacking the presumptive nominee of the other party;[62] in 2008, however, outside money was also a factor in the internecine Democratic struggle between Obama and Clinton.[63]

---

[59] *See generally* Paul Ryan, *"Testing the Waters" or Diving Right In? How Candidates Bend and Break Campaign Finance Laws in Presidential Campaigns*, COMMON CAUSE (January 2019), www.commoncause.org/wp-content/uploads/2019/01/TestingtheWatersFINAL.pdf.

[60] *Id.* at 13.

[61] *See* Green & Bigelow, *supra* note 51, at 56–58.

[62] *See, e.g.*, Green, *supra* note 45, at 108–11.

[63] *See* Green & Kingsbury, *supra* note 37, at 102–06.

In 2012, the role of outside money in nomination campaigns took a quantum leap with the emergence of the Super PAC. In 2010, the U.S. Court of Appeals for the District of Columbia Circuit held that donations to political committees that engage only in independent spending—that is, spending that is not coordinated with any candidate—cannot be limited.[64] With the Supreme Court having previously held that such independent spending could not be limited, the D.C. Circuit decision—soon followed by other courts of appeals[65]—meant that independent-expenditure-only groups could both take and spend money to expressly support or oppose candidates without limits. That is what makes them "super." The Federal Election Commission subsequently determined that even a group that makes donations to candidates can become "super" if it creates a segregated account that makes only independent expenditures; it can then accept unlimited donations to that account.[66]

In 2012, virtually every major candidate had a supportive Super PAC working for him or her. Typically established and run by operatives who had previously been on the candidate's government or campaign staff, the fundraising of these Super PACs made it clear that the contributions they received would be used to advance the political fortunes of that candidate. Indeed, candidates were free to fundraise for their supportive Super PACs, and did so. Super PACs were crucial to the campaigns of many of the 2012 Republican contenders, particularly Mitt Romney, Newt Gingrich, Rick Santorum, Jon Huntsman, and Rick Perry.[67] Indeed, Newt Gingrich's affiliated Super PAC raised more money than his official campaign committee.[68] And these Super PACs were funded by very large contributions: the vast majority of the contributions to the Obama, Romney, Gingrich, Santorum, Huntsman, and Perry Super PACs came in amounts of $50,000 or more.[69]

Super PACs were also major players in 2016. Jeb Bush's Super PAC raised a primary season record $121.1 million dollars—or nearly four times the sum donated to his campaign committee.[70] The sum is particularly striking as Bush effectively withdrew from the race after coming in fourth in the South Carolina primary in late February. The Super PACs supporting Marco Rubio, Scott Walker, Chris Christie, Carly Fiorina, Rick Perry, Bobby Jindal, and George Pataki all raised more money than did the formal

---

[64] SpeechNow.org v. FEC, 599 F.3d 686 (D.C. Cir. 2010).
[65] *See generally* Richard Briffault, *Super PACs*, 96 MINN. L. REV. 1644, 1663–65 (2012).
[66] *Id.* at 1665–72.
[67] *See* Green, Kohler & Schwarber, *supra* note 58, at 97–101.
[68] *See* MALBIN & GLAVIN, *supra* note 22, at 29 (Table 1-3).
[69] *See* Green, Kohler & Schwarber, *supra* note 58, at 98.
[70] *See* MALBIN & GLAVIN, *supra* note 22, at 29 (Table 1-3).

campaign committees of these candidates, and the receipts of the Super PACs supporting Ted Cruz and John Kasich closely approached the volume of donations to those candidates' official committees.[71] On the Democratic side, although there was no Super PAC supporting Bernie Sanders, the one supporting Hillary Clinton raised $106.4 million, or more than a quarter of the aggregate of what her campaign committee and the Super PAC collected.[72]

Of course, not all of the dramatic expansion in private money funding of presidential nomination campaigns over the past two decades has come from large donations. The last several presidential nominating contests have witnessed a remarkable surge in the number of low-dollar donors. Federal law requires candidates to obtain the name, address, and other information from any donor of more than $200. Donors who give $200 or less are known as "unitemized donors." Due in significant part to the growing and increasingly sophisticated use of the Internet for fundraising, campaigns in the twenty-first century have raised unprecedented amounts from unitemized donors. John McCain's 2000 campaign was the first to turn to the Internet; Howard Dean in 2004 was the first to rely primarily on the Internet, and to forego public funds while so doing; and Barack Obama was the first successful candidate to make significant use of the Internet to raise low-dollar donations. Although Internet fundraising requires a substantial start-up investment in personnel, equipment infrastructure, data collection, and database maintenance, once underway it is a relatively cheap way of reaching large numbers of potential small donors and is certainly far more cost-effective than earlier fundraising targeted at small donors such as direct mail. About 30 percent of the funds Obama received in the 2008 primary season came from unitemized donors. Although Howard Dean in 2004 received an even higher percentage of his funds from small donors (38 percent), and Rand Paul in the 2008 Republican primaries received an even higher fraction (39 percent), Obama obtained an impressive $122 million in small donations[73]—nearly triple what he could have obtained in public funds. Obama raised even more in small donations in 2012—$147 million—while the campaign committees of most of the Republican also-rans in 2012—Rand Paul, Newt Gingrich, Rick Santorum, Herman Cain, and Michele Bachmann—were also heavily small-donor funded, although given their limited fundraising success they might have been better off participating in the public funding system.[74]

---

[71] *Id.*
[72] *Id.*
[73] *See* Malbin, *supra* note 28, at 16.
[74] *See* Green, Kohler & Schwarber, *supra* note 58, at 89, 93.

Small donations were also a big factor in 2016. Bernie Sanders was able to go the distance against Hillary Clinton, campaigning until June, with 44 percent of his funds (almost $100 million) coming from unitemized donors.[75] Even one-quarter of Clinton's funds (almost $64 million) came from such low-dollar donors.[76] On the Republican side, a third or more of the value of individual contributions to the Donald Trump, Ben Carson, Rand Paul, Carly Fiorina, Scott Walker, and Mike Huckabee campaigns came from low-dollar donors, although the aggregate amounts were relative small, as these campaigns either raised relatively little money (Paul, Fiorina, Walker, Huckabee) or, in Trump's case, relied more on self-funding than donors.[77]

Trump's successful campaign for the 2016 Republican nomination is a useful reminder that the amount of money a candidate has or spends is not dispositive of the election's outcome. Three of the candidates Trump defeated—Jeb Bush, Ted Cruz, and Marco Rubio—spent more, or had more spent on their behalf than he did.[78] Trump, of course, benefited tremendously from his pre-campaign celebrity and the massive amount of free media coverage he received.[79] And he did give or lend more than $66 million to his campaign, which was roughly half of his total pre-nomination receipts.[80] Indeed, he was roughly 75 percent self-funded during the crucial early primary phase of the contest.[81] His self-financing was far more than he—or any candidate—could have obtained from public matching funds, or than he would have been allowed to spend in private and matching funds together if he had opted for public funds.

---

[75] Sanders may have received an even greater fraction of his funds from small donors in 2020. As of March 31, 2020, shortly before he suspended his campaign on April 8, unitemized donations made up more than 53% of his contributions. *See 2020 Presidential Race: Bernie Sanders (D)*, CTR. FOR RESPONSIVE POL., www.opensecrets.org/2020-presidential-race/candidate?id=N00000528.

[76] Early indications are that in 2020, an even greater share of the donations to Joe Biden's campaign committee—a little under 40% (or $53 million)—came from unitemized individual contributions as of March 31, 2020. *See 2020 Presidential Candidates: Joe Biden (D)*, CTR. FOR RESPONSIVE POL., www.opensecrets.org/2020-presidential-race/candidate?id=N00001669.

[77] *See* MALBIN & GLAVIN, *supra* note 22, at 29 (Table 1-3) and 31 (Table 1-4A).

[78] *Id.* at 8.

[79] *See, e.g.*, Robin Kolodny, *The Presidential Nominating Process, Campaign Money, and Popular Love*, 53 SOC. 487, 490 (2016).

[80] *Presidential Table 1: Presidential Pre-Nomination Campaign Receipts Through December 31, 2016*, *supra* note 39.

[81] *See* Kolodny, *supra* note 79, at 489.

III. GOING FORWARD: SHOULD PUBLIC FINANCING BE SAVED, AND IF SO, HOW?

A. *Why Public Funding?*

There are reasons to question whether public funding should be re-established. A primary goal of public financing is to reduce barriers to entry and thereby make elections more competitive by making it easier for candidates to raise the money necessary to compete. Yet, the recent privately funded presidential nomination contests have been marked by intensive competition. In 2012, there were nearly a dozen Republican candidates who contested one or more primaries. In 2016, there were so many Republican candidates that they had to be divided into two groups for the pre-primary debates. There were a dozen who contested at least one primary, and eight who raised more than $10 million in individual contributions (not counting their supportive Super PACs).[82] On the Democratic side, although the initial 2016 field of six quickly dropped to two, the Clinton–Sanders race was hotly and closely contested throughout the entire primary season. Moreover, by the time the 2020 Iowa caucuses were held, there were a record number of candidates for the 2020 Democratic nomination—nearly two dozen. New contenders like Senator Elizabeth Warren, Pete Buttigieg and Senator Amy Klobuchar were able to raise substantial funds—more than $125 million for Warren,[83] more than $99 million for Buttigieg,[84] and more than $52 million for Klobuchar[85]—which enabled them to make their mark in the early contests. As both the 2016 and 2020 elections demonstrate, there has been no lack of competition for the nominations of the major parties when they do not have incumbents seeking reelection.

A second major justification for public financing is to democratize campaign finance by reducing the impact of large and powerful donors and increasing the role of ordinary voters. Again, as already noted, elections over the last two decades have been marked by a striking increase in the number of donors and, especially, in the role of low-dollar donors. More than 784,000 people made itemized donations—that is, donations of more than $200—to

---

[82] *Presidential Table 1: Presidential Pre-Nomination Campaign Receipts Through December 31, 2016, supra* note 39.

[83] *2020 Presidential Candidates: Elizabeth Warren (D)*, Ctr. for Responsive Pol., www.opensecrets.org/2020-presidential-race/candidate?id=N00033492.

[84] *2020 Presidential Candidates: Peter Buttigieg (D)*, Ctr. for Responsive Pol., www.opensecrets.org/2020-presidential-race/candidate?id=N00044183.

[85] *2020 Presidential Candidates: Amy Klobuchar (D)*, Ctr. for Responsive Pol., www.opensecrets.org/2020-presidential-race/candidate?id=N00027500.

contenders for presidential nominations in 2007–08. Although that number dropped to 505,000 in 2012 (when there was no Democratic contest, although President Obama still received contributions), it returned to almost 735,000 in 2016.[86] Although the precise number of unitemized donors (giving $200 and under) is not recorded, they accounted for roughly 24 percent of the value of individual donations to the candidates of both parties in 2008; 25 percent of the value of individual donations to the Republican candidates in 2012; and 33 percent of the individual donations to the candidates of both parties in 2016.[87] As previously noted, Bernie Sanders received 44 percent of his contributions from low-dollar donors. For Sanders, at least, participation in the public funding system would have *reduced* his ability to raise small donations and would have capped the ability of small donors to participate in his campaign. Moreover, in the opening months of the 2020 campaign, many of the Democratic contenders emphasized the importance of small donors to their campaign or asserted that they would not turn to lobbyists, interest groups, or Super PACs for support.[88] The Democratic National Committee also made the ability to raise contributions from a large number of donors one of the criteria for eligibility to participate in candidate debates.[89]

Despite these developments, the traditional arguments for public financing, as articulated by Joe Biden in 1974—and Theodore Roosevelt in 1907—still apply to the presidential nomination contests. First, limited access to funds may still operate to limit the ability of candidates to compete. In 2016, there

---

[86] *See* Malbin & Glavin, *supra* note 22, at 31–33 (Tables 1-4A to 1-4C).

[87] *Id.*

[88] As of March 31, 2020, shortly before they suspended their campaigns, both Sanders and Warren had received a majority of their contributions from small donors. *See* 2020 *Presidential Race: Bernie Sanders (D), supra* note 75; 2020 *Presidential Candidates: Elizabeth Warren (D), supra* note 83.

[89] *See, e.g.,* Shane Goldmacher, 2020 *Democrats Face a Vexing Issue: Big Money from the Rich,* N.Y. Times, Dec. 11, 2018, www.nytimes.com/2018/12/11/us/politics/democrats-2020-super-pac.html; Peter Overby, *Democratic Hopefuls Compete to Spurn Establishment Cash,* NPR, Feb. 2, 2019, www.npr.org/2019/02/02/690156001/democratic-presidential-hopefuls-compete-to-spurn-establishment-cash; Kate Ackley, *Small-Dollar Donors Could Hold the Balance in 2020,* Roll Call, Mar. 15, 2019, www.rollcall.com/news/congress/small-dollar-donors-2020-democrats-president-money; Shane Goldmacher, *Inside Kamala Harris's Small-Dollar Donor Fund-Raising Operation,* N.Y. Times, Mar. 26, 2019, www.nytimes.com/2019/03/26/us/politics/kamala-harris-fundraising.html; Alex Gangitano, *Opposition to PACs Puts 2020 Democrats in a Bind,* The Hill, April 3, 20–19, https://thehill.com/homenews/campaign/437063-opposition-to-pacs-puts-2020-democrats-in-a-bind, Carrie Levine, *Why Democrats Are Falling Over Themselves to Find Small-Dollar Donors,* FiveThirtyEight, Apr. 17, 2109, https://fivethirtyeight.com/features/why-democrats-are-falling-over-themselves-to-find-small-dollar-donors/; Elena Schneider & Theodoric Meyer, *Buttigieg Renounces Lobbyist Donations, Refunding over $30,000,* Politico, Apr. 26, 2019, www.politico.com/story/2019/04/26/buttigieg-lobbyist-donations-2020-1291202.

was no incumbent in the Democratic contest, but the six declared candidates quickly dropped to two as none other than Clinton and Sanders were able to raise the necessary funds. Similarly, in the 2012 Republican contest, lack of funds drove a number of contenders out of the race early, and crippled the ability of Romney's principal rivals—Gingrich and Santorum—to compete.[90] It is less clear what role money played in the 2016 Republican race, in which Trump benefited enormously from free media and a number of his opponents, particularly Bush, Cruz, and Rubio were very well-funded. Nonetheless, several of the candidates in that large field, such as Christie and Huckabee, clearly lacked the funds necessary to mount sustained campaigns.[91] In the run-up to the 2020 Democratic nomination contest, a number of prominent Democrats—such as Senator Cory Booker or former cabinet secretary Julián Castro—dropped out before any votes were cast at least in part because of a lack of funds.[92] It's not clear the current public funding system could have done much for these candidates. Democrat Martin O'Malley did participate in the public funding program in 2016, much as Joe Biden, Christopher Dodd, and John Edwards did in 2008, and all were out of the running early in the primary season. The quality of the candidates and the dynamic of the particular election matter as much as the financing system. But a lack of adequate candidate funding tends to constrain the choices available to voters.

Moreover, while the volume of small donations has grown tremendously since the turn of the century, the volume of very large donations has also grown significantly. In 2008, individuals who each donated $1,000 or more to a presidential nomination campaign collectively provided candidates with nearly $500 million and accounted for more than half of the dollar value of all donations to candidates in each party's contest. For all of his success with small donors, Barack Obama received 44 percent of his individual primary campaign donations from $1,000+ donors, and John McCain received an even more significant 71 percent of his individual primary contributions from $1,000+ donors. Indeed, 27 percent of Obama's donations ($87.3 million) and 49 percent of McCain's donations ($60.8 million) came from individuals who "maxed out"—that is, they gave the maximum legally permissible amount. Obama's receipts from maxed-out donations was almost as large as what he obtained from unitemized low-dollar donors.[93] Moreover, as Michael

[90] *See* Green, Kohler & Schwarber, *supra* note 58, at 103-05.

[91] *See* MALBIN & GLAVIN, *supra* note 22, at 29 (Table 3).

[92] Booker raised a total of $25 million, www.opensecrets.org/2020-presidential-race/candidate?id=N00035267; Castro raised just $10 million, www.opensecrets.org/2020-presidential-race/candidate?id=N00043955.

[93] *See* MALBIN & GLAVIN, *supra* note 22, at 33 (Table 1-4C).

Malbin has pointed out, the very large donations that Obama received during the so-called "invisible primary" period—that is, the first three-quarters of 2007, long before any actual primary votes were cast—were crucial in establishing him as a serious candidate. His small donations surged later, only as he began to win primaries.[94]

Large donors were prominent again in 2012. On the Republican side, 56 percent of the value of individual donations came from individuals who gave $1,000 or more, with 40 percent coming from maxed-out donors who gave $2,500 each. The nomination winner Mitt Romney actually obtained 55 percent of his individual contributions from maxed-out donors.[95] The significance of large donors is even greater once Super PAC funds are taken into account. This makes sense, as an important reason an individual may give to a Super PAC is that he or she has maxed out on the direct contribution to the candidate. Large donors—actually, very large donors, using a $50,000 minimum contribution threshold—provided an average of 82 percent of nomination campaign Super PAC contributions, including 87 percent of the contributions to the Romney-, Santorum-, and Perry-linked Super PACs, 88 percent of the Huntsman-supporting Super PAC, and 99 percent of the pro-Gingrich Super PAC. On the Democratic side, 91 percent of the funds contributed to the Obama-affiliated Super PAC came from $50,000+ donors.[96]

Similarly, in 2016, large ($1,000+) donors accounted for 55 percent of Hillary Clinton's pre-nomination contributions; 40 percent came from maxed-out donors. On the Republican side, the candidates received on average 41 percent of their individual contributions from large donors and 25 percent from maxed-out donors, and that takes into account Donald Trump, who received a below-average share of his contributions from large donors. A number of the other major contenders—including Rubio, Bush, and Kasich—received between 60 percent and 87 percent of their funds from large donors, and 36 percent to 72 percent from maxed-out donors.[97] And, again, many of the candidates—Bush, Clinton, Rubio, and Cruz in particular—received massive support from Super PACs, which are financed almost entirely by very large donors.[98] Large donors often hold views on economic or social issues that diverge from those of average party voters,[99]

---

[94]   See Malbin, *supra* note 28, at 10–15.
[95]   See MALBIN & GLAVIN, *supra* note 22, at 32 (Table 1-4B).
[96]   See Green, Kohler & Schwarber, *supra* note 58, at 91–101.
[97]   See MALBIN & GLAVIN, *supra* note 22, at 31 (Table 1-4B).
[98]   *Id.* at 29 (Table 3).
[99]   See, e.g., David Broockman & Neil Malhotra, *What Do Donors Want? Heterogeneity by Party and Policy Domain (Research Note)*, Stanford Graduate School of Business Working Papers,

so that candidate—and, ultimately, officeholder—dependence on large donors can skew party policies and government actions away from the preferences of the voters.

In short, despite the surge in the number of donors, and especially of low-dollar donors, in recent presidential elections, the impact of the very wealthy may actually be greater than ever. Looking at federal elections in the aggregate—that is, congressional and presidential elections together—one study found that although in the 2000 election cycle just 73,926 individuals accounted for half of all donations, in 2016, a mere 15,810 individuals provided half of all campaign money.[100] The longstanding goals of public financing—promoting competition by enabling serious candidates to obtain the funds they need to sustain their campaigns, reducing the dependence of candidates (and future officeholders) on large donors, and reducing the disproportionate impact of the wealthy on public policy[101]—remain unmet by our twenty-first-century private nomination campaign finance system. But given the unhappy experience with the current public financing system, can a system be created that accomplishes public funding's goals?

B. *The State and Local Public Financing Experience*

Even as the federal presidential public financing system has gone into eclipse, states and local governments have created new programs that have had some success in advancing public funding's goals. Currently, at least fourteen states provide some form of public financing option for campaigns,[102] and another dozen local governments—most prominently New York City, Los Angeles, and Seattle—have implemented or are in the process of implementing some system of public funding for candidates.[103] These programs take a variety of

---

Working Paper No. 3757 (Nov. 30, 2018), www.gsb.stanford.edu/faculty-research/working-papers/what-do-donors-want-heterogeneity-party-policy-domain-research-note.

[100] *Campaign Finance in the United States: Assessing an Era of Fundamental Change*, BIPARTISAN POLICY CENTER, at 22–23 (January 2018), https://bipartisanpolicy.org/wp-content/uploads/2018/01/BPC-Democracy-Campaign-Finance-in-the-United-States.pdf.

[101] For further development of the arguments for public funding, see Briffault, *supra* note 3, at 117–20.

[102] *Overview of State Laws on Public Financing*, NAT'L CONF. STATE LEGISLATURES, www.ncsl.org/research/elections-and-campaigns/public-financing-of-campaigns-overview.aspx.

[103] *See, e.g.*, Michael J. Malbin & Michael Parrott, *Small Donor Empowerment Depends on the Details: Comparing Matching Fund Programs in New York and Los Angeles*, 15 THE FORUM 219, 220 (2017); *The Case for Small Donor Public Financing in New York State*, BRENNAN CENTER FOR JUSTICE, at 12–13 (Feb. 26, 2019), www.brennancenter.org/sites/default/files/publications/CaseforPublicFinancingNY_0.pdf.

forms, but three patterns dominate: (1) "clean money" programs that provide a qualifying candidate with a grant intended to fully fund the candidate's campaign; (2) matching funds programs that, like the current presidential primary system, provide public funds that match small donations but that unlike the presidential system provide funds that are a multiple of the matched small donation; and (3) voucher programs, under which voters are given vouchers that have a certain value, which they can donate to candidates, who then redeem the vouchers for public funds.[104]

A number of these programs have significant track records. The "clean elections" systems in Arizona, Connecticut, and Maine have been in place for several election cycles—Maine's program was adopted in 1996, Arizona's in 1998, and Connecticut's in 2006—and have been credited with increasing the competitiveness of elections, increasing the number of candidates able to run for office, diversifying the candidate pool, expanding voter participation in the campaign finance process, and reducing the burdens of fundraising.[105] New York City's multiple-match system has also been praised for similarly expanding the number and diversity of candidates, increasing electoral competition, and, especially, broadening and diversifying the donor pool. New York's experience has also shown the significance of the match rate. Over nearly three decades, New York City has increased the match rate from 1-to-1 to 2-to-1 then 3-to-1, 4-to-1, and in the three most recent general elections 6-to-1, while lowering the maximum matched contribution from $1,000 to $250 and finally to $175.[106] In future elections, the match rate will rise to 8-to-1, and the maximum matchable amount will go back to $250. These changes have increased candidate participation in the program, while diversifying the donor pool. In the most recent New York City elections in 2017, 84 percent of candidates in the primaries participated. The program enjoyed a high level of support, and the participating candidates won the three city-wide elected positions, four of the five borough presidencies, and 36 of 51 City Council seats. Moreover, the program succeeded in stimulating low-dollar

[104] *See generally* Briffault, *supra* note 3, at 107–10.
[105] *See, e.g.*, J. Mijin Cha & Miles Rapoport, *Fresh Start: The Impact of Public Campaign Financing in Connecticut*, DEMOS (2013), www.demos.org/sites/default/files/publications/Fr eshStart_PublicFinancingCT_0.pdf; GAO, *Campaign Finance Reform: Experiences of Two States that Offered Full Public Funding for Political Candidates*, U.S. Government Accountability Office, GAO Publication No. GAO-10-390 (May 28, 2010), www.gao.gov/ass ets/310/305079.pdf; Neil Malhotra, *The Impact of Public Financing on Electoral Competition: Evidence from Arizona and Maine*, 8 ST. POL. & POL'Y Q. 263 (2008).
[106] Malbin & Parrott, *supra* note 103, at 224–25.

contributions for participating candidates, and in generating contributions from neighborhoods around the city.[107]

So far, only one jurisdiction in the United States has adopted a voucher program — Seattle. Under the program, each Seattle resident is eligible to receive four $25 "democracy vouchers," which the resident may contribute to qualifying candidates, who may then cash them in with Seattle's elections agency for public funds.[108] The program was adopted by the city's voters in 2015, and first used in 2017 for two citywide at-large council races and in the election for city attorney. The winning candidates in all three races qualified for vouchers, as did the principal runners-up in the council races. And voucher proceeds accounted for a majority of total individual contributions in the council elections and a majority of the contributions to the winner of the city attorney race. According to the Seattle Ethics and Elections Commission, the introduction of vouchers increased the number of residents contributing, lowered the size of the average contribution, increased the percentage of contributions coming from within Seattle, and spread the sources of contributions "more equitably" across the city's neighborhoods.[109]

Each type of public funding program has its own strengths and weaknesses. Small donor multi-match and voucher programs are better than clean money's flat grant at increasing public participation in the campaign finance process. On the other hand, clean money is better at freeing candidates from the burdens of fundraising. Voucher programs enable each resident to determine which candidates get his or her public funds, but that is also true of small-donor matching. With vouchers, there is considerable uncertainty as to how many residents will actually donate their vouchers and when they will do so. It appears that in the first Seattle election in which vouchers were used, only about 4 percent were contributed to an office-seeker and most were returned just before the election, which could limit their usefulness to candidates.[110] It may be that the differences across jurisdictions in the specific provisions of a category of program are as important as the differences in the types of

---

[107] *See* New York City Campaign Finance Board, Keeping Democracy Strong: New York City's Campaign Finance Program in the 2017 Citywide Elections, at 1, 45, 52–57 (2018), www.nyccfb.info/pdf/2017_Post-Election_Report_2.pdf.

[108] *See Democracy Voucher Program*, Seattle.gov (last visited May 22, 2019), www.seattle.gov /democracyvoucher/i-am-a-seattle-resident.

[109] *2017 Election Report*, Seattle Ethics & Elections Commission (March 9, 2018), www.seattle.gov/ethics/meetings/2018-03-09/item4.pdf.

[110] *See Democracy Voucher Program: Biennial Report 2017*, Seattle Ethics & Elections Commission, at 14, www.seattle.gov/Documents/Departments/EthicsElections/Democracy Voucher/Final%20-%20Biennial%20report%20-%2003_15_2018.pdf.

programs.[111] But studies of these systems do indicate that a properly crafted public financing program can draw the participation of viable candidates, provide them with sufficient funding, and increase both the competitiveness of elections and the funding role of ordinary voters.[112]

IV. TOWARD A BETTER FINANCING SYSTEM

The presidential nomination public funding program created in 1974 played an important role in sustaining competition and reducing dependence on large donors for more than two decades, but it is effectively moribund. There have been calls for its outright abolition.[113] Instead, it should be restored to life. But any new system must draw on the lessons learned from the collapse of the old, as well as from the experiences of the many state and local public funding programs. Most importantly, the campaign finance system must be attuned to the structure of the nomination process and the concerns of the candidates who participate in it.

First, public funds must be provided on a timely basis. The provision of the 1974 law delaying the first payment until the start of the election year is entirely out-of-step with the calendar of today's nomination process. Payments should be available throughout the year preceding the year of the election. Second, and relatedly, the state-specific spending limits make no sense in what has become essentially a national election in which the importance of the early states is often far out of proportion to their voting population. Third, the system must provide enough money to sustain a viable campaign so that it is more attractive to serious candidates than the private funding route. It is hard to say exactly what that amount should be, but it is surely far more than the $24 million funding cap that applied in 2016. It is almost certainly more than $100 million, and $200 million could be appropriate. Of course, not every candidate should receive that much public money. The amount any candidate receives should reflect her seriousness as a candidate, which may be measured by her success in grassroots fundraising or the votes she obtains in primaries and caucuses. The law could also certainly raise the initial conditions for eligibility above the minimal fundraising threshold set in 1974, and index that level to inflation thereafter.

---

[111] *See* Malbin & Parrott, *supra* note 103, at 224–45.

[112] Recently, the Washington Supreme Court rejected a claim that the voucher program was a compelled subsidy of political speech in violation of the First Amendment rights of Seattle property owners whose taxes were funding the program. Elster v. City of Seattle, 444 P.3d 590 (Wash. 2019). On March 30, 2020, the U.S. Supreme Court denied a petition for writ of certiorari, thereby declining to hear the case.

[113] R. Sam Garrett, Proposals to Eliminate the Public Financing of Presidential Campaigns, Cong. Res. Serv., Report No. R41604 (Feb. 7, 2017), https://fas.org/sgp/crs/misc/R41604.pdf.

Finally, candidates should not be required to accept spending limits as a condition for public funds. Spending limits are counterproductive. As long as candidates with access to their own personal wealth or the fundraising of high-dollar bundlers are free to rely on private funding without limits, and as long as independent groups are also free to raise and spend money without limits—and current constitutional doctrine indicates that these conditions are likely to obtain for the foreseeable future—spending limits will disadvantage publicly funded candidates and are likely to discourage serious candidates who can raise substantial private funds from participating in a public funding program. Public funding can achieve its goals of increasing electoral competitiveness and reducing the role of large donors without spending limits.

That does not mean that public funding should be unlimited. A workable system could include a sizeable public grant—allotted on a small-donation-multiple-match basis—up to a maximum amount, with candidates who reach that ceiling free to raise and spend additional private contributions, perhaps limited to low-dollar donations. Such a program would lower barriers to entry for candidates without access to large donors and provide incentives to reaching out widely to small donors, without handicapping participating candidates' ability to compete against their privately funded opponents.

H.R. 1—the "For the People Act of 2019"—passed by the House of Representatives in March 2019 provides an appropriate model. Proposed to take effect with the 2028 presidential election, it would provide qualifying candidates a 6-to-1 match for the first $200 of contributions received from any individual, up to a maximum of $250 million, subject to future cost-of-living indexation. There would be no spending limit for publicly funded candidates; however, the candidate would have to agree to accept no more than $1,000 in the aggregate from any donor. H.R. 1 contains many other specific limitations and requirements dealing with the financing of nomination campaigns that would need to be considered. The Senate has not taken up the measure, and it is highly unlikely it would pass the current Senate or be signed by the current President. But it does lay out some of the elements that are critical to a successful public financing program.

As young Senator Biden recognized in 1974, public financing is "not a cure-all for all the ills besetting our present political system."[114] But a viable public financing program for the presidential nomination process could address the concerns about political inequality and wealth-based barriers to electoral competition that he raised more than four decades ago and that continue to remain troubling features of our political system.

---

[114] Biden, *supra* note 1, at 70.

11

Campaign Finance Deregulation and the Hyperpolarization of Presidential Nominations in the Super PAC Era

Michael S. Kang[*]

By virtually every measure, American politics are more polarized today along political party lines than they have been in decades. In Congress, Republicans and Democrats are more sharply differentiated and internally homogeneous than they have been since the late-nineteenth century. This polarization has occurred in both houses of Congress and mirrors similar trends at the state level and among executive officers throughout American politics. The presidential nomination process is no exception. We live in a time of "hyperpolarization."[1]

Campaign finance may be partly to blame for modern hyperpolarization. Although today's levels of partisan polarization began building long ago, the deregulation of campaign finance under the Roberts Court has likely accelerated the ongoing process of polarization even further. Deregulation of campaign finance permitted wealthy donors to channel more money into presidential elections and gave them greater influence over the political process. Wealthy donors now can exercise influence not only through direct contributions to presidential candidates and their parties, but also through powerful Super PACs and 501(c) organizations largely free from legal restriction. Because wealthy donors tend to be ideologically extreme and motivated in their giving by their ideological preferences, this wider legal capacity to contribute financially to candidates, both directly and through outside groups, has empowered wealthy donors with ever more leverage to push the parties

[*] Michael S. Kang is the William G. and Virginia K. Karnes Research Professor of Law at the Northwestern Pritzker School of Law. Many thanks to Amanda Parris, Katherine Surma, and Amanda Wells for indispensable research assistance. Part of this chapter draws from my articles *The Brave New World of Party Campaign Finance Law*, 101 CORNELL L. REV. 531 (2016), and *The End of Campaign Finance Law*, 98 VA. L. REV. 1 (2012).
[1] Richard H. Pildes, *Why the Center Does Not Hold: The Causes of Hyperpolarized Democracy in America*, 99 CAL. L. REV. 273 (2011).

toward increasingly polarized positions. And big-money campaign finance in today's Super PAC age is never more prominent than in presidential election campaigns when fundraising and spending are at their highest.

Some critics of partisan polarization propose to counteract this consequence of campaign finance deregulation with *more* deregulation.[2] The underlying logic is surprising but simple. Deregulation empowered activist donors by freeing up their financing and control of outside groups like Super PACs and 501(c) organizations. Super PACs today have become standard issue for modern presidential candidates and can keep a candidate in the primary race on the strength of a single donor's immense wealth and support. If restrictions on fundraising by the major parties likewise were relaxed, then parties would be able to acquire new financial capacity to resist the influence of these donors and their outside groups. Presidential nominees, in particular, from both parties rely on the national party committees to fundraise and spend on their behalf as part of joint party efforts. Deregulation of the major parties therefore might restore balance to the system by revitalizing the parties as a counterweight against donors and their outside groups. Parties, with their strong electoral incentives to satisfy the median voter, could use these resources to encourage their presidential nominees to toe a more moderate party line that better serves their parties' national aspirations.

A worry about this logic is that deregulation of party campaign finance might instead encourage parties to depend on wealthy donors even more than they already do. Largely the same donors who encourage polarization through Super PACs and 501(c) organizations likely would account for new party fundraising under relaxed restrictions. Under liberalized campaign finance rules, the parties would look for additional money from the same ideologically motivated donors who fund Super PACs for presidential candidates and pressurize party politics toward ideological extremes in the first place. So, it is not clear that richer parties under these circumstances would counteract the influence of these wealthy donors if their newfound money comes largely from those same wealthy donors and the dollars involved grow significantly.

However, I suggest a slightly different approach for those worried about partisan polarization and looking to campaign finance law for help. In considering potential reforms, it will be productive to distinguish between restrictions on party spending from those on party fundraising. Partial deregulation of

[2] *See* RAYMOND LA RAJA & BRIAN SCHAFFNER, CAMPAIGN FINANCE AND POLITICAL POLARIZATION: WHEN PURISTS PREVAIL (2015); Pildes, *supra* note 1; Nathaniel Persily, *Stronger Parties as a Solution to Polarization, in* SOLUTIONS TO POLITICAL POLARIZATION IN AMERICA 125 (Nathaniel Persily ed., 2015).

party spending, while maintaining restrictions on party fundraising, may achieve the aim of strengthening the major parties without simultaneously increasing the sway of wealthy donors at the same time. A cautious, bifurcated approach to deregulation would better counteract partisan polarization by strengthening the parties without expanding the influence of polarizing big-money donors who are a source of the problem in the first place. The parties' greater spending capacity and flexibility could give them greater influence to counteract Super PACs in the presidential nomination process, for instance, but without at the same time increasing the leverage of big-money donors over the parties themselves.

I. THE RELATIONSHIP BETWEEN CAMPAIGN FINANCE AND POLARIZATION

What role does campaign finance law plausibly play in partisan polarization? Without question, a much larger array of sociopolitical forces converged to generate today's hyperpolarized politics. Many have already documented the historical inputs that helped transmogrify the partisan calm of the 1950s into the intense tribal party warfare of the Trump presidency.[3] Whatever role campaign finance plays in hyperpolarization, it is a comparatively small one in the overarching story of race, economics, and realignment, well-documented elsewhere. Nevertheless, campaign finance law has played an important, if localized, supporting role in polarization over what has been a past decade of enormous change in campaign finance law and practice.

Begin with the fact that wealthy campaign contributors are highly ideological. Surveys of campaign contributors establish that contributors are ideologically extreme relative to average voters and rank ideological concerns highly in deciding when and where to give.[4] While business groups are more interested in access and regularly donate to both parties in that spirit, high-level individual contributors are more likely to donate almost exclusively to one major party and contribute disproportionately to candidates who are ideologically extreme.[5]

---

[3] *See* Michael S. Kang, *Hyperpartisan Gerrymandering*, 61 B.C. L. Rev. 1380 (2020).

[4] *See* Peter L. Francia, Paul S. Herrnson, John C. Green, Lynda W. Powell & Clyde Wilcox, The Financiers of Congressional Elections (2003); Clifford W. Brown, Lynda W. Powell & Clyde Wilcox, Serious Money: Fundraising and Contributing in Presidential Nomination Campaigns (1995); Michael Barber, *Ideological Donors, Contribution Limits, and the Polarization of State Legislatures*, 78 J. Pol. 296 (2016).

[5] *See* Adam Bonica, *Ideology and Interests in the Political Marketplace*, 57 Am. J. Pol. Sci. 294, 301–07 (2013); Michael Barber, *Ideological Donors, Contribution Limits, and the Polarization*

Individual campaign contributors thus help polarize the major parties, channeling resources to more extreme candidates and coaxing candidates and parties in more ideological directions as the need for their money grows. As a result, ideological polarization increases when legal limits on individual contributions to candidates are higher or not imposed at all.[6] When contributors are legally free to give more, they do. And when they do, their ideological influence also increases and in turn produces more polarized politics in those jurisdictions. This pattern is particularly pronounced within the Republican Party, whose donors give disproportionately to candidates and whose candidates and donors are more ideologically extreme than the Democrats' candidates and donors.[7]

Freeing high-level contributors to give more money is exactly what has happened over the past decade of campaign finance law. A U.S. Supreme Court under Chief Justice William Rehnquist that routinely upheld campaign finance regulation against constitutional challenge gave way to a new Court under Chief Justice John Roberts that consistently struck down nearly every campaign finance regulation it reviewed, from aggregate contribution limits, to restrictions on corporate electioneering, to public financing. This series reached its apex in *Citizens United v. FEC*,[8] when the Court overruled Rehnquist Court precedent in striking down federal prohibitions on corporate electioneering that stood in some form for longer than a century. The immediate effect of *Citizens United* was to enable corporations and unions to spend on independent expenditures and therefore finance campaign advocacy in federal elections.

Although the immediate public outcry about *Citizens United* focused on corporate electioneering, the decision's most important consequence was a different result, if only a little less obvious. Two months later, taking its cue from *Citizens United*, the D.C. Circuit Court of Appeals decided *Speechnow.org v. FEC*.[9] The decision struck down as unconstitutional contribution limits on a non-connected group, Speechnow.org, that planned to

---

of American Legislatures, 78 AM. J. POL. 296 (2016); Lee Drutman, *Are the 1% of the 1% Pulling Politics in a Conservative Direction?*, SUNLIGHT FOUNDATION (June 26, 2013), http://sunlight foundation.com/blow/2013/06/26/1pct_of_the_1pct_polarization/ [https://perma.cc/46U9-3UVU].

6   LA RAJA & SCHAFFNER, *supra* note 2; Michael Barber & Nolan M. McCarty, *Causes and Consequences of Polarization, in* SOLUTIONS TO POLITICAL POLARIZATION IN AMERICA 15 (Nathaniel Persily ed., 2015).

7   See LA RAJA & SCHAFFNER, *supra* note 2, at 59.

8   558 U.S. 310 (2010).

9   599 F.3d 686 (D.C. Cir. 2010).

engage only in independent expenditures without making contributions to, or coordinating with candidates for federal office. Reasoning directly from *Citizens United*, the D.C. Circuit ruled in *Speechnow.org* that "the government has *no* anti-corruption interest in limiting independent expenditures" and invalidated federal contribution limits that would have applied to Speechnow.org's fundraising for its campaign activities.[10]

The basic result from *Speechnow.org* was that outside groups suddenly faced dramatically less campaign finance regulation than they once did.[11] Non-connected groups like Speechnow.org are popularly known and regulated today as Super PACs provided they engage only in independent expenditures without making contributions. Super PACs can fund their independent expenditures with unrestricted contributions from individuals, as well as unrestricted contributions from corporations and unions. Along the same lines, 501(c) organizations ostensibly cannot contribute to candidates and parties, nor make campaigning their "major purpose." But subject to those conditions, many 501(c) organizations claim not to qualify as regulated political committees under federal campaign finance law and therefore make independent expenditures without restriction, unhindered by even basic campaign finance disclosure requirements.[12]

The rapid deregulation of campaign finance under the Roberts Court created a dramatic expansion of opportunities for the very wealthy to fund electioneering, particularly for the presidential nomination process. After these court decisions cleared the way, money flowed to newly created Super PACs in a matter of months for the 2010 elections.[13] Eighty-three newly minted Super PACs quickly raised more than $60 million for the 2010 elections.[14] Election spending by all outside groups, including 501(c) organizations, increased dramatically from nearly $70 million for the previous midterm elections in 2006 to more than $300 million for 2010.[15]

---

[10]   *Id.* at 693 (emphasis in original).
[11]   *See generally* Michael S. Kang, *The End of Campaign Finance Law*, 98 VA. L. REV. 1, 27–40 (2012).
[12]   *See* Richard Briffault, *Two Challenges for Campaign Finance Disclosure After* Citizens United *and* Doe v. Reed, 19 WM. & MARY BILL RTS. J. 983, 1007–08 (2011).
[13]   *See* Richard Briffault, *Super PACS*, 96 MINN. L. REV. 1644, 1672–75 (2012).
[14]   *See 2010 Outside Spending, by Group*, CTR. FOR RESPONSIVE POLITICS (2010), www.open secrets.org/outsidespending/summ.php?cycle=2010&disp=O&type=I&chrt=P [http://perma.cc/2 VQ4-L2GR]; *see also* Kang, *supra* note 11, at 34–38 (commenting on the amount of money raised by Super PACs leading up to the 2010 election).
[15]   *See Total Outside Spending by Election Cycle, Excluding Party Committees*, CTR. FOR RESPONSIVE POLITICS (2012), www.opensecrets.org/outsidespending/cycle_tots.php [http://perma.cc/M53S-28RA].

By the 2012 presidential nomination process, these trends only accelerated. In presidential years, federal campaign fundraising and spending always peak. Super PACs sprouted up to support individual presidential candidates, so-called alter ego Super PACs, funded almost wholly by one ultra-wealthy donor who, post–*Citizens United*, could contribute an unlimited amount to organized efforts allied with their favored candidate. Through these Super PACs, a single wealthy donor was able to fund nearly an entire presidential campaign and thus sustain unpopular primary candidates with continuing financial support long after their candidacies would have petered out from lack of popular support.

In 2012, this new legal landscape meant presidential candidates like Newt Gingrich, Jon Huntsman, and Rick Santorum relied overwhelmingly on a single Super PAC sponsor, only to be outspent by other Super PACs supporting eventual Republican nominee Mitt Romney. The result was an elongated, expensive Republican presidential primary process that some blamed in part for Romney's eventual loss in the general election.[16] All told, outside groups raised and spent more than $1 billion for the 2012 elections, with 1,310 Super PACs raising more than $800 million and accounting for more than $600 million of the total spending.[17] These trends only continued upward into the following presidential election cycle in 2016, during which 2,393 Super PACs raised almost $2 billion.[18]

However, throughout this deregulatory transformation of campaign finance law, candidates and political parties remained as regulated as they had been. Even while outside groups like Super PACs were largely liberated from regulation, and 501(c) organizations even more so, federal candidates and parties were subject to the traditional regulatory panoply of source restrictions, contribution limits, and comprehensive disclosure. The regulatory differential between candidates and party committees on the one hand, and outside groups on the other hand, created pressure for money to flow toward these outside groups that face less regulation. Campaign money in politics is fungible and tends to adapt to the regulatory landscape by finding less regulated outlets, like water finding its own level.

Although these hydraulics of campaign finance have certainly played out with respect to new regulation in the past, the recent deregulation of campaign

---

[16] See Michael S. Kang, *The Year of the Super PAC*, 81 GEO. WASH. L. REV. 1902 (2013).

[17] See *2012 Outside Spending, by Super PAC*, CTR. FOR RESPONSIVE POLITICS (2012), www.opensecrets.org/outsidespending/summ.php?cycle=2012&chrt=V&type=S [http://perm a.cc/DGE4-L24K].

[18] See Madi Alexander, *PACs Made Up Nearly Half of 2016 Election Spending*, BLOOMBERG LAW (April 18, 2017).

finance produced a pattern that I have described as the "reverse hydraulics" of campaign finance.[19] As campaign finance regulation peeled back, money channeled toward outside groups freed up by court decisions, perhaps at the expense of parties who were not. Big-money donors were eager to spend more than what contribution limits permitted and poured millions into outside groups in support of their favored presidential candidates. This newly decentralized primary environment meant lots of well-funded presidential candidates and Super PACs largely outside the influence of the major party establishment.

II. A POST–*CITIZENS UNITED* CASE FOR DEREGULATION OF PARTY CAMPAIGN FINANCE?

In response to this new Super PAC era of campaign finance, a growing chorus of prominent commentators are now arguing for the deregulation of party campaign finance as a counterweight to the ascent of well-funded outside groups.[20] The basic argument is that the reverse hydraulics feeding campaign finance money to outside groups can be undone by deregulating the major parties from their current contribution limits and other restrictions. If campaign finance money is currently directed to Super PACs and 501(c) organizations because they are less regulated than the formal party committees, then deregulation of the party committees ought to induce a redirection of that money back to the parties. Such redirection of money to the major parties would reinvigorate the parties and candidates vis-a-vis the burgeoning power of outside groups. Newly empowered parties, according to this view, could counterbalance the centrifugal influence of these outside groups and the high-level contributors who fund them. When it comes to the presidential race, parties might be able to centralize the primary process and deter primary also-ran

---

[19] See Kang, *supra* note 11, at 40–52.

[20] See Persily, *supra* note 2; Raymond J. La Raja, *Campaign Finance and Partisan Polarization in the United States*, 9 DUKE J. CONST. L. & PUB. POL'Y 223, 236–37 (2014); Richard H. Pildes, *Romanticizing Democracy, Political Fragmentation, and the Decline of American Government*, 124 YALE L.J. 804, 836–45 (2014); Nicholas O. Stephanopoulos, *Aligning Campaign Finance Law*, 101 VA. L. REV. 1425, 1425 (2015); Ray La Raja & Brian Schaffner, *Want to Reduce Polarization? Give Parties More Money*, WASH. POST (July 21, 2014), http:// washingtonpost.com/blogs/monkey-cage/wp/2014/07/21/want-to-reduce-polarization-give-parties-more-money/ [http://perma.cc/R5XA-QQRN]; *see also* PETER J. WALLISON & JOEL M. GORA, BETTER PARTIES, BETTER GOVERNMENT: A REALISTIC PROGRAM FOR CAMPAIGN FINANCE REFORM 52–57 (2009) (suggesting that eliminating restrictions on party campaign finance creates a more level political playing field).

candidates from damaging the eventual nominee's general election prospects, Super-PAC support notwithstanding.

For campaign finance purposes, the "party" could be fairly conceptualized at several different levels of generality. In the UCLA School view of parties articulated by political scientist John Zaller and his colleagues,[21] the party writ large is a broad, far-flung network of political actors that includes not only the formal party committees, officeholders, and candidates, but high-level party donors, party-allied interest groups, intellectual leaders and pundits, and even grassroots volunteers and sympathetic voters.[22] This broadest conception of the party writ large as a sprawling network certainly includes outside groups such as Super PACs and 501(c) organizations aligned with one major party or the other.[23] But commentators in favor of deregulating the major parties in campaign finance are focused narrowly on the "party" as represented by the formal party campaign finance entities, mainly the national party committees, and perhaps leadership PACs, and a few other types of party vehicles thoroughly regulated under federal campaign finance law.[24] Deregulation could take various forms, from substantially higher contribution limits, to the reintroduction of party soft money, to party-sponsored Super PACs that could collect uncapped money from individuals, corporations, and unions for independent expenditures.

This distinction between the formal party committees and the party writ large is a meaningful one in understanding the intraparty contestation at the heart of the deregulatory logic. The party committees are directly controlled by the party leadership, while the broader party is a polyphonic network in which intraparty contestation over the party's political direction occurs among a diversity of players.[25] Consistent with the UCLA School view of parties, the activists and donors behind the outside groups are policy demanders who pull

---

[21]   *See, e.g.*, Kathleen Bawn et al., *A Theory of Political Parties: Groups, Policy Demands, and Nominations in American Politics*, 10 PERSP. ON POL. 571, 572–75 (2012).

[22]   *See, e.g.*, Paul S. Herrnson, *The Roles of Party Organizations, Party-Connected Committees, and Party Allies in Elections*, 71 J. POL. 1207, 1209–16 (2009) (describing this multilayered composition of the party coalition).

[23]   *See* Kang, *supra* note 16, at 1923–27; *see also* SETH MASKET, CTR. FOR EFFECTIVE PUB. MGMT. AT BROOKINGS INST., MITIGATING EXTREME PARTNERSHIP IN AN ERA OF NETWORKED PARTIES: AN EXAMINATION OF VARIOUS REFORM STRATEGIES 3 (Mar. 2014) (characterizing the broader party as a "polycephalous creature with ambiguous boundaries") (citing Michael Heaney et al., *Polarized Networks: The Organizational Affiliations of National Party Convention Delegates*, 56 AM. BEHAV. SCIENTIST 1654, 1654–76 (2012)).

[24]   *See* Michael S. Kang, *The Hydraulics and Politics of Party Regulation*, 91 IOWA L. REV. 131, 133–35 (2005); Joseph Fishkin & Heather K. Gerken, *The Two Trends that Matter for Party Politics*, 89 N.Y.U. L. REV ONLINE 32 (2014).

[25]   *See* Bawn et al., *supra* note 21, at 572–75.

the parties toward the ideological edges, while party leadership and office-holders should pragmatically prefer centrist positions that protect the party's electoral viability. Worry about the rise of outside groups stems from the activists' and donors' centrifugal influence within this intraparty contestation for control. When there is little or no intraparty contestation about the party's immediate goals, as during a general election, the broad party network unites across its diverse membership, from the party leadership to activists and donors, against the common enemy.

But when the party is politically divided, as during presidential primary elections, activists and donors behind party-allied Super PACs and 501(c) organizations can fuel internal dissension, exacerbate polarization, and fracture the formal party leadership's influence.[26] This is what certainly occurred in the Republican presidential primaries for the 2012 and 2016 presidential elections. Arguably the inability of the Republican Party to organize neatly behind a more mainstream candidate facilitated the rise of outsider Donald Trump as the eventual party nominee in 2016. The intraparty tension between the party establishment and more ideological party donors, played out in campaign finance, controls the party's ideological direction and is therefore central to the concerns about party polarization. Ideologically extreme candidates, who enjoy fundraising advantages with ideologically motivated donors, may become more common as they and their big-money contributors become emboldened by campaign finance deregulation and the inability of the party establishments to shape their presidential nomination processes.

Richard Pildes recently championed the re-assertion of party leadership within this UCLA School-style intraparty struggle as the key to reducing hyperpolarization.[27] Drawing from political science and other advocates of campaign finance deregulation, Pildes contends that party leaders tend to be ideological middlemen with internalized incentives to broaden the electoral appeal of their parties and broker effective governance across party lines. However, across a landscape of fragmented, polarized party politics, "party leaders can play this role only if they have the tools and leverage to bring along their caucuses in the direction that [they] believe best positions the party as a whole."[28] For this reason, he proposes further deregulation of party-related campaign finance by removing restrictions from coordination between party spending and candidates and

---

[26] *See* Kang, *supra* note 16, at 1919–27 (explaining these dynamics and describing the role of Super PACs in the 2012 Republican primaries as illustration); *see also* Nicholas Confessore, *G.O.P. Donors Seek Early Call on '16 Nominee*, N.Y. TIMES (Dec. 8, 2014), at A1 (discussing the Republican Party's efforts to avoid a Super PAC-driven party split in 2016).

[27] Pildes, *supra* note 20, at 845–51.

[28] *Id.* at 833.

significantly raising contribution limits on party committees. He claims that parties donate twice as much to centrist candidates than to ideological extreme ones and thus are "a force for moderation compared to individual contributions," which are ideologically motivated and highly polarized.[29]

III. A SKEPTICAL RESPONSE TO NEW DEREGULATION

The critical question is whether deregulation of party campaign finance will enable the major parties to serve as a counterweight to outside groups as Pildes and others predict, or whether the influx of new money from the donor class will further co-opt the parties. Any notion that such deregulation will boost the formal party leadership's influence assumes that deregulation allows the formal party committees to collect and spend more campaign finance money. The questions are where that new money comes from and whether increased contributions from those sources affects how the parties subsequently behave. It would be one thing if we could assume the parties will receive new money from new sources indifferent to its use and thus allow the parties to deploy it freely as the parties wish. But this assumption would violate the overarching premise in the first place that campaign finance contributors, whether parties or individuals, care about how the money is used and thoughtfully deploy their money to achieve their strategic aims. If we assume that under deregulation the parties will strategically use new campaign finance money to gain greater leverage over their presidential candidates and achieve certain ideological ends, we ought also to expect, one step further back, that the original sources of the parties' new money also will gain greater leverage over the parties.

Most proposed deregulation simply encourages the major parties to rely even more heavily on their wealthiest donors for financial support. For instance, deregulation that authorizes political parties to operate their own Super PACs or raise soft money again would enable the parties to collect campaign money in larger chunks from very wealthy donors. So too would higher contribution limits for party-related vehicles, or the elimination of the aggregate limit on total contributions to the national parties. The so-called Cromnibus of 2014, as an example, increased the maximum an individual donor may give to each national party's committees to an aggregate of more than $1.5 million over an election cycle.[30] Apart from a few spending-side

---

[29] *Id.* at 829.

[30] *See* Hannah Hess, *Campaign Finance Provisions Causing "Cromnibus" Heartburn*, Roll Call (Dec. 10, 2014), http://blogs.rollcall.com/hill-blotter/campaign-finance-provisions-causing-cromnibus-heartburn/ [http://perma.cc/LQK2-Q27L].

exceptions, proposals for party deregulation thus encourage parties to depend even more on their wealthiest donors than they already do.

A current approximation of a party-sponsored Super PAC has been Senate Majority PAC, which is operated by former senior staffers of Democratic Senate leader Harry Reid. Senate Majority PAC spent more than $44 million for the 2014 midterm elections, $19.3 million of which came in individual contributions of at least $500,000, including a $5 million contribution from Tom Steyer and a $4 million contribution from Fred Eychaner.[31] Senate Majority PAC's average contribution, including all donors, was $170,525, which far exceeded the average American household income of $73,000.[32] The Super PAC's defining advantage over the garden-variety political committee is its legal capacity to accept unlimited donations from the very rich. Super-PAC campaign finance is a rich man's game, relying almost entirely on the generosity of ultra-wealthy men as their reason for being. Of more than $600 million raised by Super PACs in the 2014 federal election cycle, roughly a third came from just 42 individuals, mostly men, who averaged more than $1 million in Super PAC donations for a midterm election.[33] Tom Steyer alone donated a total of almost $74 million to Super PACs for the 2014 elections.[34] It is no surprise then that the share of all campaign contributions made by the top .01 percent of the voting-age population has more than quadrupled over the past thirty years to more than 40 percent.[35] This pattern has continued ever since. Sheldon Adelson donated more than $122 million during the 2018 election cycle, almost 10 percent of total Super PAC fundraising for the cycle by himself.

---

[31] *See* Steve Tetreault, *Reid Has Plenty at Stake in Election*, LAS VEGAS REV. J. (Nov. 1, 2014), www.reviewjournal.com/politics/elections/reid-has-plenty-stake-election [http://perma.cc/W X6Q-6CGD]; Matea Gold, *Top Harry Reid Advisers Build Big-Money Firewall to Protect Senate Democrats*, WASH. POST (Sept. 16, 2014), www.washingtonpost.com/politics/top-harry-reid-advisers-build-big-money-firewall-to-protect-sentate-democrats/2014/09/16991381b6 -3cdf-11e4-9587-5dafd96295f0_story.html [http://perma.cc/C8H6-JCXH].

[32] *See* Ian Vandewalker, *Outside Spending and Dark Money in Toss-Up Senate Races: Post-election Update*, BRENNAN CTR. FOR JUSTICE 2–3 (Nov. 10, 2014), www.brennancenter.org /analysis/outside-spending-and-dark-money-toss-senate-races-post-election-update [http://per ma.cc/9N7N-F4EQ].

[33] *See* Fredreka Schouten & Christopher Schnaars, *Mega-influence: These 42 Dominate Super PAC Donations*, USA TODAY (Oct. 29, 2014), www.usatoday.com/sotry/news/politics/2014/10/ 28/top-super-pac-donors-of-the-midterms-steyer-bloomber-singer-mercer/18060219/ [http://perma.cc/PS9H-EKUH]. The article notes that only one female donor gave more than $2 million to Super PACs last cycle, former Senate candidate Linda McMahon. *Id.*

[34] *See* Katia Savchuk, *Billionaire Tom Steyer on Money in Politics, Spending $74 M on the Election*, FORBES (Nov. 3, 2014), http://onforb.es/1A5xS2R [http://perma.cc/PPN5-6L5U].

[35] *See* Bonica, *supra* note 5.

For the 2016 presidential election, Senate Majority PAC doubled its midterm fundraising to $92.8 million, this time with Eychaner giving $12 million, and James Simons giving $8 million. Senate Majority PAC accounted for more than half of Democratic spending for 2016. Notably, Senate Majority PAC informally coordinated its spending with the spending of so-called "dark money" groups. Senate Majority PAC raised and spent increased amounts of money coinciding with the 60-day Electioneering Communication Period under the Bipartisan Campaign Reform Act that require "dark money" groups to disclose their funding. Where those groups curtailed their activity, Senate Majority PAC picked up the slack.[36] Senate Majority PAC raised $19 million in the first 19 days of October 2016 alone as it assumed the fundraising load.[37]

The most prominent Republican counterpart to Senate Majority PAC, the Senate Leadership Fund, is predictably run by former senior GOP staffers, including Mitch McConnell's former chief of staff Steven Law.[38] Virtually all the Senate Leadership Fund's individual donations in 2016 came from contributions of $25,000 or more.[39] As a consequence, the parties already run a version of Super PAC, and these Super PACs rely on the same familiar wealthy donors who fund their other activity and are partially responsible for hyperpolarization in the first place.

The hope, though, that deregulated party fundraising reduces partisan polarization rests on a blind faith that, when it comes to new opportunities under deregulation, the party leadership will resist the additional influence of these wealthy donors. As established, individual contributors who constitute the donor class are overwhelmingly wealthy and motivated by ideology in their campaign finance activity. These policy demanders who already have fueled polarization through their campaign financing are the only individuals meaningfully affected by most proposed forms of party deregulation.[40] The primary purpose of most forms of deregulation is to facilitate very large, effectively

---

[36] *See* Llewellyn Hinkes-Jones, *Super PAC Spending Replaces Dark Money as Election Nears*, BLOOMBERG BNA (Oct. 17, 2016), www.bna.com/super-pac-spending-n57982078708/.

[37] *See* Seung Min Kim & Burgess Everett, *Wisconsin Senate Race Becomes a Battleground*, POLITICO (Oct. 28, 2016), www.politico.com/story/2016/10/russ-feingold-wisconsin-senate-democrats-funds-230446.

[38] *See* Ian Vandewalker, *Election Spending 2016: Just Three Interests Dominate, Shadow Parties Continue to Rise*, BRENNAN CTR. FOR JUSTICE, at 6 (Oct. 25, 2016). www.brennancenter.org /sites/default/files/publications/Election%20Spending%202016%20Three%20Interests%20Do minate.pdf.

[39] *See id.*

[40] *See, e.g.*, Clyde Wilcox et al., *With Limits Raised, Who Will Give More?: The Impact of BCRA on Individual Donors, in* LIFE AFTER REFORM: WHEN THE BIPARTISAN CAMPAIGN REFORM ACT MEETS POLITICS 61, 69–79 (Michael J. Malbin ed., 2003) (reporting the ideological motivations of the wealthy donors affected by regulation of party campaign finance).

uncapped contributions from these few individuals who can afford large donations for political causes well beyond the wherewithal of most Americans.[41] The party leadership, as the existing experience so far with party Super PACs already shows, would need to draw their new revenue from the same donor class that has funded the proliferation of outside groups in campaign finance and any resulting polarization from this decentralization of party politics.[42] What is more, any current changes to party campaign finance along these lines would occur at the very moment that this donor class appears to becoming more assertive in their control of their money for ideological, as opposed to straightforwardly partisan purposes.[43]

The deregulation of party-related campaign finance may only accelerate this distributional and ideological lurch in American campaign finance toward the concentrated interests of the very wealthy. Deregulation of party fundraising today would occur in a campaign finance system that has already been thoroughly deregulated, where fundraising and spending have already skyrocketed, and where the influence wielded by wealthy donors is unprecedented in the modern era of campaign finance since *Buckley v. Valeo*.[44] It is difficult to overstate the surging importance of very wealthy donors in this rapidly evolving system already skewed so far in favor of their interests. Martin Gilens and Larry Bartels, among others, have compellingly documented the extent to which the political system is almost singularly responsive to the stratified preferences of the richest Americans over their fellow citizens of ordinary means.[45] Gilens and Benjamin Page recently summarized that "economic elites and organized interest groups . . . play a substantial

---

[41] The first contributors to take advantage of the expanded opportunities to donate to the party committees under the Cromnibus provisions included Shelden Adelson, David Koch, and Henry Kravis. *See* Kenneth P. Doyle, *Big GOP Donors Giving to New Accounts Congress Created to Help Political Parties*, BNA DAILY REPORT, May 26, 2015, at A-6.

[42] *See* Russ Choma, *Final Tally: 2014's Midterm Was Most Expensive, with Fewer Donors*, Center for Responsive Politics, CTR. FOR RESPONSIVE POL. (Feb. 15, 2018), www.opensecrets.org/ne ws/2015/02/final-tally-2014s-midterm-was-most-expensive-with-fewer-donors/ (reporting that 2014 featured the most campaign spending ever for a federal midterm election and a decline in individual donors, which produced the highest all-time average individual contribution amount).

[43] *See* Thomas B. Edsall, *Billionaires Going Rogue*, N.Y. TIMES (Oct. 28, 2012), http://campaign stops.blogs.nytimes.com/2012/10/28/billionaires-going-rogue/ [http://perma.cc/5WSN-GTHL]; Jim Rutenberg, *Money Talks*, N.Y. TIMES (Oct. 17, 2014).

[44] 424 U.S. 1 (1976).

[45] *See* LARRY M. BARTELS, UNEQUAL DEMOCRACY: THE POLITICAL ECONOMY OF THE NEW GILDED AGE 257–65 (2008); MARTIN GILENS, AFFLUENCE AND INFLUENCE: ECONOMIC INEQUALITY AND POLITICAL POWER IN AMERICA (2012); JACOB S. HACKER & PAUL PIERSON, WINNER-TAKE-ALL POLITICS: HOW WASHINGTON MADE THE RICH RICHER AND TURNED ITS BACK ON THE MIDDLE CLASS (2010); *see also* Stephanopoulos, *supra* note 20, at 1425

part in affecting public policy, but the general public has little or no independent influence."[46] These findings make it difficult not to believe the political system is tilting precipitously toward the preferences of the wealthy. Whatever the role of campaign finance law in setting political responsiveness, the additional removal of restrictions on party fundraising may just accelerate the effects of Super PACs and other forms of deregulation in multiplying the political capacity of the very rich and their polarizing tendencies.

For this reason, further deregulation of party fundraising would not reduce partisan polarization or encourage ideological moderation.[47] The literature is ambivalent on whether party leadership are actually ideological middlemen as some contend or, instead, are more extreme than their party median.[48] Because individual donors are ideologically motivated and highly polarized, party officeholders who are themselves ideologically extreme enjoy increasing advantages in fundraising and therefore exercise growing leverage because of their financial resources.[49] Eric Heberlig and

---

(summarizing this literature and proposing campaign finance law be directed toward aligning policymaking with public opinion).

[46] Martin Gilens & Benjamin I. Page, *Testing Theories of American Politics: Elites, Interest Groups, and Average Citizens*, 12 PERSP. ON POL. 564, 572 (2014).

[47] *See* THOMAS E. MANN & ANTHONY CORRADO, CTR. FOR EFFECTIVE PUB. MGMT. AT BROOKINGS INST., PARTY POLARIZATION AND CAMPAIGN FINANCE 17 (2014); Fishkin & Gerken, *supra* note 24, at 39–46.

[48] *Compare* Pildes, *supra* note 20, at 832 (arguing that party leadership comprises ideological middlemen) *with* Bernard Grofman et al., *Congressional Leadership 1965–96: A New Look at the Extremism versus Centrality Debate*, 27 LEGIS. STUD. Q. 87,98 (2002) ("[P]arty leaders (in both parties) tend to be drawn from the part of the ideological spectrum where the greatest concentration of their members lies, the area beyond the median toward the party mode."); *see also* Eric Heberlig et al., *The Price of Leadership: Campaign Money and the Polarization of Congressional Parties*, 68 J. POL. 992, 993–95 (2006) ("[B]oth the elected leadership itself and the farm system for elected leaders are increasingly populated by ideologues."); A. J. McGann et al., *Why Party Leaders Are More Extreme Than Their Members: Modeling Sequential Elimination Elections in the U.S. House of Representatives*, 113 PUB. CHOICE 337, 351–52 (2002) (finding that "party leaders tend to be more extreme that their median members . . . ."). For a neutral assessment, see Douglas B. Harris & Garrison Nelson, *Middlemen No More? Emergent Patterns in Congressional Leadership Selection*, 41 PS: POL. SCI. & POL. 49, 51 (2008) (noting that leaders from the 107th to 110th Congress were equally likely to be middlemen as they were extremists); Stephen Jessee & Neil Malhotra, *Are Congressional Leaders Middlepersons or Extremists? Yes*, 35 LEGIS. STUD. Q. 361, 380–84 (2010) (finding that elected leaders are usually close to their party's ideological median, but also display extremist tendencies). *See also* Stephanie Stamm, *Paul Ryan Would Be the Most Conservative House Speaker in Recent History*, NAT'L J., Oct. 21, 2015 (reporting that new House Speaker Paul Ryan has the most polarized DW-NOMINATE score among the last 11 Speakers and ranks in the top quintile for conservatism in the House).

[49] *See* Michael J. Ensley, *Individual Campaign Contributions and Candidate Ideology*, 138 PUB. CHOICE 221, 227 (2009) (finding that Republican and Democratic candidates could raise

his co-authors contend that this fundraising advantage actually imparts an edge to ideologues when it comes to party leadership selection, particularly as the emphasis on fundraising increases.[50] Ideologues in party leadership have incentives not only to broaden the party's mainstream appeal, which does not seem the current priority of the Republican Party,[51] but are also charged with realizing the median preferences of polarized, increasingly cohesive caucuses as a matter of conditional party government.[52] In this alternative telling, party polarization may have increased not because party leadership is weak right now, but because the party leadership represents ideologically cohesive, historically extreme caucuses and reflects the strength of those polarized preferences.[53] This dynamic is exacerbated by divided government, which makes party accountability even more difficult for independent voters to sort out.[54] As a result, how deregulation of party fundraising plays out is far from obvious and not likely to result in depolarization.[55]

---

more money if they deviated from their respective parties' ideological centers); Heberlig et al., *supra* note 48; Bertram Johnson, *Individual Contributions: A Fundraising Advantage for the Ideologically Extreme?*, 38 AM. POL. RES. 890, 903–06 (2010) (noting the advantages candidates can obtain from appealing to ideologically extreme individual donors); Walter J. Stone & Elizabeth N. Simas, *Candidate Valence and Ideological Positions in U.S. House Elections*, 54 AM. J. POL. SCI. 371, 380–82 (2010) (finding that candidates have an electoral incentive to move ideologically away from their districts and speculating that this finding is linked to campaign contributions by ideologically extreme individual contributors).

[50] *See* Heberlig et al., *supra* note 48, at 1002–04.

[51] *See generally* THOMAS E. MANN & NORMAN J. ORNSTEIN, IT'S EVEN WORSE THAN IT LOOKS: HOW THE AMERICAN CONSTITUTIONAL SYSTEM COLLIDED WITH THE NEW POLITICS OF EXTREMISM 51–59 (2012) (criticizing the Republican Party's rightward shift and developing this argument).

[52] *See* DAVID W. ROHDE, PARTIES AND LEADERS IN THE POSTREFORM HOUSE 105 (1991).

[53] *See* MANN & CORRADO, *supra* note 47, at 14 ("Parties today are strong in the electorate, strong in their vast organizational networks, and strong in government."); *see also id.* at 18 ("Inadequate resources are among the least important problems facing party leaders in Congress on either side of the aisle."). It may be that advocates of stronger party leadership today are simply nostalgic for bygone post-war bipartisanship that was itself historically exceptional. *See* Hahrie Han & David W. Brady, *A Delayed Return to Historical Norms: Congressional Party Polarization After the Second World War*, 37 BRIT. J. POL. SCI. 505, 507–12 (2007).

[54] *See* Morris P. Fiorina, *An Era of Divided Government*, 107 POL. SCI. Q. 387, 408 (1992) ("In obscuring responsibility for government actions and the results thereof, divided control exacerbates the already serious problems of responsibility that are inherent in American politics.").

[55] *See* MASKET, *supra* note 23, at 13 ("[T]here is little reason to believe that a change in the campaign finance system would substantially hurt or help parties or change the voting behavior of the politicians they nominate.").

IV. DEREGULATION OF PARTY *SPENDING*, NOT FUNDRAISING

Is there any hope of addressing hyperpolarization through party campaign finance? A key pivot, I propose, is to deregulate party campaign finance in a way that tilts intraparty contestation toward the party leadership and away from policy-demanding activists and donors. Any deregulation therefore should centralize party politics in the party leadership, but without increasing the sway of major contributors in the same process. For this reason, I suggest that the most promising approach may be the deregulation of party *spending* without deregulation of party *fundraising*. Federal law, for instance, comprehensively regulates party fundraising through a broad set of source restrictions, contribution limits, and disclosure requirements that condition how parties receive campaign money, from whom, and in what amounts. However, federal law likewise regulates party campaign spending in a variety of ways. It regulates how and when money can be spent, to whom it can be given and in what amounts, and what and how often spending must be disclosed. Deregulation of party spending need not entail the deregulation of party fundraising.

Political scientists Ray La Raja and Brian Schaffner are the foremost spokesmen for the deregulation of party campaign finance at the state level, and so far, their work on the polarizing effects of party campaign finance does not distinguish between party fundraising and spending.[56] They study the relationship between state levels of campaign finance regulation with the respective state's partisan polarization and find greater regulation of party campaign finance associated with greater polarization. While La Raja and Schaffner agree about the polarizing influence of individual contributors, they compare only those states "that allow parties to raise and contribute unlimited sums" to states with any limits on either fundraising or spending.

But it is plausible that limitations on fundraising and limitations on spending have different effects on polarization. When La Raja and Schaffner bifurcate their analysis between states that (1) limit contributions to parties but not contributions by parties; and (2) limit contributions by parties but not contributions to parties, they find that the former but not the latter resemble states that limit both types of contributions in terms of independent expenditures.[57] This finding hints at a possibility their postulated association between party campaign finance laws and polarization turns more on restrictions of party contributions to their candidates than of individual contributions to parties, as I hypothesize. Admittedly this is speculative for now, but also

---

[56] *See generally* LA RAJA & SCHAFFNER, *supra* note 2.
[57] *Id.* at 123.

grounded logically in assumptions that proponents of deregulation themselves confidently assert.

The advantage in deregulating party spending, by contrast from party fundraising, is that it frees parties to do more with their money without, at the same time, opening the door to more money from policy demanding donors. As donors are legally free to inject more money into politics, their influence increases, and since *Citizens United*, there has been dramatic deregulation of campaign finance, almost entirely on this fundraising side of party politics. *Randall v. Sorrell* struck down low contribution limits.[58] *Citizens United* and *Speechnow.org* opened the door to Super PACs without contribution limits. *McCutcheon v. FEC* struck down the aggregate contribution limit on individuals.[59] The deregulation of campaign finance likely has encouraged polarized party politics because it allows ideologically extreme contributors greater political influence through more and more opportunities to spend. However, any deregulation of the parties need not follow the same path of loosening fundraising instead of the party spending side.

A good example is raising the federal limits on coordinated party expenditures.[60] Although party committees are free to engage in independent expenditures without legal limit, federal law still caps the amount that they may spend on expenditures in formal coordination with their candidates. The limits ranged from almost $24 million in the 2016 presidential race, to anywhere from $101,900 to $3.1 million on 2020 Senate races depending on the state's voting age population, to $50,900 for most individual 2020 House races. Raising limits on coordinated party expenditures would increase the parties' leverage over party politics without significantly expanding the power of major contributors. Parties would be able to make greater use of its money to support candidates. Because they would have more resources to deploy on behalf of candidates, parties would potentially have more influence over candidates who hoped to benefit from party coordinated spending and perhaps deflect candidate loyalties from their biggest donors instead to the party and its leadership. For the presidential nomination process, for example, parties might wield a bigger financial stick in support of centrist candidates and deter more extreme candidates to offset the outsized influence of big-money donors and Super PACs. However, raising limits on coordinated expenditures would not change the parties' fundraising capacity or increase contributors'

---

[58] 548 U.S. 230 (2006).
[59] 572 U.S. 185 (2014).
[60] *See* RAYMOND LA RAJA, SMALL CHANGE: MONEY, POLITICAL PARTIES, AND CAMPAIGN FINANCE REFORM (2008); Pildes, *supra* note 20.

ability to funnel more money into party politics. Although the enhanced usefulness of party money might encourage donors to give more money to the parties, the applicable contribution limits on individual contributions to the party, as well as ancillary restrictions on earmarking, would remain in place.

The policy justification for limits on coordinated party expenditures is tenuous to start. The rationale for limiting coordinated expenditures is grounded in general campaign finance theory about coordinated expenditures. Coordination of expenditures with the candidate threatens circumvention of applicable contribution limits on donations directly to the candidate and therefore raises a corruption risk. With a coordinated expenditure, the candidate does not actually receive and spend the money herself, but she still may achieve the same end use of the money by coordinating with the financial sponsor. The sponsor and candidate could thus still execute a similar quid pro quo through coordinated expenditures as they could through a contribution. But the resulting corruption risk, however plausible between individual donor and candidate, is attenuated when postulated between a party and its candidate. Candidates are the party flagbearers who define what the party stands for and execute the party's agenda such that it is hard to conceive what it would mean for a party itself to "corrupt" its candidates through coordinated expenditures. Indeed, the motivation for deregulation would be to increase the party's leverage over its candidates, not to corrupt them in any pernicious sense, but to encourage them toward the party line and therefore counteract the otherwise polarizing influence of high-level federal campaign finance.

A focus on party spending is more promising and more cautious than the wholesale embrace of deregulation of party campaign finance so far proposed. If increasing limits on coordinated expenditures is the most obvious suggestion, there are others. A similar proposal is raising limits on the party committees' own contributions to their candidates, which La Raja and Schaffner specifically associate with lower polarization at the state legislative level.[61] Former FEC Commissioner Lee Goodman argues for the deregulation of party voter registration drives and volunteer activities such as mail drives, phone banking, and literature distribution.[62] Allison Hayward argues along similar lines for simplification of the federal rules for Levin funds to encourage state and local parties currently crowded out by the national parties in election activity.[63] Measures that expand the reach of parties while resisting an

---

[61] LA RAJA & SCHAFFNER, *supra* note 2.

[62] Lee E. Goodman, *A Time to Revive the Party*, WASH. EXAMINER (Nov. 16, 2015).

[63] Allison R. Hayward, *Revisiting the Fable of Reform*, 45 HARV. J. LEGIS. 421 (2008).

increased role for contributors best serves the goal of strengthening parties against hyperpolarization through campaign finance deregulation.

These measures would help address hyperpolarization across national politics, but the challenges for the major parties in campaign finance are magnified in presidential elections. Super PACs have their biggest impact in presidential primary elections where their unregulated financial resources can defy the party establishment, sustain insurgent candidates, and prolong a divisive primary process. The presidential primary process therefore may be where the major parties need the most help in containing the fragmentation of the Super PAC era. But by the same measure, the presidential primary process in the Super PAC era also underscores the growing and already outsized influence of big-money donors, who have emerged as new kingmakers in presidential politics as a result.[64] Presidential elections are where the big-money donors really come out to play. Deregulating party campaign finance, without attending to the risk of further fortifying this big-money donor influence, may only worsen hyperpolarization despite the best of reform intention.

V. CONCLUSION

A distinction between party campaign finance fundraising on the one hand and party campaign finance spending has not been a focus of party reform efforts, but I think it should be. It offers a better possibility for boosting the major parties and their leverage over all candidates, including presidential candidates, without necessarily boosting campaign finance donors and their leverage over the major parties. Super PACs are a permanent feature of the federal campaign-finance landscape for the foreseeable future and particularly important in presidential campaigns. Super PACs form shadow campaign fundraising and media operations for individual presidential candidates who can operate in defiance of the party leadership through the primary process. But counteracting Super PAC influence and the concomitant factionalization of the major parties will not succeed by inflating the power of wealthy mega-donors who have fueled hyperpolarization in the first place. There must be ways to strengthen party leadership without further strengthening the hold of these wealthy donors over the leadership, and our presidential candidates, at the same time.

---

[64] *See, e.g.,* Alex Isenstadt, *Rubio Takes the Lead in Sheldon Adelson Primary*, POLITICO (April 23, 2015); Michael Isikoff, *Millions at Stake, the "Adelson Primary" Is Neck and Neck*, YAHOO NEWS (Dec. 2, 2015).

12

Democratizing the Presidential Debates

Ann M. Ravel and Charlotte Hill[*]

I. INTRODUCTION

When it comes to electing the chief executive of the United States, the presidential debates play an important role in shaping public opinion and the choices facing voters. Having a fair process in place to determine who is eligible to participate in the debates and to guarantee that the debates are conducted neutrally is crucial to ensuring the integrity of the electoral process as a whole. In the past, controversies have arisen concerning which candidates should be invited to participate, which political parties should be represented, and whether the debates have been conducted in a way that is fair and neutral. Most of these controversies have never been resolved satisfactorily. Today, much more work needs to be done to ensure that our presidential primary and general election debates live up to their potential to provide truly diverse policy views to the public and are conducted in a manner that is wholly free from bias. Gender bias in terms of the questions asked of the candidates was evident in 2016, and other kinds of biases may appear in the future. Problematically, the eligibility rules for the general presidential debates have remained unchanged for decades. Meanwhile, government oversight of the debates remains virtually non-existent. The time has come to rethink how the presidential debates are conducted and how they should be regulated in the United States.

This chapter argues that we must change how the presidential debates are run and liberalize their eligibility rules so that the debates include a broader cross section of candidates who will promote a wide range of viewpoints and

[*] Ann M. Ravel is Lecturer in Law at the University of California, Berkeley, School of Law and a former commissioner of the Federal Election Commission. Charlotte Hill is a Ph.D. candidate at the Goldman School of Public Policy at the University of California, Berkeley.

policy ideas. Only once this happens will more women, more people of color, and more minor-party candidates have a true shot at winning the presidency. For non-traditional candidates to participate and effectively communicate their ideas to the American public, the format of the presidential debates need to be radically altered. Only by changing the rules governing the debates will we be able to rewrite the formula for what makes a winning candidate in the first place. Debate reform is an essential step in achieving this goal. Debates are meant to serve twin goals: they inform voters about who is running for office, while at the same time the foster a national conversation about important policy issues. However, today's American presidential debates fall short on both counts.

This chapter articulates the many functions of presidential debates and demonstrates how our current presidential debate system fails to meet them. It offers a series of reforms that would make the presidential debates more diverse and inclusive, both in terms of the types of candidates who participate and the types of ideas they espouse. The chapter concludes by offering some broad recommendations for the individuals and institutions responsible for planning and broadcasting the presidential debates, and for the journalists who then typically break down and summarize what happens at the debates for the general public.

II. WHY THE DEBATES MATTER

Debates are commonly portrayed by national media as competitions—either among candidates vying for a party's nomination in the primary debates or between two major-party candidates in the general election debates.[1] Pundits declare winners on the basis of who serves up the best one-liners and who keeps his or her opponent on the defensive. When Donald Trump chastised Hillary Clinton during their first presidential debate in 2016 for staying at home to prepare, Clinton's quipped in reply: "I think Donald just criticized me for preparing for this debate. And, yes, I did. And you know what else I prepared for? I prepared to be president."[2] Clinton's response prompted

---

[1] This can be seen in coverage of the first 2016 presidential debate. *See Who won the presidential debate?*, CNN (Sept. 27, 2016), www.cnn.com/2016/09/27/opinions/hillary-clinton-donald-trump-debate-opinion-roundup/index.html; Anthony Zurcher, *Presidential debate: Who won – Trump or Clinton?*, BBC (Oct. 20, 2016), www.bbc.com/news/election-us-2016-37711218 ; *Vote: Who won the first presidential debate?*, CNBC (Sept. 26, 2016), www.cnbc.com/2016/09/26/vote-who-won-the-first-presidential-debate.html.

[2] Tory Newmyer, *Who Won the First Presidential Debate?*, FORTUNE (Sept. 27, 2016), http://fortune.com/2016/09/26/presidential-debate-who-won/.

applause from the audience, which had been asked to stay quiet, and it thereafter received widespread coverage from the media on national television.[3]

Of course, presidential debates do more than merely demonstrate candidates' rhetorical prowess. With their large television and Internet audiences, the presidential debates are unparalleled vehicles for involving ordinary citizens in the political process. In 2016, a grand total of 259 million people watched the presidential debates, including the three live debates between Clinton and Trump and the many debates between vice-presidential candidates Tim Kaine and Mike Pence.[4] That was a national record. The first Republican primary debate of the 2016 election cycle similarly broke historical records, reaching 25 million people.[5] On the Democratic side in 2016, the first debate attracted 15 million viewers.[6] In 2019, the first Democratic primary debate reached more than 18 million viewers on live television, while another nine million streamed the debate online, setting another record.[7] That record was broken in February 2020, when the Democratic primary debate held just ahead of the Nevada caucuses attracted more than 33 million viewers, including 19.5 million who watched it on television and another 13 million who watched it online.[8] Many more Americans absorbed the ample post-debate media coverage, even if they did not watch the debates themselves.

Debates play a number of important roles in the run-up to a presidential election. First, they expose the candidates' core policy disagreements and help shape voters' own policy preferences. During the presidential debates, as Amber Boydstun, Rebecca Anne Glazier, and Matthew Pietryka explain, candidates strategically answer debate questions in order to "draw or redraw the lines of conflict" and "to draw attention to their advantaged

---

[3] *Id.*

[4] A. J. Katz, *The Presidential Debates Set Ratings Records in 2016*, TVNEWSER (Oct. 24, 2016), www.adweek.com/tvnewser/the-presidential-debates-set-ratings-records-in-2016/309089.

[5] Brian Stelter, *Democratic debate hits record 15.3 million viewers*, CNN (Oct. 14, 2015), https://money.cnn.com/2015/10/14/media/cnn-democratic-debate-ratings-record/.

[6] *Id.*

[7] Caitlin Oprysko, *Thursday's Debate Ratings Shatter Previous Dem Record, NBC Says*, POLITICO (June 28, 2019), www.politico.com/story/2019/06/28/democratic-debate-ratings-record-1390382.

[8] *See* Rick Porter, *TV Ratings: Ninth Democratic Debate Breaks Viewer Record for Party*, HOLLYWOOD REP. (February 20, 2020), www.hollywoodreporter.com/live-feed/democratic-debate-criminal-minds-tv-ratings-wednesday-feb-19-2020-1280119; Yelena Dzhanova, *Bloomberg's addition to the Democratic debate stage leads to record viewership*, CNBC.COM (February 20, 2020), www.cnbc.com/2020/02/20/bloombergs-addition-to-the-democratic-debate-stage-leads-to-record-viewership.html.

topics."[9] The media, in turn, highlights the policy disagreements among candidates in its post-debate coverage. A *Washington Post* article recapping the fourth Republican primary debate of 2016 remarked, for example, on how the Republican candidates "finally began to differentiate themselves on [the] specifics of their policies."[10] It went on to cluster the GOP candidates according to their stances on a range of issues, from raising the minimum wage (Kasich was the only "yes"), to deporting undocumented immigrants (Trump stood alone in his embrace of deportation), to bailing out the banks (Kasich would do so, while Cruz would not).[11]

By exposing policy disagreements among candidates, the debates play a critical role in informing voters about important policy choices. This is a well-established finding in both the political science and communications literatures. More than four decades of research, according to Kenneth Winneg and Kathleen Hall Jamieson, has found that presidential debates inform viewers about political issues.[12] Similarly, as James Lemert reports, scholars of mass communication generally agree, with few exceptions, that broadcasted debates inform viewers about policies.[13] In turn, this helps shape voters' own policy priorities. This process starts with the very questions that moderators ask of candidates on the stage. Although these questions are not necessarily reflective of voters' own policy concerns (indeed, research shows that debate questions are often shaped more by the interests of journalists),[14] these questions undoubtedly influence ordinary viewers. A study of this phenomenon by William Benoit and Glenn Hansen found that, after watching the debates, viewers reported caring more about the issues highlighted by the moderators and the candidates.[15]

Second, presidential debates help voters make a more informed choice in picking a presidential candidate.[16] While political scientists are largely skeptical of the influence of late-stage general debates between the Republican and

---

9   Amber E. Boydstun, Rebecca Anne Glazier & Matthew T. Pietryka, *Agenda Control in the 2008 Presidential Debates*, 41 AM. POL. RES. 863, 870 (2013).
10 *Where Candidates Stood on the Issues in Tuesday's GOP Debate*, WASH. POST (Nov. 11, 2015), www.washingtonpost.com/graphics/politics/2016-election/debates/nov-10-speakers/.
11 *Id.*
12 Kenneth Winneg & Kathleen Hall Jamieson, *Learning From the 2016 U.S. General Election Presidential Debates*, 61 AM. BEHAV. SCIENTIST 362, 364 (2017).
13 *See generally* James B. Lemert, *Do Televised Presidential Debates Help Inform Voters?*, 37 J. OF BROADCASTING & ELECTRONIC MEDIA 83 (1992).
14 William L. Benoit & Glenn J. Hansen, *Presidential Debate Questions and the Public Agenda*, 49 COMM. Q. 130, 134–36 (2009).
15 R. Lance Holbert, et al., *The Role of Communication in the Formation of an Issue-Based Citizenry*, 69 COMM. MONOGRAPHS 296 (2010).
16 *Id.*

Democratic nominees,[17] they agree that primary debates do shift voter preferences. A study by Mitchell McKinney found that a full 60 percent of primary debate viewers "changed their pre-debate candidate preferences, including more than one-third of all primary viewers switching their allegiance from one candidate to another, and nearly one-quarter of our primary viewers switching from undecided to a particular candidate following debate viewing."[18] For their part, voters certainly believe that the debates influence their decisions. According to a 2008 Pew Research Center poll, a full two-thirds of voters said that year's presidential debates shaped their vote.[19]

Relatedly, the debates also serve the important role of informing the public about lesser-known candidates. Political scientist Thomas Holbook has found that debates help the public learn more about lesser-known candidates than about frontrunners.[20] In this sense, the debates serve to level the playing field between candidates, some of whom will have received more media attention and coverage than others or been in the public eye for a longer period of time before the debate. Excluding a lesser-known candidate from the debates, meanwhile, can be a death blow to one's candidacy, as this prevents a candidate from ever building the name recognition necessary to clinch an electoral victory.

Finally, the debates play a role in shaping the long-term perceptions of the office of the presidency and in building confidence in American democracy. Just as the debates influence voters' policy agendas, they also influence what voters believe it means to be presidential—that is, they highlight what sort of traits, both personal and professional, are necessary to succeed at the job. In a related vein, the presidential debates also serve to build confidence and trust in American democracy. Given the precipitous decline in public trust in government since the 1960s, this function of the debates is arguably one of the most critical. By presenting candidates on the same stage, requiring them to engage in a shared discussion about key policy topics, and broadcasting this discussion to the electorate, the debates embody and reify key tenets of American democracy: that presidential hopefuls must compete on an even

[17] Dylan Matthews, *Do Presidential Debates Usually Matter? Political Scientists Say No*, WASH. POST (Oct. 3, 2012), www.washingtonpost.com/news/wonk/wp/2012/10/03/what-political-scientists-know-about-debates/?utm_term=.ea322bd2ace3.

[18] Mitchell S. McKinney, *Do Presidential Debates Matter? Examining a Decade of Campaign Debate Effects*, 49 ARGUMENTATION & ADVOC. 238, 252 (2017).

[19] Russell Heimlich, *Most Say Presidential Debates Influence Their Vote*, PEW RESEARCH CTR. (Sept. 11, 2012), www.pewresearch.org/fact-tank/2012/09/11/most-say-presidential-debates-influence-their-vote/.

[20] Thomas M. Holbrook, *Political Learning from Presidential Debates*, 21 POL. BEHAV. 67 (1999).

playing field, must prove themselves worthy of the office by virtue of their ideas, and must ultimately be chosen for duty by the people.

III. A BRIEF HISTORY OF THE PRESIDENTIAL DEBATES

Leading up to the 1928 presidential election, the League of Women Voters, which was then a new organization, held a year-long series of national political debates that were broadcast to the nation on the radio. However, the presidential candidates did not participate in these debates directly. Rather, they had surrogates, including journalists, scholars, and other politicians, who argued for their policy positions on their behalf.[21] However, the advent of the medium of television would change the course of the presidential debates. Starting in 1960 with the debates between Richard Nixon and John F. Kennedy, the public was able to see the candidates, who now squared off against each other face-to-face. In 1960, Nixon and Kennedy held a series of four televised debates, with over 70 million people watching the first one alone.[22]

Over the next thirty years, the rules and structure of the debates changed. In order to conduct the 1960 Nixon–Kennedy debate, Congress found it necessary to suspend its long-standing "equal time" rule, which guaranteed all candidates equal time on television. First articulated in the Communications Act of 1934, the equal time rule originally required television stations that allowed a candidate to appear on their airwaves to extend the same opportunity to the candidate's opponents.[23] The 1960 debates would not afford equal time to all candidates, just to the two frontrunners; accordingly, in order to conduct the 1960 Nixon–Kennedy debate without running afoul of the law, Congress found it necessary to suspend the equal time rule for the 1960 election.[24] With the assassination of President Kennedy, however, who was a supporter of the congressional suspension, the desire for debates waned. President Johnson did not seek, and Congress did not provide, a suspension from the equal time rule for the 1964 election, with the result being that the candidates never debated face to face. The same was true for the 1968 and 1972 elections.[25] Thus, there were no general election presidential debates held between 1964 and 1972.

---

[21] Newton N. Minow & Craig L. LaMay, Inside the Presidential Debates: Their Improbable Past and Promising Future 9 (2008).

[22] *Id.* at 14.

[23] Anne Kramer Ricchiuto, *The End of Time for Equal Time?: Revealing the Statutory Myth of Fair Election Coverage*, 38 Indiana L. Rev. 267, 267–68 (2005).

[24] *Political Broadcasts*, CQ Almanac, at 352 (15th ed. 1959).

[25] Minow & LaMay, *supra* note 21, at 2.

By 1976, the Federal Communications Commission reinterpreted the equal time rule and defined presidential debates as "bona fide news events," which allowed them to be exempt from equal time.[26] Thus, the presidential debates resumed in 1976. The debates were then conducted under the sponsorship of the League of Women Voters until 1988. However, in 1988, the League voted to withdraw from sponsoring the debates. Its concern was that the major parties were meeting behind closed doors to negotiate terms for how the debates would be conducted, and these were not in the public's interest. Specifically, these terms sought to give the campaigns unprecedented control over the debate proceedings, including the selection of questioners, the composition of the audience, and the access that the press would have to the debates.[27]

After the League withdrew, control of the debates was assumed by the two major political parties, which jointly formed the Commission on Presidential Debates (CPD). The CPD required debate participants to have achieved at least 15 percent support in opinion polling in order to participate in the debates —a rule frequently subjected to criticism. While the 15 percent rule technically existed before the formation of the CPD, it was not always set in stone. In 1980, when the presidential debates were still hosted by the League of Women Voters, independent candidate John B. Anderson was invited to participate in the first presidential debate, despite many polls showing him below the 15 percent threshold. Additional polling by the ABC News-Harris Survey had found that a majority of voters wanted Anderson on the debate stage, even if they did not plan to vote for him. As the League explained in a press release, the survey results "clearly indicate that big majorities of the voters would feel sorely let down if the League of Women Voters does not invite Anderson to debate because of an arbitrary stipulation that he must achieve at least 15 percent in the opinion polls."[28]

What the League apparently did not anticipate, however, was that Anderson's inclusion would stoke the ire of then-President and Democratic nominee Jimmy Carter, who had little desire to debate a rival candidate in public who had little hope of winning the election. Upon learning of the League's decision to include Anderson in the first debate,

[26] *See* Ricchiuto, *supra* note 23, at 271.

[27] League of Women Voters, *League Refuses to "Help Perpetrate a Fraud,"* LVW.ORG (October 3, 1988), www.lwv.org/newsroom/press-releases/league-refuses-help-perpetrate-fraud.

[28] Louis Harris, *Majority Favors Inclusion of Anderson In League of Women Voters' Debates,* ABC NEWS – HARRIS SURVEY (Aug. 21, 1980), https://theharrispoll.com/wp-content/uploads/2017/12/Harris-Interactive-Poll-Research-MAJORITY-FAVORS-INCLUSION-OF-ANDERSON-IN-LEAGUE-OF-WOMEN-VOTERS-DEBATES-1980–08.pdf.

Carter refused to participate.[29] By the time the second debate rolled around, the League had changed tactics; Carter and his Republican opponent, Ronald Reagan, were invited to participate, but Anderson was not.[30] From that point on, the 15 percent rule became a formal litmus test that candidates had to pass in order to participate in the general election presidential debates. Thus far, not a single minor-party candidate has managed to satisfy this test.

The history of the presidential primary debates is more recent and less well-defined than the history of the general election debates. There were Democratic primary debates in 1972 between Hubert Humphrey and George McGovern. Some of these involved just Humphrey and McGovern, while others involved additional candidates for the nomination.[31] In 1980, a New Hampshire newspaper limited a Republican primary debate to frontrunners George H. W. Bush and Ronald Reagan, while the other candidates for the Republican nomination were forced to watch from the audience.[32] In 1987, a joint primary debate was held, with Democratic primary candidates included alongside Republican primary candidates. In that debate, one party would provide answers to questions, with critiques from candidates from the opposing party.[33]

This ad-hoc approach to primary presidential debates, in a process largely run by the media, continued until the 2016 election cycle. But in 2016, the Republican Party, which had fielded an unusually large number of candidates, became concerned over the lack of a satisfactory debate process. It thus decided to take over its primary debates. It scheduled a total of twelve intra-party debates, making efforts to ensure a wide range of questions were asked.[34] However, because the candidate field was so large, Republicans divided debate participants into an upper tier and a lower tier and forced the candidates to participate in separate debates.[35]

---

[29] Hendrick Smith, *Carter Declines to Debate After Anderson Is Invited; First Clear-Cut Test Anderson Gets Invitation to Debate So President Declines to Take Part 3 Other Invitations Cited Carter Called "Reluctant Debater" Three Polling Specialists Used*, N.Y. Times (Sept. 10, 1980), https://timesmachine.nytimes.com/timesmachine/1980/09/10/111290136.pdf.

[30] Randy Shipp, *Anderson to debate, too, via cable-TV network*, Christian Sci. Monitor (Oct. 27, 1980), www.csmonitor.com/1980/1027/102722.html.

[31] Seth Masket & Julia Azari, *How the Parties Took Over the Primary Debates*, Vox (Aug. 30, 2016), www.vox.com/mischiefs-of-faction/2016/8/30/12679346/parties-took-over-debates.

[32] *Id.*

[33] *Id.*

[34] *Id.*

[35] *Id.*

Democrats faced similar challenges in the primary elections for the 2020 presidential nomination after more than two dozen candidates declared they would run. To ensure fair participation, the Democratic Party established a series of new qualification rules. It would allow a maximum of twenty candidates to participate in each primary debate. To qualify, a Democratic candidate had to attract at least 1 percent support in three national polls, or in polls conducted in the early primary states. Alternately, the candidate had to raise money from a minimum of 65,000 donors located in twenty different states, and to have at least two hundred separate donors in each state.[36] If more than twenty candidates qualified under these criteria, only those candidates who had met both the polling and fundraising thresholds would be allowed to participate. If there were still more than twenty candidates qualifying, the Democratic Party would invite only those candidates with the highest polling averages. Finally, if there still wound up being too many candidates, the Democratic Party decided it would randomly assign candidates to debates and hold multiple debates on different days.[37] As the primary debates progressed, the Democratic Party raised the donation threshold so that the qualifying candidate had to have 130,000 donors located in at least twenty different states. Under this new threshold, at least 400 unique donors had to contribute to the qualifying candidate from each of these twenty states. Campaigns began spending large amounts of money to attract new individual donors, with some reportedly spending $60 or more on online advertising aimed at new donors for every $1 they received in contributions.[38] In late January 2020, the Democratic National Committee (DNC) changed its rules again to create a path for Michael Bloomberg to participate in the debates. Because Bloomberg had been self-funding his presidential campaign, he could not meet the numerical donor threshold needed to qualify for the debates. The revised DNC rules dropped the donor threshold entirely and instead began to require that candidates earn at least 10 percent support in four different national polls conducted between mid-January and mid-February, or at least 12 percent support in two polls conducted only in the states of Nevada or South Carolina.[39] By the time of the tenth

---

[36] Julia Azari & Seth Masket, *The DNC's Debate Rules Won't Make the 2020 Primaries Any Less Chaotic*, FIVETHIRTYEIGHT (Feb. 20, 2019), https://fivethirtyeight.com/features/the-dncs-debate-rules-wont-make-the-2020-primaries-any-less-chaotic/.

[37] *Id.*

[38] Edward-Isaac Dovere, *The Democratic Debates Aren't Pleasing Anyone*, ATLANTIC (Sept. 19, 2019), www.theatlantic.com/politics/archive/2019/09/2020-democratic-debates-arent-pleasing-anyone/598306/.

[39] Zach Montellaro, Sally Goldenberg & Christopher Cadelago, *DNC Overhauls Debate Requirements, Opening Door for Bloomberg*, POLITICO (Jan. 31, 2020), www.politico.com/news/2020/01/31/dnc-shifts-debate-requirements-opening-door-for-bloomberg-110017/.

Democratic debate, held ahead of the South Carolina primary on February 29, the debate rules had changed yet again. Candidates could not qualify for this debate unless they met yet another new polling threshold or had been allocated at least one pledged delegate to the Democratic National Convention from the earlier primary and caucus contests held in Iowa, New Hampshire, or Nevada.[40]

IV. HOW THE DEBATES ARE FALLING SHORT

Given that the primary and general presidential debates have been around for a few decades now, it is surprising that there has not been a more robust effort to improve how they are organized and conducted. Because the presidential candidate debates play such a vital role in shaping people's policy preferences, choice of candidates, and trust in the political process, outstanding problems with the debates must be identified and rectified.

A. *Problems with Polling*

Both the general and primary debates suffer from a fatal flaw: their reliance on public polling data to determine which candidates make it onto the debate stage. Pre-election polls can be imprecise, as evidenced by the 2016 presidential election (and, earlier that year, the United Kingdom's surprising Brexit vote). More importantly, even the most accurate polls do not capture Americans' preferences around which candidates should participate in the debates. Instead, these polls focus on the less relevant question of which candidate voters intend to support on Election Day. This relentless focus on inviting only the most electable candidates ultimately skews voters' issue and electoral preferences while depriving them of important policy information.

Modern polling has become a complicated endeavor, making it increasingly difficult to achieve accurate, reliable results. There is perhaps no better demonstration of this than the 2016 presidential election. In the lead-up to the election, polls consistently forecast a loss for Donald Trump, the Republican nominee. Predictions of Hillary Clinton's likelihood of victory typically hovered around 90 percent; even Trump's own pollsters were surprised to learn

---

[40] Sarah Ewall-Wice, *DNC Announces Qualifications for South Carolina Democratic Presidential Debate Hosted by CBS News*, CBSNEWS.COM (Feb. 24, 2020), www.cbsnews.co m/news/south-carolina-debate-dnc-announces-qualifications-for-south-carolina-democratic-presidential-debate-hosted-by-cbs/.

that he had won the presidency.[41] The result, as the American Association for Public Opinion Research (AAPOR) put it, "was (and continues to be) widespread consensus that the polls failed."[42]

In the aggregate, the national polls were not that far off from the actual result, according to a postmortem on election polling conducted on behalf of AAPOR.[43] Clinton was predicted to have a 3-point lead in the national popular vote — just a point off from her eventual 2-point lead on Election Day.[44] Polling also predicted a close race in the Electoral College. However, Clinton's predicted lead was overinflated in the Upper Midwest, a region critical to Trump's ultimate victory. "Polls showed Hillary Clinton leading, if narrowly, in Pennsylvania, Michigan and Wisconsin, which had voted Democratic for president six elections running," explained the AAPOR's report. "Those leads fed predictions that the Democratic *Blue Wall* would hold. Come Election Day, however, Trump edged out victories in all three."[45]

The AAPOR's report identified at least three reasons for this underestimation of Trump's support: pollsters failed to adjust their results for the overrepresentation of college-educated respondents, some respondents "did not reveal themselves as Trump voters"[46] until the election was over, and a meaningful number of people changed their minds about which candidate to support in the final days of the campaign. Because of these (and possibly other) problems, an otherwise robust polling apparatus failed to anticipate Trump's surprising Election Day upset.

These sorts of polling challenges were not unique to the 2016 election. Polling is incredibly difficult, in part because it is seldom feasible to contact every likely voter. Instead, pollsters typically contact a sample of likely voters, doing their best to ensure that the sample is representative of the broader group of people who will turn out on Election Day. But depending on the circumstances, this is sometimes easier said than done. One challenge has to do with modern technological advancements; polling that used to be conducted by contacting people on landline phones must now be conducted by contacting them through cell phones and the Internet, technologies disproportionately

---

[41] Jennifer Jacobs, *Trump Says He Expected to Lose Election Because of Poll Results*, BLOOMBERG (Dec. 13, 2016), www.bloomberg.com/news/articles/2016–12-14/trump-says-he-expected-to-lose-election-because-of-poll-results.

[42] Ad Hoc Committee on 2016 Election Polling, *An Evaluation of 2016 Election Polls in the U.S.*, AAPOR, at 2 (May 4, 2017), www.aapor.org/getattachment/Education-Resources/Reports/AAPOR-2016-Election-Polling-Report.pdf.aspx.

[43] *Id.*

[44] *Id.*

[45] *Id.*

[46] *Id.* at 3.

used by certain segments of the population. This poses a challenge to ensuring that a true sample of the voting population is reached.[47] Even the best pollsters must also make difficult decisions about how to weight the responses of certain demographics over others.[48]

Other challenges have to do with the responses people give when answering survey questions. People do not always reveal their true voting preferences to pollsters, often out of a desire for social acceptance.[49] Some research suggests this was the case for many Trump voters, who hid their preference for Trump from pollsters.[50] And, critically, people's minds change over time. People responding to polls may say they intend to vote for someone one day, but that may not be the candidate they eventually support at the ballot box on Election Day.

To the extent that polling does accurately reflect public opinion, it succeeds only in identifying which candidates likely voters intend to support in the presidential election—which is a different issue from which candidates Americans want to see on the debate stage. In 1980, when the League of Women Voters asked likely voters whether they thought John Anderson should be included in the first presidential debate, 63 percent said yes, despite fewer than 15 percent saying they intended to vote for him on Election Day.[51] In 2000, more than half of American voters told pollsters that they wished Ralph Nader had been invited to participate in the first debate.[52] In 2016, in an election without an especially strong minor-party candidate, nearly half of voters supported including Green Party candidate Jill Stein and independent candidate Gary Johnson in the first debate; only 39 percent wanted the debate restricted to the two major-party candidates.[53] Another 2016 poll found that

---

[47] D. Sunshine Hillygus, *The Evolution of Election Polling in the United States*, 75 Pub. Op. Q. 962 (2011).

[48] *See, e.g.*, Cliff Zukin, et al., *Sources of Variation in Published Election Polling: A Primer*, AAPOR, at 7 (Dec. 2015), www.aapor.org/getattachment/Education-Resources/Election-Polling-Resources/Election-Polling-AAPOR-2015-primary_cz120215-FINAL.pdf.aspx.

[49] Norman Bradburn et al., Asking Questions: The Definitive Guide to Questionnaire Design – For Market Research, Political Polls, and Social and Health Questionnaires 11 (rev. ed. 2004).

[50] *See, e.g.*, Peter K. Enns, et al., *Understanding the 2016 US Presidential Polls: The Importance of Hidden Trump Supporters*, 8 St. Pol. & Pol'y 41 (2017).

[51] *See* Harris, *supra* note 28.

[52] Keating Holland, *Poll: Presidential race a dead heat. Two point Bush lead within margin of error*, CNN (Oct. 6, 2000), www.cnn.com/2000/ALLPOLITICS/stories/10/06/cnn.poll/index.html.

[53] Monmouth University Poll, *National: Prez Race Narrows on Debate Eve*, Monmouth Univ. (Sept. 26, 2016), www.monmouth.edu/polling-institute/documents/monmouthpoll_us_092616.pdf/.

nine in ten people would be just as likely or more likely to watch a debate that was "more inclusive of independent or third party candidates."[54] Voters consistently say they prefer a more inclusive debate environment—just the opposite of what the two major parties, which jointly organize the debates, prefer.

B. *Exclusion of Candidates*

The organizations responsible for planning and hosting the presidential primary and general election debates tend to assume that because alternative candidates are extremely unlikely to win the primary or general election, they do not belong on the debate stage. As Keith Darren Eisner has argued, this narrow conception of "who belongs" misses the ways in which "third-party and independent candidates play a vital role in the American political process, a role independent of electoral success."[55] Eisner identifies at least three important roles that alternative candidates play in elections: they push for innovative policies, reassure voters that "major parties will be held accountable," and ultimately influence electoral outcomes (even if they do not themselves get elected as President).[56]

The exclusion of certain candidates from the debates has the perverse effect of limiting the range of policy issues discussed by the candidates. When the major candidates only debate one another, rather than also having to respond to the ideas of other contenders, they ignore any issues on which they already agree. These often include the most transformative policy proposals, such as those concerning overhauling the nation's campaign finance system,[57] declaring a national state of emergency over climate change,[58] or abolishing major government programs.[59] These issues may be popular among the general

---

[54] Harvard IOP Spring 2016 Poll, *Clinton in Commanding Lead over Trump Among Young Voters, Harvard Youth Poll Finds*, HARV. KENNEDY SCH. INST. OF POL. (Apr. 25, 2016), https://iop.harvard.edu/youth-poll/past/harvard-iop-spring-2016-poll.

[55] Keith Darren Eisner, *Non-Major-Party Candidates and Televised Presidential Debates: The Merits of Legislative Inclusion*, 141 U. PA. L. REV. 973, 979 (1993).

[56] *Id.* at 977–79.

[57] *Ralph Nader on Campaign Finance Reform*, ON THE ISSUES (Sept. 9, 2018), www.ontheissues.org/Celeb/Ralph_Nader_Government_Reform.htm#Campaign_Finance_Reform.

[58] Edward Helmore, *Green Party Candidate Jill Stein Calls for Climate State of Emergency*, GUARDIAN (Aug. 20, 2016), www.theguardian.com/us-news/2016/aug/20/jill-stein-green-party-climate-state-of-emergency.

[59] Maureen Sullivan, *Gary Johnson on Education: 5 Things the Presidential Candidate Wants You to Know*, FORBES (May 30, 2016), www.forbes.com/sites/maureensullivan/2016/05/30/gary-johnson-on-education-5-things-the-presidential-candidate-wants-you-to-know/#48f1e14826bb.

voting public—for instance, 85 percent of Americans believe our country's system for funding political campaigns needs to be either fundamentally changed or completely rebuilt[60]—but if the major-party candidates have similar stances on them, they will not score political points by highlighting them. Instead, divisiveness sells. Accordingly, each major party candidate focuses on a narrower set of issues on which they believe they have the upper hand over an opponent.

The result is that voters are hindered from learning where the candidates stand on the full range of issues that matter to them and, more generally, from encountering innovative policy ideas that they may not have considered before. If history is any indication, this has negative consequences for America's social and economic development. As Gregory Magarian writes, minor-party candidates "have often proposed and popularized new substantive policies which the major parties have lacked the political awareness or fore-sight to develop."[61] This includes policies for how to implement "free public education, tougher child labor laws, federal regulation of railroads and other corporations, civil service reform, flexibility in the currency supply, an end to antilabor injunctions, progressive income taxation, and social insurance for the aged and unemployed."[62] When some candidates are denied the opportunity to promote their policies at the most widely viewed political event of election season, the entire country suffers the cost.

Voters also may become increasingly disillusioned with the political system when a broad range of candidates do not appear on the debate stage. Political trust is at a near-historic low in the United States today; in 2019, only 18 percent of Americans said they trusted government to do what is right just about always or most of the time.[63] This distrust extends to the parties themselves, with distrustful voters less likely to vote for a major-party candidate.[64] Overly restricting the debates likely perpetuates voters' sense that the two-party system is "rigged" to serve politicians and their vested interests, not the interests of voters.

---

[60] *Americans' Views on Money in Politics*, N.Y. TIMES (Jun. 2, 2015), www.nytimes.com/inter active/2015/06/02/us/politics/money-in-politics-poll.html.

[61] Gregory P. Magarian, *Fighting Exclusion from Televised Presidential Debates: Minor-Party Candidates' Standing to Challenge Sponsoring Organizations' Tax-Exempt Status*, 90 MICH. L. REV. 838, 879 (1992).

[62] *Id.*

[63] *Public Trust in Government: 1958–2019*, PEW RESEARCH CTR. (Apr. 11, 2019), www.people-press.org/2017/12/14/public-trust-in-government-1958–2017/.

[64] Geoff Peterson & J. Mark Wrighton, *Expressions of Distrust: Third-Party Voting and Cynicism in Government*, 20 POL. BEHAV. 17, 20 (1998).

By excluding alternative candidates, the Commission on Presidential Debates withholds "a critical source of the mass exposure upon which campaigns depend for legitimacy."[65] To be clear, this "legitimacy" is not necessarily dependent upon a candidate's ability to win the presidential election. Non-traditional candidates may join the presidential race in order to raise awareness of an issue, to pull the closest major-party nominee in a more liberal or conservative direction, or even to play the role of "spoiler" for one of the major parties.

In America's winner-take-all voting system, an alternative candidate can impact electoral outcomes by siphoning enough votes away from a similar major-party nominee to swing the election to the opposing candidate. This phenomenon, commonly referred to as "the spoiler effect," has played a significant role in several major presidential elections throughout U.S. history, most notably ensuring that George W. Bush defeated Al Gore in the 2000 election. Research shows that if Florida voters who supported Green Party nominee Ralph Nader had instead been forced to support either Bush or Gore, most would have supported Gore, and the state—and the country—would have elected a Democrat to the presidency.[66]

When a full range of candidates are prevented from participating in the debates, then, they are denied the opportunity to influence electoral outcomes via their critical role as both advocates and spoilers. Chief Judge Abner Mikva of the U.S. Court of Appeals for the D.C. Circuit emphasized this point in his dissent in *Fulani v. Brady*, a case brought by Lenora Fulani of the New Alliance Party after she had been excluded from the presidential debates.[67] The first woman and first African-American to appear on the ballot as a presidential candidate in all fifty states,[68] Fulani sued the IRS to challenge the tax-exempt status given to the Commission on Presidential Debates. She argued that the CPD did not meet the qualifications for tax-exempt status because it presented a partisan political viewpoint by excluding her from the presidential debates as a minor-party candidate. The CPD argued that Fulani did not have "a realistic chance of being elected to the Presidency or Vice-Presidency,"[69] a determination it made after examining a candidate's "ballot

---

[65] *See* Magarian, *supra* note 61, at 856.

[66] Michael C. Herron & Jeffrey B. Lewis, Did Ralph Nader Spoil a Gore Presidency? A Ballot-Level Study of Green and Reform Party Voters in the 2000 Presidential Election (Apr. 24, 2006) (unpublished manuscript), www.sscnet.ucla.edu/polisci/faculty/lewis/pdf/greenreform9.pdf.

[67] Fulani v. Brady, 935 F.2d 1324 (1991).

[68] *About Lenora B. Fulani, Ph.D.*, ALL STARS PROJECT, https://allstars.org/members/lenora-fulani-ph-d/ (last visited May 22, 2019).

[69] *Fulani*, 935 F. 2d at 1235.

listings; professional opinions of the media, campaign managers, and political scientists; column inches of news coverage; and findings of national pollsters."[70]

Although the D.C. Circuit denied Fulani's ability to advance her lawsuit against the IRS for lack of standing, it did not do so without a dissent. In his dissent, Judge Mikva argued that the political communication of minor-party candidates is important, even if it does not lead to electoral victory. Fulani suffered broad injuries because she lost a critical opportunity to communicate her political ideas to the electorate. As Judge Mikva wrote:

> Fulani does *not* assert that she could have won the 1988 election if she had participated in the presidential debates. Instead, she claims 1) that her credibility as a 'spoiler' and public advocate was undermined by the Commission's refusal to invite her, and 2) that allowing then-Vice President Bush and Governor Dukakis to debate alone boosted their campaigns in comparison to hers.
>
> It follows from Fulani's allegations that whatever advantage major-party candidates have going into two-candidate presidential debates is exaggerated by the debates themselves, and that such debates disadvantage minor-party candidates.... . This disadvantage constitutes sufficient injury to support a finding of standing.[71]

Going forward, the CPD and the primary debate organizers should give consideration to the inclusion of a broad range of perspectives. This can help restore the eroding trust in government and provide voters with fuller choices and information on the issues that matter most to them.

C. *Lack of Governmental Oversight*

Government oversight of the candidate debates has traditionally been minimal. In recent years, however, the Federal Election Commission (FEC) has promulgated some regulations regarding presidential debates. These regulations stem from the Federal Election Campaign Act (FECA), which prohibits any corporation, or any labor organization, from making a contribution or expenditure in connection with any election at which presidential or vice-presidential electors are to be selected.[72] However, there are important

---

[70] *Id.* at 1236.
[71] *Id.* at 1332–33.
[72] 52 U.S.C. § 30118(a).

exemptions for non-partisan activity, especially of those organizations designed to educate voters or encourage voting.[73]

The task of the FEC has been to clarify this exemption. Its approach has been to exempt non-profits that avoid endorsing, supporting, or opposing political candidates or parties, allowing them to receive corporate or labor union funds to educate voters about issues, or in the case of the CPD, which is a non-profit, to defray the cost of staging the debates. The FEC's regulations also state that the presidential debates may not be structured to promote one candidate over another, and that tagging organizations use "pre-established objective criteria to determine which candidates may participate in a debate."[74] And for general election debates, staging organizations cannot use nomination by a particular party as the sole objective criterion to include a candidate in a debate. The purpose of the FEC requirement for objective criteria is "to avoid the real or apparent potential for a quid pro quo, and to ensure the integrity of fairness of the process."[75] Accordingly, criteria cannot be "designed to promote or advance one candidate over another,"[76] and the "rule contains an implied reasonableness requirement."[77] If a debate were to fail to comply with the regulations, the value of the debate would construed as a campaign contribution or expenditure made in violation of the law.[78]

In September 2014 and June 2015, administrative complaints were filed with the FEC against the CPD.[79] The complaints took issue with the CPD's "Non-Partisan Candidate Selection Criteria," which state that candidates will be invited to participate in debates if they are constitutionally eligible to run, appear on a sufficient number of state ballots to have a mathematical chance of winning a majority vote in the Electoral College, and attract the support of at least 15 percent of the national electorate (as determined by five national polling organizations). The complaints alleged that, in the 2012 presidential election, the CPD was not, in fact, a non-partisan debate-staging organization, because its candidate selection criteria amounted to endorsing, supporting, or opposing certain political parties. In particular, the 15 percent polling threshold had the effect of barring participation from minor-party and independent candidates. (This alleged preferential treatment of major-party candidates has continued to

---

[73] 52 U.S.C. § 30101(9)(A)(i).

[74] 11 C.F.R. § 110.13.

[75] *Commission disposition of debate rulemaking* (2017), Fed. Election Comm'n (March 29, 2017), www.fec.gov/updates/commission-disposition-debate-rulemaking/.

[76] 11 C.F.R. § 110.13.

[77] 60 C.F.R. § 260; 64 C.F.R. § 262.

[78] *Id.*

[79] *Level the Playing Field v. FEC (LPF II)(New)*, Fed. Election Comm'n (Sept. 9, 2015), www.fec.gov/updates/level-the-playing-field-v-fec-lpf-ii/.

be a criticism leveled at the CPD. For its part, the CPD disputes this allegation, saying that its selection criteria have only sought to identify the candidates whose widespread public support makes them the leading contenders for president.) The complainants asked the FEC to revise its regulations to bar debate-staging organizations from using a polling threshold to help determine who could participate in general-election debates. The FEC dismissed the complaints and decided not to initiate any new rulemaking on the issue.

This was not the end of the story, however. In *Level the Playing Field v. FEC*, the Green Party, the Libertarian National Committee, and Dr. Peter Ackerman sued the FEC in the U.S. District Court for the District of Columbia over the FEC's complaint dismissals and the FEC's refusal to engage in rulemaking on these issues.[80] In 2017, the district court issued a decision in which it found that the FEC acted arbitrarily and capriciously when it determined that the CPD did not endorse, support, or oppose political parties during the 2012 president election.[81] The court also acknowledged the difficulty of any independent candidate in reaching a 15 percent approval rating in the polls, and it noted that polling involving minor-party candidates suffers from errors that makes the results less reliable.

At the court's direction, the FEC reconsidered the allegations brought by the plaintiffs. Nonetheless, it again found no basis to rule that the CPD made prohibited contributions or expenditures to certain candidates by bestowing a debate platform to them, as the CPD used "objective criteria" to determine who participated in debates. Further, the Commission again chose not to enter into new rulemaking. When the case came back to the U.S. District Court for a second time, the court granted the FEC's motion to dismiss.[82] For now, the CPD's approach to deciding who can participate in the presidential debates continues without any meaningful government oversight or without an eye toward broadening its participation rules. The FEC, an agency long hamstrung by its bureaucratic paralysis, is unlikely to pass additional regulations that provide meaningful change in this area. Either future litigation or activist pressure is needed for the CPD to re-examine its policies and for change to occur.

D. *Gender and Racial Bias in Debates*

Hillary Clinton was not the first woman to run for president of the United States. Since 1940, forty women have been nominated by various political

---

[80] Level the Playing Field v. FEC, 232 F. Supp. 3d 130 (2017).
[81] *Id.* at 140.
[82] *See* Level the Playing Field v. FEC, 381 F. Supp.3d 78 (2019).

parties for the highest office in America. Many of these women managed to get on the general election ballot in various states, and ten of them attracted at least 40,000 votes in the general election. Female contenders have been similarly active in presidential primaries. Since 1964, ten women have campaigned in a major-party primary or caucus and received at least 5,000 votes.[83]

Despite this long history of women aspiring to the presidency, 2016 marked the first time that a female candidate participated in a general presidential debate.[84] While election-year primaries and caucuses have certainly made the nomination process more democratic, the primary and general election debates still play a central role in shaping public perceptions and determining the ultimate success of presidential candidates. Because only one woman candidate, Hillary Clinton, has ever received the nomination of a major party for the presidency, only one woman has ever been invited to participate in a general presidential debate.

The story is similarly bleak for African-American candidates. Since the Voting Rights Act of 1965 enshrined into federal law the right of African-Americans to participate equally in the electoral process, particularly in the South, nine black candidates have received at least 40,000 popular votes in the general election.[85] In 1984, Reverend Jesse Jackson attracted three million primary votes as the first black candidate to compete nationally in a major-party primary.[86] Yet it was not until Barack Obama made history by clinching the Democratic nomination that a black candidate appeared on the general presidential debate stage.

We need to make the presidential nomination process more welcoming for non-traditional candidates if we want to increase the diversity of the candidates who appear in the presidential debates. Public perceptions of the presidency are shaped by who appears on the debate stage. Any rules or practices that exclude or disadvantage women and people of color from the debates

---

[83] *List of female United States presidential and vice-presidential candidates*, WIKIWAND, www.wikiwand.com/en/List_of_female_United_States_presidential_and_vice-presidential_ candidates (last updated May 20, 2019).

[84] WITW Staff, *Hillary Clinton goes where no woman has ever gone before in 1st presidential debate*, WOMEN IN THE WORLD (Sept. 26, 2016), https://womenintheworld.com/2016/09/26/ hillary-clinton-goes-where-no-woman-has-ever-gone-before-in-1st-presidential-debate/.

[85] *List of African-American United States presidential and vice-presidential candidates*, WIKIWAND, www.wikiwand.com/en/List_of_African-American_United_States_presidential_and_vice_pres idential_candidates (last updated May 30, 2019).

[86] Eudie Pak, *Jesse Jackson and 6 Black Politicians Who Ran for President of the United States*, BIOGRAPHY (May 30, 2019), www.biography.com/news/jesse-jackson-black-politicians-ran-president.

perpetuate a social perception that white men are better suited for the presidency. Though many voters have made up their minds between the two
major parties before debate season, a surprising number also report that they
rely on the debates to help them choose a candidate; according to the Pew
Research Center, a full two-thirds of voters in 2008 said that year's presidential
debates between Barack Obama and John McCain were "very helpful" or
"somewhat helpful" as they decided whom to support at the ballot box.[87]

Thus, the way the presidential debates are run today leads to a vicious cycle.
The parties, cognizant of the impact of the debates, are most comfortable
throwing resources behind candidates they deem likely to thrive in
a traditional debate setting. The candidates who lack these "winning" characteristics—which historically have included whiteness, maleness, and
a dominating television personality—are often relegated to second-tier status,
and are ultimately prevented from fairly participating on the debate stage. This
lack of participation only reinforces the parties' notion that women and people
of color are not presidential material. Obama's presidency and Hillary
Clinton's two high-profile campaigns almost certainly broadened people's
sense of who belongs in the White House. It was little surprise, then, that
the 2020 presidential debates featured a more diverse slate of candidates, with
more women running for president than in any previous election. Yet the
format of the Democratic primary debates remained particularly problematic
for women. Candidates were incentivized to engage in back-and-forth personal attacks in order to gain speaking time and attract media attention,[88]
resulting in debates that were "combative"[89] and "rife with insults and
interruptions.[90] This made it difficult for the women candidates to showcase
critical leadership skills such as collaboration and relationship-
building—areas in which women tend to excel relative to men.[91] It also left
women candidates uncertain over how to engage with their opponents without

---

[87] Russell Heimlich, *Most Say Presidential Debates Influence Their Vote*, PEW RESEARCH CTR.
      (Sept. 11, 2012), www.pewresearch.org/fact-tank/2012/09/11/most-say-presidential-debates-
      influence-their-vote/.
[88] Mark Preston, *CNN Announces Rules for Next Democratic Presidential Debates*, CNN (July 9,
      2019), www.cnn.com/2019/07/09/politics/cnn-debate-rules/index.html.
[89] Max Greenwood & Jonathan Easley, *5 Takeaways from Combative Democratic Debate*, THE
      HILL (July 30, 2019), https://thehill.com/homenews/campaign/455475-5-takeaways-from-
      democratic-debate-slugfest.
[90] Jonathan Martin & Alexander Burns, *Amid Insults and Interruptions, Sanders Absorbs Burst of
      Attacks in Debate*, N.Y. TIMES (Feb. 25, 2020), www.nytimes.com/2020/02/25/us/politics/sou
      th-carolina-debate-recap.html.
[91] Jack Zenger & Joseph Folkman, *Are Women Better Leaders Than Men?*, HARV. BUSINESS
      REV. (March 15, 2012), https://hbr.org/2012/03/a-study-in-leadership-women-do.

facing public blowback, as gender stereotypes often lead women who assert themselves to be interpreted as mean or pushy. As Adam Grant explains, "Male candidates are free to interrupt, while female candidates face a double bind: stay silent and fail to be heard, or speak up and get judged as too aggressive."[92] This is not a new problem. As Gloria Steinem commented forty years ago, "If you are assertive and aggressive enough to do the job, you're unfeminine and therefore unacceptable; if you're not aggressive, you can't do the job—and in either case, goodbye."[93]

Gender bias is not limited to the question of who makes it onto the debate stage or the rules structuring candidate engagement. The questions asked at the debates themselves also need to be free of bias. When past debates, including the vice-presidential and primary debates, have featured women candidates, they have been plagued by biased questions. If we are to seek ways to improve in the future, it is critical to examine how issues of gender bias have impacted our past debates. In a 2015 study, researchers Jason Turcotte and Newly Paul examined all of the questions that have been asked at every past presidential debate.[94] One of the findings of their study was that debate moderators tended to focus their questions more on policy issues that mattered to them personally and less on issues that mattered to the public generally and to women in particular.

There are several reasons why this happens. First, the journalists who moderate the debates have different goals than the public; the media focuses on questions designed to generate conflict, while members of the public want questions answered about their everyday concerns. Sometimes when journalists ask questions to generate conflict, the question becomes biased toward women, which is particularly problematic. As another study found, women politicians are "more likely to make bills dealing with women's issues and [make] children and family issues a priority."[95] When they are not given the opportunity to highlight these issues in the debates, women must instead play

---

[92] Stephanie Saul, *Interrupting Is Different for Men and Women, Even on a Debate Stage*, N.Y. TIMES (June 27, 2019), www.nytimes.com/2019/06/27/us/politics/debate-interruptions.html.

[93] Leslie Bennetts, *On Aggression in Politics: Are Women Judged by a Double Standard?*, N.Y. TIMES (Feb. 12, 1979), www.nytimes.com/1979/02/12/archives/on-aggression-in-politics-are-women-judged-by-a-double-standard-one.html.

[94] Jason Turcotte & Newly Paul, *A Case of More Is Less: The Role of Gender in U.S. Presidential Debates*, 68 POL'Y RES. Q. 773 (2015).

[95] Kira Sanbonmatsu, *Why Women? The Impact of Women in Elective Office*, POL. PARITY (Oct. 2017), www.politicalparity.org/wp-content/uploads/2017/10/Parity-Research-Women-Impact.pdf.

on their opponents' issue turf. This denies a key opportunity for women candidates to differentiate themselves from their male opponents.

Second, because most debate moderators tend to be men, Turcotte and Paul's study found these moderators inadvertently deprioritize policy issues that resonate more with women. Turcotte and Paul found not only that more debate moderators were men than women,[96] but also that the media entourage covering presidential campaigns in general was much more likely to consist of men. And, frequently, this media will cover an issue differently for a woman than for a man. For example, Senator Amy Klobuchar, a 2020 presidential candidate, received substantial, ongoing critical media attention due to her "reputation" as an abusive boss in the Senate. Senator Bernie Sanders, however, was celebrated for his "curmudgeon" style as a boss, despite allegedly engaging in similar behavior.[97]

Finally, post-debate media analysis plays an important role in shaping public opinion of who "won" a debate, and such post-debate analysis has been shown to be especially biased against women. As Jennifer Brubaker and Gary Hanson noted recently, "Research has suggested that media coverage does not give voters an accurate portrayal of the debates." They cite Benoit, Hansen, and Stein, who "found that newspaper coverage of primary debates accentuated the negative, emphasized character over policy and told voters relatively little of the content of these debates," and highlight additional research drawing similar conclusions in regards to television coverage of debates.[98] Not surprisingly, post-debate news coverage has tended to have more male than female participation. This has been improving in recent election cycles. However, both male and female media commentators tend to skew toward discussing conflict instead of substance. Further, as Brubaker and Hanson found, the media uses post-debate analysis to view the debate as a horse race, with the purpose of trying to determine a winner, rather than providing a full analysis of what was said substantively.

Improvements need to be made to the format of the presidential debates, to the selection of questions asked, and to the media analysis that takes place afterward to allow for greater public consideration of female candidates. Ideas

---

[96] Turcotte & Paul, *supra* note 94, at 776.

[97] Laura McGann, *The Suspiciously Sexist Views of Amy Klobuchar's Management Style, Explained*, Vox (Feb. 24, 2019), www.vox.com/2019/2/24/18218279/amy-klobuchar-fork-comb-bad-boss-binder-staffers-angry-management-style-explained.

[98] Jennifer Brubaker & Gary Hanson, *The Effect of Fox News and CNN's Postdebate Commentator Analysis on Viewer's Perceptions of Presidential Candidate Performance*, 74 SOUTH. COMM. J. 339, 341 (2009).

such as involving more unscripted questions from the general public during the debates must be considered to address these issues.

E. *Audience Reaction Bias*

Both primary and general election presidential debates have generally been conducted in front of a live audience. This audience is typically admonished by debate moderators not to provide either a positive or negative reaction to questions or responses, out of a fear that audience reactions will bias home viewers. Yet this admonition is frequently ignored. As a result, live audiences may be harmful to the goal of providing an informative, fair debate.

There are several historical examples of how audience reaction has impacted a presidential debate. Perhaps the most famous took place in 1984, during the debate between Ronald Reagan and Walter Mondale. When Reagan was asked by the debate moderator if he thought age should be an issue in the campaign, he replied, "I will not make age an issue of this campaign. I am not going to exploit, for political purposes, my opponent's youth and inexperience."[99] The debate audience erupted in laughter, creating the impression that Reagan had "won" the debate and dispelling concerns that his age would affect his ability to serve as President. Similarly, in the 2012 presidential debate, Mitt Romney asserted that Barack Obama had hesitated for weeks before denouncing the attack on the American embassy in Benghazi, Libya, as an "act of terror." This erroneous assertion was quickly corrected by the debate moderator, Candy Crowley, and then followed by a joking request from Barack Obama: "Can you say that a little louder, Candy?" This comment drew immediate audience laughter and applause, becoming a signature moment in the campaign.

Experimental research confirms that home viewers of debates are influenced by audience reactions. In a 2007 study, Steven Fein, George Goethals, and Matthew Kugler conducted an experiment in which participants watched one of three versions of the 1984 Reagan-Mondale presidential debate: a version with no editing, a version that removed audience reactions, or a version that removed the candidates' "soundbite" one-liners (including Reagan's aforementioned quip about Mondale's age).[100] Participants who viewed the unedited version of the debate felt that Reagan and Mondale

---

[99] Steven Fein et al., *Social Influence on Political Judgments: The Case of Presidential Debates*, 28 POL. PSYCHOL. 165, 165 (2007).

[100] *Id.* at 175.

performed "virtually equally." However, in the other two experimental conditions, "Reagan tended to be rated more negatively than Mondale ... particularly in the condition in which the soundbite remained but the audience
reaction was deleted."[101] In other words, audience reactions had a large impact
on how participants perceived candidate performance.

F. Post-Debate Media Coverage

The presidential debates are susceptible to media influence and media bias,
which in turn shapes the beliefs and voting patterns of viewers at home. This
runs contrary to the ostensible purpose of the debates: to inform voters about
the issues and candidates that matter most to them, and to let the voters make
up their own minds. The problem of media influence begins with the questions that the moderators choose to ask of debate participants. While the
process of how the moderators determine which questions to ask is somewhat
opaque, a leaked 2004 memo from the CPD indicates that the moderators
themselves, rather than the Commission or the parties, have control over
which questions they pose to which candidates and in which order they ask
them. At first glance, this makes sense as a question-selection strategy. Highly
esteemed journalists must be approved as moderators in advance by the
debate's participants, and these journalists have every incentive to ask both
hard-hitting and well-balanced questions during their moment in the
spotlight.

However, research indicates that this choice has a major downside: it results
in candidates being asked questions on issues that matter to journalists, not to
voters.[102] Moderators are not required to demonstrate beforehand that their
lines of inquiry reflect the public interest, much less to solicit questions from
voters themselves. Moreover, as members of the media establishment, journalists are especially attuned to—and often personally interested in—whichever
hot scandals may be creating a current buzz in news circles. In an era of
manufactured controversies pushed by parties, interest groups, and foreign
actors alike, moderators who craft debate questions around scandalous material risk unintentionally propagating misleading or overly sensationalized
information to home viewers.

This is precisely what happened in the second general presidential
debate of 2016. In that debate, moderator Martha Raddatz asked Hillary
Clinton whether Clinton thought "it was acceptable for a politician to be

---

[101]   *Id.* at 176.
[102]   Benoit & Hansen, *supra*, note 14, at 134–36.

two-faced?"[103] This was a thinly veiled reference to a passage from one of Clinton's newly released paid speeches to a large financial institution. She faced a similar question in the third debate, when moderator Chris Wallace cited a snippet from a 2013 speech Clinton had given to a Brazilian bank to suggest that she supported "open borders." As Jane Mayer of *The New Yorker* explained, both questions misrepresented Clinton's speeches. But the result of being asked these questions, coupled with Clinton's defensive answers, was that "viewers who watched the second and third debates subsequently saw Clinton as less forthright, and Trump as *more* forthright."[104] As Kathleen Hall Jamieson also explained to Mayer, strategic actors on the right (including Wikileaks and Russian hackers) ensured that an anti-Clinton narrative dominated the media during the weeks of the presidential debates; the debate moderators and the media, in turn, promulgated this narrative before a national audience of millions.[105]

The influence of the media is not limited to the questions asked of the presidential candidates. Journalists also shape public perception through their broad framing of the debates as competitions, and their coverage of the debates often encourages viewers to value clever zingers above informative policy content. In their post-debate coverage, reporters declare winners and losers, going so far as to report the results of temperature-tracking polls conducted during the debates. This polling almost certainly contributes to groupthink, making it harder for viewers to make up their own minds as to their assessment of each candidate and his or her ideas.

Finally, the media's notorious tendency to disproportionately cover the negative aspects of elections and campaigns extends to its reporting on presidential debates, likely leading to greater public negativity toward candidates and toward the government at large.[106] The negativity of media coverage during presidential campaigns has been well-documented.[107] A study by the Shorenstein Center at Harvard University found that every week of the 2016

---

[103] Jane Mayer, *How Russia Helped Swing the Election for Trump*, NEW YORKER (Oct. 1, 2018), www.newyorker.com/magazine/2018/10/01/how-russia-helped-to-swing-the-election-for-trump.

[104] *Id.* (emphasis in original).

[105] *Id.*

[106] Research has found that watching political television leads to greater cynicism and distrust toward government. *See* Michael J. Robinson, *Public Affairs Television and the Growth of Political Malaise: The Case of "The Selling of the Pentagon,"* 70 AM. POL. SCI. REV. 409 (1976).

[107] David Niven, *Bias in the News: Partisanship and Negativity in Media Coverage of Presidents George Bush and Bill Clinton*, 6 HARV. INT'L J. OF PRESS/POL. 31 (2001).

presidential election saw the average presidential candidate receive at least 64 percent negative media coverage, including during the weeks of the primary and general election debates.[108] In fact, the percentage of negative coverage has increased while the percentage of positive coverage has declined steadily since 1960, when presidential candidates received an average of 76 percent positive coverage.[109]

The study by Fein, Goethals, and Kugler, discussed above, explains how people's perceptions of the presidential debates are influenced by the expressed opinions put forth by others.[110] This is undoubtedly true as well for the negative media coverage of the presidential debates; though research on the effect of debate coverage on public opinion is sparse, related research on media coverage of the President's State of the Union addresses finds that "conflict-laden television coverage decreases public evaluations of political institutions, trust in leadership, and overall support for political parties and the system as a whole."[111]

Certainly, free speech and press rights cannot be infringed, especially in terms of political commentary. But greater awareness of these issues may lead the media to adjust how they cover the presidential debates, so as to foster greater political trust and avoid biasing viewers watching at home.

G. *Debate Format*

The traditional debate format is also problematic for several reasons. In the traditional format, there is a typical back-and-forth debate style that privileges candidates who thrive in an "us-versus-them" environment. A clear example of this occurred during the 2016 presidential debates, where Donald Trump "stalked" Hillary Clinton on stage, exacerbating an already antagonistic format. This is likely to have particularly negative consequences for women candidates, who are disproportionately penalized for appearing aggressive.[112]

Alternative formats should be explored—not only to avoid privileging certain candidates, but also to give voters what they want. According to a study by

---

[108] Thomas E. Patterson, *News Coverage of the 2016 General Election: How the Press Failed the Voters*, HARV. KENNEDY SCH., SHORENSTEIN CTR. ON MEDIA POL. & PUB. POL'Y (Dec. 7, 2016), https://shorensteincenter.org/news-coverage-2016-general-election/.

[109] *Id.*

[110] Fein et al., *supra* note 99, at 187–90.

[111] Richard Forgette & Jonathan S. Morris, *High-Conflict Television News and Public Opinion*, 59 POL. RES. Q. 447, 447 (2006).

[112] Rebecca Adams, *People Reward Angry Men but Punish Angry Women, Study Suggests*, HUFFPOST (Oct. 16, 2015), www.huffpost.com/entry/people-reward-angry-men-but-punish-angry-women-study-suggests_n_561fb57be4b050c6c4a47743.

the Annenberg Public Policy Center, voters would prefer debates that limit the number of topics discussed, that vary the topics from debate to debate, that adjust time limits to allow for more in-depth discussion on each issue, and that allow candidates to more clearly flesh out their differences.[113]

The Annenberg study discussed several alternative models for the debate format, including a "chess clock" model, a "reformed standard" model, and a continuation of the "town hall" model.[114] In the "chess clock" model, each of the candidates has an equal, finite amount of time to use during the debate. Each time they speak, their clock runs down. Once it reaches zero, candidates cannot offer additional comments, ensuring equal speaking time to all participants. The model also features questions drawn from a broader pool of sources than just the moderators, and it allows candidates to ask follow-up questions of each other.

The "reformed standard" model is closer to the existing back-and-forth debate format, with several key distinctions. The time for question and response is similar to that currently used, with short periods for response and rebuttal. However, the questions are pulled from sources other than the moderator, and each candidate is allowed to choose to have additional time on a select number of issues. The model also affords each candidate two in-depth questions, provided in advance, and gives him or her more time during the debate for response, allowing for greater clarity and understanding on a few key issues.[115]

V. HOW TO IMPROVE PRESIDENTIAL DEBATES

Given the many challenges faced by the presidential debates, reform is needed. All revisions to the existing debate process should be undertaken with an eye to fulfilling the many important purposes of presidential debates, from informing voters about the full spectrum of presidential candidates and their policy ideas to building deeper trust in the political process.

First, the use of polls as a determining factor of who gets to participate in primary or general election debates should be re-examined. Beyond being conducted fairly and accurately, polls should also capture general public interest in candidates and their ideas, not simply whether people intend to

---

[113] *Democratizing The Debates: A Report of the Annenberg Working Group on Presidential Campaign Debate Reform*, ANNENBERG DEBATE REFORM WORKING GROUP 10 (2015), https://cdn.annen bergpublicpolicycenter.org/wp-content/uploads/Democratizing-The-Debates.pdf.
[114] *Id.* at 10–11.
[115] *Id.* at 11.

vote for a given candidate on Election Day. Polling to determine which candidates voters want to see participate in the debates is one possible reform.

Second, all gender and racial bias must be eliminated from the presidential debates. Beyond expanding the selection criteria for participants include more diverse candidates, the audiences and questioners at the debates should themselves be representative of the American public. This might be done through an audience quota to ensure representation of women, people of color, and other underrepresented groups. Alternatively, the CPD could hold a random lottery to determine who will be in the audience. Debate moderators should be more diverse, as well, helping ensure that candidates are asked a more balanced and representative set of questions. Finally, all candidates should each be asked the same questions. If, for example, female candidates are asked how they will balance family with the role of the presidency, male candidates should be asked this, too.

Third, moderators should be required to ask questions centered around the public's concerns, not their personal interests. Debate questions should be solicited from diverse media outlets and from the general public. Research finds that soliciting questions from voters improves the diversity of questions; as one study's authors explained, people generally support "using town hall forums to create debate agendas that are more in line with public priorities."[116]

Fourth, the debate format should change to ensure that voters learn more substantive information and that candidates have an equal opportunity to express their ideas. Most importantly, the format must avoid biasing debate outcomes, with all candidates treated the same way. Since each debate format is likely to reward certain skills above others, there should be multiple debates in different styles, so there are opportunities for different candidate qualities to come through and shine. For example, town halls allow audience members to ask questions directly to candidates, privileging a relational communication style that may come more naturally to women candidates (and that voters might reward more in women than men). Again, the key is having a variety of debate formats so that the same candidate's strengths are not privileged each time. Speaking time must also be equitably distributed across candidates; this can be accomplished by adopting a "chess clock model" that gives each candidate an equal amount of time and then mutes the microphones of those whose time has run out.

Fifth, we need to find ways to allow voters to make up their own minds about debate outcomes, instead of being influenced by outside actors. A first step in

[116]   Turcotte & Paul, *supra* note 94, at 781.

this direction would be to ensure that more people can access the debates in real time, even without a cable or network TV subscription. The direct viewing audience could be greatly expanded by distributing the debates on social media. This will result in more people having direct knowledge of the content communicated in the debates and, presumably, would somewhat mitigate the influence of the "hot takes" offered by media pundits and political campaigns on the major TV networks. Additionally, the CPD should consider eliminating the on-site audience for debates, thereby eliminating any chance of audience reactions biasing home viewers.

Other reforms could be instituted directly by media organizations. These might include eliminating on-screen displays of temperature-tracking polls during debate coverage and, importantly, requesting that political pundits and journalists refrain from declaring for their viewers who the debate's winners or losers were. The latter reform would be similar to the existing widespread prohibition on journalists declaring electoral winners before an election is over; in both cases, the goal is to prevent media outlets from skewing election outcomes.

VI. CONCLUSION

The primary and general election debates have become critically important events leading up to the election of an American president. This is particularly true in today's world, where information about candidates is disseminated to the public not only through newspapers and television but also through the Internet and social media. This increased access serves to enhance the importance of the presidential debates and solidifies their role as a defining event in the life of a presidential campaign. Given that the debates play such a vital role, it is crucial that they be used as a platform to share a multitude of policy ideas and reflect fundamental fairness.

The FEC and the courts should take a second look at their assessment of the current debate structure. They could start by re-examining the requirement that candidates must meet a 15 percent polling threshold to participate in the debates. This requirement may be a self-fulfilling prophecy, as it withholds from lesser-known candidates the very exposure they would need to increase their polling numbers. The Commission on Presidential Debates and the media must also make a more concerted effort to provide fairness to women and people of color, both in the format of the debates and in the questions that are posed to candidates. The media must also re-examine its post-debate coverage, guiding its programs toward more substantive analysis and moving away from horse-race commentary.

Debates will always be an imperfect way of informing voters about candidates and issues. There is simply not enough time or space for every presidential contender to make his or her case on stage. But the perfect should not be the enemy of the good. The reforms recommended above will move us toward a better system in which candidates are treated fairly, policy is taken seriously, and voters are given the information they need to make the most educated choice possible on Election Day.

13

The Influence of Technology
on Presidential Primary Campaigns

Anthony J. Gaughan[*]

I. INTRODUCTION

The disruptive power of technological innovation is one of the defining features of modern life. The presidential nomination process is no exception. Changes in communication technology have profoundly shaped how presidential candidates conduct their campaigns. First radio, then television, and more recently the internet have successively emerged as essential tools for effective political communication. A presidential candidate cannot compete without embracing the new communication technologies of the day. But the adoption of new technology has relentlessly increased campaign costs for more than a century. This chapter examines how technology has shaped the presidential nomination process, making the pursuit of the White House an ever more expensive proposition.

II. THE AGE OF RADIO

The presidential primary system began in 1912, when former president Theodore Roosevelt challenged incumbent President William Howard Taft for the Republican nomination.[1] In an era before commercial aviation, Roosevelt traveled by train from city to city, personally making his case to Republican primary voters.[2] Rapid travel via train enabled Roosevelt to

---

[*] Anthony J. Gaughan is Professor of Law at Drake University Law School. He would like to thank Gene Mazo for his extremely helpful editorial advice on this chapter.
[1] JOHN MILTON COOPER, JR., PIVOTAL DECADES: THE UNITED STATES, 1900–1920, at 169–70 (1990).
[2] DORIS KEARNS GOODWIN, THE BULLY PULPIT: THEODORE ROOSEVELT, WILLIAM HOWARD TAFT, AND THE GOLDEN AGE OF JOURNALISM 688–89 (2013).

campaign in multiple primary states and thus directly contributed to his remarkable string of upset victories.[3]

The threat posed by Roosevelt prompted Taft to become the first sitting president to actively campaign for his party's nomination.[4] Boarding a train with great fanfare, he conducted a whistle-stop tour that rivaled Roosevelt's.[5] The two candidates ultimately traveled thousands of miles by rail before Taft finally prevailed in the nomination race.[6] The candidates' reliance on retail politics heralded a new era of personal campaigning.[7] The Taft–Roosevelt race also anticipated the modern era of escalating campaign costs. Roosevelt spent $550,000 while Taft spent $450,000, extraordinary figures for a nomination battle in the 1910s.[8]

Shortly after the presidential primary system began, the invention of radio revolutionized political campaigns, driving costs up dramatically. In 1912, Taft and Roosevelt had no choice but to crisscross the country if they wanted audiences to hear their speeches. But the invention of radio broadcasting enabled presidential candidates to speak directly to millions of voters simultaneously. The political power of the new medium became increasingly obvious in the 1920s as radio stations proliferated across the country.[9] By the early 1930s radio reached two out of every three American homes.[10]

Even in its earliest days, radio shaped the public's perception of the candidates and the parties. In 1924, the Democratic Party broadcast its presidential convention on radio, but soon came to regret the decision.[11] Held before a raucous crowd in New York's Madison Square Garden, the convention was one of the most divisive in the party's history, with the delegates clashing along regional, ideological, and religious lines.[12] Party leaders required the assistance of 1,000 New York police officers to maintain order.[13] For the first

---

[3] GOODWIN, *supra* note 2, at 689–90; WILLIAM H. HARBAUGH, THE LIFE AND TIMES OF THEODORE ROOSEVELT 403–05 (1975).

[4] GOODWIN, *supra* note 2, at 693.

[5] *Id.*

[6] *Id.* at 696.

[7] *Id.* at 695.

[8] LOUISE OVERACKER, MONEY IN ELECTIONS 69–70, 122–23 (1932).

[9] CHRISTOPHER H. STERLING & JOHN MICHAEL KITTROSS, STAY TUNED: A HISTORY OF AMERICAN BROADCASTING 63–69, 137 (3rd ed. 2002); EDWARD W. CHESTER, RADIO, TELEVISION AND AMERICAN POLITICS 3 (1969).

[10] STERLING & KITTROSS, *supra* note 9, at 139.

[11] CHESTER, *supra* note 9, at 17.

[12] DAVID BURNER, THE POLITICS OF PROVINCIALISM: THE DEMOCRATIC PARTY IN TRANSITION, 1918–1932, at 114–28 (1968).

[13] JOHN D. HICKS, REPUBLICAN ASCENDANCY, 1921–1933, at 96 (1960).

time in history, Americans around the country listened to radio accounts of the chaotic scene on the convention floor.[14] Only after 103 ballots did the Democrats finally settle on West Virginia attorney John W. Davis as their nominee, a compromise that pleased none of the party's warring factions.[15] As the *New Republic* observed, "The Democrats have a well-grounded suspicion that the broadcasting of their Donneybrook Fair in Madison Square Garden may have done them more harm than good."[16] Those fears proved well-founded indeed. In November 1924, President Calvin Coolidge defeated Davis in a landslide.[17]

The 1932 election demonstrated how radio boosted some campaigns while undermining others. The Democratic nomination contest that year came down to two candidates: New York Governor Franklin Roosevelt and former New York Governor Al Smith, the party's standard-bearer four years before. After his defeat in the 1928 presidential election, Smith hoped the Democrats would give him a second chance in 1932. But Smith's stumbling approach to radio broadcasts doomed his comeback efforts. Raised in an Irish immigrant neighborhood in New York City, Smith's heavy accent and habit of mispronouncing words came across poorly on radio.[18] As the historian John Hicks explained, radio gave listeners a distorted picture of the Irish-American politician:

> Smith in person was an eloquent public speaker who moved his audiences, but he could not stand still before a stationary microphone, the only kind then available, and for his radio listeners the effect was sometimes appalling. Moreover he talked with an exaggerated East Side New York accent that western and southern Americans could not always understand.[19]

Roosevelt, in contrast, thrived on the radio.[20] Stricken by polio at age 39, he was confined to a wheelchair for the rest of his life.[21] But radio gave the charismatic Roosevelt the ability to project strength, confidence, and personal magnetism.[22] Industry professionals marveled at his reassuring voice, his clear

---

[14]   *Id.*

[15]   BURNER, *supra* note 12, at 124–27, 130–31; HICKS, *supra* note 13, at 97.

[16]   CHESTER, *supra* note 9, at 17.

[17]   HICKS, *supra* note 13, at 102–03.

[18]   DOUGLAS B. CRAIG, FIRESIDE POLITICS: RADIO AND POLITICAL CULTURE IN THE UNITED STATES, 1920–1940, at 149 (2000); STERLING & KITTROSS, *supra* note 9, at 137.

[19]   HICKS, *supra* note 13, at 211.

[20]   CRAIG, *supra* note 18, at 154.

[21]   GEOFFREY C. WARD, A FIRST-CLASS TEMPERAMENT: THE EMERGENCE OF FRANKLIN ROOSEVELT 781 (1989).

[22]   CRAIG, *supra* note 18, at 157; JAMES MACGREGOR BURNS, ROOSEVELT: THE LION AND THE FOX 167–68, 203 (1984); H. W. BRANDS, TRAITOR TO HIS CLASS: THE PRIVILEGED LIFE AND RADICAL PRESIDENCY OF FRANKLIN DELANO ROOSEVELT 225 (2008); WILLIAM

diction and his "tone of perfect sincerity."[23] When he gave a speech supporting Smith for the nomination at the 1928 Democratic Convention, the radio broadcast made Roosevelt a national figure.[24] Later, as governor of New York, Roosevelt used radio addresses to build public support for his legislative priorities.[25] The medium also gave him crucial momentum during the 1932 Democratic nomination campaign. In a radio address, he called on the government to assist "the forgotten man at the bottom of the economic pyramid."[26] The broadcast became known as the "Forgotten Man Speech," and it helped Roosevelt persuade progressive voters to support his nomination.[27] As the historian H. W. Brands explained, "[o]ver time Roosevelt's radio audience would come to feel they knew him as they had known no other executive."[28] Roosevelt won the Democratic nomination in 1932 and went on to win a record four presidential elections. Radio helped make him the dominant American political leader of his time.

In the 1930s, as the nation's population surged past 120 million, it was no longer possible for candidates to rely on direct contact with voters.[29] In a continent-sized nation, radio provided an indispensable medium for mass communication. But it did not come cheap as the networks charged parties and candidates as much as $10,000 an hour for air time and the use of the radio studios.[30] Radio broadcasting became the single largest expense for presidential campaigns and costs rose steadily.[31] In 1928, the candidates and parties spent a combined total of $2 million on national and local radio broadcasts; in 1932 campaign spending on radio rose to $5 million.[32]

E. Leuchtenburg, Franklin D. Roosevelt and the New Deal, 1932–1940, at 330–31 (1963).

[23] James David Barber, The Pulse of Politics: Electing Presidents in the Media Age 247 (1980); Craig, *supra* note 18, at 155.

[24] Brands, *supra* note 22, at 206.

[25] Arthur M. Schlesinger, Jr., The Crisis of the Old Order, 1919–1933, at 393 (1957); Craig, *supra* note 18, at 154.

[26] Burns, *supra* note 22, at 133.

[27] Robert S. McElvaine, The Great Depression: America 1929–1941, at 125 (1984); Brands, *supra* note 22, at 238–39; Burns, *supra* note 22, at 133.

[28] Brands, *supra* note 22, at 225.

[29] Overacker, *supra* note 8, at 374. The population of the United States reached 123 million in 1930. *See* 1930 *Census*, United States Census Bureau, www.census.gov/history/www/throu gh_the_decades/fast_facts/1930_fast_facts.html.

[30] Craig, *supra* note 18, at 146.

[31] Overacker, *supra* note 8, at 28–29.

[32] Sterling & Kittross, *supra* note 9, at 137–38.

With radio making up the lion's share of campaign spending, election expenditures relentlessly increased.[33] The 1944 presidential campaign, for example, cost a record total of $20 million.[34] The insatiable demand for money to buy radio advertisements strengthened party control over the presidential candidates. As the historian Zachary Karabell explained, "The cost of radio time alone made it extraordinarily hard for any candidate to run outside of the party system."[35]

Campaigns that failed to appreciate the importance of radio paid dearly for it on Election Day. New York Governor Thomas Dewey learned that lesson the hard way. During the 1948 Republican nomination campaign, Dewey debated former Minnesota Governor Harold Stassen in a radio broadcast before the crucial Oregon primary.[36] The national radio audience exceeded forty million listeners.[37] Dewey won the debate so decisively that he not only prevailed in the Oregon primary but also gained crucial momentum that helped him clinch the Republican nomination later that summer.[38] But despite his success on the radio, he disdained broadcasting as a communication medium. During his general election campaign against President Harry Truman, Dewey gave national radio addresses, but he refused to authorize an aggressive radio advertising blitz.[39] He viewed such campaign tactics as undignified, but the decision backfired.[40] Dewey, who entered the fall campaign as a heavy favorite, lost to Truman in one of the biggest upsets in presidential history.[41] Some Republican campaign advisers blamed Dewey's failure to mount a full-blown radio campaign as a major reason for his defeat.[42]

One of the last presidential candidates to rely heavily on radio was Minnesota Senator Eugene McCarthy.[43] In his unsuccessful effort to win

[33] Louise Overacker, *Campaign Finance in the Presidential Election of 1944*, 39 AM. POL. SCI. REV. 899, 906 (1945); ZACHARY KARABELL, THE LAST CAMPAIGN: HOW HARRY TRUMAN WON THE 1948 ELECTION, at 73–74 (2001); RAYMOND J. LA RAJA, MONEY, POLITICAL PARTIES, AND CAMPAIGN FINANCE REFORM 62 (2010).

[34] Overacker, *supra* note 33, at 901.

[35] KARABELL, *supra* note 33, at 74.

[36] RICHARD NORTON SMITH, THOMAS E. DEWEY AND HIS TIMES 26–27, 492–94 (1982); STERLING & KITTROSS, *supra* note 9, at 313; CHESTER, *supra* note 9, at 53; SIG MICKELSON, THE ELECTRIC MIRROR: POLITICS IN AN AGE OF TELEVISION 194–95 (1972).

[37] SMITH, *supra* note 36, at 492.

[38] CHESTER, *supra* note 9, at 53; SMITH, *supra* note 36, at 492–94; STERLING & KITTROSS, *supra* note 9, at 313.

[39] DAVID HALBERSTAM, THE FIFTIES, at 227 (1993); SMITH, *supra* note 36, at 531.

[40] HALBERSTAM, *supra* note 39, at 227.

[41] See DAVID MCCULLOUGH, TRUMAN 710–11 (1992).

[42] HALBERSTAM, *supra* note 39, at 227.

[43] CHESTER, *supra* note 9, at 59.

the 1968 Democratic nomination, McCarthy devoted most of his advertising to radio advertisements.[44] But radio's time as the leading communication method had passed. In the 1950s, a new medium emerged that brought far more than just a candidate's voice into voters' homes.

III. THE RISE OF TELEVISION

The broadcasting of televised images influenced presidential campaigns even more profoundly than radio had thirty years before. Television arrived as a force in American politics in the early 1950s and immediately became the dominant means of political communication.[45] In 1952, about one-third of American homes had televisions; by 1961, that figure rose to 89 percent of homes; and by 1976, the percentage of homes with television reached 97 - percent.[46] Television made a candidate's appearance, mannerisms, and charisma a factor in elections like never before. One thing, however, stayed the same in the television age: the candidates' need for ever larger sums of money to make effective use of new communication technology.

Television shaped election outcomes as early as the 1952 election.[47] Among the Democratic candidates, Illinois Governor Adlai Stevenson performed poorly on television because he never developed a comfortable presence before the cameras.[48] Voters had a more favorable impression of the governor if they heard him on radio rather than watched him on television.[49] Although he managed to secure the Democratic nomination anyway, Stevenson's lack of telegenic appeal would gravely undermine his candidacy during the general election.[50]

In contrast, a Miami University study found that General Dwight Eisenhower was the most telegenic of the Republican candidates.[51] Eisenhower's sophisticated use of television during the Republican nomination race presaged his successful campaign against Stevenson in the general election. As former CBS News executive Sig Mickelson observed, the

---

[44] *Id.* at 59–60.
[45] *Id.* at 58 ("By 1956, television definitely had become a more important source of information during the Presidential campaign than radio"); HALBERSTAM, *supra* note 39, at 180 ("By 1949, radio was on the verge of being overtaken by television as a commercial vehicle").
[46] STERLING & KITTROSS, *supra* note 9, at 382, 455.
[47] MICKELSON, *supra* note 36, at 99–100.
[48] NELSON W. POLSBY & AARON WILDAVSKY, PRESIDENTIAL ELECTIONS: STRATEGIES OF AMERICAN ELECTORAL POLITICS 177 (5th ed. 1980); BARBER, *supra* note 23, at 271.
[49] POLSBY & WILDAVSKY, *supra* note 48, at 177.
[50] GARY R. EDGERTON, THE COLUMBIA HISTORY OF AMERICAN TELEVISION 211–13 (2007).
[51] CHESTER, *supra* note 9, at 79.

Eisenhower campaign employed "television-oriented" strategists who "from the beginning were quick to take advantage of the medium's capacity to aid in upsetting the Republican party's old order."[52] The retired general's advisers ushered in the use of 20-, 30-, and 60-second television advertisements as mainstays of presidential campaigns.[53] After clinching the Republican nomination, Eisenhower used the same advertising tactics in the general election, spending twice as much on television as the Stevenson campaign.[54] Eisenhower's decisive victory in the 1952 election made clear the power of television.[55] As the industry journal *Broadcasting-Telecasting* observed of the 1952 New Hampshire primary campaign: "If a viewer watched a reasonable percentage of the nightly newsreel programs, the discussion forums, and special primary presentations, the chances are that he saw a great deal more of the principal campaigners than the New Hampshire resident without TV."[56] Two other campaign-related innovations came into their own in the 1950s. Commercial air travel permitted candidates to travel thousands of miles in a matter of hours. During a key period in the 1952 nomination race, Eisenhower flew to six southern cities in two days, covering more ground more quickly than rail travel would ever have permitted.[57] The other major development was the rise of advertising agencies and public relations firms, which became indispensable to television-centric presidential campaigns.[58] A consumer ethos took hold in politics, as campaigns packaged candidates using marketing tactics identical to those of commercial advertising.[59] But the innovations came with a steep price tag. The cost of television advertisements, marketing firms, and commercial air travel drove the cost of presidential campaigns to unprecedented levels. As the 1960s dawned, candidates with superior financial resources possessed a clear and growing advantage.

The 1960 Democratic nomination race, in particular, revealed how wealth and telegenic appeal could propel an unknown candidate to victory in the television age. Senator John F. Kennedy entered the 1960 campaign with a long list of political liabilities. He was only 42 years old, he had an undistinguished legislative record, and he was a Roman Catholic in a Protestant-majority nation that had never before elected a Catholic

[52] MICKELSON, *supra* note 36, at 99; BARBER, *supra* note 23, at 269–71.
[53] EDGERTON, *supra* note 50, at 211–13; CHESTER, *supra* note 9, at 79, 83; MICKELSON, *supra* note 36, at 99–101, 104.
[54] EDGERTON, *supra* note 50, at 211–12; MICKELSON, *supra* note 36, at 103–04.
[55] CHESTER, *supra* note 9, at 78, 83.
[56] *Id.* at 78.
[57] MICKELSON, *supra* note 36, at 101.
[58] EDGERTON, *supra* note 50, at 211–13; MICKELSON, *supra* note 36, at 108.
[59] EDGERTON, *supra* note 50, at 211–13; MICKELSON, *supra* note 36, at 108–09.

president.[60] But Kennedy used television and his family wealth to stun the political world and win the Democratic nomination.

No primary played a bigger role in Kennedy's victory than West Virginia, an overwhelmingly Protestant state that became a test case of the Catholic senator's ability to win over Protestant voters.[61] The stakes could not have been higher for the Massachusetts senator. He knew that if he lost the primary, Democratic delegates would interpret his defeat as evidence that the nation was still not ready for a Catholic president.[62]

To prevail in West Virginia, the Kennedy campaign blanketed the state with television advertisements.[63] As the veteran journalist Theodore White observed, "Over and over again there was the handsome, open-faced candidate on the TV screen, showing himself, proving that a Catholic wears no horns."[64] A televised debate against Minnesota Senator Hubert Humphrey, the other major candidate in the race, helped move public opinion in Kennedy's favor.[65] Then, shortly before the primary election, Kennedy appeared in a televised interview to answer questions on his religious views.[66] In strong and persuasive fashion, he assured West Virginia viewers that he "would not take orders from any Pope, Cardinal, Bishop or priest."[67] White described the address as "[t]he finest TV broadcast I have ever heard any political candidate make."[68] The television strategy worked so well that Kennedy won 60 percent of the popular vote in West Virginia, a margin so large it created momentum for his campaign that carried him to the nomination.[69] "I think we have now buried the religious issue once and for all," he accurately observed the day after his victory.[70]

The 1960 West Virginia primary demonstrated the power of television-centric campaigns. Whereas Humphrey's campaign spent a total of $25,000 overall in the state, the Kennedy campaign spent $34,000 on television alone in West Virginia.[71] Humphrey lacked the funds to maintain a significant

---

[60] ROBERT DALLEK, AN UNFINISHED LIFE: JOHN F. KENNEDY, 1917–1963, at 231–33 (2003).
[61] THEODORE H. WHITE, THE MAKING OF THE PRESIDENT 1960, at 101, 106 (1962); DALLEK, *supra* note 60, at 257.
[62] DALLEK, *supra* note 60, at 252.
[63] *Id.* at 253.
[64] WHITE, *supra* note 61, at 108.
[65] THEODORE C. SORENSEN, KENNEDY 140–41 (1965); CHESTER, *supra* note 9, at 116.
[66] SORENSEN, *supra* note 65, at 145.
[67] *Id.*
[68] CHESTER, *supra* note 9, at 116.
[69] DALLEK, *supra* note 60, at 257; SORENSEN, *supra* note 65, at 146.
[70] WHITE, *supra* note 61, at 114.
[71] DALLEK, *supra* note 60, at 257; WHITE, *supra* note 61, at 110, 112.

television presence, and he also looked uncomfortable during the few times he appeared before the television cameras.[72] It was a combination fatal to his campaign.[73] In disgust, Humphrey dropped out of the race, declaring, "You can't beat a million dollars. The way Jack Kennedy and his old man [Joseph P. Kennedy, Sr.] threw the money around, the people of West Virginia won't need any public relief for the next fifteen years."[74] One of the lessons of West Virginia, White concluded, was that "TV is no medium for a poor man."[75] After clinching the Democratic nomination, Kennedy defeated Vice President Richard Nixon in the general election.[76] Television again played a key role in Kennedy's success, as Nixon's stiff awkwardness before the cameras hurt him much as the stiff performances of Stevenson and Humphrey had hurt them.[77]

Ironically, eight years later Nixon would use television to pull off one of the great comebacks in American political history. As he planned his return to politics in 1968, he knew only too well that television would determine the fate of his comeback.[78] In order to avoid the mistakes of his 1960 campaign, Nixon hired a campaign staff filled with marketing and television experts.[79] Among his top advisers was Roger Ailes, a young television producer tasked with changing Nixon's dour public image.[80] Ailes recognized that his client was not a "natural" on television.[81] In a 1969 interview with the *Washington Post*, Ailes said of Nixon:

> Now you put him on television, you've got a problem right away. He's a funny-looking guy. He looks like somebody hung him in a closet overnight, and he jumps out in the morning with his suit all bunched up and starts running around saying, "I want to be President." I mean this is how he strikes some people.[82]

---

[72]   WHITE, *supra* note 61, at 110–11.

[73]   *Id.* at 113, 169–70.

[74]   JAMES T. PATTERSON, GRAND EXPECTATIONS: THE UNITED STATES, 1945–1974, at 435 (1996).

[75]   WHITE, *supra* note 61, at 112.

[76]   DALLEK, *supra* note 60, at 294–96.

[77]   JOE MCGINNISS, THE SELLING OF THE PRESIDENT 32–34 (1969); PATTERSON, *supra* note 74, at 437–38; EDGERTON, *supra* note 50, at 223–24.

[78]   MCGINNISS, *supra* note 77, at 34; STEPHEN E. AMBROSE, NIXON: THE TRIUMPH OF A POLITICIAN, 1962–1972, at 138–39 (1989).

[79]   MCGINNISS, *supra* note 77, at 171–72, 178–89, 195–56, 205–06; AMBROSE, *supra* note 78, at 137–40; EVAN THOMAS, BEING NIXON: A MAN DIVIDED 154–55 (2015).

[80]   MCGINNISS, *supra* note 77, at 63–65.

[81]   THOMAS, *supra* note 79, at 163.

[82]   Alyssa Rosenberg, *Before Roger Ailes Created Fox News, He Made Richard Nixon the Star of His Own Show*, WASH. POST (May 18, 2017), www.washingtonpost.com/news/act-four/wp/20

To improve Nixon's television presence, his advisers carefully crafted photo opportunities and staged interviews designed to remind voters of the candidate's expertise in domestic and foreign policy.[83] In creating the public image of a "New" Nixon, the campaign filmed him in informal settings with an "arresting sound track" and used "only the most flattering pictures."[84] Above all, the advertisements sought to persuade voters that he was the candidate best prepared to serve as president.[85] As Nixon aide Harry Treleaven emphasized in an internal campaign memo, every television advertisement promoted a central theme:

> [O]f all the Republicans, the most qualified for the job by far is Richard M. Nixon. More than any other Republican candidate for the Presidency, Richard Nixon will know what has to be done—and he'll know the best way to get it done. We'll all feel a whole lot better knowing he's there in Washington running things instead of somebody else.[86]

The strategy worked. Nixon dominated the Republican primaries and caucuses, easily defeating his principal opponents, New York Governor Nelson Rockefeller and California Governor Ronald Reagan.[87] In the fall, Nixon narrowly defeated Hubert Humphrey, whose campaign never recovered from televised images of chaos during the 1968 Democratic convention in Chicago.[88]

Nixon would not have been able to reshape his public image without a massive campaign war chest. The cost of television commercials reached a new high in 1968, but Nixon had the resources to pay for them.[89] Maurice Stans, Nixon's campaign finance chairman, raised over $9 million during the primary and caucus season.[90] Much of the money came from wealthy donors. For example, 26 individual contributors each gave $100,000 or more for

17/05/18/before-roger-ailes-created-fox-news-he-made-richard-nixon-the-star-of-his-own-show/ ?utm_term=.8bd9f5bfa4of.

[83] McGinniss, *supra* note 77, at 173, 178–79; Ambrose, *supra* note 78, at 138–39; Thomas, *supra* note 79, at 163.

[84] McGinniss, *supra* note 77, at 179; Thomas, *supra* note 79, at 155; Ambrose, *supra* note 78, at 138–39.

[85] McGinniss, *supra* note 77, at 173; Ambrose, *supra* note 78, at 138–39.

[86] McGinniss, *supra* note 77, at 173.

[87] Ambrose, *supra* note 78, at 162, 169–70; Thomas, *supra* note 79, at 157, 158–60; Scott John Hammond, Robert North Roberts & Valerie A. Sulfaro, Campaigning for President in America, 1788–2016, at 743–44 (2016).

[88] Patterson, *supra* note 74, at 694–97; Ambrose, *supra* note 78, at 181–82, 220; Thomas, *supra* note 79, at 173, 187.

[89] Ambrose, *supra* note 78, at 140.

[90] *Id.*

Nixon's nomination campaign.[91] Nixon was not alone in receiving large donations. The Democratic candidates Robert Kennedy and Eugene McCarthy each received contributions of $500,000 or more from individual donors during the 1968 primary campaign.[92]

The skyrocketing cost of television required ever larger campaign budgets.[93] Between 1956 and 1968, campaign costs almost doubled, rising from $155 million to $300 million.[94] By 2000, the presidential election cost $1.4 billion; by 2008, it reached $2.8 billion.[95] In every election between 1952 and 2016, television-related costs represented the largest single line item of campaign budgets.[96] The journalist Haynes Johnson described how television dominated campaign strategy during the 1980 election: "All national campaign events were scheduled with television in mind. All presidential candidates structured their appearances to try and gain maximum network exposure on the morning and evening news programs. All campaign financial planning, all strategy sessions begin with television."[97] But television can be a two-edged sword, as Howard Dean learned in 2004. In the early stages of the presidential race, the Vermont governor jumped out to an early polling lead among Democratic voters.[98] On the night of the Iowa caucuses, however, he finished in third place behind Senator John Kerry and Senator John Edwards.[99] In an effort to inspire his disappointed supporters, Dean gave

---

[91] *Id.*

[92] Anthony J. Gaughan, *Trump, Twitter, and the Russians: The Growing Obsolescence of Federal Campaign Finance Law*, 27 S. CAL. INTERDISC. L.J. 79, 115 (2017); HERBERT E. ALEXANDER, FINANCING POLITICS: MONEY, ELECTIONS, AND REFORM 49 (2nd ed. 1980).

[93] MICKELSON, *supra* note 36, at 242–43; Anthony J. Gaughan, *The Forty-Year War on Money in Politics: Watergate, FECA, and the Future of Campaign Finance Reform*, 71 OHIO ST. L.J. 791, 808–23 (2016).

[94] Anthony Corrado, *Money and Politics: A History of Federal Campaign Finance Law, in* THE NEW CAMPAIGN FINANCE SOURCEBOOK 20 (Anthony Corrado et al. eds., 2005).

[95] *Total Cost of Elections, 1998-2018*, CTR. FOR RESPONSIVE POL., www.opensecrets.org/over view/cost.php.

[96] Derek Willis, *Why Television Is Still King for Campaign Spending*, N.Y. TIMES (June 30, 2015), www.nytimes.com/2015/07/01/upshot/why-television-is-still-king-for-campaign-spending .html?abt=0002&abg=1; Elisa Shearer, *Social Media Outpaces Print Newspapers in the U.S. as a News Source*, PEW RES. CTR. (Dec. 10, 2018), www.pewresearch.org/fact-tank/2018/12/10/social-media-outpaces-print-newspapers-in-the-u-s-as-a-news-source/; *The Total Audience Report: Q1 2015*, NIELSEN, at 8 (June 23, 2015), www.nielsen.com/content/dam/corporate/us/en/reports-do wnloads/2015-reports/total-audience-report-q1-2015.pdf.

[97] Haynes Johnson, *Media, in* THE PURSUIT OF THE PRESIDENCY 1980, at 39 (Richard Harwood ed., 1980).

[98] Keating Holland, *Poll: Dean starts 2004 leading Dems*, CNN (Jan. 5, 2004), www.cnn.com /2004/ALLPOLITICS/01/05/elec04.poll.democrats.poll/.

[99] Kenneth T. Walsh, *The Battle Cry That Backfired on Howard "The Scream" Dean*, U.S. NEWS & WORLD REPORT (Jan. 17, 2008), www.usnews.com/news/articles/2008/01/17/the-battle-cry-that-backfired; HAMMOND, *supra* note 87, at 823.

a televised speech from his Iowa campaign headquarters in which he predicted future victories, declaring: "And then we're going to Washington, D.C.— to take back the White House—YEEEEEAAAH!"[100] The "Dean scream," as it came to be known, sounded more hysterical and undignified on television than it did to those in the room, especially when constantly replayed on the cable news networks.[101] But the perception created by television mattered far more than the reality in the room. Late night talk show hosts had a field day mocking the "Scream" and the Vermont governor soon became a national laughingstock.[102] Dean's campaign was already sinking in the polls before the "Scream," but the television-created image of an unhinged candidate ended whatever chance he had of a comeback.[103]

Conversely, television saved Bill Clinton's presidential campaign in 1992. Shortly before the New Hampshire primary, two scandals rocked the Clinton campaign: allegations that he had dodged the draft during the Vietnam War and allegations that he had an affair with Gennifer Flowers while he was governor of Arkansas.[104] In previous elections candidates facing similar scandals had withdrawn, such as Gary Hart in 1988.[105] But Clinton realized that he could use television to speak directly to voters and thereby gain supporters, rather than lose them because of the scandals.[106] In a series of high-stakes televised interviews, he simultaneously denied the allegations and used the opportunity to bring national attention to his campaign.[107] The strategy worked. In a crowded Democratic field, Clinton emerged as the frontrunner in March 1992 and clinched the nomination in June, earning in the process the nickname the "Comeback Kid."[108]

[100]   Walsh, *supra* note 99; Jody Avirgan & Clare Malone, *Why the Dean Scream Sounded so Different on TV*, FIVETHIRTYEIGHT (Feb. 4, 2016), https://fivethirtyeight.com/features/why-the-dean-scream-sounded-so-different-on-tv/; HAMMOND, *supra* note 87, at 823–24.

[101]   Avirgan & Malone, *supra* note 100; HAMMOND, *supra* note 87, at 823–24.

[102]   Walsh, *supra* note 99; HAMMOND, *supra* note 87, at 823–24.

[103]   *What Howard Dean Can Teach Us About 2016*, FIVETHIRTYEIGHT (Feb. 4, 2016), https://fivethirtyeight.com/features/what-howard-dean-can-teach-us-about-2016/; HAMMOND, *supra* note 87, at 823–24.

[104]   Patrick Healy, *Resurrection: How New Hampshire Saved the 1992 Clinton Campaign*, N.Y. TIMES (Feb. 8, 2016), www.nytimes.com/interactive/2016/02/08/us/politics/bill-hillary-clinton-new-hampshire.html.

[105]   HAMMOND, *supra* note 87, at 787, 797.

[106]   Healy, *supra* note 104; HAMMOND, *supra* note 87, at 797.

[107]   Michael Kruse, *The TV Interview That Haunts Hillary Clinton*, POLITICO (Sept. 23, 2016), www.politico.com/magazine/story/2016/09/hillary-clinton-2016-60-minutes-1992-214275; HAMMOND, *supra* note 87, at 796–97.

[108]   HAMMOND, *supra* note 87, at 796–98; Dan Balz & E. J. Dionne Jr., *Clinton Secures Party Nomination*, WASH. POST (June 3, 1992), www.washingtonpost.com/archive/politics/1992/0

A quarter-century later a Republican candidate used an even bolder communications strategy to overcome seemingly insurmountable obstacles. When the reality-television star Donald Trump announced his candidacy for the Republican nomination in 2015, Politico described his campaign as "quixotic,"[109] and the Washington Post noted that he faced "an uphill battle to be taken seriously by his rivals."[110] Trump's campaign seemed unlikely to succeed because of the extraordinary number of liabilities that dogged him, including his questionable business record[111] and his complete lack of military and government experience.[112] But Trump's skilled use of television overcame his political vulnerabilities. Years before he entered the race, Trump's NBC television show "The Apprentice" made him a household name across the country.[113] The show thus not only helped him promote an image as a billionaire businessman but also gave him an invaluable platform from which to run for president.[114]

The free publicity that came with his fame proved critical to Trump's stunning success in the 2016 race. Contrary to popular belief, Trump did not use his wealth to outspend his rivals. During the primary and general campaigns, he spent a total of $66 million of his own money, a relatively modest figure when compared to the $2.4 billion raised in the 2016 presidential

6/03/clinton-secures-party-nomination/af895d8f-d08a-4dde-b640-89444f0e52e9/?utm_term= .e0d4d2e6ae21.

[109] Adam B. Lerner, *The 10 Best Lines from Donald Trump's Announcement Speech*, POLITICO (June 16, 2015), www.politico.com/story/2015/06/donald-trump-2016-announcement-10-best-lines-119066.

[110] Jose Delreal, *Donald Trump Announces Presidential Bid*, WASH. POST (June 16, 2015), www.washingtonpost.com/news/post-politics/wp/2015/06/16/donald-trump-to-announce-his-presidential-plans-today/?utm_term=.e365951e202a.

[111] Susanne Craig, *Trump's Empire: A Maze of Debts and Opaque Ties*, N.Y. TIMES (Aug. 20, 2016), www.nytimes.com/2016/08/21/us/politics/donald-trump-debt.html.

[112] Matt Flegenheimer & Michael Barbaro, *Donald Trump Is Elected President in Stunning Repudiation of the Establishment*, N.Y. TIMES (Nov. 9, 2016), www.nytimes.com/2016/11/09/us/politics/hillary-clinton-donald-trump-president.html; Jesse Yomtov, *Where Trump Ranks Among Least Experienced Presidents*, USA TODAY (Nov. 8, 2016), www.usatoday.com/story/news/politics/onpolitics/2016/11/08/donald-trump-experience-president/93504134/.

[113] Patrick Radden Keefe, *How Mark Burnett Resurrected Donald Trump as an Icon of American Success*, NEW YORKER (Jan. 7, 2019), www.newyorker.com/magazine/2019/01/07/how-mark-burnett-resurrected-donald-trump-as-an-icon-of-american-success; Jackie Calmes, *Donald Trump: Life Before The Presidency*, MILLER CTR., UNIV. OF VIRGINIA, https://millercenter .org/president/trump/life-presidency.

[114] Hank Steuver, *How Reality TV Gave Us Reality Candidate Donald Trump*, WASH. POST (July 17, 2016), www.washingtonpost.com/entertainment/tv/how-reality-tv-gave-us-reality-candidate-donald-trump/2016/07/16/0ebc597e-4454-11e6-8856-f26de2537a9d_story.html?ut m_term=.535fd637ce1a; Keefe, *supra* note 113.

campaign overall.[115] Even more remarkably, Trump's opponents outspent him in both the primary and the general election. During the Republican nomination race, Trump's campaign spent $63 million whereas his leading opponent, Ted Cruz, spent $86 million.[116] Trump's modest spending during the primary campaign made for a particularly stark contrast with the Democratic candidates, Hillary Clinton and Bernie Sanders, who spent $196 million and $219 million respectively.[117] The pattern continued during the fall campaign. The Clinton campaign spent $563 million during the general election, whereas the Trump campaign spent only $333 million.[118] Super PAC spending gave Clinton an even greater financial advantage. Pro-Clinton outside groups spent $206 million in the general election, while pro-Trump outside groups only spent $104 million.[119]

But Trump's high name-recognition and his deep understanding of the television news media enabled him to attract far more attention than any other candidate. For example, in a field of more than a dozen Republican candidates, Trump received 37 percent of all media coverage of the Republican race in January and February 2016.[120] By March he consumed 44 percent of all coverage.[121] That same month a study found that Trump received the equivalent of $2 billion in free media coverage during the first two months of the

---

[115] Ginger Gibson & Grant Smith, *Figures show Trump spent $66 million of his own cash on election campaign*, Reuters (Dec. 8, 2016), www.reuters.com/article/us-usa-election-trump/ figures-show-trump-spent-66-million-of-his-own-cash-on-election-campaign-idUSKBN13Y0 AE; Christopher Ingraham, *Somebody Just Put a Price Tag on the 2016 Election. It's a Doozy*, Wash. Post (April 14, 2017), www.washingtonpost.com/news/wonk/wp/2017/04/14/some body-just-put-a-price-tag-on-the-2016-election-its-a-doozy/?utm_term=.148ea7 411b61.

[116] *Which Presidential Candidates Are Winning the Money Race*, N.Y. Times (June 22, 2016), www.nytimes.com/interactive/2016/us/elections/election-2016-campaign-money-race.html.

[117] Dan Clark, *Trump Was Outspent by His Closest Primary Opponents*, PolitiFact (July 1, 2016), www.politifact.com/new-york/statements/2016/jul/01/michael-caputo/trump-was-out spent-his-closest-primary-opponents/; *Which Presidential Candidates Are Winning the Money Race, supra* note 116.

[118] *2016 Presidential Election*, Ctr. for Responsive Pol. (Nov. 27, 2017), www.opensecrets.org/ pres16; Jeremy W. Peters & Rachel Shorey, *Trump Spent Far Less Than Clinton, but Paid His Companies Well*, N.Y. Times (Dec. 9, 2016), www.nytimes.com/2016/12/09/us/politics/cam paign-spending-donald-trump-hillary-clinton.html.

[119] *2016 Presidential Election, supra* note 118.

[120] Thomas E. Patterson, *News Coverage of the 2016 Presidential Primaries: Horse Race Reporting Has Consequences*, Harv. Kennedy Sch., Shorenstein Ctr. on Media, Politics & Pub. Pol'y, at 13 (July 11, 2016), https://shorensteincenter.org/news-coverage-2016-presidential-primaries/.

[121] *Id.* at 14.

primary and caucus season.[122] No other candidate in either party came close to his free airtime.[123]

Trump's extraordinary command of television communication thus played a critical role in his successful presidential campaign.[124] But he also relied on another medium to reach voters and shape news coverage of the election. In 2016 the internet proved just as critical as television to Trump's extraordinarily successful communications strategy.

IV. THE EMERGENCE OF THE INTERNET

The internet first arrived as a major political force in the 2008 primaries. When the Democratic presidential race began, Senator Hillary Clinton enjoyed a large lead in the polls.[125] But in January 2008 Senator Barack Obama shocked the political world by defeating Clinton in the Iowa caucuses, an upset victory that set the stage for one of the closest nomination races in history.[126] Obama ultimately won the nomination, and one of the reasons why was the internet. His campaign used websites such as Facebook and MySpace to build a volunteer infrastructure that far outstripped Clinton's organization.[127] Obama also pioneered the use of big data to identify potential supporters and he embraced the internet as a major fundraising platform.[128]

Perhaps most important of all, the internet helped Obama deal with the most serious crisis of his campaign. In March 2008, ABC News broadcast video of Jeremiah Wright, Obama's mentor and pastor, declaring from the pulpit,

[122] Nicholas Confessore & Karen Yourish, *$2 Billion Worth of Free Media for Donald Trump*, N.Y. TIMES (March 15, 2016), www.nytimes.com/2016/03/16/upshot/measuring-donald-trumps-mammoth-advantage-in-free-media.html; Rhodes Cook, *Presidential Primaries: A Hit at the Ballot Box*, in TRUMPED: THE 2016 ELECTION THAT BROKE ALL THE RULES 85 (Larry J. Sabato, Kyle Kondik & Geoffrey Skelley eds., 2017).

[123] Confessore & Yourish, *supra* note 122.

[124] Karen Tumulty, Philip Rucker & Anne Gearan, *Donald Trump Wins the Presidency in Stunning Upset over Clinton*, WASH. POST (Nov. 9, 2016), www.washingtonpost.com/poli tics/election-day-an-acrimonious-race-reaches-its-end-point/2016/11/08/32b96c72-a557-11e6-ba59-a7d93165c6d4_story.html?utm_term=.6e3e1d130ef4.

[125] *Dems favor Hillary Clinton for 2008, poll shows*, CNN (March 19, 2007), www.cnn.com/2007/POLITICS/03/14/democrats.poll/; HAMMOND, *supra* note 87, at 830–31.

[126] Alicia Parlapiano & Karen Yourish, *If You Think the Democratic Primary Race Is Close, the 2008 One Was Even Tighter*, N.Y. TIMES (June 8, 2016), www.nytimes.com/interactive/2016/06/07/us/elections/clinton-sanders-delegate-fight.html; HAMMOND, *supra* note 87, at 832–35.

[127] DAN BALZ & HAYNES JOHNSON, THE BATTLE FOR AMERICA 2008: THE STORY OF AN EXTRAORDINARY ELECTION 184, 365–66 (2009).

[128] DAN BALZ, COLLISION 2012: OBAMA VS. ROMNEY AND THE FUTURE OF ELECTIONS IN AMERICA 76–77 (2013); BALZ & JOHNSON, *supra* note 127, at 222, 366.

"Not God bless America. God damn America," during a 2003 sermon.[129] The video became a national story and Obama's poll numbers fell precipitously.[130] The viability of his campaign suddenly appeared in doubt. To address the controversy, Obama gave a speech in Philadelphia in which he condemned Wright's remarks but also confronted America's long history of racial injustice.[131] The speech, which was extremely well-received, was viewed over five million times on YouTube, an all-time record.[132] The *New York Times* reported that the broadcast represented "YouTube's emergence as a vehicle for substantive discourse, not just silly clips."[133] By so quickly disseminating the Philadelphia speech, YouTube gave Obama a critical boost, enabling him to regain momentum and eventually win the nomination.[134]

The Obama campaign's pioneering use of digital communication methods would be essential to Obama's victories in both the 2008 and 2012 general elections.[135] In 2008, for example, over half of all American adults went online to get political news or share politics-related information or views.[136]

The full potential of the internet, however, would not be felt until the 2016 election. When the primary campaign began, it looked like an ordinary election year. The conventional wisdom viewed the establishment candidates Hillary Clinton and Jeb Bush as heavy favorites to win their respective party nominations.[137] Early fundraising numbers seemed to confirm that impression. Bush and his Super PAC led the Republican money race with $130 million while Clinton led the Democratic race with $115 million.[138]

---

[129] KATE KANSKI, BRUCE W. HARDY & KATHLEEN HALL JAMIESON, THE OBAMA VICTORY: HOW MEDIA, MONEY, AND MESSAGE SHAPED THE 2008 ELECTION 83–84 (2010).
[130] *Id.* at 83–87.
[131] *Id.* at 86–87.
[132] *Id.* at 86.
[133] *Id.*
[134] HAMMOND, *supra* note 87, at 834–35.
[135] Bruce Bimber, *Digital Media in the Obama Campaigns of 2008 and 2012: Adaptation to the Personalized Political Communication Environment,* 11 J. OF INFORMATION TECH. & POL. 130 (2014).
[136] Aaron Smith, *The Internet's Role in Campaign 2008,* PEW RESEARCH CTR. (April 15, 2009), www.pewinternet.org/2009/04/15/the-internets-role-in-campaign-2008/.
[137] John Cassidy, *Jeb and Hillary: A Tale of Two Establishment Favorites,* NEW YORKER (Oct. 25, 2015), www.newyorker.com/news/john-cassidy/jeb-and-hillary-a-tale-of-two-frontrunners.
[138] Nicholas Confessore & Sarah Cohen, *How Jeb Bush Spent $130 Million Running for President with Nothing to Show for It,* N.Y. TIMES (Feb. 22, 2016), www.nytimes.com/2016/02/23/us/pol itics/jeb-bush-campaign.html; Daniel White, *Hillary Clinton's Campaign Exceeds 2015 Fundraising Goal,* TIME (Jan. 1, 2016), http://time.com/4165391/hillary-clinton-campaign-fundraising/.

Two of their rivals, however, would use the internet to revolutionize presidential campaigning. The first was Vermont Senator Bernie Sanders, a self-described democratic socialist who used the internet to raise tens of millions of dollars from like-minded progressive voters.[139] With extraordinary effectiveness, the Sanders campaign targeted small donors through emails, texts, social media, and digital advertisements.[140] In the end, Clinton carried 3.7 million more votes and 359 more pledged delegates than Sanders,[141] but the Vermont senator nearly matched her in total fundraising, amassing $229 million to her $238 million.[142] Online fundraising was the key to his success.[143] As his campaign manager, Tad Devine, acknowledged, Sanders could not have stayed in the race "had we not developed this incredible mechanism of fundraising."[144] Although he lost the nomination to Clinton, Sanders demonstrated that a highly ideological and charismatic candidate could use the internet to raise money on a massive scale from small, ideologically motivated donors.[145]

[139] Kenneth P. Vogel, *How Bernie Built a Fundraising Juggernaut*, POLITICO (Feb. 10, 2016), www.politico.com/story/2016/02/bernie-sanders-fundraising-219112.

[140] Walter Shapiro, *The Limits of Bernie Sanders' Fundraising Juggernaut*, BRENNAN CTR. FOR JUSTICE (June 21, 2016), www.brennancenter.org/blog/limits-bernie-sanders-fundraising-juggernaut; Vogel, *supra* note 139; Politico Staff, *Sanders Raises $33M in Final Quarter, $73M Total for 2015*, POLITICO (Jan. 3, 2016), www.politico.com/story/2016/01/sanders-fundraising-final-quarter-2015-217288; Matea Gold, *Bernie Sanders's Campaign Brings in Jaw-Dropping $20 Million in January*, WASH. POST (Jan. 31, 2016), www.washingtonpost.com/news/post-politics/wp/2016/01/31/bernie-sanderss-campaign-brings-in-jaw-dropping-20-million-in-january/?utm_term=.d49d4c049a4e; Clare Foran, *Bernie Sanders's Big Money*, ATLANTIC (March 1, 2016), www.theatlantic.com/politics/archive/2016/03/bernie-sanders-fundraising/471648/.

[141] Boris Heersink, *No, the DNC Didn't "Rig" the Democratic Primary for Hillary Clinton*, WASH. POST (Nov. 2017), www.washingtonpost.com/news/monkey-cage/wp/2017/11/04/no-the-dnc-didnt-rig-the-democratic-primary-for-hillary-clinton/?utm_term=.55a9a49f830b; Nate Silver, *Was the Democratic Primary a Close Call or a Landslide?*, FIVETHIRTYEIGHT (July 27, 2016), http://fivethirtyeight.com/features/was-the-democratic-primary-a-close-call-or-a-landslide/; William G. Mayer, *The Nominations: The Road to a Much-Disliked General Election*, in THE ELECTIONS OF 2016, at 40, 43 (Michael C. Nelson ed., 2018).

[142] Philip Bump, *Bernie Sanders Is Outraising, Outspending and Outadvertising Hillary Clinton's Campaign*, WASH. POST (April 26, 2016), www.washingtonpost.com/news/the-fix/wp/2016/04/26/bernie-sanders-is-outraising-outspending-and-outadvertising-hillary-clintons-campaign/?utm_term=.d9e8a04a8d83; *Which Presidential Candidates Are Winning the Money Race*, *supra* note 116.

[143] Jonathan Swan, *Sanders Breaks New Ground in Fundraising*, THE HILL (April 2, 2016), https://thehill.com/homenews/campaign/274948-sanders-breaks-new-ground-in-fundraising.

[144] *Id.*

[145] Peter Overby, *Will the Millions of People Who Gave Money to Bernie Sanders Give to Democrats?*, NPR (June 15, 2016), www.npr.org/2016/06/15/482206235/will-future-candidates-be-able-to-raise-money-the-sanders-way; Alex Roarty, *How online money is reshaping the Democratic Party*, MCCLATCHY (Aug. 23, 2018), www.mcclatchydc.com/news/politics-government/election/article217164250.html; Vogel, *supra* note 139; Foran, *supra* note 140.

The Republican primary demonstrated the power of the internet in a quite different way. As discussed in Section III Part III, Donald Trump began the Republican campaign as the longest of long shots. From the opening day of his campaign, he faced opposition from the party's establishment.[146] He entered the primary season without a single endorsement from any Republican Senator or House member or any sitting Republican governor.[147] Trump also ranked ninth among Republican candidates in fundraising.[148]

But in the end, none of the conventional measures of candidate strength mattered. Although he trailed in the endorsement and fundraising race, Trump dominated Twitter, an online social networking and communication service.[149] His pre-existing celebrity proved more important than any endorsement because it meant he began the race with millions more Twitter followers than his opponents.[150] Taking full advantage of his superior social media presence, he tweeted 6,000 times during the nomination contest.[151] An analysis by the data scientist David Robinson found that Trump's "celebrity-style" tweeting helped him win both the nomination and the general election by generating far more interest in his campaign than a presidential candidate would normally receive from the general public.[152]

Twitter also became a crucial vehicle for Trump to launch high-publicity attacks on his opponents.[153] With relentless intensity, he used Twitter to direct

---

[146] M.J. Lee, *Donald Trump vs. the Republican establishment*, CNN (Oct. 26, 2015), www.cnn.com/2015/10/26/politics/donald-trump-republican-establishment/index.html.

[147] Peter L. Francia, *Free Media and Twitter in the 2016 Presidential Election: The Unconventional Campaign of Donald Trump*, 36 Soc. Sci. Computer Rev. 440, 442 (2017).

[148] *Id.* at 443.

[149] Oren Tsur, Katherine Ognyanova & David Lazer, *The Data Behind Trump's Twitter Takeover*, Politico (April 29, 2016), www.politico.com/magazine/story/2016/04/donald-trump-2016-twitter-takeover-213861; Jessica Guynn, *Forget Trump: Election's Big Winner Was Twitter*, USA Today (Nov. 8, 2016), www.usatoday.com/story/tech/news/2016/11/08/election-winner-twitter/93509896/. For an analysis of Trump's use of Twitter during the campaign, *see* Gaughan, *supra* note 92, at 96–99.

[150] Tsur, Ognyanova & Lazer, *supra* note 149.

[151] Sam Petulla, *One Year of Donald Trump's Tweets, Analyzed*, NBC News (June 24, 2016), www.nbcnews.com/politics/2016-election/donald-trump-s-campaign-tweets-n593846.

[152] May Bulman, *Donald Trump's "Celebrity-style" Tweets Helped Him Win US Presidential Election, Says Data Scientist*, Independent (Nov. 28, 2016), www.independent.co.uk/news/world/americas/donald-trump-twitter-account-election-victory-president-elect-david-robinson-statistical-analysis-a7443071.html; David Robinson, *Two People Write Trump's Tweets. He Writes the Angrier Ones*, Wash. Post (Aug. 12, 2016), www.washingtonpost.com/posteverything/wp/2016/08/12/two-people-write-trumps-tweets-he-writes-the-angrier-ones/?utm_term=.4cb49d33daa4.

[153] Tsur, Ognyanova & Lazer, *supra* note 149.

insults and inflammatory remarks at anyone who stood in his campaign's way, including not only opposing candidates but also their family members as well as journalists, athletes, actors, government officials, and foreign leaders.[154] The television news media reported on each controversial Trump tweet, magnifying the national circulation of Trump's original attack.[155] Millions of television viewers without Twitter accounts thus saw Trump's tweets.[156] The news media in effect became Trump's press agent, publicizing his attacks without limitation and completely free of charge. As Thomas Patterson of Harvard's Shorenstein Center observed, "Reporters are attracted to the new, the unusual, the sensational, the outrageous—the type of story material that can catch and hold an audience's attention. Trump fit that interest as has no other candidate in recent memory."[157]

Consequently, Trump dominated news coverage throughout the primaries, receiving more press attention by far than any other Republican candidate.[158] In the Republican primaries, Trump ultimately received $2.8 billion in free media coverage, almost four times as much as any other Republican.[159] During the general election campaign he continued to benefit from media coverage of his controversial remarks and provocative Tweets. By October 2016, Trump had received $5.9 billion in free media coverage, double the amount received by his Democratic opponent, Hillary Clinton.[160]

---

[154]   Sonam Sheth, *The New York Times Used 2 Full Pages to Print All of Donald Trump's Insults from the Campaign*, BUSINESS INSIDER (Oct. 24, 2016), www.businessinsider.com/new-york-times-prints-donald-trump-campaign-insults-2016-10; Jasmine C. Lee & Kevin Quealy, *The 551 People, Places and Things Donald Trump Has Insulted on Twitter: A Complete List*, N.Y. TIMES (Dec. 28, 2018), www.nytimes.com/interactive/2016/01/28/upshot/donald-trump-twitter-insults.html; Josh Hafner, *After Insulting Tweet, Cruz Tells Trump: Leave My Wife "the Hell Alone"*, USA TODAY (March 24, 2016), www.usatoday.com/story/news/politics/on politics/2016/03/24/donald-trump-posted-photo-ted-heidi-cruz/82210692/; Abby Ohlheiser, *A Look at the 170 Times Donald Trump Has Tweeted About the "Losers"*, WASH. POST (Sept. 22, 2016), www.washingtonpost.com/news/the-intersect/wp/2016/09/22/a-look-at-the-17 0-times-donald-trump-has-tweeted-about-the-losers/?utm_term=.43b1b471ae9a.

[155]   Shontavia Johnson, *Donald Trump Tweeted Himself into the White House*, THE CONVERSATION (Nov. 10, 2016), https://theconversation.com/donald-trump-tweeted-himself-into-the-white-house-68561.

[156]   *Id.*

[157]   Patterson, *supra* note 120.

[158]   *Id.* at 4.

[159]   Robert Schroeder, *Trump Has Gotten Nearly $3 Billion in "Free" Advertising*, MARKETWATCH (May 6, 2016), www.marketwatch.com/story/trump-has-gotten-nearly-3-billion-in-free-advertising -2016-05-06.

[160]   Niv M. Sultan, *Election 2016: Trump's free media helped keep cost down, but fewer donors provided more of the cash*, CTR. FOR RESPONSIVE POL. (April 13, 2017), www.opensecrets.org/news/2017/ 04/election-2016-trump-fewer-donors-provided-more-of-the-cash/.

After his victory in the November election, Trump gave much of the credit to social media, which enabled him to control the news narrative throughout the election. In an interview with Lesley Stahl of *60 Minutes*, Trump described his internet-focused communications strategy as key to his victory:

> I have such power in terms of numbers with Facebook, Twitter, Instagram, et cetera, I think it helped me win all of these races where they're spending much more money than I spent. You know, I spent my money. A lot of my money. And I won. I think that social media has more power than the money they spent, and I think maybe to a certain extent, I proved that.[161]

Trump's internet-focused campaign is a harbinger of things to come.[162] Although television has stood for years as the principal means of communicating with the electorate, a 2018 Pew Research Center study found that social media is rapidly gaining ground and recently surpassed print newspapers as the primary new source for more Americans.[163] If recent trends continue, internet communication will be crucial to all presidential campaigns for decades to come.

V. CONCLUSION

There is no doubt that the American people would like to see Congress impose limits on the cost of federal election campaigns. For example, a 2018 Pew poll found that 77 percent of Americans would support laws to restrict the total amount of campaign spending.[164] Support crosses partisan lines. The idea of legal restraints on campaign spending receives the support of 85 percent of Democrats and 71 percent of Republicans.[165]

But four decades ago the United States Supreme Court ruled that expenditure limits violate the Constitution.[166] In the 1976 case of *Buckley v. Valeo*, the Supreme Court held that "the mere growth in the cost of federal election

---

[161] *President-elect Trump speaks to a divided country*, CBS NEWS (Nov. 13, 2016), www.cbsnews.com/news/60-minutes-donald-trump-family-melania-ivanka-lesley-stahl/.

[162] Francia, *supra* note 147, at 451.

[163] Elisa Shearer, *Social Media Outpaces Print Newspapers in the U.S. as a News Source*, PEW RESEARCH CTR. (Dec. 10, 2018), www.pewresearch.org/fact-tank/2018/12/10/social-media-outpaces-print-newspapers-in-the-u-s-as-a-news-source/.

[164] Bradley Jones, *Most Americans Want to Limit Campaign Spending, Say Big Donors Have Greater Political Influence*, PEW RESEARCH CTR. (May 8, 2018), www.pewresearch.org/fact-tank/2018/05/08/most-americans-want-to-limit-campaign-spending-say-big-donors-have-greater-political-influence/.

[165] *Id.*

[166] Buckley v. Valeo, 424 U.S. 1, 57–58 (1976).

campaigns in and of itself provides no basis for governmental restrictions on the quantity of campaign spending and the resulting limitation on the scope of federal campaigns."[167] The Court asserted that "[i]n the free society ordained by our Constitution it is not the government, but the people individually as citizens and candidates and collectively as associations and political committees who must retain control over the quantity and range of debate on public issues in a political campaign."[168] The *Buckley* ruling means that there are no legal solutions to the relentless escalation in campaign costs, at least absent a dramatic new direction in the Supreme Court's campaign finance jurisprudence.

Accordingly, skyrocketing campaign costs are here to stay. In 2018, the congressional elections cost over $5 billion, an all-time record for a midterm election.[169] The 2020 presidential election will likely be even more expensive.[170] By the end of 2019, Donald Trump had already raised $143 million, the largest campaign war chest ever amassed prior to a presidential election year.[171] The march of technological progress has driven up campaign costs for more than one hundred years, and recent elections suggest the trends will continue into the indefinite future.

[167] *Id.* at 57.

[168] *Id.*

[169] Bill Theobald, *In Most Expensive Midterm Elections in History, the Biggest Spender Didn't Always Win*, USA TODAY (Nov. 16, 2018), www.usatoday.com/story/news/politics/2018/11/16/2018-midterm-election-results-record-billion-campaign-spending-house-senate-candidates-fundraising/2017289002/.

[170] Rob Garver, *Why 2020 US Presidential Race Will Be Costliest in History*, VOICE OF AMERICA (Feb. 14, 2019), www.voanews.com/a/why-2020-us-presidential-race-will-be-the-costliest-in-history/4786316.html.

[171] Julie Bykowicz & Catherine Lucey, *Trump's Campaign War Chest Tops $100 Million Heading Into Election Year*, WALL ST. J. (Jan. 2, 2020), www.wsj.com/articles/trump-campaignraised-46-million-infourth-quarter-11577970640; Josh Dawsey & Michelle Ye Hee Lee, *Trump and the RNC Raised Almost Half a Billion Dollars Last Year—and Still Had Nearly $200 Million Heading into 2020*, WASH. POST (Jan. 3, 2020), www.washingtonpost.com/politics/trump-and-the-gop-raised-almost-half-a-billion-dollars-last-year–and-still-had-nearly-200-million-heading-into-2020/2020/01/03/10ba1612-2dad-11ea-bcd4-24597950008f_story.html; Michelle Ye Hee Lee & Anu Narayanswamy, *Trump's 2016 Campaign Was Run on a Shoestring. His Reelection Machine Is Huge—and Armed with Consultants*, WASH. POST (Oct. 8, 2019), www.washingtonpost.com/nation/2019/10/08/trumps-campaign-was-run-shoestring-his-reelection-machine-is-huge-armed-with-consultants/.

14

Women and the Presidency

Cynthia Richie Terrell[*]

I. INTRODUCTION

As six women entered the field of Democratic presidential candidates in 2019, the political media rushed to declare 2020 a new "year of the woman." In the *Washington Post*, one political commentator proclaimed that "2020 may be historic for women in more ways than one"[1] given that four of these woman presidential candidates were already holding a U.S. Senate seat. A writer for *Vox* similarly hailed the "unprecedented range of solid women" seeking the nomination and urged Democrats to nominate one of them.[2] *Politico* ran a piece definitively declaring that "2020 will be the year of the woman" and went on to suggest that the "Democratic primary landscape looks to be tilted to another woman presidential nominee."[3] The excited tone projected by the media carried an air of inevitability: after Hillary Clinton lost in 2016, despite receiving 2.8 million more popular votes than her opponent, ever more women were running for the presidency.

---

[*] Cynthia Richie Terrell is the founder and executive director of RepresentWomen, an organization dedicated to advancing women's representation and leadership in the United States. She acknowledges the research that Gilda Geist put into this chapter, as well as the contributions made by Courtney Lamendola, Maura Reilly, and McKenna Donegan. She further thanks Gene Mazo for his invaluable editorial assistance and support.

[1] Jamie Stiehm, *2020 May Be Historic for Women in More Ways Than One*, WASH. POST (Feb. 10, 2019), www.washingtonpost.com/opinions/2020-may-be-historic-for-women-in-more-ways-than-one/2019/02/10/cf43698e-2bcf-11e9-b2fc-721718903bfc_story.html.
[2] Matthew Yglesias, *The Case for Making 2020 the Real Year of the Woman*, VOX (May 21, 2019), www.vox.com/policy-and-politics/2019/3/21/18273565/women-president-2020-electability.
[3] Bill Scher, *Why 2020 Will Be the Year of the Woman*, POLITICO (Nov. 24, 2017), www.politico.com/magazine/story/2017/11/24/2020-year-of-woman-democrats-post-weinstein-kamala-harris-klobuchar-gillibrand-warren-215860.

There is a reason, however, why historical inevitably has not yet been realized. Although Americans have selected a president 58 times, a man has won every one of these contests. Before 2019, a major party's presidential debates had never featured more than one woman. Progress toward gender balance in politics has moved at a glacial pace. In 1937, seventeen years after passage of the Nineteenth Amendment, Gallup conducted a poll in which Americans were asked whether they would support a woman for president "if she were qualified in every other respect?"[4] Only 33 percent of Americans said they were prepared to vote for a woman president at that time.[5] In 2012, by contrast, 95 percent of Gallup's respondents said they would vote for a woman president.[6] Now that almost all Americans are willing to cast a ballot for a woman, what will it take to elect a woman to the nation's highest office? More importantly, how can women's success in politics be sustained?[7] The goal of the women's movement is not just to shatter the presidential glass ceiling. Rather, it is to design structural reforms that will create a continuous stream of women candidates from both major parties who can win major political races year after year. Real equality for women candidates will only be achieved when women's success at the polls becomes routine.

The media's focus on the growing number of women on the presidential debate stage in 2019 and 2020 masks the structural inequities of our political system, which remain heavily tilted toward men at every level of government. Overwhelming evidence suggests that women face an uphill battle in the U.S. political system. Until we fix the rules of the game, we will not change the outcome.[8] For women to be considered viable candidates for the presidency, we need more women to be elected at all levels of government and across the partisan spectrum. To make Americans accustomed to having women in power, we need to pay special attention to executive offices. However, the goal of the women's movement in politics is not to elect *one* woman as president. Rather, it is to create a political

---

[4] *See* Matthew J. Streb, Barbara Burrell, Brian Frederick & Michael A. Genovese, *Social Desirability Effects and Support for a Female American President*, 72 PUB. OP. Q. 76, 77 (2008).

[5] *Id.*

[6] Jeffrey M. Jones, *Gender Gap in 2012 Vote Is Largest in Gallup's History*, GALLUP (Nov. 9, 2012), https://news.gallup.com/poll/158588/gender-gap-2012-vote-largest-gallup-history.aspx.

[7] At the state level, after all, an elected woman governor has been succeeded by another elected woman governor only once. *See History of Women Governors*, CTR. FOR AM. WOMEN & POL., RUTGERS UNIV., https://cawp.rutgers.edu/history-women-governors.

[8] For example, political parties and other gatekeepers recruit fewer women candidates to run for office in winnable districts, while donors and political action committees (PACs) also give less money to women candidates. *See generally* CTR. FOR RESPONSIVE POL. ET AL., INDIVIDUAL AND PAC GIVING TO WOMEN CANDIDATES (Nov. 2016), https://d3n8a8pro7vhmx .cloudfront.net/fairvote/pages/4542/attachments/original/1480388175/Giving_to_Female_Can didates_November_14_final_draft.pdf?1480388175.

system that equitably elects women up and down the ballot. Nothing less than fixing the system itself will accelerate progress. Structural reforms are needed to address cultural barriers and mitigate the differences in the genders' aspirations for political office. More women will be encouraged to pursue a career in politics if they see other women with similar qualifications and backgrounds serving in office. In turn, more women in office are needed to advance reforms that make it easier for future women candidates to succeed.

This chapter looks at the women who have run for the presidency and vice presidency of the United States. Some of these women were qualified candidates who were never given a fair shot. Others were people who should never have sought executive office in the first place. After examining this history, this chapter provides a closer examination of the structural barriers that women in the United States face in politics, as well as the innovative strategies that will enable more women to run, win, serve, and lead at all levels of government. These strategies include reforming how women's campaigns are financed, changing the candidate recruitment rules used by parties, implementing ranked choice voting, and promoting balanced media coverage. The strategies discussed in this chapter are designed to expand the pool of women candidates and to translate that success into the likelihood that a woman will eventually attain the highest office in the land.

II. WOMEN CANDIDATES FOR THE PRESIDENCY AND VICE PRESIDENCY

A. *Notable Nineteenth-Century Firsts*

The first woman to have her name placed in a nomination contest for national executive office was Lucretia Mott.[9] A well-known abolitionist and women's rights activist, Mott's name was put forth as a vice-presidential candidate by the Liberty Party in 1848. Of the 84 votes cast that year at the Liberty Party's nominating convention, Mott received five votes.[10] Though that was too few to be considered a serious contender, Mott received sufficient support to place her fourth at her party's presidential nomination contest, ahead of five other male candidates.[11]

---

[9] Walter Gable, *Timeline of Events in Securing Woman Suffrage in New York State*, THEHISTORYCENTER.NET (Feb. 2017), https://thehistorycenter.net/sites/default/files/docu ments/updated_timeline_in_securing_woman_suffrage_in_nys.pdf.

[10] *Lucretia Coffin Mott*, HERHATWASINTHERING.ORG, www.herhatwasinthering.org/biogra phy.php?id=4906.

[11] *Id.*

Throughout her life, Mott was a strong orator and an influential leader, although her outspokenness against racism and gender injustice earned her criticism for behaving in ways that were considered inappropriate for women at the time. Such outspokenness stemmed from Mott's upbringing as a Quaker. Equality among all people is a core tenet of Quaker belief, and Mott's faith led her to a life of fighting for equal rights for women.[12] Mott's interest in the women's rights movement was sparked at the 1840 World Anti-Slavery Convention. It was there that Mott met women's rights activist Elizabeth Cady Stanton, and together they came up with the idea of holding a women's rights convention. Eight years later, in 1848, Mott and Stanton organized the Seneca Falls Convention in New York, where the American women's suffrage movement was born.

In 1870, suffragist Victoria Woodhull became the first woman to become a political party's presidential nominee.[13] Woodhull was also the first woman who actively campaigned for the presidency. Woodhull announced her candidacy in April of 1870, in a letter published in *The New York Herald*.[14] In May of 1872, Woodhull was nominated for the presidency by the People's Convention of the Equal Rights Party.[15] According to an article published by *Woodhull & Claflin's Weekly*, her nomination was met with "thunderous" approval, and Woodhull accepted the party's support.[16] The Equal Rights Party nominated Frederick Douglass to be her running mate,[17] although it is unclear whether Douglass himself ever officially recognized his nomination.[18]

While many agree that Woodhull was the first woman to run for the presidency, some scholars nevertheless do not consider her to have been a true candidate because of her age. Woodhull was only 33 years old at the

---

[12] Mott was raised Quaker in Massachusetts and attended a Quaker boarding school in upstate New York. *See* Debra Michals, *Lucretia Mott*, NAT'L WOMEN'S HIST. MUSEUM (2017), www.womenshistory.org/education -resources/biographies/lucretia-mott.

[13] *See* Jeff Wallenfeldt, *Who Was the First Woman to Run for President of the United States?*, ENCYCLOPAEDIA BRITANNICA, www.britannica.com/story/who-was-the-first-woman-to-run-for-president-of-the-united-states.

[14] Victoria C. Woodhull, *The Coming Woman*, N.Y. HERALD (April 2, 1870), www.newspapers.com/clip/6836678/victoria_woodhull_announces_her/.

[15] *Spirit of the Press; Extraordinary Politics*, VICTORIA-WOODHALL.COM (May 11, 1872), www.victoria-woodhull.com/wc060100.htm.

[16] *Id.*

[17] Unlike Woodhull, Douglass's name was one of many brought forward at the national convention, and the half dozen or so speeches made on his behalf ultimately earned him the Equal Rights Party's vote. *Id.*

[18] It is uncertain whether Douglass ignored or declined the nomination. No one has been able to locate the letter he supposedly wrote to reject the party's nomination. *See* Mary L. Shearer, *Frequently Asked Questions About Victoria Woodhull*, VICTORIA-WOODHULL.COM, www.victoria-woodhull.com/faq.htm .

time of her nomination, whereas the Constitution requires the president to be 35.[19] Born on September 23, 1838, Woodhull would have been only 34 on election day (November 5, 1872) and on inauguration day (March 4, 1873), had she won.[20] In the end, many of the votes Woodhull received in the 1872 general election were not counted because of her gender, and the total she received remains unknown; it was likely a negligible number.[21]

For those who do not count Woodhull as the first woman to have run for president because of her age, Belva Lockwood is considered to be the first woman presidential candidate. Lockwood went to law school and was admitted to the bar in the District of Columbia, and before running for president Lockwood spent many years teaching.[22] In 1876, the Supreme Court refused to admit Lockwood to its bar because of her gender. Lockwood lobbied Congress to pass legislation that would allow her to be admitted to the Supreme Court bar, and she later became the first woman to argue before the Supreme Court. In 1884, Lockwood was nominated for the presidency by the Equal Rights Party and ran with Marietta Stow as her vice-presidential running mate.[23] Lockwood launched her candidacy under the theory that although she could not legally vote, there was nothing in the law that prevented men from voting for her. She raised money for her campaign by delivering paid speeches. Lockwood succeeded in gaining ballot access in six states but garnered fewer than 5,000 votes in the general election.[24] In 1888, she ran again but received even fewer votes.[25]

B. *Minor-Party Women Candidates*

Lucretia Mott, Victoria Woodhull, and Belva Lockwood were all nominated for the presidency by minor political parties. Minor parties have demonstrated

---

[19] U.S. CONST. art. II, § 1, cl. 5.

[20] *See* Shearer, *supra* note 18.

[21] Woodhull is not recorded to have received any electoral or popular votes. Election records show there were 2,000 "scattering votes," but it is unknown whether any were rightfully hers, as ballots at the time were printed by the individual parties. Some sources claim that the popular votes Woodhull received were discounted because of her gender, though this is again disputed, and the evidence of this is limited. *See* Maggie MacLean, *Victoria Woodhull*, EHISTORY, https://ehistory.osu.edu/biographies/victoria-woodhull.

[22] *Id. See also* Jill Norgren, *Belva Lockwood: Blazing the Trail for Women in Law*, 37(1) PROLOGUE MAG. (2005), www.archives.gov/publications/prologue/2005/spring/belva-lockwood-1.html.

[23] *Belva Ann Lockwood*, ENCYCLOPAEDIA BRITANNICA, www.britannica.com/biography/Belva-Ann-Lockwood.

[24] *See* Norgren, *supra* note 22.

[25] The exact number of votes earned by Lockwood in the second election is unclear, given the evidence. *See id.*

a particular willingness to nominate women candidates for the presidency and vice presidency, and they continued to do so regularly throughout much of the twentieth century. However, some of the women nominated by these parties were not strong candidates—and some were not serious candidates, either.

In 1940, comedian Gracie Allen announced her candidacy as a publicity stunt for her radio show, "The Burns and Allen Show."[26] She ran as a member of the "Surprise Party," and kept the bit up for several months, until she gave a speech saying she would stop her campaign and let the serious candidates continue without her.[27] Despite the fact that she ran as a joke and discontinued her campaign, she received many write-in votes in the general election.[28]

In 1968, Charlene Mitchell became the first African-American woman to run for president, when she received the nomination of the Communist Party.[29] Mitchell's running mate was Michael Zagarell, the National Youth Director of the Communist Party.[30] Mitchell and Zagarell only gained ballot access in two states, and they received no more than 1,075 votes in the 1968 general election.[31] Unlike the campaigns of today, Mitchell's campaign was scaled down; she operated out of a bookstore in Boston and spoke at trade union meetings, on street corners, and in parks.[32]

In 1972, a woman received an Electoral College vote for the first time.[33] That year, Theodora "Tonie" Nathan was the vice-presidential nominee of the Libertarian Party. A single faithless elector named Roger MacBride cast his vote for her to be vice president. Although a Republican from Virginia, MacBride chose to vote for Nathan and her presidential running mate John

---

[26] Cristen Conger, 5 *Strangest Political Parties*, HowStuffWorks.com, https://people.how stuffworks.com/5-strange-political-parties5.htm.

[27] *Remembering Gracie Allen's White House Run*, NPR (Nov. 4, 2008), www.npr.org/templates/ transcript/transcript.php?storyId=96588557.

[28] *See* Josh Compton, *Political Humor on the Radio, Image Repair, and Gracie Allen's 1940 Presidential Campaign*, 22 J. OF RADIO & AUDIO MEDIA 255, 255–58 (2015); *see also* DARRYL J. LITTLETON & TUEZDAE LITTLETON, COMEDIENNES: LAUGH BE A LADY, ch. 2 (2012).

[29] Nadra Kareem Nittle, *Black Women Who Have Run for President of the United States*, THOUGHTCo.COM (Mar. 18, 2017), www.thoughtco.com/black-women-who-have-run-for-president-4068508.

[30] *Id.*

[31] Richard Winger, *Women Running for President in the General Election*, BALLOT ACCESS NEWS (Jan. 22, 2007), http://ballot-access.org/2007/01/22/women-running-for-president-in-the-general-election/.

[32] Nicholas Gagarin, *Charlene Mitchell*, HARV. CRIMSON (Nov. 5, 1968), www.thecrimson.com/ article/1968/11/5/charlene-mitchell-pbtbhe-frederick-douglas-book/.

[33] *Libertarian Tonie Nathan, first woman in U.S. history to receive an electoral vote, dies at 91*, LIBERTARIAN (Mar. 20, 2014), www.lp.org/blogs-staff-libertarian-tonie-nathan-dies-at-91/.

Hospers over Richard Nixon and Spiro Agnew.[34] Four years later, MacBride would change his party affiliation to Libertarian and become the Libertarian Party's presidential nominee.[35]

In 1972, Linda Jenness ran for the presidency as a member of the Socialist Workers Party. Despite being too young to be president constitutionally, Jenness made it onto the ballot in 25 states. She received fewer than 70,000 votes in the 1972 general election.[36] Her running mate was Andrew Pulley, a 22-year-old African-American man who helped organize G.I.s United Against the War in Vietnam.[37] Jenness also ran for governor of Georgia, her home state, in 1970.[38]

Civil rights advocate and Los Angeles community activist Margaret Wright ran for president as the nominee of the socialist People's Party in 1976. Wright's running mate was Dr. Benjamin Spock, who had been the People's Party's presidential candidate in the previous election.[39] Appearing on only six state ballots, Wright won 49,016 votes in the general election.[40]

Sonia Johnson, who founded Mormons for the Equal Rights Amendment, ran for president with the Citizens Party in 1984. The Mormon Church had excommunicated her in 1979 for her feminism and political activism. Nonetheless, Johnson got on the ballot in twenty states, received write-in votes in six states, and garnered 72,200 votes nationally in the 1984 general election.[41]

In 1988, Lenora Fulani of Pennsylvania became the first African-American and first woman to gain ballot access in all fifty states for a presidential election. With Joyce Dattner as her running mate in most states and the New Alliance Party as her political affiliation, Fulani received 217,219 votes in the general election that year.[42] This is the fourth most votes ever cast for a woman

[34] Brian Doherty, *Tonie Nathan, R.I.P. (The First Woman to Receive an Electoral Vote for Vice President)*, REASON (Mar. 20, 2014), https://reason.com/2014/03/20/tonie-nathan-rip-the-first-woman-to-rece/.

[35] *Libertarian Tonie Nathan, supra* note 33.

[36] Jone Johnson Lewis, *All the Women Who Have Run for President of the U.S.*, THOUGHTCO.COM (Oct. 20, 2017), www.thoughtco.com/women-who-ran-for-president-3529994.

[37] *1972 Campaign*, N.Y. TIMES (Oct. 29, 1972), www.nytimes.com/1972/10/29/archives/other-presidential-aspirants-offer-wide-choice.html.

[38] Judy Flander, *Another Woman's Hat in the Ring – Linda Jenness Is the Socialist Party's Candidate for U.S. President*, MEDIUM (Jun. 19, 2017), https://judyflander.org/another-womans-hat-in-the-ring-linda-jenness-is-the-socialist-party-s-candidate-for-u-s-3328e8b111d0.

[39] Lewis, *supra* note 36.

[40] Jacqueline Antonovich, *Rosie the Riveter for President: Margaret Wright, the People's Party, and Black Feminism*, NURSING CLIO (Nov. 8, 2016), https://nursingclio.org/2016/11/08/rosie-the-riveter-for-president-margaret-wright-the-peoples-party-and-black-feminism/.

[41] Lewis, *supra* note 36.

[42] *Lenora B Fulani*, CARRIE CHAPMAN CATT CTR. FOR WOMEN & POL., IOWA ST. UNIV., https://awpc.cattcenter.iastate.edu/directory/lenora-b-fulani/.

presidential candidate in a general election. Fulani ran again in 1992, and this time received only 73,714 votes in the general election.[43] In both races, she qualified for federal matching funds.[44]

Cynthia McKinney, the first African-American woman to represent Georgia in Congress, ran as the presidential candidate of the Green Party in 2008. She received 161,797 votes in the 2008 general election.[45] Her political career began in 1986, when her father registered her as a candidate for the Georgia state house, without her knowing, and she won 20 percent of the vote against the incumbent. Two years later she became an at-large state representative in Georgia.[46]

The Green Party has been especially hospitable to women candidates. When Ralph Nader ran for president in 1996 and 2000 as the Green Party's nominee, his vice presidential running mate was Winona LaDuke. In 2000, LaDuke received 2.9 million popular votes in the general election, which is the most votes that any woman has received—apart from major-party presidential and vice-presidential nominees Hillary Clinton, Sarah Palin, and Geraldine Ferraro.

Sometimes, multiple women have sought the Green Party's nomination. Comedian Roseanne Barr ran as a Green Party candidate in 2012 but lost the nomination to Jill Stein. Barr then decided to run for president with the Peace and Freedom Party.[47] She received a total of 49,534 votes in the 2012 general election, placing her in sixth place in terms of the popular vote.[48] Her campaign was the focus of Eric Weinrib's documentary *Roseanne for President*.

Jill Stein ran for president as the Green Party's nominee in 2012 and 2016. She received 468,907 and 1.4 million popular votes in the general election, respectively. Despite running as the nominee of a minor party, Stein was one of the most successful woman presidential candidates in a general election.

---

[43] John Paul Hill, *The New Alliance Party, in* ENCYCLOPEDIA OF AMERICAN POLITICAL PARTIES AND ELECTIONS 241, 242 (Larry J. Sabato & Howard R. Ernst eds., 2006).

[44] *Women Presidential and Vice Presidential Candidates: A Selected List*, CTR. FOR AM. WOMEN & POL., RUTGERS UNIV., https://cawp.rutgers.edu/levels_of_office/women-presidential-and-vice-presidential-candidates-selected-list.

[45] *2008 Presidential Popular Vote Summary*, FED. ELECTION COMM'N, https://transition.fec.gov/pubrec/fe2008/tables2008.pdf.

[46] *McKinney, Cynthia Ann*, HISTORY, ART & ARCHIVES, U.S. HOUSE OF REP., https://history.house.gov/People/Detail/17982#biography.

[47] Larry Fitzmaurice, *Remember When Roseanne Ran for President?*, VULTURE (Apr. 6, 2018), www.vulture.com/2018/04/remember-when-roseanne-ran-for-president.html.

[48] Cavan Sieczkowski, *Roseanne Barr Places 6th In Presidential Election*, HUFF. POST (Nov. 7, 2012), www.huffpost.com/entry/roseanne-barr-president-fifth-place-presidential-election-2012_n_2088588.

Originally from Chicago, Stein became involved with the anti-Vietnam War movement in the late 1960s while a student at Harvard University. Later, she became a doctor, and after treating patients with asthma, disabilities, cancer, and other ailments that she believed pollution caused, she became an environmentalist. In 1998, she campaigned to close five dirty coal plants in Massachusetts and eventually joined the Green Party. Stein spoke at a rally for Ralph Nader in 2000, after which the Green Party asked her to run for governor of Massachusetts. Stein lost, but the experience led her to run as a Green Party candidate in eight other elections.

It is disputed whether Stein was a spoiler in the 2016 presidential election. Although she did well in states like Michigan and Wisconsin, where Trump won by a very small margin, it is not clear whether Stein's voters would have voted for Clinton, Trump, or neither had Stein not run.[49] Her campaign in 2016 also received criticism because of its relationship with the Russian media group *Russia Today*, which was the only news network to cover Stein's candidacy consistently.[50] Despite Stein's many electoral losses, she received the second and third most votes of all women presidential candidates in the general election in 2016 and 2012. The only woman presidential candidate to have received more votes in a general election was Hillary Clinton.

C. *Major-Party Women Candidates*

Although minor-party women candidates found some success in securing presidential nominations, it took more than forty years after the ratification of the Nineteenth Amendment for a woman to seek a major party's endorsement in earnest. When they have sought the presidential or vice-presidential nomination of the two major parties, women have had a much harder time.

In 1964, Margaret Chase Smith became the first woman to seek the presidential nomination of a major party when she declared her candidacy for the Republican Party's nomination.[51] At that point, Smith had already held the distinction of being the first woman elected to both houses of Congress.[52] Smith participated in at least five Republican primaries and received 27

---

[49] Eve Peyser, *Everybody Hates Jill*, VICE (Nov. 28, 2017), www.vice.com/en_us/article/8x5pw3/jill-stein-profile.

[50] Ben Schreckinger, *Jill Stein Isn't Sorry*, POLITICO (June 20, 2017), politico.com/magazine/story/2017/06/20/jill-stein-green-party-no-regrets-2016-215281.

[51] Audrey Amidon, *Cracking the Glass Ceiling: Margaret Chase Smith and Shirley Chisholm*, UNWRITTEN RECORD, https://unwritten-record.blogs.archives.gov/2016/07/26/cracking-the-glass-ceiling-margaret-chase-smith-and-shirley-chisholm/.

[52] *First Woman Elected to Both Houses of Congress*, SENATE HIST. OFF., U.S. SENATE www.senate.gov/artandhistory/history/minute/First_Woman_Both_Houses.htm.

delegate votes on the first ballot at the Republican National Convention in 1964. After the first ballot, she removed herself from contention, and the party's nomination went to Barry Goldwater.[53] Another woman, Fay Carpenter Swain, also sought the Democratic Party's nomination in 1964, although she did not get very far, receiving only a few thousand votes in the Indiana primary.

In 1972, three women vied for the Democratic Party's presidential nomination.[54] They were Shirley Chisholm, Patsy Mink, and Bella Abzug. By the time of the party's national convention, only Chisholm and Mink remained in the race, and neither would receive the party's nomination.[55] Chisholm was the first African-American woman to be elected to Congress, in 1968, and in 1972 she also became the first African-American woman to seek a major party's presidential nomination.[56] Chisholm faced many barriers to her presidential candidacy,[57] including a lack of funding, few endorsements,[58] and poor access to the debate stage.[59] But even with little support from the media or from powerful groups, Chisholm successfully entered 12 Democratic primaries and won 28 delegates ahead of the Democratic National

---

[53] *Women Presidential and Vice Presidential Candidates: A Selected List*, Ctr. for Am. Women & Pol., Rutgers Univ., https://cawp.rutgers.edu/levels_of_office/women-presidential-and-vice-presidential-candidates-selected-list.

[54] Adrienne Lafrance, *The Women Who Paved the Way for Hillary Clinton*, Atlantic (Nov. 3, 2016), www.theatlantic.com/politics/archive/2016/11/the-women-who-ran-before-hillary-clinton/506336/.

[55] Bella Savitzky Abzug stood as a candidate for nomination but withdrew before the Democratic Party's national convention in 1972. Martin Iversen Christensen, *Female Presidential Candidates 1870–1990*, Worldwide Guide to Women in Leadership (2017), www.guide2womenleaders.com/Candidates1870.htm.

[56] Megan Snyder, *12 Facts About Shirley Chisholm, The First African-American to Run For President*, Mental Floss (Jan. 21, 2019), http://mentalfloss.com/article/87244/12-facts-about-shirley-chisholm-first-african-american-run-president.

[57] As an African-American woman, Chisholm faced many barriers to running, which defined the degree to which she could campaign successfully. Politicians and journalists were constantly making judgments about her ability to lead and often focused their criticism on her gender rather than her policies. People said she was partaking in "female meddling," "just ego tripping," and "playing 'vaginal politics.'" *See* Erin Blakemore, *Here's What People Once Said About How a Woman Would Never Be the Democratic Nominee*, Time (June 7, 2016), https://time.com/4359610/shirley-chisholm-nominee/.

[58] The Congressional Black Caucus and the National Organization for Women, which Chisholm helped found, chose not to endorse her bid for the presidency. *See* Jenn M. Jackson, *Congresswoman Shirley Chisholm's Historic Presidential Run Was "Unbought and Unbossed,"* Teen Vogue (Feb. 8, 2019), www.teenvogue.com/story/congresswoman-shirley-chisholm-unbought-and-unbossed.

[59] Chisholm was also barred from participating in the primary debates. She filed a complaint with the Federal Communications Commission, after which she was allowed to make just one televised speech. *See* Debra Michals, *Shirley Chisholm*, Nat'l Women's Hist. Month, www.womenshistory.org/education-resources/biographies/shirley-chisholm.

Convention, where she garnered 152 delegate votes (10 percent of the total).[60] Though this was insufficient to secure the party's nomination, Chisholm won enough votes to come in fourth place at the convention.[61]

Like Chisholm, Mink was also a path-breaker. Mink was the first Asian-American woman to be elected to Congress, where she was one of the authors of Title IX. Before announcing her candidacy for the Democratic party's 1972 nomination, Mink received an invitation to appear on the primary ballot in Oregon as part of an anti-war campaign which that state's Democratic party had launched in 1971.[62] Mink received 5,082 votes in the Oregon primary but soon dropped out of the race.[63] Despite this, Mink later received votes in Maryland's and in Wisconsin's state primaries.[64] Overall, 1972 was a pivotal year for women—in every election since 1972, there has been at least one woman seeking a major party's nomination for president or vice president.[65]

Anti-abortion activist Ellen McCormack ran for the Democratic Party's presidential nomination in 1976. She got on the ballot in twenty states, was the first woman to receive protection from the Secret Service, and was the first woman to qualify for federal matching funds.[66] She ran again in 1980 with the Right to Life Party and garnered 32,327 votes in the general election.[67]

In 1996, Heather Harder and Elvena Lloyd-Duffie both sought the Democratic Party's presidential nomination. Harder was an author, speaker, spiritual advisor, and life coach who received a cumulative 29,149 votes in the primaries of three states, though she received by far the most votes (28,772) in Texas.[68] Harder ran again in 2000, when she won fewer than 2,000 votes in the primaries. In 2000, Harder issued a controversial statement saying that "UFOs exist and have always existed . . . No amount of government denial will change

---

[60] Snyder, *supra* note 56.

[61] Michals, *supra* note 59.

[62] *Mink, Patsy Takemoto*, HISTORY, ART & ARCHIVES, U.S. SENATE, https://history.house.gov /People/detail/18329.

[63] Jo Freeman, *The Women Who Ran for President*, JOFREEMAN.COM, www.jofreeman.com/ politics/womprez03.htm.

[64] *Id.*

[65] *See* Jo FREEMAN, WE WILL BE HEARD: WOMEN'S STRUGGLES FOR POLITICAL POWER IN THE UNITED STATES 89, 85–102 (2008); *see also* Lafrance, *supra* note 54.

[66] Valerie J. Nelson, *Ellen McCormack Dies at 84; Antiabortion Presidential Candidate*, L.A. TIMES (Apr. 2, 2011), www.latimes.com/local/obituaries/la-xpm-2011-apr-02-la-me-ellen-mccormack-20110402-story.html.

[67] *Ellen McCormack becomes first woman to receive federal funds for presidential race*, NAT'L CONST. CTR., https://constitutioncenter.org/timeline/html/cw12_12310.html.

[68] *1996 Presidential Primary Election Results*, FED. ELECTION COMM'N, https://transition.fec.gov/ pubrec/fe1996/presprim.htm.

my beliefs."[69] Lloyd-Duffie was also a relatively controversial candidate in the 1996 presidential election. She won over 90,000 votes across five state primaries,[70] notably claimed that she could balance the budget in "three to four days,"[71] and went on the record as saying that welfare is "a disgusting and disgraceful thing."[72]

In 2004, the Democrats had a more serious woman seek the party's nomination: Carol Moseley Braun, who had previously been the first African-American woman to be elected to the U.S. Senate in 1993. Moseley Braun was endorsed by a number of women's groups and garnered more than 100,000 votes in the primaries. Notably, this was after she had withdrawn from the race in January of 2004,[73] after deciding that her campaign was not picking up enough steam. At that point, Moseley Braun backed the Democrat Howard Dean, the former governor of Vermont.[74]

In 2012, Michele Bachmann sought the Republican Party's presidential nomination.[75] Like Moseley Braun, Bachman was an experienced politician and was at the time considered to be a serious candidate for the presidency. In 2006, Bachman became the first Republican woman from Minnesota to be elected to the U.S. House of Representatives, where she had been one of the founders of the Tea Party Caucus in 2010. However, Bachmann dropped out of the Republican race after the Iowa caucus, where she finished in sixth place with only 6,046 votes.[76]

In 2016, Carly Fiorina ran for the Republican Party's nomination but withdrew from the race after placing seventh in the New Hampshire primary.[77] Born in Texas, Fiorina started her career in the private sector and became CEO of Hewlett-Packard. She was the first woman to head a Fortune 500

[69]   Lewis, *supra* note 36.

[70]   *Lloyd-Duffie, Elvena E.*, OUR CAMPAIGNS, www.ourcampaigns.com/CandidateDetail.html? CandidateID=19329.

[71]   Lewis, *supra* note 36.

[72]   David Ruisard, *Democractic presidential candidates differ from Clinton*, LARIAT ARCHIVES, BAYLOR UNIV. (March 1, 1996) www.baylor.edu/lariatarchives/news.php? action=story&story=9306.

[73]   Moseley Bruan withdrew from the race ahead of the primaries, but she was already on the ballot in several states, which enabled her to win 100,000 votes regardless. Lewis, *supra* note 36.

[74]   Candy Crowley et al., *Braun backs Dean in tight Iowa race*, CNN (Jan. 16, 2004), www.cnn .com/2004/ALLPOLITICS/01/15/eleco4.prez.main/index.html?iref=mpstoryview.

[75]   *Iowa Republican Caucuses*, N.Y. TIMES (Jan. 3, 2012), www.nytimes.com/elections/2012/pri maries/states/iowa.html.

[76]   *Michele Bachmann fast facts*, CNN (Apr. 10, 2019), www.cnn.com/2013/02/01/us/michele-bachmann-fast-facts/index.html.

[77]   *Carly Fiorina*, BALLOTPEDIA, https://ballotpedia.org/Carly_Fiorina.

company. Fiorina also served as John McCain's economic advisor during his presidential campaign in 2008.[78] She was one of three women in American history to seek the Republican presidential nomination and to receive more than 5,000 votes.[79] During her presidential campaign, Fiorina received many sexist comments about her looks.[80] Although Fiorina was considered a longshot for the presidency in 2016 — her only political experience had been a failed run for the U.S. Senate — her presence as the only woman in a crowded field of Republican Party candidates was impactful.[81] Fiorina became Ted Cruz's running mate after she dropped out, although Cruz suspended his campaign a few days after choosing Fiorina as his running mate.[82] A single faithless elector later cast a vote Fiorina for vice president in the Electoral College.[83]

D. *Women Candidates Who Have Won a Major Party's Nomination*

Despite all of the women who have run for federal executive office, only three have managed to win the nomination of the two major parties: the Democratic Party nominated Geraldine Ferraro for vice president in 1984, the Republican Party nominated Sarah Palin for vice president in 2008, and the Democratic Party nominated Hillary Clinton for president in 2016. However, none of these women were victorious in the general election in November.

In 1984, Ferraro became the first woman to win the vice-presidential nomination of a major party. She ran with Democratic Party presidential nominee Walter Mondale. Ferraro's nomination came after pressure was placed on the Democratic Party to nominate a woman to the ticket.

---

[78] *Carly Fiorina fast facts*, CNN (Sept. 8, 2019), www.cnn.com/2015/05/28/us/carly-fiorina-fast-facts/index.html.

[79] Richard E. Berg-Anderson, *2016 Presidential Primaries, Caucuses, and Conventions*, THE GREEN PAPERS, www.thegreenpapers.com/P16/R; *see also* JAY NEWTON-SMALL, BROAD INFLUENCE: HOW WOMEN ARE CHANGING THE WAY WASHINGTON WORKS (2016).

[80] Donald Trump famously said the following about Fiorina in an interview with *Rolling Stone*: "Look at that face! Would anyone vote for that? Can you imagine that, the face of our next president?" Julianne Pepitone, *Carly Fiorina: "Leaders look different. Leadership is always the same"*, NBC NEWS (Apr. 16, 2019), www.nbcnews.com/know-your-value/feature/carly-fiorina-leaders-look-different-leadership-always-same-ncna995201.

[81] *Carly Fiorina*, NBC NEWS, www.nbcnews.com/politics/2016-election/candidates/carly-fiorina.

[82] Rachel Frazin, *Carly Fiorina Slams Trump: "He Views Women as Something to Be Used"*, THE HILL (May 14, 2019), https://thehill.com/blogs/blog-briefing-room/news/443569-carly-fiorina-slams-trump-he-views-women-as-something-to-be.

[83] Ben Kamisar, *Trump Loses 2 Electoral Votes Because of "Faithless" Electors*, THE HILL (Dec. 19, 2016), https://thehill.com/homenews/campaign/311107-two-texas-electors-abandoned-trump.

Feminist organizations and political strategists argued that nominating a woman would help the Democratic Party attract women voters and defeat Ronald Reagan. This pressure worked, and in July of 1984 Mondale announced Ferraro as his running mate.[84] But Mondale and Ferraro carried only Minnesota and the District of Columbia, and Republicans Reagan and George W. Bush won that year's general election. In the end, Ferraro received more than 37.5 million popular votes and thirteen Electoral College votes. At that time, that was the most any woman had ever received.

In 2008, Sarah Palin became the first woman to secure the Republican Party's nomination for vice president after Republican presidential candidate John McCain selected her as his running mate. Palin had been elected mayor of Wasilla, Alaska, her hometown, at a young age and then became the first woman and the youngest person ever to serve as governor of Alaska. She enjoyed a notable but ultimately unsuccessful run as the Republican Party's vice-presidential nominee. Although McCain and Palin lost to Barack Obama and Joe Biden in the general election, Palin received almost 59.9 million popular votes and 173 Electoral College votes. Until Hillary Clinton's nomination in 2016, this was the greatest number of Electoral College votes ever received by a woman.

Another woman was also seeking a major party's nomination in 2008: Hillary Clinton. That year, Clinton ran for the Democratic Party's presidential nomination against Barack Obama. Clinton won 17.8 million primary votes and a total of 23 different primary contests, although she placed third in the all-important Iowa caucus. In the Democratic primaries, Clinton received 48.0 percent of the total votes cast, while Barack Obama received 48.1 percent.[85] Which candidate won the party's popular primary vote is disputed due to a number of complications that arose during the primaries, including the fact that Obama's name did not appear on the ballot in Michigan.[86] Regardless, Clinton lost the nomination, but her serious attempt to win a major party's nomination remained a milestone. In 2008, she became the first woman to win a major party's presidential primary.[87]

---

[84] *Ferraro, Geraldine Anne*, History, Art & Archives, U.S. Senate, https://history.house.gov /People/Detail/13081.

[85] *2008 Democratic Popular Vote*, RealClearPolitics.com, www.realclearpolitics.com/epolls/ 2008/president/democratic_vote_count.html.

[86] Brooks Jackson, *Clinton and the Popular Vote*, FactCheck.org (June 5, 2008), www.factcheck.org/2008/06/clinton-and-the-popular-vote/.

[87] Rachel Balik, *Hillary Rodham Clinton, First Woman to Be a Presidential Candidate in Every Primary and Caucus*, Finding Dulcinea (Oct. 26, 2010), www.findingdulcinea.com/fea tures/profiles/c/hillary-clinton.html.

In 2016, Clinton sought the Democratic Party's presidential nomination again. This time, she successfully secured it, outlasting Democratic rival Bernie Sanders in the primaries. Clinton became the first woman to secure the presidential nomination of a major party, and she later became the first woman to win the popular vote for the presidency. In total, she received 65.8 million popular votes in the general election and 227 Electoral College votes — the most of any woman candidate in history. But this was not enough to get her into the White House,[88] as Clinton lost the Electoral College vote to Donald Trump. Throughout the presidential campaign, Trump regularly expressed sexist attitudes. Rather than elect a woman with an impressive political resume, American voters instead elected a man who bragged about sexually assaulting women.

A number of different factors contributed to Clinton's loss, and sexism was one of them. Research suggests that men running for leadership positions are favored over women because leadership roles are typically male-dominated. This dynamic was likely at play in the 2016 presidential election, since this was the first time a woman was close to being elected to a position that has always been held by men.[89] Research suggests that the presence of a woman running for a powerful male-dominated role is enough to bring both tradi-tional (blatant) and modern (subtle) sexism to the forefront in an election. One recent study found that a high percentage of Americans see feminism as negative, believe that women do not face sexism, and negatively characterize women as being overly sensitive to sexism. According to this study, 20 percent of Clinton's voters were categorized as sexist, while 58 percent of Trump's voters were considered sexist. These sexist attitudes combined with the correlation between sexism and political affiliation suggest that Clinton's gender may have played a role in choices voters made during the 2016 presidential election.[90]

Even after losing the election, the double standards against Clinton did not stop. Clinton expressed surprise at the number of people who wanted her to exit the political realm after her loss. She pointed out that men in her position were never told to leave politics, recalling that Al Gore, John Kerry, John McCain, and Mitt Romney all remained involved in politics after their failed

---

[88]   *Presidential election, 2016*, BALLOTPEDIA, https://ballotpedia.org/Presidential_election,_2016.

[89]   Jonathan Knuckey, *"I Just Don't Think She Has a Presidential Look"*: *Sexism and Vote Choice in the 2016 Election*, 100 Soc. Sci. Q. 342, 346–47 (2019).

[90]   Angie Maxwell & Todd Shields, *The Impact of "Modern Sexism" on the 2016 Presidential Election*, DIANE D. BLAIR CTR. OF SOUTH. POL. & SOC., U. OF ARK., https://blaircenter .uark.edu/the-impact-of-modern-sexism/.

bids to win the presidency.[91] Women are criticized for things that are seen as normal for men—reflecting on electoral losses, speaking their minds, and running for president. These double standards contributed to Clinton's campaign challenges, and they threaten to hold back any woman who tries to challenge the status quo by running for president in the future.

On a positive note, it is worth mentioning that several women, apart from Hillary Clinton, received Electoral College votes in 2016, although in each case these came from faithless electors. Elizabeth Warren received two electoral votes for vice president: one from a faithless elector in Hawaii, and one from a faithless elector in the state of Washington. Meanwhile, Maine's Republican Senator Susan Collins, Washington's Democratic Senator Maria Cantwell, former Green Party vice-presidential nominee Winona LaDuke, and Republican vice-presidential candidate Carly Fiorina each also received a single Electoral College vote for vice president from faithless electors. The Electoral College votes cast for Collins, Cantwell, and LaDuke came from faithless electors in Washington, while Fiorina's vote came from a faithless elector in Texas.

E. *Women Running for the Presidency in 2020*

Considering the challenges that women have historically faced while running for federal executive office, it is no wonder the media has been excited by the prospect of having another woman secure a major party's presidential nomination in 2020. In 2019, six women vied for the Democratic Party's presidential nomination. These women were Tulsi Gabbard, Kirsten Gillibrand, Kamala Harris, Amy Klobuchar, Elizabeth Warren, and Marianne Williamson.

These six women candidates, as with other women who have run for the presidency in the past, could be separated into two groups: some of them were longshots, and some were serious contenders. Of the four women who fell into the first category, Gabbard, a member of the House Representatives from Hawaii, was known for her military background and political experience at the city, state, and federal levels.[92] However, she tended to lag in the polls.[93] Gillibrand was a U.S. Senator from New York who had repeatedly branded

[91] Veronica Stracqualursi, *Hillary Clinton cites sexism in criticism she should exit political stage*, CNN (March 30, 2018), www.cnn.com/2018/03/30/politics/hillary-clinton-election-loss/index .html.

[92] Gabbard was a member of the Honolulu City Council (2011–12), Hawaii House of Representatives (2002–04), and the U.S. House of Representatives (2013–present). Edward-Isaac Dovere, *The Enduring Mystery of Tulsi Gabbard*, ATLANTIC (Sept. 5, 2019), www.theatlantic.com/poli tics/archive/2019/09/tulsi-gabbard-2020-candidate/597226/.

[93] *Id.*

herself as a feminist, although she struggled to resonate with progressives beyond topics surrounding women's equality.[94] Harris was a Senator from California and the district attorney of San Francisco.[95] And Williamson, a self-help author, had no political experience beyond a failed campaign for the U.S. House of Representatives in 2014. Williamson insisted that the United States was lacking moral leadership and her campaign was centered on offering that kind of leadership to the American public.[96]

While these four women were crucial to women's representation because they showed that women in politics are not an anomaly, voters and analysts alike saw them as presidential longshots. Klobuchar and Warren, by contrast, were real contenders for the nomination. Klobuchar, a U.S. Senator from Minnesota, emphasized her centrism as key to helping Democrats win swing states in the Midwest and picked up support in early contests. Before announcing her candidacy, Klobuchar was best known for her work in combating the opioid crisis and her questioning of Justice Brett Kavanaugh during his Supreme Court confirmation hearings. Warren was a former law professor and the senior U.S. Senator from Massachusetts. Though Warren was a Republican before 1996, in 2020 many Americans saw her as one of the most progressive candidates in the Democratic presidential field. She was known for her meticulous policy planning and focus on income inequality.[97]

Klobuchar and Warren performed better during the presidential debates than many of their male opponents. Yet their abilities continued to be called into question. One of the excuses people made for not voting for them is that women like Klobuchar and Warren were not "electable" or "not able to beat Trump." In other words, voters often say they want to vote for someone whom they are sure can win, and by implication that person is not a woman. This logic is based on implicit gender bias.[98] History and statistics show that women win elections as often as white men do.[99] At times, women even perform

---

94 *Which Woman Running for President Is Your Candidate?*, REFINERY29 (June 12, 2019), www.refinery29.com/en-us/2019/06/234860/women-running-for-president-2020-candidates.
95 Alexander Burns et al., *Who's Running for President in 2020?*, N.Y. TIMES (Sept. 11, 2019), www.nytimes.com/interactive/2019/us/politics/2020-presidential-candidates.html.
96 *Id.*
97 *Id.*
98 Li Zhou, *Women Candidates Are Constantly Asked About Their Electability. Here Are 5 Reasons That's Misguided*, VOX (Aug. 15, 2019), www.vox.com/policy-and-politics/2019/8/15/18525308/elect ability-women-candidates-2020-elizabeth-warren-kamala-harris-amy-klobuchar-kirsten-gilli brand?fbclid=IwAR3Vv-iw9bGAyrJTYwkHhaHCofhDA4jDNDHH6331v70tz946NkDpl ZbUFPY.
99 Brenda Choresi Carter, *White Men's Electability Advantage Is a Myth*, NEWSWEEK (July 8, 2019), www.newsweek.com/white-men-electability-advantage-myth-1448089.

better. Before running for the Democratic presidential nomination, Kirsten Gillibrand, Kamala Harris, Amy Klobuchar, and Elizabeth Warren had won every single political race they entered, which their male rivals for the democratic nomination certainly could not say of themselves: Cory Booker lost his first mayoral race in Newark in 2002, Bernie Sanders lost his bid for the Democratic nomination in 2016, and Biden had sought the Democratic Party's presidential nomination twice before, in 1998 and 2008, and lost in the primaries each time.[100]

III. CHALLENGES AND SOLUTIONS

The American electorate does not know what a woman presidential candidate is supposed to look like. Indeed, one reason why some voters do not see women candidates as viable is because they have seen so few viable women candidates before. If voters keep choosing candidates based on who they think can win, we will never elect a woman as president. The logic is circular here: if some American voters refuse to vote for a woman for president because there has never been a woman in the White House before, then how can a woman ever be elected to the presidency?

The only solution is to start at the bottom of the system and to begin to make changes to the American electoral system as a whole. Before we can discuss what needs to change, however, we need to determine what is wrong with our current system and to investigate exactly which obstacles women face when running for an executive office such as the presidency.

A. *Campaign Finance*

Fundraising challenges exist that are unique to women. Some of these fundraising challenges are different from what people assume them to be. We can begin by debunking a common misconception about gender in campaign fundraising: studies show that women raise just as much money as men when running for office. This becomes especially true in general elections. One explanation for why women do as well as men is that political action committees dedicated to women candidates offset the negative effects of gender discrimination in fundraising.[101]

---

[100] Jeff Simon, *A peek at Joe Biden's past presidential campaigns*, CNN (Oct. 21, 2015), www.cnn.com/2015/10/21/politics/joe-biden-presidential-campaigns-1988-2008/index.html.

[101] Kira Sanbonmatsu, *Money and Women Candidates*, POL. PARITY, at 1, www.politicalparity.org/wp-content/uploads/2017/10/Parity-Research-Women-Money.pdf.

The main problem women face with fundraising has to do with how women perceive their abilities to raise money. A study found that 56 percent of women state legislators believed that it was more difficult for women to raise money than for men.[102] Other studies have found that women candidates view fundraising more negatively than men do. This perceived barrier, even if it does not conform with empirical reality, deters women from running.[103] While there is not enough evidence to support the claim that the availability of public funding would lead to greater success for women candidates, women's reservations about their ability to engage in robust fundraising suggests that public funding might at least encourage more women to run for office. This is because public funding would allow women to worry less about the need to fundraise. Women should be educated to understand that they have as much fundraising ability as men. In the meantime, public funding could be used to help change the perception that gender impacts fundraising abilities.

When it comes to fundraising, one of the problems women candidates face is that they typically have a relatively wide base of small donors, compared to the typical donor base for men candidates, which tends to be smaller but is comprised of larger donors. Securing a greater number of small contributions takes more time and effort, meaning that women typically have to work harder to be on par with men in their fundraising.[104] We can see how different donor bases affect elections. During a U.S. House election in Kentucky in 2018, for example, Democrat Amy McGrath raised the second largest amount of money of all women candidates competing for a House seat that year, with 24 percent of her funds coming from small donors and 4 percent from PACs. Her opponent, Republican Andy Barr, raised 4 percent of his funding from small donors and 40 percent from PACs. Barr beat McGrath by fewer than four percentage points.[105] This example demonstrates that some differences in fundraising by gender exist, even at the higher levels of campaign fundraising.[106]

Studies also suggest that, although men and women candidates generally are able to raise the same amount of total money, women need to spend more

---

[102]   *Id.* at 2.

[103]   *Id.* at 2–3.

[104]   *Id.* at 3.

[105]   *Rep. Garland "Andy" Barr Wins Kentucky's 6th Congressional District Seat*, WASH. Post (Apr. 8, 2019), www.washingtonpost.com/election-results/kentucky-6th-congressional-district/.

[106]   Kate Zernike, *Female Candidates Break Barriers, Except When It Comes to Money*, N.Y. TIMES (Oct. 30, 2018), www.nytimes.com/2018/10/30/us/politics/women-campaign-fundraising.html.

to counteract the effects of gender discrimination.[107] Although more research is needed to reach a definitive conclusion on this issue, it seems that women candidates' money may translate into fewer secured votes than that of men candidates.[108] Problems with fundraising affect certain women candidates more than others. One study of the 2018 midterm election found that women of color receive the least amount of money from donors of any other group. One reason for this disparity is that donors usually base how much money they give to a candidate on how much money that candidate is likely to raise. Many donors will wait until they see that a candidate has reached a fundraising threshold before donating themselves. This dynamic disproportionately favors established candidates with white, wealthy, and male networks, and it makes it more difficult for women of color to raise money.[109] The evidence suggests that Republican women candidates also disproportionately fall behind when it comes to fundraising. A recent study found that not only are Republican women underfunded by PACs, but they also tend to be some of the biggest targets of oppositional spending.[110]

The final problem women candidates face is that PACs tend to underfund women running for open seats. Open seat races are important to getting more women elected to federal office because incumbents tend to be difficult to unseat—and, of course, most of them are men. For this reason, women's groups often encourage strong women candidates to run for open seats. Women candidates in open seat races are consistently underfunded by PACs, however. While PACs usually give about 18 percent of their funds for open seats to women, it is also the case that women make up more than 18 percent of open seat candidates.[111] Putting money toward women who are challenging incumbents is far less strategic, as these women are highly unlikely to win in these races.

The key to getting more funding for women candidates—especially women of color, Republican women, and women running in open seats—is PAC funding. PACs need to be educated on how they can make a more conscious effort to fund women candidates. PACs that give to and endorse candidates—especially those with member-driven priorities such as the Sierra Club, the

---

[107] NAT'L COUNCIL FOR RESEARCH ON WOMEN ET AL., MONEY IN POLITICS WITH A GENDER LENS 16–17 (Jan. 2014), www.icrw.org/wp-content/uploads/2016/11/moneyinpoliticswithagen derlens_0.pdf.

[108] Sanbonmatsu, *supra* note 101, at 3.

[109] CTR. FOR RESPONSIVE POL. ET AL., INDIVIDUAL AND PAC GIVING TO WOMEN CANDIDATES, *supra* note 8, at 12.

[110] *Id.* at 4, 20.

[111] *Id.* at 13.

Chamber of Commerce, and those supported by organized labor and the faith community—can establish rules that set targets for intentional action in endorsements and in political giving. While women-oriented PACs like EMILY's List support only women candidates, other PACs deserve to be educated about how they can contribute a larger share of their funds to women. Gender targets cannot be mandated by the government, but they can be adopted by individual PACs and they can be set to increase with each election cycle. PACs should be encouraged to consider gender targets for donations for all levels of elected office. With public attention, balanced funding of men and women candidates may develop into a comparative advantage for PACs and might enable PACs to become agents of change in the struggle for equality.[112]

B. *Party Recruitment*

Another barrier for women candidates is political party recruitment. The major political parties in the United States serve as gatekeepers, and their failure to recruit more women candidates preserves the status quo. Political parties can take a number of proactive steps to change this. One step that has been proven to work is to have parties implement voluntary party quotas. For example, party rules should be changed to require that women make up a certain proportion of the party leadership that controls candidate recruitment. Voluntary party quotas, which are not legally mandated but instead adopted voluntarily on an individual basis by party organizations, would go a long way in ensuring that more women have a positive voice in recruitment practices.[113]

Political parties can also implement parity grants. These would entail higher levels of the party organization incentivizing the recruitment of women candidates at lower levels of the party. State or national party organizations would voluntarily set goals for the proportion of women candidates recruited during each election cycle, and local party organizations that met this goal would receive grant money. The goals could increase slowly over time in order to bring party recruitment gradually closer to parity.[114] Although parity grants incentivize recruiting women at the local level, having more

---

[112] SASKIA BRECHENMACHER, TACKLING WOMEN'S UNDERREPRESENTATION IN U.S. POLITICS: COMPARATIVE PERSPECTIVES FROM EUROPE 20–23 (Feb. 2018), https://carnegieendowment .org/files/CP_323_Brechenmacher_Gender_web.pdf.

[113] *See* Anisa A. Somani, *The Use of Gender Quotas in America: Are Voluntary Party Quotas the Way to Go?*, 54 WM. & MARY L. REV. 1451, 1466–68 (2013).

[114] *Id.* at 1468–69.

women entering politics at the local level is essential; such recruitment would have ripple effects all the way up to the presidency by creating a larger pool of experienced women candidates for the national party to choose from. Also, having more women in local office would help voters become more comfortable with the idea that women can be leaders.

C. *Electoral Reforms*

Another reform that would help more women get elected, this time in the public sector, is the implementation of ranked choice voting (RCV). Plurality winner-take-all voting rules for the election of presidential electors, state governors, and members of the House and Senate often result in vote splitting among multiple women candidates. Winner-take-all voting rules also fuel negative campaigning, and they lead to plurality winners being elected who lack majority support—all of which are particularly damaging to women candidates trying to break into the political establishment. The consequences of our antiquated plurality winner-take-all voting rules are perfectly clear: as a result of them, there have been only 44 women governors in 30 states in the history of the United States, and currently only 9 women serve as governors.[115] Women also represent only 25 percent of the seats in the U.S. Senate, and only 56 women have served as U.S. Senators.[116] With so few women being elected to these high-profile offices, it is not surprising that there have been so few women presidential candidates. A solution to this structural barrier is for states to adopt ranked choice voting. This system would allow voters to rank their candidates in order of preference.

RCV is easy to implement. Voters rank candidates in order of their choice. If no candidate among the first-choice selections receives majority support, the candidate with the fewest votes is eliminated. Those who ranked this last-place candidate as their first choice have their ballots redistributed to their second choice candidate. This process of elimination and redistribution continues until one candidate wins a majority of the vote. This type of voting system ensures a fair election outcome, and it eliminates the concerns of "vote-splitting" among candidates who may have common perspectives—for example, if the race features more than one woman.[117] RCV also minimizes

---

[115] *Women in Statewide Elective Executive Office 2019*, CTR. FOR AM. WOMEN & POL., RUTGERS UNIV., https://cawp.rutgers.edu/women-statewide-elective-executive-office-2019.

[116] *Women in the U.S. Senate 2019*, CTR. FOR AM. WOMEN & POL., RUTGERS UNIV. https://cawp.rutgers.edu/women-us-senate-2019.

[117] REPRESENTATION2020, THE STATE OF WOMEN'S REPRESENTATION 2013–2014: AMERICAN WOMEN IN ELECTED OFFICE & PROSPECTS FOR CHANGE 37 (Oct. 2013), http://d3n8a8pr

strategic voting, eliminates the need for runoffs, and promotes civil campaign-ing. These benefits can help create a more level playing field for women candidates at all levels.

RCV is currently already used in one form or another in over twenty jurisdictions throughout the United States, for student government elections at over 75 colleges and universities, and for military and overseas voters in a number of Southern states.[118] In 2018, Maine adopted ranked choice voting and used RCV to elect its members of the House of Representatives, its U.S. Senator, and its first woman governor, who won an RCV primary from among a large field of candidates. Cities that use RCV tend to have more diverse city governments and a greater proportion of women holding public office. Currently, nine cities use RCV for their city council elections, and ten additional cities are slated to begin using RCV in the near future. Of the cities that currently use RCV, the average share of women serving on city councils is 49 percent, which is more than twice the average in non-RCV cities. Additionally, 50 percent of cities with RCV have women mayors, compared to an average of 23 percent in the one hundred most populous cities in the United States without RCV.

In 2016, RepresentWomen conducted a study to assess the impact of ranked choice voting on the representation of women and people of color. Controlling for the impact of socioeconomic, political, and electoral factors, the study found that implementing RCV for the races of 53 local political offices in the San Francisco Bay Area led to an increase in the percentage of city council candidates who are women and people of color.[119] When RCV was adopted in the four cities that were the subject of this study—San Francisco, Oakland, Berkeley, and San Leandro—they all had white men serving as mayors. Their mayors now are two white women, an African-American woman, and a Hispanic man. When several strong women are running in the same election, such as we saw during the Democratic primaries in 2020, there is some concern that they could split the vote. The use of RCV would avoid vote-splitting and elevate whoever can better unite the electorate. In total, six states used RCV for their primaries and caucuses in 2020: Alaska, Hawaii, Iowa, Kansas, Nevada, and Wyoming. These contests were run by

o7vhmx.cloudfront.net/themes/5707f5a06a21dbdb81000001/attachments/original/1467134849 /rep2020Report-2013-14.pdf?1467134849.

[118] *Ranked Choice Voting/Instant Runoff*, FAIRVOTE, www.fairvote.org/rcv.

[119] REPRESENTATION2020, THE IMPACT OF RANKED CHOICE VOTING ON REPRESENTATION: HOW RANKED CHOICE VOTING AFFECTS WOMEN AND PEOPLE OF COLOR IN CALIFORNIA 24 (Aug. 2016), https://d3n8a8pro7vhmx.cloudfront.net/fairvote/pages/4541/attachments/origi nal/1476462696/RCV-Representation-BayArea.pdf?1476462696.

political parties, so the parties adopted RCV, not the states.[120] But the data gathered from these elections will allow researchers to examine how ranked choice voting affects the presidential nomination process.

D. Media Coverage

Women candidates are also hurt by gendered media coverage. Media coverage of women running for office disproportionately focuses on the family roles of women, on the appearance of these candidates, and on women's issues, all of which have an effect on how the public views these candidates. A study was recently conducted about how subtly sexist word choice can affect voters' perceptions of women candidates. The study asked 269 students to read variations of an article about a mayoral race. Different versions of the article varied the gender of the candidate and the words used to describe that candidate, although these versions were otherwise identical in every way. The students were asked to rank the mayoral candidate based on her qualification and how much they liked her. The results showed that a woman politician described using masculine-coded adjectives, such as "ambitious" and "assertive," was seen as being nearly 10 percent more qualified and 7 percent more competent than a women candidate described using feminine-coded adjectives, such as "compassionate" and "loyal." This study found that gendercoded language, even if seemingly harmless, could have an effect on how the electorate views women candidates.[121]

Coded language is not the only thing that has a negative impact. The same is true for the questions that women candidates receive. In her 2010 book *Women for President*, Erika Falk takes note of the gendered nature of questions often posed to women candidates. "By asking women to answer questions 'as females,' the press consistently portrays women as gendered beings," Falk writes. "Men are never asked, 'What is it like to be a man in office?' because men are the norm and as such are free to be individuals or political beings."[122] The differences in press coverage that men and women candidates receive is often attributed, at least in part, to the disproportionate number of men in the journalism industry. In the United States, women comprise 41.7 percent of newsrooms and own only 7.4 percent of commercial television stations. Additionally, men are given 63 percent of the bylines and reporting credits

---

[120] *Ranked Choice Voting/Instant Runoff, supra* note 118.

[121] Rachel Garrett & Dominik Stecula, *Subtle sexism in political coverage can have a real impact on candidates*, COLUM. JOURNALISM REV. (Sept. 4, 2018), www.cjr.org/analysis/pink-wavecandidates.php.

[122] ERICA FALK, WOMEN FOR PRESIDENT: MEDIA BIAS IN NINE CAMPAIGNS 86 (2010).

in print, online, wire, and TV news. When women reporters get bylines, the topics they tend to write about often focus on health, lifestyle, and leisure, while male reporting tends to dominate topics relating to U.S. policy and elections.[123]

Because more men work in the journalism industry, subconscious sexism is more likely to seep into news coverage—including news coverage of women presidential candidates. To make press coverage of women candidates fairer, newsrooms must make a conscious effort to recruit and hire more women and decrease the amount of subconscious bias and sexism that is present in our news. Also, in order to retain women staff, media organizations must be willing to promote women to leadership roles and close the pay gap that exists in journalism. With more women in the newsroom, coverage of women candidates will tend to be more accurate and equitable, and this will translate into giving more women candidates a fairer shot at winning office.

IV. WOMEN'S LEADERSHIP IN COMPARATIVE PERSPECTIVE

Many of these solutions proposed here are already in place abroad—and they have yielded clear, positive results. RepresentWomen's 2019 International Report ranked all countries based on the level of women's representation found in their national legislatures. The United States currently ranks 83rd. There are currently only fourteen women heads of government in the world; nine of them are in countries that are doing better than the United States in terms of women's representation. In countries ranking above the United States in terms of women's representation in their national legislatures, 12 percent of heads of government are women. In countries ranking below the United States, only 4 percent of heads of government are women. Also, 50 percent of the world's countries with women heads of government are in the top thirty countries for women's representation.

Of countries where women head the government, 71 percent have some form of gender quota in place. Of the countries where men head the government, only 58 percent have such gender quotas. There are two important takeaways here. One is that the majority of countries have gender quotas in place by now. This fact indicates that such quotas should not be brushed off as a kind of aberrant political practice, but rather embraced as the new frontier. The other key takeaway is that countries with gender quotas are more likely to have women heading up their government.

---

[123] *The Status of Women in U.S. Media 2019*, WOMEN'S MEDIA CTR. (Feb. 21, 2019), www.womensmediacenter.com/reports/the-status-of-women-in-u-s-media-2019.

Gender quotas are not the only reform foreign governments are using to increase women's representation in politics. Most of the countries ranked above the United States in terms of women's representation in their national legislatures also use proportional or mixed representation voting systems, while most of the countries ranking below the United States use majoritarian systems. RepresentWomen's research shows that proportional and mixed systems are associated with greater women's representation because these systems allow parties more opportunities to nominate women to run—and when more women run for office, more women win.

While the data on these countries concern mostly national legislatures, there are also connections to the executive branch. Of the countries that have women heads of government, 71 percent have mixed or proportional representation systems. Meanwhile, of the countries with male heads of government, only 57 percent have mixed or proportional representation systems. This suggests that countries with mixed or proportional representation systems are somewhat more likely to have a woman heading their executive branch of government. It is reasonable to hypothesize that in countries with mixed or proportional representation electoral systems, more women are able to win legislative seats, and the result of this is that the concept of women holding positions of power becomes normalized. Reforming voting systems has the power to change culture, and a culture of equality for women further amplifies the positive results of these systemic changes.

A look at other countries reveals the root of the problem in the United States: it's not that the United States lacks qualified women who have what it takes to win elections, including the presidential election. Rather, the problem is that antiquated rules shut these women out of having an equal shot at winning the presidency. In order to have more women candidates run for the presidency, Americans do not need women candidates to change what they are doing. Instead, they need to change the county's laws and electoral practices to normalize women's political power.

V. LOOKING AHEAD

The next woman who wins the presidential nomination will be continuing the legacy of Victoria Woodhull, Belva Lockwood, Shirley Chisholm, Hillary Clinton, and so many other women presidential candidates. Each of these women opened doors for the next woman. But if a woman were actually elected to the highest office in the United States, she would do more than open another door. Rather, she would open floodgates. Her win would catalyze a substantial change for all women in American society. The next generation would grow up seeing a woman in the very highest political office. It would set a monumental precedent, and women who have spent their entire lives being represented by men would finally be represented by a woman.

15

The Nomination of Presidential Candidates by Minor Political Parties

Richard Winger[*]

I. INTRODUCTION

In many democratic countries, talented individuals run for the nation's top elected office under the banner of newly formed parties. Once in a while, these individuals manage to win. In France, for example, a new party called En Marche! was formed on April 6, 2016. The party's full name, "La République En Marche!" roughly translates as "The Republic on the Move!" This party backed Emmanuel Macron for the French presidency in 2017.[1] Macron received 24 percent of the vote in the first round of the French presidential election on April 23, placing first out of five candidates.[2] A second-round runoff with the top two candidates was then held, and Macron was elected President with 66.1 percent of the vote.[3] In the legislative elections of June 2017, En Marche! also won a majority of the seats in the National Assembly, the French parliament.

In Mexico, a new party, the National Regeneration Movement, was formed in January 2014. It was nicknamed "Morena," which means "brown-skinned." During Mexico's presidential election of July 1, 2018, the party's presidential nominee, Andres Manuel Lopez Obrador, was elected with 53 percent of the

[*] Richard Winger is the editor of *Ballot Access News*, a monthly print publication published since 1985. He gratefully acknowledges Eugene Mazo for his help in getting this chapter ready for publication.

[1] Laura Smith-Spark, *France: Ex-economy minister announces presidential run*, CNN (Nov. 16, 2016), www.cnn.com/2016/11/16/europe/france-presidential-race-emmanuel-macron/index .html.

[2] *French election poll tracker*, BBC News (May 5, 2017), www.bbc.com/news/world-europe -39641442.

[3] Seán Clarke & Josh Holder, *French Presidential Election May 2017 – Full Second Round Results and Analysis*, GUARDIAN (May 26, 2017), www.theguardian.com/world/ng-interactive /2017/may/07/french-presidential-election-results-latest.

vote, placing first among five candidates.[4] The party also won a majority of seats in the Chamber of Deputies, the lower house of Mexico's parliament. Similarly, in Ukraine, a new party, Servant of the People, was formed on March 31, 2018. It nominated Volodymyr Zelensky for the presidency. He was elected with 73 percent of the vote, defeating the country's incumbent president, on April 21, 2019. Zelensky's party then won the parliamentary elections in July 2019, marking the first time a party had won a majority of seats in Ukraine's parliament, the Verkhovna Rada, since the country gained its independence in 1991.

In the United States, by contrast, third-party candidates have virtually no chance of winning the presidency. When it comes to the presidential election, third parties are often an afterthought. Indeed, the legitimacy of third-party presidential candidates is often questioned by mainstream political commentators who argue that these candidates should not even run in the first place because they siphon votes from the two major parties and have the potential to "spoil" the outcome of the general election. Of course, those who make these arguments tend to ignore the fact that close to a majority of voters in the United States hold negative views of the two major parties,[5] and that many Americans do not fully support their policy platforms either.[6]

Countries are better off when their laws permit candidates from minor or new parties to compete against candidates from major or old parties. Elections should provide a meaningful choice to all voters, not just to a subset of them. When minor-party candidates are excluded, a portion of voters feel disenfranchised.[7]

---

[4] Azam Ahmed & Paulina Villegas, *López Orbrador, an Atypical Leftist, Wins Mexico Presidency in Landslide*, N.Y. TIMES (July 1, 2018), www.nytimes.com/2018/07/01/world/americas/mexico-election-andres-manuel-lopez-obrador.html.

[5] *See* R. J. Reinhart, *Majority in U.S. Still Say a Third Party Is Needed*, GALLUP (Oct. 26, 2018), https://news.gallup.com/poll/244094/majority-say-third-party-needed.aspx. Gallup does a poll every October asking if there is a need for a new major party. In the latest poll conducted in October 2018, 38% of respondents said they believe the current two-party system does an adequate job of representing the people. On the other hand, 57% said they believed there is a need for a third major party. *Id.*

[6] They also ignore the fact that the United States happens to have been a signatory to the Copenhagen Meeting Document, part of the Helsinki Accords, since 1990. In that agreement, the United States pledged to "respect the right of individuals and groups to establish, in full freedom, their own political parties or other political organizations and provide such political parties and organizations with the necessary legal guarantees to enable them to compete with each other on a basis of equal treatment before the law," as well as to "respect the right of citizens to seek political or public office, individually or as representatives of political parties or organizations, without discrimination." *See* Document of the Copenhagen Meeting of the Conference on the Human Dimension of the CSCE, §§7.5–7.6, www.osce.org/odihr/elections/14304?download=true,.

[7] *See, e.g.*, Lubin v. Panish, 415 U.S. 709, 716 (1974) ("It is to be expected that a voter hopes to find on the ballot a candidate who comes near to reflecting his policy preferences on contemporary issues.").

Although presidential candidates from minor political parties in the United States rarely receive the media attention or monetary backing that the two major-party candidates enjoy, minor-party candidates nonetheless offer Americans something meaningful. They offer novel policy ideas, and thus give hope to those who are disenchanted with the status quo. For this reason, America's minor political parties have consistently nominated their own candidates to compete in the presidential election. These minor parties know that public attitudes toward old parties harden over time, just as public attitudes toward old manufacturing and retail companies harden. True competition requires that new entrants be allowed to enter the market, regardless of whether it is an economic market or a political market.

U.S. election laws and practices make it virtually impossible for candidates from third parties to win a presidential election, however. A number of obstacles face third-party candidates. Some of these are the product of state laws, some arise from federal law, and some are embedded in the Constitution. Republicans and Democrats purposefully make it difficult for new policy ideas to be introduced to the American public by third-party presidential candidates who have any serious chance of winning. By lowering the barriers to third-party candidates, new ideas and insights could be made attractive to the American electorate and gain the support of a sizable portion of voters, as happened recently in France, Mexico, and Ukraine. This chapter surveys the numerous challenges that third-party candidates face in the United States when they run for the presidency. It first begins by recounting how several prominent American third parties nominate their presidential candidates. It then explains why a third-party candidate has little chance of winning the presidential election, no matter how qualified he or she may be.

II. THE PRESIDENTIAL NOMINEES OF MINOR PARTIES

The United States has three nationally organized minor parties that regularly place their presidential nominees on the ballot in enough states to be able to win a presidential election, at least in theory. These minor parties are the Libertarian Party, the Green Party, and the Constitution Party. All three of these parties nominate their presidential candidates using a method similar to that pioneered by the Democrats and Republicans in the nineteenth century and first half of the twentieth century. First, each party holds state conventions that meet in the first few months of a presidential election year. At these state conventions, delegates are chosen to attend the party's national convention. Next, these delegates meet at a national convention and choose a nominee to represent the party on the general election ballot in November. Sometimes the outcome of these minor-party presidential conventions cannot be predicted in advance, so the delegates actually exercise genuine power over the party's choice at the national convention.

Individuals campaign for the presidential nomination of a minor party by appearing at the parties' state conventions. It is often the case that individuals campaigning for the nomination will also obtain a list of national convention delegates and will reach out to those delegates in advance by postal mail, electronic mail, and telephone. The Libertarian Party, the Green Party, and the Constitution Party typically hold their presidential nominating conventions in April, May, June, July, or August of a presidential election year. Because the rules of these parties provide that no presidential candidate may be nominated without a majority of the vote of the convention delegates, often multiple convention ballots need to be held before the nominee is chosen.

During the presidential elections of 1996 and 2000, the Reform Party and the Natural Law Party also placed their presidential candidates on the ballot in states containing a majority of the Electoral College vote. The presidential selection process of these parties was slightly different. The Natural Law Party ceased to exist in 2004, and the Reform Party has now virtually ceased to exist, given that it has not placed a nominee on the ballot in most states since the 2000 election.

A. *The Libertarian Party*

Since 1976, the Libertarian Party has always placed its presidential candidate on the ballot in enough states to be able to win a majority of the Electoral College vote. For election years 1976 through 1992, the party always held its presidential convention on the Labor Day weekend of the year before the presidential election. The party did so because it was easier to get on the November ballot if it chose its candidate early, since some states require the name of a third party's presidential nominee to be listed on the petition a minor party must file with the state seeking ballot access. But holding such an early convention also had disadvantages. It forced the party's potential presidential candidates to begin their campaigns very early, and it forced the Libertarian Party to choose a nominee before it was clear who the major-party nominees would be—and before anyone knew what issues would be debated by the major-party candidates. In 1993, the party decided that it would hold its 1996 convention on July 4 weekend of the year of the election itself. The party obtained rulings from election officials in many states permitting it to use a stand-in nominee on its ballot access petition, and permitting that stand-in to withdraw and be replaced by the actual nominee once he or she was chosen.[8]

The later convention date permitted the Libertarian Party to run its presidential candidates in government-administered primaries, at least in states that allowed the Libertarian Party to appear on the presidential primary ballot. However, the party decided as a matter of policy that these presidential primaries would be "beauty contests" and that their outcomes would not be binding on the party's national convention delegates. Libertarian delegates would continue to be chosen through state conventions, regardless of the outcome of the government-administered primaries.

The party's convention dates were in early July in 1996 and 2000, and ever since then have been in May. Generally, there is a frontrunner for the nomination and only one or two ballots have been needed before that person has won a majority of the votes of the convention delegates. That was certainly the case in 1996 and 2000, when party leaders recruited bestselling author Harry Browne to run for President, and he managed to obtain the Libertarian Party's nomination on the first ballot. In 2004, however, the Libertarian Party's presidential candidate, Michael Badnarik, was only nominated on the third ballot, beating out the candidacies of movie producer Aaron Russo and talk show host Gary Nolan. And in 2008, it took six ballots for anyone to win a majority of the Libertarian delegates' votes.[9] Former Georgia Congressman Bob Barr eventually won the nomination. However, because Barr had taken stands in the past that were clearly not libertarian (especially regarding the legal status of marijuana), he faced determined opposition, despite his insistence that he had changed his views, from runners up Mary Ruwart and Wayne A. Root. One must look all the way back to 1940 to find an instance when either a Republican or Democratic presidential convention needed to hold as many as six ballots to choose a presidential nominee (the Republican Party needed six votes to choose Wendell Willkie in 1940). In 2012, the Libertarian Party nominated Gary Johnson for President on the first ballot. In 2016, the party nominated Gary Johnson once again, though this time only on the second ballot.

B. *The Green Party*

Although Green Party candidates for lesser office began running in the United States in 1984, the Green Party did not nominate anyone for the presidency

---

8   *Libertarians Revise Presidential Choice Date*, 8(11) BALLOT ACCESS NEWS, at 1 (Jan. 8, 1993).
9   Richard Winger, *Libertarian Presidential Convention Vote*, 24(2) BALLOT ACCESS NEWS, at 3–4 (June 1, 2008) (providing the state roll call for each vote).

until 1996. The Green Party's rules say that government-administered presidential primary outcomes bind the votes of delegates at the party's national
convention on the first ballot only. As is the case for the Libertarian Party,
generally there is a frontrunner before the convention who is easily nominated
on the first ballot. In 1996, the Green Party nominated Ralph Nader as its
presidential candidate. Green Party leaders had wooed him, and no one else
declared for the nomination. The party let Nader choose his own vice-
presidential nominee, which he did, picking Winona LaDuke. In 2000, the
party again nominated Nader and LaDuke, and the nomination was virtually
unanimous.

In the first round of voting, David Cobb, who wanted the nomination,
received 308 votes. Peter Camejo received 119, and Nader received 117.5.

However, in 2004, the Green Party had a messier presidential selection
process. In October 2003, Nader said he would not seek the 2004 Green Party
nomination. On February 22, 2004, he declared that he would run for the
presidency as an independent. Nader believed that the message he wanted to
present to voters would be clearer if he were an independent candidate, rather
than the nominee of the Green Party. Yet he gave some indication that he
hoped the Green Party convention would *endorse* him. Under the party's rules,
that would have made it possible for individual state Green parties to nominate
him, which would have helped him with ballot access. The Green Party
delegates were sharply divided on their attitudes toward Nader's strategy. At
the national convention in Milwaukee on June 26, 2004, two ballots were
needed before the party managed to settle on its presidential nominee.

In the first round of voting, David Cobb, who wanted the nomination,
received 308 votes. Peter Camejo received 119, and Nader received 117.5.
Camejo did not actually wish to run for President, but he formally let his
name be entered as a placeholder for Nader. Because Camejo had won the
Green Party primary in California, the large California delegation was
required by the party's rules to vote for Camejo in the first round. In
the second round (unlike the first), however, Nader could not be listed as
a candidate, because the party's rules stated that the second round of balloting
had to be reserved for candidates who had declared for the nomination. Cobb
narrowly won the nomination with 408 votes, while 308 votes were cast for "no
nominee," and 55 votes were cast for others. "No nominee" was a stand-in for
a Nader endorsement.[10]

In 2008, the Green Party nominated former Georgia Congresswoman
Cynthia McKinney as its presidential candidate, and in 2012 and again in

[10]   Richard Winger, *Green Party National Convention*, 20(4) BALLOT ACCESS NEWS, at 5
       (August 1, 2004); *see also* Richard Winger, *Greens Nominate Cobb*, 20(4) BALLOT ACCESS
       NEWS, at 8 (August 1, 2004).

2016, the party nominated Jill Stein, a physician from Massachusetts. Only one ballot was needed during these years at the national convention to secure the party's nomination. Stein had also won each of the party's government-administered primaries.

C. *The Constitution Party*

The Constitution Party was founded in 1992 by Howard Phillips, a prominent conservative who had run two federal agencies during Richard Nixon's presidency. The original name of the Constitution Party was the U.S. Taxpayers Party, but the current name was adopted at the party's national convention in 1999. Under the party's rules, the outcomes of any government-administered presidential primaries are not binding on the party's delegates. The Constitution Party, unlike any other U.S. political party, also allows delegates at national conventions to cast proxy votes for other delegates who are not present. In addition, the party allows fractional voting.

Like the Libertarian Party and the Green Party, the Constitution Party's presidential conventions are generally won by the frontrunner with little suspense. That was the case in 1992, 1996, and 2000, when the party nominated Phillips as its presidential candidate, and again in 2004, when the party unanimously nominated Michael Peroutka, a Maryland attorney, also on the first ballot. The only exception was the 2008 convention, when Alan Keyes, a former Republican candidate for the U.S. Senate from Maryland in 1988 and 1992, and also a former Republican candidate for the U.S. Senate in Illinois in 2004 (he was Barack Obama's Republican opponent) deserted the Republican Party a few weeks before the Constitution Party's national convention and sought the Constitution Party's presidential nomination. Keyes expected to win. But the party's founder, Howard Phillips, made an impassioned speech at the convention in support of Reverend Chuck Baldwin, the other candidate who wanted the nomination. Phillips argued that Keyes's foreign policy ideas were at odds with the party's stance of opposing U.S. intervention in the affairs of other countries. Baldwin defeated Keyes by 383.8 votes to 125.7 votes. Keyes then promptly left the convention hall. He later managed to persuade the party's California affiliate, the American Independent Party, to throw its backing behind him instead of Baldwin.[11]

---

[11]   Richard Winger, *Constitution Party Roll Call Vote*, 24(1) BALLOT ACCESS NEWS, at 5 (May 1, 2008); Richard Winger, *Constitution Party Convention*, 24(1) BALLOT ACCESS NEWS, at 8 (May 1, 2008). The American Independent Party nomination was contested in court, but the Alan Keyes faction won that lawsuit. *See* Richard Winger, *Alan Keyes Wins National Convention*, 24(5) BALLOT ACCESS NEWS, at 3 (Sept. 1, 2008).

Still, Baldwin secured the party's presidential nomination. In 2012, Virginia Congressman Virgil Goode received the party's presidential nomination, beating out second place finisher Darrell Castle, although Castle officially managed to secure the party's nomination in 2016.

D. *The Reform Party*

Ross Perot, who had run for President as an independent in 1992, formed the Reform Party in September 1995. He first said he would not seek the Reform Party's presidential nomination for 1996. Former Colorado Governor Dick Lamm then declared for the nomination on July 9. Two days later, Perot said he would also accept the nomination if the party wanted him. The party had decided that voters who had either registered as members of the Reform Party or who had signed a petition to put the party on the ballot would be eligible to vote in the party's national, privately funded presidential primary, which would be held by U.S. mail. The ballots were mailed in July, and they did not name any candidates. Instead, all voters were to cast a write-in vote. However, material enclosed with these ballots said that the only two candidates were Lamm and Perot. The party announced the results on August 17, with Perot receiving 32,145 votes and Lamm 17,121. Lamm only carried Alaska, Colorado, the District of Columbia, and Minnesota. Thus the party did not need a national convention to choose its nominee. Its single government-administered presidential primary had been held in California, where no one filed to be on the ballot, and which Ralph Nader actually won based on the write-in votes he received.

In 2000, the only other presidential election year in which the Reform Party was on the ballot in enough states to win the majority of the Electoral College vote, the party again had a national, privately funded presidential primary, again using postal ballots. Pat Buchanan had declared for the nomination on October 25, 1999. On the same day, Donald Trump joined the Reform Party and said he was thinking about seeking its presidential nomination. The nomination was attractive to Trump because under federal campaign finance law, the party was entitled to receive approximately $16 million in public funding. Trump was placed on the Reform Party's government-administered primary ballots in California and Michigan, even though he had not formally declared for the nomination, because the laws of those states required state election officials to place presidential candidates on the government's primary ballots if they were mentioned in the major news media as candidates. Buchanan asked not to be listed in either of those government-run primaries, and Trump won both of those contests. Trump then said he was not going to seek the Reform Party's nomination. The only other government-administered presidential primary the Reform Party had was in Missouri, and Buchanan won that primary.

At the end of December 1999, John Hagelin also declared for the Reform Party's nomination, and he was listed, along with Buchanan, on the Reform Party's government-administered primary in Missouri. Hagelin was a founder of the Natural Law Party and the only presidential candidate that party ever had; he ran for the Natural Law Party's nomination in 1992, 1996, and 2000. Thus, in 2000, Hagelin sought the presidential nomination of two minor parties.

The postal ballot was very expensive, but the Federal Election Commission allowed the Reform Party to use public funding to pay for it. The results of the postal ballot were that Buchanan received 49,529 votes, as compared to Hagelin's 28,539 votes. The results were contested, however, because Pat Buchanan had sent out as many as 500,000 ballots. As mentioned, the party's rules held that ballots should only be mailed to registered Reform Party members or to people who had signed a petition to put the Reform Party on the ballot, and a state-by-state analysis showed that Buchanan had sent out hundreds of thousands of ballots to ineligible voters.

In 2000, the Reform Party held its national convention in Long Beach, California. The Reform Party's rules allowed the national convention to override the results of the party's privately administered postal presidential primary. However, a majority of the national convention delegates that year were Buchanan supporters. When it was clear to Hagelin's supporters that Buchanan had a majority, the Hagelin delegates found a nearby alternate venue; they quickly left the original location and relocated to their own new location. The delegates at the original location then nominated Buchanan to be their presidential candidate with 453 votes; only six votes were cast for anyone else. The Hagelin delegates cast a unanimous vote for Hagelin at their new location, but only 223 delegates at that meeting voted.

Although rival groups in many states filed Reform Party petitions either for Buchanan or for Hagelin, generally state authorities recognized Buchanan as the Reform Party's actual presidential candidate. The Federal Election Commission had sent the party's public funding to the Buchanan campaign, not to the Hagelin campaign, and that influenced states to recognize Buchanan as well. In Minnesota, however, Buchanan and Hagelin both appeared on the November general election ballot under the "Reform" label.[12]

---

[12]   Richard Winger, 2000 *Reform Party Presidential Ballot*, 16(6) BALLOT ACCESS NEWS, at 5 (Sept. 1, 2000) (providing the state-by-state Reform Party mail ballot results); *see also* Richard Winger, *Reform Conventions: Voter for President, Vice President*, 16(6) BALLOT

E. *The Natural Law Party*

The Natural Law Party was formed in April 1992.[13] Although it was not able to get on the ballot in states containing a majority of the Electoral College vote in 1992, it did do so in 1996 and 2000. Unlike the other minor parties described above, the Natural Law Party always nominated its presidential candidate by a consensus of the party's top leadership. The party was based on the Transcendental Meditation movement. Its devotees did not believe in conflict, and most members of the party were content to let a handful of national party leaders determine the party's presidential nominee. Although the party did hold national conventions, the vote was always unanimous for John Hagelin. Hagelin was a physicist at a college located in Fairfield, Iowa, which happened to be owned by the Transcendental Meditation movement. Although the party participated in a few government-administered primaries, the only person whose name was ever listed on those primary ballots was Hagelin's.

The five minor parties above, together with the Democrats and Republicans, are the only parties that have managed to place their presidential nominees on the ballot in states containing a majority of the votes of the Electoral College in presidential elections from 1996 to 2016.

III. WHY MINOR-PARTY CANDIDATES DON'T WIN

The United States makes it virtually impossible for the nominees of minor parties to win a presidential election. There are many obstacles standing in the way of these candidates. Most of these are unique to the electoral system of the United States. Some of these obstacles are the product of state laws, some arise from federal law, and some are embedded in the Constitution.

A. *State Restrictions*

One obstacle that minor-party candidates face is that the election laws of many states make it difficult and expensive for a minor-party presidential candidate to get on the ballot. State ballot access laws pose many challenges for candidates who run for the presidency outside of the two major parties. State laws

ACCESS NEWS, at 6 (Sept. 1, 2000) (providing the vote cast by convention delegates at both Long Beach conventions, and the number of delegates each state was allotted).

[13] For a description of the Natural Law Party written by one of the party's activists, see ROBERT ROTH, A REASON TO VOTE: BREAKING THE TWO-PARTY STRANGLEHOLD—AND THE REMARKABLE RISE OF AMERICA'S FASTEST GROWING POLITICAL PARTY (1998).

often require minor-party candidates and independent candidates to file a petition to get on the government-regulated ballot, and the number of signatures required for such petitions to be successful tends to be very high. Many states also impose petition filing deadlines on minor-party candidates that come too early for a late-announcing candidate to be able to get on the ballot. Sometimes these state ballot access laws also force minor-party candidates to choose a vice-presidential running mate before the minor-party presidential candidate may be able or ready to do so. Finally, some states have "sore loser" laws that work to prevent minor-party candidates from qualifying for the general election ballot as an independent or as a third-party candidate if that minor-party candidate has already run for the presidency earlier in the year in any major party's presidential primary and lost the primary election.

1. Ballot Access Petitions

In almost every state, minor-party presidential candidates have two choices for gaining access to the ballot. First, they can run either as an independent candidate or as the candidate of a minor third party. Second, they can run as the presidential candidate of a new party, after that new party has formed and registers with the state. Either way, the candidate must petition to get on the ballot. Every state has a procedure for how an independent party can gain access to the ballot, and every state has a procedure for how a new party can be registered and its candidate can get on the ballot. Generally, the procedures in each state for these two routes to the ballot are equally difficult. However, some states make it slightly easier for an independent or minor party's presidential nominee to gain access the ballot relative to the nominee of a new party, while other states do the opposite and make it slightly easier for a new party's nominee to get on the ballot.

Given that every state's general presidential election is really an election to choose the members of the Electoral College for that state, the United States does not really have a single general presidential election. Instead, it runs 51 separate presidential elections. For the past one hundred years, every candidate who has run for president outside the two major parties has tried to qualify for a state ballot either as an independent or minor-party candidate or as the candidate of a new party. There is no barrier to choosing either of the two procedures to qualify, so a minor-party candidate will generally pick whichever happens to be easier of the two in a particular state. In states where it is far easier to get a new party on the ballot, the minor-party candidate will form a new party inside the state and run on its ballot. Conversely, in states where it is easier for the minor-party candidate to run as the nominee of an independent party, he or she will do that. The following table sets out the minor-party ballot access requirements for the 2020 election. In each case, the easier of the two methods for getting on the ballot is listed.

The states in the table are arranged in order of difficulty, with those that make ballot access easiest listed at the top. As should be obvious from the table, there is no such thing as a typical minor-party ballot access requirement. Extreme variability exists among the states. In some states, qualifying for the ballot is quite easy. In others, it is extremely difficult, so much so, in fact, that the state's minor-party ballot access requirements are almost never satisfied.

Slowly, over time, ballot access requirements have loosened for minor-party presidential candidates. In 2017, North Carolina lowered the number of petition signatures required for a new party to qualify for the ballot from 2 percent of the total votes cast in the last gubernatorial election to 0.25 percent.[14] In 2020, this will lower the number of petition signatures required for a new party to gain access to the ballot from 94,221 signatures to 11,778.[15] Also in 2017, North Carolina lowered the number of signatures required for an independent candidate to qualify for the ballot from 2 percent of the total votes cast in the last gubernatorial election to 1.5 percent.[16] Given that North Carolina is now more generous to new party candidates than to independent party candidates, any sensible minor-party presidential candidate running in North Carolina will choose to form a new party inside North Carolina to take advantage of the easier ballot access requirement for new parties.

This has been done before. In 1980, when a new party petition required 10,000 signatures but the independent party petition required 166,383 signatures to gain access to the presidential ballot, presidential candidate John B. Anderson merely formed the "Independent Party" in North Carolina and appeared on the ballot as that party's presidential candidate. However, from 1983 to 2017, North Carolina proved to be one of the nation's most difficult states for ballot access for minor-party candidates. Ralph Nader, who placed third in the presidential elections of 2000, 2004, and 2008, never succeeded in getting on North Carolina's presidential ballot. North Carolina was one of only four states in which Nader's name never appeared on the ballot. The other three were Oklahoma, Georgia, and Indiana.[17]

Another state that eased its requirements for minor-party candidates in 2017 was Oklahoma, which passed a new law that allows minor-party presidential

---

[14]   S. Res. 656, 2017 Gen. Assemb. Reg. Sess. (N.C. 2017) (enacted over a gubernatorial veto).
[15]   *Id.*
[16]   *Id.*
[17]   Ben Adler, *Nader, Barr Muscle onto the Nov. Ballots*, POLITICO (Sept. 19, 2008), www.politico.com/story/2008/09/nader-barr-muscle-onto-the-nov-ballots-013595.

TABLE 15.1 *Ballot access requirements for new party or independent presidential candidates, 2020*

State	Legal Requirement to Qualify for the Ballot	State's Election Code Section	Signatures Required	As Percent of State Votes Cast for Pres. in 2016
Vt	no petition; no fee	Title 17, § 2402(b)	—	—
Colo	pay $1,000; no petition needed	1-4-801(b)	—	—
La	pay $500; no petition needed	Title 18, § 465C	—	—
Fla	file for FEC recognition	97.021(12)	—	—
Ok	pay $35,000; no petition needed	Title 26, 1-108	—	—
Tenn	number stated in law	2-505	275	.01
NJ	number stated in law	19:13-5	800	.02
Wash	number stated in law	29.24.030	1,000	.03
Ill	number from court order	Libertarian Party of Illinois v. Pritzker	2,500	.05
Mn	number stated in law	204B.08	2,000	.07
Wi	number stated in law	Title 2, § 8.20(4)	2,000	.07
Miss	number stated in law	23-15-359	1,000	.08
Pa	number from court order	Constitution Party v. Cortes	5,000	.08
Ark	number stated in law	7-302(5)(B)	1,000	.09
Ohio	number stated in law	3513.257	5,000	.09
Utah	number stated in law	20-3-38	1,000	.09
Iowa	number stated in law	Title 4, § 45.1	1,500	.10
Va	number stated in law	24.2-543	5,000	.13
Id	number stated in law	34-708A	1,000	.14
Del	1% of reg. voters, Dec. 2019	Title 15, § 3001	720	.16
Hi	1% of reg. voters, Nov. 2018	Title 2, § 11-62	757	.17
Ga	number from court order	Green Party of Georgia v. Kemp	7,500	.18
Md	number from court settlement	Maryland Green Party v. Hogan	5,000	.18
NY	number stated in law	Chap. 17, § 6-142	15,000	.19
RI	number stated in law	17-14-7	1,000	.22
Ala	number stated in law	17-19-2(a)	5,000	.24
NC	25% of 2016 gub. vote	163-96(2)	11,171	.24
Ky	number stated in law	Title 10, § 118.315(2)	5,000	.26

TABLE 15.1 *(continued)*

State	Legal Requirement to Qualify for the Ballot	State's Election Code Section	Signatures Required	As Percent of State Votes Cast for Pres. in 2016
Neb	number stated in law	32-504(2)(c)	2,500	.30
Mass	number stated in law	Chapter 53, § 6	10,000	.30
Ct	stated in exec. order	9–453(d)	5,250	.32
Mo	number stated in law	Title 9, § 115.321	10,000	.36
NH	number stated in law	Title 4, § 655:42	3,000	.40
Ks	number stated in law	25-303	5,000	.42
NM	½ of 1% of 2018 gub. vote	1-8-2.B & 1-7-2.A	3,483	.43
SC	number stated in law	7-9-10	10,000	.48
Me	number stated in law	Title 21, § 494.5	4,000	.52
Mi	number stated in law	168.544(f)	30,000	.63
Nv	1% of 2018 US House vote	Title 24, § 293.1715	9,608	.85
SD	1% of 2018 gub. vote	12-7-1	3,393	.92
Tex	1% of 2018 gub. vote	181.005	83,435	.93
WV	1% of 2016 pres. vote	3-5-23	7,145	1.00
Or	1% of 2016 pres. vote	Title 23, § 249.735	20,014	1.00
Alas	1% of 2016 pres. vote	15.30.025	3,187	1.00
Mt	number stated in law	13-10-601	5,000	1.01
ND	number stated in law	16.1-12-02	4,000	1.16
Az	1.33% of 2018 gub. vote	16-802	31,685	1.23
Cal	1% of reg. voters as of Oct. 2018	8400	196,964	1.39
Wy	2% of 2018 U.S. House vote	22-4-402(d)	4,018	1.57
Ind	2% of 2018 Sec. of State vote	3-8-6-3	44,934	1.64

candidates to get on the ballot simply by paying a filing fee of $35,000, without filing a petition.[18] Oklahoma's new law applies to both independent candidates and the nominees of new political parties.[19] Although $35,000 is a great deal of money, it is still cheaper than gathering petition signatures. Oklahoma law requires petition signatures amounting to 3 percent of the votes cast

---

[18] S. Res. 145, 56th Leg., 1st Sess. (Okla. 2017); *see also* Richard Winger, *Oklahoma Eases Presidential Ballot Access*, 33 (1) BALLOT ACCESS NEWS, at 1 (June 1, 2017).

[19] *Id.*

statewide in the last presidential election. In 2020, that would be 43,590 signatures. Paid petition signature gatherers who work during an election year earn about $3 per signature, and generally a successful petition must collect 50 percent more signatures than required by law to get on the ballot to allow for challenges.

The three states that require the highest number of signatures for minor-party candidates to qualify for the presidential ballot are California, Florida, and Texas. California has always had harsh ballot access for independent candidates or for candidates supported by new parties. The original California ballot access law required a petition with signatures equal to 5 percent of the last statewide vote cast. In 1893, however, California changed its petition requirement and asked minor parties to provide signatures amounting to 3 percent of the number of votes cast in the last gubernatorial election. At the time, that was the nation's second-most severe petition requirement. Nevada's ballot access law, originally passed in 1891, required a petition containing 3 percent of the last vote cast, but in 1893 that amount was raised to 10 percent.[20]

California now requires an independent party presidential candidate to obtain signatures equal to 1 percent of the number of registered voters in the state as of the last general election (rather than signatures equal to a percentage of the number of votes cast).[21] For 2020, that will be 196,964 valid signatures. These signatures, moreover, must be collected in 105 days.[22] Also, the ballot petition cannot start to circulate until the independent presidential candidate has chosen his or her 55 California presidential electors, whose names and addresses must be printed on the signature petitions. A recent case challenging the large number of signatures and the short petitioning period required for independent candidates to qualify for the presidential ballot was dismissed by the U.S. Court of Appeals for the Ninth Circuit.[23] That case was brought by plaintiff Roque De La Fuente, who, after losing the 2016 Democratic primary in California, wanted to continue his candidacy in the general election as an independent candidate. He argued that California's petition requirement was "cost prohibitive," but he lost his case.[24]

---

[20] The original California ballot access law required a petition of 5% of the last vote cast. See 1891 State Session Laws, ch. 130, p. 166. In 1893 it was lowered to 3%, but that was still the most severe requirement in the nation, except for Nevada. 1893 Session Laws, ch. 220, p. 303. The original Nevada law, passed in 1891, required a petition of 3% of the last vote cast. 1891 Session Laws, ch. 40, p. 40. But it was raised in 1893 to 10%. Session Laws 1893, ch. 106, p. 113.

[21] Cal. Elec. Code § 8400 (2018); Cal. Elec. Code § 8403 (2018).

[22] Richard Winger, *High Turnout Causes Higher Petition Requirements*, 34(7) BALLOT ACCESS NEWS, at 2 (Dec. 1, 2018).

[23] De La Fuente v. Padilla, 930 F.3d 1101 (9th Cir. 2019).

[24] *Id.* at 1104.

For California to recognize a new party, that new party, unlike an independent candidate, needs to have a membership base equal to 0.33 percent of the state's registered voters.[25] New parties obtain registered members by asking potential members to fill out a new voter registration application, listing themselves as members of the new party. Currently, a new party needs to have approximately 64,000 members for it to be recognized by the state. As the number of registered voters continues to rise in California, however, this requirement obviously increases as well.

In contrast to California, Texas had a relatively easy ballot access requirement on the books for minor parties and new parties — at least until 1967. A new party merely had to hold a state convention and also county conventions in at least twenty counties in the state. In 1967, the law was stiffened to require a ballot access petition to be circulated with signatures equal to 1 percent of the votes cast during the last statewide gubernatorial election.[26] No signatory was allowed to sign the petition if he voted in that year's primary elections.[27] Before obtaining a signature, moreover, the new law required the signature gatherer to read a long statement to each petition signer.[28] In 2010, the Green Party managed to get a candidate on the Texas state ballot through Texas's petition process. The party's success was made possible by a donation it received for $600,000, which gave it the ability to hire paid signature gatherers.

Currently, under Texas law, a new party petition requires 83,435 signatures, which have to be collected in 75 days. An independent party petition requires signatures equal to 1 percent of the votes cast during the last presidential election. For 2020, that would amount to 79,939 signatures, which have to be gathered within a 68-day circulation period.[29]

Florida made ballot access very easy for new and minor parties between 1999 and 2016. During that time period, a minor party could get on the ballot

---

[25]   Cal. Elec. Code § 5100 (2016).

[26]   Elec. Code. Revision, ch. 723, 1967 Tex. Laws 1, 1921 (1967).

[27]   *Id.*

[28]   Tex. Elec. Code § 141.064 (1997). The petitioner must tell everyone he approaches: "I know that the purpose of this petition is to entitle the (whatever) Party to have its nominees placed on the ballot in the general election for state and county officers. I have not voted in a primary election or participated in a convention of another party during this voting year, and I understand that I become ineligible to do so by signing this petition. I understand that signing more than one petition to entitle a party to have its nominees placed on the general election ballot in the same election is prohibited." The legislature tried to repeal this requirement in 2003, but Governor Rick Perry vetoed the bill. H.R. Res. 1274, 78th Leg., Reg. Sess. (Tex. 2003).

[29]   *Filing deadlines and signature requirements for independent presidential candidates,* 2016, Ballotpedia, https://ballotpedia.org/Filing_deadlines_and_signature_requirements_for_inde pendent_presidential_candidates,_2016.

merely by filing a list of its officers and a copy of its bylaws with the state, and also by showing that it had a relatively low level of contributions and expenditures. But in 2016, the Florida secretary of state began enforcing a dormant state law that prevented a minor third party from gaining access to the presidential ballot unless the FEC classified that party as a "national committee" for campaign finance purposes. This law had been passed in 2011, but Florida's secretary of state at the time decided not enforce it because his office had no official knowledge of which parties were recognized by the FEC.[30] In September 2016, a new Florida secretary of state began enforcing the law.[31] This resulted in three presidential candidates suddenly seeing their names removed from the presidential ballot, after they thought they had qualified for it. These candidates were Evan McMullin, the presidential candidate of the Independent Party; Gloria La Riva, the candidate of the Socialism and Liberation Party, and Thomas Hoefling, candidate of America's Party. Because the FEC has a policy of refusing national committee status to a party until after it has participated in at least one federal election, the Florida law is discriminatory against newly formed parties. If a qualified party is not recognized by the FEC, the only other way for it to place a presidential candidate on the ballot under Florida law is to submit a petition signed by 1 percent of the state's registered voters, which in 2020 would amount to a petition that contains 132,781 signatures.[32]

Another problem with linking a state's recognition of a political party with regulations imposed by the FEC is that the FEC will not recognize a party that only exists in a single state.[33] There are many such parties in the United States, including the well-known Conservative Party of New York State, the oldest continuously ballot-qualified party in any state, other than the Democrats and Republicans. The Conservative Party of New York State has qualified for the ballot in every election since 1962. The Conservative Party of New York State, like most other ballot-qualified parties that exist in only one state, has always participated in the presidential election within its own state, except in 1964.

---

[30]   The secretary of state's letter saying he would not enforce that law is dated September 1, 2011. It was addressed to Dan Winslow, the counsel for Americans Elect, a new party in Florida that did not have FEC recognition.

[31]   *See* Richard Winger, *Florida Changes Rules to Remove Presidential Candidates*, 32(5) BALLOT ACCESS NEWS, at 3 (October 1, 2016).

[32]   *Filing deadlines and signature requirements for independent presidential candidates*, 2016, Ballotpedia, https://ballotpedia.org/Filing_deadlines_and_signature_requirements_for_independent_presidential_candidates,_2016.

[33]   *See* FEC Advisory Op. 1976–95 (Oct. 28, 1975), www.fec.gov/files/legal/aos/1976-95/1976-95 .pdf (denying national committee status to the Liberal Party, which only existed in New York state).

But if the Conservative Party of New York State were a party in Florida, the new Florida law would not allow it to nominate a presidential candidate, unless it submitted a petition containing more than 120,000 signatures supporting its presidential candidate.[34]

2. Early Filing Deadlines

The states have traditionally imposed early petition filing deadlines on independent and minor-party presidential candidates. That this practice persists is surprising. After all, in 1983, in striking down an Ohio statute that imposed an early petition filing deadline on independent presidential candidates, the Supreme Court held said that such a deadline violates the First Amendment.[35] The challenge to the Ohio statute and to that state's early filing deadline was brought by John B. Anderson, an independent presidential candidate who had declared his run for the presidency after the ballot qualifying deadlines for independent candidates had already passed in five states. Anderson sued, and he won all five cases before the 1980 election. He then managed to appear on the ballot in 51 jurisdictions.[36] In 1984, various independent presidential candidates sued states that imposed early filing deadlines in April, May, and June of the presidential election year, and for a brief moment, in 1987, every state had a filing deadline that was either in July, August, or September.[37]

But since then, some states have backslid. In 2017, North Carolina moved its independent petition deadline for all elected offices to February.[38] In 1986, Texas moved its deadlines from July to May, for all types of petitions.[39] In 1999, Illinois moved its deadline, again for all types of petitions, from August to June.[40] In 2019, New York moved its deadlines for all types of petitions from August to May.[41] Many other states still impose very early filing deadlines for new parties, but at least they have late deadlines for independent presidential candidates.[42]

---

[34] Fla. Elec. Code § 99.0955 (2017).
[35] Anderson v. Celebrezze, 460 U.S. 780 (1983).
[36] *Id.*
[37] Richard Winger, *How Many Parties Ought to Be on the Ballot?: An Analysis of Nader v. Keith*, 5 ELECTION L.J. 193 (2006).
[38] H.R. Res. 100, 2017 Leg., Reg. Sess. (N.C. 2017) (adopted over a gubernatorial veto).
[39] 1986 session laws, ch. 14, 3rd called session, p. 577.
[40] H.R. Res. 1790, 91st Gen. Assemb., Reg. Sess. (Ill. 1999).
[41] S. Res. 779, 2019 Gen. Assemb., Reg. Sess. (N.Y. 2019).
[42] The Utah deadline for a new party petition is November 30 of the year before the election.

As the U.S. Supreme Court explained in *Anderson v. Celebrezze*, early petition deadlines injure independent candidates and minor parties, and the voters who are interested in voting for them, in several ways. First, it has been common in U.S. history for voters to organize new parties, or to boost independent presidential candidacies, during the election year itself. The Republican Party was formed on July 6, 1854, in reaction to Congress passing the Kansas-Nebraska Act in May of that year. That federal law converted the Nebraska and Kansas territories from jurisdictions in which slavery was banned to jurisdictions in which voters would be allowed to decide whether slavery should be banned or not. This unexpected change enraged anti-slavery voters of the North. Back in 1854, because there were no government-printed ballots, the law did not impose any impediment to forming a new party in July of an election year. Anti-slavery voters gave solid support to the formation of a new party that year, and that new party elected a plurality of the U.S. House of Representatives. This revolutionary change would not have been possible if election laws at the time would have prevented a party formed in July from getting on the ballot.

It is very common for voters in democracies around the world to form new parties in election years, as the examples of France, Mexico, and Ukraine with which this chapter began all suggest. In fact, this practice is so common that the State Department filed a human rights complaint against Azerbajian after that country passed a law banning political parties from appearing on the ballot if they had been formed less than six months before an election. In the United States, however, many states impose various kinds of early filing deadlines on new and minor parties. These deadlines hamper minor parties because it is difficult for these parties to raise enough money to pay petition circulators during non-election years. In 2016, the Green Party managed to place its presidential candidate on the ballot in all but six states, but this was only possible because Jill Stein had qualified for primary season matching funds, and she used that money for petition gathering. However, it is not possible for a presidential candidate to receive primary matching funds earlier than the election year. When petition deadlines come as early as February of an election year, or even earlier, the money for petitioning is not yet available.

3. The Vice-Presidential Choice

Major parties almost never know who their vice-presidential candidates will be until their national conventions take place, or at the very least until shortly before the national conventions, at which point the leading major-party presidential candidates will announce their choice for a vice president. However, many states require independent presidential candidates, as well as the nominees of new or minor parties who must petition to get on the ballot, to choose their vice-presidential candidates before they can even begin the petition process. This is so because, under the laws of many states, all of the names of a minor or new party's candidates must be printed on the ballot petition, including the name of the party's candidate for the vice presidency.

In 1980, John B. Anderson did not manage to find a suitable running mate until August 27, when he chose former Wisconsin Governor Patrick Lucey to be his vice president. In the meantime, his ballot access petitions were almost all complete, and had been submitted. Anderson's petitions in almost all of states listed Milton Eisenhower as a "stand-in" for vice president. At the time, Milton Eisenhower was 90 years old and was unwilling to serve as vice president. Anderson's attorneys persuaded almost all of the states to let Eisenhower withdraw, and to be replaced by Lucey. Florida and Pennsylvania refused, however, so Anderson had to sue those states to have Lucey listed.[43] Today, one would think that this problem should no longer exist. But that is not the case, as many states that agreed to a substitution in 1980 have changed their policies since. In 2008, the Libertarian Party had to petition to get on the presidential ballot in Massachusetts. At the time, it did not know who its presidential and vice-presidential nominees would be, so it used stand-ins.[44] When it submitted its petition, the Massachusetts secretary of state refused to let the party substitute the names on its petition with name of the party's eventual nominee.[45] The Libertarian Party sued and won, in part because the state had frequently permitted such substitution in the past, and had even told the Libertarian Party in 2008 that it could use stand-ins.[46] Massachusetts appealed to the U.S. Court of Appeals for the First Circuit after the 2008 election was over, however, and the First Circuit reversed, finding that nothing in the Constitution required states to permit stand-ins on candidate petitions.[47] This area of the law is now unsettled, thanks to several conflicting court decisions.

---

[43]   *See* Anderson v. Firestone, 499 F.Supp. 1027 (N.D. Fla. 1980); Anderson v. Davis, 419 A.2d 806 (Pa. Commonw. Ct. 1980). Anderson also sued Indiana over vice-presidential substitution, but the state compromised by extending its deadline from September 1 to September 16, giving him time to circulate an entirely new petition listing Lucey. The petition required 6,982 signatures.

[44]   Carla Howell, *Libertarian Party wins court case against FEC and CPD*, LP NEWS (Apr. 2017), www.lp.org/wp-content/uploads/2017-2_LP_News.pdf.

[45]   *Id.*

[46]   Barr v. Galvin, 626 F.3d 99 (1st Cir. 2010).

[47]   *Id.*

4. Sore Loser Laws

A few of the most successful independent presidential candidates in American history had run as Democrat or Republican candidates earlier in the same election year. In 1912, Theodore Roosevelt competed in almost all of the Republican presidential primaries, and he won almost all of them. However, at the Democratic National Convention, he lost the battle for his party's nomination to William Howard Taft, the incumbent President. Unwilling to admit defeat, Roosevelt organized a new party, the Progressive Party, and proceeded to get this new party, or else just himself as an independent candidate, onto the general election ballot of every single state except for Oklahoma. Roosevelt did not make it onto the Oklahoma ballot because that state had a June filing deadline for a new party to qualify for the ballot, and meanwhile it had no qualification provision allowing for an independent presidential candidate to qualify.[48]

No state had tried to keep Roosevelt off the general election ballot on the grounds that he was a "sore loser," though he may have been just that. Some states at the time had laws on the books that prevented a candidate who had lost a primary from running again under a different party's label in the general election in November. However, in practice, these laws did not affect pre-sidential candidates. That is because, in 1912, the names voters saw printed on their general election ballots were the names of individuals vying to become members of the Electoral College. Since every state printed the names of each candidate for presidential elector on the November ballot and let voters pick and choose among these candidates, a presidential candidate who lost the primaries still had a shot at winning the general election if enough citizens voted for his presidential electors.

In 1980, John B. Anderson, then a member of Congress from Illinois, duplicated Roosevelt's maneuver from earlier in the century. Anderson ran in most of the Republican presidential primaries, which he did not win. Then, on April 23, Anderson, perceiving that he had no chance to win the Republican nomination against Ronald Reagan, declared his run for president as an independent.[49] Anderson got on the ballot in every jurisdiction. No one

---

[48] Roosevelt sued Oklahoma, but the Oklahoma Supreme Court upheld the early deadline. All new parties had to have their state primaries in August, and the court said the early deadline was required by the state for administrative reasons. Persons v. Penn, 127 P. 384 (Okla. 1912).

[49] Richard Winger, *Thirty-Six Years Ago Today, John B. Anderson Dropped out of Republican Race and Declared as an Independent*, BALLOT ACCESS NEWS (Apr. 23, 2016), http://ballot-access.org/2016/04/24/thirty-six-years-ago-today-john-b-anderson-dropped-out-of-republican-race-and-declared-as-an-independent/.

kept him off, despite the fact that he had earlier been a candidate in twenty Republican presidential primaries.[50]

Roosevelt and Anderson were not the only American presidential candidates whose names appeared first on a presidential primary ballot and then, as third-party or independent candidates, on the general election ballot in November. Jacob Coxey ran in a few Republican presidential primaries in 1932 and then appeared on the ballot in November as the presidential nominee of Farmer-Labor Party.[51] Douglas MacArthur was listed in a few Republican presidential primaries in 1952 and then his name appeared on the general election ballot in a few states in November as the nominee of the Constitution Party and also of the Christian Nationalist Party. David Duke ran in some Democratic presidential primaries in 1988 and then, in that same year, his name appeared on the November general election ballot as the nominee of the Populist Party.[52] Similarly, Lenora Fulani ran in New Hampshire's Democratic presidential primary in 1992, and then in the general election as the nominee of the New Alliance Party.[53] In 2008, after Ron Paul ran in most of the Republican primaries, he appeared on the November ballot under a different label in two states, Montana and Louisiana, even though he did not officially campaign in the general election.[54] That was also true in 2008 for Alan Keyes, who ran in several Republican primaries and then appeared on the general election ballot in three states in November as the nominee of the American Independent Party.[55] Finally, Lyndon LaRouche ran in many Democratic primaries in 1984, 1988, and 1992, and then appeared on many general election ballots as an independent candidate. The American tradition that a third-party candidate could run first in a major party's primary, and then outside the major parties in the general election, was well-established.

For more than one hundred years, no state had kept a presidential candidate off its November ballot because of a "sore loser" law until Michigan's secretary of state removed Gary Johnson, the Libertarian Party's nominee, from

---

[50] *Id.*

[51] *Massillon History: General Jacob Coxey*, MASSILLON MUSEUM, www.massillonmuseum.org /jacob-coxey.

[52] Bill Turque, *The Real David Duke*, NEWSWEEK (Nov. 17, 1991), www.newsweek.com/real-david-duke-201998.

[53] Gwen Ifill, *New Alliance Party Leader Attacks Arkansas Governor*, N.Y. TIMES (Mar. 29, 1992), www.nytimes.com/1992/03/29/us/the-1992-campaign-new-york-new-alliance-party-leader-attacks-arkansas-governor.html.

[54] Ron Paul was nominated by the Constitution Party of Montana and appeared on Montana's general election ballot, and some people also placed him on the Louisiana ballot as an independent.

[55] *Presidency 2008*, Politics 1, www.politics1.com/p2008.htm (last updated Nov. 2, 2008).

Michigan's general election ballot in 2012. Michigan decided to do that because Johnson's name had been printed on Michigan's Republican primary ballot in February 2012.[56] Johnson had withdrawn from the race for the Republican Party's nomination on November 29, 2011, and he entered the race to be the Libertarian Party's nominee instead.[57] Unfortunately, his application to withdraw from that year's Michigan Republican primary was faxed to the secretary of state's office, and it arrived two minutes after the deadline for withdrawal had passed. On May 5, 2012, after he won the Libertarian Party's nomination, Johnson challenged the Michigan secretary of state's determination that his name could not appear on the general election ballot. Johnson pointed out that Michigan had allowed John B. Anderson's name to be listed on Michigan's general election ballot, even though Anderson had also been a candidate in the Republican primary in 1980.[58] The courts sided with the state.[59] Both the U.S. District Court and the U.S. Court of Appeals for the Sixth Circuit were reluctant to give Johnson relief, in part because Johnson's campaign had been so slow to file his lawsuit.[60]

In 2016, two states that had previously permitted presidential candidates to appear on the general election ballot either as independents or minor-party nominees, even though these candidate had run in a major-party presidential primary previously, retracted their old policies and denied ballot access to these candidates in the general presidential election. Roque De La Fuente had run in the Democratic presidential primary in Alabama and Arkansas in 2016, and later submitted petitions to run as an independent candidate in those states. Although both petitions had the required number of signatures, De La Fuente was denied ballot access on the grounds that the state's "sore loser" law applied to presidential elections.[61] In 1992, these same states had placed Lyndon LaRouche on the November ballot as an independent presidential candidate even though LaRouche had run in the Democratic primaries earlier that year. The law had not changed in either state since. De La Fuente sued the state of Alabama, but the court upheld his exclusion.[62] De La Fuente did not sue Arkansas because the Arkansas secretary of state removed his name just prior to the ballot-printing deadline, and there was little that a victory in court

---

[56] Richard Winger, *Sixth Circuit Rules that Sore Lose Laws Apply to Presidential Primaries*, 29(1) Ballot Access News, at 1 (June 1, 2013).

[57] *Id.*

[58] *Id.*

[59] Libertarian Party of Michigan v. Johnson, 714 F.3d 929 (6th Cir. 2013).

[60] *Id.*

[61] *Id.*

[62] De La Fuente v. Merrill, 214 F.Supp.3d 1241 (N.D. Ala. 2016).

could have done for him. Later in 2016, Pennsylvania also barred De La Fuente from appearing on its general presidential election ballot in November because he had run in the Pennsylvania Democratic primary earlier, even though De La Fuente submitted a petition with enough valid signatures for his name to appear on the November ballot. De La Fuente sued Pennsylvania over the issue but lost.[63]

B. Federal Restrictions

Federal restrictions also serve to hamper minor-party candidates from winning the presidency. At the federal level, these restrictions are not always imposed by law, but rather come in other forms as well. For example, federal campaign finance law imposes certain barriers to minor-party candidates, as does the electoral system. But not all hurdles are legal in nature. For example, the presidential debates also disadvantage minor-party candidates.

1. Public Funding

In 1976, the federal government instituted a scheme that could offer public funding to presidential candidates running in the general election if they happened to be the nominees of political parties that had received 5 percent or more of the popular vote in the preceding presidential election.[64] In 1976, the presidential nominee of each major political party received $21.8 million to be used for the general presidential election. In 2008, the last year that a major-party candidate chose to accept a general election grant, that amount, adjusted for inflation, had risen to $84.1 million.[65] (In 2016, the general election grant would have been $96.14 million, though no major-party nominee chose to accept public funding.)

However, independent presidential candidates and candidates nominated by new parties do not qualify to receive this public funding or any equivalent funding from the government. The presidential candidates of new parties cannot get general election funding before an election, and nor can independent presidential candidates. Such funding can only come after the election is over, and only if these parties received 5 percent or more of the vote.[66] Even

---

[63] De La Fuente v. Cortés, 261 F.Supp.3d 543 (M.D. Pa. 2017).
[64] *Public funding of presidential elections*, FED. ELECTION COMM'N, www.fec.gov/introduction-campaign-finance/understanding-ways-support-federal-candidates/presidential-elections/public-funding-presidential-elections/.
[65] *Id.*
[66] *Id.*

that threshold does not put new and minor parties on an equal playing field, as the amount of general election funding given to parties is much greater if they polled at least 25 percent of the vote in the preceding election.

It takes a great deal of money to be elected President. A federal public funding system that denies such general election public funding to new parties makes it difficult for new parties to have enough money to complete with established parties. This is one reason why the news media has become accustomed to the idea that presidential candidates who are not the nominees of the Democrats or Republicans will not be competitive — unless they happens to be extremely wealthy.[67] From 1970 to the present day, Ross Perot is the only minor-party or independent candidate who has received 10 percent of support in the polls prior to the general election, and he happened to be very wealthy. Michael Bloomberg, the former mayor of New York City, always got press attention when he suggested that he might run for president as an independent because he was also very wealthy. Howard Schultz, another wealthy individual who happens to be the CEO of Starbucks, got a lot of publicity in 2019 when he was deciding whether or not he would run for the presidency as an independent in 2020 — again because he was very wealthy.

There seems to be no realistic chance that the existing federal laws that regulate public funding will be altered to be more favorable to the presidential candidates of new parties, minor parties, or for independent candidates. The existing law was upheld by the U.S. Supreme Court in 1976 in *Buckley v. Valeo*.[68] Since then, no member of Congress has ever introduced a bill to allow new parties to receive general election funding in advance of a particular election.

2. The National Presidential Debates

State ballot access laws and the federal public funding scheme are not the only barriers that minor-party candidates face. The Commission on Presidential Debates (CPD), a private organization, maintains criteria for which candidates gets invited to the presidential debates. In theory, the CPD's criteria make it impossible for someone other than the Democratic or Republican candidate to be invited. To qualify for the debates, the CPD requires a presidential candidate to have a 15 percent approval rating in national polls in September of an election year. Since World War II, only one minor-party

---

[67]   Micah L. Sifry, *Why America Is Stuck with Only Two Parties*, NEW REPUBLIC (Feb. 2, 2018), https://newrepublic.com/article/146884/america-stuck-two-parties.

[68]   424 U.S. 1 (1976). The vote on general election public funding was 7–2. Only Justices Warren Berger and William Rehnquist felt that the unequal aspect of general election public funding was unconstitutional.

candidate has polled high enough to satisfy this criterion. That was George Wallace in 1968.[69] In 1992, Ross Perot, who ran as an independent candidate, polled 7 percent nationally.[70] In September 1996, when Perot ran again and sought the Reform Party's nomination, he was polling well below 15 percent.[71] Henry Wallace in 1948, John Anderson in 1980, and Gary Johnson in 2016 also did not come close to polling at 15 percent by September.[72]

The CPD maintains a monopoly over the general election presidential debates. Presidential candidates who are invited to the CPD's debates must agree not to participate in any other general election debates. In practice, no minor-party candidate will be able to satisfy the CPD's polling requirement. When George Wallace did so in 1968, he polled at 18 percent in September,[73] but back then there was no general election presidential debate and no CPD. Lawsuits have been filed to try to force the CPD to ease its barriers to entry for minor parties and third parties.[74] In 2014 and 2015, the Green Party, the Libertarian National Committee, and an organization called Level the Playing Field filed two complaints with the FEC alleging improprieties by the CPD. However, so far this litigation has not been successful.

3. Lack of Ranked Choice Voting and Runoff Elections

No state uses ranked choice voting for president in the general election, and there is no general election runoff in any state for presidential elections. As a result, whenever an otherwise strong outsider is perceived as someone who is likely to "spoil" the election for one of the major-party nominees, that candidate is attacked. Republican orators in 1924 denounced Progressive Party nominee Robert La Follette for this reason.

Although no state currently uses ranked choice voting its general presidential election, a bill is pending in the Maine legislature that would use ranked choice voting for the presidential contest.[75] If Maine were to pass its bill, and

---

[69] George Wallace polled 18% in September 1968. *See* Kate Stohr, *Before You Vote for a Third-Party Candidate, Here's What You Need to Know*, SPLINTER NEWS (Aug. 23, 2016), https://splinternews.com/before-you-vote-for-a-third-party-candidate-heres-what-1793861329

[70] Robin Toner, *The 1992 Campaign: The Overview; Perot Re-enters the Campaign, Saying Bush and Clinton Fail to Address Government "Mess,"* N.Y. TIMES (Oct. 2, 1992), www.nytimes.com/1992/10/02/us/1992-campaign-overview-perot-re-enters-campaign-saying-bush-clinton-fail-address.html.

[71] *See* Stohr, *supra* note 69.

[72] *Id.*

[73] *Id.*

[74] *See* Level the Playing Field v. FEC, 381 F.Supp.3d 78 (D.D.C. 2019).

[75] S. Res. 315, 129th Leg., 1st Reg. Sess. (Me. 2019).

use ranked choice voting for its presidential election in November 2020, other states may follow.

It is not feasible for states to hold old-fashioned runoff elections for president, because Congress, since 1845, has required all states to choose their presidential electors by the first Tuesday after the first Monday in November. Thus there is no easy way for any state to be able to organize a second-round runoff in a way that is administratively feasible. Of course, if a constitutional amendment ever passes to alter or abolish the Electoral College, that amendment could also provide either for a second-round runoff presidential election, or could provide that the states must use a ranked choice voting system for their general presidential elections.

C. *Constitutional Restrictions*

The U.S. Constitution spells out that if no presidential candidate wins a majority of the votes in the Electoral College, the House of Representatives chooses the President.[76] Almost every member of the House is either a Democrat or a Republican, however. That means that unless an independent or new party's presidential candidate is so popular that he or she can win a majority of the Electoral College, or can persuade the Republican and Democratic members of the House to support him or her, the independent or new party's candidate has virtually no chance of winning an election decided by the House of Representatives. Bills are from time to time introduced in Congress proposing a constitutional amendment to abolish the Electoral College, but since 1969, none of these has come close to passing. Currently, the House bill to abolish the Electoral College, introduced by Congressman Steve Cohen of Tennessee, has only nine co-sponsors.[77] The Senate bill to do the same, sponsored by Senator Brian Schatz of Hawaii, has only three co-sponsors.[78]

There is a movement called the National Popular Vote Interstate Compact that seeks to alter the way the Electoral College works, via changes to state laws. The National Popular Vote Interstate Compact would require the states that signed onto it to award their presidential electors to the candidate who wins the national popular vote. Maryland was the first state to adopt this plan into state law. Since then, New Jersey, Illinois, Hawaii, Washington,

---

[76] U.S. Const. art. II, § 1, cl. 4.
[77] H.R.J. Res. 7, 116th Cong., 1st Sess. (2019) (introduced by Congressman Steve Cohen of Tennessee).
[78] S.J. Res. 17, 116th Cong., 1st Sess. (2019) (introduced by Senate Brian Schatz of Hawaii).

Massachusetts, the District of Columbia, Vermont, California, Rhode Island, New York, Connecticut, Colorado, Delaware, New Mexico, and Nevada have also signed on.[79] The compact will not go into effect until states with a majority of Electoral College votes have joined.[80] A 2015 Supreme Court opinion held that states may use the statewide initiative process to amend laws governing federal elections.[81] Public opinion polls show that the National Popular Vote Interstate Compact has majority support,[82] so it is possible that supporters of the plan will begin to use the initiative process to add more states as signatories of the compact.[83]

So far, the states that have joined hold 189 electoral votes, which falls short of the 270 electoral votes needed to elect the President. Once states containing 250 electoral votes join, it is possible that members of Congress and state legislators will begin taking a serious interest in passing a constitutional amendment to alter or abolish the Electoral College. If politicians in the United States seriously consider amending Article II of the Constitution to change the method we use to elect the nation's President, it is conceivable that the same amendment would alter the provision of the Constitution that allows the House of Representatives to select the President when no one candidate receives the majority of the Electoral College vote.

IV. CONCLUSION

There are many barriers to victory for presidential candidates who run outside of the two major parties. Of them all, the one where some progress has been made is with ballot access laws. In some ways, these laws are now easier to satisfy, although in other ways they are not. The number of signatures required to get on the ballot has been getting lower in many states across the country. But the rules for choosing a vice-presidential running mate have become

---

[79] *Status of National Popular Vote Bill in Each State*, National Popular Vote, www.nationalpopularvote.com/state-status.

[80] Matthew S. Schwartz, *Nevada Poised to Become 15th State to Sidestep Traditional Electoral College Outcome*, NPR (May 22, 2019), www.npr.org/2019/05/22/725616541/nevada-poised-to-become-15th-state-to-ditch-electoral-college.

[81] Ariz. State Legis. v. Ariz. Indep. Redistricting Comm'n, 135 S. Ct. 2652 (2015).

[82] *See* Steven Shepard, *Poll: Voters Prefer Popular Vote over Electoral College*, POLITICO (March 27, 2019), www.politico.com/story/2019/03/27/poll-popular-vote-electoral-college-1238346

[83] *See National Popular Vote Bill in Each State, supra* note 79. States that have not joined, but which have the statewide initiative, are Alaska, Arizona, Arkansas, Florida, Idaho, Maine, Michigan, Mississippi, Missouri, Montana, Nebraska, North Dakota, Ohio, Oregon, South Dakota, Utah, and Wyoming.

substantially more restrictive. And candidates who first run in a major-party presidential primary and then hope to run outside of the major parties in the general election face ballot access barriers that did not exist before 2012. While it is unlikely the Americans will elect an independent candidate or the nominee of a minor party to the presidency anytime soon, it is important to note that minor parties do consistently nominate candidates for the U.S. presidency, and that these candidates do compete in the general election. And minor parties will continue to run their own candidates in the future. Their efforts deserve to be understood, and also celebrated, because these minor parties are part of the fabric of American democracy, and because they play a crucial role in introducing Americans to policy ideas that they might not find anywhere else.

16

Reforming the Presidential Nominating Process: A Curmudgeon's View

Bradley A. Smith[*]

I. INTRODUCTION

With the conclusion of each presidential election, scholars, commentators, and political junkies begin the quadrennial exercise of discussing reform of the presidential nomination system. If we could alter the process in just the right way, goes the thinking, we would get better nominees, a more informative campaign, and everyone, or at least a lot of people, would be happier with their choices on the next presidential ballot.[1]

And why not? How hard can it be to improve our presidential nominating system? After all, in 2016, both Gallup and Pew reported that voters had historically negative impressions of both major party nominees,[2] so changes

[*] Bradley A. Smith is the Josiah H. Blackmore II/Shirley M. Naught Professor of Law at Capital University. He thanks Eugene Mazo for his encouragement, comments, and editorial assistance, Akhil Rajasekar for research assistance, and the authors in this volume for sharing their thoughts and ideas.

[1] See, e.g., Walter Shapiro, *The Chosen One: Thoughts on a Better, Fairer, and Smarter Way to Pick Presidential Nominees* (Brennan Ctr. for Justice, 2017); Jay Cost, *Our Presidential Nomination Process Is an Embarrassing Mess*, NAT'L REV. (Dec. 11, 2017), www.nationalreview.com/2017/12/democrats-limit-superdelegates-role-more-democracy-not-answer/; Jeffrey H. Anderson & Jay Cost, *A Republican Nomination Process*, 16 J. NAT'L AFFAIRS (Summer 2013); Scott Piroth, *Selecting Presidential Nominees*, 64 SOC. EDUC. 278 (2000); John Haskell, *Reforming Presidential Primaries: Three Steps for Improving the Campaign Environment*, 26 PRES. STUD. Q. 380 (1996); Edward N. Kearny, *Presidential Nominations and Representative Democracy: Proposals for Change*, 14 PRES. STUD. Q. 348 (1984); Cyrus R. Vance, *Reforming the Electoral Reforms*, N.Y. TIMES MAG. at 357 (Feb. 22, 1981); Reid Peyton Chambers & Ronald T. Rotunda, *Reform of Presidential Nominating Conventions*, 56 VA. L. REV. 179 (1970); Paul T. David, *Reforming the Presidential Nominating Process*, 27 L. & CONTEMP. PROB. 159 (1962).

[2] See Lydia Saad, *Trump and Clinton Finish with Historically Poor Images*, GALLUP, Nov. 8, 2016, https://news.gallup.com/poll/197231/trump-clinton-finish-historically-poor-images.aspx?g_source=scalometer&g_medium=search&g_campaign=tiles; PEW RESEARCH CTR., VOTER SATISFACTION WITH CHOICE OF CANDIDATES AT LOWEST POINT IN DECADES, Sept

that would improve voter satisfaction must be low-hanging fruit. Indeed, the authors in this volume have offered up a number of thoughtful, intelligent suggestions for reform.

Yet, if past performance is any predictor of future success, the answer may be that it is quite hard. In fact, we have been tinkering with the nomination process, through statutes, judicial interpretations of statutes and the Constitution, and party rules, for well over a century, and particularly so for the past fifty years, only to end up with the great voter discontent of the 2016 election. The problem is probably not the want of thoughtful ideas for reform. Rather, the difficulties lie in determining whether any proposals can realistically anticipate the changing nature of campaigns and the electorate, and whether they will have unintended side effects that make things worse. Assuming we are satisfied with our answers to those questions, we then must determine how to get from here to there. Our current system, with which we are so dissatisfied, is, after all, itself a product of often carefully orchestrated change aimed at improvements.

II. SOME INTRODUCTORY PROBLEMS

Because the nomination process is so big and sprawling, it is difficult to focus on merely one change. Any single change to one part of the system will likely affect other aspects of the nomination system, not always in predictable ways, and any one change that doesn't affect other parts is likely to be trivial. Yet the obstacles to systematic reform are substantial. Developing a more rational presidential nomination system through legal means is extremely difficult because of the decentralized nature of the American electoral system, and the constitutional protections political parties retain as private associations.

The first problem is the lack of legal authority for any overarching, national reform. The Constitution gives the federal government very little control over presidential elections. While Congress has the power to set the "Times, Places, and Manner" of elections for the House and Senate, it has power only to set the "Time" of choosing presidential electors.[3] Perhaps this objection is overstated — we may note that, with Supreme Court approval, Congress has regulated the

---

9, 2016, www.pewresearch.org/fact-tank/2016/09/12/already-low-voter-satisfaction-with-choice-of-candidates-falls-even-further/satisfaction_1/.

[3] *Compare* U.S. CONST. art. I, § 4, providing, "The Times, Places, and Manner of holding Elections for Senators and Representatives, shall be prescribed in each state by the Legislature thereof; but the Congress may at any time by Law make or alter such regulations," *with* U.S. CONST. art. II, § 1, granting Congress the authority to "determine the Time of chusing the Electors, and the Day on which they shall give their votes."

manner in which presidential candidates finance their campaigns, and how private citizens can promote their views on presidential candidates.[4] Still, even if the courts granted Congress some added leeway, for the most part, this will remain a show run by candidates themselves, political parties, and the fifty states,[5] each of which has particular interests that may not jibe with what others perceive to be a better nomination system. And it is difficult for parties themselves to impose a rational system because of their own decentralized structure, and because our legal regime—especially in campaign finance regulation—is heavily oriented toward individual candidates.

In the end, however, the biggest problem may be that we don't really know how to reform the system, and we may not know how to reform the system precisely because every election is different. This means that no system will ever be the "best" for any given election, for most elections, or even for the next election. In practice, past efforts at reform have not been very successful at achieving their stated goals.

III. A BRIEF LOOK BACK

The presidential nomination "process" has now gone through three distinct phases: the congressional caucus phase, the national convention phase, and now, the primary phase.

The founders made no plans for political parties in the Constitution, and were somewhat surprised when parties quickly sprouted. The "nomination" of presidential candidates was expected to take place in conjunction with the Electoral College. State legislators—or at the legislature's discretion, voters— would select presidential electors, unpledged to any particular candidate. These electors would then cast votes for president. Early on, congressional leaders in each faction, the nascent parties, simply got together and, perhaps after some debate and bargaining, agreed on a candidate. Their faction would

---

[4]   *See* Title 52, United States Code (the "Federal Election Campaign Act"); Buckley v. Valeo, 424 U.S. 1. In *Smith v. Allright*, 321 U.S. 649 (1944), the Supreme Court held that primary elections were subject to constitutional requirements of due process and equal protection. The case, however, turned on the fact that the state was a participant in the primary process. *See also* Terry v. Adams, 345 U.S. 461 (1953) (extending *Allright* to a private, non-party organization "in which county election officials have participated in and condoned a continued effort effectively to exclude Negroes from voting") (Frankfurter, J., concurring). For an argument that the regulation of "campaigns" are distinct from "elections," and that only the latter may be regulated under Congress's enumerated powers, or consistent with the First Amendment, *see* Bradley A. Smith, *Separation of Campaign and State*, 81 GEO. WASH. L. REV. 2038 (2013).

[5]   We might note here that, in fact, there are not even any truly "federal" elections in the United States. Rather, there are state elections for federal office, including that of presidential elector.

then support the selection of presidential electors known as supporters of the party and its chosen nominee in the states. When these legislators headed home, they rallied local sympathizers around the agreed-upon candidate. The process made sense — in those days when travel was arduous, Congress was one of the few places where influential political leaders from different states could meet and discuss the presidency, and plan efforts to get their preferred choice elected nationally. Most states did not have popular voting for electors,[6] and the congressmen were highly influential in the selection of electors.

The first national party nominating convention came in 1831, when the Anti-Masonic Party met in Baltimore and nominated William Wirt for president in the 1832 election. By then, the increase in popular voting for the office[7] diminished the ability of a handful of congressmen to influence the selection of presidential electors. Furthermore, the Party, founded only in 1828, had a negligible presence in Congress.[8] Both the National Republican Party, forerunner to the Whigs, and the Democratic Party later held conventions at which they selected presidential nominees for 1832. Party conventions would remain at the core of the process until well into the second half of the twentieth century.[9]

In an extremely large country, yet one in which travel remained slow and dangerous and communication slow and intermittent, national conventions served many purposes in the selection process. They were often the only opportunity for party leaders from different parts of the country to meet and discuss national politics directly. Leaders could discuss both the policy and electoral needs and demands of their states, and it was a rare opportunity for state and local party leaders to see potential candidates first hand. If the modern image of the nineteenth- or early-twentieth-century nominating convention is one of smoke-filled rooms and backroom deals, it is because they were exactly that. Leaders from around the country gathered together, often met and sized one another up for the first time, pled their respective cases, considered alternatives, negotiated, compromised, and politicked. They were

---

6   For popular vote totals and information on where and when popular voting took place for presidential electors prior to 1828, see The American Antiquarian Society and Tufts University Digital Collections and Archives, A New Nation Voters: American Election Returns 1787–1825, https://elections.lib.tufts.edu/.

7   By 1828, only Delaware and South Carolina did not hold popular elections for the office of elector. *See* David Leip, Atlas of U.S. Presidential Elections, https://uselectionatlas.org/RESULTS/.

8   It held 17 seats in the then-213 member House. *See* Office of the Historian, U.S. House of Representatives, Party Divisions of the House of Representatives, https://history.house.gov/Institution/Party-Divisions/Party-Divisions/.

9   Piroth, *supra* note 1.

citizens, engaged in the affairs of state. With our modern mania for "transparency," we tend to forget that deals for compromises and solutions are often best struck in quiet, out of the limelight.[10]

Nominating conventions might be conducive to backroom deals and, therefore, some element of corruption, but they were not especially conducive to the bombast of a Theodore Roosevelt or the uncompromising self-righteousness of a Woodrow Wilson. This was frustrating for the first generation of "progressives," who needed some way to wrest control of the nominating process from party veterans. The progressives argued that not only the general election, but the process of party nomination itself should be subject to democratic control as determined by government. Generally speaking, it is not unfair to say that they sought government intervention into the affairs of political parties—historically viewed as private organizations—in order help assure the nomination and election of their preferred candidates for president and lower offices. Primaries would break the grip of party elites—in which progressives were not well represented—on the nominating process. Simultaneously, selective restrictions on political speech, in the form of campaign finance laws, would limit the ability of their opponents to make a case to the public.[11]

The first presidential primaries were held 1912, in the Republican Party, when twelve states held primaries. By 1916, 26 states held presidential primaries. However, turnout in primaries was generally low, and holding primary elections is expensive. States quickly began to trim back, and from 1924 through 1968 no more than 20 states used presidential primaries in any election—usually, the number was a fair bit less.[12] The selection of unpledged delegates through state conventions and caucuses remained the dominant mode for selecting delegates to the national conventions through 1968. Candidates—often the weaker candidates—might enter a few primaries in an effort to show voter appeal. But that was merely an effort to strengthen their position for the real action at the national convention.[13] For example, in 1952, Senator Estes Kefauver defeated President Harry Truman in the New Hampshire Democratic primary, convincing Truman to drop out of the

---

[10] The Constitutional Convention of 1787 famously took, as one of its first acts, to close its doors to the public, so that the delegates could debate, argue, and compromise freely. *See* JOHN P. KAMINSKI, SECRECY AND THE CONSTITUTIONAL CONVENTION 7 (2005).

[11] *See* United States v. Newberry, 256 U.S. 232 (1921); PAULA BAKER, CURBING CAMPAIGN CASH: HENRY FORD, TRUMAN NEWBERRY, AND THE POLITICS OF PROGRESSIVE REFORM (2012).

[12] Stephen Gardbaum & Richard H. Pildes, *Populism and Institutional Design: Methods of Selecting Candidates for Chief Executive*, 93 N.Y.U. L. REV. 647, 656–57 (2018).

[13] NELSON POLSBY & AARON WILDAVSKY, PRESIDENTIAL ELECTIONS 230 (1971).

race. In fact, Kefauver won 12 of 15 Democratic primaries that year. Yet in the end, Adlai Stevenson, who had not entered any primaries, won the Democratic nomination.[14]

The third, and current, era of presidential nominations is the primary era. In 1968, two Democratic senators opposed to the Vietnam War, Robert Kennedy and Eugene McCarthy, won over two-thirds of the vote in Democratic primaries. Vice President Hubert Humphrey, whom, it was perceived, would carry on the war policies of President Lyndon Johnson, did not contest any primaries. Yet at the national convention, Humphrey emerged with the nomination. After Humphrey lost in the fall to Richard Nixon, Democrats established new rules, requiring all national convention delegates to be chosen in primaries or open caucuses, and providing for proportional representation of delegates. Seeing the popularity of primaries, and not wanting to be left behind, Republicans followed suit, although they did not immediately adopt proportional representation. By 2000, each major party held at least forty primaries, and states without primaries typically held open caucuses.[15] In 2020, 42 states will select delegates to the Democratic National Convention through primaries.[16]

Since 1972, most proposals for reform have assumed that primaries will remain the dominant factor in the nomination process. The few reformers who suggest a retreat from primaries, or more radically, the abolition of primaries, may simply be tilting at windmills. Instead, proposed reforms have generally focused on altering the "primary calendar," or order of primaries; attempting to maintain a role for party officeholders and elites within a system in which primaries are dominant; adjusting delegate selection formulas (proportional or winner-take-all); adjusting the financing of primaries; and changing the candidate debates that take place before and around primaries.

---

[14] ELAINE KAMARCK, PRIMARY POLITICS 9–10 (3rd ed. 2019). Piroth, *supra* note 1, at 280. That year, however, Dwight Eisenhower used a victory in the Republican primary in New Hampshire to demonstrate his vote-getting ability, which was instrumental to his ultimate convention win over party stalwart William Taft. *See* RHODES COOK, RACE FOR THE PRESIDENCY: WINNING THE 2000 NOMINATION 5 (2000).

[15] Piroth, *supra* note 1, at 281.

[16] David Weigel, *The Trailer: What We Learned from All the 2018 Results: The Winners, Losers, Flippers, Voters and Spenders*, WASH. POST (Dec. 9, 2018), www.washingtonpost.com/politics/paloma/the-trailer/2018/12/09/the-trailer-what-we-learned-from-all-the-2018-results-the-winners-losers-flippers-voters-and-spenders/5c0ae53a1b326b67caba2b49/?utm_term=.c120121caa49.

IV. SOME DIFFICULTIES WITH REFORM

Let us consider just one area in which proposals for reform are often floated: the primary calendar. Here, the early dates of the New Hampshire primary and Iowa caucuses are a source of regular criticism. Because of their early position in the selection process, these two small and demographically atypical states (but is there a truly typical state?)[17] are said to wield excessive influence. But any state that tries to jump ahead of New Hampshire in the primary line merely causes the latter, by state law, to move its primary earlier in the season.[18] This seems, then, to merely lengthen a process that many complain is already too long and must be shortened.[19] Others have suggested greater changes to the primary calendar, including specific orders of states, regional primaries, the times between primaries, and so on. Even assuming "objective" observers could agree on an order, any such scheme would require the unlikely agreement of large numbers of self-interested states—including Iowa and New Hampshire. So individual action by states is unlikely to be effective. Some national approach is necessary.

On the face of it, however, the federal government would seem to lack any authority to impose primary dates on the states, and historically it has been conceded that a constitutional amendment would be required.[20] But even if such an amendment were passed, or the federal government were able to convince a court that setting a national presidential primary calendar was

---

[17] One study suggests Illinois is the most typical demographic state. Andy Kiersz, *Revealed: The Most Normal States in America*, BUSINESS INSIDER (Apr. 14, 2014), www.businessinsider.com/ the-most-average-states-in-america-2014-4. But in recent decades, Illinois has hardly been typical in its choice for president. No Republican has won so much as 45 percent of the vote in the general election in Illinois since 1988, even though every Republican nominee has won at least that percentage nationally in every election since 2000. Leip, *supra* note 7. Moreover, in 2016, Illinois primary voters gave wins to Donald Trump and Hillary Clinton, the two candidates who were, supposedly, so disappointing to the electorate. *See Illinois Primary Results*, N.Y. TIMES (March 15, 2016), www.nytimes.com/elections/2016/results/ primaries/illinois.

[18] *See* N.H. REV. STAT. § 653:9.

[19] *See, e.g.,* Jay Cost, *Our Sick Body Politic*, NAT'L REV. (Jan. 7, 2019), www.nationalreview.com /2019/01/politics-mean-spirited-omnipresent-presidential-campaign/; Seth Masket, *How to Improve the Primary Process? Make It Less Democratic*, PACIFIC STANDARD (Aug. 11, 2017), https://psmag.com/magazine/how-to-improve-the-primary-process; *but see* Shapiro, *supra* note 1, at 11 ("Primaries should stretch over several months.").

[20] *See, e.g.,* SUBCOMMITTEE ON CONSTITUTIONAL AMENDMENTS OF THE SENATE COMMITTEE ON THE JUDICIARY, HEARINGS ON NOMINATION AND ELECTION OF PRESIDENT AND VICE PRESIDENT, 87th Cong., 1st Sess. (1961); SUBCOMMITTEE ON CONSTITUTIONAL AMENDMENTS OF THE SENATE COMMITTEE ON THE JUDICIARY, HEARINGS ON NOMINATION AND ELECTION OF PRESIDENT AND VICE PRESIDENT, 84th Cong., 1st Sess. (1955).

a legitimate extension of its power to set the time for choosing presidential electors,[21] its seems unlikely that members of Congress would agree on the best order for primaries any more than the states, when left to their own devices.

The parties have found it equally difficult to impose calendar reform. For example, suppose it were decided by great election law minds that in a more rational system, the first primaries would be held on the same date, and involve Georgia, Ohio, Connecticut, and Arizona. The parties could presumably enforce this by refusing to seat delegates from any state that held its primaries or caucuses earlier, which the courts have held they have a right to do as private associations.[22] In practice, however, the parties have been unable to institute such discipline. Efforts in the 1980s by the parties to force New Hampshire and Iowa out of their first-in-the-nation status through party rules failed miserably, in part because the politicians don't want to alienate general election voters in those two competitive states.[23]

More recently, in 2008, the Democratic Party adopted rules penalizing states which had their primaries outside of a master plan approved by party officials, by stripping them of their delegates. Florida and Michigan held early primaries anyway. When push came to shove, candidate Hillary Clinton needed those delegates, and pushed for their inclusion at the convention. Further, both states were considered key "battleground" states in the upcoming election, and it was almost inconceivable that the party would simply stiff their delegations and potentially offend voters in those states. Eventually, the party seated the delegations, though it did reduce their voting power.[24] The parties clearly have the authority to decide which delegations to seat, and what their voting power will be, at the national conventions, even if contrary to the selection process specified by state law.[25] The problem is that, politically, it is too costly to use that power.

---

[21] The Supreme Court has held that party primaries are subject to constitutional limitations on state action as part of state run elections. United States v. Classic, 313 U.S. 299 (1941), and upheld some, though by no means all, state regulation of party primaries. *Compare, e.g.,* Clingman v. Beaver, 544 U.S. 581 (2005) (upholding a state law prohibiting a party from opening its primary to members of other parties), *with* Tashjian v. Connecticut, 479 U.S. 208 (1986) (striking down a state law prohibiting a party from opening its primary to independent voters, as violating the associational rights of the party).

[22] Democratic Party of the United States v. Wisconsin ex rel. La Follette, 450 U.S. 107 (1981).

[23] For a detailed discussion of the Democrats' failed effort to alter their place in the primary calendar, see KAMARCK, *supra* note 14, at 57–75.

[24] *Id.* at 3.

[25] *La Follette*, 450 U.S. 107 (1981); Cousins v. Wigoda, 419 U.S. 477 (1975).

Meanwhile, the parties' rights of association, as private organizations, make many efforts to impose some specific vision of a good nomination process quite difficult. For example, many believe that the best primary system would limit the selection of national convention delegates to party members. But the parties don't always agree, and the states may not impose by law a "closed" primary in which only party members may vote.[26] Others think the system would benefit from "open" primaries, in which all voters could participate in either party's primary. But that, too, may not be imposed by law.[27] And that merely begs the question of which is best—obviously, various party officials and leaders disagree, and such disagreements will often be affected by the particular time, place, and situation of the party. In *Tashjian v. Republican Party of Connecticut*, the Connecticut Republican Party was the clear minority party in the state. It wanted to open its primary to non-members. It's hope was that doing so would lead to the selection of a nominee with strong appeal to independent voters, a necessity for any Republican to win election in that state. That, in turn, might gradually draw those voters into the party. In *California Democratic Party v. Jones*, however, the California Democratic Party—a majority party—wanted to restrict the nomination to its members, precisely to select a candidate with strong appeal to its members. There is no real agreement on which system is best, and it may vary in time and place. In any event, the states lack the ability to command one or the other. At the same time, the parties themselves have had difficulty imposing one or the other system over the electorate's objections. Political parties, almost by definition, are unlikely to take steps that alienate voters in states where voters are particularly inclined to one type of primary or another.

The self-interests of candidates and other actors also come into play, as we have seen with the 2008 effort by the Democratic National Committee to control the primary calendar. In another example, in 2016, both major parties made some effort to control the timing and number of candidate debates.[28] But in the United States, party hierarchies have very little power over what candidates choose to do. If, for example, an entity wishes to sponsor an "unsanctioned" debate, and if a candidate wishes to participate, there is very little the party can do about it. Nor can it do much if candidates choose not to participate in an "approved" debate. Candidates will participate in debates if they see the debates as a way to gain net votes (or minimize losses versus non-participation).

---

[26] Tashjian v. Connecticut, 479 U.S. 208 (1986).
[27] California Democratic Party v. Jones, 530 U.S. 567 (2000).
[28] Bob Bauer, *A Debatable Role in the Process: Political Parties and the Candidate Debates*, 93 N.Y.U. L. REV. 589, 600 (2018).

And if one candidate participates, it becomes very risky for others to bypass the event. The party has few options if the candidates don't conform to its wishes. It can adopt rules making it harder for an uncooperative candidate to gain the party's nomination,[29] but it is hard to imagine a party trying to deny the nomination to its most popular candidates. Similarly, the party can threaten to withhold party support from such a nominee. But fat chance of that happening if the offending candidate actually wins the nomination.[30] No major party is about to forfeit a presidential election.

What we see, then, is that most sweeping proposals to create some national system of primaries, or some predictable pattern of debates, are non-starters. There are too many actors—candidates, parties, states, and even the electorate—who have their own ideas and will pursue their own interests.

In the end, this is probably all for the good. It would be bad for political parties to become mere appendages of the state, subject to state dominance. It is good that candidates have the freedom to make campaign decisions, rather than have them dictated by government. And, having put the matter before the voters, it is generally good that parties respond to the desires of voters, even if the experts might prefer a different primary system.

V. WHAT'S A BETTER SYSTEM, ANYWAY?

Even if it were possible to impose a "better" nominating system across the board, we should be very skeptical of our ability to do so. For example, after losing landslide elections in 1972 and 1980, and barely winning in the post-Watergate election of 1976, Democrats were increasingly concerned about the dominant positions of New Hampshire and Iowa in the delegate selection process. The states were atypical of the general population. They made it too easy for less-vetted, long shot candidates—such as Carter and McGovern—to claim the nomination by winning over these small state electorates and riding the ensuing free media and "momentum" to a broader victory, despite their weaknesses as general election candidates. In the words of AFL-CIO President Lane Kirkland, it was time to "put the bosses back in charge" because they would "pick winners."[31] Though unable to force Iowa and New Hampshire out of their poll positions, the party adopted a number of rules to encourage states to hold primaries within a particular window, and reserved seats for

---

[29] *See* LaRouche v. Fowler, 152 F.3d 974 (D.C. Cir. 1998); Duke v. Massey, 87 F.3d 1226 (11th Cir. 1996).

[30] Bauer, *supra* note 28.

[31] Quoted in KAMARCK, *supra* note 14, at 62.

"superdelegates," longtime party officials, activists, and officeholders.[32] It was thought that these changes would empower party regulars to choose candidates with broader national appeal. But in the end, the hapless, establishment-backed liberal Walter Mondale won the 1984 nomination, only to lose 49 states in November.

Another failed effort was "Super Tuesday." Facing a difficult primary challenge from Senator Edward Kennedy, in 1980 President Jimmy Carter successfully lobbied many southern states—where he was more popular than the Massachusetts liberal—to move their primaries forward. Conservative southern Democrats happily complied. The thinking was that, by assuring a major role relatively early in the process for the party's moderate, southern wing, Democrats would arrest the party's leftward drift and nominate a candidate with broader appeal for the general election.[33] By 1988, "Super Tuesday" was explicitly a southern phenomenon. But the gadfly Reverend Jesse Jackson, no moderate he, swept most of the deep south with plurality votes fueled by liberal African-American voters. Meanwhile, the northeastern liberal Michael Dukakis won the Florida primary, with its somewhat atypical (for the South) electorate, and went on to win the nomination.[34] Dukakis then lost a none-too-close race to George H. W. Bush.

Setting the calendar has not been the only problematic area. In the 1970s, Democrats changed their rules to provide for proportional representation in most primaries and caucuses. The goal was, in part, to assure that former segregationist Alabama Governor George Wallace did not pick up the nomination by winning pluralities in various states and sweeping up disproportionate numbers of delegates as a result.[35] The end result was that George McGovern, who was generally viewed by the American public as too far left, won the 1972 nomination, only to be crushed in the general election by Richard Nixon. Forty years later the proportional system continues, dragging on nomination contests long after their usefulness is over, because it takes so long for the frontrunner to officially clinch the nomination.

The Democrats democratization of their nomination process after 1968 also created a scenario in which it was perceived that party officeholders and leaders had too little influence over the nominee. Under the post-1968 delegate selection system, the party lost the elections of 1972 and 1980 in landslides, and barely eked out a win in the post-Watergate year of 1976. Moreover, in

---

[32]   *Id.* at 115–16.
[33]   *Id.* at 32.
[34]   *Id.* at 123.
[35]   *Id.* at 94, 124.

1980 the party lost its majority in the U.S. Senate for the first time in 26 years. Democratic House members, as "the last vestige of Democratic control at the national level," therefore demanded a greater role in the nominating process.[36] The result was the creation of the aforementioned "super delegates." These were uncommitted delegate spots set aside for elected office-holders and party leaders, whom, it was thought, would have a greater interest in seeing that the party nominated electable candidates with appeal in the general election.

In fact, it didn't really work out that way. In 1984, it was these super delegates who clinched the nomination for Walter Mondale,[37] who would lose 49 states in the fall. Of course, Mondale's main opponent was the charismatic but callow and flawed Senator Gary Hart, so maybe the "super delegates" did make the right choice. The answer may depend on whether the primary qualification for a nominee should be electability, or experience in actually governing. But since the latter requires the former, perhaps the balance changes with each election. In any event, by 2008, Democratic party activists were nearly apoplectic over the prospect that super delegates would award the party nomination to Hillary Clinton over Barack Obama, who had won the most delegates in primary and caucus contests. By 2016, the very existence of super delegates was considered corrupt, and in 2018, Democrats stripped super delegates of a vote on the first ballot for the nomination.[38]

Republicans have had their own misadventures. For example, after 2012, Republicans tweaked their delegate selection system to encourage winner-take-all primaries after March 15. They hoped the change would avoid the type of long, drawn-out challenge that had sapped Mitt Romney's strength in 2012. What they got was Donald Trump, who despite winning the presidency (so perhaps the change worked?) is supposedly one of two big reasons voters were so dissatisfied in 2016. Indeed, it is hard to think of a "change," "reform," or "improvement" to the nomination process that has not, within a cycle or two, boomeranged on the party implementing it, or at least not worked as anticipated.

One area where Congress has been able to intervene in the nominating process is in the financing of campaigns. As we have seen, primaries came to dominate nominee selection with the elections of 1972 and 1976. The Federal Election Campaign Act was passed in 1971, and given major amendments in

---

[36] *Id.* at 173–74.

[37] *Id.* at 177.

[38] *Id.* at 182. *See also* Daniel Marans, *Democrats Strip Superdelegates of Power in Historic Reform Vote*, THE HILL, Aug. 25, 2018, www.huffingtonpost.com/entry/dnc-approves-historic-reforms-strips-superdelegates-power_us_5b8165d0e4b034858600dcff.

1974, including the implementation of a system of government financing for a portion of candidate primary campaigns.[39] This experience again shows the difficulty of perfecting the process. By offering free government money, the process attracted corruption and publicity seekers. Indeed, in the very first presidential campaign with government-subsidized primary campaigns, exuberant fundraisers for Pennsylvania Governor Milton Shaap's campaign submitted false statements of contributions to qualify for the government money.[40] Numerous candidacies have lived on government subsidies, including fringe third party candidates such as Lenora Fulani of the New Alliance Party, and major party "contenders" such as Al Sharpton and Lyndon LaRouche. Many of these candidates seem drawn into the race by little more than the opportunity for government-subsidized publicity. The program was obsolete almost from its inception, since it imposed constraints on spending money that did not correspond to the realities of campaigns. Today, the program limps on, but no candidate seriously interested in winning a major party nomination participates. Meanwhile, the accompanying regulatory system of the Federal Election Campaign Act placed the locus of fundraising on candidates. This caused candidates — even those accepting the subsidies — to spend more time fundraising, and placed a premium on fundraising ability as opposed to other, perhaps more valuable attributes in a potential officeholder.[41]

It's not that changes are impossible. As this brief narrative shows, they are routinely made. We just shouldn't expect too much. Yet who can resist playing kingmaker?

I, too, have ideas for what I would have done differently in 2016. If I were to offer any one change going forward, without knowing the candidates or the shape of future races, it would be to do away with what we call primary "debates," at least in their current format.[42] Though few would go quite so far, I am not alone in my dissatisfaction, as debates are a regular subject for proposed change.[43] But I put the term "debate" in quotes quite deliberately, for these events have none of the

---

[39] 95 U.S.C. § 9001 *et. seq.*

[40] FED. ELECTION COMM'N, MUR 256 (1977); FED. ELECTION COMM'N, REPORT OF THE AUDIT DIVISION ON THE SHAPP FOR PRESIDENT COMMITTEE 5–6 (1976). For a general discussion of corruption caused by government financed campaigns, see, e.g., David M. Mason, *No Cure for Corruption: Public Financing Under Constitutional Constraints*, 10 ENGAGE 89 (2009).

[41] Many of these problems are discussed in James Sample, *The Last Rites of Public Campaign Financing?*, 92 NEB. L. REV. 349 (2013).

[42] *See* Bradley A. Smith, *A Most Uncommon Cause: Some Thoughts on Campaign Finance Reform and a Response to Professor Paul*, 30 U. CONN. L. REV. 831, 851–62 (1998).

[43] *See, e.g.*, Shapiro, *supra* note 1, at 17–18; Jeremy Paul, *Campaign Reform for the 21st Century: Putting Mouth Where Money Is*, 30 U. CONN. L. REV. 779 (1998).

structure of traditional debate (as the term might have been used at the time of the famous Lincoln-Douglas debates, or in American high school debate clubs and competitions today). There are no formulated resolutions or questions to be debated (for example, "Resolved: The United States benefits from multilateral free trade pacts such as NAFTA and the Trans-Pacific Partnership"; "Resolved: "The Affordable Care Act Should be Repealed"; or "Resolved: Health Care is a Right that Should be Guaranteed by the Federal Government"). Rather, the events are actually joint press conferences, in which journalists ask a series of questions, and the candidates are given the bare minimum of time needed to regurgitate talking points, but not enough time to explore the issue in depth, or engage in meaningful give and take and discussion. Further, the journalists, in an effort to get ratings, will tend to focus on areas of conflict rather than enlightenment, and often on the trivial but easily understood rather than the important but complex. These problems are exacerbated in the primaries, when large numbers of candidates on stage make it particularly difficult to have in-depth discussion. "Analysis" after these "debates" tends to be trivial and facile, focused on who "won" or "lost" (usually based on style or some ultimately meaningless "gaffe").[44] Worse, the extensive attention given to debates may cause some voters to disengage from more meaningful exploration of the candidates and issues, figuring their job is done with watching a simple 90-minute joint press conference. And it is possible that news coverage focused on debates may cause a reduction in overall campaign coverage and readership.[45]

Curiously, such "debates" are almost never used in state and local elections, or for U.S. Senate or House, and Americans seem more satisfied with their choices in those races.[46] Yet it is obvious that, at least for the immediate future, the idea that we would not have these "debates" is a non-starter likely to be met with gasps of disbelief.

[44] Jennifer Brubaker & Gary Hansen, *The Effect of Fox News and CNN's Post-debate Commentator Analysis on Viewers' Perceptions of Presidential Candidate Performance*, 74 SOUTHERN COMM. J. 339 (2009).

[45] Roughly a third of debate viewers consider the debates the most important information in the campaign. *See* JO HOLZ, HEATHER AKIN & KATHLEEN HALL JAMIESON, PRESIDENTIAL DEBATES: WHAT'S BEHIND THE NUMBERS, WHITE PAPER OF ANNENBERG PUBLIC POLICY CENTER AT UNIVERSITY OF PENNSYLVANIA 7–9 (2016). Debate viewing then leads to partisan reinforcement. Jaeho Cho & Yerheen Ha, *On the Communicative Underpinnings of Campaign Effects: Presidential Debates, Citizen Communication, and Polarization in Evaluations of Candidates*, 29 POL. COMM. 184, 185–86, 193–96 (2012). Cho and Ha, however, also find that debate viewing stimulates more information consumption, but that this, too, led to further polarization. *Id.* at 199.

[46] *Compare* PEW RESEARCH CTR., *supra* note 2, *with* PEW RESEARCH CTR., LITTLE PARTISAN AGREEMENT ON PRESSING PROBLEMS FACING U.S. 8 (Oct. 15, 2018) (showing 66% satisfied with their choice of candidates for House and Senate).

But having said all that, the truth is that I don't know if any of my suggestions will even be applicable in 2020 or 2024. Even if you agree with my recommendations, the rise of Twitter as a form of communication, the ongoing decline of mass broadcast media, the increasing partisanship of mainstream journalism, potentially the number and nature of candidates, and possibly other factors could make my brilliant ideas obsolete in a cycle or two. Writing them into the rules, where they are likely to stay for at least two or three elections beyond any usefulness they might have had, may simply lead to worse candidates in 2028 or future years. This all illustrates my larger point: either we experts don't have all of the answers, or we can't persuade others that we do, or our answers will become obsolete before we know it. We're always fixing the last cycle.

VI. TWO ALTERNATIVE HYPOTHESES

Let me conclude by offering two hypotheses. First, perhaps the U.S. nominating system isn't so bad. After all, look at our fellow democracies.

In 2017, the French offered up a presidential election in which the runoff candidates were Emmanuel Macron, a 39-year-old investment banker who had never held elective office and who got to the final round by end-running the traditional nomination process; and Marine Le Pen, candidate of the National Front, a party whose first leader, her father Jean-Marie Le Pen, was thrice convicted of Holocaust denial in France.[47] The National Front also made the runoff in 2002, with the elder Le Pen losing badly to Jacques Chirac, whose career would end some years later with a conviction for diversion of public funds while serving as Mayor of Paris before that 2002 election.[48] Of course, Macron won in 2017, but by late 2018 his technocratic government was being roiled by mass protests throughout the country.[49] Across the Channel, our cousins in the U.K. had a 2017 general election in which the two major party leaders were the self-proclaimed socialist Jeremy Corbyn,[50] who had gained and held leadership of the Labour Party through a somewhat flukish

---

[47] Angelique Chrisafis, *Jean-Marie Le Pen Fined Again for Dismissing Holocaust as "Detail,"* THE GUARDIAN (Apr. 6, 2016), www.theguardian.com/world/2016/apr/06/jean-marie-le-pen-fined-again-dismissing-holocaust-detail.

[48] Edward Cody, *French Ex-President Chirac Convicted of Corruption,* WASH. POST (Dec. 15, 2011), www.washingtonpost.com/world/french-ex-president-chirac-convicted-of-corruption/2011/12/15/gIQAfp97vO_story.html?utm_term=.646920cabdc4.

[49] Alissa J. Rubin, *Hundreds of Thousands in France Protest Taxes by Blocking Roads,* N.Y. TIMES (Nov. 17, 2018), www.nytimes.com/2018/11/17/world/europe/french-drivers-protest-fuel-taxes.html.

[50] *See, e.g.,* Michael Settle, *Corbyn: I'm a Socialist, Not a Unionist,* THE HERALD (Aug. 17, 2015), at www.heraldscotland.com/news/13609421.Corbyn__I_m_a_Socialist_not_a_Unionist/

series of events, and the colorless Tory Theresa May, whose issue-free campaign managed to lose seats to Corbyn's Labour Party despite entering as heavy favorites. Italy's longest serving post–World War II Prime Minister is Silvio Berlusconi, who was convicted of tax evasion in 2013.[51] So, when we complain about our process for choosing nominees, we might ask, "compared to what?" Indeed, it bears mentioning that as recently as 2008 Gallup found that Americans were *more* satisfied with their major party candidates for president than in any election going back to at least 1988. And 2004 ranked second on that score.[52]

Second, democracy's discontents appear to extend far beyond the presidential nomination process, and it is a mistake to think that they can solved with a few more tweaks of that process. The problem may be that we expect more of democracy and the electoral process than either is able to bear. Kenneth Arrow long ago demonstrated that there is simply no electoral system that is able to perfectly synthesize voter desires.[53] Moreover, voter desires themselves are often inchoate and even contradictory. The data demonstrate a remarkable degree of voter ignorance or confusion about many basic facts and issues.[54] This doesn't mean that voters lack a basic sense of the direction in which they'd like to go, or the ability to discern if their own situation, or that of their neighbors, has improved or worsened under the incumbent government. But it does suggest that any system is going to leave large numbers of voters dissatisfied with their choices, and the larger the scope of government—that is, the more government factors into our daily lives—the greater the room for disappointment, and the more regularly is that disappointment felt.

Democratic elections are obviously a critical element of self-governance, important to protecting individual freedom and political equality. But perhaps they function best as mere insurance against despotism. In theory, at least,

---

("Mr Corbyn, asked if he would describe himself as a Unionist, said: 'No. I would describe myself as a Socialist.'"); Catherine Boyle, *People's QE? Left-Wing Leader's Plans for the UK*, CNBC (Aug. 18, 2015), www.cnbc.com/2015/08/18/peoples-qe-left-wing-leaders-plans-for-the-uk.html ("I'm very proud to call myself a socialist").

[51] Rachel Donadio, *Berlusconi Is Found Guilty of Tax Fraud*, N.Y. TIMES (Oct. 26, 2012), www.nytimes.com/2012/10/27/world/europe/berlusconi-convicted-and-sentenced-in-tax-fraud.html.

[52] Frank Newport, *Voters Not Clamoring for Third-Party Candidate This Year*, GALLUP (Jan. 22, 2008), https://news.gallup.com/poll/103846/Voters-Clamoring-ThirdParty-Candidacy-Year.aspx.

[53] KENNETH J. ARROW, SOCIAL CHOICE AND INDIVIDUAL VALUES (1951).

[54] *See, e.g.*, ILYA SOMIN, DEMOCRACY AND POLITICAL IGNORANCE (2016); MICHAEL X. DELLI CARPINI & SCOTT KEETER, WHAT AMERICANS KNOW ABOUT POLITICS AND WHY IT MATTERS (1996).

would-be tyrants can be voted out, and government can be held accountable. Democratic elections help to assure that a government enters office with at least some significant degree of popular support, and that government will usually at least try to pursue policies it thinks congenial to the public. But elections are not a very effective means of determining the finer points of public policy or selecting a platonic philosopher-king, and as a means of dividing economic spoils or enforcing lifestyle preferences, they are bound to create conflict and disappoint large numbers of the electorate. The success of the United States and the European democracies may be found less in democratic elections—as important as those may be—than in the rule of law, constitutional protection for civil liberties, respect for property rights, and independent judiciaries. Constant efforts to jigger the system to produce the best candidates may be a fruitless exercise, if not a mistake. If governments now seem unresponsive to public opinion, perhaps it is not reform of the nominating or election process that is needed, but a major overhaul of the institutions of what is dubbed "the administrative state," the huge, faceless bureaucracy that now governs so much of life, and seems relatively uninterested in who wins electoral office.

Public confidence in government has been in decline for a considerable time, a decline starting at about the same time that we began ongoing efforts to perfect our electoral systems through law. Perhaps we are barking up the wrong tree.

VII. CONCLUSION

While we certainly should be willing to try to improve our nominating systems—as we should be open to ideas to improve almost anything—it is probably best that such efforts come in small doses and in individual states and parties, rather than through a singular, top-down design. Correspondingly, such reform will be best if implemented by parties as rules for private associations of people, rather than through binding law. Presumably, parties have their own long-term interest at heart; presumably, that long-term interest is in nominating candidates who are palatable to the electorate; and presumably, good government makes future nominees palatable to the electorate. Legislatures are more likely to adopt rules aimed at harming, or at least ignoring the unique circumstances of the opposition party, and legislative rules, once adopted, are much more difficult to change, even after they have outlived whatever usefulness they might once have had.

Experience, rather than theory, should probably be our guide. But experience suggests that we did pretty well with presidential nominations in the days when party conventions, rather than primaries, selected the nominees—at least if voter satisfaction is the issue. Yet the public seems dead set against any change that would reduce the role of primaries—indeed, primaries seem destined to play an increasingly prominent role, as indicated by the recent decision of the Democratic Party to strip super delegates of their power, and the fact that both major parties have adopted "robot rules," requiring delegates to vote as pledged on at least the first ballot at the convention, even if circumstances have changed dramatically in the months since their selection.[55] Of course, smoke-filled rooms were not perfect either. In the end, we may simply have reached the limits of what the nominating process can be expected to do, and may find better targets for reform elsewhere, particularly in the structures of government, rather than elections.

[55] KAMARCK, *supra* note 14, at 168–70.

Index

For EU product safety concerns, contact us at Calle de José Abascal, 56–1°,
28003 Madrid, Spain or eugpsr@cambridge.org.

www.ingramcontent.com/pod-product-compliance
Ingram Content Group UK Ltd.
Pitfield, Milton Keynes, MK11 3LW, UK
UKHW010248140625
459647UK00013BA/1733